S0-BYW-366

THE ASTORS
1763–1992

Landscape with Millionaires

By the same author:

Rothschild: A Story of Wealth and Power
Sweet Robin: A Biography of Robert Dudley Earl of Leicester 1533–1588
The Circumnavigators
The Tower 1078–1979
The World Encompassed: Drake's Great Voyage 1577–1580
A Tudor Tapestry: Men, Women, and Society in Reformation England

THE ASTORS
1763–1992

Landscape with Millionaires

DEREK WILSON

Weidenfeld and Nicolson
London

First published in Great Britain in 1993 by
Weidenfeld & Nicolson, a division of
the Orion Publishing Group Limited,
5 Upper St Martin's Lane, London WC2H 9EA

A catalogue record for this book is available
from the British Library

ISBN 0 297 81261 0

Filmset by Selwood Systems, Midsomer Norton

Printed in Great Britain by
Butler & Tanner Ltd, Frome and London

Contents

Illustrations

Selective Astor Genealogy I (c. 1600–c. 1850)

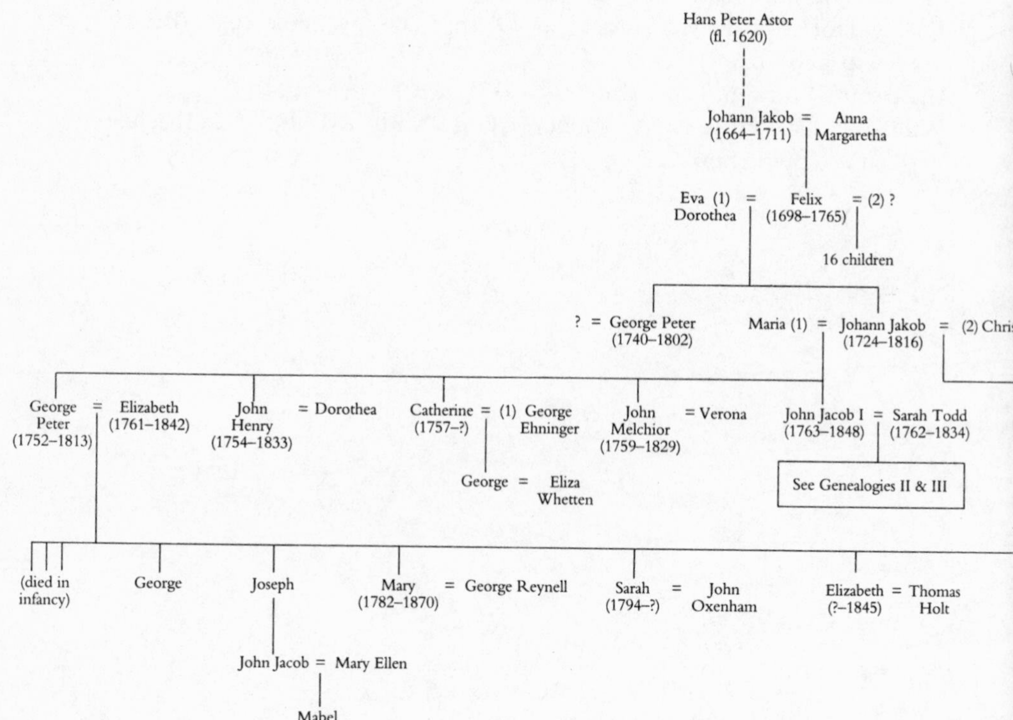

Hans Peter Astor
(fl. 1620)
Johann Jakob =
(1664–1711)
Anna
Margaretha
Eva (1) =
Dorothea
Felix
(1698–1765)
= (2) ?
16 children
? = George Peter
(1740–1802)
Maria (1) =
Johann Jakob
(1724–1816)
= (2) Chris
George
Peter
(1752–1813)
= Elizabeth
(1761–1842)
John
Henry
(1754–1833)
= Dorothea
Catherine = (1) George
(1757–?)
Ehninger
George = Eliza
Whetten
John
Melchior
(1759–1829)
= Verona
John Jacob I = Sarah Todd
(1763–1848)
(1762–1834)
See Genealogies II & III
(died in
infancy)
George
Joseph
John Jacob = Mary Ellen
Mabel
Mary
(1782–1870)
= George Reynell
Sarah
(1794–?)
= John
Oxenham
Elizabeth = Thomas
(?–1845)
Holt

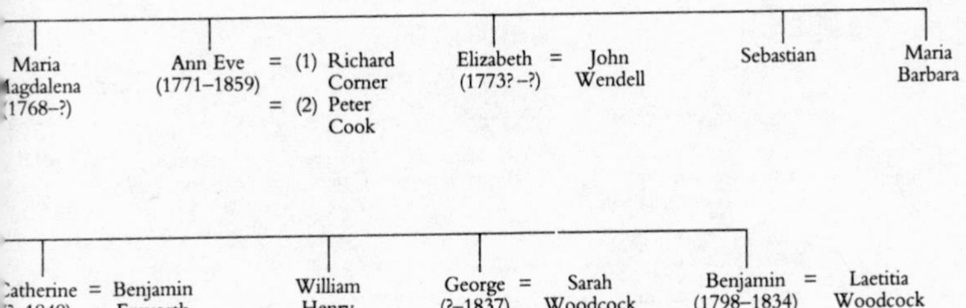

Maria
Magdalena
(1768–?)
Ann Eve
(1771–1859)
= (1) Richard Corner
= (2) Peter Cook
Elizabeth
(1773?–?)
= John Wendell
Sebastian
Maria Barbara
Catherine
(?–1849)
= Benjamin Epworth
William Henry
George
(?–1837)
= Sarah Woodcock
Benjamin
(1798–1834)
= Laetitia Woodcock

Selective Astor Genealogy II
The American Astors
From 1848

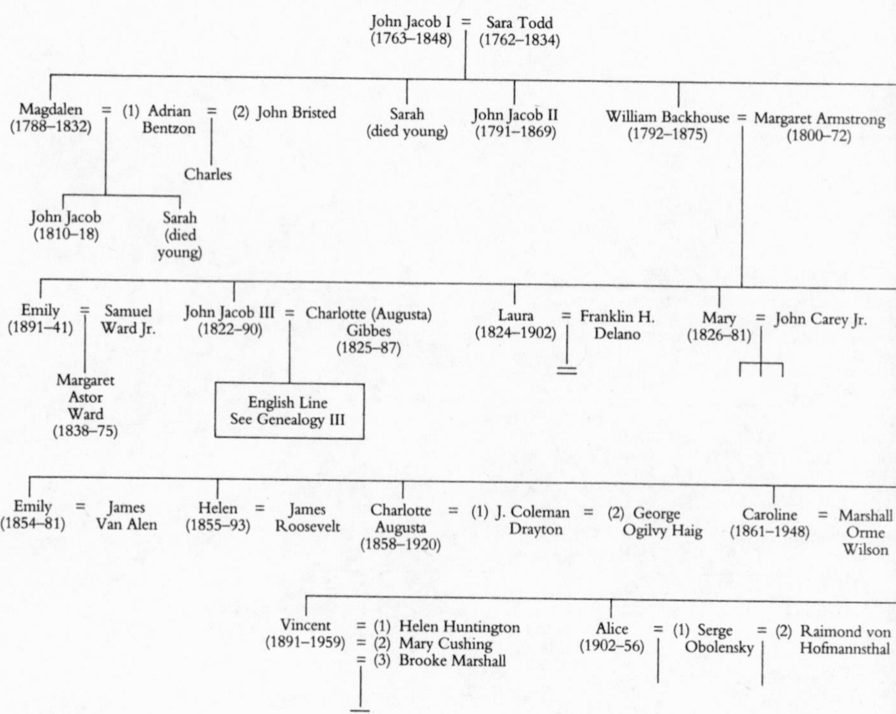

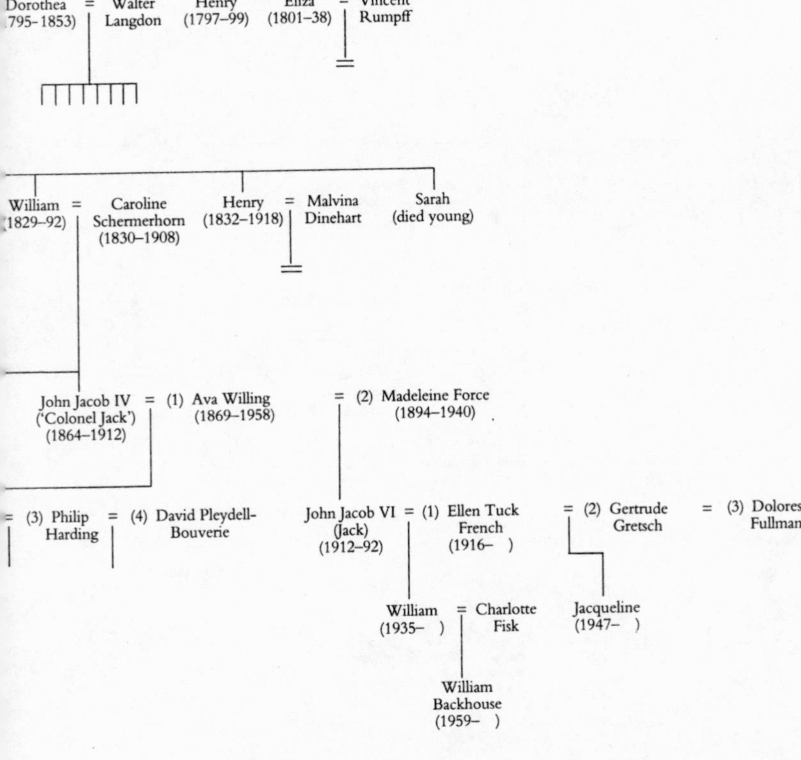
Dorothea = Walter Langdon
795–1853)
Henry (1797–99)
Eliza = Vincent Rumpff
(1801–38)
William = Caroline Schermerhorn
(1829–92)
(1830–1908)
Henry = Malvina Dinehart
(1832–1918)
Sarah (died young)
John Jacob IV ('Colonel Jack') (1864–1912)
= (1) Ava Willing (1869–1958)
= (2) Madeleine Force (1894–1940)
= (3) Philip Harding
= (4) David Pleydell-Bouverie
John Jacob VI (Jack) (1912–92)
= (1) Ellen Tuck French (1916–)
= (2) Gertrude Gretsch
= (3) Dolores Fullman
William (1935–)
= Charlotte Fisk
Jacqueline (1947–)
William Backhouse (1959–)

Selective Astor Genealogy III
The English Astors
From 1848

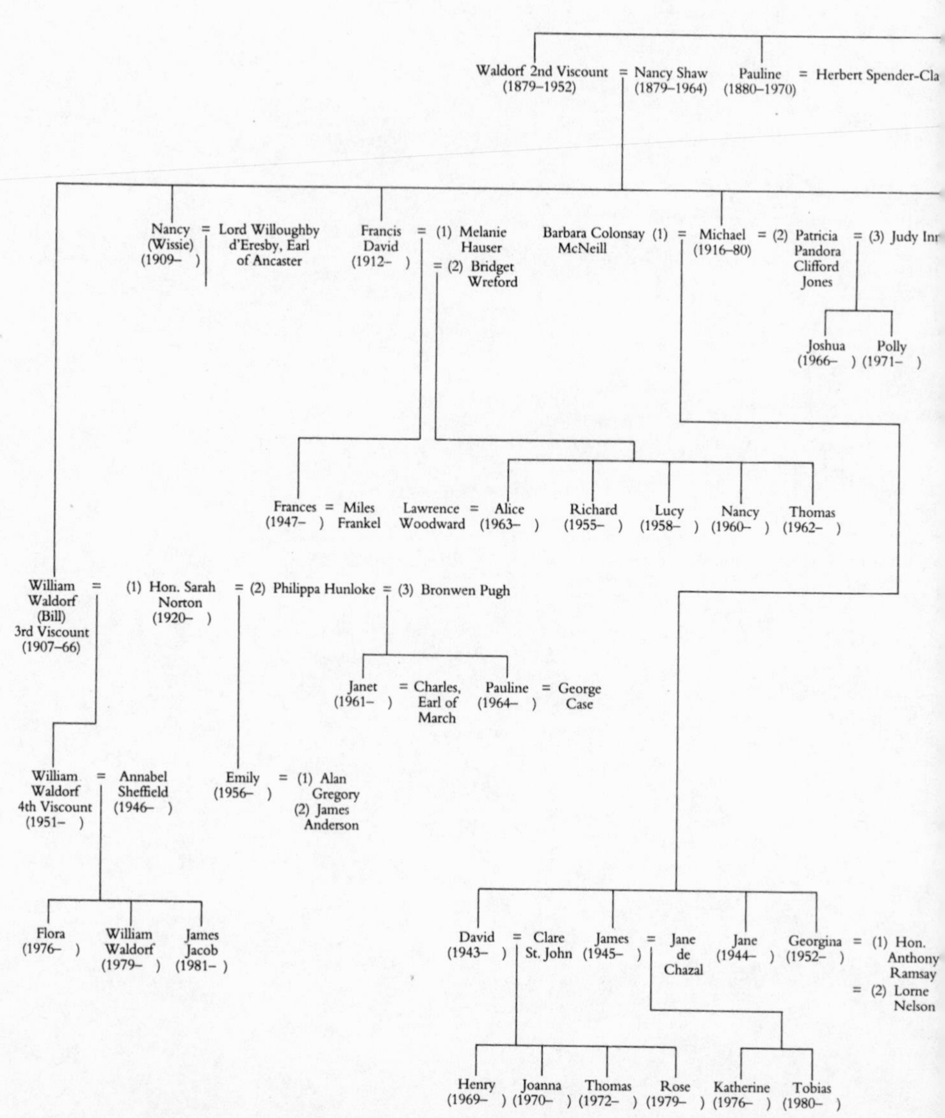

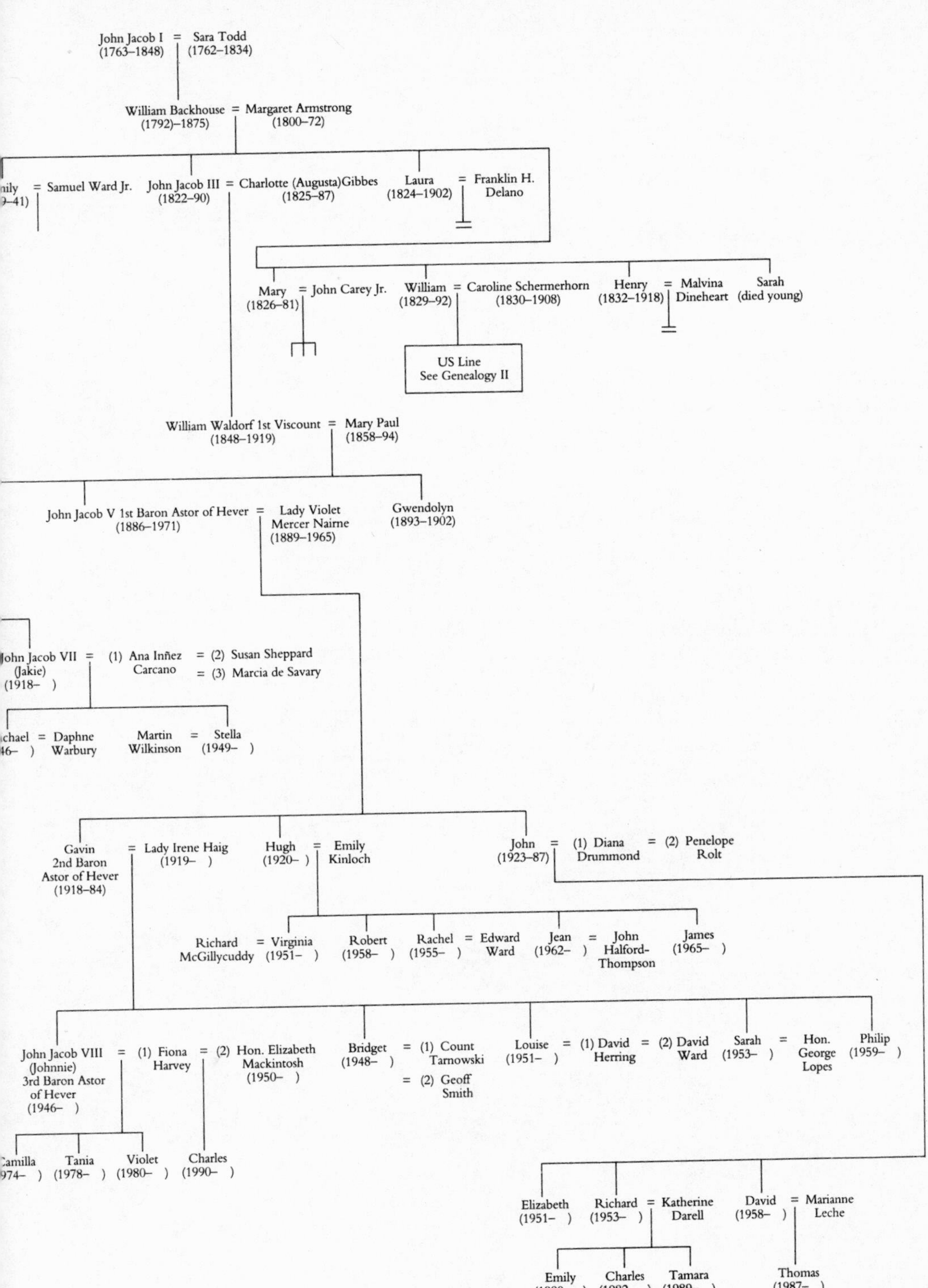

John Jacob I = Sara Todd
(1763–1848) (1762–1834)
William Backhouse = Margaret Armstrong
(1792)–1875) (1800–72)
nily = Samuel Ward Jr.
)–41)
John Jacob III = Charlotte (Augusta)Gibbes
(1822–90) (1825–87)
Laura = Franklin H. Delano
(1824–1902)
Mary = John Carey Jr.
(1826–81)
William = Caroline Schermerhorn
(1829–92) (1830–1908)
Henry = Malvina Dineheart
(1832–1918)
Sarah
(died young)
US Line
See Genealogy II
William Waldorf 1st Viscount = Mary Paul
(1848–1919) (1858–94)
John Jacob V 1st Baron Astor of Hever = Lady Violet Mercer Nairne
(1886–1971) (1889–1965)
Gwendolyn
(1893–1902)
John Jacob VII = (1) Ana Inñez Carcano = (2) Susan Sheppard = (3) Marcia de Savary
(Jakie)
(1918–)
chael = Daphne Warbury
46–)
Martin Wilkinson = Stella
(1949–)
Gavin
2nd Baron
Astor of Hever
(1918–84)
= Lady Irene Haig
(1919–)
Hugh = Emily Kinloch
(1920–)
John = (1) Diana Drummond = (2) Penelope Rolt
(1923–87)
Richard McGillycuddy = Virginia
(1951–)
Robert
(1958–)
Rachel = Edward Ward
(1955–)
Jean = John Halford-Thompson
(1962–)
James
(1965–)
John Jacob VIII
(Johnnie)
3rd Baron Astor
of Hever
(1946–)
= (1) Fiona Harvey = (2) Hon. Elizabeth Mackintosh
(1950–)
Bridget = (1) Count Tarnowski = (2) Geoff Smith
(1948–)
Louise = (1) David Herring = (2) David Ward
(1951–)
Sarah = Hon. George Lopes
(1953–)
Philip
(1959–)
Camilla
974–)
Tania
(1978–)
Violet
(1980–)
Charles
(1990–)
Elizabeth
(1951–)
Richard = Katherine Darell
(1953–)
David = Marianne Leche
(1958–)
Emily
(1980–)
Charles
(1982–)
Tamara
(1989–)
Thomas
(1987–)

Introduction

There are a number of reasons why I should want to write and you might feel disposed to read an Astor family history. For many people wealth itself holds a fascination. It is intriguing and, perhaps, instructive to discover how a vast fortune was made, retained and spent, and to observe the good and ill effects of inherited riches. A moneyed dynasty inevitably produces more than its fair share of eccentric characters, for conformity is usually the child of economic constraint, and where such restriction is removed we are likely to encounter people like Henry, who floored one room of his house with silver dollars, or Alice, who believed herself to be the reincarnation of an ancient Egyptian princess. People like the Astors are different from most of us. Their lifestyle is fuller and more varied. Irrespective of their own talents, they mix freely with the great and are on familiar terms with the famous. And to this privileged world wealth is the passport. Yet of itself it does not entitle its holders to have their deeds recorded for posterity. There have been many thousands of very rich families whose quirks and achievements are of no interest to anyone outside the narrow circle of their descendants. Were the Astors to fall into this category you and I could spend our time more profitably than in studying their lives.

For the historian part of the challenge about the Astor chronicles is to eliminate the distortions of past scribes. The Astor story has often been told in terms of an extended gossip column, in which all that is noteworthy is scandal, outrageous expenditure, humorous anecdote and meaningless rows of noughts. Such accounts move from one 'memorable' episode to the next, regardless of authenticity. Perhaps the most notorious example of the uncritical retelling of tales is the one concerning Captain Kidd's treasure. In 1894, a certain Frederic L. Olmstead invented what he later referred to as a 'burlesque hoax'. He set forth in bogus detail an account of how one of John Jacob I's captains stumbled across the pirate's celebrated hoard on Gardiner's Island and how this became the basis of the Astor fortune. The fraud succeeded too well, perhaps because it was more romantic than the truth, or because it was easier to believe that John Jacob owed his wealth to serendipity rather than to industry, commercial expertise and good luck. By 1923, the myth had become such an embarrassment to its perpetrator that he decided to come clean. On 28 October, in the *New York World*, Olmstead described minutely how he and a few friends had devised the hoax. But you cannot keep a good story down. Nearly a century after its invention the Captain Kidd yarn is still retold, often with the suspicion that there could be 'something in it'. Similar embellishments to fact have been set forth to make characters and incidents conform to easily understood stereotypes. Thus one of the first 'biographies' of John Jacob I, in *Hunt's Merchant Magazine* of July 1840, determined to tell a rags-to-riches tale, depicted the young German taking a tearful farewell of his home town with his few worldly possessions wrapped in a bundle tied to a stick over his shoulder.

Other chroniclers have been inspired by quite opposite motives. Convinced that the Astors had made their money at the expense of slum tenants and the poorer citizens of New York, they accumulated an apocrypha of legends which displayed John Jacob I and his heirs as insensitive money-grubbers – and crass into the bargain. The diary of James Gallatin became a much-worked seam of disreputable detail. James was the son of Albert Gallatin, John Jacob I's great friend. His diary was published in 1914, a century after the events which it relates, by a descendant of the writer. The picture it gives of the middle-aged businessman is of a coarse, uncivilized boor who thought of nothing but money and whose manners were so deplorable that he could wipe his greasy fingers on the lace sleeves of a lady sitting next to him at dinner. Such, quite uncorroborated, slurs seemed to have unimpeachable provenance – until 1957. That was the year in which Raymond Walters subjected to close scrutiny *A Great Peace Maker, the Diary of James Gallatin, Secretary to Albert Gallatin* and revealed that not only was James a hostile witness, in that he despised his father's friend, but that large parts of the supposed diary were fabrications. This, however, has not stopped the colourful tales being retold. Faced with such accretions to the truth, the historian is called upon to be like a picture restorer, removing layers of over-painting and discoloured varnish so that characters and events can be seen in something approaching their original colours.

One result of this process is the regaining of some of the subtler hues. In traditional tellings of the Astor story certain characters and events stand out boldly while others have been lost in shadow. Thus we know a great deal about John Jacob, the 'founder of the fortune', Caroline, 'the queen of New York', and Nancy, 'the first lady MP'. Other individuals now emerge as equally fascinating. John Jacob's brother Henry was every bit as canny an entrepreneur as his more famous sibling. William Waldorf was an outstanding connoisseur and antiquarian. And Nancy's husband, Waldorf, far excelled her as a political analyst. Indeed, the man whom we shall see clearly in the following pages was almost prophetic in his grasp of the movement of national and international events. As a result of a fresh study of the archival material, and the work of other scholars, several new areas of Astor activity can now be seen properly for the first time. Among them are John Jacob I's travels in Europe in the 1820s and 1830s, Vincent's membership of F. D. Roosevelt's private intelligence service, the sad disintegration of Waldorf and Nancy's relationship after 1945, Bill's work on Lord Lytton's commission to Manchuria and a detailed assessment of his contribution to worldwide refugee relief.

It has been particularly important to try to show Bill, the third Viscount Astor, in his true colours. The world remembers him, if it remembers him at all, as the peer who got mixed up in the Profumo affair; but he was very much more. The sordid scandal of the sixties, which hastened his early death, cut short not only a life which had more than its fair share of sorrows, but also a notable career in public service. Thanks to the generous assistance of Bill's widow and his son, who have given me exclusive access to Bill's papers, the truth about his disastrous connection with Stephen Ward can now be told for the first time and set in the context of his other activities and friendships.

Context is everything. A shrub removed from the border may be admired for its brilliant blossoms or glistening foliage. Set back in place among its companions, its appearance changes radically as it enhances and is enhanced by the whole. That brings me to my main reason for undertaking the Astor story and also to the sub-title of this book. 'Landscape with Millionaires' has a double meaning. The first is quite literal. The Astors are a family who have left their mark upon the landscape. John Jacob I helped to shape Manhattan and gave Astoria, on the opposite seaboard, its *raison d'être*. John Jacob IV and William Waldorf provided New Yorkers with a new meaning for the word 'hotel'. Transferring his attention to Europe, William Waldorf created his own romantic fantasies at Hever, Temple Place and Sorrento. Waldorf pioneered the plans for a new city centre in Blitz-battered Plymouth. Yet even more important is the metaphorical connotation of 'Landscape with Millionaires'. From the close of the War of Independence to the ending of the Cold War, the Astors have been a transatlantic family. As relationships between Europe and the USA worsened, improved, changed and developed, they were at the heart of things. Astor boys studied in Germany. Astor girls married European noblemen and diplomats. The family tried to prevent America going to war with Britain in 1812 and encouraged her to open hostilities with Germany in 1917 and 1941. At home on both sides of the ocean, they frequently found themselves explaining the New World to the old and vice versa. They were evangelists for the special relationship, not only in good times but also in bad. Thus they were openly critical of America's lukewarm attitude towards the League of Nations and just as vigorously condemned the Anglo-French invasion of Egypt in 1956. They were very active figures in the changing landscape of international events – through their social contacts and marriages; through their diplomatic and political activity; through the columns of their newspapers. They helped to shape transatlantic relations and were shaped by them. In the last analysis, it is that which, in my view, makes the Astor story worth the telling.

This fresh recounting of the chronicles of Astor has only been possible because of the access I have enjoyed to several public and private archives. Some important primary sources have only become available in recent years. The New York Historical Society has microfilmed and catalogued the extensive Albert Gallatin Papers, which include a correspondence with John Jacob I spanning more than three decades. The New York Public Library's Monroe Papers contain informative letters between John Jacob and the president. The Library of Congress in Washington, DC, possesses a small deposit of letters written from William Waldorf Astor to Amy Richardson. Mrs Richardson was a chance acquaintance whom William Waldorf met on shipboard between Britain and America, yet it was to her that this strange man chose to pour out – in elegant prose – some of his deepest feelings. The House of Lords Archive contains material dealing with Waldorf's parliamentary career between 1908 and 1920. Most of Waldorf and Nancy's extensive papers are in the possession of Reading University Library. The West Devon Record Office houses valuable papers dealing principally with Waldorf and Nancy's Plymouth constituency. *The Times* Archives provided details of John Astor's proprietorship of the newspaper. The Scottish Record Office houses Lord Lothian's correspondence. To the staff of these and other archives acknowledged in the notes I am extremely grateful for their courteous assistance and for permission to quote from the documents in their care. My thanks are especially extended to Viscount Astor and Lord Astor of Hever for the rarely granted permission to research in their family archives.

Several members of the Astor family have helped me with my work. Viscount Astor, Lord Astor of Hever, Bronwen Viscountess Astor, the Hon. Hugh Astor, the Hon. David Astor, Major the Hon. Sir John Astor, the Marquess of Lansdowne, Lady Margaret Myddelton, Countess Colletti and others who have asked not to be acknowledged by name have given generously of their hospitality and time. While the judgements and opinions in the book remain mine, these members and friends of the family have helped me to avoid at least some gaffes.

The ready co-operation of so many people has made the researching and writing of this book a pleasure. I hope some of my enjoyment communicates itself. The only real reasons for reading a book are to be informed and entertained. I hope *Landscape with Millionaires* will perform for you this double function.

CHAPTER 1

'A never wavering confidence of signal success'

It was quite a party. The streets were decked with flags and crowded with people. The celebrations went on for three days. There was dancing, singing, displays of parachuting, swimming and fireworks, a concert, a fair and a pageant, church services, presentations and speeches, and a great deal of feasting and drinking. It was June 1988. The place was the small German town of Walldorf. The occasion was the twenty-fifth anniversary of the twinning of Walldorf with the city of Astoria on the Pacific coast of the United States of America. However, the principal guest of honour was neither German nor American. John Jacob Astor VIII, third Baron Hever, had come from the very English county of Kent. The communities in both Baden and Oregon had good reason to be grateful to Lord Astor's family; he and his ancestors over several generations had made generous benefactions to the two towns. For their part the members of the dynasty felt strong sentimental and historical attachments to these foreign locations, which were highly significant in building up one of the world's biggest private fortunes and in prospering a remarkable Anglo-American family. The saga of that family ran parallel to and formed a commentary upon the ever-changing chronicle of relations between the New World and the old from the War of Independence down to the ending of the Cold War. That is the saga on which we now embark.

If we say that the story has its beginnings in Walldorf, we immediately have to qualify that statement. When and where may a family be said to 'begin'? The answer must be, as far back as we can reliably trace it. Astor genealogists who wished to flatter their employer drew an extremely dubious line to a thirteenth-century Castilian grandee. More reliable research neither carries us so far back nor provides the Astors with such an impressive origin. Documentary evidence points us to the Italian town of Chiavenna, which lies at the foot of the Alps close to the Swiss border. In the seventeenth century it was an important staging post. Here goods were unloaded from waggons and packed on to mules for the journey through the Splügenpass. The religious wars which erupted in 1618 provoked fierce persecution, and in nearby Valtellina there was an appalling massacre of Protestants. This led to a hurried exodus from the district of several families who fled northwards to escape the fury of the Counter-Reformation. One such was the household of Giovan Pietro Astor, who arrived in Zurich in 1620. He settled in the city with his wife and two children, found work with the silk-maker Holzbalb, and changed his name to Hans Peter Astor. The family were still living in Switzerland in 1664 when Johann Jakob Astor, presumably a grandson of Hans Peter, was born. He moved to Nussloch in Baden, where he pursued the trade of tiler and was head of the Calvinist presbytery. He died there on 2 April 1711. The only child of Johann Jakob and his wife Anna Margaretha of whom we know anything was Felix, but here, at last, we are on firmer ground, for the records provide us with at least the bare bones of Felix's life. He moved to Walldorf, some thirty kilometres south of Heidelberg, in 1713 on his marriage to Eva Dorothea Freund, almost certainly because he came into property settled on his wife. He achieved the honoured position of churchwarden and died in 1765. He may also have been the 'Mr Astor' who owned the Lion Inn and who bought a vineyard in nearby Wiesloch.

From these meagre records the Astors emerge as enterprising members of the entrepreneurial class. They were men and women of some substance in the small community of Walldorf (about a thousand souls in the mid-eighteenth century). However, Felix's vineyard notwithstanding, they never quite made it into the landowning class. Their fortunes remained subject to the vagaries of trade and their own commercial skills. And their fertility. Felix married twice and sired twenty children. Whatever wealth he had amassed would have been spread very thinly among his progeny. They had to make their own way in the world. Most of them must have dispersed. One son, Georg Peter (1740–1802), certainly migrated to England to seek his fortune there. Another, Johann Jakob, stayed and became the town butcher of Walldorf, and struggled in his turn to bring up a large family on his profits from the sale of meat and skins.

The Europe within which this unremarkable domestic chronicle had its setting was a continent rippling with social and political disturbances and heading, unwittingly, towards a quarter of a century of revolution and war. Ordinary people were, to some extent at least, aware of the myriad dislocations in the politico-economic framework. Border disputes, trade disruption, minor wars had their effect at all social levels. The old idea that the inhabitants of the past were much more static than ourselves, that they lived, loved, worked and died in their own town or village and seldom travelled more than a few miles beyond its limits, is one which requires considerable qualification. We have already seen that it was not true of the Astors. It was not true of many in eighteenth-century Germany. The territory between France and Austria, the Alps and the Baltic was divided up into over three hundred principalities, duchies, free cities and estates constantly subject to change as a result of land deals, dynastic marriages and warfare. Even at the end of the century the population had not fully recovered numerically from the devastations of the Thirty Years War which had ended in 1648. Peasants, merchants and craftsmen might go about their daily lives largely oblivious of shifting political realities, but there was, nevertheless, an undercurrent of instability which could tug at family and local bonds and weaken the sense of identity.

Baden, in the extreme south-west, was a long strip of territory bordering the Rhine between Mannheim and the Swiss border. From the mid-sixteenth century it had been divided into two states. Their separation was more than political: Baden-Baden was Catholic, Baden-Durlach was Protestant. The two margraviates only came together again under one ruler in 1771. All this provided little incentive for the development of commerce and industry, and Baden was in the doldrums economically.

If the state was a backwater, little Walldorf was a stagnant pond. There was not much employment to be had locally, and it is not, therefore, surprising that, as the butcher's sons grew to maturity, they one by one left home in search of a better future. Three of them proved to be enterprising and skilful entrepreneurs. The eldest, George, migrated to England. For most young Europeans wishing to improve their lot this was the land of promise. Generally speaking, wages were higher than on the Continent. The Industrial Revolution was under way. Farming techniques were being improved. In both town and country a large, wealthy élite was emerging and demanding an ever-widening variety of luxuries, amenities and services. There was, therefore, steadily increasing scope for men with skills and ingenuity. From Holland, France, Germany and farther afield they came, drawn by the magnet of opportunity.

No fashionable home was complete without at least one keyboard instrument, and John Broadwood, of Messrs Tschudi and Broadwood of Great Pulteney Street, was the most famous English manufacturer. He was also a leading developer of new and improved pianoforte actions. In connection with this side of his work, he brought over a number of German craftsmen. One of these was young George's uncle, Georg Peter Astor, and it was he who found an opening for his nephew. Young George was evidently musical and a gifted craftsman and seems to have done well in the busy workshop. But he was also ambitious, and it was not long before the young man wanted to branch out on his own. In 1777 he borrowed fifty gulden from Dr Nebel, one of Walldorf's wealthier citizens (the loan was not completely repaid until 1822), and set out to make his own way in the vigorous London music scene, dominated then by such figures as J.C. Bach and Thomas Arne. He understood the market for musical instruments and had met some of Mr Broadwood's fashionable clientele. His resources would not stretch to setting up a keyboard workshop, but he could, he believed, make a start as a flute maker. He was soon doing sufficiently well to contemplate matrimony. He wooed a young girl called Elizabeth Wright. Because she was below the age of consent, her father had to agree to their union. The fact that he did so suggests that George was not regarded as a 'penniless foreigner'. The wedding took place in the church of St George the Martyr, Queen Street, on 9 November 1779.

The most adventurous of the older Astor boys was the second son, Henry. He fetched up in distant New York, and thus walked straight into a war. Britain's American colonies had just begun (in 1775) their struggle for independence, so the New World was scarcely the most obvious place for a young man to go to make his fortune. Perhaps he was an idealist. In the 1770s Europe was buzzing with new political theories. *Ancien régime* France, already agitated by the first tremors of unrest, was just across the Rhine from Walldorf. It is unlikely that a butcher's boy would have heard much about the revolutionary theories advocated by Jean-Jacques Rousseau and other radicals, though he may have had friends at the university in nearby Heidelberg. But he would certainly have known about the brave colonists, for their defiance was the *cause célèbre* of the day. Like most men throughout continental Europe, he probably sided with the rebels. Whatever his motives, at the age of twenty-one Henry Astor set out to cross the Atlantic. He travelled in a British naval vessel, the captured French frigate *Belle Poule*, in a non-combatant capacity, as assistant to one of the officers. At journey's end, he decamped. Whether this had been his intention all along, or whether he simply tired of shipboard life and the jibes of rough British sailors, we do not know. What matters is that he quickly established himself in his adopted land. He stuck to the trade he knew, and by 1777 he was running his own butchery, dealing in meat, hides and skins.

Meanwhile in little Walldorf life followed its humdrum routine. Old Johann Jakob had five surviving children by his first wife, Maria, and four by his second, Christina. He had two older boys still at home in 1775, Melchior (sixteen) and John Jacob. Born on 17 July 1763, the latter was destined to become the most famous member of the family and one of the most famous men in the world. But there was no hint of future greatness as the teenage boy grew up with his father and stepmother and the annually increasing tally of brothers and sisters in the cottage attached to the slaughterhouse and the shop. He passed through early adolescence with the smell of blood and sawdust in his nostrils, the squeals of animals and children in his ears. And at fourteen (in 1777) he became a man. He was confirmed in the local Lutheran church. He left the village school but stayed in Walldorf, to help his father and brother in the family trade – skinning animals, jointing carcasses, serving customers and delivering orders.

It was not a very congenial life, and the occasional letters telling of the successful exploits of his brothers living abroad can have done nothing to calm John Jacob's restless spirit. He yearned to follow their example. After little more than a year at his father's shop counter he made the break. It is at this point that the romantic stories about him really begin. The 'rags-to-riches' legend demands that the hopeful teenager should have left home with 'only the clothes he stood up in'. One such account confidently, and totally without authority, informs us that 'It was on a warm Spring day in 1779 that young John Jacob left Walldorf, the equivalent of two dollars in his pocket and a bundle of clothes slung from a stick across his shoulder, his eyes blurred with tears.' The author details the sorrowful farewells, the young man's striding out along the dusty highway and his pausing at the first hilltop, 'whence he might see the red tiles of the village roofs gleaming amongst the trees, wiping his eyes dry, and . . . making three resolutions: To be honest, to be industrious, and not to gamble.'[1] The more prosaic truth is that his going to London was something of an accident.

George was prospering and he needed help with his flute-making business. He was also in a position to assure his father that the prospects for one of his younger brothers in Britain were excellent. But he did not have John Jacob in mind. He proposed that Melchior should come over to help in his new venture. But Melchior could not or would not leave home. Either he was not interested or his father could not spare him from the business. For whatever reason, it was decided that fifteen-year-old John Jacob should go to London and be taken into partnership by George. The lad was eager to grab the opportunity, and his father probably concluded that, with George and his wife, Elizabeth, to look after him, he would be safe enough in a foreign land. To complete the story of the brothers, we should record that, five years later, Melchior left home to join a community of the evangelistic Moravian church at Neuwied, near Koblenz, where he is variously reported to have lived by farming and by managing the community schools.

In 1778 the firm of George and John Astor began trading at 26 Wych Street, off Drury Lane, in the heart of London's fashionable quarter. They made wooden flutes and other wind instruments, gradually widening their range as business developed. The partnership remained in being for five years. During that time the younger brother grew to manhood, learned the basics of business practice and became fluent in English, though to the end of his days he spoke it with a heavy, guttural accent and wrote the language less than perfectly. Instrument-making seems to have been reasonably profitable.

The number of Astor flutes, clarinets and oboes which have survived suggests that the products of the brothers' workshop were eagerly sought after. John Jacob proved to be a born salesman, and George was an intelligent entrepreneur whose business expanded and diversified over the years. But in 1783 the brothers amicably parted company. The reason was that John Jacob was strongly drawn to America.

Meanwhile, across the Atlantic the war raged fiercely. News (always several weeks out of date) arrived in batches and told a confused story of the progress of hostilities. The turning point had come about the time of John Jacob's emigration to England. In 1778 France entered the war on the side of the colonists. Succoured by his new allies on land and at sea, General George Washington's resistance to Britain's veteran troops was strengthened. But the result of the war was by no means a foregone conclusion, and in London those who read the newspapers were regaled with bewildering information of victories and defeats. Even the surrender of Cornwallis at Yorktown, in November 1781, did not establish the outcome of the conflict. Almost two years of negotiations followed before a formal peace treaty laid out the boundaries of the new nation on 3 September 1783. But more interesting to John Jacob than war news were the letters from Henry which indicated that he was prospering and that there were, in the new nation, unprecedented openings for industrious and ambitious young men. His American brother urged young John Jacob to come over and try his luck. It is no coincidence that, within weeks of the signing of the Treaty of Paris, John Jacob Astor embarked on a ship for the infant republic.

A whole new nation had come into existence, bounded by the Atlantic, the Mississippi, the Great Lakes and Spanish Florida. It was a country the size of Germany, France, Spain and Britain rolled into one. Most of it was unexplored and, as yet, untenanted by white men. There was commerce to be established, a new society to be structured. And the men who would do it would be the settler families already dwelling along the eastern seaboard and the immigrants hastening thither by the shipload. They were freemen all, whose connections in the Old World (or lack of connections) counted for little. What mattered were personal initiative, industry, ingenuity – and sufficient working capital to get a man started.

It was no mere starry-eyed enthusiasm which prompted John Jacob's dramatic move. Astor's subsequent career shows him to have possessed two balancing qualities – a soaring imagination and a restraining prudence. As he prepared for his migration and discussed it with George, he must have calculated carefully the opportunities awaiting in the new nation. Now that the struggle for freedom was behind them, the ex-colonists would be cultivating the arts of peace and civilization. That would mean, among other things, that they would want musical instruments. John Jacob knew about the music trade. Moreover, thanks to brother Henry, he was sure of a secure base in New York. Therefore, if he crossed the ocean with a small consignment of flutes and tried his luck at selling them, he would certainly not be burning his bridges behind him. And, of course, he always had another string to his bow. At the age of twenty, John Jacob was master of two trades. If the music business failed, there was always butchery; flutes were a luxury but people always needed meat, leather and furs.

John Jacob left for America as an entrepreneur in his own right. He took a selection of Astor instruments (legend says five guineas' worth), but he was not, as has been previously assumed, simply setting up an overseas branch of the London firm. The partnership was dissolved and George reverted to trading under his own name.[2] The young man set off fully independent. With his own slender resources he booked a cheap passage aboard the *North Carolina* or *Carolina*, which weighed anchor for America in late November 1783. So impatient was he to be away that he took a winter passage to Baltimore, although his eventual destination was New York. This was in the hope of avoiding the pack ice which clogged up the more northerly ports in January.

A cheap passage aboard an emigrant ship was not a pleasant experience. Conditions may not have been as bad in the early period as they were in the migration boom years half a century later (in 1847, 100,000 emigrants set sail for New York; 17,000 died at sea, most of them from disease) but Astor's five guineas bought a cramped berth, meagre fare and minimal privacy. His voyage was prolonged and rendered still more uncomfortable by bad weather. The ship was four months at sea and, because of an unusually severe winter, did not avoid the pack ice. She ended up held fast in the frozen waters of Chesapeake Bay. But John Jacob was a healthy young man and able to withstand better than most the rigours of life on board ship. Indeed, in February and March 1784, when other passengers chose to leave the vessel and complete their journey across the ice, he elected to stay behind. After all, the shipping company were obliged to provide his bed and board until the end of the voyage, whereas, once ashore, he would have to fend for himself. Not until 24 or 25 March, when there was still no sign of an imminent thaw, did he make his way over frozen Chesapeake Bay to the thriving port town of Baltimore.

After a brief stay, Astor completed his journey to New York and sought out his brother. Henry was hard-working and ambitious but his means were still very modest. He had recently advanced from a wheel-barrow to a horse and cart for deliveries, and about this time he acquired the added responsibility of a wife. If the records are correct, the bride was still in her early teens, and the marriage appears to have been a purely commercial arrangement.

Dorothea was the stepdaughter of another German immigrant butcher, John Pessinger, who was much better established than his son-in-law. He had reached the status of being a stall-holder in the busy Fly Market, close to the waterfront. Having no sons of his own to inherit his business, he was happy to bring into the family a fellow-countryman who was showing great promise in the trade. If John Jacob needed an object lesson in shrewdness and opportunism, brother Henry certainly provided it. Marrying into the family of a senior member of the craft was his first step up the ladder of success. Within a few years he had his own stall in nearby Maiden Lane. In no time at all, he was doing a roaring trade, presumably by undercutting the competition – so much so that there were complaints about the throng of his customers blocking the thoroughfare. Further evidence of Henry's business enterprise comes from a petition presented to the Common Council in 1801. It is a complaint that 'Henry Astor and certain others who are licensed butchers, leaving their stalls and the selling of their meats to journeymen who are not licensed butchers, are in the constant practice of forestalling the market by riding into the country to meet the droves of cattle coming to the New York markets, and purchasing cattle for other stalls besides his own'.[3] However, in 1783 when his brother called upon him, Henry was still in a modest way of business. His accommodation was apparently too restricted to permit space for a lodger, so John Jacob was found digs with a nearby friend, the baker George Dieterich.

Those first few years in New York were a time of 'testing the water'.

When Astor became the richest man in America people, inevitably, wanted to know the 'secret' of his success. All manner of stories about his early business life were in circulation and were confidently written into books and articles about him. They could not all be right, because they could not be made to fit into a coherent timetable of John Jacob's first years in New York. Their existence and the paucity of hard documentary evidence bedevil any attempts to chronicle accurately the start of Astor's commercial career. Perhaps all that we really need to know is that John Jacob was a natural entrepreneur. He could sell anything. Therefore, all he had to do was discover, through his growing circle of acquaintances on the waterfront and in the city's business houses, just what would sell most profitably. The legends of his peddling imported trinkets in the streets, working for a fur merchant and operating as an independent trader of musical items need not unduly bother us. Doubtless there is some truth in all of them. Astor was nothing if not an opportunist, and he used every means that came to hand to build up his working capital.

It took him only a matter of months to dispose of his original stock-in-trade. In a remarkably short space of time he was able to return to London to accumulate a new consignment of goods specifically chosen for the New

York market. It was much more ambitious than his original box of flutes. By 22 May 1786 he was back to inform readers of the *New York Packet* that he had imported from London

An elegant assortment of Musical Instruments, such as piano fortes, spinnets, piano forte guittars, the best of violins, German flutes, clarinets, hautboys, fifes, the best Roman violin strings, and all other kinds of strings, music books and paper, and every other article in the musical line, which he will dispose of on very low terms for cash.[4]

Clearly, John Jacob was not just buying from Wych Street. He was making use of George's contacts with other manufacturers to provide his customers with a very varied stock of instruments. Within the space of little more than two years this thrusting young immigrant had built up a business capable of rivalling that of New York's two established music dealers, Messrs Dodd and Wilks of 66 and 235 Queen Street respectively. The profit margin on instruments was huge. A new fashionable élite was emerging which demanded all the luxurious trappings of sophisticated European society. In the fullness of time the new nation would have its own craftsmen, able to meet this demand, but in the fledgling years goods from the ateliers of the Old World had a considerable cachet – and therefore commanded a high price. And yet John Jacob was soon to forsake this trade for another, even more profitable, one.

Astor's musical emporium was established, like those of his rivals, in Queen Street. Number 81 was the home of Mrs Sarah Todd, a widow of modest means. This brings us to another important strand in the young immigrant's life. Astor had made the acquaintance of the Todd family soon after his arrival in New York, and on 19 September 1785 he was married to the youngest member of the household, also named Sarah. There was a considerable degree of calculation about marriages in those days, and the young John Jacob was a particularly calculating man. Whatever his feelings were towards the young lady, who was slightly older than himself, she possessed at least three other attractions. Her family had strong maritime connections: her brother, Adam, was a captain and the family had married relations in the ship-owning community. Mrs Todd was also acquainted with several of the leading members of New York society, which was obviously advantageous to the sort of business in which her son-in-law was involved. Thirdly, Sarah brought with her a dowry of $300, which was invaluable in setting up and stocking the new shop. She became a useful junior partner who, in addition to bringing up her family, was fully conversant with the day-to-day running of the business. Sarah thus had plenty to keep her occupied, and she had a wide circle of relatives and friends to fulfil her social needs. It was just as well, for she was destined to see little of her husband during the forty-nine years of their married life. John Jacob travelled widely in America and made several trips to Europe. In later years he sometimes took one or more of his children with him, but Sarah, it seems, never accompanied him on his travels.

Mrs Astor was, in fact, soon running the shop herself. Her husband had already discovered a potentially more profitable merchandise to which he increasingly gave more of his time. Like musical instruments, this other commodity was one of which he had a good basic understanding. His early years in the butcher's shop had made him adept at skinning animals and taught him something of the curing and marketing of hides and furs. He now added to this knowledge by working, possibly on a casual basis, for some of the city's established furriers.

Legends abound explaining how John Jacob got into the fur trade. According to one, the young Astor spent much time during his 1783 crossing deep in converse with Jonas (or Hans) Gollow, a fellow traveller. Gollow was a retired furrier on his way to visit his three sons who had emigrated to New York, and he was able to explain in detail how the lucrative trade worked. Such stories may or may not be true. We may be sure John Jacob picked up useful information wherever he could find it. But he needed no special sources of intelligence about the fur business. He spent most of his life on the waterfront. He knew how valuable this commodity was, and that there were considerable profits to be made from it once one could establish oneself. Rare animal skins are historically on a par with gold, ivory, spices and other precious commodities. They have always been sought after by the wealthier classes in the civilized world. In England, for example, the wearing of sable and ermine had, since the Middle Ages, been a privilege reserved for royal and noble families, and other furs also conveyed status on their owners. At the same time the hunting and trapping of animals for their pelts required courage, skill and endurance and took men into the remoter regions of the northern hemisphere. Fur trading, therefore, was doubly romantic: it was a hazardous, adventurous occupation, and it brought great financial rewards.

The wealth obtainable from the acquisition of animal skins had been the chief commercial reason for the opening up of North America. The French were the pioneers. Operating out of Quebec and Montreal, merchants built up a highly profitable trade with the Indians who arrived at the trading posts every spring, their canoes laden with pelts, which they exchanged for knives, pots, blankets, liquor and imported trinkets. At the end of the Seven Years War, in 1762, the French lost control of Canada, and this fabulous trade fell into British hands. Life along the fur trails had the rough-and-ready character of any frontier situation – white men, Indians and half-castes cheating, fighting and outwitting one another in uncontrolled competition. Not until around the time of Astor's arrival in New York did the leading merchants in

Canada get together to regularize commercial procedures. They formed the North West Company, which soon monopolized the trade north and east of the Great Lakes. There, they rapidly evolved a class system as rigidly graded as the social hierarchies of the Old World. The trappers – European adventurers and half-castes – were hard men, used to living in the wild and enjoying a precarious symbiosis with the Indians. The depots were staffed by clerks and merchants – men with a practical education and a grasp of figures, men who understood market forces and considered themselves the guardians of the frontiers of civilization, ambitious men who looked for better things in the service of the company. At the top of the socio-economic pyramid were the partners, who presided over their wealthy commerce from warehouses in Montreal. They were the aristocrats of the fur trade. Here is how Washington Irving describes their journey to the annual meeting with their up-country representatives at Fort William:

> They ascended the rivers in great state, like sovereigns making a progress: or rather like highland chieftains navigating their subject lakes. They were wrapped in rich furs, their huge canoes freighted with every convenience and luxury and manned by Canadian voyageurs, as obedient as highland clansmen. They carried up with them cooks, and bakers, together with delicacies of every kind and abundance of choice wines for the banquets which attended this great convocation. Happy were they, too, if they could meet with some distinguished stranger, above all some titled member of the British nobility, to accompany them on this stately occasion, and grace their high solemnities.[5]

While the North West Company was establishing its control north of the lakes, vast tracts of unexplored territory to the south were just waiting to be exploited. Another band of merchants, the Mackinaw Company, was not slow in setting up trade in this virgin land. From their entrepôt at Michilimackinac on the straits between Lake Huron and Lake Michigan the Mackinaw traders made their way along the network of rivers feeding the Wabash, Ohio and Mississippi.

The hinterland of the confederated American States was thus dominated by agents of the old enemy, Britain. Its commercial avenues led northwards into Canada. The ex-colonists benefited little from the prosperity generated beyond the frontier. The trading concerns operating through the east coast ports were, by comparison, small. Indians exchanged furs for everyday commodities in backwoods stores from which the furs were bought by dealers from the cities. Some trappers came down to the docks in New York to barter their wares directly with American merchants or with ships' captains. Established furriers did send their representatives on forays into the interior, but for serious trading they were dependent on the Montreal market. This had the additional disadvantage that direct transit of goods from Canada to the United States was prohibited by the British government, so that consignments for New York had to be routed via London. The American legislators resented the fact that the lion's share of the fur business was diverted from their territory but, in the absence of any determined national consortium, they had to accept the realities of the situation.

One advantage of the loosely structured mercantile system was that small businessmen could share in it. This is precisely what John Jacob Astor did. On 23 October 1788 his occasional newspaper advertisement of musical instruments carried the additional information:

> He gives cash for all kinds of Furs; and has for sale a quantity of Canada Furs, such as beaver, beaver coating; raccoon skins, raccoon blankets, and spring musk rat skins; which he sells by large or small quantities – a considerable allowance will be made to every person who buys a quantity.[6]

Astor was an impatient young man. He could see the immense profits which could be made from the fur trade – as much as 1,000 per cent by buying from Indian trappers and selling in Europe. The only problem that held him back from making a quick fortune was lack of capital. In the early days, Henry lent him money. The brothers were very close and frequently gave one another practical help. In January 1792, for example, when Henry was out of town his sibling successfully represented him before the commissioners of the almshouse when they met to decide on awarding the meat concession for the institution. John Jacob employed whatever cash he could spare to buy pelts on the waterfront. He made forays into the remoter regions of New York State to obtain them from rural trading posts. He acquired them across the counter at 81 Queen Street. But this was all exceedingly small beer. The fragmentary documents covering Astor's early business dealings hint at brief partnerships with established furriers and attempts to raise capital for major deals. In his impatience to get on he sometimes put severe strains on his relationship with Henry. An often-told story relates how young John Jacob tried his elder brother's patience with frequent requests for loans. At last, Henry, well on the way to becoming a 'solid' member of the mercantile community, delivered a strong lecture. He warned his headstrong sibling about what happened to businessmen who tried to run before they could walk, and ended up by making a proposition. He would not advance John Jacob another penny. What he would do was give him $100 on the strict understanding that John Jacob never again approached him for money.

Yet, somehow, this 'aspiring spirit that always looked upward' (as Washington Irving labelled him) had scraped together sufficient capital by 1787 – a mere two years after opening his shop – to make the journey to Montreal and buy a major consignment of furs. It was the first of many such visits.

The Canadian fur capital had been an important goal ever since he began in the business. His forays into the interior took him northwards along the Hudson Valley towards the territory of the North West Company. They were hard journeys. By day he drove his waggon through swamps and along forest trails. By night he slept beneath the stars. At each stopping place he not only had to gauge the quality of the pelts on offer and bargain hard for them, he had to beat and bale the evil-smelling skins and often carry heavy bags on his back for several miles. He may well have felt that his profit was well earned. It would make much better commercial sense to press on to the border, do business with the sophisticated Canadian merchants and buy furs already expertly dressed and bundled ready for export. The only obstacle was cash and, by 1787, he had overcome that particular hurdle. He made what was to become the first of several annual visits to Montreal. Every summer, in late June or July, he set off northwards from New York, along the Hudson and the shore of Lake Champlain, trading all the way. He reached Montreal in August, stayed for several weeks, retraced his steps in the autumn and reached home in late October or early November.

With various members of the North West Company he regularly concluded deals running into thousands of dollars. The 'secret' of this rapid advancement is no secret. John Jacob achieved his success by applying the prosaic virtues of frugality, thrift and industry. He and Sarah lived simply and worked long hours. Astor frequently spoke of his wife as a business partner and acknowledged that, when it came to gauging the quality of pelts, she was a better judge than himself. The couple worked hard, John Jacob occasionally finding employment with other furriers to gain both extra capital and experience, and ploughed every penny back into stock.

Astor expanded his business interests rapidly, hungrily, in every possible direction, making the most of whatever opportunities presented themselves. By the end of the decade he was regularly shipping barrels of furs back and forth across the Atlantic (in compliance with British regulations), largely in association with Thomas Backhouse and Co. of London. He was importing an ever-widening range of general trade goods. He was making annual forays into upstate New York and had established his own depot at Schenectady on the Mohawk River, twenty miles above its confluence with the Hudson. Here he was often to be seen, sleeves rolled up, beating, cleaning and packing furs in person. And he had begun to speculate in real estate.

It was his brother, and not John Jacob, who was the pioneer in this aspect of fortune-building. Henry worked hard at his butcher's trade and prospered. He and his wife lived simply. The years of their youth slipped past and Dorothea produced no children. With little to spend his profits on, Henry's capital began to build up very satisfactorily. He could have increased the size of his business, but that would have entailed even more work and, with no sons to inherit, may well have seemed rather pointless. New York lacked the financial institutions which managed cash in Old World capitals. Banking was in its infancy (the First Bank of the United States came into being in 1791, but there was much political disagreement as to its future and its relationship with private banks), and the New York Stock Exchange did not establish its tentative beginnings until 1792. Anyway, there was an easier and more productive way of putting spare cash to work. It was obvious to anyone with an eye for a bargain.

New York was a boom town. As well as being an important port and commercial centre, it was the state capital until 1797 (when the legislature moved to Albany), and from 1785 to 1790 it was also the federal capital (the Congress met in City Hall before removing to Philadelphia in the latter year). For a few years New York was the heart of the nation upon which the arteries and veins of its political, social and mercantile life centred. In 1786 the population was 23,614. By the end of the century it had more than doubled to 60,489. Steadily the city limits advanced over the farms and wasteland of Lower Manhattan. Henry Astor could not miss the chance of buying in on the ground floor.

As early as the 1780s he bought his own house at 31 Bowery Lane and began acquiring adjacent properties. Over the years he accumulated a considerable amount of real estate on the east side of town. On 18 May 1789 he sold on to his brother two lots and four half-lots near the junction of Bowery Lane and Elizabeth Street for £250. Perhaps he was trying to steer young John Jacob into a safer form of speculation than furs. If so, he was only partially successful. Unlike cautious, solid-citizen Henry, John Jacob had little interest at this stage in sinking money in land. Fur trading demanded maximum liquidity and most of his cash was tied up in stock. Although he was, by now, buying and selling a wide range of merchandise, he had to watch turnover very carefully. Bearing in mind the immense real estate fortune he later built up, it is tempting to see this initial purchase as proof of great commercial vision. The truth is more prosaic and more revealing. Manhattan property speculation was, indeed, his first foray into long-term trading, and, within the next couple of years, John Jacob did lay out nearly $7,000 for plots concentrated in two outlying areas. But he was initially looking for short-term profit from rising land values. In this he was not very successful. Some parcels of land which he sold had not shown a marked increase in value. On others he had to be content with the rents he collected from his tenants (mostly farmers). But the bug had bitten and John Jacob's appetite for real estate soon took him beyond the bounds of his adopted city. In 1792 we find him bidding for land in Lower Canada. Since the war with the American colonies there had been a steady flow of British immigrants as well as Loyalists from south of the border. The Crown now made available large tracts of virgin territory for settlement. Once again, the prospects for increasing land values looked excellent and Astor, though not a British subject, applied for 1,200 acres. In the event, bureaucratic complications deterred him from proceeding with the purchase, but the aborted negotiations show clearly which way Astor's mind was working.

In the midst of this real estate dealing John Jacob bought a property for himself. The accommodation in Queen Street was very cramped. It had served well enough for a young childless couple, and the shop premises had been adequate for the Astors' modest stock-in-trade in the early days. But now both business and family were growing. Magdalen was born in 1788; 1790 saw the birth and early death of a second daughter; the following year Sarah was pregnant again. So the couple moved to 40 Little Dock Street. The new premises still served a double function, so that Sarah and the children had to live over the store. But the accommodation for both family and goods was much more spacious and reflected the status of 'Astor, John J., fur trader', as he now appeared in the city directory.

In the small world of New York business and fashion the young German with the rough manner and Midas touch now counted for something. He was not greatly given to parties, balls, theatre outings and lavish dinners. For her part, Sarah was a serious, religious woman with even less taste for such frivolities. But they appeared at functions where convention or business required their presence. John Jacob became a Freemason and this ensured regular contact with many of New York's leading citizens. In 1793 he thought it not inappropriate to have his portrait painted by the fashionable Gilbert Stuart.

Stuart had just returned to his native America after a chequered career in fashionable London and Dublin society. He worked for a year in New York before moving to Philadelphia, the cultural capital of the new union. In both cities the social élite and the aspiring élite flocked to his studio, and Stuart soon became the leading American portraitist of his day. Most members of fashionable society were delighted to possess the status symbol of their image captured for posterity by the man who had numbered several of the English nobility and gentry among his clients. But Stuart's satisfied customers did *not* include the thirty-one-year-old John Jacob Astor. When his portrait was delivered, Astor took one look at it and sent it back. He demanded a new painting at no extra cost.

The accomplished artist read his sitter well – perhaps too well.

Dealing with all manner of men from Indians and rough trappers to wealthy businessmen and government officials had developed resilience, resolution and a thick skin. Astor had acquired the reputation of being a hard and canny negotiator; a man not to be shifted once he had named his price; a man careful to tie up every creditor securely with legal cords while avoiding, whenever possible, putting his own obligations in writing. Everyone who had commercial dealings with John Jacob learned to accord him great respect. Few, it seems, felt any affection for him. He was naturally extrovert and could be amiable, charming, generous. But his was a calculated geniality. Unable to lay out his money without carefully reckoning the return it would bring, he became unable to give himself in acts of disinterested love and friendship.

All this came out in Stuart's first portrait, which gives the viewer a distinctly uncomfortable feeling. The subject is shown half-length in a seated but restless pose. The hands, loosely clasped in Astor's lap, seem impatient to be otherwise occupied. The eyes look shrewdly, almost calculatingly, out on the world and avoid the viewer's direct gaze. The thin lips lack any trace of humour.

Stuart knew better than to argue with his patron. If he wanted payment he would have to produce a picture more to Mr Astor's taste. The second attempt apparently satisfied John Jacob, but it is hard for us to believe that it is a representation of the same man. Perhaps we might imagine it having been executed a few years later when age and experience had mellowed the sitter. In this head-and-shoulders study the face is fuller, the eyes less hooded, the expression, openly directed at the viewer, is one of smiling candour.

Which was the true John Jacob Astor I? When he died, fifty-four years later, few tears were shed and the *New York Herald* described the multi-millionaire as 'a self-invented money-making machine'.[7] On the other hand Washington Irving, the 'father of American literature', regarded Astor as a generous friend, a man of 'persevering industry, rigid economy and strict integrity', possessed of 'an aspiring spirit that always looked upward, a genius bold, fertile and expansive, a sagacity quick to grasp and convert every circumstance to its advantage, and a singular and never wavering confidence of signal success'.[8] Success draws its admirers and its detractors.

CHAPTER 2

'A grand and beneficial stroke of genius'

During the months when John Jacob was making the first tentative moves in the New York property market, an American whaling captain, Daniel Greene, became the first citizen of his country to circumnavigate the globe. The connection between these two events is not immediately obvious. The link can be defined in one word: Canton.

The great eighteenth-century surge of maritime exploration which had led to the discovery of Australia, New Zealand and most of the islands of the Pacific inevitably quickened the interest of the western mercantile community. The opening up of new, fast sea routes to south-east Asia, the new-found lands and the Pacific seaboards of Russia and North America meant that merchants and captains were soon seeking out new commercial opportunities. Intrepid mariners braved the Horn, the Roaring Forties and the Antarctic pack-ice in search of whale oil and sealskins. Others ventured to the new Russian colonies round Kamchatka, traded with Amerindians for furs and with the Chinese for silks, tea and porcelain. The key to successful enterprise in these waters was Canton.

The introspective Chinese empire permitted one point of contact only with the outside world. This had been the situation since the sixteenth century. First the Portuguese had obtained a toehold at Macao, then the British, French, Dutch and Russians had set up factories (or *hongs*) along the mouth of the Xijiang, the river leading to Canton. The trade had consisted of exchanging gold bullion, manufactured goods and textiles for highly prized Chinese luxury items. But merchants were always looking for other commodities with which to tempt their Asian counterparts. This is what makes Captain Greene's visit to Canton significant. He completed a highly profitable voyage by trading for China wares with Cantonese merchants in exchange for sealskins.

Greene did not discover the Chinese demand for furs; these had long constituted a valued import. But only in the closing years of the eighteenth century did foreign merchants find means of supplying the Canton market with pelts in bulk. One method was the hazardous one of plundering the seal colonies in the high southern latitudes. But the Russians had established a direct commerce by setting up trading posts on the coast and islands of Alaska (then known as Russian America) and conveying furs from there to China. Yet the most popular means of exploiting this market, and the one favoured by Europe's leading maritime nations, was the triangular trade: cheap goods from Europe to the Pacific coast of North America, where they traded with the Indians in exchange for furs. These in turn were conveyed to Canton, whence the merchantmen returned laden with tea, silks, and so on. Such voyages, when safely concluded, showed an immense profit. Now, into this complex system, a new mercantile nation entered, a nation rich in its own native furs. It was inconceivable that one of the United States' leading furriers would not soon be drawn into the Cantonese trade.

Astor was a master of what today would be called lateral thinking. He had established a reputation as a leading dealer in furs and skins. No one knew the business better (sometimes even customs officers called on his expertise for valuing consignments of pelts), but that did not mean that he was *only* a fur dealer. He had already diversified into land. He kept up his music business. In 1795 he was back in London, partly to order fresh musical stock, some of it custom-built:

14 March 1795

City Coffee House, Cheapside

To Messrs J. Broadwood

Gentlemen, Please to make me one of the best grand pianofortes you can. I rely on your honors to let it be a good one. I wish to have it plain in every respect and the case of hornbeam wood. The pedals may be screwed fast when done. Call on Mr George Astor for the payment. I shall wish to have it shipped in July or August by the ship *Hope* for New York or any other good ship, to be sent John J. Astor.

I am, Gentlemen, with respects, Yours

John Jacob Astor[1]

Whether this fine instrument was to adorn his own home or that of an affluent customer is not known.

In addition to what had become traditional Astor commerce, John Jacob was constantly expanding the range of his general imports. In the closing years of the century, for example, he emerged as a substantial arms dealer. On 12 November 1799, he could offer his customers:

22 tons London Patent Shot, 5 Musquet and Cannon Powder, 2,000 lb Refined Salt Petre, 500 Musquets with Bayonets, 200 Pistols, for ships use, 5 pair double fortified 6-pounders with Carriages, Shot, Spunges, etc – complete, 5 pair double fortified 4-pounders . . .[2]

It would be interesting to know who was buying ordnance and small arms from John Jacob. These were, of course, turbulent times for the young nation, especially for those Americans who were settling the frontier. But such pioneers can scarcely have had much use for minor artillery pieces. The clue may be in the phrase describing pistols as 'for ships use'. The small-bore cannon also suggest naval armament.

If this assumption is correct, Astor had perceived another important market. After the War of Independence, Congress had decided that there was no call for a standing navy, but the troubled times soon proved this to be a mistaken policy. Barbary corsairs inflicted severe damage on American ships in the Mediterranean. During the Revolutionary and Napoleonic wars rival fleets patrolled the Atlantic. They were not noted for respecting the flags of neutral nations, nor were the pirates and privateers who prowled from their Caribbean bases. In 1794 the United States began building warships, and four years later the government set up a navy board. In this climate captains and owners were especially conscious about the security of their vessels at sea and there was a brisk trade in small arms and naval artillery.

Trouble on the transatlantic routes may have been a contributing factor in directing Astor's attention increasingly to the Orient, but it would only have been a marginal consideration. What drew him irresistibly to Canton was the high profit margin on China goods. A dramatic change had already come over his fur business. In 1796, by the terms of Jay's Treaty, restrictions on direct trade between Canada and the USA were lifted, and John Jacob could now bring large consignments of pelts from Montreal to New York without the delay and expense of having to route them via London. From that moment no American furrier was better placed to take advantage of the lucrative China trade – and lucrative it certainly was. Tea, for example, was both expensive and popular (protests at the duty on tea had, after all, been one of the sparks that ignited the revolt of the colonists). At $1.50–$2 (depending on quality), a pound of tea was about the same price as a man's shirt and much more costly than sugar (16 cents), rice (7 cents), tobacco (15 cents) or salt ($4 a barrel). The low cost price at Canton made possible a huge mark-up.

Yet he eased his way into the trade carefully. He bought consignments of tea and silk from other merchants. He discussed the workings of the Canton market with captains on the waterfront, and particularly, perhaps, with his kinsman by marriage, Stewart Dean, who had been one of the first American captains to visit the Xijiang River. When unemployed at sea, Dean sometimes acted as an agent for Astor and certainly represented the merchant at Albany, a staging post on the route to Montreal. When, in 1800, John Jacob was ready for his first large orient venture, Dean was master of the ship which carried his cargo. Astor and three other New York merchants fitted out the *Severn* with furs, textiles, cochineal and ginseng. She sailed in the spring and was back just over a year later with silks, satins, nankeens, taffetas, Souchong teas, fans, nutmegs, cloves, porcelain and other exotic goods which the owners disposed of to New York retailers or re-exported to Europe. Other ventures followed. By May 1804 Astor was the sole owner of the *Severn*, and two other vessels, the *Beaver* and the *Magdalen*, were being built to his specification.

Now one of the most substantial merchants in New York, Astor no longer lived over the shop. His business premises moved several times in response to the scale of his activities and, in 1803, he took up residence in a fashionable town house at 223 Broadway. By this time the family was complete. Of the eight children born to Sarah, five survived infancy. That was about par for the course in well-to-do households of the time. Sadly, such documents as have survived allow us very few glimpses of the Astors' home life. There may not have been much of it. John Jacob's annual business trips, the long hours he spent at his desk, the evenings passed in the company of merchants, mariners, politicians and other 'useful' acquaintances, and his periodic trips to England left him little time to spend with Sarah and the children.

Among John Jacob's 'useful acquaintances' one name stands out well above the rest. Albert Gallatin became a firm, lifelong friend, achieved high government office and was one of the leading diplomats of the age. He was two years John Jacob's senior. He came from a distinguished Genevan family, migrated to America in 1780, made an unsuccessful foray into business, and then took to a political career. In 1795 he was elected to the House of Representatives, which for most of the next five years met in Philadelphia. Thomas Jefferson appointed him Secretary to the Treasury in 1801 and he remained in that post until 1814 (by which time James Madison was President), wrestling with the economy of the expanding nation and trying hard to keep it out of expensive foreign entanglements. Gallatin was one of the most honest, conscientious and clear-thinking political figures of his day. Despite the many financial offers and temptations that came his way, he maintained an unsullied reputation, often remarking that it would be unseemly for someone in his position to die a wealthy man. Gallatin had his share of enemies, but none of them ever accused him of corruption.

John Jacob and Albert met in the early 1790s, long before either had risen to prominence, and forged a friendship which only grew stronger the more widely their paths diverged. They met through their maritime friends, the Nicholsons. John Jacob had many dealings with 'Commodore' James Nicholson, who had extensive interests in commerce and shipping. Around 1795 Albert began courting Nicholson's daughter, Hannah. Gallatin had been married before, shortly after his arrival in America, but his first wife had fallen ill and died suddenly within months of the wedding. His second marriage, to Hannah, was destined to be long and happy. The Gallatins and Astors lived close together in New York until Albert's removal to Philadelphia, and the children of the two families frequently played together. The correspondence between the two men begins after the relocation of the capital in 1800, and early letters are full of personal and domestic references: John Jacob has made a fur tippet for Hannah; little John was sorry Albert Gallatin Jr had not come up to New York for some sledging, etc. When Gallatin received his Treasury appointment and was known to be intimate with the thrusting and successful furrier this 'inevitably set a-wagging the tongues of people inclined to imagine and believe the worst',[3] but Albert was scrupulous in guarding government secrets and his honesty was one of the traits John Jacob most admired in him. Hannah seems to have been less enthusiastic about the Astors than her husband. Her elder son, James, was, in later years, quite rude about the Astors, whom he regarded as mere 'German tradespeople'. But nothing ever disturbed the mutual regard in which the two men held each other, and their extant correspondence, spanning over thirty years, provides a fascinating view of both domestic and political life in the early years of the nation.

In later years John Jacob observed, 'My life's purpose is fulfilled when I see my children happy.' If we were to take him literally at his own valuation we would have to conclude that he was a failure. With one exception, his sons and daughters grew up to experience few periods of real 'happiness'. They wanted for little in material terms, but they lacked a father's hand in their upbringing and they had no grandfather to provide them with the role model of a 'normal' patriarch. Thanks to her Scottish Calvinist upbringing, Sarah was strict with the children, but her efforts were often spoiled by her husband who, in his rare moments with them, tended to be sentimentally indulgent.

Fate also intervened cruelly among those destined to inherit the vast Astor fortune. It was the boys for whom the Astor inheritance proved most tragic. John Jacob intended to pass on his wealth to future generations. He knew that a fortune without a future was futile. He did not want to see all the effort which had gone into building up his various enterprises dissipated on worthless sons-in-law. Therefore the birth of his first son, in 1791, was an occasion of great jubilation. The infant, confidently christened John Jacob Jr, would be the heir of the Astor commercial empire. Such hopes were very soon dashed, for it became clear that the baby was mentally defective. He did not respond to various stimuli, but lay inert for long periods with seemingly unseeing eyes. Medical knowledge at the time (and Astor could and did afford the best) was unable to diagnose or treat the condition. It is impossible, now, to know whether the affliction was hereditary or caused by problems during pregnancy or delivery. All that is clear is that, as the child grew up, he alternated between phases of lucidity and complete torpor. (The irony is that, while three of his siblings died in infancy, John Jacob II outlived almost all his generation, dying, still insane, at the ripe old age of seventy-eight.)

All was not lost. Sarah was still under thirty and there might yet be more sons. In fact, William Backhouse (named after one of Astor's close trading associates) was born little more than a year after his unfortunate brother. How anxiously his parents must have surveyed his early progress. How relieved they must have been when the child appeared to be, in all respects, normal. John Jacob had to wait another five years for his third son, but Henry was not destined to carry the family name and prosperity into the future. A letter dated 7 December 1799, in John Jacob's poor written English (it improved considerably over the years), gives us one of our few sightings of him as father at this time:

> Dear Peter
>
> I Recie' Severel Letters from you that of the 11 ulto is the Last you might well esspected Some from me for you ought to have had tham but youil esuse me when I tell you that on my Return from Canada I found my famely at Albany and my 3 Childrin Ill one of whom I Lost a fine Little boy 23 Months old Died 14 Days ago in this Situation I could not think mush of business ...[4]

The entire weight of John Jacob's plans and expectations thus devolved upon the shoulders of William Backhouse. Whether the responsibility stifled him or whether he would not have amounted to much anyway is difficult to say. The only clear fact is that by the time he reached maturity the guardian of the Astor millions was almost totally devoid of personality and character.

The three girls were the only ones with any sparkle. John Jacob certainly enjoyed their company. As they grew into rather plain teenagers he adopted the habit of taking one or other of them on his journeys. He liked showing them off and sometimes he needed a consort at dinner parties, banquets and balls arranged by his business associates. We must assume that Sarah either had no taste for the peripatetic life or could not be spared from the nursery and the counting house. Two of her daughters inherited John Jacob's determination and strength of personality. Magdalen doted on her father and was proud of his wealth and success. He, for his part, was over-indulgent. As a result, Magdalen grew into a spoiled and unhappy woman (though, in fairness, it must be acknowledged that personal tragedies shadowed her life). Dorothea went the other way. 'Fat Dolly', as someone unkindly dubbed her, felt the need to escape from her parents' control. At the age of seventeen she did this with a vengeance (see below p. 34). Eliza, the youngest (born in 1801), inherited her mother's gentle and pious nature. She was loved and admired by all who knew her but sadly did not live long enough to fulfil her early promise.

Meanwhile Astor's orient trade grew and diversified. If we take just one voyage we shall see how extensive his international contacts were becoming. In May 1805 the *Beaver* left on her maiden voyage carrying a cargo of which the most valuable item was $62,000 in bullion. The only furs carried were a few hundred otter, sea otter and fox pelts. This uncharacteristically small consignment probably reflects Astor's readiness to adapt quickly to the mercurial situation at Canton. With western merchants vying with each other to do business, the requirements of the indigenous market altered from month to month and the most successful traders were those who could anticipate changes in demand and correctly read the whims of their oriental opposite numbers. Clearly, in 1805 the primary need was for gold. In the spring Astor advertised his desire to buy Spanish dollars in order to make up a large consignment of specie. The other items in the cargo were ginseng, brandy, madeira and quicksilver. The *Beaver* reached Canton on 18 September, began her return journey on 4 December and docked in her home port on 26 March 1806. Within a few weeks Astor had transshipped a large part of the cargo: 298 chests and 50 half-chests of tea and 190 bales of nankeens were directed to Baltimore; 50 bales of nankeens were sent to Tenerife. On the following 7 January Astor dispatched a similar batch of silks to Livorno, but this was destined never to reach the consignee. On 14 March the vessel carrying Astor's goods was intercepted and seized by a French man-of-war.[5]

Trade with Europe had now become extremely hazardous. As Britain emerged as France's only remaining unconquered and determined enemy a state of total war developed between the two nations. Having failed, in 1805, to batter his island foes into submission, Napoleon resolved to starve them out. In 1806 he imposed his Continental System, theoretically closing to British ships all ports from the Mediterranean to the Baltic. His Britannic Majesty's government countered by declaring their own blockade of all harbours participating in this system. Both sides issued warnings to neutral nations that any trade carried on with the enemy would be regarded as collaboration. Nor was it only Astor's trade with Europe which was disrupted by the distant war; two of his vessels were boarded and searched by British naval personnel in Canton. Worse was to follow. President Jefferson, incensed by the way peaceful American shipping was being harassed, decided to retaliate. His somewhat dog-in-the-manger response was to forbid his own citizens to trade with *any* foreign port.

Soon, every waterfront along the east coast was littered with idle shipping, out-of-work mariners, and frustrated merchants and shipowners. John Jacob was furious. He took the embargo almost as a personal affront. Every story told about Astor, true or apocryphal, shows him as a man who was determined to get his own way, who seldom backed down and who enjoyed a battle of wits, whether it was over a big land deal or the modest equipping of a ship. Take, for example, the dispute he had with one of his best captains, either John Cowman or Frederick De Peyster. The insurance company insisted that his vessel must be fitted with a chronometer at a cost of $500. When the master put this to Astor, John Jacob told him bluntly that such expenditure was the responsibility of the captain, not the owner. The mariner, not unnaturally, disagreed. Neither man would yield and the captain eventually resigned. With some difficulty Astor found a replacement and the ship duly left for Canton. The disgruntled master obtained another command on the China run and, by dint of superior seamanship, brought his vessel back to port only one week after Astor's ship. John Jacob had not yet unloaded his tea because he was waiting for an upturn in the market. His rival showed no such restraint. He discharged his cargo at the best price available, thus flooding the market and cutting still further the value of Astor's tea. Next time master and merchant came face to face on the quayside, John Jacob admitted, 'I should have paid for that chronometer.' It was the nearest he came to an apology, though the story concludes with the captain rejoining Astor's employ.[6] This was one of the rare occasions on which John Jacob's 'take it or leave it' attitude rebounded.

Intransigence based on the power of wealth was all very well when Astor was dealing with employees and commercial rivals. It counted for nothing when he found himself up against the high-principled resolve of the philosopher-President. So John Jacob decided to play upon Jefferson's humanity and fair-mindedness. The result was the celebrated 'mandarin' episode. Astor set it in motion with the collaboration of a Chinese friend and the gullibility of a US Senator. On 12 July 1808, the latter, Samuel Latham, wrote a letter to the President.

> Punqua Wingchong, a Chinese merchant, will be the bearer of this note of introduction. He came to New York about nine months ago, on business of a commercial nature, and has resided during that time, partly here and partly in Nantuck[et. H]aving completed the object of his visit to the [Unit]ed States, he is desirous of returning to Canton, where the affairs of his family and particularly the funeral obsequies of his grandfather, require his solemn attention.
>
> This stranger is represented to me as a man of respectability and good standing in his own Country; and is consequently intitled to a corresponding regard and treatment in ours.
>
> The chief object of his visit to Washington is to sollicit the means of departure, in some way or other, to China; but he feels at the same time a strong desire to see the Chief executive officer of the United States . . .[7]

Jefferson, who had already left the capital for his estate at Monticello, did not meet Punqua Wingchong, but he was touched by the letter and another from the 'mandarin' in person which were sent to him. He saw distinct diplomatic advantages in acceding to the request of what he supposed to be a high-born Cantonese, and he gave written permission for Punqua Wingchong to commission a vessel at New York for his homeward voyage. Needless to say, the ship selected was one of Astor's, the *Beaver*. When it departed on 17 August its hold was not, of course, empty. Despite letters of protest from his competitors, who pointed out that the 'mandarin' was a mere waterfront coolie, John Jacob's vessel was the only one allowed to break the embargo, giving him a temporary monopoly in the China trade. Legend has it that his profit on the round trip exceeded $200,000. It was one more proof of the old maxim that an ordinary man's problem is an extraordinary man's opportunity. But for Astor such a victory could only be symbolic. The trade disruptions of these years were extremely frustrating. This was probably when he resolved to execute a grandiose scheme he had long been contemplating.

What Astor planned was to bring the greater part of the North American fur trade under his own personal control by setting up a chain of posts right across the continent. The lynchpin of this enterprise would be a depot near the Pacific coast on the lower reaches of the Columbia River. It would be named Astoria. The project was not original. Alexander Mackenzie of the North West Company had explored direct routes across Canada in 1789 and 1793 and had urged the British government to set up a chain of posts, but such grandiose visions were regarded in London as unnecessary and expensive. Astor, of course, knew of these schemes, but not until 1806 did he realize that the plan could be amended to create a trade trail across the continent *south* of Canadian territory. The concept was breathtaking in its scope, for it took every aspect of the existing American fur trade and carried it through to its logical conclusion. It would end the monopoly of the Canadian companies in the vast unoccupied lands to the west; it would free Astor from interference by his own and other governments; and it would provide him with a Pacific base for direct trade with Canton.

Commercial activity along the western seaboard was by now very well established and vigorous. Several western nations were involved, but the main rivals were the Russians and a number of Boston-based Americans. The latter sent their captains direct to the west coast, either via the Horn or the longer Cape of Good Hope route, carrying trade goods for the Indians. They spent the summer months on the California coast, gradually working their way farther and farther northwards. If they could not accumulate a full cargo of pelts in one season they would winter at Hawaii. This arrangement had advantages for both sides. Kamehameha I was in the process of extending his power and he did so with the indispensable aid of the white men. In 1782 he ascended the throne of one of Hawaii's four kingdoms. By 1810 he was master of all the islands and he had achieved this by buying firearms from the European traders. He gave in exchange the sweet-smelling sandalwood in which his territory abounded and which was highly prized in Canton. Two seasons on the American coast were usually sufficient for gathering enough furs. Then the ships made their way to China and returned to their home port laden with luxury goods. One of these Bostonian captains, Robert Gray, had, in 1792, discovered and named the Columbia River, and it was on the lower reaches of this waterway that Astor planned to set up his great outpost.

The Russians had not been idle while all this was going on. The pressures of foreign competition and rivalries between their own merchants led them to set up the Russian-American Company in 1799. In 1804 the company made its main base at New Archangel (modern Sitka) on Baranof Island, close to the 57°N parallel. The settlement grew rapidly into a flourishing commercial and even an industrial centre. Ships operated northwards and southwards from New Archangel, and the company claimed a monopoly of fur trading over an unspecified stretch of coastline. But the Russians were never in a position to exclude competitors totally from their preserves, because they were dependent on the ships of other nations for their supplies. Regular succour from their own Baltic ports (ice-bound throughout the winter) was impossible, and attempts to set up agricultural colonies on the Californian coast failed. Therefore there grew up between the inhabitants of New Archangel and the crews of visiting foreign ships a love–hate relationship. Each resented the other's presence but, at the same time, relied upon it.

Of course, the white visitors were not the only active partners in the fur trade. The Europeans were involved with indigenous peoples whom they found unpredictable and difficult to understand (if, indeed, they ever tried to understand them). Failure of communication meant that a group would sometimes be friendly and at other times hostile. Certainly when it came to trade the Amerindians were far from being simpletons. They had had years and, in some cases, centuries to adjust themselves to the needs of the white man. Spaniards had been trading along the Californian coast since the mid-1500s, and by the end of the eighteenth century foreigners had penetrated most of the larger bays, inlets and islands well into the higher latitudes. In 1791, for example, the Frenchman Etienne Marchand had visited Queen Charlotte Islands and found the people extremely experienced in bartering furs for European goods. They knew precisely what they wanted. They were not fobbed off with decorative items and cheap trinkets; they would only accept utilitarian metalware – pots, pans, tools and weapons. They were prepared to haggle for hours and, if one of their number concluded a particularly advantageous deal, his colleagues would immediately engage him to treat on their behalf.

The seaward approach was therefore well established, but what about the more than 3,000 miles which any land expedition would have to cross? The basic answer is that attitudes to the vast tract of unexplored territory to the west were changing rapidly as the new century got under way. Nothing indicates this more clearly than the terminology used. What used to be called the 'back-country' was now the 'frontier', a movable and moving line of settlement, and there seemed to be no limit to the area which could be carved out for habitation. By 1803 only half of the territory between the east coast and the Mississippi had been occupied, yet in that year the remarkable Louisiana Purchase doubled the size of the nation. It was in 1803 also that Jefferson projected a trans-continental expedition to discover the potential of the areas still farther west for agriculture, industry and commerce. The result was the famous journey (1804–6) of Meriwether Lewis and William Clark up the Missouri, across the continental divide, and down the Columbia.

John Jacob Astor was among the thousands of excited Americans who read the reports of the explorers' activities after their return in September 1806. Within months he was engaged in confidential discussions with government officials about the possibility of setting up a commercial enterprise to be called the American Fur Company which would establish trading posts along the route staked out by Lewis and Clark. It is clear that he dressed up his proposal in patriotic language for the consumption of the politicians. The activities of the company would ensure that the American hinterland would be exploited by Americans and not foreigners. It would expedite the settlement of the interior and the west coast. It would open up avenues of commerce for other entrepreneurs to travel. The President and his advisers were impressed. Years later Jefferson recalled:

> I considered as a great public acquisition the commencement of a settlement on that point of the Western Coast of America, and looked forward with gratification to the time when its descendants should have spread themselves thro' the whole length of that coast, covering it with free and independent Americans, unconnected with us but by the ties of blood and interest, and enjoying like us the rights of self government.[8]

It would be pleasant to believe that Astor was truly inspired by altruism and patriotic idealism in submitting his ideas to government. The facts, however, do not support such an interpretation. What he was trying to obtain was commercial concessions and even military protection for a private trading company. John Jacob actually made his specific applications relating to the American Fur Company at precisely the same time (the summer of 1808) that he was shamelessly hoodwinking the President in the 'mandarin' episode. He outlined an elaborate scheme covering the rights and duties of the shareholders when it was his intention to be the sole proprietor. The American Fur Company, which was incorporated in 1810, had a board of directors entirely made up of Astor's nominees. Two years later he bought out the Mackinaw Company, merging it with his own in a new entity known as the South West Company. Had these arrangements come to fruition, all the assets of the Mackinaw Company would have passed into his hands. He would have owned a large concern rivalling the splendid North West Company. He would, in fact, have been the undisputed king of the North American fur trade.

As to the development of Astoria into a dominant base on the west coast, that, too, was in the founder's mind from the outset. The project came under the auspices of the Pacific Fur Company, set up in 1810. Astor now had three corporate entities covering his fur business, in each of which he was the major shareholder. There seems little doubt that his ultimate objective was to merge the other concerns with the American Fur Company and to buy out most of his colleagues, thus setting up a gigantic, continent-spanning monopoly. Bold though the plan was, Astor prepared the ground with his usual caution and care. One plank in his platform was a diplomatic approach to the Russians. The newly arrived consul-general, Andrej Daschkov, was under instruction from his government to make strong representations about the behaviour of US citizens on the north-west coast. American fur traders had been selling guns to the Indians and seriously destabilizing the local situation. There was little the executive in Washington DC (which had become the federal capital in 1800) could do. Astor was quick to seize his opportunity. What government could not achieve, private enterprise could, he suggested. If the Russian-American Company and his own enterprise could reach an agreement as to trading rights, Astor's agents would regulate the conduct of American traders (by forcing out all competitors). What was more, Astor would guarantee regular deliveries of supplies to New Archangel by his own captains. Daschkov was impressed and provided for Astor's agents letters of introduction to Alexander Baranov, director of the Russian American Company at Archangel. But John Jacob wanted to buttress this loose arrangement with more impressive support. He needed someone to go to St Petersburg to gain official sanction from the tsarist government and from the principals of the Russian company. And he had the ideal emissary – his son-in-law.

In 1807, the British West Indian fleet took control of Danish colonies in the Virgin Islands to prevent them falling into French hands. The ousted governor of Santa Cruz, Adrian Bentzon, found himself in New York and out of a job. Within weeks his engagement to Magdalen Astor had been announced. The match had obvious advantages for both parties. Bentzon was marrying money, and the German immigrant's daughter achieved the respectability of being part of the international diplomatic community. The couple certainly did not delay; the wedding took place on 14 September 1807. Astor found his new son-in-law a valuable asset when it came to negotiating with government departments and the representatives of foreign nations. Specifically, he employed Bentzon in discussions with the Russian representatives in Washington. The Dane was the obvious person to be dispatched to St Petersburg.

Nothing could better illustrate the prominence Astor had by now achieved than the arrangements made for his envoy. The government was sending to Denmark an official delegation led by George Irving aboard the naval vessel *John Adams*. Astor made representations to his political friends, including the new President, James Madison. He pointed out how vital his projected expansion of the fur trade was to the national interest. He hinted at financial assistance to the government. The result was that he obtained a passage for Bentzon and his wife aboard the *John Adams*, which sailed on 21 January 1811. It seems likely that the couple also took with them their baby son, who was born in 1810 and christened John Jacob – some solace for the tragic disappointment of Astor's own elder son. Not only did Mr and Mrs Bentzon gain a passage on the official ship; they were also offered the best accommodation. The indignant George Irving was ordered to relinquish his cabin and was obliged to sleep on a sofa throughout the entire voyage.

The negotiations with Count Rumiantzov, Minister for Foreign Affairs and Commerce, and with the director of the Russian company proceeded satisfactorily. It was agreed that the two concerns would co-operate, respect each other's territory and support the monopolistic principle by excluding all others from the fur trade.

So much for the top-level preparations. John Jacob devoted just as much energy to exploring the commercial possibilities on the ground. In September 1809 he bought a fine two-year-old ship, the *Enterprise*, and on 15 November he dispatched her on a thirty-one-month voyage to the Pacific. She carried two of the most experienced men in the Canton trade. Her captain, John Ebbets, had made several expeditions to the north-west coast and was used to dealing with Baranov and the Russians. The ship's supercargo was none other than Daniel Greene, the mariner who had pioneered American commerce with China, knew well the stormy waters that thundered around the Horn and had plied often between Canton and Boston.

Ebbets's investigation of the commercial and political situation on the far side of the continent was thorough. He visited several Indian settlements; he made contact with some of the Spanish colonies in California; he entered the mouth of the Columbia and assessed the prospects for Astor's projected trading post. While engaging in lengthy discussions with Baranov at New Archangel he assessed the strengths and weaknesses of the Russians' position. But Baranov was no fool. He understood perfectly what his American rivals were trying to do. He knew that if they succeeded in establishing posts on the coast and in keeping them well supplied by sea and land it would only be a matter of time before they attempted to oust all competition. He therefore refused to endorse the long-term arrangements Astor was establishing at the diplomatic level. All he would do was make certain *ad hoc* trade agreements with Ebbets. He bought part of the cargo of supplies the *Enterprise* had brought from New York. He also asked Ebbets to sell for him in Canton $65,000 worth of furs on a commission basis. This was forced on him by a breakdown in relations between the Russian and Chinese governments which had temporarily closed Canton to ships from New Archangel. The *Enterprise* sailed to China and then returned to New Archangel, loaded a fresh supply of pelts bought from the Russian American Company, disposed of these, too, in Canton and finally embarked for home in January 1812. Ebbets was able not only to show his employer a handsome profit on the voyage, but also to provide detailed information on the workings of trans-Pacific commerce.

Some aspects of the grand Astoria project had thus progressed very favourably. They were the ones which the originator either presided over in person or delegated to well-chosen subordinates. Unfortunately, not all the men to whom he entrusted aspects of this ambitious enterprise were equal to the task. The good fortune which had graced so many Astor enterprises was about to change.

CHAPTER 3

'Would you have me . . . weep for what I cannot help?'

The years 1811–15 were not easy ones for John Jacob and his family – and 'family' extended far beyond his own offspring. He maintained contact with his relatives in Germany and England. They, for their part, were not slow to take advantage of his continuing concern. 'Uncle John Jacob' received many appeals for financial aid. As the years passed, a veritable flock of Astors settled in America, and most of them looked to the millionaire furrier to give them a start in life. We can trace at least eight siblings, half-siblings, nephews and nieces who moved to New York, most of whom married there to produce yet more family members with expectations of a share in John Jacob's bounty. This must often have been exasperating for the great man, who wanted to do his best for his kindred, without pampering them and certainly without encouraging spongers.

He provided for his father throughout a prolonged old age (Johann Jakob died in 1816 at the age of ninety-one). He felt a particularly strong affinity with his eldest brother. George had given him his start in life and he continued to do business with him. Poor George lacked either the entrepreneurial skills or the good luck of his American brothers. He was a good, honest craftsman, and after John Jacob's departure he combined with or employed other instrument makers, in order to extend the service on offer to his customers. He also brought in other financial partners and took every opportunity to expand. By 1796 he had premises at 79 Cornhill, in the heart of the City, and at 27 Tottenham Street. By this time Astor and Co. was producing not only a range of woodwind instruments, but also instruction manuals, sheet music and even pianos. The firm made a still more ambitious move in 1801 when it acquired a factory at Sun Street, Bishopsgate, and began building organs. George was trading regularly in America and, presumably at the instigation of his brothers, he sank some of his profits in Manhattan property. Subsequently he exchanged this with John Jacob for 10,000 acres of wild land in Canada. By 1880, when this property had passed down to George's only English descendant, Mabel Astor, it was worth the not inconsiderable sum of £4,000. But this nest egg seems to have been of little help to George. Though, to the casual observer, his business must have looked like a flourishing concern, George had run into difficulties, partly by expanding too fast and partly by accumulating bad debts. Some goods sent to America in 1812 were impounded when war broke out between the two countries. In these circumstances, George now looked to his younger brother and he did not look in vain. In 1813–14 alone John Jacob sent £3,000 to London. None of George Peter's sons entered the family business: either they lacked the inclination or Astor and Co. could not support them. Three of them, as we shall see, arrived on their uncle's doorstep, looking for jobs. At the end of 1813 George Peter died. His brother, naturally, wrote to express what were heartfelt condolences, but he also took the opportunity to give the widow some business advice. It would be as well, he suggested, to sell up the firm and realize what capital she could. Elizabeth declined. The doors of the shop in Cornhill remained open and she took on other partners. For some years the sign above read Astor and Horwood, and from 1824 to 1831 the firm traded as Gerock Astor and Co. It was presumably in the latter year that Elizabeth finally relinquished her interest. To the end of her days (she died in 1842) she received periodic and generous gifts from her brother-in-law.

Meanwhile, three of her sons, George junior, Benjamin and William, had all taken up residence in New York. William seems to have been the only one to have found a niche for himself without his uncle's financial underpinning. He made a living as a music teacher. Benjamin looked to find a place in the Astor empire but was adjudged by John Jacob to be lacking in talent. He worked for some years as a porter, and when he died several years later it was said that he left his wife penniless. John Jacob did, however, take the eldest nephew under his wing. George junior was estranged from his father, who specifically excluded him from his will. He set up his own business but this failed and, in 1813 his uncle gave him a job as one of his agents in Canada. By 1816 he had opened his own store, probably with family help, at 144 Water Street. He seems to have made a reasonable success of life in the twenty years remaining to him. Like many self-made men, Astor was ready to help relatives who were prepared to help themselves but would not indulge those who simply wanted to grow fat and indolent on his money. Apparently it did not worry him that other Astors were performing humble, even menial, tasks a few blocks from his own opulent residence. George Peter's remaining son, and the one he designated as his heir (having disinherited George), was Joseph. He remained in Britain and, perhaps because he refrained from seeking financial aid, John Jacob bestowed on him $50,000, some of which was for the education of his children. On the strength of this, Joseph was able to retire to St Helier, where he lived many years in comfort.

John Jacob was also prudently generous towards some of those who were less closely related to him. His sister Catherine and her husband, George Ehninger, settled first of all in New Jersey, where George pursued his career as a distiller. The couple soon discovered that there was no guarantee of success in America. In 1795 George was imprisoned for insolvency. He made a fresh start in New York (having probably been bailed out by his brother-in-law). But misfortune dogged him: the poor man died as the result of 'an accident caused while burning spirits'. The couple had one son, and John Jacob gave the boy, also christened George, a chance by sending him on voyages to Canton. Young George married the daughter of John Whetten, one of the Astor captains. His mother, meanwhile, married again and her husband, Michael Miller, continued the cordial distillery at 11 Barley Street (off Broadway). Catherine's son eventually joined him, and the family business continued until 1846. Elizabeth, John Jacob's half-sister, married John Gottlieb Wendell, one of Astor's employees. Wendell pleased John Jacob, and it was doubtless for this reason, rather than to satisfy Elizabeth, that he set up the couple in their own business, in which they prospered. In the early years of the nineteenth century there thus grew up in New York quite an Astor colony. Henry and Dorothea did not add to it, for they were childless, but they did send forth into the world a bevy of 'proxy-Astors'. It became their philanthropic habit to adopt young orphan girls, see them properly educated and brought up and then dower them handsomely on the occasion of their marriage.

As he entered his fiftieth year John Jacob was therefore the centre of one of New York's leading families. He was, by now, a millionaire, as was Henry (although by no means as rich as John Jacob), and one of the leading citizens. The name Astor ensured instant respect. People pointed to him and his relatives on the streets. In the privacy of their Broadway home the family experienced the joys and sorrows common to most households, but the consciousness of being celebrities somehow exaggerated them. It was difficult for them to keep their disputes, jealousies and tragedies to themselves. They became common property. For example, street urchins would climb the garden wall hoping to glimpse 'mad Mr Astor'. There were some pleasant, relaxed family occasions. Sarah and her daughters were never fashionable hostesses committed to the high society circuit and they were not admitted to the exclusive circle of 'old' families, but nor were they cut off from the world of fashionable New York. They enjoyed outings to the theatre (John Jacob was half-owner of the Park Theater on Broadway), and they sometimes had musical evenings at home at which they entertained one another or hired professional performers.

But it was not a happy family. All the children grew up with problems, the resolution of which was not helped by their high public profile. Magdalen was a termagant who made her husband's life a misery. In 1810 they had a son (John Jacob) on whom his grandfather doted. As we have seen, Magdalen and her husband, Adrian Bentzon, spent much of 1811–12 on a journey to Denmark and Russia. In 1813 the couple had a second child, a daughter named after her grandmother; unfortunately the baby survived only a few months. Perhaps the marriage was already showing signs of strain, for when, at the conclusion of the European peace, in 1815, Denmark's colonies were restored, Bentzon hurried to resume his former position in Santa Cruz. He did not take his wife and son with him. In effect he disappeared from their lives, only too pleased to have made good his escape from a difficult woman. In the West Indies he took up with another lady, made no attempt to conceal his adultery and cheerfully co-operated when Magdalen sought a divorce in 1819. Since divorce at that time was exceedingly rare, the case inevitably created a sensation. Thus, for a few years, John Jacob and Sarah had a very unhappy daughter back under their roof and had to endure the whisperings of neighbours and acquaintances.

Another daughter had already left home, under equally unhappy circumstances. In 1812, when Dorothea was seventeen, she was invited to stay in Washington with the family of her father's influential friend Albert Gallatin, Secretary of the US Treasury. There the impressionable girl met a dashing young soldier, Colonel Walter Langdon, who swept her off her feet. The gallant Gallatin was alarmed. Fearing that Langdon was a fortune hunter, he urged John Jacob to come and fetch his daughter home – but it was too late. The couple eloped and were wed. Dorothea's parents were, naturally, distraught, and John Jacob lost no time in disinheriting his daughter. It may be that this was the making of the marriage. The young people had forsaken all for love and had to work at their relationship without the enervating comfort of Astor wealth. They had thirty-five years of happiness and raised eight children. Of course, in time, John Jacob was reconciled to the match. He set the Langdons up with a fine town house, a country estate and enough money to enjoy both.

As to the Astor boys, John Jacob Jr's condition had not improved. His parents never ceased to hope for a miracle, but their deranged son needed special attendants to care for him and, when necessary, to restrain him. As much as possible he was kept from contact with anyone outside the family circle. William Backhouse Astor, now in his formative, student years, was away in Europe. He was developing into a shy, bookish young man, quite unlike his commercially aggressive father. In 1808 John Jacob sent him to complete his education first at Heidelberg University and then at Göttingen, currently enjoying a reputation as one of the civilized world's more prestigious centres of learning. It must have given John Jacob much personal satisfaction to know that the son of the poor boy from Walldorf was now in Germany studying and roistering with the wealthy young élite of Europe in their gowns and tasselled caps – except that it is difficult to imagine anyone as dull as William actually 'roistering'.

Yet even his spirit cannot have failed to be stirred by the events of those years when the armies of Napoleon and his enemies were marching to and fro across the continent. William Backhouse certainly did not lack for stimulating company. In the autumn of 1810, John Jacob engaged as his son's tutor and companion Christian Bunsen, a considerable scholar and, later, one of the finest diplomats of his day. Bunsen received, between October 1810 and March 1811, thirty louis d'or for giving his pupil instruction in 'German and other things'. John Jacob obviously intended that his son should not neglect his heritage. William Backhouse and Christian became close friends, and the young Prussian subsequently accompanied his charge on the Grand Tour. In April 1813 they set out for Frankfurt, Würzburg, Vienna, Milan and the North Italian lakes, 'receiving intelligence of the great events by which the French armies were driven out of Germany, like indistinct echoes from a distance, listened for with intense interest'.[1]

The military campaigns which were bringing a tumultuous quarter of a century to a close had played their part in stoking the intellectual furnace to white heat. Europe, and especially the German-speaking areas of Europe, rang with debates on politics, religion and art, with arguments about freedom, justice, tyranny and democracy. These were the years of Beethoven and Schubert, of the aged Goethe, of the philosophers Hegel, Niebuhr and Schleiermacher. A student from the land of the great democratic experiment could hardly avoid being caught up in these vibrant issues. In Bunsen he had a first-class mentor. The scholar's circle included the cleverer and more radical young men in Göttingen. In 1810–11 its most remarkable member was Arthur Schopenhauer, an intense, introverted young man destined to become one of the giants of nineteenth-century thought.

Back home William Backhouse's father was emerging, somewhat reluctantly, into the limelight of United States politics. The years during which the furrier and international merchant had been building his business had marked also the infancy of national political parties. Various interest groups gradually coalesced and gave themselves labels. The 'Federalists' were pro-British, traditionalist and believed in strong central government. The 'Republicans' were radicals and democrats who looked to France for their political ideals. In New York the Federalist nucleus was provided by the 'aristocratic' old families such as the De Lanceys, Schuylers, Van Rensselaers and their leader Alexander Hamilton. This exclusivist group looked down on 'new' men of inferior social status, like Astor. John Jacob, who was a stranger to political idealism, temperamentally found himself in opposition to the Federalists, though he was sympathetic to many of their policies. Particularly, he mistrusted the French and was in favour of maintaining good relations with Britannia who manifestly ruled the waves.

If Astor inclined to either party, it was, somewhat reluctantly, to the Republicans, among whom Thomas Jefferson emerged as leader. In New York the radical focus was Tammany Hall, the popular name of the Society of St Tammany, an organization of businessmen and middle-class citizens set up to challenge the pretensions of the 'aristocrats'. John Jacob was a member from quite early in his residency. He even provided the buck tails Tammanyites wore in their hats on ceremonial occasions. Tammany Hall, freemasonry and his day-to-day business brought him into contact with the most powerful men in the state – particularly members of the Clinton family. George Clinton was Governor of New York from 1777 to 1795 and from 1801 to 1804. From 1804 until his death in 1812 he was Vice-President of the United States of America. George's nephew, De Witt Clinton, served first as his uncle's secretary, then followed a political career on his own account, in the state legislature and the US Senate, before becoming Mayor of New York (1803–15). John Jacob knew the younger Clinton very well. The two men were admitted to the same prestigious masonic lodge (Holland No. 8) in 1790 and passed together through the various grades of membership. De Witt was a vital link to the federal government in 1808 when Astor was forming his ambitious plans for a trans-continental chain of trading posts. The advantages in this association were far from being one-sided, for politics was an expensive business. Even wealthy men like the Clintons were, from time to time, desperate for ready cash. John Jacob was willing to oblige. In 1805, for example, he paid George Clinton $75,000 for a half-interest in the Vice-President's property in Greenwich Village.

A more flamboyant associate was Aaron Burr, an extravagant socialite, a lawyer and an ambitious, devious-minded politician. In 1789 Governor Clinton appointed him Attorney-General for New York. John Jacob knew him well. Burr was a Tammany Hall activist and also performed valuable professional services for Astor in various pieces of property litigation. Burr's political expenses and his natural extravagance made him, like George Clinton, a candidate for John Jacob's financial support. In various property deals with Astor, Burr received almost $75,000.

It is highly significant that the money John Jacob paid to Clinton, Burr and associates was vastly more than he had invested in property up to that time. In fact it accounted for over half of all the cash he put into Manhattan real estate between 1800 and 1820. The sums involved were huge. They had to come out of Astor's international trading operations and so were not available for ploughing back into fresh cargo. And they were paid out at a time when John Jacob was actively planning the westward expansion of the American Fur Company, an operation which would, as he knew, soak up capital. There can be no doubt that the main motivation for this enormous diversification into real estate was commercial. We shall return later to chronicle the development of the Manhattan property empire. What we must note here is that there was a political element present in John Jacob's early purchases. By obliging Burr and Clinton, whose stars were very much in the ascendant, he was tying some of the nation's leaders to him with strong bonds of obligation. That could only bode well for the furtherance of all his plans.

In fact, he may well have come to regret his help to Aaron Burr. That turbulent politician reached the height of power and then, through scheming and intrigue, threw everything away. In 1800 he was named as Jefferson's running-mate in the elections. In New York the Tammany Hall caucus overthrew the Federalists and this spearheaded a Republican victory in the nation at large. Burr duly became Vice-President, but Jefferson found him too unstable a colleague: he chose George Clinton to share the presidential ticket in the next election. Furious, Burr threw in his lot with the Federalists, but it was not long before he fell out with his new allies. He actually picked a duel with Alexander Hamilton. When the two men met, on a sunlit July morning, Hamilton was killed. That, effectively, was the end of Burr's political career. The rest of his long life was spent in the muddy shallows of wild, sometimes treasonable, schemes and impracticable plots.

These domestic conflicts were taking place against a worsening international situation. Memories of the colonial past, rivalry along the Canadian border and frustration with the economic dislocation caused by the European conflict all contributed to a heightening of tension between Britain and America. In June 1812, as a result of political bluster, diplomatic incompetence and an element of bad luck, the two countries were brought to war. Hostilities continued until January 1815 (although peace terms were actually agreed on Christmas Eve 1814). Although casualties were, mercifully, light, bitter battles were fought by land and sea, Washington, the new capital of the United States, was sacked and opinion within the country was deeply divided.

John Jacob was among those opposed to the war, although he gave the government strong financial support. Any man's politics is a mixture of idealism and self-interest, and Astor was not heavily endowed with the former. What was blatantly obvious to him was that armed conflict was bad for business. Making an enemy of the world's leading naval power must further disrupt his commerce with China and Europe. Making the northern border a battle line would be disastrous for the fur trade with Canada and would inflame the more restless Indian tribes.

For all these reasons war was, to Astor, inconceivable. But President James Madison and the Republicans seemed hellbent on what they regarded as a second war of independence which would drive the last redcoat from the North American continent and bring Canada into the Union. In 1811 the administration imposed a total boycott on trade with Britain and everywhere political arsonists were to be found starting nationalist fires. It took a year for Astor's complacency to be broken down. Then, on 9 June 1812, he helped draw up a petition signed by fifty-six New York merchants urging the government not to go beyond embargo as an expression of hostility towards Britain. A few days later he decided to back this up with personal representations to the nation's leaders. He set out to ride the 250 miles to Washington. He arrived in the capital on 19 June. War had been declared the day before.

Having failed in his peace mission, there was nothing John Jacob could do except try to salvage as much of his property as possible before fighting actually started on the Canadian border. He had consignments of furs in various depots and he sent off a flurry of messages from Washington with instructions for them to be dispatched southwards without delay. Gallatin allowed his friend to use the government frank, which ensured swift transit for his letters. John Jacob also dispatched duplicate orders by different routes so that as many as possible would get through before communications with the enemy were stopped. He succeeded too well for his own reputation.

As a direct result of Astor's action the first campaign of the war was won by the British. His message reached Montreal before official notice of the declaration of war was received in the area. The military commander in Upper Canada, General Isaac Brock, immediately marched on the US garrison at Michilimackinac, on the strait between Lakes Huron and Michigan, and overwhelmed it. A relief force sent north from Fort Dearborn (Chicago) was massacred by Indians. Brock, meanwhile, had marched on to Detroit with a small force to confront the main army of invasion. By a combination of bluff and surprise he induced the Americans to surrender.

Members of the war party were not slow to accuse Astor of treachery. It was not a charge to be taken lightly. These were tense and difficult times. Supporters and opponents of 'Mr Madison's War' frequently clashed and it was not unknown for lynch law to take over on such occasions. John Jacob was probably too well known and too well connected to be seriously in danger of his life, but he did find himself forced into a Janus-like attitude, looking out for his own interests as assiduously as possible while showing a public face of ostentatious loyalty.

Having done all that he could in Washington, Astor hurried to Montreal to salvage as much of his stock as possible. Once more he had the help of his friend. In these tense days when Albert Gallatin was carrying the entire financial burden of an unpopular war, he put his reputation at stake for the sake of John Jacob. He gave the furrier letters authorizing him to enter Canadian territory for the purpose of recovering his property. Astor paused at Plattsburg on Lake Champlain, and there news reached him of a mutiny of Canadian militia at Lachine. To show his patriotism, Astor hastened to pass the information to government forces at Albany.

This anxious facing both ways marked his attitude throughout the conflict. He supported the war effort while maintaining his contacts in enemy territory and using every method, including subterfuge and bribery, to keep trade on the move. There was, however, little that Astor could do to salvage his overseas commerce. In mid-1813 a British naval blockade became effective in all the major ports. A few ships carrying John Jacob's goods managed to break out, but such escapades were gestures rather than serious attempts to resume trade. He did gain in the short term from the rapid price rise of imported goods. In a few months the value of the tea stocks held in his warehouses doubled and it was much the same with other commodities. But once his existing supplies were used up, Astor had nothing to sell. By early in 1814 he was complaining that he was 'almost out of business, as I do not wish to speculate and there is nothing else to be done'.[2]

Such protestations should not be taken entirely at face value: Astor was prone to claiming that he was on the verge of bankruptcy, especially when confronted by hopeful suitors or creditors. One of the stories often told about him which is less likely than most to be apocryphal concerns his later patronage of the remarkably talented artist and ornithologist John James Audubon. He was one of the wealthy subscribers to the latter's superb publication, *The Birds of America*, which comprised four volumes of hand-coloured plates and six volumes of text. When the artist came to collect from John Jacob the $1,000 which was his promised share of this expensive undertaking he found the great man ready with a stock of excuses. Whenever he called, Astor had 'nothing in the bank' or all his money 'invested' or was suffering from a 'downturn in the market'. On his sixth, patient visit he discovered Astor and his son William Backhouse in earnest conversation on some important business matter. As the latter withdrew to an adjacent room, John Jacob greeted his guest. 'Ah, M. Audubon, so you have come again after your money. Hard times, M. Audubon – money scarce!' Seeking confirmation, he called out to his son, 'Have we any money at all in the bank?' William promptly replied, assuming that the enquiry related to the business they had just been discussing, 'Yes, Father. We have $220,000 in the

Bank of New York, $70,000 in the City Bank, $90,000 in the Merchants', $98,400 in the Mechanics', $83,000 ...' 'That'll do!' John Jacob shouted hastily. 'Well, it seems, M. Audubon, that William can give you a cheque.'[3]

There is no doubt, however, that the war made life very difficult for Astor, which renders all the more impressive the service he performed in 1813 for his old friend and for his country. By this time the nation's finances were in a parlous state. A pre-war run on gold had pushed the Bank of America's reserves down to $5.5 million. Madison had turned to Congress for extra taxation and had been turned down. Gallatin faced the prospect of seeing all that he had patiently achieved over the last decade torn to pieces. He took the only action open to him to provide the President with a war chest: he floated a government loan. It failed. The business community was in no mood to finance a costly and unnecessary conflict. The Federalists were delighted. They expected the administration to go bankrupt and be forced to resign. In March 1813 Tsar Alexander offered to mediate a settlement and Madison jumped at the chance of peace with honour. He appointed Gallatin a member of the commission to talk with the Russians. But the financial crisis remained. The Treasury Secretary had failed to interest major businessmen and banks in the $16,000,000 loan and now he opened it to the public. It flopped. Gallatin felt he could not leave the country without making one final effort to salvage the flotation. In this extremity he asked Astor to use his best endeavours on the government's behalf.

On 3 April, John Jacob went to Philadelphia to discuss the situation with the city's two leading financiers, David Parish and Stephen Girard. Both men were wealthier than Astor. Parish was a member of a famous Hamburg banking house, who had come to America in 1806 and within two years made a million dollars exporting Spanish gold and silver to Europe. Much of this he had invested in land along the St Lawrence River. This, of course, had lost value since the start of the war, and he was anxious to see a speedy end to hostilities. His inclination was to let the war effort fail through lack of funds; it was, in fact, his opposition which had destroyed the earlier loan negotiations. Girard had come from France before the War of Independence, established himself as a shipowner and merchant and now commanded the largest American mercantile fleet. He had as much reason as the others for desiring a return to peace.

Although he was not in the same league as these two financial giants, it seems that in the discussions John Jacob made the running. It is likely that he used purely commercial arguments: with Russian mediation the war would soon be over, so the value of any stock they acquired would appreciate handsomely. When Gallatin joined them two days later, the backers were quickly able to conclude a deal. Parish and Girard between them took up $8 million of the loan. Astor subscribed for himself and some of his friends $2,056,000. They paid eighty-eight dollars in the hundred for stock at 6 per cent. The issue, which had a term of thirteen years, eventually paid 7.487 per cent and was a long-term success. It is no exaggeration to say that four men saved the United States government. That is certainly how contemporaries saw it. The Federalists were furious. They vilified the four foreigners and sought the first opportunity to vent their anger on Gallatin. For his part, the Treasury Secretary was immensely grateful to his old friend and commended him to Madison. Parish and Girard, he explained, had the government over a barrel and could have dictated conditions, but Astor 'came out with a subscription of more than two millions of dollars bottomed exclusively on his own resources and credit, and enabled me, by that competition, to obtain better terms from Parish and Girard'.[4] Gallatin was able to sail for Europe on 9 May with a lighter heart.

His enemies were quick to stir up trouble, however. Determined to force Gallatin out of office, they persuaded the Senate to refuse to ratify his new diplomatic appointment on the grounds that he was Secretary of the Treasury – a thin stratagem barely covering the true political motivation. When John Jacob heard how his friend was being treated he was outraged. He rushed to Washington, talked with Albert's friends, lobbied Congressmen and had an interview with the President. Within days he dispatched to Gallatin 'an account of the strange, if not wicked, proceedings of the Senate'. He explained that the conspirators had held a pistol to Madison's head: 'If he would renominate, with an understanding to appoint another secretary then the nomination should be confirmed.' This had thrown the President into great mental anguish. On principle, he did not want to yield to the Senate's blackmail. He valued Gallatin's financial expertise at the Treasury, and he knew that his mission to Europe was vitally important. John Jacob described the sordid intrigues which went on behind the scenes – manoeuvres, incidentally, confirmed in a letter from Madison's wife to Mrs Gallatin: 'Mr Astor will tell you many particulars that I ought not to write of the desertion of some whose support we had a right to expect, and of the manoeuvring of others always hostile to superior merit.'[5]

Astor's own feelings agreed with those of the President: he valued Gallatin's work at the Treasury and he also wanted a speedy end to the war. On balance, however, he was in favour of his friend retaining his old office, even if it meant relinquishing his diplomatic assignment. He was convinced that Gallatin could do valuable work on the diplomatic scene, even in an unofficial capacity:

> I pray to God that you may have laid the basis of an honourable and lasting peace before this comes to hand and that, when you can no longer act by power of authority derived from government, you will still exert your own powers with . . . your

colleagues. Do not, at this critical moment, withdraw your services from the country. I have a consolation in the firm belief that you are fully above resentment against those who from personal or political motives can sacrifice the good of our country . . . the most complete triumph you could possibly wish for over these pitiful enemies will be the doing good to our country . . .[6]

In fact, Gallatin was content to yield to the Senate's decision. He exchanged an administrative career for a diplomatic one and, for the next fourteen years, he served America as effectively in foreign lands as he had in Washington. He remained in Europe and helped to negotiate the final peace between Britain and America concluded in Ghent on Christmas Eve 1814. The following day the delegates were entertained to roast beef and plum pudding at the British embassy. James Gallatin, Albert's son and secretary, recorded the mood of the occasion in his diary:

The band played first 'God Save the King', to the toast of the King, and 'Yankie Doodle', to the toast of the President. Congratulations on all sides and a general atmosphere of serenity; it was a scene to be remarked. God grant there may be always peace between the two nations.[7]

The prayer was answered. Gallatin and his family spent the next few tumultuous months in Europe. They were actually in Paris when Napoleon made his triumphant return from Elba in March 1815, and in London a hundred days later when the capital went wild with the news from Waterloo.

Meanwhile, life in America was, if less exciting, certainly no less worrying. The war with Britain dragged on longer than people had hoped. That was particularly bad for the businessmen and the financiers. John Jacob through all his political contacts urged on the peace-making process. Thus in July 1814 we find him advising Secretary of State James Monroe that all his mercantile friends were agreed that the government should concede to Britain the right to search US ships for their own nationals, otherwise the war would drag on for months.[8] After an early increase, the value of government loan stock dropped, reaching a nadir in the middle of 1814. Astor had laid out for a short war and a quick profit. In the event, he was obliged to sell off most of his holdings at around or slightly above what he had paid. When the government floated a larger loan in 1814 John Jacob's attitude towards it vacillated sharply, but he did eventually buy some parcels of stock. By September he was complaining, 'I find at this moment such difficulty in getting money that I am disgusted with money transactions and I wish now more than ever to be completely out of debt and free from engagements.'[9] Once again, we have to be careful not to take him too seriously. Although he was a relative newcomer to the world of pure financial speculation, and although juggling funds in the uncertain war years was a hazardous pastime, it is unlikely that Astor lost out. Indeed, he probably made a healthy profit from government securities. What is beyond doubt is that his prestige was appreciably enhanced by his direct involvement in national affairs.

At the same time that all this was happening he was involved in the establishment of the Second Bank of the United States. In 1811 the charter of the First Bank of the United States fell due for renewal, and unfortunately it had made many powerful enemies by its firm control of the flow of specie and notes. One of those enemies was John Jacob Astor. A few months earlier the furrier had withdrawn an unusually large consignment of gold. This so much annoyed the directors of the bank that they closed his account and demanded the prompt repayment of existing loans as they fell due. Astor was absolutely furious at this slight and made the whole affair public in the press. It is hardly surprising that his voice was among those demanding the non-renewal of the bank's charter. Indeed, he dispatched Bentzon to Gallatin with a strongly worded message to that effect. The result was a compromise: the First Bank ceased business, but the directors were permitted to continue in New York as operators of a state bank. The premises in Philadelphia were bought by Stephen Girard, who established his own bank.

Without some kind of central institution the nation's finances were in a very precarious state. Astor and other major capitalists feared for the fate of their government securities and, indeed, of all other investments whose value would fall if there was a serious loss of public confidence. By the spring of 1814 the man who had told Gallatin that he would 'go to great lengths . . . to see the bank down'[10] was campaigning for the foundation of an institution to succeed it. He threw himself into the task – holding meetings, writing to the nation's leaders, organizing petitions, lobbying senators and preparing a detailed scheme for the funding and running of the new bank. For the next two years he watched with growing frustration as the politicians argued, throwing out one bank bill after another. Sometimes he travelled to the capital to bring personal influence to bear. 'If you think it will do any good,' he wrote to a colleague in October 1814, 'I'll come to Washington and make any arrangements so as to leave here the day after I receive your letter . . . It is very inconvenient for me to go but I suppose I must do it.'[11] After a few unproductive days talking with members of the government and their Federalist opponents, he returned abruptly to New York. 'I am now more than ever satisfied, that I could not have done any good,' he wrote tetchily on his return home. 'It appears to me that it will take some weeks before Congress get to pass the Bank bill and if they go on Mr Calhoune's plan they must fail and ruin the country and themselves.'[12] Fifteen months later he was still protesting impatiently, 'I wish to God we might get a national Bank and that quickly. Do you think it would do any good if I was now to go to

Washington?'[13] These were the words of a man of action who had no sympathy with debates and party hacks. The Second Bank of the United States came into being, at long last, in April 1816. John Jacob Astor's name appeared on the list of directors.

All this formed the political background to the central tragedy of John Jacob's life, the Astoria failure, to which we must now return. By midsummer of 1810 the corporate structure for his grand design was in place and Astor lost no time in dispatching his pioneers to the west coast. There were two parties: a land expedition which set out by canoe up the Missouri from St Louis in October, and a sea expedition which left New York on 8 September carrying all the supplies necessary for the establishment of Astoria. One failed for lack of strong leadership. The other ended disastrously because the leadership was too strong.

The calamitous voyage of the *Tonquin* makes that of the *Bounty* look like a pleasure cruise. When the 300-ton armed merchantman slipped her cable she carried four directors of the company, eleven junior members and a small crew under the captaincy of Jonathan Thorn, a young officer in his first command. Most of the subsequent problems arose from the fact that the parameters of authority had not been clearly established. The company men regarded Thorn as their subordinate. They expected him to defer to their wishes and show them respect. The captain, for his part, looked upon his passengers as a vainglorious, disorderly rabble who would wreck Mr Astor's bold enterprise if they were not firmly controlled. Thorn was a first lieutenant in the US Navy, raised in a hard disciplinary school to believe that the commander of a vessel at sea was due unquestioning obedience from everyone else aboard. Both sides claimed the privileges of rank and failed to grasp the fact that in the claustrophobic atmosphere of a small ship life is intolerable without flexibility and mutual understanding. Traditionally blame for the *Tonquin* disaster has been attributed to Thorn's mounting paranoia. We have to remember, however, that he was a young, inexperienced officer; that he was responsible for the safety of his ship, cargo, crew and passengers; that he was taking his vessel round the Horn, the most feared of all stretches of ocean; and that he was answerable to John Jacob Astor, an owner who expected the highest standards from employees and was intolerant of failure. For their part, some of the passengers had an ambiguous attitude to the enterprise. These were Astor's Canadian friends who had come in from the North West Company and were not wholehearted supporters of an American venture. Unknown to Astor, they had called on the British representative in New York to clarify the attitude of the London government towards their participation in the Astoria scheme. They were a tough bunch of French and British individualists, backwoodsmen used to hardship, to fighting for survival and to disposing of opposition with scant regard for law. John Jacob himself was clearly aware that the *Tonquin* was carrying a highly unstable and combustible human cargo, for he wrote anxious letters to both Thorn and his colleagues, urging harmony.

Any such prospect was dashed before the ship had been more than a few hours at sea. Thorn, perhaps in order to make an early demonstration of his authority, ordered 'lights out' at 8 p.m. Duncan McDougall, one of the partners, protested at this demeaning treatment. The captain threatened to clap him in irons for insubordination. McDougall brandished a pistol. The antagonists were calmed down by onlookers but no one slept easily that first night out. There were several other petty quarrels, and if open mutiny was avoided during the early part of the voyage it was only because most of the company men spent several days groaning in their berths with sea-sickness. They received little sympathy from the captain who, in the interests of health and hygiene, made them turn out on the deck for fresh air and exercise and keep their quarters clean. When they recovered and were ready to fill their empty stomachs with food their voracious but finicky appetites provided another cause of friction, as Thorn reported to his employer: 'When thwarted in their cravings for delicacies they would exclaim that it was d—d hard they could not live as they pleased upon their own property, being on board of their own ship, freighted with their own merchandize.'[14]

Eventually, the passengers decided that the only way to live with their tetchy captain was, as far as possible, to ignore him. This only exacerbated the poor man's insecurity. He watched them lying about the deck chatting, laughing, smoking, singing, scribbling away in their personal journals, while he worked and worried over the progress of the expedition. He felt himself despised, a mere hack mariner paid to deliver them to their destination. He had turned his back on the possibility of friendship. They had rejected a subordinate role. There remained inevitable enmity, which could only deepen as the *Tonquin* crossed the tropics and headed for the rigours of the Horn. Thorn took delight in refusing every request to land, or sail farther inshore to observe the coast and its inhabitants. The passengers sought solace in their superiority.

At last they reached the Falklands, where the *Tonquin* was to reprovision and take on fresh water. Now the landlubbers could go ashore, explore, hunt wild animals for the table, and, above all, escape the rigorous and surly regime of Jonathan Thorn. But even here there were disputes, culminating in a nasty incident when the *Tonquin* was ready to weigh anchor. Thorn signalled for the shore party to return aboard. The eight gentlemen enjoying themselves in various ways on the island either did not see or chose to ignore the flags and the unfurled canvas. The captain's patience (and, perhaps, his reason) finally snapped. He ordered full sail and steered away from the anchorage. The alarmed company men jumped into their boat and rowed feverishly after the *Tonquin*. For three and a half hours they chased the diminishing vessel towards the empty horizon. On board there was no less alarm. One of the passengers threatened Thorn with a gun if he did not go about but the captain called his bluff. Had not the weather taken a hand he would certainly have carried out his threat to abandon the troublemakers. He said as much in a letter to Astor:

> Had the wind (unfortunately) not hauled ahead soon after leaving the harbour's mouth, I should positively have left them; and indeed I cannot but think it an unfortunate circumstance for you that it so happened, for the loss in this instance, would, in my opinion, have proved the best, as they seem to have no idea of the value of property nor any apparent regard for your interests, although interwoven with their own.[15]

From this point there was virtually no communication between passengers and crew. Thorn smelled conspiracy every time he saw groups of company men talking together, especially when some of them reverted to their native Gaelic.

The weather did not help the situation. Although the Horn, which the *Tonquin* rounded on Christmas Day, was reasonably kind, light and contrary winds beset her as soon as she entered the Pacific and another seven weeks passed before her next landfall at Hawaii. Here the passengers and crew were eager to explore the delights of the islands, and McDougall and his colleagues were anxious to establish good relations with the king. They held several meetings with him and his representatives and sought to impress him with their own importance. Thorn watched these antics with absolute disgust:

> It would be difficult to imagine the frantic gambols that are daily played off here; sometimes dressing in red coats, and otherwise very fantastically, and collecting a number of ignorant natives around them, telling them they are the great [chiefs] of the northwest, and making arrangements for sending three or four vessels yearly to them from the coast with spars etc ... Then dressing in Highland plaids and Kelts and making similar arrangements, with presents of rum, wine, or any thing that is at hand. Then taking a number of clerks and men on shore to the very spot on which Captain Cook was killed ... Then sitting down with some white man or some native who can be a little understood, and collecting the history of those islands ... [all this] is indeed ridiculously contemptible. – To enumerate the thousand instances of ignorance, filth etc, or to particularize all the frantic gambols that are daily practised, would require volumes.[16]

Thorn also had to deal with sailors who attempted to desert (a common problem experienced when ships called at these Pacific island 'paradises'). He savagely vented his anger on the culprits, having them all flogged, and even ordering one man to be beaten insensible and flung overboard. It is clear that by this stage of the voyage the captain's grasp of reality had become very weak.

On 22 March the *Tonquin* reached the mouth of the Columbia River. Three attempts to discover a channel deep enough for the ship by sending boats through the heavy breakers cost the lives of eight men. The company agents could not wait to get ashore and rid themselves of the detestable Thorn. They set up a temporary base and unloaded the supplies. The whole company spent several weeks exploring the region, establishing relations with the local people and beginning the construction of a fortified trading post. Then, on 1 June, the settlers thankfully bade farewell to Captain Jonathan Thorn and his crew. But even they would not have wished upon the mariners the fate which soon befell them.

The *Tonquin* now embarked on the second phase of her voyage. Astor could not allow any of his ships to sail without bringing back a profit. Therefore, having laid the foundations of the Columbia River depot, Thorn was charged with carrying out his own trading venture. Unfortunately for the Astorians, he took with him the lion's share of the expedition's trade goods. Thorn was a man singularly ill-equipped for the sensitive business of bargaining for furs. Not only was he totally inexperienced in bartering with the Indians, he held the 'savages' in utter contempt. John Jacob had given him precise instructions regarding his relations with the natives. They were not to be trusted, and particular care was to be exercised over permitting any of them to board the vessel. Both men were convinced of the superiority of the white man, but long dealing with the Indians had given Astor a healthy respect for them. Thorn made the fatal error of underestimating them.

He sailed to Vancouver Island, anchored in one of its many harbours and, while Astor's representative, Alexander McKay, went ashore to establish relations with the local chief, began trading with several Indians whom he allowed *aboard the ship*. Exactly what happened next will never be known, but Washington Irving pieced together a narrative from the second- or third-hand accounts of company men who later reported back to Astor. It is vivid and colourful and probably not far from the truth. Having failed to drive a satisfactory bargain with Nookamis, an elderly Indian well-versed in bartering with white men,

> [Thorn] thrust his hands into his pockets and paced up and down the deck in sullen silence. The cunning old Indian followed him to and fro, holding out a sea otter skin to him at every turn, and pestering him to trade. Finding other means unavailing, he suddenly changed his tone and began to jeer and banter him upon the mean prices he offered. This was too much for the patience of the Captain, who was never remarkable for relishing a joke, especially when at his own expense. Turning suddenly

upon his persecutor, he snatched the proffered otter skin from his hands, rubbed it in his face, and dismissed him over the side of the ship with no very complimentary application to accelerate his exit. He then kicked the peltries to the right and left about the deck and broke up the market in the most ignominious manner. Old Nookamis made for shore in a furious passion, in which he was joined by Shewish, one of the sons of Wicananish [the local chief], who went off breathing vengeance, and the ship was soon abandoned by the natives.[17]

When McKay returned and heard what had happened he was extremely alarmed. He urged Thorn to weigh anchor immediately. The captain brushed aside his anxieties. After all the fierce disagreements of the last nine months, he was not now going to let one of the troublesome landlubbers tell him how to run his ship. Before dawn the Indians were back – first just a canoe-load, then more and more. They feigned goodwill and were soon vigorously engaged in trade. Then, at a sudden signal, they turned on the *Tonquin*'s small complement and butchered all but five who barricaded themselves into the cabin. Jonathan Thorn was one of the first to fall.

The remnant of the *Tonquin*'s crew were too few to get the ship safely out to sea. Four of them took to the longboat under cover of darkness in the hope of reaching Astoria. Within hours they were captured and put to death, after suffering appalling torture. The last survivor of the expedition remained aboard because he was too badly wounded to attempt the journey, and also because he had planned an ending to the '*Tonquin* Incident' worthy of a 1950s Hollywood epic. The following morning he dragged himself on deck and motioned to the Indians to come aboard. In a little while the vessel was swarming with Wicananish's people, cheerfully plundering the ship of everything that took their fancy. They did not notice that the last white man had disappeared below. Suddenly the bay was rent by a colossal explosion. As the smoke cleared, the water where the *Tonquin* had floated was seen to be littered with debris and bodies.

Meanwhile, the overland expedition had run into problems which, if less dramatic, were scarcely less disastrous. Inexperienced leadership and divided counsels led the party to take a route through barren and inhospitable territory. A year after setting out, one of the five partners resigned. The remaining leaders split the company into four groups which travelled separately. After suffering many privations and warding off Indian attacks, they arrived at Astoria between January and May 1812. Discouraged by the difficulties of the journey and the state in which he found the settlement, another of the partners promptly gave up his stake in the company.

However, the remainder made the best of the situation, established good relations with some of the Indian groups over a wide area and began trading. In May 1812 another of John Jacob's ships, the *Beaver*, arrived with fresh supplies and it seemed that the great enterprise might yet succeed. There were problems, to be sure. Some of the local chiefs were unpredictable and others hostile. Agents of the North West Company resented the newcomers. They now made strenuous efforts to establish their own Pacific coast base and did everything possible to discourage their rivals. But with determination and frequent contact by sea and land with New York, the colony might have survived. Then, in January 1813, the devastating news reached Astoria that America and Britain (and, therefore, Canada) were at war.

In New York, Astor made several attempts to dispatch ships to the west coast, but all his efforts were frustrated by the blockade. A brig, the *Lark*, did clear the harbour *en route* for Astoria, but she came to grief off Hawaii. John Jacob used every diplomatic and political channel at his disposal to get succour to his settlement, but the government in Washington were too preoccupied with the war to worry about a few of their citizens on the far side of the continent. By contrast, the Canadian traders were much more successful in petitioning their political superiors in London. The Admiralty dispatched a convoy to reinforce the North West Company's presence and expel the enemy.

None of these activities were known on the Columbia. The settlers were simply faced with the bleak prospect of no supply ships arriving from the USA, while their Canadian rivals became steadily more obstructive. Several of the Pacific Fur Company's representatives were, as we have seen, old North West men. They had no stomach for a fight with their former colleagues. To most of the leaders at Astoria the situation seemed hopeless, but a minority was in favour of staying on. After much argument they reached a compromise: they would wait until the summer of 1814. If the situation had not improved by then, they would abandon Astoria. The traders struggled on for a few more months, but in October they heard about the imminent arrival of the British warships. This was the last straw. The remaining partners hastened to sell their stock and equipment to the North West Company. Winding up the Pacific Fur Company almost certainly lay beyond their legal powers, but they were acting in an emergency and there was nothing Mr Astor, in distant New York, could do about it. On 30 November a British sloop arrived. Her captain claimed the territory around the lower Columbia in the name of His Britannic Majesty and renamed Astoria, Fort George.

Information reached New York in dribs and drabs, and Astor's mood fluctuated with each piece of intelligence. In July 1814 he wrote to a friend in London that the war had 'not only caused me great loss but ruined my favourite plan by which I should have done all I wished or ought to have desired'.[18] But in December, before he heard of the demise of the Pacific Fur Company, John Jacob's belief in the Astoria venture seemed undimmed. He poured out his heart to Albert Gallatin. How could the government be so blind to the importance of staking a claim to a Pacific base?

> It is of great national importance and will prove a new source of wealth. There is no person who possesses the information which I do and there is yet but little known of the importance of it in Europe. But it soon will be, when we shall find it more and more difficult to accomplish an advantageous arrangement on that subject. The present is the time![19]

As soon as the full extent of the disaster became known Astor spent months urgently petitioning the government to send troops to reclaim the settlement, but it seems there was no one in authority who could see the importance of Astoria.

The whole lamentable venture cost John Jacob tens of thousands of dollars. Contemporaries observed that he was taciturn in the face of the collapse of his grand scheme. When the news of the loss of the *Tonquin* reached him he is reported to have made no change in his plans and to have visited the theatre that very evening. When a friend remarked upon this behaviour Astor is said to have replied, 'What would you have me do? Would you have me stay at home and weep for what I cannot help?'[20] That pretended nonchalance covered the profoundest emotions – anger, disillusionment, frustration. In a very real sense he never recovered from this great disappointment. He knew that he had been right, and that if the government had glimpsed only a fraction of his vision the effect on the growth of the United States would have been dramatic. That thought obsessed him for years to come. 'If the government had sent 50 men in 1815 and 1816 it would have been as good as 5000,' he insisted in 1827.[21] Even Albert Gallatin did not see the significance of the Columbia territory. John Jacob's grandson recalled a conversation between the two friends in which Gallatin remarked, 'It will be time enough for our great-grandchildren to talk about that in two hundred years.' John Jacob responded, 'If we live, we shall see trouble about it in less than forty years.'[22] The failure of Astoria marked a turning point in John Jacob's career. Thereafter, his appetite for business waned. He thought less about increasing the size of his empire and even began talking about withdrawing from commerce altogether. For years he brooded over what might have been, and not until his final years, when he commissioned Washington Irving to write an account of the Astoria venture, did he finally exorcise the ghosts that haunted him from the desolate mountain trail and the shattered, sunken remnants of the *Tonquin*.

This brave, failed adventure made, in years to come, an important psychological impact and was not without its influence in determining the eventual boundary of the USA. Writing to a member of the government in 1826, Gallatin observed: 'Of the great merits of Mr Astor there can be no doubt.

The United States are indebted exclusively to him for the settlement of Astoria, which constitutes our only right *of possession* to the Columbia territory.'[23] Astoria had been restored to America in the peace treaty of 1814, and this paper claim to a Pacific outpost was to prove vitally important, even though the fort remained unoccupied for thirty years. It encouraged the 'Oregon Trail' migration of the 1840s and strengthened the government's bargaining position with Britain over the frontier. Although the Hudson's Bay Company provided the only effective government on the northern Pacific coast for many years, Canada never laid claim to any territory south of the Columbia River. In 1846 the boundary was finally agreed running along the 49th parallel, though not before, as Astor had prophesied, the two nations had come close to war. By this time Astoria had been permanently settled. In August 1848, five months after John Jacob's death, the state of Oregon officially came into being.

1815 did bring some consolations. It was a year of homecomings. Having successfully concluded the work for which he had been sent to Europe, Albert Gallatin brought his family back to America. The old friends met up again and had a great deal of news to exchange about events on both sides of the Atlantic. But when talk turned to the future neither man viewed it with optimism. Gallatin had no job and needed some way of earning a living. John Jacob was disillusioned with trade and could find little comfort in business prospects. It was in these circumstances that he made a determined attempt to bind the houses of Astor and Gallatin closer together. First, he invited Albert to join him in his commercial undertakings. To show that he was serious, he set down all the relevant facts and figures, estimating his trading capital at $800,000 and his net annual profit at between $150,000 and $160,000. Gallatin could have a one-fifth share of all this, to be paid for out of profits over as long a period as he wished, and Astor would charge him the legal rate of interest.

At the same time, he proposed another kind of union – the marriage of Albert's elder son, James, and his own youngest daughter, Eliza (eighteen and fifteen respectively). Both offers were declined. Albert gave the business proposition long and hard consideration, but he was, at the same time, being hard pressed by the President to accept a posting as Minister (Ambassador) to Paris. Eventually, knowing how eager his wife and children were to return to Europe, he accepted the diplomatic appointment. As to the other suggestion, whatever the menfolk felt, it failed to win the approval of Mrs Gallatin or her son. Hannah thought the Astor women 'shrewish', and James had no desire to be united with the daughter of a man who had come to America 'with a pack on his back and peddled furs'.[24] James Gallatin was a foppish, self-opinionated snob and one cannot help feeling that little Eliza had a very narrow escape.

The other returnee was William Backhouse Astor. He came home from war-shattered Europe in the spring of 1815 (much to his father's relief), but he planned to spend no more than a year in New York. His main concern seems to have been to persuade his father to agree to a protracted – perhaps permanent – absence from America. John Jacob reluctantly agreed to his son's return to Europe, but he wanted him to have some definite employment. How fortunate that his good friends the Gallatins were now returning to Paris. In August he wrote to Hannah urging her to intercede with her husband:

> . . . my son, William, seems absolutely fixed to return to Europe and, as I believe it will be for his best, I must consent to let him go, but I wish him to be engaged in some honourable employment and as at present I know of none so much so as that of Secretary of Legation and being persuaded that he would derive great advantage and pleasure from the society of Mr Gallatin I would be greatly pleased if he could accompany him on his mission as Secretary of Legation.

John Jacob offered Mrs Gallatin two inducements. The first was financial: he would pay $4,000 per annum for William to be lodged with her family. Secondly he would reciprocate by taking young James Gallatin (who was also at a loose end) under his wing, providing him with a commercial training and, in all ways, 'to do for him as if he were my son'.[25] It is very unlikely that either James or his mother relished the prospect of the refined 'courtier' being apprenticed to the man they regarded as a mere German tradesman. Certainly, nothing came of the suggestion.

But William did return to live and enjoy the life of a rich, culture-hungry student. He reached Paris at the end of the year and found the city much changed since the final overthrow of Napoleon. He noted with disapproval that the country seemed to be declining rapidly into a pre-Revolution state under the restored monarchy. The Louvre had been virtually emptied of its treasures as aristocratic families reclaimed their looted possessions. Prices were high and services poor. His gloomy outlook was obviously influenced by his experience of discrimination against English-speaking visitors. Frenchmen, he discovered, blamed the British and, by extension, the Americans for the restoration of the *ancien régime* and took their revenge by fleecing travellers. As he indignantly reported to a friend, he had had to pay through the nose for post horses, and 'a miserable bed on the third floor' cost him five guineas a week.[26] However, William Backhouse cheerfully tolerated such annoyances as the price to be paid for being a free agent, able to come and go in Europe as he pleased.

John Jacob's attitude towards his son's chosen lifestyle was ambivalent. On the one hand he was proud of the cultured, cosmopolitan young man William was becoming. Yet he also worried about his heir turning into a dilettante.

William came home, his head full of the ideas of young Schopenhauer: 'Philosophy is an Alpine road ... The higher you climb, the lonelier, the more desolate grows the way. But he who treads it must know no fear; he must leave everything behind him ... the world will soon lie far beneath him; its deserts and bogs will disappear from view.'[27] Such concepts were beyond John Jacob's comprehension and he fretted that his son showed no inclination to settle to some 'serious' career. It would not be long before he had second thoughts about allowing his son to wander round Europe with no ambition and a long purse.

Closer to home John Jacob suffered other anxieties. His involvement with the Second Bank of the United States constantly provoked his anger and indignation. He was fully in accord with his friend and fellow-director, Stephen Girard: 'intrigue and Corruption formed a ticket for twenty Directors ... who I am sorry to say appear to have been selected for the purpose of securing the presidency to Wm. Jones, the Cashir's office to Jonn. A. Smith and for other pecuniary views.'[28] It was not just jobbery that upset Astor; he believed that banks should be run by businessmen, not politicians. Events bore him out: for its first few years the Second Bank was disastrously mismanaged. John Jacob soon gave up his directorship. He did not allow his name to go forward for selection in 1817, but he was appointed president of the New York branch. Doubtless it was more convenient for him to serve in this capacity, and he may well have felt that he could exercise more influence as the biggest fish in a smaller pool. He resigned his position in 1819.

That was when he decided to make a long-postponed visit to Europe and escape from the pressures and disappointments of America. When Gallatin was proposing to resign his embassy in Paris his friend wrote with sad, sage advice, 'I really think you will not like it so much in this country as you did, and I believe you had better remain where you are.'[29] Certainly in 1819 Astor was growing tired of the country where he had made his fortune and was contemplating leaving it – possibly for good.

CHAPTER 4

'I would buy every foot of land on the Island of Manhattan'

By 1815 John Jacob Astor headed a business empire that spanned the world and employed several hundred people. He still supervised every aspect of it himself. He was fifty-two, had devoted thirty years to business and enjoyed success beyond his wildest dreams. If he had ever been a workaholic, a sequence of events now cured him of this obsession and enabled him to escape from the daily drudgery of the counting house. Once he had obtained that freedom, he elected to go back to Europe. There he spent most of his time between 1819 and 1834, and only returned to America when old age and poor health had begun to restrict his activities.

The main event which precipitated this move was the failure of Astoria. The winding up of the Pacific Fur Company in 1814 marked John Jacob's first major setback. When all his efforts to obtain government aid were thwarted, he decided both to contract and to concentrate his activities. He withdrew from the Far West and from the St Louis and upper Missouri territories and focused his attention on the Great Lakes region. He persuaded Congress to bring in a law whereby trade in the interior was only permitted under licence, and such licences would only be granted to US citizens. On the strength of this Astor was able to buy out his Canadian partners in 1817, on his own terms. After this the South West Fur Company was owned and capitalized entirely by himself.

Only one obstacle now prevented Astor from becoming the unchallenged commercial king in his chosen area of activity. Along the trails hundreds of government trading posts had been set up. They existed to protect the Indians from exploitation and to maintain good relations between them and the settlers. They provided goods at cost price and they sold no alcohol to the local people. The existence of this network of government depots was a constant irritant to the private traders, one of whom referred to it as a 'pious monster'. It effectively prevented them from charging exorbitant prices for trade goods and from using strong drink and credit to control the local people. Astor now set out to smash this system. Washington had failed to come to his aid over Astoria: he would recoup some of his losses at Washington's expense. John Jacob's carefully executed campaign operated at two levels. In the interior he used his superior financial muscle to undercut the prices charged for certain staples (any loss was, of course, more than recouped once Astor's agents had established their monopoly in the area). He also authorized his traders to undermine the Indians' confidence in the government by spreading false rumours, and to win their friendship by lavish gifts of whisky. Once this strategy was well under way, John Jacob had his friends in Congress call for the abolition of the government posts on the grounds that *they* were responsible for the breakdown of peace and stability in the interior. In 1822 the government factory system was officially wound up. Effective control of the wild men who plied the trails had never been strong. Now it was non-existent.

Another critical question concerned the future of William Backhouse. The young man had eagerly returned to Paris in December 1815, three months earlier than he had originally planned. He proposed to pay a long visit with Bunsen to Berlin, which was fast becoming the intellectual centre of Europe. But first he intended to set off for a tour of Rome and Florence with a group of American friends. The arrangement was that Bunsen should join him in Italy, where they would resume their travels and studies. However, when the Prussian eventually reached Florence in June he found awaiting him a devastating letter from his American friend 'announcing that all was at an end between us'.[1] Young Astor had dropped everything and hurried home, too distressed (or too inconsiderate) to contact his old friend.

In point of fact, William had left Europe in March. The decision was a very hurried one. He did not leave Paris until the end of January and was planning a very leisurely tour. He wrote to one of his friends, J. A. Smith, offering his services as a guide and laconically suggesting, 'let me know what parts of Europe you want to see.' The next time he wrote to Smith, a mere two months later, he was already on board ship in Liverpool docks.[2] The most likely reason for this sudden change of plan is that John Jacob had peremptorily summoned his son home, intending to put an end to William's extended education.

His father probably reasoned that the time had come for William to settle down to a career. If he could not decide on a vocation himself, then he would have to return home and relieve John Jacob of some of his commercial concerns.

The Astor business interests were becoming so complex that John Jacob needed the help of someone he could trust. He had approached Albert Gallatin, but his friend had declined the offer. He had then suggested that Albert's son James might like to be trained for leadership of the Astor enterprises. This, too, had been turned down. Apparently, there was no one else he could trust to ease the burden of day-to-day administration. One fact that is clear from John Jacob's correspondence is that he had no deep-laid plans to establish a commercial dynasty. He wanted to make a lot of money and secure it as far as possible for future Astor generations, but that did not necessarily involve setting up a family business. There was no sense in which William was 'groomed and doomed' to succeed his father as most family biographers have suggested.

Whatever crisis or sudden decision brought William scurrying back to New York, he was released again after a few months. Early in 1817 Albert Gallatin reported to John Jacob his son's safe arrival in Paris. His friend thanked him for the information, confirmed that William would be spending about two months in France and hoped that 'his conduct will continue to win your approbation'. This trip seems to have been planned as William's European swan song. It was short and was perhaps designed to enable the Astor heir to make his tender farewells to the friends and haunts of his youth. It appears that father and son had, at last, reached an agreement about William's future and that the initiative had come from William. John Jacob confessed to Albert in March:

> I am rather sorry to find that he will become a merchant. I would have liked him to have been in public employ but he says that he can not be idle and must have something to do.[3]

Fathers frequently live out their unfulfilled ambitions in their sons. John Jacob idolized his friend Gallatin as a man of culture and principle, a sophisticated and incorruptible public servant. Nothing would have made him more proud than to see William emulating the minister and diplomat. But a prominent career in national or international life was not to William's taste. He knew, perhaps, that he was not a 'big' enough man for the task. His suggestion that the diplomatic life was one of idleness sounds like a defensive self-justification (and one wonders how Gallatin reacted to it). William seems to have accepted his father's suggestion that, at the age of twenty-four, the time had come for him to settle down. Since he could think of nothing else to do with his life he would help his father to rule the Astor empire.

John Jacob's disappointment is unlikely to have run very deep. William's decision freed him to lead a more exciting life and to make the extended visit to Europe which he had looked forward to for so long. It was now over twenty years since he had crossed the Atlantic. He had planned an extensive tour of the Old World in 1802–3 to show Magdalen the sights, but this had had to be aborted. Ever since then the demands of business had stood in the way of pleasure. Other friends and relatives made extensive visits to Europe, among them John Jacob's lively nephew, Henry Brevoort (a son of Sarah's sister). In the early days Henry had served his uncle in the fur trade, enjoying the excitements of the frontier life, but subsequently he had decided upon more refined adventures across the Atlantic. He had spent many years in London and Paris during the tumultuous period of the Napoleonic Wars, living a Bohemian existence and numbering among his friends many of the leading political, literary and theatrical personages of the day. He had recently returned to New York to marry and raise a family, but he maintained contact with his European friends and his heart really lay on the other side of the Atlantic. As soon as possible he planned to return. In 1830 he wrote to tell his friend Washington Irving that he was, at last, making good his escape from the dullness of New York.

> My children are now sufficiently advanced in life to be benefited by a residence in Europe and we ourselves have not yet passed that melancholy crisis of existence when novelty ceases to be enjoyment . . . I am tired with the sameness of this nutshell circle of existence, and unless I break from it now, I shall be doomed to walk in it to the end of my days.[4]

There can be little doubt that the same *ennui* afflicted John Jacob in the years after the war with Britain. He, too, was conscious of life slipping by and was determined to return to the continent of his birth to enjoy its undoubtedly superior refinements. Now, with Gallatin strategically placed in Paris, would be a good time to make the long-postponed voyage – and William Backhouse would be in the office to keep an eye on things in his absence.

The wanderer finally returned in the spring of 1817. A year later William was satisfactorily married off to Margaret Armstrong, a young lady of impeccable pedigree and small fortune. Her father, General John Armstrong, was a member of the Republican élite centred on Madison. He had been a belligerent and unsuccessful Secretary for War during the recent conflict and, before that, US Minister to Napoleonic France. Possibly the two young people had first become acquainted in Paris, but whether or not this was so William and Margaret shared a cosmopolitan upbringing and were sufficiently compatible to suggest that their union might be reasonably happy and successful. After the traumas surrounding his elder daughters' marriages John Jacob must have been sensitive to the couple's feelings, although there can be little doubt that social and financial considerations weighed more heavily with both fathers. To mark William Backhouse's entry to the ranks of respectable householder, John Jacob took him into partnership. The firm of John Jacob Astor and Son was set up to control all the overseas trading activities.

The year 1818 should have been a happy one for the Astor family but, unfortunately, black shadows hung over it. Magdalen was difficult to live with. She had started drinking heavily to anaesthetize herself against the pain of desertion and the stigma attached to her divorce proceedings. There was no doubt that she was, technically at least, the wronged party. In an affidavit which Adrian Bentzon cheerfully swore in November 1818, he confirmed that Magdalen had offered to accompany him to the West Indies and that he had refused the offer. He admitted that since then he had consorted with several women and primarily with a Creole girl called Susanna, or Sukey, who lived openly with him, had assumed his name and borne him children.[5] However, Magdalen found herself on the wrong end of the prevailing dual morality. Wives were expected patiently to endure their spouses' infidelities and to live, if necessary, in lonely virtue. That did not suit the high-spirited Magdalen. On the principle that what was sauce for the gander was sauce for the goose she freely sought male company. Tongues were soon wagging about her relationship with John Bristed, a dilettante Englishman who divided his time between practising law, lecturing and sundry literary pursuits.

The tragedy which really shook the family and irretrievably soured relations occurred in February 1818. Magdalen's seven-year-old son, young John Jacob, was her one consolation. He was also the chief delight of his grandfather's life. John Jacob often spent time with the boy and tried to fill part of the gap left by his absent father. At the beginning of 1818 he made a journey to Baltimore, Philadelphia and Washington with his daughter Eliza, and took his grandson in the hope that the boy would benefit from the slightly warmer climate. It was in the capital that there befell 'so great a misfortune which has and keeps me in such distress of mind that I can scarcely think, much less act [and] that I fear it will take years if I should live before my grief will abate'. On 2 February the mishap occurred which John Jacob described in a letter to Gallatin:

> I was changing my clothes for to dine and while Bentzon [his grandson] was sitting by the street door at or near 5 in the afternoon a boy of 17 years of age came by with his skates and persuaded Bentzon to go with him to the Tiber [Creek]. Bentzon was not 5 minutes absent before I missed him but before we could hear where he had gone, both he and the boy with him were drowned. No one had seen them on the ice and we met while looking about only a little boy who had seen them walking towards it. Bentzon had never been on ice before. I cannot describe to you the distress the misfortune has occasioned.[6]

The tragedy dominated John Jacob's thoughts for months and, though this made planning more difficult, it can only have strengthened his resolve to go.

He spent a long time preparing for the journey. He compiled a dossier of detailed business information for his son, urging him 'occasionally to look over the notes which will here follow as I propose to note some points which may otherwise be forgotten'. John Jacob was under no illusions about the complexities of the task he was leaving to William's charge:

I have some considerable anxiety about the business of the American Fur Company, having considerable interest therein and as I think not a person who is capable to direct or manage the whole so as to prevent a loss or to make the most of it.[7]

He also took pains to cover the eventuality of his not returning. Travel, especially on the high seas, was a hazardous activity, and there was always the threat of disease when journeying in foreign lands. Should he meet an untimely end, John Jacob knew that his multifarious commercial and financial undertakings would be very difficult to unravel. Therefore, he produced another lengthy memorandum with this explanation:

Supposing it may be useful to those of my family which will survive me, I propose to make some notes of some transactions which are not entered in my books and to explain some which are entered more fully than appear on my books.[8]

John Jacob Astor left New York on 2 June 1819 on a new ship, the *Stephania*, landed in Le Havre and made straight for Paris. He took with him his elder son, John, and his youngest daughter, Eliza. John Jacob was hopeful that a change of scene might jolt poor John's distracted mind into some semblance of normality; so, despite the embarrassment his behaviour caused, he took his son to Europe with a nurse who was in constant attendance on him. Astor left him in the hands of leading experts on mental disorder but the experiment, of course, failed. The unfortunate John Jacob II gained nothing from his sojourn in Europe. All accounts of eighteen-year-old Eliza agree that she was the pleasantest of the Astor brood, though she was on the plump side and could not be called beautiful. She was quiet and studious by nature and had inherited her mother's Calvinistic piety. In the French capital father and daughter met up with the Gallatins. Since their friends were shortly leaving to spend the summer in Geneva, whither all the Parisian élite annually flocked to escape the oppressive heat of the city, the Astors too made for Switzerland.

Through the Gallatins they had the entrée to prominent figures in the world of diplomacy and politics. One couple who made a particular impression on them were the Duc and Duchesse de Broglie. Albert de Broglie was a moderate member of the French parliament who strove to counteract the forces of reaction during the reigns of Louis XVIII and Charles X. His wife, Albertine, was the daughter of the formidable novelist Madame de Staël, who had attracted widespread admiration by her opposition to Napoleon and had been forced into exile by the emperor. The de Broglies were intimate friends of the Gallatins and entertained the Americans often at their lovely château at Coppet on Lake Geneva. Here the Astors were also received. Eliza and

Albertine, who were much of an age, discovered a ready affinity. Both were natural and unaffected; both were serious young women who shared a lively Christian faith and a disposition to charity.

John Jacob revelled in all this activity, but he was strangely nervous and unsure of himself in his new surroundings. When Gallatin returned to Paris, and Eliza and her new friends wanted to go to Italy, he was thrown into a mild panic. He wrote to his old friend:

> To have the pleasure of your society at Paris was an inducement to me to come to Europe. Independent of this it appears to me as if we would have some uncertain if not unpleasant times in Italy . . . my interests may require me at home or as near as possible. In Paris my situation on this account would be much better than Italy. However, it appears to be decided that we go to Italy . . .[9]

He had some cause for anxiety. In the post-Napoleonic settlement the greater part of Italy had fallen under direct or indirect Austrian rule. As a result revolutionary and nationalist groups were active everywhere – holding protest meetings, distributing pamphlets, committing minor terrorist outrages and plotting revolt. As the Astors moved about the country, they moved from court to court, bearing letters of introduction to men and women of the ruling élite. Small wonder that John Jacob felt vulnerable.

Between November 1819 and June 1820 their itinerary took father and daughter to Rome, Naples, Florence and Milan. From Rome John Jacob reported to the US President on the state of affairs in Europe. Monroe was acutely interested. America might be thousands of miles away, but many of her people thought of the country as a champion against tyranny everywhere. More specifically, the government was involved in sensitive negotiations with Spain. As the effective strength of the imperial power weakened, her agents could not maintain their hold over Florida and, one by one, the dependencies of Latin America grasped their independence. In Cadiz a mutiny inspired by the sending of troops against the rebellious colonies quickly grew into a revolution. It was a difficult time in US foreign relations and Astor obviously thought that Monroe would welcome his observations. 'It appears to me', he wrote,

> that all Europe is threatened with revolution. The example of Spain will, I have no doubt, be followed and I am persuaded that those in power are trembling, but none can or dare to act. Whatever their feelings and wishes be, they must be still and look on . . . All men of sense and information have a hope and look to our dear country for a place of safety. It is expected by all Europe, generally speaking, that your recommendations to Congress as respects the Floridas [Monroe moved the purchase of the territory from Spain in 1819] have been adopted. I rather think of remaining yet some time in Europe, where, if I can be of any use to you I would be most happy by being informed of the manner.[10]

Despite the general ferment, the Astor progress was trouble-free and John Jacob enjoyed meeting several celebrities on his travels. In Rome, for example, he had long discussions with the beautiful and outrageous Pauline Bonaparte, Princess Borghese and Duchess of Guantalla. Pauline was the most beautiful of Napoleon's sisters, though she was already afflicted with the cancer that would kill her in 1825. The better to be received in such exalted society, John Jacob learned a little Italian. He paid careful attention to the political situation in the countries where he stayed, and detected everywhere bubbling unrest and the promise of more revolutions against the established order.

John Jacob concluded his Italian tour in June 1820 and spent high summer in Switzerland. Then he left the palaces and mansions of the wealthy and powerful to seek out his German relatives and introduce Eliza to the cousins she had never met. She was particularly interested when they visited Uncle Melchior, Aunt Verona and their two daughters in the Moravian community at Neuvied. The members of this Protestant church were committed to personal faith and to evangelism: the Moravians dispatched missions all over the world, including America. What Melchior thought of brother John's worship of mammon is not recorded, but there is no doubt that the life of his family and neighbours made an impression on Eliza.

The winter of 1820–21 saw the Astors' party in a very different environment. They were back in Paris, enjoying the gaiety of court and aristocratic circles and receiving introductions to Albert Gallatin's friends in the fields of politics and diplomacy. The French capital was the centre of the fashionable world, a magnet which drew wealthy and cultured people from all over Europe and beyond. There were always prominent Americans staying or passing through. It was here that John Jacob met Washington Irving, with whom he was to have a close relationship. Here, too, he made friends with one of the most remarkable women in Paris, Elizabeth Patterson Bonaparte. This lady, now in her mid-thirties, was a great beauty and wit. She was the daughter of a Baltimore merchant. In 1803, she fell in love with and married Jerome Bonaparte, youngest brother of the First Consul (and later emperor) who was serving in the French navy and had stopped to make a courtesy call in Baltimore. Napoleon was furious at this unauthorized match and subsequently annulled the marriage by imperial decree. The discarded lady elected to be known as Madame Patterson Bonaparte and, after the downfall of her brother-in-law's regime, although long since formally divorced from her exalted husband, devoted her time and energies to achieving for herself and her son the recognition and fortune she considered their due. She cultivated Mr Astor as a sympathetic compatriot who was an expert in financial affairs. He liaised for her with her in-laws in Rome, from whom Elizabeth hoped, vainly, for monetary assistance, and he advised her on her

American investments. Though he was unable to do much for her, he was certainly flattered by the confidence she reposed in him.

James Gallatin, who liked to consider himself a sophisticated *beau*, looked down his nose at the Astors. In his diary he, *reputedly*, recorded highly unflattering remarks about the businessman's dining habits: he ate his peas with a knife and he wiped his greasy fingers on the sleeve of Miss Gallatin's dress. Almost all later writers have pounced on this seemingly impeccable source and used it as evidence that Astor never mastered the arts of polite society and remained, to the end of his days, somewhat boorish. However, as long ago as 1957, the Gallatin diary was exposed, at least in part, as a fraud.[11] In the absence of any corroborative evidence we are, therefore, well advised to take these colourful stories with a very large pinch of salt. There was a tendency in Europe, and particularly in Britain, to be condescending towards *all* Americans. It may seem perverse, in the light of the above comments, to quote another anecdote from James Gallatin's diary, but this is supported, in general, if not in particular, by what we know of its principal character.

Madame Bonaparte had arrived late at a dinner party and thus delayed the start of the meal. She was seated next to an English guest, Mr Dundas, who was most put out at having to wait.

> After the soup had been served he turned to Madame Bonaparte and asked her if she had read the book of Captain Basil Hall on America. She replied in the affirmative. 'Well, madame, did you notice that Hall said all Americans are vulgarians?' 'Quite true,' calmly answered Madame Bonaparte, 'I am not in the least surprised. If the Americans had been the descendants of the Indians or the Esquimaux there might have been some reason to be astonished, but as they are the direct descendants of the English it is perfectly natural that they should be vulgarians.' After this Mr Dundas did not open his mouth again and left at the first opportunity.[12]

Madame Bonaparte's own letters reveal how conscious she was that her country was 'on approval' among the older nations of Europe, and its representatives regarded with some curiosity. 'The Americans begin to excite respect and interest,' she informed her father in 1815. 'American institutions, government, manners, climate, etc., etc., have become the subject of enquiry and concern ... every one seems to think [the USA] will one day be great.' However, at present 'the British are, as they modestly confess, the greatest nation in the world'.[13] James Gallatin, who considered himself a European by parentage and culture, would certainly have wanted to distance himself from his less-refined countrymen. He may also have been jealous of Astor. The merchant was immensely rich, while his own father was constantly beset by money problems. How insufferably patronizing John Jacob's offers of financial aid and business opportunities must have seemed to his friend's over-sensitive son.

As to Astor's manners, no one would have called them polished. He never, for example, mastered the intricacies of court etiquette. As his letters show, he was a plain-spoken man, not given to disguising his real feelings with a mask of insincere praise or diplomatic euphemism. On the other hand, he certainly appreciated the finer things of life – music, painting, intelligent conversation – and this was one reason why he spent so many years in Europe. He was also well aware of his own limitations. For example, when, in 1817, he wished to buy a 'handsome service of plate', he asked Albert to make the necessary arrangements because he reposed complete confidence in his friend's taste. He simply specified that the service should contain 'a pair of handsome salvers and a plateau' and should cost between three and four thousand pounds.[14]

If Astor's behaviour had fallen below an acceptable standard, some doors would certainly have been closed to him, but it is clear that John Jacob was in no way shunned by the leaders of society. However limited Astor's accomplishments were in the field of complicated Parisian etiquette, much was forgiven to a man of his great wealth. He and Eliza were greatly sought after and enjoyed a busy round of concerts, banquets, soirées, theatrical performances and salons. Yet never, amidst all the pleasant distractions of his new and exciting life, did Astor allow himself to forget the progress of his business interests. He kept up a steady correspondence with William and with his other colleagues. However, although he was as sharp as ever in his attention to details, it is possible to detect a different tone in his letters. He is content to leave decisions to subordinates. He speaks of withdrawing from some areas of the market and selling major interests to his partners. In 1821 he was still trying to persuade Albert Gallatin to take a one-fifth share in John Jacob Astor and Son. From the vantage point of cultured Paris, the New York counting house and the frontier trading posts seemed somehow less important.

John Jacob also received news from home. It did not make pleasant reading. In January 1820, Magdalen had become pregnant, and on 9 March she and John Bristed were married. Magdalen's second matrimonial adventure was briefer and ended more abruptly than her first. Within eighteen months Bristed decided that life with such a 'maniac' was intolerable. Like Bentzon, he hastened to put as much distance as possible between himself and his wife. He returned to his native England. There must have been something very weird and unpleasant about Magdalen for two men to have renounced a portion of the Astor fortune rather than continue under the same roof with her. It seems more than likely that something of the mental instability that plagued John Jacob II marred the life of his eldest sister. Bristed certainly appears to have been pleasant enough. He subsequently returned to America, where he served as rector to the church of St Michael, Bristol, Rhode Island, from 1830 to 1843. After his death in 1855 the grateful parishioners raised a monument to his memory.

Meanwhile, John Jacob and his daughter continued their European tour. After wintering in Paris and spending July 1821 in Switzerland, they travelled to England. John Jacob found the air of London in August 'not the most desirable to breathe' and he was still anxious about his business affairs in New York. 'Every letter I get from home', he told Gallatin, 'is more and more pressing for me to come home.' Yet he was reluctant to put an end to the holiday and eagerly sought reasons to delay his departure. One was his son John. The doctors were holding out hope of a successful outcome to his current treatment. 'Should I get good news of him in the course of next month I may then remain till spring,' he informed his friend.[15] Another reason for delay was his desire to fit in with Gallatin's plans. The diplomat had it in mind to relinquish his mission early in 1822 and Astor wanted to travel on the same ship. By December, he and Eliza were in Manchester and had definitely decided to book their passage to New York in the spring.

They sailed the following May. In the event they were unable to accompany the Gallatins, who postponed their return to America for a further year. But no sooner had John Jacob set foot in New York than he longed to be away again. By September, he was already making plans to spend a few years in Europe for 'here my health is not good'.[16] Astor's problem had little to do with his physical well-being; the plain fact is that he was bored with business. In October 1822 he wrote lugubriously to Gallatin:

> Matters here go on irregular enough. It's all the while up and down. So soon as people have a little money they run into extravagancy, get in debt and down it goes. Exchange is again $12\frac{1}{2}$ to 13, and people will again ship specie, the bank again curtail discounts, bankruptcy ensues, exchange will fall for a short time, and then we have the same scene over again. You know so well this country and character of the people that I need say no more.[17]

The pessimistic tone of this letter was partly due to the fact that Gallatin seemed finally resolved to return to America and his friend was trying to dissuade him. 'Your leaving Paris will be a great loss to me,' he confessed. James could not resist noting in his diary, 'Mr Astor, with great courage, has written begging [Father] to remain. Rather amusing as it is evidently for his own interests, as he is shortly coming to Paris.'[18]

Once again, we have to modify the cynicism of Gallatin *fils*. John Jacob was certainly dismayed at the prospect of being in Paris without his friend, and he readily confessed as much. But his motives in recommending Albert to remain in Europe were far from being entirely selfish. He was jealous for Gallatin's reputation and he knew, probably better than the diplomat himself, how widely he was respected. When Gallatin, weighed down by the financial burdens of his office, had asked his friend's advice over a possible move in 1819, Astor had been quite frank:

> As to the utility of your remaining in Europe till our matters with Spain are settled I think in all probability it will be very important that you do remain and in this opinion I know that I am not alone. You have acquired great fame as a public man and it would be a pity that by any means it should be lessened.[19]

John Jacob's high opinion of his friend was certainly shared by other American expatriates. 'Mr Gallatin is highly respected by everyone in Europe,' wrote Madame Bonaparte on the eve of what she hoped would not be the minister's final departure in 1823, 'and excessively admired for his talents. I fear it would be difficult to represent the country half as well if he should decline continuing minister.'[20]

Whether or not Gallatin remained in Paris, John Jacob was determined to return to Europe – and to leave America. 'Here I cannot pass my time but by being constantly engaged in business, which is a trouble to me and causes anxieties which I wish to avoid . . . I can do better in Europe or more pleasantly.'[21] John Jacob's mind was so firmly set by the end of 1822 that he declined an honour conveyed to him by Gallatin. William I, King of Württemberg, was one of Germany's more liberal rulers. He now offered Mr Astor the post of Consul in New York. John Jacob had considerable admiration and respect for the denizens of the diplomatic world, but if he was thrilled at the prospect of joining their ranks, his reply to his friend certainly did not show it. He was, he wrote, very conscious of the honour His Majesty was paying him and he would love to be in a position to help some of the poor immigrants who arrived from Württemberg every year. Unfortunately his imminent departure from the USA rendered it impossible to accept the consulship.[22]

Clearly we have to revise the traditional picture of John Jacob Astor as the compulsive entrepreneur, dominated by the making of money. That is certainly the impression he gave to most contemporaries, and doubtless he did not reveal to colleagues and rivals that he was weary of the demands and intricacies of commerce. Such, however, is the truth that emerges from his private correspondence. His own desire to return to Europe was reinforced by Eliza, who had hugely enjoyed her travels in 1819–21 and made many friends in Paris and Geneva. Thus it was that father and daughter set sail again in June 1823. Their ship crossed in mid-Atlantic with the one bearing the Gallatins home.

John Jacob and Eliza now had well-placed friends in Europe and were not reliant on their country's representative. They were not, this time, taking John with them, and once again there seems to have been no question of Sarah accompanying her husband on this trip, to sample the delights of high society in the old world. John Jacob's letters to other members of the family make affectionate references to Sarah, but clearly the couple could view long separation with equanimity. John Jacob had, apparently, no desire to share with his wife the pleasures of his extended holiday. Perhaps she, as a good Calvinist, had no desire to be involved in the frivolities of foreign courts. Whatever the truth – and it is unlikely that we shall ever know it – Astor was able to contemplate, even if only temporarily in moments of high enthusiasm for his new environment, making a life for himself in Europe far away from the pressures of family and business.

The itinerary that father and daughter planned this time was intended to cover northern Europe and some of the capitals and commercial centres they had not visited on their earlier journey. From Le Havre they went to Antwerp, The Hague, Amsterdam, Hanover and Frankfurt. From there John Jacob intended to travel south to Heidelberg and pay another call on his relatives in Walldorf. Unfortunately, Eliza was taken ill in Frankfurt and doctors prescribed mountain air for her. As soon as she was strong enough to travel John Jacob took her to Geneva, which they reached in December 1823. It was good to be back in Switzerland, which held such happy memories, even though most of their fashionable friends would have been in Paris for the winter. Now it was John Jacob's health which suffered a reverse. The malady, whatever it was, does not seem to have been too debilitating but he decided to curtail his travelling for the present. He bought a lovely villa at Genthod on the north shore of the lake and there father and daughter settled for several months.

One lady of their acquaintance who was in Switzerland because she could not afford the social demands of the French capital was Madame Bonaparte. It is to her somewhat acerbic pen that we owe a description of the Astors at this time:

> Mr A and daughter are here. He seems, poor man, afflicted by the possession of a fortune which he had greater pleasure in amassing than he can ever find in spending. He is ambitious, too, I fancy, for his daughter, to whom nature has been as penurious as fortune has been the reverse. She may marry by the weight of her person, but any idea of disposing of her except to some painstaking man of business, or ruined French or Italian nobleman, would be absurd. She is not handsome, and sense cannot be bought; therefore they will wander from place to place a long time before their object is accomplished. The father has no small portion of natural sense, and, could he have commanded the advantages of instruction which he gives his children, he might have made that figure which he desires, but will never attain for his family.

Education improves, but can never give capacity – a truth some people never discover.[23]

We have to be careful in picking the bones from this description, worthy almost of one of Jane Austen's less agreeable *grandes dames*. Elizabeth Patterson Bonaparte's judgements had certainly been distorted by her sad experiences. She lived in self-imposed exile, aspiring to a place in society she lacked the resources to sustain. There was more than a little envy in her contempt for the Astors' wealth and her observations about their lack of style. As to her assertion that Eliza was being hawked around the European marriage circuit, this was coloured by the fact that she was doing precisely that with her son. Elizabeth spent years seeking a 'suitable' match for her 'darling Bo' and was enraged when the young man ended up marrying an ordinary *American* girl. Nevertheless, Madame Bonaparte's pen portrait, more refined than James Gallatin's arrogant diary entries, does reveal some of the subtleties of the relationship between wealthy American visitors and the European élite at this early period.

If there is any truth in the assertion that Eliza and her father were husband hunting, their efforts were crowned with success far sooner than Madame Bonaparte prophesied. Within a few months John Jacob reported to Dorothea, 'Eliza is very well and very happy, I never knew her so much so.'[24] One reason for the twenty-three-year-old girl's good humour was the company of Vincent Rumpff. This Swiss-born diplomat was the representative in Paris of the Free Cities of Germany, a post which made up in commercial importance what it lacked in prestige. Rumpff was a cultured and accomplished man and very popular in the French capital. How and when he came into Eliza's life is not clear. They may have met earlier in Paris or on the Astors' brief stay in Frankfurt (for this was the *de facto* capital of Germany and by far the most important city Rumpff represented) or on their arrival in Geneva. However they met, their friendship quickly blossomed into something deeper. Inevitably, money had its part to play in furthering the romance. Rumpff had no fortune of his own, and the $300,000 John Jacob was prepared to settle on his daughter must have added considerably to Eliza's attractions. It would remove financial anxiety from him for the rest of his days, and there was always the promise of further benefactions from Astor's seemingly bottomless purse. As for John Jacob and Eliza, they had every reason to congratulate themselves on the match. The redoubtable Madame Bonaparte informs us that Rumpff 'is a handsome man of thirty-five, and we all think she has been very fortunate in getting him, as she is no beauty . . . He . . . is well connected, and has it in his power to introduce her into the best company.'[25]

John Jacob was very happy about this eminently suitable match, although the only comment of his which survives is his laconic observation to a business associate, 'I have nothing to regret but that Mr Rumpff is not an American, altho he is a good Republican and a respectable man.'[26] He and Eliza fell back into the fashionable habit of wintering in Paris and passing the warmer months with their Genevan friends. On 10 December 1825, Vincent and Eliza were married in Paris. By this time, the bride had, of course, spent all her young womanhood in Europe. The life of French high society to which she now happily settled was in no way new and she was soon a great favourite at court.

Early the following March she bade farewell to her father. John Jacob had spent an enjoyable winter in Paris, during which he had met most of the current celebrities of court and capital. Now, however, he was deprived of his travelling companion and had less to occupy his mind. His thoughts turned once more to business. It was time to get back to New York to see how well William was managing. He sailed from Le Havre on 10 March 1826.

There were by now compelling business reasons for his return. During his absence the firm of John Jacob Astor and Son had gradually and deliberately withdrawn from the China trade. The impressive fleet of clippers had been disbanded, the warehouse space sold off. There were two reasons for this drastic retraction. John Jacob's mercantile antennae sensed a new climate. His sojourns in Europe had revealed to him that fashions were changing. Smart gentlemen were now wearing silk hats. 'Beavers' were disappearing because it was now cheaper to make the felt from the skins of rabbits and hares. Chinese silk lost its cachet as the textile mills of Europe produced ever more varied materials. Even the taste in tea was changing as leaf from Japan and Java and, within a few years, India reached the West. In China internal disturbances and increasing competition made for difficult relationships with suppliers. The old, comparatively simple trading patterns were breaking down. That in itself was not a sufficient reason for abandoning a commerce in which John Jacob had been very profitably engaged for a quarter of a century, however. There had always been fluctuations in supply and demand; this was part of the challenge of the China trade. John Jacob had been successful because of his remarkable understanding of this volatile market and his ability to anticipate sudden shifts of direction. The second, and compelling, reason was that William Backhouse Astor lacked his father's entrepreneurial genius. He was a competent enough businessman, but he was not blessed with the imagination, audacity and the kaleidoscopic mind necessary to hold together an international network of trade. The family business had reached a crossroads and, at the age of sixty-three, John Jacob had to go home to plot its new route.

The aggressive policies of the American Fur Company and its subsidiary the South West Fur Company continued. Wherever possible, Astor's tough and ruthless agents forced competitors out of business. But they were under strict instructions not to ruin trade by creating conditions of destructive rivalry. Where necessary John Jacob was always ready to buy out other concerns. Having established commercial control over a vast tract of territory from the lower Mississippi to the Canadian border, the traders, trappers and trailblazers exploited it systematically. And they used the latest technology. In 1831 the American Fur Company launched the first steamboat service. For a decade these remarkable vessels had been revolutionizing the life and trade of the Southern cotton states. Astor realized that they could perform the same service for the more inaccessible lands to the north and west. Soon the *Yellowstone* was regularly plying between St Louis and Fort Union, a thousand miles away at the junction of the Missouri and the Yellowstone rivers, providing the company's trading posts with supplies and rushing their pelts to market.

Fort Union (reconstructed in recent years as a tourist attraction) was a symbol of the final phase of the Astor fur business. It was John Jacob's most distant depot, and it was an impressive demonstration to the Indians and the semi-civilized white men of the frontier of the owner's wealth and sophistication. Within its twenty-foot-high cottonwood palisade the manager lived in some state. The large 'Bourgeois House' was the scene of many grand gatherings and sumptuous dinners given in honour of visiting dignitaries. Here the indigenous people and the traders from the East met in profitable, and for the most part peaceful, transactions. The Indian wars, to which the American Fur Company's opening up of the waterways inevitably contributed, still lay in the future. For a few years Fort Union represented the partial realization of John Jacob's dream of a continent-spanning network of settlements which would be centres for the diffusion of trade and civilization – but only for a few years. By 1835 the American Fur Company's flag no longer flew over Fort Union, nor over any of the frontier trading posts. John Jacob Astor had withdrawn from the fur business.

During his second long visit to Europe the great furrier was not altogether satisfied with the way business was being handled in his absence. In his letters to various colleagues he found much to complain about: 'I have been vexed and I am not pleased with the expense the company has been put to in buildings.' 'The more I see it, the more I am convinced that we have ever imported too many goods and been induced to give them too freely to people who are unable to pay for them.' 'Mr Crooks is clever as an Indian trader . . . but he is not a merchant. His ideas . . . as to the trade are fallacious and extravagant.'[27] Much as he longed to distance himself from his business interests, John Jacob found it difficult to delegate. Not without some justification, he was convinced that no one could possibly understand as well as he the workings of the American Fur Company. He returned home in 1826 and threw himself into the task of reorganizing and tightening up the administration of his empire. All this was very daunting for thirty-four-year-old William, who, having made all the day-to-day decisions and borne the burden of responsibility for seven years, now found his father breathing down his neck and complaining that he had let things slip. John Jacob was becoming increasingly tetchy in old age. He was given to muttering, and sometimes writing in letters to associates, that the fur business was becoming so troublesome that he didn't know why he bothered with it. His threats to quit became more frequent with the passing months but no one took them seriously. As one colleague remarked, 'the business seems to him like an only child and he cannot muster courage to part with it.'[28]

Yet part with it he did, and at the very time when it seemed to have reached its peak of efficient organization. Probably the underlying reason was that he was conscious of his own failing powers. The fluctuations of the worldwide trade in pelts demanded an astute and energetic mind, but the business computer which served Astor as brain was past its prime. The fine calculations which had once provided him with exciting challenges now wearied him. Then again, the abandonment of the fur business was an almost inevitable corollary of the winding down of John Jacob's general overseas trade. The two had become intricately interwoven. Now that Astor had no ocean-going ships of his own for the transport of furs, he had to pay freight and warehousing costs which, of course, cut down his profit margins.

Then, in 1832, John Jacob received a very nasty shock. His beloved Eliza and her husband were both brought close to death. A great cholera epidemic, beginning in India in 1826, spread inexorably across Asia and Europe and eventually reached Paris, where the Rumpffs were among those struck down by the disease. Fortunately, they recovered, but it was only after weeks of worry that the family in New York received the welcome news. Meanwhile, the contagion was spreading along the shipping lanes and reached the American seaboard that summer. By this time John Jacob had once more departed for Europe (the two events may not be unrelated). Now, it was widely believed that animal skins were among the major carriers of the contagion. Understandably, there was a general slump in demand for furs. Understandably, also, Astor may have decided that he no longer wanted to be involved with the business. Like most elderly people he had become very preoccupied (one might almost say obsessed) with his health. To all these reasons for quitting the fur trade we can add one more. John Jacob by now had many other means at his disposal for increasing his capital by investment. By far the most important was Manhattan real estate – and, unlike furs and tea and shipping, land was a commodity that William Backhouse *understood.* In his declining years, therefore, John Jacob Astor turned his attention increasingly to New York property. To this activity we must shortly return.

The years 1826–32 were uneventful in the life of the New York family. William's wife, Margaret, had by the latter date provided John Jacob with six healthy grandchildren. Dorothea brought her total of Langdon children to four boys and four girls. In 1827 Eliza and Vincent arrived for a visit, taking the opportunity of a diplomatic mission that Rumpff had to undertake in Washington. It can be imagined with what excitement the ladies of the family gathered to be introduced to Eliza's elegant husband and to appraise her 'catch'. Three years later John Jacob's youngest daughter was back, alone and in less happy circumstances. In Paris, the autocratic Bourbon monarch Charles x had tried to put the clock back and strip away many of the rights won by the lower orders between 1789 and 1815. Opposition mounted over the years and came to a head in 1830 when the king dismissed an unco-operative parliament. In July the barricades went up in the streets of Paris and the palace was under siege. Before the crisis reached its peak Vincent Rumpff sent his wife back to her family for safety. He stayed in the capital and endured several uncomfortable days before the insurrectionists triumphed and ejected Charles x in favour of the Orleanist Louis-Philippe, the 'Citizen King'.

By the time Eliza reached New York order had been restored in France. As soon as the news reached her she was, of course, anxious to get back to her husband, but she stayed a few weeks to help nurse her sick sister. Dorothea was very ill after the birth of her last child, Eugene, but Eliza's gentle ministrations aided her recovery. To complete her cure the doctors recommended a change of air, and it was agreed that she and the children should return to Europe with Eliza. They took with them young Charles Bristed. Magdalen was now too ill, physically and mentally, to look after her son, and she, in fact, died within a few months.

Dorothea Langdon spent four years in Paris. It was a sojourn that radically changed her sister's life. Nothing is recorded of Dorothea's religious sentiments, but she had in her entourage a lady of most fervent Christian faith. This domestic, who gloried in the name of Phoebe Maybee, had a profound effect on Eliza. She made open profession of an intensified zeal for evangelical Protestantism and from that time became a generous patroness and enthusiastic instigator of missionary and educational work. Without abandoning her position at court (she was a great favourite with Louis-Philippe and his queen), she radically changed her lifestyle. Balls, outings to the theatre and to the opera were things of the past. Nor was she alone. She belonged to a group of ladies (including the Duchesse de Broglie) who met regularly for prayer and Bible study and who promoted charitable works. Eliza had improving books sent from America in order to establish a library for the children of British and American residents in Paris. This proved so popular that, within a few years, similar facilities had been set up in Le Havre, Nantes, Brussels, Naples, Florence and even St Petersburg. John Jacob had made over to her the villa at Genthod and this became another centre for Eliza's religious industry. She opened a school and even invented 'bussing', for she had children brought in by horse and cart from quite a wide region. All this was very expensive and would certainly have far exceeded her husband's ambassadorial stipend – but Eliza, of course, was an Astor. She had a large marriage settlement, and from time to time her father sent her further sums, all of which, we are told, 'she appropriated wholly to the promotion of religious and charitable objects'.[29] Doubtless it gave her considerable satisfaction to divert to God's work money tainted by the moral dubiety of trade. Certainly, she had found something which had eluded other members of her family – a purpose for living. Nature denied her children of her own, but she was able to serve hundreds of other people's offspring because of the advantages brought to her by her husband's position and her father's wealth.

John Jacob never learned the joy of giving money away with a light heart. His life's energies had been concentrated too much on acquiring a fortune. It was too late for him to learn the nobler art of dispensing it. This does not mean that he lacked generosity or affection for those he considered deserving of his aid. We have seen how even distant relatives benefited from his charity. Similarly, he did not forget his old friend Albert Gallatin. In 1826 the aged diplomat was prevailed upon by the government to undertake one more mission, this time to London. He returned at the end of the following year, looking forward at last (at the age of sixty-six) to retirement. Astor knew that the honest public servant had expended more than he had received in the representation of his country and he was determined to help.

He had never totally relinquished the idea of joining in a business venture with his friend. Advancing age rendered this a dream rather than a possibility – but, nevertheless, a dream he sometimes shared with Albert:

> At the moment, when there is not in all this city any mercantile house which may be considered as of very high and first rate standing here and in Europe, I am more than ever sorry not to be 10 or 15 years younger. With my capital and your friends and [good] name we could get all the good business of Europe. Such an establishment would be the height of my ambition and a great fortune could be [gained?] but, as it is, I feel as if I were too old and require too much time for the preservation of my health to attend much to business and I feel, also, as if I had fortune enough.[30]

Writing to Gallatin in London in 1827 he urged him to approach Barings to see if the bank would help him establish a New York-based business. The diplomat lacked both the commercial skill and the inclination to follow such advice. Astor knew this would be the case, so he took a hand himself to secure his friend's future. In 1829 the promoters of a new bank, to be called the National Bank of New York, came to John Jacob for help with funding. He agreed to provide it on one condition: that Albert Gallatin be appointed president, with a salary of $2,000 a year. The institution duly came into being. It was named the Gallatin Bank, and Astor's friend was president until 1839 (his salary was increased to $2,500 in 1836). At the same time, John Jacob also set up Albert's two sons in their own trading business – Gallatin Bros – on Wall Street. Thus did Astor privately take care of a public servant who might more appropriately have been rewarded by the government for his unstinting service to the nation.

Even in such acts as this one detects in John Jacob's attitude a want of sensitivity. *He* decided how best to help Albert and his family. *He* would be the munificent benefactor. *He* would provide for a friend who was too unworldly to feather his own nest. There is no indication that much consideration was given to Gallatin's opinions and feelings. There could scarcely be a greater contrast between two men whose circumstances were so similar. Astor and Gallatin were almost exact contemporaries. Both had left Europe to find a better life in a new country. Each in his own way had prospered. Gallatin ended his days serene in the knowledge that he had done the state some service. Astor could calculate his achievements more precisely, simply by opening a ledger and running his eyes over the columns of figures. The retired diplomat devoted his final years to a seminal study of the Indian tribes of the North American continent and became known as the 'father of American ethnology'. Astor's simple sobriquet was the 'richest man in America'. It would be several decades before scholars rescued Gallatin from comparative obscurity and assessed his true importance as a statesman and diplomat. Astor's legacy was obvious to anyone who walked the streets of Manhattan or read the gossip columns of the New York papers.

John Jacob had reached the age when the possible verdict of posterity began to be important to him. The first signs of this were observed around 1831. It was then that he decided to provide his city with its finest hotel. The central site he earmarked for this prestigious development was the block on Broadway between what were then Barclay and Vesey Streets. Gradually, surreptitiously, he bought up individual properties which came on the market. One he already owned, for it was his own mansion. It is not recorded that he asked Sarah how she felt about moving so that her home could be demolished in the furtherance of her husband's business ambitions.

Despite all these activities, Europe still beckoned and, in 1832, John Jacob set out for what he must have known would be his last visit to Europe. After an interval of six years, he longed to be back in his old haunts in Paris and

Geneva, to bask once more in the gentility of royal courts and the splendour of ancient capitals. Eliza, Vincent, Dorothea and the children welcomed him warmly. He renewed old friendships and, it is said, secured an introduction to Louis-Philippe.

John Jacob found France much changed. The new, liberal regime of the Citizen King still enjoyed much popularity and seemed to be establishing good relations with neighbouring nations. Yet not everyone was in favour of the enlightened monarchy. Astor had a long conversation with Lafayette, the seventy-five-year-old republican warhorse, the last great link with the French and American revolutions, the man regarded as 'the hero of two worlds'. Lafayette had originally supported the Orleanist cause, but now Astor had to report sadly that 'in politics he is out with most of his old friends as well as with the King. He charges them [with] having deviated from the cause and is understood to be *passé*.'[31] John Jacob found Paris much less gay but considered the change of style a considerable improvement. Perhaps he was influenced by his sober-minded daughter, who had now foresworn the frivolities of high society.

Astor had intended his stay to be a short one, principally because he had finally decided to close down his fur business. That would mean terminating contracts and selling off parts of the enterprise to other concerns. All this would require his personal attention. But as on previous occasions, when it came to the point, he could not tear himself away.

Yet he could not ignore the news which arrived by every mail from America. John Jacob's twenty-one months in France and Switzerland were months of mounting anxiety and sadness. He had to dispatch a stream of letters to New York with instructions for the winding up of the American Fur Company. He consulted a succession of Parisian doctors about his health. But on top of all this, unhappy news from home fell like repeated hammer blows. Hardly had he arrived in France when a letter from New York told him of Magdalen's death. It was followed over the ensuing months by further tragic information. William's infant daughter died, then John Jacob's sister, Catherine Ehninger, and in 1833 Henry, his last surviving brother, passed away (Melchior had died in 1829).

For months John Jacob hovered between duty and inclination. When, in March 1834, he did at last make up his mind to leave, the decision was a hurried one. By the time he applied for his ticket, all the state rooms on the *Utica* (the first available ship) were taken. However, the captain sacrificed his cabin for the wealthy passenger and John Jacob duly embarked. Yet he was still torn between the security of the family he had left and the responsibilities awaiting him in New York. Part of him certainly wanted to stay longer in France. Apart from anything else, he wished to be present at the wedding of his favourite granddaughter, Sarah Langdon, to Baron Robert Boreel, First Secretary of the Dutch legation in France, which was scheduled for 2 May. Such seems to have been his state of mind when he embarked.

Nothing else can explain the extraordinary events of the next couple of weeks, as related in one of the more bizarre anecdotes to have gathered around the name of John Jacob Astor. The story first appeared in *Harper's Magazine* in 1865 and the author was ostensibly given it by the captain of the *Utica*. Probably we should make some allowance for exaggeration: the seaman's tale had doubtless grown with much telling. However, here is the narrative, for what it is worth.

John Jacob was a seasoned traveller – over the years he had crossed the Atlantic in all weathers – yet when the *Utica* hit storms in the Channel he panicked. He scrambled up to the poop deck and assailed the captain with a demand to be put ashore in England. He offered a thousand dollars to be placed aboard a pilot boat. So importunate was he that the master agreed to alter course if the ship failed to reach the open ocean in the next few hours. During the night a change of wind took them out into the Atlantic, but the gales had not yet done their worst and the *Utica* was forced towards the Irish coast. Again Astor begged to be put ashore – *anywhere.* He now raised his offer to $10,000 to be delivered from the bucking vessel. The captain explained that if he tried to put into an unfamiliar harbour he would lose his insurance cover. 'But I'll insure you!' the demented Astor shouted. He rushed below and emerged waving a piece of paper covered in illegible scrawl. 'What's this?' the captain asked. 'It's a draft on my son for $10,000.' 'But no one can read it.' 'That's all right, my son will understand it.' Not surprisingly, the captain failed to be reassured by that assertion. He suggested the obvious answer (and the one which would rid him of his troublesome passenger): 'Let one of the other gentlemen draw up a proper draft. You sign it. Then I'll get you to land.' Suddenly, Astor changed his tune. Perhaps the shock of having his money refused brought him to his senses. He turned down the offer, stamped back to his cabin and sulked. Within hours the wind abated and the *Utica* was able to resume her course. But Astor's strange behaviour was not at an end. When the ship was off the Newfoundland Banks the master hailed an outward-bound vessel. Once more Astor was at his side. 'Tell them I'll pay a thousand dollars for a passage to Europe,' he urged.

The story has, in its bare elements, the ring of truth. It certainly fits with what we know of Astor's feelings for Europe and America. If we accept it, we can see Astor's odd behaviour arising, not from a bad bout of seasickness or the fear of impending shipwreck (as the original author suggested), but from a sudden change of heart about returning to the USA. The nightmare crossing ended, at last, on 4 April, when the *Utica* berthed in New York.

On the quayside John Jacob learned that his wife had died eight days earlier.

He returned to an empty house – or, at least, a house peopled only by servants. Doubtless William and Margaret did their best to comfort him, but any grieving he did, he did alone. When Dorothea heard of her mother's death she hurried home with the younger children, but it was autumn before the Langdons were back in New York. The only family John Jacob had around him for the crucial first weeks of his bereavement were William and his wife. Whether through force of habit or because he knew work was the best antidote for grief, Astor was soon back at his desk. On 4 May he described to a friend something of what he felt.

> I am getting some better, but slowly . . . while absent, I lost wife, brother, daughter, sister, grandchildren and many friends and I expect to follow very soon. I often wish you were near me. I should find much in your society which I am in need of, being no longer disposed to business, or rather not able to attend to it . . .[32]

His heart may not have been in his work, but the practised mechanism of his business brain ticked on. Over the next few months he attended to the detailed obsequies of the American Fur Company. As the assets were disposed of money poured into his various bank accounts – money for which a use had to be found. Some of it was invested in securities, but they did not bring much return. Land was considerably more interesting and potentially more profitable. Soon John Jacob was well on the way towards creating the third, and biggest, Astor fortune.

The present Viscount Astor has in his possession a book, made in 1840, in which his ancestor recorded all his New York property transactions. Each right-hand page has a coloured drawing showing exactly the boundaries of every plot bought and sold. On the opposite leaf, in tiny handwriting, are the details of purchase or lease, buildings and rents. From this squat leather-bound volume it is easy to see that John Jacob approached the task of building up his Manhattan land holdings very scientifically. There is an old story that, until quite late in life, he combined business with his favourite form of exercise by regularly riding round the outlying areas of the growing city and noting down any acreage that was likely to be coming on the market. As New York spread, so did the Astor holdings. However, the bulk of John Jacob's properties were in the prime development areas now bounded approximately by Fifth Avenue, 42nd Street, the Hudson River and Central Park.

As we have seen, John Jacob had been involved in land speculation since the beginning of the century, but his strategy changed around 1819. This coincided with the winding down of his other business interests and the entry of William Backhouse into full partnership. For the first twenty years or so John Jacob had looked to land to yield short-term profit rather than long-term security. Property transactions were simply a part of his total commercial activity; a means of increasing his working capital or providing collateral for raising business finance. Sometimes, when there was no alternative, Astor acquired blocks of land on long lease. His profit then came from splitting such blocks into lots and sub-leasing them for short terms. Since these blocks were usually in new residential districts the arrangement was that the lessees would erect their own houses on the land they had acquired. At the end of the term, Astor either granted a new lease at an increased rental or bought the buildings. Either way, the value of his holdings had been increased largely at someone else's cost and bother. The 'landlord' is never a popular figure, especially if he proves himself unsympathetic to hard-pressed tenants in difficult times. John Jacob and his immediate descendants certainly had a bad name among the New York citizenry. By and large the reputation seems to have been deserved. John Jacob certainly had no compunction about foreclosing when rents or mortgage payments (he sometimes granted mortgages to his tenants) fell into arrears.

After 1819 the balance of his property speculations was reversed. Now he bought, not for quick profit, but for long-term appreciation. Now he dealt in land, not as part of his overall business activity, but as his principal commercial interest. In the last twenty-nine years of his life he invested $1.25 million in real estate. This compares with about $700,000 previously expended, most of which Astor spent during the first decade of the century. Some of the purchase money came from business profits and the sale of his other concerns, but by about 1835 the Astor property empire was wholly self-financing. In 1815 John Jacob had told Gallatin that his net annual profit from the China trade fluctuated between fifty and a hundred thousand dollars. The following yearly rental returns show that real estate soon became a more rewarding, as well as less hazardous, commodity than furs and tea.

1830/31	$ 46,000
1840/41	$128,000
1847/48	$200,000

To these figures can be added income from direct sales of freeholds and leases. The bulk of this profit went into acquiring yet more property. Shortly before his death Astor calculated that his Manhattan land holdings had cost him two and a half million dollars and were then worth twice that figure. Small wonder that he remarked to a friend in his last months, 'Could I begin life again, knowing what I now know, and had money to invest, I would buy every foot of land on the Island of Manhattan.'[33]

It would be pleasant to be able to record that John Jacob Astor was possessed of some sort of vision for the future of the city; that he worked with construction companies and architects to impose a shape on the rapidly growing metropolis. In fact, there is little evidence that he was anything other than a speculator in land. He leased or sold many plots to builders and, in some cases, helped to finance their work, but it was they who drew up the plans and raised the town houses, tenements, offices and shops that, bit by bit, gave New York its shape. By the law of averages some of these edifices were impressive and well-constructed while others were shoddy, hastily built and destined to degenerate into slums.

The one exception was John Jacob's grand hotel project. When he returned from Europe in 1834 and discovered that his wife had died there was no longer anything to stop him pressing ahead with the demolition of the existing properties. He was probably quite glad to see his own house disappear. Its now empty rooms held too many memories. Within weeks the site was cleared and, on Independence Day, John Jacob laid the foundation stone for the Park Hotel. It opened its doors in May 1836 and New Yorkers discovered that they had, as well as eighteen new high-class shops, a modern, luxuriously appointed building with three hundred bedrooms and *seventeen* bathrooms! Such magnificence could, of course, only be afforded by the wealthier Americans and foreign visitors, but it certainly added to the prestige of the city and, as soon as its success was obvious, its name was changed from Park Hotel to Astor House. John Jacob, however, did not run it. Like all his properties, it was leased, in this case to professional hoteliers.

If the property tycoon scores low marks for public-spiritedness, he comes near the top of the class for benevolence to his family. In 1819 John Jacob gave some advice to a friend experiencing family problems:

> Remember, my dear friend, how soon you may have to leave this world and remember that, like all men, you will seek forgiveness. Forgive your children, as you wish our father in heaven to forgive you. Let them come to you and support them . . . for all your wealth will do you no good in your grave. Divide some of it with them. See them happy and comfortable and you will be so yourself. Don't tell me that it is easy to give advice. I say to you that I do divide with my children. Like you, I worked for them and I wish them to have all the good of it. The more they enjoy it, the more happy am I.[34]

This was no empty boast. A glance through John Jacob's property inventory shows on almost every page individual plots and blocks of land which he made over to members of his family. Thus, for example, Astor House was given to William as soon as it was built, and a whole row of plots at the northern end of the Bowery (now Park Avenue) was given to the Langdons. In his will, drawn up in 1836, John Jacob completed the dividing of his real estate among his children, grandchildren, nephews and nieces. While it is true that he kept the greater part of his estate intact for William, it is also true that the head of the family ensured that all those relatives to whom he was well disposed would be very comfortably provided with capital and income. It may even be that he invested the bulk of his money in property in his later years with the specific intention of devising it to his descendants. Certainly, he was careful to set up trusts to administer some of his legacies in order to keep any tax liability to a minimum.

By the time Astor House opened its doors John Jacob was comfortably past the age of threescore years and ten and his thoughts frequently turned to his reputation. The public only knew him as a grasping landlord and a ruthless man of business. For most of his life he had been proud to be seen as such. It was precisely because competitors, tenants and employees knew him to be shrewd, parsimonious and unscrupulous that they respected him and thought twice about trying to cheat him. But now that the money-chasing years were behind him, John Jacob wanted to be remembered for other things. He wanted to be seen as a man of culture, a public benefactor and an adventurous spirit. He believed he was all these things. The world would take some convincing.

When Astor returned to New York he found an old friend already ensconced there and enjoying considerable public acclaim. After seventeen years of European wanderings, Washington Irving had returned to his homeland in 1832, and immediately became a literary lion. The two men met up again and John Jacob realized that his own name would be enhanced if he could persuade this celebrated author to write something for him. What he had in mind was the great Astoria adventure. Accordingly, he offered to put all his documents at Irving's disposal and to pay for assistants to sort them out in readiness for Irving to take up his pen. The author agreed and soon his nephew, Pierre Irving, and Astor's personal secretary, Fitz-Green Halleck, were poring over letters, bills and account books at Hell Gate, John Jacob's modest thirteen-acre estate on the banks of the East River. When their work was done, Irving set to work and early in 1836 he completed *Astoria, or Anecdotes of an Enterprize Beyond the Rocky Mountains*. It is an exciting and well-told account that does justice to its subject. Of course, it presents Irving's patron in the best possible light and places all the blame for the expedition's failure on other shoulders. Further, it perpetuates Astor's criticism of the nation's leaders for refusing to support the great vision.

> We repeat, therefore, our sincere regret that our government should have neglected the overture of Mr. Astor and suffered the moment to pass by when full possession of this region might have been taken quietly as a matter of course, and a military post established without disputes at Astoria. Our statesmen have become sensible when too late, of the importance of this measure. Bills have repeatedly been brought into Congress for the purpose, but without success, and our rightful possessions on

that coast, as well as our trade on the Pacific, have no rallying point protected by the national flag and by a military force.

History and the march of human events, Irving concludes, will vindicate John Jacob Astor and condemn the faint hearts which doomed the great adventure.

As one wave of emigration after another rolls into the vast regions of the west, and our settlements stretch towards the Rocky Mountains, the eager eyes of our pioneers will pry beyond, and they will become impatient of any barrier or impediment in the way of what they consider a grand outlet of our empire.[35]

For all its biased political intent, however, *Astoria* is an important piece of historical literature based on materials most of which are no longer available.

Whatever it did for his reputation as a man of affairs, *Astoria* did not win for John Jacob a place among New York's cultural élite. For his part, he patronized literary men. Washington Irving was a frequent guest in his home and he supported some of the less-established poets and authors of the day. He erected for himself a splendid new town house further along Broadway at number 585 and filled it with the finest works of art and furniture which he had brought back from Europe over the years. Here he held occasional musical evenings, engaging the best performers to entertain his guests. His circle of friends and acquaintances was wide, embracing merchants and sea captains, politicians and literati. Those who knew him well found the old man good company, full of fascinating stories about early days on the fur trail and the great men and women he had met in Paris. For all that, entry to the club eluded him. New York, like every other city, had its inner circle, membership of which was only by common consent and governed by no formal rules. Wealth was only one qualification and not an overmastering one. Despite his millions, John Jacob Astor was never 'in'.

There were many reasons for this. One obvious one was that he had no hostess, no one to accompany him to soirées or organize her own balls and 'at homes'. He kept a bachelor establishment with his secretary, a companion, Joseph Cogswell, and with his grandson Charles Bristed. Astor brought the latter up as his son, educated him, sending him to Yale and subsequently to Trinity College, Cambridge, and finally bequeathed to him both his residences and also enough money to enable him to live the life of an independent gentleman. Bristed, it is pleasant to record, always revered his grandfather's memory and was ever ready to come to his defence when the old man's name was under attack. And there were always those ready to disparage John Jacob. Stories of his meanness and sharp practice were common currency in the smart clubs and salons. Moreover the Astor name was seldom out of the courts. John Jacob was involved in frequent litigation with tenants and lessees, creditors and debtors. Where his financial interests were involved he was tenacious, and most people in New York society knew someone who had been involved in unpleasant legal proceedings with John Jacob Astor.

What most of his fellow citizens did *not* know was that in his latter years John Jacob Astor was making plans for something that would prove of inestimable benefit to New York for generations to come. The project had a long gestation period and a difficult birth, and would not have come into the world at all but for the patient and determined pre-natal nursing of Cogswell. Joseph Green Cogswell was a prominent American man of letters and a graduate of Harvard and Göttingen. He was already fifty-one when, in 1837, he first came to the attention of John Jacob. Cogswell was a friend of Washington Irving and was currently employed by (or, more accurately, enjoying the patronage of) the banker Samuel Ward. It was Irving who effected the introduction, and Cogswell's reaction was similar to that of many who actually got to know the man, rather than his reputation. Astor was, the scholar explained to a friend, 'not the mere accumulator of dollars, as I had supposed him; he talks well on many subjects and shows a great interest in the arts and literature'.[36]

As the friendship of the two men grew, Astor confided to Cogswell that he wished to devote part of his fortune to a major enterprise for the city of New York. The words were music to Cogswell's ears, for he had long nursed an ambition to see the city provided with a public library which would enhance its status and give its citizens access to the cultural heritage of the world. John Jacob agreed to provide this facility and by the end of July 1837 the whole scheme was agreed in principle. Then the magnificent plan was leaked to the press. That changed everything. Cogswell was on a visit to Boston and did not return until early October.

> As soon as Mr Astor heard of my being in New York, he sent a messenger into the city to beg me to call upon him. I went out [to Hell Gate] the next day and found him very cordial but feeble. I learnt that he had been beset by innumerable applications for money, in all possible amounts from five to five thousand dollars, since his great act of munificence had been made known ... This his own penetrating mind had foreseen, and it had induced him to change his intended donation to a legacy.[37]

It was a disappointment, but Cogswell could see no reason to slow down the pace of the planning process. There was, after all, much to be arranged – land, architects, drawings, staffing, the purchase of books, etc. Over the course of the next few months the basic details were worked out. On 22 August 1839, John Jacob added a codicil to his will by which $400,000 was to be set aside for the Astor Library ($120,000 of which was to be spent on books) to be built on a plot provided by him at the corner of Lafayette Place and Arts Street.

In the autumn of 1839 Cogswell travelled to Europe at the behest of William Backhouse, to see his son, John Jacob III, well settled into Göttingen University. The scholar went reluctantly and only agreed when John Jacob provided him with substantial funds to buy up any private European libraries which might happen to come onto the market.

When Cogswell returned, Astor urged him to join his household. The old man was now quite unscrupulously using the project as a form of blackmail. He was lonely. He enjoyed Cogswell's cultured company. Knowing the other man's absolute commitment to the library, he deliberately spun out the negotiations. Cogswell knew perfectly well that he was being used, but he submitted because that was the only way to ensure that John Jacob did not change his will. He moved into the Astor ménage. In 1842 there was a showdown. Washington Irving was appointed US Minister to Spain and invited Cogswell to accompany him as secretary of legation. Naturally, John Jacob did not want him to go. Cogswell said he would stay only on condition that work on the library was set in hand immediately. The old fur merchant was adept at striking bargains. 'What consideration will induce you to stay with me,' he asked, 'and leave the question of the library to my future decision?' Cogswell's answer was brief: 'None whatever.' He had Astor over a barrel – or so he thought. John Jacob agreed to his friend's terms and immediately summoned architects and builders to set the work in hand. Cogswell stayed – and nothing happened. Having gained his objective, Astor went back to prevarication.

Only after John Jacob's death did work on the library get under way. As soon as the will was proved, Cogswell set off on the first of several buying sprees in Europe, and acquired several of the rarities for which the New York Public Library is now world famous. He was the Astor Library's first director. He saw the original building opened in 1854, housing some 80,000 volumes.*

By the last years of his life John Jacob Astor had become a phenomenon, an institution. He conformed to none of the accepted conventions. His manners were not polished. He was brusque to the point of eccentricity. But there was more to it than that. He was the Richest Man In America, a living legend. People stood on the sidewalk to stare as he passed in his elegant carriage or, in winter, in his open, horse-drawn sleigh. And, because lesser men always feel uncomfortable in the presence of great success, they told stories about him. Thus sprang up a wide apocrypha of tales, some amusing, some vicious, and only a few grounded in truth. In order to tie Gulliver

* The library benefited from subsequent Astor bequests over the next two generations and was substantially extended twice. In 1895 it was consolidated with other private trusts to form the New York Public Library. It moved to its present site on Sixth Avenue in 1911.

down his Lilliputian fellow countrymen used the cynical cords of satire and broad humour.

In reality, there was nothing very risible about John Jacob's last years. In 1838 he received the dismal news that the beloved, *très pieuse* Eliza had died in Switzerland after a short, painful illness. He still had William and Dorothea and their extensive families as well as scores of nephews and nieces. He presided over this clan like a fond patriarch and especially enjoyed the company of the children. But many of them found him an embarrassment. Wealth and education had distanced them from the man who had provided these things. With his heavily accented speech and his rough-and-ready ways, John Jacob was a relic from another age, another world. His descendants, the younger Astors, Langdons, Wilks and Kanes, enjoyed the fashionable life of a New York that had changed radically since the pioneer days of half a century earlier. It was bigger, busier and more socially stratified. The new generation had their own preoccupations: there were parties to plan, clothes to buy and gossip to spread. For the more serious-minded there was the growing friction between North and South over the issues of slavery and states' rights to worry about.

In his beautiful homes with nothing left to plan but the bequeathing of his millions, old John Jacob lingered too long. He entered his eighties with an alert mind in a decaying body. He relied heavily on Cogswell who, as the months passed, became more a nursemaid than a companion. In 1843 Cogswell told a friend, 'Mr Astor has now no one but myself to amuse him, and I am chiefly occupied with doing that . . . Every pleasant day we take a steamboat and while away some three or four hours in the inner or outer bay.'[38] John Jacob loved boats. He would sit for hours watching them pass up and down the East River, doubtless reliving the days when heavily laden vessels had crossed the world's oceans at his behest. The following year, a dinner guest recorded:

> He sat at the dinner table with his head down upon his breast, saying very little, and in a voice almost unintelligible . . . a servant behind him to guide the victuals which he was eating, and to watch him as an infant is watched. His mind is good, his observation acute, and he seems to know everything that is going on. But the machinery is all broken up, and there are some people, no doubt, who think he has lived long enough.[39]

The nights were the worst time for John Jacob. In the sleepless hours he would summon Cogswell and other members of the household to his bedside and keep them engaged in conversation till their eyelids drooped and their heads throbbed.

John Jacob Astor I maintained his tenacious grip on life until 29 March 1848, three and a half months short of his eighty-fifth birthday. The only question most men asked and speculated about after his death was 'Just how rich was he?' His executors conservatively put the figure at $8 million. The wilder press elements suggested $150 million. The *Illustrated London News* cautiously calculated: 'The estimates of the value of his property are various; those knowing his affairs best placing it at 30,000,000 dollars, and some as high as 50,000,000 dollars. His income on a moderate estimate must have been of late 2,000,000 dollars a year.'[40] Since most of his money was tied up in property there can be no precise assessment, but most biographers have been happy to accept a total estate of between twenty and thirty million dollars. When one is dealing in such astronomical sums an odd million or two is neither here nor there. Few outside the Astor circle benefited from the old man's will. His largest public benefaction was the $400,000 towards the building and equipping of the Astor Library. The German Society of New York received $20,000. And in his last years the thoughts of the butcher's son from Baden turned back to his roots. Perhaps, like the fictional Citizen Kane, John Jacob sat in his mansion and dreamed of happier, simpler days. The $50,000 he left to the town of Walldorf was earmarked to provide a foundation to care for the frail and elderly and also to provide education for poor and orphaned children. He impressed on his family the importance of this particular donation and, within two years of his death, his eldest grandson travelled to Germany to oversee the setting up of a trust to administer it. The richest American remained to the end of his days a man whose heart lay in large measure on the other side of the Atlantic. That was to be a part of his legacy.

The prospect of a citizen becoming enormously successful and passing on the fruits of his success to future generations created problems for many commentators in the land of equality and opportunity. During the years when John Jacob had been acquiring his fortune he had been widely admired, even though some disliked his business methods. This was, after all, what America was about. It was the land where a poor immigrant could become a millionaire by solid industry and honest endeavour. But when that millionaire bequeathed the bulk of his estate to his son who had done nothing to merit it, alarmed critics could see the evil class divisions of the Old World replicating themselves in the new. 'The millionaire is as dangerous to the welfare of the community in our day, as the baronial lord of the Middle Ages,' one writer complained,[41] and another protested that the object of John Jacob's will was 'to create an Astor dynasty – and to keep up this dynasty by entailing the property upon the regular successors of the individual for ages to come'.[42]

Horace Mann, a noted social reformer, put into words (in *A Few Thoughts for a Young Man*, 1850) what many Americans probably vaguely felt, that the Astor fortune should, in large measure, be used for the benefit of the country in which it had been made. He contrasted Astor's will with that of Stephen Girard, who had died in 1831 leaving his millions for the founding and endowing of a school. It was Charles Bristed who sprang to his grandfather's defence in *A Letter to the Hon. Horace Mann* (1850). He pointed out that there was one enormous difference between Girard and Astor. Whereas the former died a childless bachelor, John Jacob had a large family which looked to him for succour. As to Mr Girard's college, surely Mann knew that the terms of the foundation stated that 'no ecclesiastic, missionary, or minister of any sect whatsoever, is ever to be admitted for any purpose'.[43] Did Mr Mann really approve the use of garnered wealth for the purpose of spreading atheism? If one accepted the probate valuation of the Astor estate (which was certainly far too low) Bristed argued, it would be seen that the late millionaire had bequeathed a sixteenth of his fortune for the public well-being – no niggardly bequest. The apologist went on to point out that if the government had supported Mr Astor's far-sighted Columbia territory project the nation would have reaped incalculable rewards.

When later generations formed assessments of John Jacob Astor and the Manhattan property snowball he set rolling, they were, inevitably, influenced by the lives of the furrier's descendants. Some were not very talented, some were exceedingly dull, some were outrageously arrogant dilettantes. There was something wrong about open American democracy, critics reasoned, when such people were allowed to strut around like *ancien régime aristos* who did not earn their keep.

The fact is that both America and the Astors were unprepared for the phenomenon of inherited wealth. The nation's rulers lacked the means to achieve a degree of social levelling. Indeed, the very idea was anathema to those who believed that all men are endowed with the inalienable rights of 'Life, Liberty and the pursuit of Happiness'. As for John Jacob and his immediate descendants, they had not been brought up in a paternalistic tradition which sought to balance the privileges of wealth with its obligations. The Astors – and other families who had prospered in the early years of the republic – constituted an upper class in an avowedly classless society. Some, like John Jacob, would be constantly drawn towards Europe, where the concepts of élitism and wealth differential were understood. Some would try to create an American version of a stratified society. All would, to a greater or lesser extent, find their inheritance uncomfortable.

CHAPTER 5

'The parsimonies and the squanderings of wealth'

All human beings are selfish, unless and until they find in self-giving a path to fulfilment and happiness. The only thing that marks out a millionaire like William Backhouse Astor from the rest of the race is the sheer scale of his meanness. From the mid-nineteenth century onwards commentators and biographers have hypocritically castigated the heir to John Jacob I's wealth. In December 1875 *Appleton's Journal* complained:

> No schools, no academies, no churches, no public pleasure grounds bear his name. The wealth of this great millionaire is not even evidenced in useful or economical things. The best form of house for the laboring man is one of the problems of the day. Mr Astor, with all his great resources, made no effort to solve it. No model tenements went up under his inspiration; no pretty or tasteful rows of cottages were devised by his hand; no contribution whatever toward the solution of questions in the economy of the home ever came from him. He made no experiments, acquired no experience, contributed no results, set no needed example even in the domain of house-building, into which his accumulated wealth ever steadily went.

That is typical of the verdicts expressed and repeated down the years. Great riches certainly open up great opportunities. The hypocrisy lies in insisting that it is more reprehensible for a rich man to husband his resources than for a poorer man to do so. It is as though the writer, envious of the Astor millions, were saying, 'Of course, if I possessed such resources, I would be generous in my benefactions' – an assertion as unlikely as it is incapable of proof. William Backhouse Astor believed, as most people believe, that his own property was his to do with as he pleased. He was a narrow man who could not see far beyond his own immediate interest. His only achievement lay in doubling the fortune he inherited. Even that was less the result of skilful investment than of the natural increase of property values. The biographer's task is to try to explain why this should be so and what its results were.

The first of those twin responsibilities is made difficult by the fact that William ordered all his personal papers to be destroyed after his death. We are therefore denied any glimpses of his deeper thoughts or finer feelings.

Such must have existed, for William as a young man had delighted in the company of profound and sensitive thinkers such as Schopenhauer and Bunsen. These men had gone on to make significant contributions to European philosophy and politics, as William must have been aware. What was it that stamped out the youthful fires of idealism and intellectual speculation, leaving only the dull grey ash of a self-absorbed reactionary?

At the time of his father's death William was fifty-six and he had spent thirty-two years in the estate office. Throughout the first half of that period he had been in sole command for much of the time while John Jacob enjoyed the delights of Europe which his son had been obliged to relinquish. Yet his had been an illusory authority. Every ship from France brought letters from John Jacob conveying instructions and countermanding orders, and whenever the head of the company returned there were inquisitions over his son's conduct of affairs. In the final analysis John Jacob had made it clear to his heir that he lacked the initiative and business acumen necessary to sustain a complex and multi-faceted commercial operation. This had been a major reason for the channelling of the Astor millions into that safest, most idiot-proof of all commodities – land. During those years of early manhood William grew up knowing – as everyone around him knew but seldom said to his face – that he was but a pale shadow of the old man.

There were three possible ways he could react to the common verdict. He could accept it and become the humdrum creature of low self-worth that others proclaimed him to be. He could confound his detractors by throwing himself enthusiastically into the work of Astor and Son and making an original contribution to its functioning. Or he could turn his back on it and strike out on his own path (perhaps in Europe) as his father and uncles had done.

If the third alternative was ever a real option it was firmly and, doubtless, deliberately squashed by William's father. Between 1810 and 1817, John Jacob took various longstanding colleagues into partnership in the American Fur Co. and the Pacific Fur Co. They all had minor shareholdings but they enjoyed considerable authority in different parts of the interior. As we have seen, he also made repeated attempts to draw Albert Gallatin into his overseas trading concern. He certainly envisaged the possibility of his various undertakings being entrusted to other hands. He would scarcely, otherwise, have sent his only sane son to complete his education in war-dislocated Europe. (At one time, in fact, he convinced himself that William had been killed.) He spoke frequently about retirement and his long sojourns in France and Switzerland were, indeed, a semi-retirement. So it seems clear that passing on his empire intact to a hereditary heir was far from being a fixed resolve. John Jacob might well have been content to see his children and grandchildren set up as ladies and gentlemen of independent means. But Gallatin turned him down, the fur business became more precarious at the precise time that the Astor companies achieved paramountcy and John Jacob conceived a passion to return to Europe. For all these reasons he needed William at the centre of his operations in New York. William bowed to his father's will, although it is not clear how hard he found the decision. It does not place much strain upon our imagination to see John Jacob ruthlessly playing the 'filial obligation' card. There was no-one else to look after the business in his absence; William must shoulder his family responsibilities. And, of course, John Jacob always had the financial ace up his sleeve. He had already disinherited Dolly, albeit only temporarily, for displeasing him. William would not have relished the thought of going out into the world without a penny to his name. In any case, he was soon married and that effectively ruled out an act of defiance which might have monetary consequences.

With the third option ruled out, William seems to have settled for a combination of the other two. He certainly accepted that the mantle of his father's greatness had not fallen upon him; that he was a man of very modest talents. He suppressed his youthful enthusiasms and settled to the dull routine of the Astor office. At the same time, he played an active part in steering the business towards a preoccupation with Manhattan property. As well as his major interests, John Jacob had fingers in several other pies – banking, insurance, government securities. He held tracts of land in Canada and the interior and he even flirted briefly with speculation in railroads. William could not cope with all these activities, but he did understand New York real estate and he encouraged his father to put more and more of his eggs into this particular basket. William's genuine interest in property investment probably explains one otherwise puzzling fact. He shared his interest in land with his Uncle Henry. As we have seen, Henry Astor was a pioneer investor in Manhattan real estate and introduced John Jacob to it. Henry died, a childless millionaire, in 1833. Most of his money was tied up in property and he left the bulk of it to William. Several of his relatives were angered and disappointed. They felt that they were more in need of Henry's bounty than the heir to John Jacob's vast fortune. Henry, who was certainly neither unkind nor stupid, seems to have felt that his nephew was the one member of the family who really understood the property market and was the best equipped to administer the portfolio he had carefully built up.

After 1834 William found himself *de facto* head of the business but liable to be overruled at any time by the man who was still in command *de jure* and whose will was as strong as his body was increasingly frail. The office was adjacent to John Jacob's town house, so there was no escaping the old man, who lingered on, his behaviour sometimes an embarrassment, his interest in the business keen to the end. By the time William was eventually free of this encumbrance any creative energy he might once have possessed had long since evaporated. He would continue for the rest of his life doing what had become habit – poring daily over rent books, leases, deeds and ledgers.

The work could have been done by a handful of competent clerks, but that would have involved reorganization and training. It would have meant trusting subordinates. Above all, it would have obliged William to find some other way of filling his days. Since he had few friends and fewer interests this would have posed quite a problem. Despite his wife's efforts to coax him out into society, William disliked the glitter and frivolity of balls, parties and dinners. The man who could have afforded lavish entertainment, gambling, spirited horses or any other fashionable pursuit asked nothing more than to sit by the fire with a good book. Books had always been his main solace and his refuge from the counting house since student days. He maintained throughout his life the fascination with facts and ideas that had been kindled in the earnest discussions far into the night with Bunsen, Schopenhauer and the friends of his youth.

William Backhouse was a man afflicted with progressive spiritual blindness. As year followed year his field of vision narrowed. Eventually, the only fact that he could see clearly was that he was the richest man in America, and that dominated every aspect of life for himself and his family. The estate office was run with a cold, profit-conscious efficiency which shrugged off allegations of exploitation and the ownership of slum tenements. It was not that the Astors were crassly immoral; the Calvinistic strain in their upbringing was too strong for that. William and Margaret were diligent Episcopalians (a more respectable form of Protestantism than that of their parents). They brought up their children with a strict regimen of personal ethics whose vertebral column was made up of duty, hard work, self-reliance and self-control. Duty was an extension of their own enterprising individualism. So was industry: 'God helps those who help themselves' might well have been their watchword.

Assured of divine approval, the Astors cared not a jot for the opinions of mere mortals. They inhabited a lonely pinnacle among New York's social élite. Others might band together in an exclusive club of wealth and self-importance. Others might found dynasties whose names were synonymous with luxury and influence – Vanderbilt, Drexel, Stuyvesant Fish and a select group of banking, shipping and railroad barons. Others might create a Manhattan set, with its own protocol and etiquette palely reflecting the court-centred hierarchies of Paris, London and Vienna. But there was only one Astor family, and they chose to remain aloof – or at least, William Astor did. Unlike European nobility, New York's financial and commercial upper crust lacked a royal household around which to revolve. The gap was very noticeable. A brittle society in which taste, fashion and culture are the vital elements needs an ultimate arbiter who decides who is 'in' and who is 'out' and what the prevailing style shall be this season. Manhattan's aristocracy would happily have crowned the Astors in order to fill the gaping hole in their social fabric. When William and his sister Dorothea built themselves palatial residences on Lafayette Place at the verdant, out-of-town extremity of Broadway, other wealthy New Yorkers fell over themselves to acquire neighbouring plots. When William bought his father-in-law's estate at Rhinebeck on the Hudson, as a weekend retreat for his family, it immediately became the fashion to have a 'country place'. When Margaret put her household servants into livery so did all her friends and acquaintances. Yet William was indifferent to all this emulation and steadfastly refused the proffered purple. This difficulty in finding a place and a role in society was to prove hereditary.

William's attitude towards Europe indicates just how completely he had turned his back on convention and cultural pretension. By the middle of the century frequent visits to Britain, France, Italy and Austria were *de rigueur* for wealthy Americans. Wives longed to be introduced in foreign courts, to collect antique furniture and works of art and – the ultimate prize – to marry their daughters into ancient aristocratic families. William for years refused to take Margaret on a transatlantic tour, having apparently lost all desire to revisit the haunts of his youth. Not until 1857 did he yield to his wife's entreaties. In that year he dispatched several letters across the ocean to reactivate long-dormant friendships. One was to Christian Bunsen, now retired after a long and distinguished diplomatic career. The sixty-five-year-old philosopher and linguist was almost pathetically touched and excited to hear from his ex-pupil after a silence of four decades. He was, he told his wife, deeply affected by Mr Astor's letter. 'I have bestowed much love upon him, and he had considered and acknowledged me as his guide. He now writes with real friendship. I shall answer him as soon as I am again at Heidelberg – using "Du" as of old.'[1] Sadly, the encounter proved a disappointment. Bunsen reorganized his schedule, cutting short his cure at Wildbad in order to reach Heidelberg by 21 August to greet the Astors. The two men had a happy reunion but William was not interested in prolonging it. He explained to his crestfallen ex-tutor that he had a tight schedule and must swiftly depart in order to keep up with the planned itinerary through Germany and Italy. Within a couple of days the Astors had moved on. Before the year was out they were safely back in New York. William and his wife were accompanied by their nineteen-year-old granddaughter, Margaret Astor Ward, whom they were bringing up as their own daughter. The young woman, as Baroness Bunsen observed, was totally enthralled by everything she saw: she 'enjoyed so enthusiastically the manifold objects of interest offered to her eagerly-grasping mind in European countries, that she promised herself and others to persuade her grandfather to repeat his journey the very next year'.[2] But, however urgent her entreaties may have been, William resisted them. Never again did he leave American soil.

Just as he shunned the social round, so the head of the Astor clan declined to take an active part in American politics. Between 1861 and 1865 the United States passed through the most traumatic years since the War of 1812, but, unlike his father, William did not court the confidence of the nation's leaders. His involvement in public affairs was confined to endorsement of the Democratic leadership of New York City. The passage of the years had done nothing to eradicate corruption from Tammany Hall, which represented a cynical alliance of politicians and businessmen intent on maintaining themselves in power and enriching themselves and their friends at the expense of the community. Party names might have changed, but not the system – and Astor went along with the system. In 1855 Fernando Wood, whose skills included mellifluous oratory, the patronage of mobs and the organization of riots, became the city's mayor. He held office until 1858 and had another term from 1860 to 1862. The Republican state legislature was determined to end, or at least curb, Wood's corrupt reign. When they replaced the municipal police board with a new metropolitan authority the mayor deliberately instigated widespread civil unrest. He went on to press for the creation of New York City as a separate state. As the nation lurched towards civil war, Wood was one of the few Democratic leaders (known as Copperheads) who opposed conflict with the South, on the grounds that it would be ruinously expensive and that the financial burden would fall heaviest on the members of the wealthy establishment. All Wood's policies were motivated by sectional interest and were directed against the forces of radical reform – and William Backhouse backed him to the hilt. He provided money for Tammany funds, and at election times he gave the mayor public endorsement. Of course, Wood made it worth his while, and William was able to buy several blocks of municipally owned land at bargain prices. That was the way the system worked.

But it was not only for financial gain that William supported the Democratic establishment. Wood represented the stability of unchallengeable power in an age threatened by change and bombarded by new ideas. Slavery was only one burning issue. It was inextricably bound up with the old argument about states' rights. More fundamental for New Yorkers was the alarming growth of the poorer element in their city. In the middle years of the century there was an unprecedented influx of immigrants as men, women and whole families fled from poverty, famine and persecution in Ireland, Germany, Austria, Hungary and Russia. Between the censuses of 1850 and 1870 the city's population rose from 515,394 to 942,292. The same pressures that increased the value of Astor land put an intolerable burden on municipal resources – health, transport, housing, law and order. They also produced demands for political power and social change from a new breed of radical orators. All this was unwelcome to the old families – among whom the Astors were now paramount.

Paramount they may have been, but the family was not large or close. William and Dorothea, despite being next-door neighbours for several years, were not on the best of terms. They fell out over their father's will, when Dorothea tried to lay claim to the interest from the trusts John Jacob had created for his grandchildren. William refused to agree and thus set off a long legal wrangle which went all the way to the appeal court before being decided in Mrs Langdon's favour. In 1853 Dorothea died, leaving William and mad John as the only representatives of their generation.

William and Margaret had six children who survived infancy – three girls and three boys. They were destined to bring their parents rather more heartaches than joys. The eldest girl, Emily, was pretty and vivacious. She filled the Astor home with two rare commodities, gaiety and laughter, and she was her parents' favourite. She was only eighteen when she was snapped up by Samuel Ward Jr, the equally lively heir to a banking fortune. The couple were wed in January 1838 and enjoyed a blissfully happy marriage – for just three years. Emily died giving birth to her second child, a boy, who followed his mother to the grave a few days later. Grief hit the Astor household like a hammer blow. Margaret, it seems, never fully recovered. To the end of her days she wore a mourning veil whenever she went out of the house. She and William took Emily's infant daughter, Margaret Astor Ward, under their roof and lavished on her the love and care of which she had been tragically deprived. Her father, Sam Ward, rapidly disappeared from the Astor ambit. He committed three crimes which exiled him from his in-laws' affections: he married again; he married a woman of dubious reputation; and he gave his new wife the house in Bond Street that had come to him as part of the settlement on Emily. 'Medora' Grymes was a wild beauty from New Orleans and the toast of the Manhattan fast set. She was an excellent match for the raffish Ward and the couple made a good, if stormy, marriage. In bestowing his name and property upon Medora, Sam had acted neither illegally nor improperly, but William, Margaret and old John Jacob were deeply distressed. They had never really approved of their son-in-law: he was too much of a free-thinker, too uninhibited to fit in with their conventional Calvinism. Now they turned against him and did their best to turn his daughter against him. When the Ward bank crashed it simply proved what they had always believed and they did not lift a finger to help him. The young man went on to live a varied and colourful life as gold prospector, journalist, traveller and man of letters, but he ceased to be part of the Astor story.

The other two daughters of William and Margaret grew up to make much more suitable marriages. Laura (born 1824) at the age of seventeen made a genuine love match with one of the most eligible bachelors on the social circuit. Franklin H. Delano was the partner in a wealthy shipping business – until he landed the Astor girl. Thereafter, he never had to work again. To his own fortune was added a huge settlement of cash, land and trusts which came with Laura. The couple eased into a comfortable – though, sadly, childless – marriage, became prominent collectors and patrons of art, and eventually settled in Europe. One of Delano's nieces, Sara, married a millionaire landowner and speculator in railway stock called James Roosevelt. In 1882 she was delivered of her only child, who was christened Franklin Delano Roosevelt. The youngest Astor girl, Mary, married a well-to-do Englishman, John Carey, and returned with him to his native land.

The boys reproduced in distinctive ways what had become established Astor characteristics. The youngest, Henry, had his Aunt Magdalen's ungovernable temper, Dorothea's rebelliousness and a certain quirkiness which reminded some people of his Uncle John. Henry (born 1832) was large, boisterous, unruly and given to whisky. Feeling unnecessarily confined within the cage of Astor expectations and uncommitted to a family ethic which was stronger on theory than practice, he simply broke out, chose roistering companions and went his own gambling, drinking, wenching way. He was almost the classic ne'er-do-well. Born to plenty and with no challenges to help him develop character, he followed his instincts. When his father tried to restrain him this red-bearded giant would fly into a rage, shouting abuse and sometimes needing to be physically restrained. By common consent Henry went into 'exile' on the family's country estate at Rhinebeck. But if William thought he was relieving himself of an embarrassment, he was mistaken. No sooner had the scapegrace taken up residence at Rokeby, than he proposed marriage to the daughter of one of the local poor farming families.

William was furious and made haste to limit the damage as far as possible. He drastically reduced the sizeable share of the Astor fortune which Henry would have inherited – though he was powerless to deprive his son of the property left in trust by John Jacob. When he came of age, Henry was a millionaire in his own right. But he was quite hopeless at administering his patrimony. He was haphazard about collecting rents, and when they were collected he would stuff the cheques into his pocket and not bother to bank them for several months. Such a complete lack of interest in business reflected badly on the family and, eventually, the Astor estate office took over the day-to-day running of Henry's property.

Meanwhile the prodigal and his wife, Malvina, had put a hundred miles and more between themselves and the Astors. They bought a farm in the Berkshire Hills of Massachusetts. At last out of the spotlight in which the family was obliged to appear, they lived a long and surprisingly happy life. They were childless, which may have been as well, for Henry remained an eccentric. He was prone to pranks such as locking Malvina and a neighbour in a room and going round the empty houses brandishing a Bible and preaching lengthy sermons. The breach between Henry and his father was complete, but younger members of the family would visit their odd uncle. In time the 'peasant girl' Malvina was accepted by her in-laws, for she was, in fact, a very genuine, outgoing person.

Henry was *only* eccentric. He was not mad. His was merely that 'oddness' of character which not infrequently occurs in wealthy families, where the ultimate restraint of limited resources is not experienced. The press, of course, loved to exaggerate and were not slow to point out that there *was* insanity in the family. But Henry's only 'lunacies' were unrestrained exuberance and a rejection of the Astor brand image. He settled down once he had escaped from the Astor orbit and was able to make a life for himself. His violence, drinking and other excesses gradually abated. He lavished considerable care on the mansion he built at West Copake, known as the Big House. Unlike his relatives, who engaged the country's leading architects to create their fine residences, he designed it himself, employed local craftsmen and supervised the construction. Not all the ideas he wanted to incorporate turned out to be practicable. He ordered one room to be paved with silver dollars, but when the effect was not what he had hoped he replaced them with a more mundane flooring material. When the house was finished, he filled it with choice furniture and works of art, most of which came from abroad. The whole effect was beautiful and tasteful.

The Big House became the centre of a thriving agricultural estate. Henry bought up several local farms and took life 'on the land' very seriously. His main achievement was building up a herd of pedigree cows. Forgetful of and forgotten by Manhattan, he settled to a long and comfortable rural life. On 6 March 1898 a letter to the *New York Times* written by a near neighbour had this to say about him: 'Henry Astor is, as far as I can learn, a quiet, intelligent old gentleman, a great reader, and one who has done a great deal of good in the community in which he lives. Stories of his mental incapacity are false.' Henry long outlived all his siblings. He died in 1918 possessed of an estate worth $5,040,000 which was divided into 360 shares and distributed unequally among his nephews and nieces. By that time five million was positively paltry by Astor standards.

The bulk of the family fortune was destined for the two older brothers, William (born 1829) and John Jacob III (born 1822). If Henry chose to play no positive role in life, it may reasonably be said that William was forced into inactivity. William Backhouse was determined to hand on the family interests intact and well-managed. This meant that there must be only one hand at the helm – and that hand must belong to the heir, John Jacob. William Backhouse had been encouraged by his father to do something 'useful' with his life, but he did not similarly encourage his own second son. William was therefore deprived of a *raison d'être* and never managed to find one. The unfortunate probability is that, had matters been arranged differently, William might well have discovered his vocation in the estate office. His elder brother, who always took an active part in national affairs, would almost certainly have found a niche in political or diplomatic life. The Astors had not been brought up to think in terms of public service, and William, who was certainly very able, could not make the conceptual leap which would have freed him for a meaningful life.

Like his father, William displayed a literary bent. He distinguished himself at Columbia. Then, again like his father, he completed his education with extensive foreign travel in Europe – and also in the Middle East. When he returned to New York in 1850 his grandfather was dead, his father had assumed full command and his elder brother had stepped into the role of second-in-command. Three years later he made an 'appropriate' marriage with Caroline Schermerhorn, one of the young ladies of Lafayette Place, who came from an old and wealthy American family. There was no love in their union and the two young people had little in common. William submitted to the arranged match out of filial duty. It was the last time he allowed that virtue to rule his life.

John Jacob III also assumed the position decreed by the family, although his own inclinations would have taken him along a different path. He was, by temperament and upbringing, a gentleman of leisure. He would have been happy to devote his life and fortune to travel and cultural pursuits and perhaps to follow a political and diplomatic career, as befitted one of his class. He followed his father to Göttingen University and was as impressed as William Backhouse had been by the ancient cultures of Europe. John seems to have been one of the few members of the family to remain on good terms with Sam Ward, and enjoyed a cheerful, bantering relationship with his good-natured brother-in-law. He corresponded with him from Germany, on one occasion enclosing a poem which he suggested, tongue-in-cheek, would not disgrace Byron. Here are a few sample lines of his 'Ode on seeing Moreau's Monument':

> . . . 'Twas on a rainy day.
> There shone no sunny ray.
> When the Emperor Nap he said,

'We'll give them some cold lead' . . .
The Gun was brought,
And quick as thought
The bullet sped
And struck him on the head.
Sam, thy pardon I beg.
'Twas not his head, but leg . . .
It cut through skin and bone,
And made the traitor groan . . .
He called for a segar,
Which he lighted from a star.
(It was a coal of fire
But the rhyme does 'star' require) . . .[3]

(It is interesting to note, in passing, that John did not take his 'literary' output at all seriously. In this respect his son was very different.)

John returned home in 1842 to spend a couple of years mastering the rudiments of law, first at Harvard and then with a firm of New York attorneys. Soon after knuckling down to work in the estate office, he married, in December 1846, Charlotte Augusta Gibbes, the twenty-one-year-old daughter of an old-established South Carolina family. The couple honeymooned in Europe, and they were back there again in 1850, when John Jacob travelled to Walldorf to superintend the execution of his grandfather's will. He set up a board of trustees, comprised largely of leading citizens of Heidelberg. With them he chose a site for the building of Astor House. John Jacob and Charlotte returned in 1854 with their six-year-old son (christened William Waldorf in honour of the German connection) for the opening of the orphanage. Initially, the home catered for the needs of thirty children between the ages of six and fourteen. This was the practical beginning of the family's involvement with its place of origin, an involvement which was to grow in scale and variety over the years. The American visitors stayed several months, travelling widely and including Italy and Britain on their itinerary. Both of them loved the Old World and its ways. Charlotte found there an ordered, class-orientated gentility which was similar to the structured society of the slave-owning South. It was a system which also appealed much more to her husband than the self-conscious egalitarianism of New York, where status counted for little and wealth, in itself, was not enough to ensure universal respect.

When the Civil War broke over the nation in 1861, John Jacob came out strongly in support of President Lincoln and the Union. This is perhaps surprising in view of his father's commitment to compromise and his wife's family ties in South Carolina, the very heartland of the secession movement. Even more surprising is the fact that, at the age of thirty-nine, the Astor heir enlisted in the Union Army, when the scions of other wealthy families were buying their way out of military service. But John Jacob's commitment to the principles of federal solidarity and freedom for the slaves was completely genuine. Right at the beginning of the conflict, he donated money for the relief of Fort Sumter, the South Carolina garrison besieged by Confederate troops. In the aftermath of the fall of Fort Sumter and the first shedding of American blood by Americans, a hero of the Mexican War, George McClellan, was appointed to lead the Army of the Potomac, defending Washington, and subsequently to overall command. John Jacob now hurried to the capital and placed himself at McClellan's disposal, while in New York Charlotte, an ardent convert to the cause of freedom, helped to raise a black regiment for the Union.

In the event John Jacob's active military involvement was short-lived and far from glorious. He was appointed aide-de-camp to McClellan with the rank of colonel (a title he retained with pride to the end of his days). His duties were entirely administrative, and for several months he enjoyed the luxury and social life of Washington and the glamour of a uniform without any of the concomitant danger. While Lincoln urged him to action, the general preferred to husband his resources and train his raw recruits. At last, in mid-February, McClellan moved his army of 110,000 men towards the enemy, having devised a grandiose strategy for the capture of Richmond, Virginia. Colonel Astor supervised the riverain supply column. There followed six months of indecisive campaigning, culminating in the army's recall to protect Washington, which was once more under threat following the Confederate victory at Second Bull Run (a mere twenty-five miles from the capital). The general revitalized his troops and halted the enemy advance, but once more he failed to press home his advantage. In November 1862 a frustrated President relieved McClellan of his command. McClellan's contribution to the Civil War has always been a subject of controversy. Certainly his lack of spectacular success was due as much to divided councils in Washington as to his own caution. He was a good organizer and was very popular with his men.

He was certainly popular with John Jacob Astor. Disgusted with the way his superior had been treated, Colonel Astor resigned his commission and went home. In January 1863, three months after McClellan's dismissal, John joined with other prominent New Yorkers to present the general and his wife with a house – 22 West 31st Street. In the following year McClellan sought his revenge on Lincoln by running against him for the presidency. He campaigned on the issue of a speedy end to the war, believing that this would win the support of the business community. He also counted on his popularity with the troops to bring in their votes. This put Astor in something of a quandary. His loyalty to McClellan clashed with his commitment to the

President and his policy of pushing the conflict to all-out victory. Furthermore, Charlotte was an even more devoted fan of Lincoln than he was. In October 1864 John wrote to his old friend and superior to explain the situation. McClellan reported to his wife: 'I had a note from John Astor, who evidently feels very badly and, as his wife sails for Europe within a week, I should not be at all surprised if he in the end came out all right.'[4] History does not record how Astor actually voted, but his commitment to the Unionist cause was unabated. Sending his son seventeenth-birthday greetings (William Waldorf had recently followed the family tradition and gone to Göttingen) in March 1865, he wrote:

> We have plenty of good news every week now from the troops in every direction. The rebels are getting dispirited and their cause is failing and I think that before my birthday (10th June) the rebel armies will be broken up except some bands of guerrillas and robbers . . . [5]

Nine days later one of the most celebrated meetings in history occurred at Appomattox court house when Robert E. Lee surrendered to Ulysses S. Grant.

The commitment of John Jacob and Charlotte to the Unionist cause was uncharacteristic of the Astors as a whole and requires some explanation. William Backhouse was so opposed to the war that he refused to pay the income tax levied to prosecute it. He complained that the impost was unconstitutional, took the matter right up to the Supreme Court – and won. He also prevented his second son from enlisting, even though William had raised a regiment. The family certainly reacted negatively to the wider implications of the conflict. The upheaval of 1861–5 was socially disturbing and for this reason was a worry to the propertied class. The abolition of slavery issue sparked off demands for rights among the packed tenements of impoverished immigrants, causing the wealthy to band more closely together and look to their own interests. But Charlotte and John Jacob were the first Astors to display a social conscience, to conceive the idea of *richesse oblige.* Imperfectly the colonel grasped the fact that he owed a debt to the nation where the Astor fortune had been raised. His visits to Europe, and especially to Britain – a country he loved – had made him aware that public service was accepted as an obligation by the representatives of 'old' money, and that this was one of the marks distinguishing them from the *nouveaux riches.* Charlotte, for her part, came from a society which was much more cohesive. The cotton plantations of the South bore a close resemblance to the semi-feudal estates of Europe with their complex, interlocking relationships of masters and servants. Mrs Astor was an active patroness of charities. She and her husband donated $250,000 for the raising of a cancer hospital. Charlotte was particularly concerned with the welfare of New York's poor. It was doubtless her enthusiasm which inspired John Jacob to build Astor House, and West Side Hostel to provide food and shelter for destitute young men.

But this benefactor was, seemingly, unable to make the connection between his private charity and his public, professional conduct. Had he done so his name would never have become linked with the notorious 'Boss' Tweed. William Marcy Tweed came to power in the city shortly before the war by engineering the overthrow of the corrupt Fernando Wood. But if New Yorkers supposed that the new regime would usher in an era of honest, conscientious government they soon discovered their mistake. They had simply replaced a hyena with a tiger (as the cartoonist Nast caricatured Tweed). Between 1858 and 1871 he held various public posts and ensured that several of his friends were appointed to others. Thus came into existence the 'Tweed ring'. Its members enriched themselves directly from public coffers to the tune of some $50 million, and this took no account of the sale of municipal contracts or the issuing of bonds at inflated rates of interest. The scandal reached alarming proportions and was publicized in influential newspapers such as *Harper's Weekly* and the *New York Times*. In 1870 Tweed was sufficiently worried to organize a whitewash operation. He opened the city's books to a committee of local businessmen, headed by John Jacob Astor. Naturally, Tweed had arranged that the public accounts he presented should reveal no irregularities, and few people can have been surprised when the *ad hoc* commission declared itself satisfied with the administration of public funds. The hounds of the radical press, however, kept up their pursuit. When a government accountant handed over pages of the fiddled city books the *New York Times* denounced the ring and the Astor cover-up and demanded that the perpetrators be brought to justice. Tweed and his associates were tried and the 'Boss' was sentenced to twelve years in the penitentiary. Even that was not the end of this unsavoury story. In 1875, Tweed broke out of jail and escaped to Spain disguised as a sailor. Unfortunately for him, his notoriety had reached across the Atlantic. He was recognized from a Nast cartoon, extradited back to the USA and died in prison in April 1878.

It was episodes such as this which turned sections of the popular press resolutely against the Astors. From the 1860s onwards, journalists took a particular delight in lampooning the family's lifestyle, disclosing or inventing scandals, and making the Astor estate the principal target in frequent campaigns against slum landlords.

William Backhouse avoided the worst of these attacks. By the time they had gathered momentum he was dead. After the war he retired from active business involvement; he was by then in his mid-seventies. In 1872 his wife died. Without the only two supports on which his life had rested – his property and his marriage – the old man's mind began to disintegrate. In November 1875 he too passed away as quietly and unobtrusively as he had lived. But he had long since stamped his negative, uncreative temperament on the estate office, and John Jacob was far too set in his ways to indulge in innovation now that he enjoyed sole command. The simple fact was that he was not very interested. Travel, collecting and the refined pleasures of a gentleman's life were more important to him than the monotonous accumulation of rents. It is significant that he erected new business premises on 26th Street and that they were more commodious and comfortable than the drab premises which had sufficed his father.

But this did not betoken a new, more dynamic attitude towards the management of Astor real estate. Indeed, John Jacob's business interest lay, as he perceived it, in resisting the mounting clamour for change. New York had reached bursting point, partly because of the population explosion and partly because corrupt administrations had sold outlying blocks of land to wealthy citizens like the Astors. Such speculators were in no hurry to release it to builders until pressure had forced the ground rents sky high. They in their turn recouped their capital by cramming as many dwelling units as possible on to their plots. Below 14th Street, therefore, tenement town began – a drab acreage of cheek-by-jowl, airless, insanitary apartment blocks, eight or ten storeys high. Municipal authorities and social reformers complained. Newspapers thundered their denunciation. All were powerless to put a stop to the evil, sprung, as it was, from the very ethos of the city. The planners were in the hands of the entrepreneurs because New York had grown to prosperity by encouraging free enterprise.

From across the ocean their ancestors had whistled up the monster of private capital and allowed it free rein. It was too late, now, to muzzle the beast. The nineteenth century boasted barely a score of American millionaires at its midway point but almost three thousand by its close. John Jacob III was not directly responsible for the squalor in which an increasing number of New York's poor were forced to live; he did not create the stifling, noxious streets where disease, despair, violence, vice and crime flourished. But, of course, he was part and parcel of the *laissez-faire* system which permitted such horrors, and he regarded as an assault upon liberty and enterprise any attempt to restrain or control the activities of landlords and tenants. By the same token he resisted plans for municipal transport systems. These were matters for private developers not public servants. Besides, they would encourage people to live outside the city, and that would have an adverse effect on property values.

In order to pass a fair judgement on John Jacob's patrician aloofness from the urban problems for which he was, in part, responsible, we have to consider his action or lack of action in context. This was a period in American life when public morality touched rock bottom. The Industrial Revolution was in full swing. The West was being opened up. Railways and roads were fanning out across the land. Natural resources were being discovered and ruthlessly exploited. Factories, shops and warehouses were springing up everywhere. America was, with a headlong rush, catching up with the Old World as an industrial, trading and agricultural nation. Fortunes were being made. A whole new class of entrepreneurs came into being untrained in the responsibilities of wealth. Untold riches were there for the grasping – by men who had tenacity of purpose and were not unduly restrained by scruples. And behind the pioneers were the financiers, the bankers and the stock speculators, greedy for quick profit. There were risks, of course. In 1873 the overheated economy exploded, hundreds of businesses failed, thousands of investors were bankrupted and the New York stock exchange closed its doors for ten days. But the possibility of failure only incited Cornelius Vanderbilt, Daniel Drew (the steamboat tycoon), August Belmont (the banker) and a host of other fortune-seekers to buttress their position by fraud, bribery and sharp practice.

The American Astors of the third generation were not in the same league as such ambitious brassnecks. Indeed, they were at pains to distance themselves from the vulgar horde. When the new money moved into Lafayette Place, the Astors moved out. William and John Jacob both built town mansions further from the centre, on Fifth Avenue near the intersection with 34th Street. When the Union Club began to accept 'undesirables', John Jacob and a few friends founded the more exclusive Knickerbocker Club. Charlotte held elegant soirées for artists, musicians and men of letters, and those of her intimate circle who alone had the taste to appreciate the finer things of life. It was not simple snobbishness which erected these barriers. In a few brief years east coast society had been transformed and vulgarized. When the historian Henry Adams returned from Europe with his family in 1868, he remarked, 'Had they been Tyrian traders of the year 1000 BC, landing from a galley fresh from Gibraltar, they could hardly have been stranger on the shore of a world, so changed from what it had been ten years before.' The Astors and their like had become – or so they liked to believe – the *ancien régime* of America, distinct from the turbulent peasantry of the tenements and the bourgeois industrialists vulgarly trying to elbow their way into the elegant world of their betters.

To emphasize their superiority and to protect themselves from encroachment, New York's old families self-consciously barricaded themselves within rigid rules of etiquette and social convention. Inside the stockade they created a world of brittle glamour and ostentatious luxury such as America had never seen. This was, in part, a reaction to the Civil War. The conflict between the Confederacy and the Union made a psychological impact on the United

States of an intensity which was not to be experienced again until the war in Vietnam. It was, in many ways, similar to the recoil of shock and horror caused in Europe by the carnage of 1914–18, and smart society reacted in much the same way as the flapper generation of the 1920s. They erased from their minds the memory of past evils and averted their gaze from contemporary ones. All the time was party time. The USA could now boast the world's wealthiest élite and, for half a century, its members flaunted their riches.

> Those were the days of magnificence, when money was poured out like water. Nothing but the best was good enough and so the best had to be procured regardless of cost ... Festoons of priceless jewels draped ample bosoms, yards of historic lace trimmed under-petticoats, the greatest dress designers of Europe vied with one another to create costumes that would grace some splendid ball for one night and then be thrown away.
>
> Gold plate gleaming on dinner-tables laid for a hundred and fifty guests ... fleets of lorries coming up from the South in depth of winter laden with orchids to decorate the ballroom of some great hostess. No one thought of the cost. Cotillions with jewel favours, diamond bracelets for the women, sapphire cravat pins for the men ... ball suppers of terrapin and quail, vintage wines, nothing but the choicest champagne ... No one would have dreamt of giving anything else! The entire entertaining floor at Sherry's redecorated and upholstered in rose brocade just for one night ... the entire staff of musicians, footmen and attendants equipped with Louis XVI liveries – a hundred thousand dollars as the price of an evening's amusement.[6]

So one authoress described the life of New York's smart set at the turn of the century, by which time the pattern had become so well established that it seemed to be eternally unchangeable.

The basic elements in that pattern were the Manhattan winter season, with balls, theatre parties, visits to concerts and the opera, dinners and soirées, and summers at Newport, Rhode Island. This lovely resort with its balmy climate, natural harbour and quaint pre-Revolution buildings was 'discovered' after the Civil War and turned into *the* fashionable second centre for wealthy New Yorkers. Here they built sumptuous summer 'cottages', enjoying wide ocean views. Here they gave elegant alfresco lunches and supper parties on spacious lawns strung with Chinese lanterns. Here they indulged the rich man's new craze – steam yachting. The denizens of these twin worlds were only released from obligatory attendance for frequent and extended visits to Europe, for it was transatlantic style that more than ever dominated the lives of the fashion-conscious. Not only did they dress in the Parisian mode and import furniture and works of art from across the ocean; they employed French maids and English butlers, they brought titled guests over to grace their opera boxes and engaged Europe's leading performers to entertain those guests. The core of

New York's cognoscenti liked to be known as the Faubourg St Germain set.

Where were the Astors in all this? Certainly not in the place that one might have expected. They still disdained to provide Manhattan society with a 'royal' family. John Jacob and Charlotte were perhaps too genuinely European to associate themselves totally with the shallow world of gossip and gaiety. They certainly enjoyed the high life. They entertained lavishly. They were among the first to build a summer residence at Newport: Beaulieu was a splendid house in the French style where Charlotte presided over extravagant balls and dinners. But pleasure was never allowed to dominate their lives. They were more conscious than most of the emptiness of a society that was at the same time vital and vulgar, successful and sordid. They shared the disdain of Walt Whitman, who wrote in *Democratic Vistas* (1871):

> Never was there, perhaps, more hollowness of heart than at present ... our New World democracy ... is so far an almost complete failure in its social aspects, and in really grand religious, moral, literary and esthetic results.

John Jacob and Charlotte were good Episcopalians with a strong sense of responsibility and duty. Much of their spare time was devoted to sitting on the boards of charitable societies. In the 1870s, their only child, William Waldorf, entered politics. It was, as we shall see, a disastrous experiment, but it demonstrated a desire, instilled by his upbringing, to make a positive contribution to national life.

The 'other' Astors were very different. John Jacob and his brother William were never on good terms, although their wives were friends. John Jacob regarded the younger man as a boor. William resented his father's favouritism for the heir and was scornful of his brother's gentility. William loathed fashionable society. In order to occupy his active mind he bought Ferncliff, another estate at Rhinebeck on the Hudson, where he concentrated on farming and breeding racehorses. He also acquired a large yacht, *Ambassadress*. In summer, when everyone else was at Newport, William was immersed in breeding charts and stock yields at Ferncliff. Most winters, while his wife and her friends were disporting themselves in Manhattan's ballrooms and parlours, William sailed for Florida with a handful of cronies. In later years he developed some of the traits of his brother Henry. He drank too much, was given to bouts of moody violence and surrounded himself with prostitutes and gamblers.

From this it will be seen that William's marriage was little more than a formality. Caroline was both strong-willed and aristocratic of bearing. Her commitment to the 'governing élite' was as deep as William's contempt for it. Their relationship was not helped by the fact that their first nine years together had produced four daughters. By dint of perseverance, William at length sired a son, who was born in July 1864 and, inevitably, named John Jacob IV. By the 1870s William and Caroline were spending only a few weeks each year together, an arrangement which suited each of them admirably. It was then that Caroline, who was only an Astor by marriage, propelled the family name into the limelight in a manner which was almost as dramatic as the way in which the first John Jacob had achieved fame. She decided that if New York society had no king it should have a queen. It needed a centre around which to cohere – and she would provide that centre.

The decision which was to transform the Manhattan *haut monde* was not made as suddenly as that, but it did stem from Caroline's concern to preserve civilized standards, ancient values, and to prevent egalitarianism and vulgarity overwhelming at least the upper reaches of society. Two events set Caroline upon her glittering crusade. Between 1872 and 1879 she had four daughters to launch into society. This obliged her to spend most of her time during those years arranging balls, parties and other functions designed to advertise Astor wealth and sophistication and attract for her girls the attentions of America's most eligible young men. It was a daunting prospect, given that Caroline's husband was not interested in such 'tomfoolery' and, anyway, was absent most of the time. This difficulty was overcome when she met the forty-four-year-old Ward McAllister.

McAllister was one of those men, like Beaux Brummell or Nash (of whom it was said he perfected 'the art of living without money'), who both created and were created by fashion. He played his part in the symbiotic relationship with the men and women of riches and culture by taking them and their extravagant fripperies immensely seriously. Any wealthy and wasteful élite determined to insulate itself from the real world needs such an *arbiter elegantiarum* to keep its eyes focused on trivialities and to protect it from painful self-knowledge. McAllister was a distant relation and kindred spirit of that Sam Ward who had flitted briefly and colourfully into the Astors' lives a few years before. He was a Southern lawyer who, like Oscar Wilde, might well have boasted that he had nothing to declare but his genius. McAllister's genius lay in flattery, organizing ability and a meticulous knowledge of the ways of polite European society (acquired during an extensive Grand Tour).

He had already begun to make a reputation for himself as an organizer of social functions before his name came to be linked with that of Caroline Astor. McAllister applied himself to his chosen task with complete professionalism.

> He read books on heraldry and precedence, studied the customs of every Court in Europe. He revelled in forms and ceremonies, his cult of snobbishness was so ardent, so sincere, that it acquired dignity; it became almost a religion. No devout parish priest ever visited his flock with more loyal devotion to duty than did Ward McAllister make his round of the opera-boxes on Monday evenings. He would listen to plans

> for forthcoming parties with the utmost gravity . . . And all the while his watchful eyes would be observing the neighbouring boxes, noting the newcomers, whom they were talking to, who was taking them up.[7]

He was a godsend to any hesitant hostess uncertain about whom to invite (or not invite) to a dance, how to engage the most celebrated visiting singers and musicians, or whom to seat next to whom at table. These services he duly performed for Mrs Astor, but soon their interrelated ambitions led them much further. They realized that Caroline's money and McAllister's flair could create social events of unparalleled brilliance and extravagance. So it proved. Caroline, thanks to her ADC, entertained in a style that others tried in vain to emulate. At her weekly dinner parties, guests were regaled with sumptuous food prepared by one of the world's greatest chefs, enticed from Paris at heaven knows what cost. They ate off gold plates and drank the finest wines from crystal goblets. They were served by waiters in powder-blue livery. Afterwards they were entertained by performers brought especially from London or Vienna, and during the intermission they could admire the latest additions to Caroline's collection of old masters, which covered almost every square inch of wall space running both sides of a long gallery.

Mrs Astor's ball, held annually in January, rapidly established itself as the pivotal event of the Manhattan season. Caroline, resplendent with so many diamonds that one observer likened her to a chandelier, received her guests in an anteroom at 350 Fifth Avenue beneath a life-size portrait of herself. Each couple then passed through into the long ballroom – lit by the massive candelabra the Astors had brought from Italy – which was large enough to accommodate four hundred couples. This gave rise to 'the Four Hundred'. The dimensions of a room came to determine the boundaries of polite New York society. Making a virtue of necessity, Caroline and her major domo asserted that everyone who was acceptable received invitations to *the* ball. There were four hundred people who came into this category. Their qualifications were wealth, ancestry (they had to number at least three American generations) and social grace. Many families aspired to inclusion, but Caroline was judge and jury. Those who passed her strict scrutiny received their 'membership cards' – the invitations to the Astor ball. Those who did not were 'out'. It seems hard now to imagine that anyone cared a fig whether or not they received the 'queen's' seal of approval, but in New York a hundred years ago it mattered very much. Aspiring matrons who had little else to occupy their minds energetically vied with each other for Mrs Astor's approval. Those who failed to gain admittance to the prescribed number of the elect deeply felt the shame of it.

But even within the Four Hundred there were inner wheels of exclusiveness and favour. At her ball Caroline presided over the proceedings from a long padded divan on a raised dais at one end of the room. It was always known as the 'throne'. Besides Mrs Astor it had room to accommodate half a dozen other ladies whose names were indicated on cards laid upon the red velvet. To be placed upon the throne was the ultimate honour. Not to be so located was regarded by some as a rebuff. One such neglected guest rushed from the ballroom in tears, screaming, 'She doesn't love me! I won't stay one minute longer in a house where I am not loved.'[8] Only with difficulty was the disconsolate socialite coaxed back into the fray.

Caroline, of course, established herself as commandingly in Newport as in the city. In 1881 she took over a classical-style house called Beechwood high on a cliff overlooking the Atlantic. It was already large, but, by the time $2 million had been spent on it, it comprised sixty-two commodious and elegantly decorated rooms. Its white and gold ballroom (inevitably, the biggest on the island) was decorated with painted mythological figures, and its banks of French windows gave on to a colonnaded terrace cooled by ocean breezes. The adjoining dining room was presided over by a portrait of John Jacob I, who would scarcely have approved of the extravagance it represented. Naturally, Caroline made frequent visits to Europe. Her headquarters there were the apartment she bought at 146 Avenue des Champs-Elysées. Here she held court among the throngs of Americans visiting Paris.

The extravagance mounted year by year. Not only did Caroline have to surpass her own standards of opulence, she also had to keep a step ahead of the opposition. As the century drew to a close the waves of new money were beating unremittingly against the bastions of the old. Fortunes larger than the Astors' were being amassed. The Vanderbilts and the Rockefellers, the Morgans and the Goulds, could all give wildly extravagant parties. Secure in their own circles of influence, they could afford to disdain Caroline's exclusive club, just as, half a century before, the Astors had been indifferent to the 'aristocrats' who looked down their noses at them. Yet, to the end of her days, Mrs Astor kept up her campaign. By 1895 a younger man, Harry Lehr, a witty and beautiful homosexual who modestly claimed to be the Christ to his predecessor's John the Baptist, had replaced Ward McAllister as her confidant. Together they planned ever more incredible diversions which made her guests gasp with surprise and kept the gossip columnists well supplied with copy. Some of her entertainments read like pages from the Arabian Nights. On one occasion she had her dining table spread with sand and bid her visitors prod with silver trowels to discover gifts of diamonds, rubies and sapphires. Thus did the frenzied quest for novelty bring Caroline perilously close to that vulgarity she so ardently despised. Her extravagance did not seem to her to be unduly wasteful. With $5 million a year coming in from rents on hotels, shops, offices, houses and tenements it was very difficult to spend money fast enough to make any kind of adverse impression on the Astor bank balance.

CHAPTER 6

'The chessboard's fascination'

Towards the end of his life, William Waldorf Astor, the only son of John Jacob III and Charlotte, wrote a brief autobiographical sketch. In it he stated baldly his attitude towards John Jacob I, the ancestor who died two days before he was born.

I am glad that my great-grandfather was a successful trader, because in all ages trade has led the way to Civilization. I have studied his life, seeking to learn its aims, grateful to him for having lifted us above the plough-shares of Baden and bent upon continuing his purpose.[1]

In so far as any simple statement can provide a key to unlock a complicated character, these few words do so. William Waldorf was very like the founder of the family's fortune. He was the first descendant to possess all the salient qualities of John Jacob I – ambition, impatience, energy, imagination, egocentricity and rigid self-discipline. His misfortune was that he never found an object worthy of his passionate dedication. 'Trade', to which John Jacob had devoted himself, was beneath William Waldorf's attention. Great-grandfather had lifted the family above that grubby avocation, just as surely as he had lifted it above 'the plough-shares of Baden'. Nor was the acquisition of wealth a spur to William Waldorf's endeavours. He grew up as the sole heir to a $170 million estate and never lacked the funds he desired for even his most extravagant schemes. How was he, then, to set his stamp upon the world? His seventy-one years were to be a restless and, ultimately, a tragic quest for meaning.

William Waldorf grew up as the lonely only child of parents who led a frenzied life devoted to business, social obligations, charity work and travel. The regimen of nannies and tutors was strict, but his mentors were, in their turn, following firm rules laid down by their employers, John Jacob III and Charlotte. It was borne in upon the boy that as the future head of the richest family in America he had enormous obligations. When he assumed his inheritance the eyes of the world would be upon him, so he must prepare himself for his public role. He must learn, above all, how to handle money.

To that end gambling was forbidden and he was given very little cash of his own. Even when he came of age, his allowance was only $1,800 a year, which certainly left him little scope for 'riotous living'. But the discipline imposed upon the boy extended also to the minutiae of life. He was not allowed to whistle. No games were permitted on Sundays – and no books, save those of a religious and improving nature.

William Waldorf read avidly and had a special love of history and biography. He admired forceful and ruthless men like Cesare Borgia and Napoleon Bonaparte. Later he would develop pretensions to authorship – though, alas, without the talent to support them. His literary diet was not entirely serious: he devoured novels, especially historical romances, and numbered among his favourite writers Walter Scott, Mark Twain, James Fenimore Cooper, Wilkie Collins, Dickens and, later, Conan Doyle. What he read, he retained, and his memory for detail was prodigious. He excelled at chess and in later life never travelled without a small pocket set. Such were his powers of concentration and memory that he could play a game blindfold, retaining in his mind the positions of all the pieces. Chess was particularly important to him, and it is easy to imagine the solitary boy sitting for hours in a quiet corner of the Fifth Avenue mansion posing and solving problems on the chequered board. As an old man he wrote warmly, if floridly, of his lifelong addiction to the game:

> Most men and women who have sailed the world possess a navigator's gathered memories: tapestry of travel; crystals of curious legends; silks and satins of courtly days; a lace or two of friendships woven; pearls and ingots of poet's fancy. Mine is only a fragment of sandalwood drift; yet it has influenced all my days. It is the chessboard's fascination. Its axioms are a fixed star of methodical procedure. The movement of its amber figures is of practical value, being the most perfect demonstration of pure force. It trains the mind to keep its pigeon-holes tidy ... The exercise of chess proves that in all things concentration is the secret of success; that time is decisive; that to one battled by the world attack may be the best defence; that a broad margin must be left for the Unforeseen which is continually present in our larger game; that in life's arena, as on the board, an astute and dramatic move works transformation. In all ages men of achievement have possessed the art to convert their pawns to pieces.[2]

Little wonder, then, that William Waldorf Astor became a man obsessed with precision, pattern, punctuality; a man whose desk was always immaculately tidy, its papers and ever-sharpened pencils arranged with parade-ground exactness; a man who imposed on himself and those around him the habits and rules of life instilled in his own childhood. He approached physical exercise in the same way. The concept of 'sport', as one of his sons later recorded, was meaningless to him. That people could hit a ball about for pleasure or feel intense rivalry over something as trivial as a race or match struck him as absurd.[3] Games were not team efforts or contests of stamina, strength and skill against friendly adversaries; they were the means of training the body, making it fit, alert and healthy. In this spirit he applied himself diligently to fencing, boxing, riding and swimming.

Over William Waldorf's entire early life brooded the figure of his lugubrious grandfather. William Backhouse did not die until his grandson was already twenty-seven. At the end of his own life William Waldorf remembered him as 'a man of iron constitution whose hand old age and illness scarcely relaxed. He carried this sense of duty beyond the grave, and by his Will sought to extend a guiding arm even after death.'[4] When, following the demise of his wife in 1872, the old man joined the Astor migration to Fifth Avenue, William Waldorf paid weekly visits to his grandfather. In those last three years of William Backhouse's life the two of them grew closer than they had ever been. They would sit late into the night over cigars and a decanter of Balaclava port, while William Waldorf recounted his modest doings and the old man, mind wandering now, recalled a lifetime's personalities and anecdotes. May it have been that during these relaxed, nocturnal debates William Backhouse inadvertently, in moments of nostalgic reverie, let slip his early love of the Old World, his meetings with men who had met Napoleon and helped to shape great events? And did the young man ask his grandfather just how, after such an exciting early life, he had come to be trapped in the Manhattan estate office?

The boy had no intention of being similarly ensnared. Not only did he fill his imagination with tales of other lands, but his parents also took him on visits to Europe. In later life he could still remember meeting, at the age of eight, the last King of Naples in pre-*Risorgimento* Italy. Later, he followed the family tradition and studied at Göttingen. He stayed on in Europe for more travel and study and while doing so experienced the greatest personal tragedy of his early years. All we know of the event is his own brief, poignant account of it written half a century later. He was still in Europe, finishing his general education wandering among the relics of ancient civilizations, when *it* happened:

> At twenty-one a love affair with a young lady of rare charm touched me ... She was a figure of statuesque beauty. It was a strange and delicious emotion, an intense dreaming and anguish ... I became humanized and lifted out of my youthful savagery ... But the fates were unkind and we were not allowed to marry ...[5]

This is all William Waldorf ever committed unequivocally to writing about the affair but clearly it was no fleeting passion, to be revalued in the truer perspective of mature age. The relationship with the woman he always referred to as his 'Princess' remained more precious to William Waldorf than the one he enjoyed with the woman he eventually married. Who the adored one was and why she was deemed unworthy to be admitted to the great Astor dynasty he would never say.

Now, however, it has been possible to piece together at least some of the story from clues which William Waldorf himself left. In June 1904, while taking a cure for gout at Kissingen, he wrote a short story, which was published in the *Pall Mall Magazine* in December of that year, under the title 'A Secret of Olympus'. To an American friend he revealed, 'It is the confession of a love adventure of my own when young.'[6] The tale, written in the first person, tells of an encounter in 1869 when Astor was studying in Rome with 'Professor Vaini'. He met an eighteen-year-old, dark-eyed, tranquil beauty named Hebe, across whose face 'floated a swift tinge of tragic passion'. The two young people fell deeply in love, but there was an obstacle to their union for Hebe was already engaged to another – inevitably a brute of a man for whom she entertained no tender feelings at all. One day, as they walked hand in hand in the professor's garden, Hebe begged her lover to run away with her. 'How often in after years,' the author noted, 'walking through beautiful solitudes – and amid the scent of flowers and the song of birds remembering Hebe – how often have I asked myself, would it have been well for us if that handclasp had been for life.'[7] William Waldorf refused, and the story moved to a tragic conclusion with Hebe making a murderous attack on her fiancé and subsequently vanishing completely.

Herein lies the kernel of William Waldorf's first and deepest love. In Homeric legend Hebe was the divine princess and goddess of youth. In Rome, in 1869, William Waldorf fell in love with a girl who, to his romantic soul, represented the very essence of classic divinity and beauty. In his brief memoir he wrote, 'Had we been allowed to marry, would life have been happiness for us both?' – a question echoing the one he posed to himself in 'A Secret of Olympus'. The more dramatic elements of the story we can dismiss as poetic licence. There may, indeed, have been a rival, but he could have been bought off had William Waldorf's parents been disposed to do so. Clearly, they were not so disposed. It was out of the question for the heir to the Astor millions to marry an Italian peasant girl. John Jacob summoned his son home immediately and nipped this youthful infatuation in the bud. Obediently, William Waldorf returned to New York; but nothing could have been more calculated to bind him closer to Italy and its culture, or to turn him against a life in the family estate office. Once again, the pull of an older culture was exerted on a new Astor generation.

William Waldorf Astor's life of seventy-one years and seven months falls almost exactly into two halves. It was in August 1882, the midway point in his earthly journey, that he left America for his first major sojourn abroad, and during that three-year sabbatical the idea of setting up home permanently in the Old World became, as he recorded, 'a settled resolve'.

That decision was far from inevitable. This dutiful Astor tried in various ways to follow the pattern set by his forbears and to extend Astor influence in the land of his birth. Not that he had a great deal of choice in the matter initially, for his course was minutely planned out for him. He began work in the estate office in October 1871 at the age of twenty-three. His training was thorough. It started at the bottom, with the young heir seated at a high clerk's desk mastering the intricacies of double-entry book-keeping. He was taken, map in hand, around all the family's properties, stretching from the Battery to Harlem. He collected rents. He dealt with correspondence. He was initiated into every detail of business in the counting room. The work was tedious and the hours long, but William Waldorf did not complain. This was his destiny. For two years he laboured thus on the 'shop floor'.

Only when his father thought that he was ready was the young man elevated to the rank of property-dealing businessman. He was introduced to all the leading Wall Street magnates and allowed to handle large sums of money. The next step in the progress mapped out by John Jacob III was a year to be spent with the Astors' lawyers – but at this William Waldorf demurred. Probably the thought of incarceration in another dusty office, learning its laborious routine, was too much for him. He asked whether he might not instead spend a few terms at the law school of Columbia College, and his father agreed. This very modest rebellion did not put much distance between William Waldorf and the Astor nerve centre – Columbia was then only a few blocks away, on the corner of 49th and Madison – but it did mean that, for a few brief months, he was able to enjoy again the more stimulating company of professors and fellow students.

The 'change of air' was cut short in December 1875 by his grandfather's death. Although William Waldorf did manage to take his barrister's degree, he had to return to the office in order to help wind up William Backhouse's estate (he was an executor of his grandfather's will). Now, his elevation to the position of regent of the Astor empire was rapid. Within a few months John Jacob executed a power of attorney in favour of his son, which gave William Waldorf effective control.

It is not difficult to see why the new head of the family so rapidly abdicated. Like some Byzantine emperor who hankered more after the monastic life than the imperial purple, John Jacob Astor III wanted to be shot of his responsibilities. Now that his father's forbidding presence was removed, he was free to follow his inclination. He must have felt that he deserved a respite. For almost thirty years he had carried the burden with no help from his brother. Now he was fifty-four and he had a weak heart. He had completed his responsibility to the family business by, in his turn, training up his own son to succeed him. Well, that son could now take over and leave him more time for the visits to Britain he so much enjoyed and for other recreations.

By now, however, William Waldorf also viewed the estate office with distaste and was looking around for other ways of fulfilling his family and social obligations. 'In the summer of 1877,' he tells us, 'I startled and amused my relatives by declaring my wish to stand for election to the New York State Legislature.'[8] The family raised no objection. It may well be that William Waldorf's father was prepared to indulge him because, in aspiring to public office, he was fulfilling an ambition that he himself had suppressed. William Waldorf's flirtation with politics lasted five years and brought him nothing but bitter disillusionment.

He could not have chosen a more dismal period to enter American public life. The Civil War lay well in the past, and no fresh, dramatic issues had emerged to stir the public imagination or provide the parties with distinctive manifestos. Not surprisingly, therefore, Republicans and Democrats were equally poised throughout the nation as a whole. Political contests at all levels were often decided by a few votes. Personalities and electioneering tactics had become more significant than policies and principles. All this placed more power than usual in the hands of fixers, faction leaders and lobbyists. Corruption and sectional interest were rife. Republican leaders like James G. Blaine of Maine, Roscoe Conkling and Chester A. Arthur in New York manipulated men and money to wed big business and politics. Since these were the rules and the rule-makers of United States government in the last quarter of the century, it is neither surprising, nor especially culpable that William Waldorf Astor should enter politics with a deep sense of responsibility, but no easily discernible philanthropic principles.

What he did espouse vigorously was élitism. As we have seen, rapid industrialization had thrust up hundreds of wealthy entrepreneurs. To William Waldorf they were anathema, as they were to his father. He longed to see their power curbed and real authority placed where it belonged, in the hands of a few well-established, educated families.

He began his brief but not uneventful political career when his Republican friends nominated him for a safe seat in the state assembly in 1877. For a while he was content to prove himself unswervingly loyal to the party bosses. In any case, another event soon dominated his life. On 6 June 1878 he married Mary Dahlgren Paul, a nineteen-year-old girl from Philadelphia.

'Mamie', as she was known to family and friends, was beautiful, charming and light-hearted in a quiet, unassuming way. She came from an established 'old' family who were based in Philadelphia and owned an estate and a fine house at Villa Nova. In all the obvious ways she was an eminently suitable choice – attractive, well-connected, popular and socially accomplished – as the consort for the future head of the Astor clan. Yet, in her upbringing, she was a complete contrast to her bridegroom. She came from a large family where everything was rumbustiousness and noise. Unlike the well-ordered and class-conscious household in which William Waldorf had grown up, the Villa Nova establishment was carefree and relaxed. When Mamie and her husband visited they were embraced, not only by a bevy of parents and siblings but also by the servants, most of whom had been with the Pauls since time out of mind. Martha Tiddley, Mamie's faithful maid, had been in the Pauls' employ since 1848, had nursed Mamie from infancy, went with her to New York (and subsequently England) and served as maid and confidante until her mistress died. Mamie's brothers were an easygoing, somewhat eccentric bunch. For example, one of them, Lawrie, was in the habit of sending himself postcards to remind him of important engagements because he could not be bothered to keep a diary.

What did William Waldorf make of this zany, laid-back family? It may be that he envied their easy self-assurance. The Pauls had to make no strenuous efforts to maintain their social superiority. It was something they – and everyone else – took for granted. They wore gentility like an old, well-fitting coat. By contrast, leading Astors tended to sport their prestige like a plumed helmet – uncomfortable but necessary. Perhaps he hoped that Mamie would bring to his household the grace, the *noblesse oblige* and that indefinable aura which attached to the older New York families, whose snobbishness matched that of the still more venerable Bostonian clans of whom it was said, 'the Lowells talk to the Cabots and the Cabots talk only to God'.[9] Possibly the truth was much simpler: William Waldorf may have been attracted by the warmth and homeliness of his prospective in-laws. Mamie and her family had scores of genuine friends who did not cultivate them for their money. William Waldorf's children, a few years later, eagerly looked forward to their visits to Villa Nova. His daughter Pauline recalled:

> My grandmother Paul was the most hospitable warm-hearted and generous person, always welcoming visitors who might drop in unexpectedly and pressing them to stay for any meal, and it was enough for me to admire any little trinket for her to give it to me.[10]

With a beautiful new wife to show off, who brought youth and gaiety to the house they moved into on East 33rd Street (a present from John Jacob III), William Waldorf threw himself vigorously into political and social life. He gave parties, balls and soirées which soon began to rival those presided over by his Aunt Caroline. The couple were happy and seemed to have the world at their feet. In the first three and a half years of marriage Mamie presented her husband with three children: Waldorf (born 1879), Pauline (born 1880), and a son who survived only a few weeks. And William Waldorf had many issues to get his teeth into in the state legislature at Albany. After two years, having proved himself unswervingly loyal to the party leaders, he was advanced, with little effort on his part, to a place in the state senate. Within a few months he began to make clear where his real interests lay. He launched a vigorous campaign against the new men. He personally introduced a bill to halve the fares on the New York elevated railway, doubtless in the hope that such a measure would force the owners of the hideous enterprise into bankruptcy; it mattered nothing to him that several of the shareholders were fellow Republican senators. The bill was heavily defeated. William Waldorf had more success with his attempt to remove another eyesore, the Croton aqueduct. He steered this measure successfully through the upper house but it failed in the assembly.

Senator Astor took such reverses very personally. He was, in fact, too thin-skinned for political life, but this did not stop him pursuing his new career with enthusiasm. At the same time that his father was declining the offer of a highly prestigious diplomatic post, William Waldorf was angling for a seat in the US Congress. In December 1879 President Hayes, one of the least distinguished holders of the supreme office, invited John Jacob III to become America's representative at the Court of St James's. Given John Jacob's known Anglophile sentiments, it was a good choice. But the head of the family declined, as his son believed, through 'sheer diffidence'.[11]

It was only months later that William Waldorf was nominated for the Republican ticket in New York's seventh congressional district. The campaign of 1880 was one of the grubbiest on record, marked not only by bitter rivalry between the evenly balanced parties, but by divisions in the Republican ranks. President Hayes had aroused opposition in New York by deliberately confronting Conkling over corruption in the city administration. As a result several members of the Conkling caucus lost their lucrative positions, including Chester A. Arthur. Not surprisingly, Conkling turned against Hayes. His nomination as the Republican candidate in 1880 was Ulysses S. Grant, a man who during his two previous presidencies had turned a blind eye to 'irregularities' and allowed the local bosses considerable scope. In the event James A. Garfield from Ohio won the Republican contest but, as a sop to Conkling, he chose Arthur as his running-mate. It took only a few weeks for the new President to fall out with members of the Conkling faction over the distribution of the spoils of victory. On 2 July 1881 Garfield went to the Baltimore and Potomac Railroad's depot in Washington to catch a train. There he was shot down by a fanatical member of the 'Stalwarts', as the members of the Conkling faction called themselves. Vice-President Arthur was immediately sworn in to succeed him. These were the depths to which

United States political life had sunk at the time William Waldorf Astor aspired to a seat in Congress.

He lacked the stomach necessary for a game played according to such rough-and-tumble rules. But he had the party's hard men behind him; Conkling and even Grant spoke at his meetings. The fixers assured him that a lavish distribution of Astor greenbacks would secure victory. The seventh district contained hundreds of Astor slum properties whose tenants might consider it advisable to vote for their landlord. Using William Waldorf's money, the campaign managers bought hundreds of local lads prepared to cheer at Republican meetings and parade the streets with torches and banners. But, of course, the candidate was expected to do more than just throw dollar bills about and make portentous speeches. He would have to visit the poverty-stricken voters in their hovels and he must be ready to 'mix it' with his adversaries. These things he could not do. Begging for votes on the doorsteps of his own tenants was beneath him, but worse was the swapping of insults and abuse with the Democrats. When he was pilloried in the newspapers as an unthinking party hack and a millionaire playing at politics, instead of bouncing back with counter-charges, he took the offensive comments to heart and sulked. His patrician sensibilities were revolted by the vulgar realities of campaigning. At some point in the electioneering process something happened which inclined him to run away from the whole rotten business. Four decades later he was able to pinpoint this new impulse with complete precision: 'On the 20th September, 1880 when I was 32 the thought occurred to me that we should fare better in another land.'[12]

It is tantalizing that we do not know the specific event which drove William Waldorf Astor to this momentous conclusion. Yet, whatever the catalyst was, it can only have been one of many happenings which combined to convince him that America was no place for a gentleman. For the moment, however, severing the links with his native land remained a distant goal. There were pressing and immediate matters to attend to. Despite his lack of commitment to the exercise, William Waldorf did remarkably well in the election. In what was traditionally a Democratic district, out of more than 23,000 votes cast he fell short of victory by only 165.

Over the next few months two debates occurred simultaneously. Within the Astor family circle William Waldorf and his father discussed the possibility of the former's emigration. The idea seems to have developed rapidly, for it was soon being referred to as 'the English Plan'. If William Waldorf's later recollections are to be trusted, John Jacob was surprisingly agreeable to his son's forsaking the day-to-day management of the business. Probably he realized that the younger man was only planning what he had dreamed about but lacked the resolve to accomplish. At the same time Conkling and Co.

were urging William Waldorf to contest another seat. A suitable vacancy soon occurred when the incumbent of the fifteenth congressional district was appointed as Minister to France. It was a safe Republican constituency in one of the wealthier parts of the city, and Astor, perhaps against his better judgement, accepted the nomination. The Democrats, determined to make a fight of it, put against him a millionaire stockbroker who could match Astor's electioneering expenditure dollar for dollar.

Once again William Waldorf became the victim both of his own sensitivities and of the chaotic state of national politics. He held aloof from the more personal aspects of campaigning. One correspondent noted that Astor even shook hands with his gloves on. Naturally the Democratic press attacked him and his family, but, because of the divisions within the party, even Republican newspapers were not very warm in their support. More than that, the public was growing increasingly disillusioned. The prospect of two wealthy citizens cynically buying votes, following on the shock of Garfield's assassination, brought home to people just how corrupt the democratic process had become. So, what should have been a low-key by-election assumed national importance as a symbol of the current state of American politics. William Waldorf was subjected to weeks of press vilification. His ancestry, his lifestyle, the Astor record as slum landlords, his character, his maverick performance in the state legislature – all were venomously attacked. Even when, to cap it all, he lost the election, William Waldorf was not left in peace. The jeering press rubbed salt into the wounds of his humiliation. It is no exaggeration to say that the experience scarred him for life. Decades later he referred bitterly to 'that atrocity called the American press', 'tobacco-spitting journalism' and 'those trained vulgarians, those thimble-riggers the American press'. He looked back ruefully on the whole episode as 'a fine roll in the mire'.[13]

It all served to strengthen his resolve to live abroad, yet even now he did not take the initiative himself. The opportunity was presented by no less a person than President Arthur. Wishing to reward Astor for his service to the Republican cause and, perhaps, to remove him from the limelight, he offered him the post of Minister to Italy. William Waldorf accepted with alacrity and called upon Secretary of State F. T. Frelinghuysen to enquire what his duties in Rome would entail. With a wave of the hand, the seasoned politician replied, 'Go and enjoy yourself, my dear boy; have a good time!' And that, for three years (1882–5), is precisely what William Waldorf Astor did.

At last he had found his ideal *métier.* In Rome, he enjoyed status and respect unencumbered with onerous mundane duties. He moved in the ordered, precise world of international protocol. He spent his time with civilized people. He attended glittering functions and hosted a succession of balls, dinners and receptions. And he had at his side a wife who was widely regarded as one of the most beautiful women in Rome. King Umberto was particularly fond of her. The Astors' stay in Italy coincided with a time of peace and national reconstruction under the premiership of the veteran statesman Agostino Depretis. There were no international incidents or diplomatic wrangles to intrude upon William Waldorf's peaceful enjoyment of office. He and Mamie toured Europe, visiting many of the places whose historical and romantic associations appealed so much to him. As well as events in the distant past, his interests now included the more recent Franco-Prussian War, and military history in general. Campaign strategy was, for this avid chess player, the life of the chequered board writ large. It was in the conducive atmosphere of Italy, and particularly of Sorrento, for which he formed a special attachment, that William Waldorf devoted himself to the creative arts: drawing, sculpture – and writing. In 1884 he published a historical novel called *Valentino*, based on the life of Cesare Borgia, and followed it up a couple of years later with *Sforza, A Story of Milan*. Alas, it soon became clear that he was no more likely to make his name as a novelist than as a politician. In an age of expanding readership, subscription libraries and cheap editions, an age which gobbled up romantic fiction, Astor's efforts did not stir the public imagination – nor, one is bound to admit, did they deserve to.

During his stay in Italy William Waldorf made exhaustive enquiries into his ancestry. He employed the London genealogists Janson, Cobb, Pearson and Co. to seek out every Astor, living or dead, of whom there remained any record. Soon their agents were scurrying all over Europe, burrowing into municipal and ecclesiastical archives in Germany, Switzerland, France, Spain and England. Their researches occupied at least five years and were expensive as well as extensive. For all their labours, they were unable to trace a direct line back beyond mid-seventeenth-century Baden. William Waldorf was obviously disappointed – but he was not discouraged. He had Messrs Janson, Cobb, Pearson and Co. explore the records of other families which had a similar name. He was very excited when they unearthed information about the French Huguenot dynasty of d'Astorg. Not only was this an interesting family of some distinction; it was also Protestant (William Waldorf had an intense dislike of Roman Catholics); and it could trace its origin back to Castile at the time of the Crusades. A certain knight and royal attendant had recaptured the queen's favourite falcon, which had escaped. In gratitude Her Majesty ennobled the young man, who took the name of Pedro d'Astorga (*azor* being Spanish for 'goshawk') and the arms 'falcon, argent, on a gloved hand, or'. This gallant subsequently enjoyed a distinguished military career and was killed at the siege of Jerusalem. Mr Astor was in no doubt that here at last he had discovered his true ancestry. In vain did the experts point out to their client that any connection between the Franco-Spanish d'Astorgs and the German Astors was highly speculative. William Waldorf thanked them for their successful and satisfactory work and paid them off.

Another activity to which William Waldorf devoted himself enthusiastically was the collecting – or perhaps it would be truer to say the *amassing* – of art and antiques. This was the time at which American high society was badly infected by the collecting virus. Men with new fortunes wanted to buy ancient respectability. They vied with each other to pay record prices in the salerooms. They patronized the premises of immigrant dealers who now swarmed to the fashionable areas of all America's leading cities. They sent agents to scour Europe for new acquisitions. Rockefellers, Vanderbilts, Henry Flagher of Standard Oil, Washington Roebling the builder of Brooklyn Bridge, California Governor Leland Stanford, and a host of *arrivistes*, all hastened to fill their mansions with imported works of art. One Philadelphia collector was reputedly obliged to hang pictures on the inside of his front door because he had run out of wall space. This was the era when Emmanuele Cesnola presided over the Metropolitan Museum, largely founded on the thousands of artefacts he had plundered while US Consul in Cyprus in the 1860s. It was the era which saw the foundation of some of the great private collections associated with the names of Andrew Mellon, Henry Frick, Isabella Stewart Gardner and others. John Jacob Astor III had begun serious collecting about 1875, relying heavily on New York's leading dealer, Michael Knoedler. Arrived in Europe, his son was soon buying on a massive scale.

He had a genuine passion for the antique and a bottomless purse. He acquired anything that took his fancy – paintings, books, tapestries, armour, architectural fittings. His largest single purchase was the balustrade and fountains fronting the magnificent Villa Borghese, whose owners had fallen on hard times and were desperate to raise money. But his most ardent pursuit at this period was of items of classical and Renaissance statuary and sculpture. The rape of Greece and Italy which had begun a century before was in full spate in the 1880s, thanks largely to the entry of American collectors into the market and the founding of new museums like the 'Met'. As he toured Italy Astor enthusiastically participated in this spoliation. We may, now, deplore such activity, but if we do so we reveal only that we are creatures of our own age. William Waldorf Astor was a creature of his. Thus, he accumulated Roman copies of Greek statues, carved friezes, sarcophagi, pottery jars from Pompeii, columns from Rome's Temple of Venus and fifteenth- and sixteenth-century Italian carvings inspired by classical models.

This acquisitiveness was not mere 'cheque-book connoisseurship'; William Waldorf brought to his collecting the enthusiasm and industry of a studious amateur antiquarian. He read avidly. He talked with scholars and collectors. He made notes and sketches of the artefacts and buildings that he saw. And he envisaged the eventual display of his treasures. These dreams did not include shipping crates of ancient objects back to America. There can be little doubt that the 'English Plan' was still maturing in his mind, though whether as a scheme for permanent emigration or occasional residence is less clear. He still had commitments and a social position in the USA, and his wife did not want to cut herself off from her family. When they returned to America in 1885, they gave every sign of returning to the old life.

The election of 1884 brought a Democrat to the White House and signalled the end of William Waldorf's sojourn in Italy. The family went back to New York and resumed their former activities. William Waldorf presided once more over the estate office and relaxed at the most fashionable clubs, the Knickerbocker, the Lawyers', the Union League and the Tuxedo. Mamie once more presided over her sumptuously spread table at 33rd Street. In May 1886 she was brought to bed of a second (surviving) son, who became the next Astor to bear the prestigious names John Jacob. Life continued on its even course. Then, within the space of little more than two years, William Waldorf lost both his parents. On 12 December 1887, Charlotte died. John Astor, now a sixty-five-year-old widower, apparently had no relish for the single state. On 27 October 1889 the *New York World* reported his engagement to a Mrs Bowler of Cincinnati. The lady in question, the paper informed its intrigued readers, was a widow of some five or six years' standing who had previously been married to a wealthy financier. She now lived in Europe with one of her children, and during the previous year Mr Astor had twice crossed the Atlantic to visit her. Alas, the romance was destined not to blossom. On 22 February 1890, John Jacob Astor III followed his wife to the grave. Seven months later William Waldorf and his family sailed back to Europe.

In his memoirs William Waldorf claimed: 'when in 1885 I returned to New York and renewed my acquaintance with its ways, "The English Plan" became a settled resolve.'[14] The contrast between American society and that of sophisticated, age-hallowed Italy was marked. The press were still sniping at the Astors, as at most wealthy citizens. There were no family ties to keep William Waldorf in New York. He actively disliked his relatives, especially domineering Aunt Caroline. Now that his parents were dead and he had complete possession of America's largest personal fortune his independence was total. He could do entirely as he wished with his life. So, by October 1890, William Waldorf, Mamie, Waldorf, Pauline, John Jacob V and their personal servants were installed in St Thomas's Hotel, London. This move was the most fateful event in Astor history since John Jacob I set foot in Baltimore. The senior branch of the family, in contrast to the line descended from William, was destined to be prolific. Had they remained on the western side of the Atlantic their fortune and their talents would have ensured the Astors a continuing position of prominence in American life. Instead, they would make their mark in Britain.

The 1890 migration was not, however, a clean break, any more than John Jacob I's transit from Europe to America had been. William Waldorf would happily have settled in Europe, but for his wife's sake he maintained the transatlantic link. Thus, Mr and Mrs Astor were back in residence at Beaulieu for the Newport season the following summer. Here William Waldorf made it clear that if Mamie wanted the east coast social life she must take her proper place in it. As wife of the head of the Astor family the only possible position for her was the pinnacle. This gave rise to the 'battle of the cards', a minor incident which delighted contemporary gossip columnists and has been resurrected by most family chroniclers as an event of significance. The insufferable Caroline, sensing a threat to her pre-eminence and determined to keep her nephew and niece in their places, changed her visiting cards to read 'Mrs Astor' (she had previously been quite content to be known as 'Mrs William Astor'). William Waldorf was furious. It was Mamie who was *the* Mrs Astor now; her calling cards and invitations proclaimed as much. The idiotic feud went on for weeks and threw the Newport postal authorities into confusion, since mail addressed to 'Mrs Astor' could not be delivered to either Beaulieu or Beechwood without upsetting one or other of the wealthy residents. The rival queens vied with each other in the lavishness of their hospitality and the illustriousness of the names on their guest lists. But toppling the formidable Caroline was a considerable undertaking and one for which Mamie had no stomach. She was too intelligent to find the contest anything other than faintly absurd. As for William Waldorf, he soon realized that the internecine feud only served to provide the hyenas of the press with more carcasses to savage in public. This just strengthened his conviction that there was nothing left in America to which he had any emotional commitment. As for his wife, well, he had tried to please her and look what had happened. Since he never took the trouble to understand the complexities of other people's feelings, he believed that Mamie would be happier in Britain. Nothing, therefore, stood in the way of carrying into effect his long-matured resolve. There was the small matter of a vast fortune in Manhattan real estate – but that could be quite adequately administered from abroad. When he and Mamie sailed again for England, in the autumn of 1891, it was for good.

Such a celebrated emigration was a juicy bone thrown to the gutter press. 'William Waldorf Ass-TOR,' bayed one Ohio leader-writer, 'an American tory whose grandfather accumulated vast sums of money in low callings in and about the city of New York, has soured on the United States and gone to England to reside. This country isn't good enough for "WILLIE old chappie", so he has emigrated to the land of lust and baccarat. His coat of arms should be a skunk rampant, on a brindle ox-hide ...' And the more restrained, if equally outraged, *Boston News* commented: 'What more natural than that the latter-day representative of three generations, which originating in a German slaughterhouse, have devoted their very souls to the getting of American money ... should ... forsake the land that has made him ... Goodbye William, we really shall not miss you much.'[15]

It is not at all difficult to understand why William Waldorf should have wanted to quit America, but it is worth pausing at this juncture to ask the question 'Why England?' The Astors had many friends in Italy, where the climate was certainly more congenial than that of foggy London. And what about Germany? That was where William Waldorf's roots were and where he still had distant relatives. Moreover, little Walldorf was very proud of its connection with the rich American family and would certainly have laid out the red carpet for him. William Waldorf's father and grandfather had made generous periodic donations to the town charities set up under John Jacob I's will, and William Waldorf continued the tradition when he sent them 65,000 marks in 1890. But if not Germany, fashioned by Bismarck, the hero of the Franco-Prussian War, there were other countries to which the history-loving Astor might be drawn. William Waldorf had already commissioned extensive genealogical enquiries about his ancestry, and England did not feature anywhere in the family tree. If it was simply a question of being at the centre of European civilization, Paris and Vienna had greater claims to pre-eminence in the 1890s than London did. William Waldorf spoke Italian, French and German and regarded himself as a cosmopolitan. So, taking up residence in Queen Victoria's realm was in no sense a 'coming home'; it was another Astor emigration. There was no obvious inevitability about the 'English Plan'.

But the Astors' move to London was not a unique phenomenon. The last quarter of the nineteenth century witnessed quite an exodus from New England of men and women who regarded themselves as belonging to the cultural élite. A fascination with things European and especially British was *de rigueur* in the literary and artistic world and that section of the *haut monde* which overlapped it. Whistler, Sargent and Henry James were only the best-known creative Americans who found their inspiration in the Old World. Everyone in the Newport set paid frequent visits to London and sought to outdo their neighbours back home with souvenirs picked up in West End shops and galleries and stories of their encounters with nobility and royalty. Some even managed to marry into the English aristocracy – most notably Jennie Jerome, who became the wife of the Duke of Marlborough's second son and the mother of Winston Churchill.

For many rich Americans who enjoyed enormous wealth and freedom to spend it wherever they pleased Britain exercised a strong magnetic attraction. Examples of families yielding to this pull are legion. We cite just one which illustrates the point and which also has a tangential relevance to our story. Mahlon Sands was a Fifth Avenue neighbour of the Astors and the inheritor of a huge fortune made from patent medicines. At twenty-six he was able to retire from business, enjoy to the full the exclusive delights permitted only to members of the Four Hundred, race his yacht every summer at Newport and dabble in politics. In 1872, at the age of thirty, he married for a second time (his first wife having died of typhoid). His choice fell upon the awesomely beautiful Mary Morton Halfpence who, at the age of eighteen, had made her debut in society the previous year and taken it by storm. William Waldorf was certainly stunned by the soulful eyes and natural grace of Miss Halfpence. It was later surmised in the family that she was the mysterious 'Princess', but it was not so. In 1874 the Sands visited London for the wedding of Mary's cousin to Ernest Chaplin, a close friend of the Prince of Wales. They stayed three years. Mary was as much a favourite in London and Cowes as she had been in New York and Newport. As well as the court circle, their friends included the Rothschilds and several leading members of the Liberal party. In 1879 they returned to England, this time for good, and took a house in Hanover Square. From this base they brought up four children, travelled widely and enjoyed an ever-increasing circle of friends, which included Sargent (who later painted Mary's portrait), Henry James and Mrs Gladstone. In 1888 Mahlon was thrown from his horse in Rotten Row and killed. Supported by friends, prominent among whom, after 1890, were the Astors, this still-young widow cared for her two sons and one daughter. The eldest boy, Alan, was a contemporary of William Waldorf's eldest son, Waldorf, at Eton and New College, Oxford. In 1896 Mary Sands died of a heart attack and her children were even more dependent on the kindness of friends. They paid frequent long visits to the Astors' country home in Buckinghamshire.

It was in 1875 that Henry James settled in London. He devoted a considerable part of his literary output thereafter to exploring the impact of the older civilization on the younger. 'The roots of it', he observed in a story published in the *Atlantic Monthly* in 1871, 'are so deeply buried in the virgin soil of our primary culture, that, without some great upheaval of experience, it would be hard to say exactly when and where and how it begins. It makes an American's enjoyment of England an emotion more fatal and sacred than his enjoyment, say, of Italy or Spain.'[16] Did William Waldorf Astor read 'A Passionate Pilgrim', in which those words appear, the story of an American travelling to England in search of his roots and finding them in a Herefordshire estate 'where great trees stood singly and the tame deer browsed along the bed of a woodland stream', where stood 'the dark Elizabethan manor among its blooming parterres and terraces'?[17] Voracious reader that he was, it seems likely that he subscribed to the *Atlantic Monthly*, where James's story first appeared and which regularly carried the work of some of his favourite authors, such as Oliver Wendell Holmes. Certainly, his subsequent career demonstrated that he was imbued with the historical romanticism of James and his fellow exiles.

So it was that considerations emotional, social and cultural drew William Waldorf to Britain rather than to those countries with which he had closer associations. Indeed, England may have drawn him precisely because he had *no* family ties there. For all his genealogical fantasies, Germany was a constant reminder of the Astors' humble origins, and Walldorf something of an embarrassment. On one occasion in the 1890s when he visited the town, the respectful citizens presented him with an elaborate illuminated address. William Waldorf subsequently gave instructions that it was to be destroyed – though it is probably unwise to try to read too much into this, just as it is to try to discover in William Waldorf a consistency towards things Germanic. For example, he considered Bismarck to be the greatest living European but, although catholic in his musical taste, he loathed Wagner.

It has been suggested that William Waldorf, having failed to receive in America the recognition he considered his due, set his heart on obtaining a British peerage. It is certainly true that, years later, he eagerly pursued this goal, but there is no evidence that coronets and ermine were in his mind from the start. It was several years before he took out British citizenship, a move he almost certainly did not contemplate while Mamie was alive.

Having made the decision to settle in England, William Waldorf threw himself wholeheartedly (perhaps *too* wholeheartedly) into becoming 'English'. His sons were entered for Eton. He rented an impressive town residence, Lansdowne House, and a country estate, Taplow Court, on the Thames near Maidenhead. These property transactions were only temporary arrangements until the American millionaire could find more suitable homes for his family. It took him very little time to locate the ideal rural retreat. He simply acquired the most magnificent estate in the Thames Valley. A mile and a half upstream from Taplow Court stood Cliveden. The forty-year-old house (the third on the site), a square Italianate mansion attached by a curved façade to large east and west wings, enjoyed one of the finest locations in the southern counties, with a superb view of the Thames. The estate, which had passed through several aristocratic hands since the seventeenth century, extended over acres of formal gardens, lawns and wooded walks studded with classical 'temples'. Cliveden belonged to one of Britain's wealthiest noblemen, Hugh Grosvenor, first Duke of Westminster. It had come to him by marriage and he had seldom lived there. In 1892 William Waldorf rented it. The following year he persuaded the duke to sell it to him for, reputedly, $1.25 million.

William Waldorf had great plans for the refurbishment and improvement of Cliveden, but this by no means exhausted his building ambitions. In 1894 he took out a lease on 18 Carlton House Terrace, a centrally placed Crown property only a stone's throw from St James's Park, as a London home for his family, and he bought a large plot of land on the Victoria Embankment for the construction of his business headquarters. At his various residences Astor entertained lavishly and made a determined effort to gain acceptance in English society. Mamie, as usual, attracted friends easily. She even achieved access to court circles through the good offices of Louisa, Duchess of Buccleuch, Mistress of the Robes, who remained close to the family for many years.

It might be thought that establishing himself and his family in a new land, keeping tabs on his American property empire and developing his new building schemes was quite enough to keep William Waldorf busy. It is indicative of the man's remarkable energy and industry that he now embarked on yet another career, that of newspaper proprietor. In 1892 he bought the respected London evening paper the *Pall Mall Gazette.* This was a vibrant epoch in the history of journalism, and owning one of the public information organs was one way for a wealthy man to obtain widespread attention and acclaim. The golden age of the press barons had not quite arrived. William Randolph Hearst was only just embarking on his career in America. The Harmsworth brothers made their first major acquisition in 1894. The Establishment maintained an ambivalent attitude towards such framers of public opinion – for instance, it would be another quarter of a century before the Harmsworths obtained peerages (as Viscounts Northcliffe and Rothermere). But established journals such as *The Times* (run by three generations of the Walter family) had a growing circulation and new papers appeared frequently. It was obvious to astute businessmen in the 1890s that, in a population that was increasingly literate and politically conscious, owning a slice of the only communications medium was a means of making money and gaining influence.

There is little doubt that Astor also saw running a newspaper as a means of 'hitting back' at those who had pilloried him and his family. He was almost paranoid in his hatred of the American press, and kept a large scrapbook of scurrilous articles which had appeared in newspapers over the years. Shortly after his arrival in London he 'leaked' to the news agencies a report of his own sudden death. The disinformation was taken up with alacrity in New York and became the subject of leaders and obituaries in most of the major papers. William Waldorf hugely enjoyed their subsequent embarrassed retractions. By owning his own journal he would show the world what a newspaper *ought* to be. This, of course, meant that he intended the *Pall Mall Gazette* to be a mouthpiece for his own views. It had begun life in 1865 as a Conservative organ, boasting that it was written 'by gentlemen for gentlemen'. A subsequent change of ownership had taken it into the Liberal camp. The *Gazette* was foursquare behind Gladstone, especially on the burning issue of the day, home rule for Ireland. William Waldorf wanted none of that. He acquired the *Gazette* anonymously through intermediaries and the editor was assured that the paper would retain its Liberal colour. He was in for a shock. Astor's first act was to dismiss members of the staff who would not go along with a complete reversal of the paper's policy. (Most of them were immediately hired by Sir George Newnes, Liberal MP and owner of the *Strand Magazine* and *Tit Bits*, to produce a rival broadsheet, the *Westminster Gazette.*)

According to legend, while this journalistic battle was going on Astor happened to meet at a luncheon a gentleman by the name of Harry Cust, liked his conversation, and offered him the editorship of the *Gazette* on the spot. Henry Cust had no experience of journalism but was just the sort of lively and unconventional man to rise to such a challenge. He was an MP, a barrister who had chosen to be called to the bar in France because it was more 'fun', and heir to a barony. He accepted the offer even though William Waldorf tried to encase him in an impossibly restricting straitjacket. Cust's terms of employment included the condition that he 'shall at all times be bound by *any instructions and directions* which may be given him by the proprietor, whose rights of *controlling the policy* and management of the paper are hereby acknowledged'.[18] Nothing could be a clearer indication of Astor's intentions.

The inevitable result was that the next three years were marked by a struggle between owner and editor for actual control of policy. Cust squarely stood up to his employer and demanded his independence. Though generally in agreement with Astor, he occasionally supported radical or progressive measures, attacked Astor's friends and resisted plain directives. Most of Astor's forthright instructions fell on deaf ears: the *Gazette* is 'not to be used for attacks such as the cordite, Harness belt, or London hospital affairs'; place the *Gazette* 'in a position of such antagonism to the Progressives as will show peradventure where we stand'; 'Lady Henry Somerset [a temperance campaigner]. For personal reasons I ask you to give her a heavy broadside. I hope you will put some more gunpowder in your cartridges.'[19] The fact that this situation continued for so long may be attributed in part to Cust's good humour and charm and in part to Astor's inability to handle insubordination. No one had ever defied him in this way before. He found it impossible to descend from his Olympian detachment to debate or argue with his recalcitrant employee. Nothing makes this clearer than the discussion which did eventually take place in February 1896 and which Cust recorded in abbreviated form:

Astor: American crisis very severe, my position very delicate. Conduct of paper of great importance to me.
Cust: On first news I telegraphed to you for instructions. You answered maintain judicious attitude. I hoped for further instructions or interview. Has the paper gone wrong?
Astor: Not at all, perfectly satisfied; moderate and judicious, but acute crisis requires new editorial arrangements. You and Iwan-Müller must go, and in a week. Salary paid, of course, in lieu of notice.
Cust: Why?
Astor: Well in such case prefer dictate policy week by week and day by day.
Cust: Why the devil didn't you say so?
Astor: Knew no use.
Cust: Why?
Astor: You wouldn't have followed my wishes.
Cust: Did you express them?
Astor: No.
Cust: How could I follow them? . . .
Astor: I do not wish to enter into details.
Cust: I do. Hasn't the paper been a success, in circulation, advertisement and position?
Astor: The greatest. Heartily congratulate you.
Cust: Well!
Astor: Well?
Cust: Pig![20]

The issue which finally brought matters to a head was a boundary dispute between Venezuela and British Guiana in which the US government felt its interests to be at stake. Astor was very sensitive on the matter of transatlantic relations. Despite having shaken the dust of America from his feet he was not going to allow his paper to lampoon the Secretary of State, Richard Olney, as Cust had done in recent leaders headed 'Drink to me Olney with Thine Eyes' and 'Fee Fo Fum'. The editor had to go.

It says something for William Waldorf's tolerance that on a matter closer to his own heart he had patiently endured Cust's snubs. One reason for acquiring the *Gazette* had been to secure an outlet for his own literary endeavours. 'I shall expect', he informed his editor, 'that anything I send – provided it is not obscene or inciting to a breach of the peace – to be immediately printed.' But when he provided short stories and articles – the dear children of his soul – Cust returned them as unpublishable. Astor did not fly into a rage. Instead he accepted his editor's suggestion that he find another organ as an outlet for purely cultural features.

Thus there came into being the *Pall Mall Magazine*, a monthly miscellany of stories and articles of a predominantly literary and historical nature (though its range later extended to include wider interests and contemporary issues in a bid to increase a dwindling circulation). It was founded to reflect William Waldorf's taste for the antique and the romantic and to ensure the publication of his own fictional efforts. Over the years several works from his pen appeared within its pages. With such titles as 'Pharaoh's Daughter', 'The Wraith of Cliveden Reach' and 'The Vengeance of Poseidon', they all gave expression to Astor's antiquarian romanticism. Many of them were good yarns, though some were still marred by the author's affectation of what he supposed to be an earlier literary style:

> Likewise, came it back to me, traversing the hall, how one evening shortly before my Lady of Shrewsbury's cheerless going hence . . . she idled in the chimney corner, drawing from her Lute its subtle chords, when behold, the clock chime struck athwart her musique with a curious tinklinge ecstasie . . .[21]

Within the covers of the *Pall Mall Magazine* Astor's prose rubbed shoulders with that of more distinguished contributors such as H. G. Wells, Laurence Housman, E. Nesbit, Algernon Blackwood, Walter de la Mare, Percy F. Westerman and Ernest Bramah. Around the turn of the century this periodical brought to the public attention for the first time several writers of note.

The most important fact to emerge from all this journalistic activity was that Britain had another trenchant, conservative, Unionist journal. From the start its stance was quite clear:

> If [Mr Gladstone] be wise, if he be just, if he be patriotic, if he have the courage to confess an error, he will abandon the vain and dangerous scheme which he so rashly undertook six years ago, grant to Ireland the local government which already obtains in England and Scotland and devote himself to urgent social reforms that are in every man's knowledge and in every man's heart.[22]

The *Gazette* rapidly developed as the mouthpiece of the most reactionary elements in British politics, the more so when the rise of the Independent Labour party caused the appalling spectre of socialism to be sighted in the land. Mr Astor's paper urged employers to stand firm against striking workers, advocated closing all museums and galleries to women in order to prevent sabotage by militant suffragettes, inveighed against attempts to engineer international armament reductions, resisted the imposition of death duties and estate taxes and vociferously supported tariffs and imperial preference. But the burning issue, year in and year out, for the *Gazette*, its proprietor and its supporters was the maintenance of the link with Ireland.

In the closing years of the century 'Home Rule' and 'Unionism' were the rival standards to which politicians rallied whose convictions on other issues varied widely. Allegiance cut right across 'Liberal' and 'Conservative' labels, making a nonsense of the two-party system to which the British Establishment, in defiance of all logic, has always stubbornly adhered. The House of Commons was made up of Gladstonian Liberals, Unionists, Irish members and a handful of MPs representing the embryonic Labour party. But the Unionists could scarcely be called a party. Most of them were Conservatives (the label was dropped for many years), but there was also a rump of anti-Home Rule Liberals. Many MPs represented the landed interest comprised of families which had estates in Ireland or relatives among the Irish ruling class. The only cement which held the Unionist edifice together was its emotional adherence to the indissolubility of the United Kingdom. The party had no clear manifesto covering a range of issues. Within its ranks were to be found reactionaries, progressives and radicals; preservers of the *status quo* and advocates of social reform. William Waldorf Astor belonged, unyieldingly, to the establishmentarian right wing, class-based and suspicious of all change.

The exercise of William Waldorf's almost manic enterprise and imagination was not confined to his adopted country. In 1891 he conceived a plan that would revolutionize the social life of New York. The idea probably occurred to him during his sojourn in Italy. One of the most marked contrasts between America and Europe was the quality of city life. The elegance of Rome, Vienna, Paris, London and other ancient centres was not restricted to the town mansions of the wealthy and the great opera houses and theatres; they boasted public rooms, parks, cafés and hotels where the élite could congregate to see and be seen. 'Café society' and 'dining out' were concepts unknown on the other side of the Atlantic, where a hotel was merely a convenient place to eat and sleep when away from home. There was no counterpart in New York of the palatial Grand Hotel in Rome, the Paris Ritz, the establishments springing up along the newly fashionable Riviera or London's recently opened Savoy with its seventy bathrooms, electric lighting and lifts, and superb cuisine presided over by Georges Auguste Escoffier (it was in 1893 that the great chef created *pêche Melba*, in honour of the opera singer). It was precisely this ambience that William Waldorf Astor decided to recreate in the city of his birth.

The site for his new enterprise was ready to hand. William Waldorf had no personal use for his father's house on the corner of Fifth Avenue and 33rd Street and it was right in the heart of fashionable New York. The fact that Aunt Caroline lived next door and would be immensely inconvenienced by the construction work was an added bonus. At the beginning of 1892, John Jacob III's mansion was demolished (some fittings being salvaged to grace the new establishment). On 14 March 1893, the Waldorf Hotel opened its doors for the first time with a charity ball in aid of St Mary's Free Hospital. All the leaders of society were present for the occasion, and a sizeable crowd endured the cold, wet evening to watch the procession of carriages draw up at the long *porte cochère*. From that moment the Waldorf became the cultural centre of the city. Hostesses vied with each other to book its sumptuous rooms for private dinner parties and elaborate *bals masqués*, and lesser mortals thronged through its portals to marvel at its marble columns, velvet drapes, antique furniture and liveried footmen and to experience a touch of real luxury.

In its first year of operation William Waldorf's brainchild grossed four and a half million dollars. The audacity and success of the venture provoked cousin John Jacob IV into retaliation. His mother had moved out of her now overshadowed residence, marking her defiance of her upstart nephew by having a much larger and more sumptuous house built at 840 Fifth Avenue (its ballroom alone could accommodate, not the old Four Hundred, but six hundred couples). John Jacob IV now decided that he too would enter the hotel business. On the site of his mother's former home he raised the Astoria Hotel, just as luxurious as its neighbour and much larger. But the cousins did not allow their rivalry to obscure their commercial good sense. The two buildings were linked by internal corridors and thus, in 1897, became the Waldorf Astoria, with 1,500 bedrooms the world's largest hotel.

This most magnificent building by no means exhausted William Waldorf's plans for New York. In the same year that the Waldorf opened, another Fifth Avenue hotel, the Netherland, was erected. Over the next decade or so the compulsive builder was responsible for a series of prestige developments – private houses, apartment blocks, and complexes of offices and shops – in the heart of Manhattan between Central Park and 17th Street.

At last, William Waldorf, with his growing family, his fine homes, his many interests and his increasing circle of cultured, fashionable friends, seemed to have found a satisfactory and meaningful life. In October 1893 he and Mamie had another daughter, Gwendolyn, thus neatly balancing their children between boys and girls. As 1894 progressed things looked good for the English Astors. There was only one cloud in their sky – but it would grow and darken with dreadful rapidity.

After Gwendolyn's birth, Mamie did not recover her old strength and vigour. Her doctors were anxious about her and ordered rest. She therefore spent long hours languishing on a sofa at Cliveden. It seems likely that her condition was a nervous rather than a physical disorder; post-natal depression, perhaps, exacerbated by enforced absence from her own family. William

Waldorf was very attentive, but his business interests took up much of his time and he was not the sort of man who could readily express his sympathy for the sufferings of others, even those close to him. Whatever the nature of Mamie's ailment, its result was to make her progressively weaker and a prey to a variety of viruses. By December she had developed peritonitis. William Waldorf summoned an American doctor in whom he had great faith from Rome, but nothing could be done. Three days before Christmas, Mamie Astor died at the age of thirty-six. Early in the New Year William Waldorf took her body back to New York for burial.

Astor had always been an introspective man, but from now on he turned in on himself almost completely. His relationship with his wife had not been one of deep love; she never replaced in his affections the 'Princess', with whom he remained in contact for many years. Yet he was deeply moved by Mamie's death. It seemed that everything he cared for was denied him or taken from him by the cruel Fates – his first love, his wife, his political ambitions, his place in American society. The conviction that 'life' was against him was reinforced when it was discovered that little Gwendolyn was suffering from a serious heart defect. She died shortly before her ninth birthday. So William Waldorf Astor became a living cliché – the unhappy millionaire. One Sunday morning this very rich man emerged from church and remarked to his daughter Pauline, 'I can never understand how we can thank God for our creation.'[23] By then, he had long since locked up his emotions and thrown away the key. Life, he thought, was a conspiracy to cause him pain and anguish. Very well, he would foil it by not exposing himself to attack. He would retreat into his own, well-ordered world, keep his contacts with other people to a minimum and allow no one access to his feelings.

It was now, in his forties, that William Waldorf Astor developed into a complete, austere eccentric. The 'chessboard's fascination' became an obsession. Order, harmony, discipline were to be the inflexible rules of his life, imposed as rigidly on others as on himself. He undoubtedly lost several friends over the years for no other reason than that they failed to come up to his own impeccable standard of punctuality. Anyone arriving a few minutes late for an appointment was likely to receive a distinctly frosty welcome. All his servants had to follow to the letter the strict routines laid down by their perfectionist employer. When 'daylight saving' was introduced during the 1914–18 War, William Waldorf simply refused to acknowledge what he considered a stupid idea – at least for the first year. Thus 'Astor time' was an hour behind everyone else's. He personally planned all meals days in advance and kept a large selection of cookery books for this purpose. Every item had to be cooked precisely to his taste. The flag carrying his armorial bearings had to be raised promptly at 9 a.m. and lowered at sunset in whichever house he was currently resident. He had a fixation about privacy and security. He had a high wall built around Cliveden, topped with broken glass, which did not endear him to local people who had been used to enjoying the walks through part of the grounds. Contact with underlings he kept to a minimum. Inevitably, the large amount of building, alterations and maintenance involved in his elaborate plans for his several houses meant that he not infrequently had to talk to staff or contractors. There was no question of discussion at such meetings. William Waldorf would take his place at the head of a long table and issue his instructions. One contractor whose firm carried out extensive gardening projects for the reclusive millionaire later recalled the invariable pattern of these briefings: 'He was very quiet and courteous, and with the minimum of words would describe what he wanted; then the invariable formula – "So will you please settle this with my agent, good-day to you gentlemen", and that was that!'[24] If he required minor changes to be made in the grounds of his country homes he would sometimes go out alone with an axe, cut down some bushes or small trees to indicate the location of the new work, then inform his head gardener, as tersely as possible, of what had to be done.

Such arrant bad manners were accepted by social underlings as no more than their due around the turn of the twentieth century, and Astor was certainly not alone in adopting an aloof posture towards servants. Unfortunately, he took a similar stance with those who regarded themselves as his equals or even his betters, and this inflexible *hauteur* landed him in several public rows. He had a long-running dispute with the Duke of Westminster. After the sale of Cliveden, the duke courteously asked if the new owner would be kind enough to return the family visitors' book which had, inadvertently, been left in the house and which contained the signatures of many important guests. Astor refused. Everything left in the house at the time of purchase, he asserted, was legally the property of the new owner. The quarrel went on for years, but William Waldorf never budged. His intractability did him no good in the society in which he craved acceptance. His insensitivity could lead him into the most appalling gaffes. He once engaged Dame Nellie Melba to perform at one of his soirées at Carlton House Terrace. The great operatic soprano naturally assumed that she would be the main attraction for a discerning and refined clientele. She was appalled to discover, on arrival, that she was expected to share star billing with a celebrity from a very different musical world, Yvette Guilbert, currently the toast of the Parisian music halls, who specialized in vulgar, risqué songs. Small wonder that the great Melba's feathers were considerably ruffled and that she was only with considerable difficulty prevented from stalking out.

William Waldorf had escaped from an egalitarian society where Astors did not receive the respect he considered to be their due, and had deliberately ensconced himself in a land dominated by class and privilege. What he could not accept was that his place within this structure involved deference towards those placed *above* him in the hierarchy – particularly the friends of the Prince of Wales. Indeed, he was openly contemptuous of many of them. 'I have never shown myself subservient,' he boasted, 'which his intimates of the smart set, the South African crowd and his Jew friends always are.'[25] In actual fact, Mr Astor seemed to go out of his way to antagonize the heir to the throne. One evening in 1898, Sir Berkeley Milne, a friend of the prince, arrived uninvited at William Waldorf's town house for one of his soirées. He had been brought by a friend who assured him that 'Mr Astor won't mind' – but Mr Astor minded very much. He hated being taken for granted. His precise mind rejected the casual manners which seemed to be the prevailing fashion, certainly in the prince's circle, and nothing made him more furious than an invasion of his privacy. Recalling the incident a few years later, he admitted that perhaps he had allowed his temper to 'carry me beyond the bounds of moderation', but of late several ladies and gentlemen had come unbidden to his concerts and he had determined to make an example of someone. Not only did he ask Sir Berkeley to leave, he published the incident in the *Gazette*. The offender sent Mr Astor a written apology, but it did not assuage his wrath. Inevitably, Mr Astor was the only loser; he was made to look pompous and ridiculous.

It was, however, three years later that William Waldorf put himself firmly beyond the bounds of royal favour. Edward, now king, took Mrs Keppel as his latest mistress. Astor was morally outraged and responded accordingly. His own recollection not only gives the facts; it indicates the venom of his attitude towards the king:

> . . . when Mrs George Keppel had sunk to the life of a public strumpet, I no longer invited her to my house. She was then commencing her relations with the King to whom she reported my omission. When I speak of her relations with the King it is only fair to add what all the world knows, that the King has been physically impotent for more than twenty years.[26]

William Waldorf was bitter because, although he genuinely disapproved of Edward's lifestyle and had felt much more at home with the more genteel ways of Victoria's court, he desperately wanted some mark of recognition – a knighthood or a peerage – that only Edward could bestow. He therefore convinced himself that his failure to achieve his ambition was entirely due to the king's spite.

The reality that William Waldorf was trying to conceal from the world behind the thick ramparts of wealth, brusqueness and reserve was that he was a lonely, middle-aged widower with four young children to bring up. It was a difficult role to play, and he did not make a success of it. He did his best for his sons and daughters. He was an indulgent, probably an over-indulgent, parent. Waldorf, Pauline, John and Gwendolyn had the best nannies, tutors and governesses. They were taken on tours of foreign galleries and museums to improve their minds. No gift was too costly for him to bestow – a covered tennis court, an indoor riding school, a rented grouse moor in Scotland when the boys were learning to shoot. He followed their progress at school with interest and pride. He was, for example, very excited when young Waldorf rowed in the Eton boat which won the Ladies' Plate at Henley. If any of the youngsters was sick he was particularly solicitous and would sit at the bedside for hours on end telling stories.

Yet there was a gulf between William Waldorf and his offspring which he could not – and perhaps did not want to – bridge. They regarded him with a certain amount of awe and did not find him a father in whom they could easily confide. Pauline recalled:

> It was not easy to discuss things freely with him, although he was always ready to listen to any problem that worried you, but having given your opinion you could not re-open the subject with an after-thought without risk of being taxed with vacillation and 'not knowing your own mind'. This made exploratory conversation difficult, and discouraged free interchange of ideas.[27]

For his part, he tried to inculcate in his children those habits of mental discipline that he regarded as essential to a well-ordered life. Occasionally, he took over their lessons and set rigorous tasks designed to train memory.

> One of these exercises was done with a sheet of paper lined up into 64 squares like a chess board. In each square he had written some historic date or a proverb, or well known fact. These we had to memorise in their proper order, and when we could reel them off correctly we were asked to work our way backwards from the 64th to the 1st square without making a mistake in their order.[28]

This was considered appropriate training for seven- and eight-year-olds.

It was Pauline, fourteen at the time of her mother's death, who bore the brunt of the resulting household changes. William Waldorf simply expected her to take over as hostess at Carlton House Terrace and Cliveden. Escorting strangers through the Astor country mansion and making grown-up conversation across the dinner table were dreadful ordeals which were certainly not lessened by the knowledge that her father expected everything to go without a hitch.

> ... his weekend parties in the country, planned many months in advance, lacked that sense of *joie de vivre* which the word 'party' is supposed to suggest. Guests were told exactly when to arrive; and when they arrived they were greeted by a secretary (or by his daughter ...) who showed them their rooms and told them where, and at

what time, they would assemble before meals. The rest of the weekend was according to a schedule, short periods set aside for walking, driving, resting, eating, and finally sleep.[29]

The poor girl was allowed few friends of her own age and was not permitted to move freely among the Astors' neighbours in London or Buckinghamshire. Even her coming-out in 1898 was not the happy and exciting experience it should have been. It goes without saying that no expense was spared for this grand occasion. If money and court connections could have made it a success it should have been a major event. Pauline was presented by the Duchess of Buccleuch and chaperoned throughout the season by the Countess of Selkirk. But her own ball which should have been the highlight of all these activities fell victim to William Waldorf's passion for organization. He had no idea of passing fashion and so modelled the evening on a successful ball he had given in Rome twenty years before. What had been regarded as the norm in the highly formal diplomatic world of an earlier epoch appeared 'stiff and starchy' to the modern young things of the gay nineties. Pauline was mortified when each of her guests was presented with a card and a pencil in order to note dance partners. The event was a flop and Pauline wept with embarrassment.

There seemed no escape from the sumptuous boredom and rigorous discipline of the life of an Astor chatelaine. As well as running the household, Pauline had to nurse her sickly sister. Relief came, at last, in 1902, and from an unexpected quarter. During the early summer the country was abuzz with the excitement of Edward VII's forthcoming coronation. Very few people could remember the last such event, sixty-four years before. During the month of June London began to fill up with foreign royalty and political leaders congregating for the great event. They all had to be housed and entertained. It was an unprecedented opportunity for the socially ambitious. Astor was delighted when Crown Prince Ferdinand of Romania accepted an invitation to stay at Cliveden with his suite. At twenty-one, Pauline had become an accomplished hostess, but the responsibility for a large royal entourage was daunting in the extreme. To cap it all the king fell ill and the coronation was postponed. The guests had to be invited to stay on and this threw the programme into confusion. Yet, in the midst of all the arranging and rearranging, Pauline made a close and lifelong friend. The crown prince's wife Princess Marie, daughter of the Duke of Edinburgh and granddaughter of Queen Victoria, was a charming and strong-minded woman of twenty-six. She loved Cliveden and she loved the young Astors. In September, as soon as she heard of Gwendolyn's death, she invited Pauline to Romania. It was the first of many visits to that lovely country where Pauline enjoyed the company of 'a true friend who helped to restore my rather shattered nerves'.[30] Free at last, at least for part of the time, she began to live her own life. At the end of the following year, her engagement was announced to a serving army officer, Captain Herbert Spender-Clay. On her marriage she moved to her husband's family home at Ford Manor, Kent, where over the years she made her mark, not only as a loved and respected member of local society but also as an accomplished amateur gardener. She transformed the grounds at Ford, particularly the woodland area where she developed new strains of rhododendrons and azaleas.

The boys fared rather better. They were destined to be brought up as typical young English gentlemen. Inevitably, that meant Eton, followed by Oxford and, for John, a commission in the Guards. It would be hard to say which of the two gave the most obvious evidence of future promise. At school, Waldorf shone both in the classroom and on the games field. He won the Prince Consort's prize for French and was captain of boats. At New College books took a low place in his priorities. He devoted most of his time to rowing, hunting, polo and steeplechasing, until a strained heart forced him to abandon his more strenuous activities. Even then, he still managed to gain a half blue for fencing. Waldorf loved horses. It had been his ambition to train and ride a Grand National winner. When that became impossible, he devoted himself to breeding thoroughbreds. For £100 he bought his first racing mare, Conjure. She only won him two races, but she was the foundation of a stud which was to make Astor one of the leading names on the turf for over seventy years.

Since sport took up so much of his time, and since he had no need of an academic qualification, it is not surprising that he emerged from Oxford after three years with a 'fourth', the lowest class of degree the university could bestow. Yet it would be a great mistake to dismiss Waldorf Astor as a typical upper-class boorish 'hearty'. Formal studies did not attract him, but there was a studious and extremely serious side to his nature and he maintained strong links with Oxford's intellectual élite. He was a quiet young man who read widely, kept abreast of current affairs and loved nothing more, when the day's excitements were over, than to sit late into the night with well-informed friends, discussing the burning issues of the day. His English upbringing had imparted to him (and also to his siblings) something which had never afflicted earlier generations of Astors – a social conscience. Almost a century later his surviving children could vividly recall the maxim he had imparted to them: 'You are lucky enough to be rich; that gives you a profound responsibility towards all those who are not so lucky.' Waldorf Astor left Oxford as a man of principle looking for a cause.

Waldorf may have been the more enterprising of William Waldorf's sons, but it was John who was his father's favourite. Perhaps because John was more conventional, less independent-minded than Waldorf, his father found the younger boy easier to understand. Waldorf grew up critical of his father's reclusiveness and reactionary politics; John was more disposed to accept them. On the rare occasions when William Waldorf shared his deeper thoughts with anyone it was John he chose as his confidant. In later years John recalled with pleasure 'intimate' meals alone with his father at the vast table in the dining hall of Temple Place, talking about books, people, current events, early reminiscences and, above all, military matters. It pleased his father that John had set his heart on a military career. He spent only a year at New College, then 'escaped' by being commissioned into the 1st Life Guards. He loved the life: camaraderie, horses, games, socializing in the mess – nothing could have suited better his genial, uncomplicated personality. Early in his military career he became something of a regimental hero when he saved a trooper from drowning during a swimming practice with the horses. At Eton he was the leading sportsman of his year and he went on to achieve national distinction. Like his brother he enjoyed steeplechasing and polo, but his real talents lay in ball games and racquets. In 1908 he participated in the London Olympic Games. With Victor Pennel he won the gold medal for racquets (the forerunner of squash) doubles and carried off the bronze medal in the singles competition. This was the first and last time that racquets featured as an Olympic sport, and Britain captured virtually all the honours. Soon after this John went to India, and in 1911 he was appointed aide-de-camp to the new Viceroy, Lord Hardinge. He was thus present at the great Delhi Durbar in December. He was joined by Pauline and her husband, Bertie Spender-Clay, for what was one of the greatest spectacles of the twentieth century and the zenith of Britain's imperial dream. Pauline wrote home excited letters minutely describing the pageantry as King George v and Queen Mary, seated on a richly appointed dais, received the homage of a cavalcade of jewel-bedecked Indian princes. John, one may imagine, was too involved in the stage management of this piece of high theatre to have much time for correspondence.

But there were plenty of other things to keep him occupied. For all the lavish show of loyalty, there was a good deal of unrest in the country. Maintaining effective control involved tact and diplomacy as well as a strong military presence. The situation was not helped by the unveiling in 1912 of a statue to the former Viceroy Lord Curzon, who had been unpopular in Bengal. The memorial had to have a constant police guard. The social side of life at the residence was full and demanding, and was punctuated by shooting expeditions on the plains which John particularly enjoyed. The most significant encounter John made during his time in India, however, was with Lady Violet Mercer Nairne. This beautiful young woman was the daughter of the Earl of Minto, who preceded Hardinge as viceroy. In 1909, at the age of nineteen, she married her father's ADC, Captain Lord Charles Mercer Nairne, a younger son of the Marquess of Lansdowne. Before and after their marriage they moved in the same circle as Captain Astor, and they all became friends. At some point, John discovered, doubtless to his dismay, that he had fallen in love with Violet. Of course, he never declared his feelings, and nothing untoward happened to mar his relationship with Charles Mercer Nairne. John worshipped from afar, never imagining that he would ever be able to do anything else. Charles and Violet soon returned to Britain and John immersed himself in his duties.

William Waldorf's children were easily finding their places within the Establishment whose acceptance he still craved. Despite his contempt for, or perhaps incomprehension of, some of the unwritten conventions of polite British society, he worked hard to cultivate the leaders of that society. Early in the new century he employed as a secretary Captain (later Lieutenant-Colonel) Gerald Tharp. This soldier who had served with distinction in South Africa came from an ancient, well-connected Cambridgeshire family, had been on the staff of the Governor-General of Canada, was an intimate of the royal family and counted many crowned and titled people throughout Europe among his friends. It was thanks to Tharp that foreign royalty and other notables graced Astor's London soirées and country house parties. He was thus on social, if not intimate, terms with Lord Salisbury, Kitchener, Austen Chamberlain, Campbell-Bannerman and even some members of the despised Edward VII's entourage.

After Mamie's death William Waldorf threw himself into his building projects with fiercely concentrated enthusiasm. This was to prove the most creative era of his life, and the one which would leave the richest heritage. To Cliveden he brought the Villa Borghese balustrade, several items from his collection of classical antiquities, pictures, tapestries and panelling from the Continent. He engaged armies of craftsmen and artists to lay mosaic floors and paint frescoed ceilings. Perhaps his most felicitous single architectural achievement was the dining room. This rococo chamber, sumptuous with green and gilded woodwork, painted panels and ceiling, was brought in its entirety from a French palace built for Madame de Pompadour and fitted with furniture of the period. Its centrepiece was, and is, a superb extending mahogany table capable of seating a small family group or thirty guests.

Even more characteristic of his whole approach to architecture was the business headquarters he built on the Embankment. This was like no other office block before or since. Astor House at 2 Temple Place was, and is, late Victorian domestic architecture at its best. William Waldorf hired the architect John Loughborough Pearson, who had already worked on the other Astor houses and was now at the height of his fame and skill. Like his employer,

Pearson was steeped in history. Most of his energy was devoted to ecclesiastical buildings. He designed many Gothic Revival churches, restored Westminster Abbey and Westminster Hall, and has the unique distinction of having drawn up the plans for two cathedrals (Truro and Brisbane). Craftsman and patron shared a common vision, and the result was one of those rare buildings in which clear conception and limitless funds combined to make a rich and unambiguous statement. Number 2 Temple Place, completed in 1895, is an ebulliently decorated Renaissance town mansion. Oriel windows, tall chimneys and crenellations confront the street, and the whole edifice is topped with a gilded weathervane in the shape of a fifteenth-century caravel such as Columbus had sailed to the New World.

The interior is a revelation of what could be achieved by unbridled romanticism and enormous wealth. The staircase hall is floored with multi-coloured marble. The newel posts of the stairs bear magnificent carvings of characters from Dumas's *Three Musketeers*. Light enters through a lofty roof of stained glass. Beneath it a plaster frieze depicts scenes from Shakespeare plays and, below that again, pillars flanking the gallery are topped by heroes and heroines from American novels. The great hall, seventy-one feet in length and rising thirty-five feet from the elaborately patterned floor to the hammer-beamed roof, was William Waldorf's office. Its frieze carries fifty-four portraits of some of the historical and fictional personages whom Astor admired, ranging from Lorenzo Medici, Bismarck and Captain Cook to Dante, Ophelia and Pocahontas. Small wonder that businessmen and officials summoned here by the great man were overawed as much by the impressive surroundings as they were by Astor himself. Elsewhere in the building there are marble fireplaces, elaborate moulded ceilings and a riot of carved doors and wood panels. The materials and craftsmanship are everywhere of the highest quality. The whole building is a testament to a man who knew precisely what he wanted and who utterly refused to compromise.

Like his great-grandfather, William Waldorf could boast that he usually got what he wanted. As constant proof of this he carried on his watch chain a large sapphire carved in the form of a ram's head. This exceedingly rare object, which he called the 'diadem of the king of the gods', was an Egyptian religious emblem dating from some fifteen hundred years BC. He bought this miniature treasure from the architect and antiquary Charles Davis (whose main claim to fame was the discovery of some of Bath's Roman baths) and proceeded to weave a romantic tale around it. 'Pharaoh's Daughter' appeared in the *Pall Mall Magazine* in 1900, and the talisman was described in William Waldorf's usual breath-holding prose:

Bound about the blackened brow [of the mummified princess], as in defiance of the grave's decay, was a sapphire ram's head of exquisite workmanship – a startling token

... of that amorous passion for the sake whereof its decorous phrase declares, 'Mortals are proud to die, and for which, alone, a god should aspire to live'.[31]

If Astor wanted something, whether a precious jewel or a craftsman's services, he could, and did, pay handsomely. But it takes more than the offer of a fat fee to induce talented, independent-minded men to give of their best. Though William Waldorf might have preferred to keep his creative employees at arm's length, he had to enter into the turbulent non-rational world of artist and patron. Thus, when Thomas Nicholls completed the Dumas carvings and then refused to deliver them, not all the millionaire's blusterings could make him change his mind. The elderly craftsman considered the figures to be his best work and he simply could not bear to part with them. William Waldorf actually had to wait until Nicholls died before he could get his hands on the carvings for which he had paid. Astor was guided in his choice of artists purely by his own estimation of their work and the extent to which they shared his vision. Thus, though he employed men with established reputations such as Pearson (and, subsequently, his son, F. L. Pearson), George Frampton RA (later Sir George, famous for statues of Queen Victoria, Edith Cavell and Peter Pan) and W. S. Frith (a frequent exhibitor at the Royal Academy), he also commissioned work from Thomas Nicholls, the metal-worker J. Starkie Gardner and other lesser-known artists.

If Temple Place is an epitaph to William Waldorf Astor's iron determination, Hever Castle, between Edenbridge and Penshurst in Kent, stands as a memorial to his imagination. Hever had everything that would attract a millionaire romantic. It was a moated manor house of Norman origin. It was connected with important events in English history, for Henry VIII had courted Anne Boleyn within its ancient walls. It was reputedly haunted; the ghost of the discarded queen was said to stalk its corridors by night. And it was in dire need of a wealthy saviour. By the end of the nineteenth century Hever was suffering from centuries of neglect. It had degenerated into an agricultural dwelling occupied by stock as well as tenant farmers. Parts of the building had collapsed. Rooms had been subdivided. Panelling had been whitewashed over. Windows had been bricked in. The gardens had reverted to wilderness. In 1895 the rot was arrested by a certain Captain Sebright, who took out a ninety-nine-year lease. He was dismissed by one contemporary as 'a gentleman of restoring proclivities of whom we will say nothing further than that he pulled down the very interesting Tudor stabling ... in order to get old timber for his work'.[32] This was somewhat unfair, for Sebright did make a serious start on the restoration of Hever; but there was a limit to what Sebright could do as a tenant, and he lacked the resources to acquire the freehold. For his part, the owner, Edmund Meade-Waldo of nearby Stonewall Park, who had inherited Hever in 1896, was not willing to spend large sums of money on a near-ruin. He was perfectly willing to sell – at a price. The stage was set for William Waldorf's entry. Negotiations began in 1901 and were concluded on 27 July 1903, when Astor, having bought out Sebright's interest, acquired the freehold of the castle and 640 acres. Thus began one of the most remarkable and controversial pieces of building and restoration. The monumental works carried out on the house and grounds took four years and cost $10 million.

The question must be asked why Astor wanted to go to all this trouble and expense on a *second* country seat. He had transformed Cliveden into a rural palace worthy to receive royalty. Was that not enough? Certainly he did not rush into buying Hever. More than once between 1901 and 1903 he had second thoughts about it. Part of the answer seems to be that Cliveden had not been an altogether happy place for him. His wife and his much-loved younger daughter had died there. The hospitality routine he had built around Pauline would come to an end with her marriage, which had been agreed by the time William Waldorf signed the contract for Hever. Thereafter, his visits to Cliveden became more and more infrequent, and in 1906 he gave it to his elder son. Probably the answer lies chiefly in William Waldorf's personality. He was a planner, a man who delighted in conceiving and executing bold schemes. Once a project was finished he inevitably experienced the sense of anticlimax that comes to every artist the moment he stands back from a masterpiece and knows that it is complete; that there is no more that his energy and talent can add to it. The artist in William Waldorf Astor needed a new, and greater, challenge. He was still passionately collecting, and he had to have another setting for the paintings, armour, tapestries, furniture and *objets d'art* that he was amassing.

What William Waldorf executed at Hever was a grand design in the long tradition of English eccentric house builders. Frederick Augustus Hervey, Earl of Bristol, raised at Ickworth an extraordinary mansion of classical severity and symmetry. Baron Ferdinand de Rothschild recreated a French Renaissance château at Waddesdon. Similarly, Mr Astor constructed in the Kent countryside something that was the expression of his personality and interests. The only difference was that he started from an existing building. Hever Castle was a medieval fortified dwelling with sixteenth-century modifications and additions. Astor took this and improved upon it. In effect he 'out-Tudored' the Tudors. The result has been hailed by some as a piece of sensitive and imaginative restoration, and condemned by others as a kind of proto-Disneyworld.

William Waldorf knew that his activities at Hever would arouse criticism. He still bitterly resented criticism. Just as he built a protective wall of aloof reserve around himself, he now enclosed his building works with a fence, diverted the main road which ran past the castle and employed eight private detectives to keep out snoopers. There have always been different schools of thought about what constitutes architectural restoration. William Waldorf, characteristically, ignored them all and did his own thing at Hever. As far as the castle was concerned, this meant preserving all the original fabric and removing later accretions. Features which had long since disappeared, such as the medieval drawbridge, were replaced with modern copies. Then came the embellishments – carved friezes, inlaid panelling, fireplaces with heraldic motifs, moulded ceilings, armorial stained glass. Every feature was either an original brought from another fine house or a careful copy of work existing elsewhere. William Waldorf cared passionately about authenticity. For example, carpenters replacing beams and panelling were obliged to use only chisels, adzes and such tools as would have been available to their Tudor ancestors. When all was done, Astor lavished as much thought and care on furnishings. He brought to Hever vast quantities of period furniture, arms and armour, paintings, tapestries, pottery, metalwork and decorative items.

But the end result was not a mid-Tudor mansion. Anne Boleyn and her family would have found it a strange place. Nor was this merely because the twentieth-century owner had installed modern conveniences, such as bathrooms, running water, heating and electricity. Hever was equipped to the highest contemporary standards. Since there was no local electricity supply William Waldorf installed his own power house. Sewage disposal was another problem on this low-lying site. To prevent waste being deposited in the nearby river, he had it pumped to farmland two miles away. Equally elaborate was the equipment for the prevention and fighting of fire, which included hydrants and a horse-drawn fire-engine. It was not merely these obvious and necessary anachronisms that would have been unfamiliar to Henry VIII's subjects. The whole feel of the place was idealized Tudor – a harsh, crude age viewed through later rose-tinted spectacles.

In the grounds William Waldorf permitted himself even more latitude. He changed the line of the river Eden, created an outer moat around the castle and had a large lake dug to the east. These measures were partly for visual effect and partly to improve drainage. He allowed his imagination to run riot in creating 'historical' features. He installed a maze, had mature trees brought in to create avenues and copses and even 'discovered' a smugglers' cave. This latter was secretly dug out of the sandstone by a couple of discreet labourers and a legend was carved into the rock:

I'll eat when I'm hungry,
I'll drink when I'm dry.

If ye king's men don't kill me,
I'll live till I die.
– Long John of By Bow

The area around Hever was rich in smugglers' tales, so of course Astor, the romantic, had to have his own legitimate 'gentlemen's' haunt. Just as he had to have yew hedges clipped into the shape of Tudor chessmen for his 'Anne Boleyn Garden'. Just as he had to have concealed doors and secret passages. Just as he had to employ psychic researchers to try to record Anne Boleyn's ghost. (They never saw her. Some of William Waldorf's critics suggested that the queen had left in disgust at his vulgar Americanizations.) The most impressive external feature, however, was the Italian Garden, designed by F. L. Pearson. This extensive area, which included a pergola, a Roman bath, marble pavements and grottoes, was designed as a setting for the large collection of classical and Renaissance sculptures Astor had amassed in Italy. It culminated in a superb loggia with a colonnaded piazza and an elaborate fountain on the edge of the lake. This feature was modelled on the Gallery of a Thousand Fountains at the Villa d'Este, Tivoli, and Astor sent his gardening contractor to Italy to make the necessary drawings, notes and measurements.

The most unusual and controversial element in the whole Hever plan was the Tudor 'village'. Astor turned on its head a famous maxim: for him an Englishman's castle was his home – and his exclusively. During his occupancy no one else lived in Hever Castle; indeed, there was only one bedroom in the castle. When he drove up in his two-horse brougham and the drawbridge was raised behind him he was alone with his superb collections and their purpose-built setting. Somewhere had to be found for servants and guests, however. Had generations of wealthy owners resided at Hever, they would without qualms have added to the building in the prevailing styles of succeeding ages. The idea of erecting a twentieth-century wing or annexe was anathema to William Waldorf. His solution was either brilliant or ludicrous, according to your point of view. He laid out what, externally, appeared to be a sprawling, huddled village of stone, brick and half-timbered houses. In reality the picturesque deception enclosed bedrooms, bathrooms, reception rooms, domestic quarters and estate offices, linked by corridors and joined to the castle by a covered bridge over the moat. It was, perhaps, the ultimate architectural folly.

Hever absorbed almost all Astor's energy and enthusiasm for over three years. That was all it took to complete the major works. Throughout that time he employed an army of labourers and craftsmen and he held every contractor to strict contract terms, hedged about with penalty clauses. Not only that; he carried out painstaking research on the history of the estate and its owners. The frenzied pace of the work perhaps reflected not only his own impatience but a sense of urgency about establishing himself in English society before he was too old. Whatever his motivation, Hever was a splendid achievement, the realization of a romantic's dream. As such it is still enjoyed by thousands of visitors every year.

Not content with these magnificent English homes, in 1905 William Waldorf bought himself a villa at Sorrento. He had formed the habit of wintering every year in his favourite spot on the Bay of Naples (and we may assume that his 'Princess' was one of the attractions). Now, he acquired one of the best properties in the region. The Villa Labonia, a three-storey nineteenth-century building perched high on the cliff, enjoyed spectacular views across the Golfo di Napoli to Vesuvius. In the blue-green waters below, the remains could still be seen of Roman temples erected for the worship of Neptune, Venus and Saturn. William Waldorf could at last feel that he rested in the shadow of the Caesars, for Julius, Nero and Antoninus had all owned winter homes here. He changed the name to Villa Sirena and set about alterations and decorations with his usual thoroughness and energy.

Each of William Waldorf's houses was a living museum. Including the Villa Sirena, he had five buildings to act as settings for his numerous acquisitions. Only at Hever can we still obtain an impression of the sheer size and quality of his collections, though even here some elements (notably the superb examples of arms and armour) have been dispersed. But it is worth attempting a mini-catalogue just to appreciate the rare feat of this latter-day Maecenas. Hever's library boasts 2,500 leather-bound volumes, most of them rare, some unique. There are portraits by Holbein, Scrots, Clouet and other sixteenth- and seventeenth-century masters. The large tapestries are the finest examples of sixteenth-century Flemish and French work. Astor scoured Europe for items connected with the court of Henry VIII, such as Anne Boleyn's prayer book (which she is reputed to have carried to the block), examples of embroidery and an autograph of the hapless queen. All this, together with the ecclesiastical vestments, furniture, Persian carpets and eighteenth-century porcelain, would be considered an impressive lifetime's accomplishment, but it accounted for less than a quarter of William Waldorf's total gleaning. An inventory made at Temple Place after his death detailed a treasure trove which would make any connoisseur drool. There were over 400 autographs, including letters by Mary Queen of Scots, the Duke of Marlborough, Pepys, George Washington, Shelley and Dickens. The library housed no less than five Shakespeare folios, an early Chaucer, thirteen illuminated books of hours dating from the fifteenth century, dozens of volumes bearing the arms or monograms of Cardinal Richelieu, Henry III, Talleyrand, Catherine de Medici, Madame du Barry, Marie Antoinette, James II and many others, and a Latin treatise with margin notes by Queen Elizabeth I. In addition to such gems there were numerous oddities, bought because they took the collector's fancy: lutes, a spinning wheel and Napoleon's hat.

In each of his homes William Waldorf created a world of taste and splendour where he could wander, usually alone, and revel in the past with all its romantic associations. At Hever he went one better by creating for himself a setting which gave the illusion of permanence and illustrious ancestry. Did it satisfy him? Probably not. He knew that it was an illusion. For all his wealth, his sensitivity, his devoted appreciation of historical continuity, he could never be accepted among that introverted class of English men and women, to whom these qualities belonged by right of inheritance, and who therefore floated effortlessly through life with a sense of unassailable superiority. In her memoirs, Lady Ottoline Morrell summed up the feelings of this caste:

> Coming of a long line of men and women who have enjoyed inherited wealth and so have been free to move about in the world – to travel hither and thither – and who have sunned themselves in the sunshine of art and culture and who, too, have taken part in weaving the tangle of history, have become conscious of what civilization and subtlety of thought and quickness of action mean, must influence one and make one more complex, more mature, and richer in comprehension, and must lay a foundation of quick perception and understanding. Think, too, what it must mean to a small child to be brought up in the midst of historical associations and treasures from every land, and to wander from early years in beautiful rooms filled with such things as other children only see in museums. How I loved to finger and caress the pearl drop from King Charles' ear, and to lock up and hide my first precious letters in a casket given by King William the Third, with keys that are a pattern of beauty and delicacy, and to play and act with King Henry VIII's ruby-studded dagger. It made the past vivid and interesting and perhaps endowed me with greater awareness and sensibility.[33]

This was the object of William Waldorf Astor's quest, his Holy Grail, which would always elude him because it could not be acquired with the profits from Manhattan real estate. His family's humble origins constantly rankled and the American newspapers never relented in their campaign of mockery. In 1904 he paid a nostalgic visit to the land of his birth. It was not a success. Journalists and gossip-mongers hounded him everywhere. The following year he wrote:

> I do not believe that anything would avail to change the ordinary acceptation in America of my great grandfather's life and character. He will go down as a 'Dutch sausage peddler' and my fate promises to be the same if the American press can make it so.[34]

Small wonder that it mattered enormously to him to establish his noble ancestry.

In 1899 he published in the *Pall Mall Magazine* the results of his genealogical researches – or rather, he published as fact the highly speculative family tree which traced his origins back through Jean Jacques d'Astorg (1664–1711), to Pedro d'Astorga, the Castilian knight who had fought with the Count of Toulouse against the Moors in 1085 and had subsequently been ennobled. The American press, who had never forgiven William Waldorf for his defection, gleefully seized upon this piece of nonsense and brought in their own academic big guns to demolish it. Astor was not a whit moved by their arguments. Half a century later a grandson would comment wryly: 'If he had a choice, if language had presented no barrier, I think he would have liked to have been a Spaniard, and certainly a grandee which in a sense he already was. In the old world there was no more backward country than Spain, no country so cut off from the feeling and fashion of the twentieth century.'[35] Yet Britain was the country he had chosen, and he was determined to blazon (literally) his ancient right to an honoured place there.

Mr Astor decided that he would have a coat of arms. As early as 1889 he had instigated researches in Europe as to what insignia might be derived from his 'ancestry'. From a scholar in Cologne he received a shield design showing a very modest arrangement of blue chevrons on a red ground. That would not do at all. He set out to discover what arms his 'ancestor' Pedro d'Astorga had borne and appropriated for himself the silver hawk on the gold gloved hand. When he came to decorate Hever, he made lavish use of this device and of a whole coat of arms based upon it. Then, while spending Christmas 1905 in Paris, a sudden thought occurred to him which caused him to rush off a note to his agent in London: 'I think my arms should be registered at the Heralds' College and ought myself to have thought of this long ago.' Garter King of Arms and his minions were expected to fall in with Mr Astor's wishes in the matter, so the ensuing correspondence with Richmond Herald was not an easy one. The armorial experts tactfully informed Mr Astor that his design did not conform with English heraldic rules. They provided an alternative. William Waldorf did not like it and continued to have his own standard unfurled on Hever's ramparts. Then, in the autumn of 1906, something happened which both immensely flattered William Waldorf and also put a stop to his cavalier attitude towards armorial convention. His name was pricked for Sheriff of Buckingham. Now it was the turn of Richmond Herald to be firm: 'As His Majesty's representative in the County [Mr Astor] could not with propriety make use of Armorial Ensigns publicly to which no legal right had been established.'[36] Thereafter, matters were put on a proper basis and the squire of Hever received a duly authorized grant of arms.

By this time the rigid pattern he had imposed on his life had become a ritual. In the spring he went to one of the German spas, usually Kissingen, for a cure. June and July were passed at Cliveden and Hever. In his Kentish castle he held those 'obligatory' house parties inspired more by a sense of duty than by any desire to share his palace with friends whose company he enjoyed. He once wrote to an American correspondent: 'I am pretty busy with Hever parties and preparations for the two dinner concerts at the end of this month. It is a nervous fretting task to me because it is a woman's work and not a man's at all. I blunder through somehow and usually come out alive.'[37] Thus wrote the misanthrope who genuinely preferred his own company to other people's. August always found Astor in Switzerland where he enjoyed walking in the mountains. September and October were spent in England. Then he escaped for the winter to his beloved Sorrento.

The Villa Sirena witnessed his last romantic building project. Since his purchase of the lovely old house overlooking the Bay of Naples he had added to the property an adjoining orange grove and the neighbouring convent and church of St George (of which he demolished all but the cloister). In 1906 he decided to recreate a Roman villa in the grounds. Once more builders were set to work with precise instructions from the owner. Once more agents were dispatched all over Italy to acquire classical statuary, mosaics, bronzes, ironwork and stoneware. William Waldorf's latest enterprise cost him half a million dollars, and his acquisitiveness and taste raised up an idealized evocation of life as it might have been lived in the region during the last days of Pompeii. The Villa Flora had its own terraced and colonnaded gardens overlooking the bay, where roses, myrtles and fig trees enjoyed the protection of walls covered with copies of Roman murals. The spacious marbled rooms were alive with carved and painted decoration and filled with the rarest original artefacts. Thus did this private aesthete evoke for himself a little fragment of the grandeur that was Rome.

But while William Waldorf was absorbed in the past, his elder son encountered someone who would profoundly affect the family's future.

CHAPTER 7

'Most important you should not lose touch with the advocates of liberty and democracy'

In one of his stories, 'The Vengeance of Poseidon', published in 1910, William Waldorf Astor described an American father and daughter travelling in Europe. The man 'had begun life as a country lad, had found employment on the nearest railway, and in twenty years had made his way into the phalanx of millionaires'. He was forever telling stories – much embellished – of his own past exploits. 'He spoke the Western nasal vernacular, and smiled so sourly at his own jokes, that in mirthful sallies his lips reminded me of a nutcracker.' As for the daughter, the narrator remarked, 'I remember pausing to observe the soulless mechanism she had caught from her father and reflected in herself.' She was attractive, in a vivacious way, and wore expensive clothes well.

> Her voice was shrill and she spoke in a leisurely drawl. She possessed a considerable stock of mixed information, inclined to an extreme nervous restlessness and adored her native belongings. 'There are many cities,' she said, 'but only one Chicago.' She habitually adorned her phrases with the split infinitive, was familiar with chance travelling folk, and shook hands with the hotel head waiter. By way of religion, both father and daughter cherished a sentiment of absolute human equality . . .

The girl espoused a militant form of Christianity, was excellent at repartee and loved debunking pomposity. Astor has her say to the narrator, 'You remind me of a man I met in a street-car a couple of years ago. I handed him our best tract, *Abide with Me*, but he looked at it stiff, same as you, and gave it back. "Thank you," he says, "I'm a married man." "Well," I says, "polite manners are getting scarce as hen's teeth." '[1] Thus, under the guise of fictional figures, did Chillie and Nancy Langhorne make their appearance in William Waldorf Astor's prose *oeuvres*.

There can be little doubt that the author modelled his characters on the woman who had become his daughter-in-law, and her father. He frequently used people and objects from real life as the building blocks of his stories, and the brash *nouveau-riche* participants in 'The Vengeance of Poseidon' certainly matched his image of his new relations. Chiswell ('Chillie') Dabney

Langhorne came from a well-established Virginia family, lost everything by fighting on the losing side in the Civil War, and worked his way back to wealth and social position. He was by turns a salesman, tobacco auctioneer, poker player and railroad builder. In all his commercial incarnations the gift of the gab was his greatest asset. He was an ebullient enthusiast with a fund of anecdotes and a ready wit. He could talk his way into opportunities and out of difficulties. In the land where self-belief was everything, it is not surprising that he prospered.

Nancy Witcher was the eighth of the eleven children born into the rumbustious Langhorne household. In childhood she experienced both poverty and plenty as her father's career pursued its switchback course. Although by the time she was in her teens the Langhornes had emerged on to the plateau of graceful living at Mirador, their estate close by the Blue Ridge Mountains, Nancy never forgot her early years in a crowded city tenement where her mother struggled to make ends meet. Life at Mirador was never dull, but it certainly was not an unsullied idyll. There were always interesting people to meet, for Chillie was greatly given to Southern hospitality. There were magnificent horses to ride, for Mr Langhorne kept an excellent stable, and Nancy loved nothing better than excursions with the local hunt. There was a serious side to life, for her parents were strict adherents of Episcopalianism, very puritan in their doctrinal thinking and this rubbed off on Nancy. There were amorous (though, of course, very proper) adventures, for the Langhorne girls were uncommonly beautiful and much sought after by the scions of Virginia's 'aristocratic' houses. But there were shadows which fell across the sunlit lawns and elegant chambers of Mirador. Chillie, like many 'hail-fellow-well-met' extroverts, had a violent, possessive side to his nature. As the children grew up they either submitted passively to his demands or asserted their independence – which led inevitably to furious rows. Nancy was never one to give in without a fight. It was harder for the boys than it was for Nancy and her sisters. Two of her brothers took to drink and died young. That made a profound impression on her.

It may have been partly a desire to assert her independence and set up her own household which lured her into marriage. On a visit to New York at the age of seventeen she formed an attachment for Robert Shaw, a wild, rich, good-looking, athletic young man. She was not altogether sure about settling down with her latest exciting admirer but she accepted his proposal, and the fact that her parents warned her against Shaw was enough to banish all doubt from her mind. Nancy and Robert were married the following year. Within two days the bride was home at Mirador pleading with her father to free her from her husband somehow. Chillie sent her back to New York, but there was no possibility of the marriage working. Shaw was sinking rapidly into alcoholism and had possibly also inherited mental instability. There were constant rows and frequent separations. By 1901 Nancy had returned to Mirador for good – with a baby son, Bobbie. Two years later the couple were divorced – but not before Nancy had undergone a long struggle with her conscience. She was deeply committed to the belief that 'what God had joined' man could not 'put asunder'. Only when Shaw precipitated a potential scandal by contracting a second, bigamous marriage did she consent to apply for a decree. She could at least claim that, on one interpretation, the Bible sanctioned divorce on the grounds of adultery.

Nancy was determined never to make the same mistake again, and to enjoy the independence she had once so rashly thrown away. The next years were spent enjoying the social life of Virginia, making occasional visits to Europe and stepping lightly over the prostrate forms of men who threw themselves at her feet. One event that clouded this high summer of reborn youth was the death of her mother. Briefly Nancy took upon herself the mantle of Mirador hostess and housekeeper. The experiment was not a success. Chillie's wife had known how to wheedle and coax and, when necessary, to give way graciously. Chillie's daughter possessed none of those skills. Two strong personalities inevitably clashed over the day-to-day running of the household, and calm was only restored when Chillie made it clear to Nancy that she could not step into his dear wife's shoes and nor should she try to do so.

Freed, now, from all restraints except her responsibility to her infant son, to whom she remained utterly devoted (and he to her) for the rest of her days, Nancy enjoyed life to the full. Especially she enjoyed visits to England, where she felt particularly at home. This was, in part, due to the kindness of friends and relatives and to a season's excellent hunting in Leicestershire, but more to her effect on English society. The younger set were bowled over by her outspokenness, her outrageous sense of humour, her unbridled gaiety and her transatlantic disregard of 'stuffy' conventions. She was – and always remained – one of those people who could enter a room and immediately become the centre of attraction. Inevitably, she upset some of the more hidebound, but the oft-told story of her exchange with Edith Cunard indicates how even the most disapproving could be won over. 'I suppose you have come over here to get one of our husbands,' Lady Cunard observed. Nancy's response was typically swift and to the point: 'If you knew how much trouble I had getting rid of my husband, you'd know I don't want yours.' The two women were firm friends from that moment. Summer 1905 found Nancy back in the USA, but England acted on her like a magnet, and in December she crossed the Atlantic again. On board ship she met Waldorf Astor. Instantly he fell under her spell. There was nothing unusual about that. What was surprising was that she fell in love with him. Thus there came into the Astor world the most remarkable outsider (including Caroline Schermerhorn) ever to enter it.

It is useless to speculate about the emotional alchemy which makes apparently unlikely relationships work surprisingly well. Nancy and Waldorf brought very different ingredients to their life together. She was American; he was British. She was wildly extrovert; he was reflective, almost to the point of shyness. He possessed an almost ascetic self-control; she was wholly governed by her emotions. For her, issues were always black and white; he agonized over their self-evident intricacies. She dominated any gathering in which she found herself (and with the passing of the years she became positively domineering); he was happy to remain in the background. Yet it is easy to be distracted by their obvious personality differences and miss the things they had in common. These were many and varied – a love of horses, a hatred of pomposity, a genuine interest in and concern for people, a disregard for convention (although Waldorf did not flout it as outrageously as Nancy, he was very impatient of those who adhered strictly and unthinkingly to predetermined attitudes). Above all, they shared a profound social concern. Nancy and Waldorf were at heart *serious* young people. Nancy's moral fervour sprang from religious conviction and the hard times she had experienced in her childhood. Waldorf's was more an amalgam of paternalism, a profound sense of 'duty' and a desire to do something useful with his life. His approach to the responsibilities of adulthood resulted partly from the absorption of the attitudes instilled by his father and partly from rejection of those attitudes. His son Michael analysed it in these words:

> He wanted to succeed in a life of public service and make amends, as he saw it, for his father's negligence in this respect. He felt particularly keenly that he owed this to the country of his father's adoption. His handicap was that he had little instinctive feeling for people. His approach to life was that of reason and he allowed his intuition very little play; consequently his methods, though admirably tenacious, were stern and not relieved by those flights of fancy and spontaneous outbursts which so enlivened my mother's life.[2]

Duty, determination, self-control and personal reserve – these were the traits Waldorf Astor inherited from his father. Autocracy, snobbishness and *folie de grandeur* were the paternal attitudes he rejected.

In 1905 Waldorf had not yet discovered how to express the concerns and social passions which were churning round disturbingly within him. Nancy would soon help him to find a direction for his life. On 9 March 1906 the couple announced their engagement, and on 3 May they were married. The ceremony was held at All Souls, Langham Place, by special permission of the Bishop of London, who waived the Church of England's ban on the remarriage of divorced people. Ecclesiastical scruples might be easily set aside, but what of the attitude of society? Here was a prominent and wealthy citizen forming a union with an American, a beautiful socialite, a divorcée and, moreover, one who was trailing in her wake a child – a beautiful, blue-eyed, curly-haired boy – by a previous husband. Such behaviour was still regarded as mildly scandalous even though the long reign of the virtuous Victoria was now over. Not until Edward VII accepted an invitation to visit the couple at Cliveden were disapproving tongues silenced. It is not without significance that William Waldorf did not attend the wedding, preferring to distance himself at Hever from the public celebration, for reasons of 'poor health'.

Not that he shunned the couple privately – far from it. Nancy was certainly not the bride he would have chosen for his heir, but he got on well with her. What was more surprising, he liked her father. Waldorf had dreaded the meeting of the austere William Waldorf and the brash Chillie Langhorne. In fact, it was a great success; the two men took to each other at once. Langhorne was, at root, a Southern gentleman. He could turn on the old-world charm when it suited him, and his new relative responded warmly to it. William Waldorf was certainly generous to the newly-weds. He gave them Cliveden and bestowed on Nancy a superb tiara containing the Sancy diamond, a 55 carat stone which had, in its chequered career, belonged to Charles I's queen, Henrietta Maria, to Louis XIV and to the Maharaja of Patiala.

Nancy reacted by going out of her way to be pleasant to the old man. She may have felt an additional responsibility to do so because of the coolness already evident between father and son. For the first ten years of her married life she kept up a frequent correspondence with William Waldorf. (Nancy was a prodigious letter writer, which goes much of the way towards explaining her almost illegible scrawl. 'Are you unwell,' John Astor once enquired in mock concern, 'I read your last letter without having to guess at every third word.') The existing fragments of their correspondence show that he responded in the same spirit. He never fails to remember her birthday or to congratulate her on the arrival of a new baby. He thanks her for the gift of a cheese which tasted like Double Gloucester only more fruity. He recalls a very pleasant day at Hever when Nancy brought Hilaire Belloc to meet him. He sends a silver porringer as a present for his latest grandson – but is careful to let her know what he paid for it. And he tells her about his travels. On a wartime trip to the Highlands he writes, characteristically: 'My chief delight is to lounge in a pine forest nearby, as St Chrisostom did when he was reviewing his life. He had much to repent of, which is not my case in the least but I delight, like him, in the rustling tree tops.'[3] Yet the dull gleam of cruelty can often be glimpsed in his letters. He basically disapproved of his daughter-in-law and much that she stood for, and sometimes he did not bother to conceal his true feelings. He promises to send her an advance copy of 'The Vengeance of Poseidon', knowing that in it she will see herself and her father lampooned. In the middle of a chatty, newsy letter he breaks off to tell her that he finds Christian Science (the religion to which Nancy, by then, passionately adhered) 'offensive' and 'blasphemous'. One scarcely has to read between the lines to discern the real situation: Nancy doing her best to revive the generous and warm responses buried deep in her father-in-law's personality; William Waldorf resisting her aggressive do-goodery.

It was not so with the rest of the family. Pauline and John were carried along on their new sister-in-law's tidal wave of gaiety. Both of them found in Nancy a sympathetic confidante. To John she was '*the very* best friend anyone could possibly have . . . I can't tell you how grateful I have always felt to you for everything'. Pauline describes her as one who has 'always done nothing but good to all of us and . . . brought so much happiness into our lives'.[4] Over the years they all had their quarrels. That was inevitable with someone like Nancy, who always said what she thought and was prone to flattening other people's plans and ideas with the steamroller of her own enthusiasm. But such estrangements never lasted, for there was little malice in Nancy and it was difficult to be cross with her for long. The whole family also had in their minds the depressing example of William Waldorf, who *did* harbour grudges, real and imaginary, and used them as the building blocks of his barrier against the world.

The already existing tensions in the father–son relationship were inevitably heightened as Waldorf and Nancy developed their own very different pattern of life. Just how different that pattern would be was symbolized by Nancy's draconian onslaught on Cliveden. It was obvious that the new mistress would want to stamp her own identity on the house, but to assert sweepingly (and wrongly) 'The Astors have no taste' was to declare war on all that William Waldorf had so lovingly created at Cliveden. Out went classical statuary, mosaic floors, painted ceilings and leather upholstery. In came parquet, chintz drapes, bookcases and French furniture. The new owners fully realized the enormity of what they were doing. When William Waldorf paid his first visit to them Nancy was so worried about his reaction that she took to her bed in order to avoid his anguished response to the 'improvements'. In fact William Waldorf was far too self-controlled to give vent to his emotions, though he did confide to an American friend, 'The house has been somewhat altered in decoration and furniture and without objecting to these changes, it is no pleasure to me to see them.'[5]

More basic differences between the 'Cliveden Astors' and old William Waldorf emerged when Waldorf entered on a political career. He could very easily have settled to the life of a country gentleman. He did, in fact, devote considerable attention to his horses in the first years of his married life. He bought his initial stock wisely and, from 1908, was able to breed all his own foals at Cliveden. He reared both jumpers, which were trained at Manton, near Newbury, and flat racers, which were sent to Newmarket. By 1910, he was the eighth most successful owner on the British turf. In that year his five horses had twenty-seven outings, won ten races, were placed in nine others and brought in almost £13,000 in prize money. By any reckoning, that was an impressive start for a newcomer, and it reflected his perfectionist attitude to the science of breeding. It was *breeding* that appealed to him, not the social side of the sport, and he often boasted that he had never bet so much as a sovereign on any of his horses – 'gambling spoils sport' was his constant motto. Buying successful horses from other owners in order to win more races never interested him. As he told a reporter years later: 'a race is only the culmination of about three or four years' effort on one particular animal. During that time to see the horse develop gives me interest, pleasure and recreation. That is how I regard racing.'[6] Yet during these same years Waldorf Astor was developing a keen interest in politics and applying to his studies the same diligence that he devoted to his stud records.

Early in their married life Waldorf and Nancy began to indulge in that pastime for which they would become famous and, at one point, notorious: surrounding themselves with interesting people. They acquired an elegant town house at 4 St James's Square (little more than a stone's throw from the old Astor residence in Carlton House Terrace), and both there and at Cliveden they entertained a wide variety of guests from the literary, political and academic worlds. Waldorf enjoyed the conversation of intelligent, well-informed men and women. He was a good listener, preferring to weigh up facts and opinions and arrive at a balanced judgement rather than to deliver himself of witty, incisive pronouncements. The lunchtime or dinnertime gatherings over which he presided were a continuation of his undergraduate debates with earnest young contemporaries. Indeed, the most influential of his friends were men he had known at Oxford – men who would later become the 'Round Table' group and who would take a very clear stance on most of the issues of the day.

The mentor and elder statesman from whom they drew their inspiration was Lord Milner. Alfred Milner (1854–1925) was one of the most remarkable public servants of his own, or any other, era. A man of immense intellect, he had swept all before him at Oxford, occupied various posts in the City, in domestic politics and in colonial administration (most notably as a controversial High Commissioner for South Africa during the Boer War), and exercised an enormous influence on generations of political thinkers. Milner was saturated with the spirit of Victorian liberalism. He and his friends, as he stated quite clearly, 'were deeply impressed with their individual duty as citizens and filled with enthusiasm for social equality which led them to bridge the gulf between the educated and the wage-earning class'.[7] But Milner was not a Liberal. He had parted company with Gladstone over Ireland and what he considered the Grand Old Man's 'flabby' imperial and foreign policy. His vision was of a Britain playing a leading world role as head of a federated empire.

In his later years Milner took on a new role in British political life as the mentor to whom many young Unionists looked for their inspiration. Some, known collectively as 'Milner's Kindergarten', had served under him in South Africa and returned to Edwardian Britain as apostles of a new political gospel. The wider group who fell under the Milner spell included such diverse people as H. G. Wells, George Bernard Shaw, J. L. Garvin (editor of the *Observer*), Lord Haldane and Sir Edward Grey. But the inner core of disciples formed a more coherent group which came to be known as the 'Round Table' and which, from 1910, produced a quarterly magazine of the same name. Members included Philip Kerr (younger son of Lord Lothian), Geoffrey Dawson (later editor of *The Times*), Robert Brand (Fellow of All Souls and member of a variety of imperial committees), Lionel Curtis (lecturer in colonial history at Oxford and later adviser to the government on Irish affairs) and Edward Grigg (*Times* journalist, later Baron Altrincham, and Governor of Kenya). These men were all close friends of Waldorf and Nancy, frequent visitors to their homes, and were destined to play important roles in the Astor story.

Within the pages of the *Round Table* magazine can be found many of the causes which Waldorf later laboured for enthusiastically – preferential tariffs, a federal solution to the Irish problem, an imperial agricultural policy, resistance to Prussian militarism while maintaining good relations with Germany, etc. The main concern of the Round Tablers and the issue which they regarded as the keystone of all British policy was an imperialism not so much jingoistic as mystical:

> . . . the Empire has succeeded in combining the establishment of peace and law with a steady growth of freedom . . . amongst those whom it unites there has suddenly come to light the amazing truth that . . . it carries with it the instinctive loyalty and practically all the trained intelligence of citizens and subjects numbering a quarter of the human race . . . To save this great system now, and to maintain it afterwards, is the most effective contribution which we can make to international progress and the general peace of the world.[8]

But Waldorf could not be content with elevated debate. He had a passionate desire, as he often said, to 'get things done'. The only way to achieve this ambition was to enter Parliament. So, within a year of his marriage, he offered his services to the Unionist party as a prospective candidate. The hierarchy were delighted. Astor was exactly the sort of young man they were looking for: bright, a member of the Establishment, and *rich* – money was always an asset in election campaigns. They found him a safe constituency. He declined it. This was not his idea of what politics were about. He wanted to win votes for the things he believed in, not slip into a comfortable seat warmed by someone else. From his father Waldorf had learned steel determination and iron self-discipline, but he was more of an ascetic than William Waldorf had ever been. He rose early, spent long hours at his desk, and devoted himself completely to mastering the task in hand. He had an almost flagellant love of enduring self-imposed hardship. One of his sons remarked that, when they were shooting on their Scottish estate, Waldorf would much rather walk with his pointers for hours and bag one grouse than stand in the butts while hundreds were driven over the guns. So he decided to serve his political apprenticeship, studying all the issues and waiting for a contest worthy of his efforts.

In the summer of 1908 he was accepted as Unionist candidate for Plymouth, a seat with a long Liberal tradition where the government had a healthy majority. It was typical of Waldorf that one of his first actions was to buy a house in the city (3 Elliot Terrace, The Hoe). Before the First World War it was by no means the norm for MPs to reside in their constituencies, but Astor was not the sort of man to use the voters for his own political ambition. He was seeking public office to *serve* the people of Plymouth; therefore he intended to pay frequent visits to the city, discover its problems, meet its leading citizens. The Plymouthians were not slow to respond. Thus began a close relationship which lasted to the end of Waldorf's and Nancy's lives and extended into the next generation. There were two elections in 1910. At the first, in January, the Liberals retained their majority. In small measure Waldorf contributed to their success, for he was too ill to canvass throughout most of the campaign. However, in the following December he and his Unionist colleague (Plymouth returned two members) wrested Plymouth from their rivals and Waldorf duly took his place in the House of Commons. A new era had begun.

William Waldorf's life took on more muted colours during these years. He spent more time pursuing his private pleasures – travel, books, collecting. The great building projects were almost things of the past. In New York the Astor Apartments were erected on 75th and Broadway in 1901, and were followed seven years later by the nearby Apthorp Apartments, the last word in luxury for a wealthy clientele who felt the need to be at the centre of American life. About the same time, William Waldorf projected a new fifteen-storey hotel on 56th Street and Fifth Avenue, but it never got off the drawing board. Thus ended a remarkable phase of building activity which had changed the face of downtown New York and with it the social life of the city.

Yet there was one other building which arguably made a greater impact on New Yorkers and visitors than even the Waldorf Astoria. In 1902, William Waldorf commissioned the architects Clinto and Russell to design a new hotel overlooking Longacre Square (now Times Square). Two years later, on 1 September 1904, the Astor opened its doors to a discerning public. It was William Waldorf's last bid to introduce old-world elegance to the brash centre of a modern American city. It was a new concept of what the life of a busy commercial centre needed and was the brainchild of William C. Muschenheim, a German-born chef who had gained a reputation as overseer of the mess at West Point military academy. What twentieth-century citizens and visitors required, he believed, was not primarily a place to sleep, but a place to eat in style. William Waldorf liked the man's ideas and agreed to pull down a row of Broadway theatrical boarding houses to make way for an $8 million hotel complex. Behind its French Renaissance façade only half of the Astor's floor space was devoted to guest accommodation. Most of the rest was given over to dining and reception rooms, of which the largest could seat 2,500 guests, and a kitchen measuring 231 by 150 feet. At its opening it could boast that it was 'the world's most electrified hotel' with such modern facilities as an internal fire warning system and a kind of 'food escalator' for conveying dishes from the kitchen to the banqueting room at maximum speed. Muschenheim's vision swiftly became reality (and showed him a handsome profit on his $500,000 per annum rent). The Astor lobby became one of the world's most famous meeting places, its roof-garden a crowded summer venue and its dining rooms an essential gathering point for pre-theatre suppers. Its larger chambers were much in demand for the city's most prestigious events. The hotel was regularly packed for the annual celebrations that brought New Yorkers thronging to Times Square – New Year's Eve and the Macy Parade on Thanksgiving Day. Regular residents included such lions of show business and politics as Toscanini, Jimmy Durante, Jack Dempsey, Woodrow Wilson and W. C. Fields, among many.

Most of this success was in the future when William Waldorf sat in baronial splendour at Temple Place reading the reports from his New York agents. He was pleased to be able to advise friends that the Astor was the best eating place in the city, although he deprecated Muschenheim's visual pun in decorating the restaurant with ceramic asters. By the end of the Edwardian era his passion for building was spent. He was now of the age when men begin to lose old friends and acquaintances to the angel of death. In 1909 he suffered a particularly distressing bereavement: his mysterious 'Princess' died. 'We walked forty years in unaltered friendship,' Astor later wrote, 'till by a singular coincidence forty years to a day from our first meeting the eyes I had loved closed forever . . . Had we been allowed to marry, would life have been happier for us both?'[9] If William Waldorf, in his private thoughts, blamed thwarted passions for the frustrations and disappointments of his life, he was certainly deluding himself. If his heart was wounded, it soon healed. Within a couple of years he was nursing a *tendresse* for another lady. It seems that William Waldorf was living partly in the world of chivalry created by his own imagination – the world of the courtly romances in which knights and princesses entertained adulterous (and usually unfulfilled) longings for one another. Many years later a secret cache of pornographic literature was discovered at Cliveden. Clearly, William Waldorf's tastes were more catholic than his family and friends realized. This introverted man kept his secrets well, and we shall never know how many of his amorous adventures were fact and how many were fantasy.

Yet we must not allow ourselves to be misled by the conventional picture of William Waldorf Astor as a lonely, embittered hermit. He certainly became such a figure, but only in the closing years of his life. In the first decade or so of the century he was, like most thinking men, caught up in the great movements of national and international events. He was closely involved with the world of politics and political journalism. For William Waldorf that world centred on the Unionist party, and the Unionist party in these years was in a state of turmoil.

In 1895, taking advantage of Liberal divisions over Home Rule, Lord Salisbury had formed a Tory/Unionist administration. In 1902 the elder statesman's nephew, Arthur Balfour, took over the leadership of the party and the country. But the alliance on which the government was based was always unstable. Internal differences over various policies, exacerbated by the Prime Minister's austere, autocratic inflexibility (his short way with insurgents while Secretary for Ireland in the 1880s earned him the nickname 'Bloody Balfour'), brought his administration down in 1905 and returned the Liberals and their allies to power with a large majority. The next few years, leading up to the First World War, were among the bitterest in British political history. Under the leadership of Henry Campbell-Bannerman (1906–8) and Herbert Asquith (1908–16), the government moved inexorably towards autonomy for Ireland and introduced sweeping social reforms (which were largely the work of David Lloyd George as President of the Board of Trade and, later, Chancellor of the Exchequer). To most Unionists it seemed that these changes were destroying the very fabric of British society.

Throughout this period the *Gazette* thundered its approval of the most extreme right-wing policies and its denunciation of Unionism's foes:

> Mr Arnold-Forster remarked this week that 'if they enquired of any of England's enemies they would find that their desire was that the Liberals should reign.' That

is a hard fact, and ... it should not be left out of the reckoning by those who are anxious to exercise their franchise. (13 January 1905)

When we try to find out what Ministers have to say for themselves, there is nothing audible except the voice of that 'specialist in offal', the Chancellor of the Exchequer [Lloyd George], who tries every day to beat his own record in vulgarity. He turns aside from vituperation of the House of Lords only to shed the practised tear of susceptibility over ... 'the poor fellows weltering in the morass' of destitution. His sympathy is not uncalled for, seeing that he is the supporter of a fiscal system which keeps the morass filled ... (28 November 1910)

Rendered impotent by the government's majority in the Commons and the support it usually received from Irish members and Labour MPs (of whom there were forty-two by 1910), the party looked increasingly towards the packed Unionist benches in the House of Lords – and this provoked the constitutional crisis of 1910. Lloyd George's first budget as Chancellor in 1909 proposed a package of reforms to be financed by new taxes on land and inherited wealth. It was the first distant trumpet call of the Welfare State, and it sent a shudder up the spine of the British Establishment. The Liberals steered the Finance Bill safely through the lower chamber, but the House of Lords threw it out. This unprecedented attack on representative government caused the most important constitutional crisis since the Reform Act of 1832. The situation was serious enough for William Waldorf to make the unthinkable sacrifice of breaking his winter sojourn in Sorrento. 'So acute have matters become,' he wrote to a friend, 'that my peace of mind requires me to return to London for the election [January 1910] ... I was doing effective work all Summer against Socialism and believe I can be of great use to my Conservative friends when the contest begins.'[10]

The crisis resulted in two elections in 1910 (after which the main parties were more evenly balanced and the Liberals were dependent on minority groups), an abortive constitutional conference, and a promise extracted from the new king, George V, that if necessary he would create 250 new peers to ensure the passage of the government's Parliament Bill (designed permanently to curb the power of the upper house). This was the turbulent moment at which Waldorf Astor arrived at Westminster. It was a time not only of conflict between the parties, but of divisions and intrigues within the Unionist ranks. Over the next few years the new MP and his father were closely involved in these behind-the-scenes manoeuvrings – and they seldom found themselves seeing exactly eye to eye.

The smoke and dust of political battle rolled until that sombre day in August 1914 when the country awoke to discover that it had a real war on its hands. As the air cleared, the most interesting fact for the family chronicler to observe is that the Astors had acquired another newspaper and its editor, James Louis Garvin.

In 1905, Baron Northcliffe (later Viscount Northcliffe) bought for a song the seriously ailing *Observer* and thus added Britain's oldest Sunday newspaper to his Fleet Street stable. Now he needed a new editor to wake the paper up, and the man for the job was James Garvin ('Garve' to his intimates), one of the brightest and most forceful men in London journalism. It took three years to persuade Garvin to occupy the editorial chair, but the results were immediate. The quality of the *Observer* improved and the circulation soon followed. Unfortunately, however, editor and proprietor seldom enjoyed editorial agreement. Northcliffe was a bully who expected his 'subordinate' to defer to his policy decisions (even though Garvin had a share in the equity), and Garve was not the sort of man to be dictated to. By 1911, their relationship had reached breaking point. Northcliffe decided to wash his hands of Garvin or the *Observer* or both. He gave the editor a week to find a purchaser. After that he would buy Garvin out, virtually on his own terms. Garve hurriedly went the rounds of his political contacts and, very quickly, a Unionist syndicate emerged prepared to come to his rescue. Then one member of that syndicate ventured an alternative plan.

Waldorf Astor knew full well the power of the press. He knew the financial difficulties the *Pall Mall Gazette* was in. And, through the Round Table, he knew Garvin, a man whose political vision he shared. The obvious solution was for the Astors to acquire the *Observer*. Garve could then save the *Gazette* as he had already saved the *Observer*. Moreover, Waldorf would secure a platform for that brand of reformist Unionism that he and Garvin espoused. In a highly revealing letter to Garvin the following year he made crystal clear his attitude towards politics and journalism, and the role he aspired to play:

> My own personal object and hope in life (including politics) is to be able to help to get certain things done with, through or under the right people. I don't wish to spend time hunting for or shaping a career – my time and energy had much better be spent in getting things done ... If the career follows and accompanies, by all means let it do so but it would be a useless end to aim for if it had to come first ... you and I agree in fundamentals. To bring about what we want and believe in some independent thought and the formation of sound public opinion is essential ...'[11]

No other words could more lucidly express Waldorf's unique mixture of modesty, idealism and determination.

Waldorf Astor the politician has been seriously underrated. Because he was devoid of personal ambition and because, from 1919 onwards, Nancy totally upstaged her husband, he has been seen as a shadowy background figure and all too easily dismissed as a lightweight. In fact, he was a man of political vision many of whose ideas were ahead of their time. In party terms he was really a 'Liberal Unionist' and stood well to the left in the opposition ranks. He supported most of Lloyd George's reforms and was a lifelong friend and admirer of the 'specialist in offal'. He mastered well those subjects which interested him (ranging from agriculture and health, political reform, and relations with America to the development of the Empire) and spoke or wrote about them with clarity and precision. Nor was he an impractical idealist. He knew that the stuff of politics was intrigue and back-room deals. He used Cliveden and 4 St James's Square to the full in bringing together public figures who could help him acquire influence and achieve his aims. His offer to buy the *Observer* was a calculated political act.

It was all very well for Waldorf to make overtures to Garvin, but they had no validity unless he could obtain William Waldorf's financial backing. Since father and son did not altogether agree on politics, this was far from being a foregone conclusion. Astor senior, as was his invariable custom, was wintering in Italy. Precise accounts and financial forecasts for the *Observer* had to be telegraphed to him. They seemed satisfactory. But then there was the matter of control. William Waldorf insisted on total ownership and the same right of editorial veto that he exercised over the staff of the *Pall Mall Gazette*. He even wanted details of Garvin's religious views. Garvin had no wish to jump out of the Harmsworth frying pan into the Astor fire, but there was no other offer available and time was running out. He could doubtless have found another job, but he had a deep emotional commitment to the *Observer* (as his daughter later wrote, 'More than his being the life and soul of it, it was the life and soul of him').[12] He needed the Astors' money and that meant accepting the maxim that he who pays the piper calls the tune. Even so, he probably would not have reached an accord with William Waldorf had it not been for the tacit agreement that it would, in fact, be Waldorf who would be keeping a proprietorial eye on the *Observer*, rather than his father.

The deal was concluded on 5 April and there thus came into being an unstable *ménage à trois*. William Waldorf was the boss. Through his agent he concerned himself largely with matters of circulation and profit, but he was no mere cypher as far as editorial policy was concerned. It was not uncommon for a telegram to arrive in the *Observer* office from Hever, Sorrento or some even more distant point of origin demanding that the paper take a reactionary line on a particular issue. Garvin, now editor of both Astor papers, was an experienced political journalist with his own very clear views, which did not always agree with those of Astor *père* or Astor *fils*. Waldorf had an immense respect for Garve and looked upon him, in the early days, as something of a political tutor, but he often found the editor's stance insufficiently progressive for his taste.

The first issue which confronted the new management was the Unionist leadership. The government's determination to force the Parliament Bill through presented their opponents with a dilemma: should they fight to the last ditch or bow gracefully to the inevitable. Waldorf and Garvin were agreed that there could be no yielding on this point of principle. The *Observer*'s editorial on 5 March 1911 staunchly upheld the view that 'there is only one path of safety, as of honour, for the Unionist Party, and it is straight and plain. Surrender to the Parliament Bill is the unthinkable course combining the maximum of folly with that of disgrace.' The Astor press became an organ for the 'Die Hards' – those who wanted the House of Lords to veto the bill and call the government's bluff. In this it was at loggerheads with Balfour and the Marquess of Lansdowne (Unionist leader in the upper house), who believed that continued intransigence would weaken the House of Lords and even risked bringing the Crown into disrepute. The Die Hards were incensed and Garvin attacked Balfour in the columns of the *Gazette*.

This was too much for Waldorf. He disliked the tone of the editorial and he disapproved of the party's divisions being made public. He wrote to Garvin to complain and to remind him of his policy obligations to the proprietor. This provoked a long, uncompromising reply. 'Nothing but a policy of extraordinary boldness and fearlessness could have made *The Observer*; nothing else can restore to the *Pall Mall Gazette* its old repute or extend its influence,' Garvin asserted. Editorial independence was vital, he suggested, not only for the newspapers, but also for the party: 'If [the *Gazette*] does not criticise Unionist leadership when that role obviously needs to be criticised, its support will not be very valuable when it thinks the leaders ought to be supported.' He ended with the request that any future difference of opinion between himself and the owners should be argued out in writing. There was no suggestion of an editorial climb-down under such circumstances.[13]

In the event, it was Waldorf who did the climbing down. He went away to Cliveden, where he always found the atmosphere 'congenial and restful', reflected at length on the whole issue, and concluded that Garvin was right. It was not an easy decision to reach, for he was in daily contact with Balfour and other major actors in the drama. (Indeed, while these letters were being exchanged the Unionist leader spent a few days at Rest Harrow, the Astors' holiday home at Sandwich, to recuperate from the strain of the previous month.) What swayed Waldorf was his sense of *duty* – in this case the duty to put the good of the party and the country above loyalty to individuals. It was because he came to believe that Garvin was similarly motivated that he was prepared to concede that his editor had been right and he had been wrong. It was an important step on the journey away from the belief instilled in him by his father that changing one's mind was a sign of weakness. It also laid the foundation for one of the most remarkable proprietor–editor relationships in the history of British journalism. The two men agreed in future to thrash out any differences face to face.

But the party was still in crisis. Factions and counter-factions met daily advocating different resolutions of the internal strife, and Waldorf, though very much a 'new boy', was in the thick of all this manoeuvring. In October he helped to found the Halsbury Club. Its leading lights were Milner, Austen Chamberlain, Edward Carson and other prominent parliamentarians, and its aim was to raise a banner around which 'forward' Unionists could rally. It was not part of its avowed objective to force Balfour's resignation, but that seemed from the beginning to be the inevitable outcome of the plotters' debates. Waldorf determined to bring the issue to a head at one meeting by suggesting that the present position of the club was 'ridiculous'. This led to a furious argument. A vote of no confidence in Balfour was passed by a sizeable majority, then dropped when Chamberlain and others threatened to boycott the club; nothing could have better illustrated the Unionists' disarray. Within weeks, however, Balfour resigned. Now the inevitable in-fighting took place to find a successor. Astor and Garvin were among those who backed the candidature of Austen Chamberlain, and Garvin tried hard to dissuade Andrew Bonar Law, a Canadian-born Nonconformist Scottish businessman, from throwing his hat into the ring. Within days of Bonar Law's victory, however, Waldorf wrote to congratulate him: 'I have now a feeling of hope and confidence in the future of our Party which I should not have imagined possible a few days ago.'[14] At the same time he observed wryly to Garvin about Chamberlain's patrician opponents and the new leader: 'It is at all events pleasing to realize that the Carlton Club Tories who refused to follow Austen because he was "middle class" now find themselves marching solidly behind a Glasgow manufacturer!'[15]

Waldorf's father had his own reasons for being pleased with the change of leadership. Although he never discussed his ambitions with anyone, least of all his children, it is clear that William Waldorf had by this time set his heart on a peerage. Furthermore, he considered that he deserved one. He had served the Unionist cause faithfully through the *Pall Mall Gazette* and also with generous financial donations. The Harmsworths and other prominent party benefactors had been rewarded, but he had been overlooked – probably, he suspected, because of Balfour's disdain for his Yankee origins and Edward VII's antipathy towards him. It was certainly soon after Balfour's resignation that William Waldorf drew the attention of Unionist leaders to his years of service. He obtained an invitation to dine with Lord Lansdowne and, in June 1912, he enjoyed a quiet lunch at the Ritz with Bonar Law. In briefing Bonar Law for this meeting, Sir Herbert Praed, chairman of the Association of Conservative Clubs and establishment figure *par excellence*, gave a very clear assessment of William Waldorf's activities and motivation:

In addition to the large sums he has given me for the Party Fund, he has contributed most generously to oppose Communism and in other ways, amongst others he gave me £4000 for the development of Conservative Clubs. He is in favour of fighting the Radicals on every feasible opportunity and admires you because you have the determination and capacity to carry out such a policy. I know he thinks he has been neglected by the Party and that his efforts have not been recognised. A few compliments will not be thrown away . . . I gather that on *some points* he does not see eye to eye with Mr Garvin . . . He thinks Balfour might have put forward his name for a peerage . . .

What Praed advises, to use modern vernacular, is: 'This man is useful to us. Keep him sweet. Listen to his grumbles but promise nothing.' He also drew Bonar Law's attention to Waldorf – 'a very bright, popular fellow with an ambitious wife who had been previously married'.[16] Bonar Law doubtless filed away the information in his mind for possible future action. For the time being William Waldorf had to be content with words of gratitude.

Another small piece of evidence illustrates how the two Astors and their politics were viewed by contemporaries. It is a fragment of correspondence between William Waldorf and Lord Curzon. The 'votes for women' campaign gathered momentum from the founding of the Women's Social and Political Union in 1903, and several Members of Parliament were sympathetic to its cause. There were various attempts to introduce bills in the Commons, and in 1910 a well-thought-out piece of legislation was set before the house which attracted much support. For the first time, reactionaries were seriously alarmed – so much so that Lord Curzon (former Viceroy of India) set up the Anti-Suffrage League. Among those he approached to boost the fighting fund was William Waldorf Astor. Curzon had high hopes of Astor's support. The two men were friends and neighbours (Curzon's town house was also in Carlton House Terrace); Curzon's wife had been an American millionairess; and the peer knew Astor's anti-socialist views. Moreover, William Waldorf had previously responded generously to appeals Curzon had made for Oxford University (of which he was Chancellor). Therefore, Curzon confidently approached the newspaper proprietor in July 1910:

This insidious Bill which is going to be carried on its second reading tomorrow is a socialistic scheme: for though it would enfranchise only 1,000,000 women, the franchise conferred is so arbitrary and grotesque that it would at once be made an argument for the grant of adult suffrage (male and female) which is socialism naked and unashamed . . . I have talked to Waldorf but he is rather wobbly.[17]

'Wobbly' Waldorf certainly was. His wife was a vociferous supporter of women's suffrage both in Britain and America (where an equally energetic campaign was being fought), and the logic of the suffragettes' case seemed to him unanswerable (although he deplored their more violent methods). What is more interesting is his father's reaction to Lord Curzon's appeal. William Waldorf politely declined to be associated with the Anti-Suffrage League and maintained this stance despite repeated pleas from Curzon. William Waldorf may have been a reactionary, but he was not a blinkered and unthinking reactionary.

Shortly after the change of Unionist leadership Waldorf made a speech in his constituency on the subject of social reform. It was full of the party rhetoric endemic to the genre, but it did make quite clear the things the MP for Plymouth believed in and wished to achieve. The speech, like others being delivered up and down the country, was part of the Unionist riposte to Lloyd George's National Insurance Act, which had just become law. This wide-ranging revolutionary measure launched a frontal attack on poverty and inadequate medical provision. It provided for the first time obligatory contributions to a fund out of which unemployment and sickness benefit would be paid to those in need. Many Unionists attacked the Act as a monstrous infringement of individual freedom. Not so Waldorf Astor: 'There are some who talk of the liberty of the subject, and who say we have no right to interfere. In my opinion interference is not half as bad as non-interference where protection is most needed . . . Science and religion have failed to stem the tide of disease and sorrow, and it is now the duty of the State to act.'[18] Waldorf was obliged to make jibes about Lloyd George and his reforms, but his complaint was not that the Chancellor's proposals were too radical, but that they were not radical enough. He outlined a programme of legislation covering housing, education, trade disputes, health and maternity provision and wage rates which he promised to campaign for at Westminster.

He was as good as his word. The National Insurance Act had transformed health care. Therefore, a great deal of planning and creative thought had to go into the modernizing of old institutions, the establishment of new ones and the allocation of public funds. It is a measure of the impact that Waldorf had already made on the back benches that he was deeply involved in this process. In 1912 he chaired a committee of medical experts set up to report and advise on the treatment of tuberculosis, one of the greatest killer diseases of the day. The following year he became treasurer to the Medical Research Committee, which was charged with co-ordinating the work of scientists, central government and local authorities and which led to the formation of the permanent Medical Research Council. This work brought him into close contact with Dr Christopher Addison who, as Liberal MP for Hoxton worked closely with Lloyd George in framing the new welfare legislation. The reformers fought, almost unaided, for the acceptance of new ideas against the entrenched vested interests of the civil servants who ran the Local Government Board (which, since 1871, had supervised local expenditure on poor relief, sanitation, health, etc.). The thinking of these experts was geared towards preventing overspending rather than encouraging enterprise and research designed to improve the health of the nation. They bitterly resented extended state control and the concomitant increase in public expenditure.

At the same time as he was helping to implement social change, Waldorf brought together a group of Unionist colleagues to hammer out a complete range of policies covering housing, education, agriculture, industrial unrest and reform of the poor law. Their findings were published in 1916 in a pamphlet entitled *The Health of the People – A New National Policy.* The group put forward its proposals 'without party interest'. (Waldorf became increasingly impatient with party conflict; all too often it stood in the way of his desire to 'get things done'.) The main thrust of all this thinking was towards a streamlining of organization and a pruning of the many overlapping authorities involved in public welfare. This activity by Astor and his colleagues led eventually, in 1919, to the establishment for the first time of a Ministry of Health.

Conservatives when not in power tend to be deeply infected by both bitterness and bewilderment, as though something has gone drastically wrong with the natural order of things. Morale on the Unionist benches was very low and was felt even by Waldorf, who liked to think issues out for himself and was no party automaton. He soon modified his first impression of Bonar Law. The Unionist leader seemed to have no consistent policy and was all too easily wrong-footed by Asquith. 'Until we have sufficient guts and sense to discover a policy,' Waldorf grumbled to a friend, 'and then have enough confidence to come forward and stand on the merits of this policy, and are not obliged to rely only on the fluctuating unpopularity of our opponents, I don't see why we should expect the man in the street or the man in the motor car to give us his support.'[19] For once the three members of the *Observer* triumvirate saw eye to eye on the political situation. Quoting Garvin with approval, William Waldorf wrote in 1913: 'the Government are more unscrupulous than we and we are more incapable than they.' (Waldorf would not have agreed with the policy recommendation his father also made: 'Old age pensions is dishonest in principle but it has come to stay and we can only aim to prevent its extension.[20])

As always, Ireland was the most contentious party issue. Never far from the surface of day-to-day politics, it now floated to the top again. A third Home Rule bill was introduced into Parliament in April 1912, passed its various Commons stages and was, predictably, vetoed in the Unionist-dominated upper chamber. Since the passage of the Parliament Act their lordships could not prevent the Home Rule measure passing into law, but they could, and did, obstruct its progress while Unionist tub-thumpers campaigned vigorously from public platforms and the pages of the press. Their campaign was not, now, for the retention of the whole of Ireland, but for the protection of the rights of the Protestant North. 'I can imagine no length of resistance to which Ulster will go, which I shall not be ready to support,' Bonar Law told a Unionist rally. Unfortunately, some Ulstermen were prepared to use violence and armed revolt to prevent themselves being coerced into accepting rule from Dublin. At Westminster the old flags of 'Democracy for Ireland' and 'No Betrayal of Fellow Countrymen' were waved with renewed vigour. Government leaders were determined to use their majority to force Home Rule through. The opposition front bench schemed on ways to force an election before the Act went for royal assent. By the spring of 1914, as the major continental powers staggered, like drunken men, towards the open pit of war, Unionist peers were seriously contemplating vetoing the annual Army Act. So blinkered were they to world realities that they were actually prepared to leave the country defenceless in order to embarrass the government.

But there were others, including Waldorf Astor and the Round Tablers, who were working behind the scenes for compromise. Meetings between Liberal and Unionist politicians were held – not a few of them at St James's Square or Cliveden. The solution urged at these gatherings was some sort of federalism, devolving some central government powers, not only to Dublin, but also to assemblies in Scotland and Wales. Waldorf, firmly committed as he was to the conviction that there is no problem so intractable that it cannot be solved by men of goodwill sitting round a table, was driven to fury by the stubbornness and obtuseness of the party hacks. He urged Garvin to try to make the federalist issue clear in the *Observer*. 'Some of our people are so thickheaded they cannot see it . . . [These] "Talk Louds" or "Talk Fasts" . . . have not begun to grasp what we mean by Federalism or Devolution – they are such fatheads that they don't see we advocate it as the least bad of the alternatives and not as an ideal policy.'[21]

The younger Astor was in a difficult position. Once again Garve was taking a more reactionary line than he would have liked. At the same time parliamentary friends and colleagues held Waldorf responsible because in their view his editor was not reactionary enough. Such assaults tried Waldorf's patience to the utmost, especially when they came from Unionist peers who had buckled under in the Parliament Act crisis. He was angry that members of the upper house who had not been prepared to 'risk their coronets' in 1911 were now calling themselves 'Die Hards' over the Irish issue. He vented his full spleen in a letter to one of these noble recalcitrants and defended his editor to the hilt:

If you had not elected to be blind and deaf and suspicious you might have grasped [the views put forward] in what you call my Press ... [As for the so-called 'Die Hards'] No action was taken; no action is being taken ... no action will be taken, because most of our friends won't take risks ... 'Gas' is their watchword ... To cover up their own failures they turn on Garvin because he is not the hopeless, unimaginative reactionary that many of them are ...[22]

It was not only parliamentary hotheads who were advocating extreme measures. Waldorf also found himself at odds with his father over the Home Rule issue. From the Villa Sirena William Waldorf dispatched letters and telegrams urging Garvin to take a tough line and do anything that might contribute to the downfall of the government.

About Bonar Law's decision to oppose the Army Act he crowed:

I have great hopes that the Government has sustained an irreparable injury and that the *Observer* and the *Gazette* are being largely instrumental in bringing public opinion to this view ... I trust ... that by a hearty pull all together we may land the Government in the ditch.[23]

Once again the *ménage à trois* was pulling the Astor press in different directions. On this occasion the editor's sympathies were with Astor *père* – or so he explained to Waldorf. But he had other reasons for wishing to placate the man who held the purse strings: the *Observer* and the *Pall Mall Gazette* were up for sale.

The first hard documentary evidence for the disintegrating relationship between William Waldorf and Waldorf Astor (and, perhaps, also Pauline) comes from Lady Sackville (mother of Vita Sackville-West), who made the following entry in her diary after a visit to William Waldorf at the Villa Sirena in March 1914: 'He has become hard on everyone, even against his own children and so self-centred and unfeeling about everything ... We are parting perfectly good friends, but things have changed, alas.'[24]

At fifty-one, Victoria Sackville-West, half Spanish, half blue-blooded English aristocracy, still had the power to fascinate men. One had left her a vast fortune. Dark-eyed and with spectacular long silken tresses, she was vital, wilful, eccentric but capable of great tenderness. William Waldorf had known her well. The Sackvilles' magnificent Tudor mansion, Knole, was only a few miles from Hever; and it was more impressive – filled with treasures, including paintings by Holbein, Rembrandt, Hals, Mytens, Gainsborough, Reynolds, Poussin and other old masters, which had accumulated there over centuries of Sackville ownership and not been bought up by one insatiable collector. Knole represented everything that William Waldorf most admired about the English great house. It was but a short step from that to persuade himself that he was in love with Knole's mistress. He knew, everyone knew, that Victoria and her husband, Lionel, were estranged and that they conducted their own discreet extra-marital liaisons. For some time, William Waldorf worshipped his new princess (or was she Queen Guinevere of Camelot?) from afar.

In 1913, he began to woo her in earnest. One July day she came to Hever and there, in the space of 'a splendid hour's excitement' (as he later wrote), their relationship passed beyond friendship. It was followed by a 'little gift' of £10,000 in fresh notes and secret assignations at Temple Place ('a little palace on the Embankment where I live in solitude. *La ci darem la mano*' – apparently he saw himself as a sixty-five-year-old Don Giovanni). In the winter William Waldorf went, as usual, to Sorrento, and he begged her to come out and spend some time with him. The eagerly awaited visit took place at the end of March. It did not go as William Waldorf had anticipated. Victoria had fallen for someone else, and she had come to see the black side of her host's nature. As gently as possible, she detached herself from his emotional coils. They continued to correspond for some months, but the affair (if such it ever was) ended the following August after Victoria had explained that it would be unwise for him to become godfather to her new grandson.[25]

This is the sad, familiar story of two lonely people discovering that they are not the answers to each other's problems. Lady Sackville's desolation was intensified in October 1913 when her only child, Vita, was married to Harold Nicolson, a young diplomat of whom she did not altogether approve. At that time William Waldorf wrote her a consoling letter, saying that he knew exactly how she felt. That was no exaggeration. There is no worse loneliness than that of the parent who fails to turn growing children into friends and discovers, too late, that they have become strangers. To Victoria, it would seem, the old man unburdened himself about his disappointment with Waldorf and Pauline and their respective spouses. But Victoria understood that it was the father who had grown away from the children, not vice versa, and that he had so hardened his heart as to make reconciliation impossible. It was a mistake she did not make with Vita.

It was in the aftermath of this broken romance that, in the winter of 1913–14, William Waldorf began negotiations for the sale of his newspapers. It may have been an act of sheer spite, designed to upset Waldorf and thwart his political ambitions, and it certainly brought relations with his elder son almost to breaking point. More likely, however, it was evidence of the almost complete lack of communication between the two men. Waldorf did not know his father was planning to sell, and his father did not know, or affected not to know, that Waldorf had a keen interest in the papers. 'Yes the "Observer" is gone,' he announced (prematurely, as it happened) in August 1914, 'a good property no doubt, and the "Gazette", which has been one of my notable failures. I bought the Observer to get rid of the Gazette but should perhaps not have sold them had it not been for disputes with the Printers Federation which created for me an intolerable situation. When Waldorf wrote me a year or two ago that he did not wish the papers I never thought of him again in connection with them.'[26]

The *Observer* was more or less viable, thanks to Garvin, but the daily paper was still losing £50,000 a year. The industrial dispute was, for William Waldorf, the last straw. Disdaining any negotiation with his 'servants', he resolved to wash his hands of them and, without bothering to inform the editor, opened negotiations of sale. When Garvin heard the news he suspected that Conservative Central Office was behind the decision. He was probably right. The Unionist top brass had long resented the refusal of the Astor press to toe the party line. Garvin was angry but, as he told Waldorf, he had a wife and family to consider. Under the circumstances he did not feel disposed to upset his boss or his possible new boss by being openly critical of the Unionist leadership.

Negotiations dragged on throughout 1914, but on New Year's Day 1915 William Waldorf was able to inform his son that the purchase would be completed within a month. Only at this stage did he deign to explain: he realized this decision would be a disappointment but 'The *Observer* is a good property but I regard the *Gazette* as brother to the Biblical ox in a pit. In my hands it has been a ponderous failure, and the incessant worries and squabbles connected with its management have brought me to regard it with deep disgust.'[27] Waldorf knew better than to argue with his father and steeled himself to the loss of his newspapers and the end of his relationship with Garvin. This seems to have been the point at which the breach with his father became unbridgeable. Then, at the last moment, the negotiations broke down. Over the next few weeks William Waldorf sought another buyer, but in March Waldorf intervened decisively. All this uncertainty, he complained, was bad for everyone connected with the papers. He reached a private understanding with his father whereby, in return for taking over complete responsibility for the Astor press, he would disembarrass the family of the *Gazette*. William Waldorf was only too happy to wash his hands of the whole business. Thus, the *Observer* was saved and its connection with the Astors was maintained for more than half a century. In 1916 Waldorf found a buyer for the *Pall Mall Gazette*.

By this time Britain was at war. The problems of Fleet Street and even of Ireland were dwarfed by the conflict between the Triple Entente nations and the Central Powers. The Astors, each in his or her own way, threw themselves into the war effort.

William Waldorf was almost literally thrown into the conflict. In August 1914 he was at Vichy, taking the waters for his gout. Suddenly his well-ordered routine was shattered. 'Before I could realize the extreme gravity of the situation, the usual conditions of travel were dislocated. Thousands fled, leaving their luggage. Most of the shops closed. Doctors, bath attendants and barbers were ordered to the front.' He hired a car, made a desperate two-day drive across central France and reached the Swiss border at Bellegarde, where he had to argue with the military authorities who tried to impound his baggage. Once safely across the frontier, he found himself in what was, for an Astor, a distressingly unfamiliar situation, 'living on tick, my cheques useless, and my French and German banknotes unavailable'. Not until he had prevailed on his Paris bank to send him a bag of gold coin was he able to make good his escape.[28]

In the next few weeks, the soldiers went off to fight. Pauline's husband, Bertie Spender-Clay, had resigned his Guards commission in 1902 and became the Unionist MP for Tonbridge in 1910, but he now re-enlisted at the age of thirty-nine and went out to France in November with the rank of captain. He served for the first half of the conflict on the headquarters staff of 19th Division but was ultimately brought home to Southern Command HQ, Salisbury. In the spring of 1917, he was sent to America following Washington's declaration of war, as part of a deputation to provide the US government with a first-hand account of the theatre of war and to persuade them to commit troops to Europe. He also found time to dine with Mrs Vincent Astor and to spend an evening at New York's celebrated Coconut Grove. He ended the war as a lieutenant-colonel and was awarded the CMG for military and political services.

The outbreak of war placed Waldorf in an agonizing dilemma. He was thirty-five and he had a younger brother serving on the western front. Jingoism was at fever pitch in the country and people looked askance at any able-bodied young man (especially any rich young man) not in uniform. The Astor press itself thundered:

> It should now be taught to the well-to-do of England that their claim to the title of gentleman rests on their willingness to do service to the State . . . the poorer classes are no longer willing to be drilled and brigaded, as they believe, for the defence and possession of the rich.[29]

Waldorf's own keen sense of responsibility compelled him to enlist, but the fact was that he was not fit enough to be sent to the front: his weak heart and other ailments sometimes prostrated him for days or weeks on end. Yet he refused to submit to a purely civilian existence, and a means was found to get him into uniform. He was appointed supervisor of training camps for Southern Command with the rank of major. He spent the early months of the war touring military establishments, reporting on food and living conditions, listening to complaints and, where necessary, organizing improvements. If he was not allowed to bear arms himself, this, at least, gave him direct contact with the fighting men, and he threw himself into the work with enthusiasm. Christopher Addison recorded in his diary how Major Astor returned to London in January 1915, looking very impressive in khaki and polished leather, eager to impress on the 'top people' the plight of the soldiers.

He tells me that in some of the Salisbury Plain camps the Tommies are slithering about in a sea of mud from six to eighteen inches deep, but that notwithstanding these horrible conditions their health is better when in camps than when billeted or in barracks. He gives a splendid account of the men of the New Army.[30]

In both his military and political capacities Waldorf was particularly concerned about conditions in Plymouth. So was Nancy. She had thrown herself one hundred and one per cent into the life of the constituency from the very beginning, canvassing at election times, making speeches, attending official functions, founding day care centres and interesting herself in a variety of social issues. In the spring of 1914 she complained to a friend in the town: 'I am being dragged away on Saturday by my husband, as he thinks I am doing too much, and I believe that you are one of those people who agree with him, but you are wrong; I haven't begun yet.'[31] In the early months of the war she sometimes accompanied Waldorf on his tours of facilities available for military and naval personnel in and around the harbour. The Astors paid out of their own pockets for mess huts at Crown Hill barracks because the existing ones were, in their opinion, sub-standard. Nancy also extended her amateur nursing activities to servicemen's hospitals in the town.

The semi-military phase of Waldorf's life did not last long. He continued his parliamentary activities, and as it became apparent that the management of the war was being badly handled he played an active part in dislodging the Asquith government. In May 1915 the Liberals had given way to a coalition, headed by Asquith. It never really worked. Other cabinet personalities, notably Lloyd George, who was proving very successful as Minister for Munitions with Addison as his under-secretary, were more prominent. There were internal clashes over such issues as the introduction of conscription, and it was generally felt that the Prime Minister was not prosecuting the war as enthusiastically as he should. When, in December 1915, Asquith made a speech in which he referred to the peace negotiations which must, at some time, take place, the Astor press pounced. Such talk, Garvin protested,

raises the vision of a 'drawn' war which would have to be fought all over again at no very distant date; of a Germany untamed in her arrogance . . . of the standards of warfare permanently debased by her brutalities; and of a pyramid of crimes and outrages left unavenged . . . [Mr Asquith] would relieve the country of a certain shade of discomfort by making it freshly explicit that no offer of peace just now which does not involve the complete submission of Germany would possess any practical interest for himself and his colleagues.[32]

At the same time plots and counter-plots were going on behind the scenes to provide the country with a more vigorous war leadership. Once again, 4 St James's Square became one of the centres of intrigue. Waldorf favoured Milner as the new head of the coalition, with Lloyd George as his second-in-command, but it rapidly became clear that Milner had too many enemies and that the Unionists had no other candidate of sufficient stature to put forward. Waldorf therefore switched his allegiance to Lloyd George. At a small dinner party in his London home in May 1916 he urged the Welshman to resign over the conscription issue and thus force a government crisis, but Lloyd George was not yet ready for a major clash.

It was in the midst of these manoeuvrings and against the background of a worsening war situation in which, like most British families, the Astors were daily losing dearly-loved friends, a massive bombshell hit the family, with the arrival of William Waldorf's long-awaited peerage. From the start of hostilities he had helped the war effort in the only way he knew how, donating hundreds of thousands of pounds to the Red Cross, to public funds and to wartime charities. He was motivated by pure sentiment, for he was genuinely moved by the sufferings of the troops in the trenches. Through his press and diplomatic contacts, and especially through his letters from John, he was better informed than most about what was happening on the battlefields of Europe, and he wanted – discreetly – to do what he could to alleviate suffering. It was for these services that he was cited to receive a barony in the 1916 New Year's Honours List.

This event finally destroyed the relationship between Waldorf and his father and soured other family relationships. It is therefore important to consider it in all its aspects. First of all, there is the motivation for William Waldorf's political, journalistic and charitable activities which secured him a title. There is no doubt that he had, for some years, hoped for a peerage, but that is not to say that personal ambition provided the only reason for his donations to party funds and charities. Contemporaries and historians unable to penetrate the mask of self-indulgence and reclusiveness were cynical about Astor's public service. Newspapers in New York and London certainly took the opportunity to rail against the purchase of honours by millionaires who were not conspicuous for adding to the sum total of human happiness. Those few people who knew him well, however, testified that his gruff manner concealed an acute awareness of the sufferings of others. Pauline, who visited him often in the years after her marriage, wrote:

My father was not at all hard hearted, in fact he was very sensitive . . . I often felt he needed help and sympathy, and yet it seemed impossible to reach him through his defences of reserve and a certain aloofness . . . It has occurred to me in recent years that the shroud of indifference coupled with slight sarcasm behind which he retired may have been his form of defence against the hurts of misunderstandings. His true self seldom appeared and his motives were often misjudged.[33]

Part of his reticence was undoubtedly due to the fact that, like all rich men, he was inundated with requests from charities. The destruction of all personal papers that he ordered in his will makes it impossible to assess just how generous he was in responding to such appeals. We are dependent on surviving scraps of information. These tell us that among his benefactions were new building works at Oxford University, the Library for the Blind, the Royal Geographical Society, the London School of Tropical Medicine and the Primrose League. Sometimes his philanthropic involvement went beyond the mere writing of cheques. Some of the at-homes and soirées held at Carlton House Terrace were fund-raising events. There were also comparatively small day-to-day disbursements, such as the 5,000 marks he sent to Walldorf in 1892 to set up a fund for the families of disabled firemen.[34] He made no charitable bequests in his will, 'all dispositions of the nature', as the probate statement declared, 'having been made by the late Peer in his lifetime'.[35]

His contributions to the war effort were constant, generous, and continued after he obtained his peerage. They were also discreet, so that, once again, details were only revealed if special circumstances – or *scandal* – threw a light upon them. In 1923 the Conservative party was trying to locate funds that it suspected Lloyd George might have appropriated during the years of the wartime coalition. What transpired was that some £80,000 of Astor money had found its way into Liberal coffers either through the incompetence or the manipulation of the aged Lord Farquhar. This Tory treasurer and one-time Master of the Household to Edward VII had administered considerable funds on behalf of the government, but when the coalition broke up in 1922 and the Conservatives came to power the Unionist cupboard was discovered to be bare. Questioned by party activists, Farquhar (suspiciously granted an earldom in Lloyd George's last honours list) claimed that Lord Astor had given him £200,000 in 1917 or 1918 (he was vague and, in Bonar Law's opinion, 'gaga') 'to do exactly what he liked with'. Some of the money had, reputedly, been given to King George V for war charities, and the rest had been divided between the funds of the two main parties. But it was nowhere to be found. William Waldorf would certainly not have considered that amusing.

When we turn from Astor's motivation to that of Asquith, who recommended the honour, we are on firmer ground. The Prime Minister may have felt that William Waldorf's services deserved recognition; he may have wanted to ensure the millionaire's continuing contributions to the war effort. What is certain is that there was a great deal of personal calculation in the decision. Given the turbulent state of coalition politics, Asquith desperately needed friends and supporters, and Astor owned two newspapers which were constantly snapping at the Prime Minister's heels. A few months previously it had seemed that the *Observer* and the *Gazette* would be sold, but the failure of negotiations left the papers in William Waldorf's hands.* There could be no harm, and might be considerable profit, in making a friendly gesture to old Astor. He was, after all, the only man capable of muzzling Garvin. And there was, of course, ample precedent for creating 'press barons': the Harmsworth brothers, Lord Burnham of the *Daily Telegraph* and Lord Glenesk of the *Morning Post* had all been ennobled during the previous decade or so. Perhaps Asquith deliberately intended to annoy Waldorf. The two men and their wives enjoyed a strange, complex relationship. They had been friends for years and the two men had a genuine respect and liking for each other, but personal feelings became soured by political differences. By 1915 the Asquiths had ceased to receive invitations to Cliveden and St James's Square. As Lloyd George emerged more clearly as a rival and was seen to be drawing talented young men like Waldorf to his camp, Asquith inevitably felt betrayed. The animosity comes out clearly in the long correspondence between Margot Asquith and Nancy which veered wildly between protestations of endearment and expressions of utter disdain. Their husbands doubtless cloaked their feelings, but Asquith may well have taken secret pleasure in the annoyance he knew Waldorf would feel at his father's summons to the Lords.

Why did this unexpected turn of events upset Waldorf and Nancy so much that it led to an almost complete breach in their relations with the new Baron Astor? The immediate reason was that it came out of the blue and was a complete and utter shock. William Waldorf had rigidly observed the secrecy to which forthcoming recipients of honours are pledged. His son had the news at third hand from a friend on the morning of 1 January and hastened to check its accuracy in the papers. He reacted with uncharacteristic haste, dashing off a letter of protest to his father (apparently he could not bring himself to telephone). It was this act which actually caused the rift.

But this does not explain what Waldorf found so exceptionable about his father accepting a peerage. The two men had been growing apart for years and this latest development must have symbolized their disagreements on social and political issues. It must also be said that at this time Waldorf did

* How ironical it would be if Waldorf's rescuing of the *Observer* had indirectly led to his father's ennoblement and the blighting of his own political career.

not have a high opinion of the House of Lords. The behaviour of several of its members in the pre-war years had angered and disgusted him (it is significant that only a few years later he introduced a bill for the reform of the upper chamber). Waldorf had become a devoted House of Commons man. He had embarked on a career as an MP. He enjoyed the work. He felt he was being useful. He had reason to believe that even broader avenues of service were opening up to him, as he explained to Garvin:

> The job which L.G. wanted for me and wh. was being considered was practically the creation of a Health Department. One has only to realise that a healthy people is a contented people (important in war) and that the country must absolutely conserve its manpower by preventing the present huge preventable wastage of disease and premature crippling and loss of life to see what a genuine chance for constructive and valuable work w'd have been before one.[36]

Waldorf had thrown himself heart and soul into the work of reforming the administration of health care. Obviously, he had discussed with Lloyd George the possibility of heading a brand new ministry. By the end of 1916 this innovation was within Lloyd George's power to make, as the new Prime Minister. Now Waldorf's Commons career had been placed in jeopardy because, sooner or later, he would inherit his father's title.

Yet even this does not fully explain his furious reaction, for he could quite easily have pursued an active political career and achieved ministerial status as a member of the upper house. Indeed, he was for many years a conscientious member of the Lords. Was it his wife's reaction which tipped the scale? Nancy was no respecter of persons or titles. She had an American's passionate commitment to equality, and a largely emotional contempt for the British class system with its inherited distinctions. But there was nothing second-hand about Waldorf's revulsion at the prospect of becoming Lord Astor. To him such titles were anachronistic and, in the context of the war, almost obscene. Europe's young men were slaughtering each other in a conflict arising directly from the bungling ineptitude of the ruling classes. As he moved among the Plymouth poor or the soldiers in the camps he did so – or felt that he did so – as a man of the people. He knew that the fighting men and their anxious families were looking, hoping, for a new order after the war. In a handwritten note scribbled on a letter to Lloyd George about government business he made the earnest appeal:

> Even to win the war it is most important you should not lose personal touch with the advanced advocates of *Liberty* and *Democracy*. There is a big movement going on in the country which has been stimulated by Russia and America.[37]

In a frustrated note to Garvin he declared, 'I have often had a suspicion that I w'd end up as a Socialist in a new young and live country.'[38]

The business of the peerage, therefore, went to the very heart of all that Waldorf stood for and believed in, so it is not surprising that he acted precipitately. He asked (almost demanded) that his father should find some way of declining the honour, and informed him that if the title descended to him he would find some way of disembarrassing himself of it. His letter shook the old man to the core. Now it was his turn to be affronted and to feel that all *he* believed in most profoundly was being trampled on.

Nancy, who had followed up Waldorf's hasty note with a calmer letter, received the following response. It is worth quoting in full, for it tells us much about the man and the situation:

January 7th XVI
HEVER CASTLE.

Dear Nancy,

On my return here this morning, I found your letter of yesterday and have read it with great appreciation of its fairness and moderation. It is in that same spirit I wish to answer.

I am sorry that Waldorf takes my promotion so bitterly hard. I cannot think that what has happened is in any sense a decadence and the course of advancement is as open to me as to him.

Several times in my long life I have seen the 'Bird in the bush' take wing and fly away. Which is why I never brag what I shall do with the pretty creature – not even to my own son – until it has become a 'Bird in the hand.'

I have never gone in pursuit of this honour, believing that in all things the honour should come to the man and not that the man should go stalking the honour.

The late Lord Salisbury wished to give me a peerage in 1902, but the late King Edward, who hated me, forbade it. Upon subjects of this kind an acute disagreement arose between them and Lord Salisbury retired from office in that year.

From that time I have never relinquished the purpose to attain what Edward's spite had withheld. But had I mentioned that purpose, visionary as it would have seemed, do you not think I should have cut a sorry figure – even to my own son?

It was painful to Waldorf to receive his first knowledge from a newspaper on the morning of New Year's day. And yet it was precisely from that same source that I acquired my own first positive knowledge of it, at 7 o'clock that morning. A few days before it was still open to doubt whether Mr Asquith would give his assent.

The love of success is in my blood and personally speaking I am delighted to have rounded these last years of my life with a distinction. I should be still more glad were it possible for me to meet Waldorf's wishes and convey it away from him at the last.

With love I am, affectionately yours,

W. W. Astor[39]

The implication that an Astor peerage had anything to do with Lord Salisbury's resignation is, of course, absurd. And then William Waldorf contradicts himself over the question of whether or not he actively sought the honour. What comes across is that he wanted a title desperately, that he felt himself cheated at not being given one years before and that he took every opportunity to commend himself as a worthy candidate. It is a measure of the man's secretiveness that no one in his family had any inkling that his ambitions lay in that direction. The realization came as a complete surprise to all his children.

One member of the family was far away from all this. In the midst of the horrors of war, John might well have felt a little impatience with the news from home. He had deliberately placed himself in a situation of danger. His connections with the army high command could have secured him a safe staff job, but he declined that soft option. At the outbreak of hostilities he went to France with the British Expeditionary Force as a Household Cavalry signalling officer. Like most of his countrymen who rushed to arms in those first months of the war, John embarked enthusiastically and almost light-heartedly upon what he thought would be a short military adventure. This was an attitude his father could never understand. William Waldorf followed the communiqués from the front with rapt and horrified attention. 'He spoke with bated breath and almost tears in his eyes of the retreat from Mons, the first battle of Ypres, the casualties of many friends and acquaintances.'[40] The first weeks of the engagement on the western front produced an open, mobile kind of warfare as the Germans pushed through Belgium in an attempt to encircle Paris, while French, Belgian and British contingents confronted the invader at various points to frustrate his advance. In this the Allies were eventually successful, and the war in the West settled into a muddy, bloody stalemate of trenches, barbed wire and artillery bombardment. Before that John was invalided home: he received an arm wound at Messines in October, serious enough for him to be removed from combat.

The father who had always found it difficult to communicate with his children now welcomed John home with effusive displays of affection. He was lodged at Hever and everything conceivable was provided to aid his swift and complete recovery. 'I might have been a hero,' John later recalled. 'Father demanded to know "was there *anything* he could do for me".'

Worse for John than his wound was the loss of his friend Charles Mercer Nairne, who was killed in the same action. 1914 was doubly tragic for his widow, Violet Mercer Nairne. The news from France reached her when she was still mourning the death of her father the previous March. It was natural that John should call on the grief-stricken Violet. But what should he say? Could he ever confess his love for her? And if so how long an interval should he leave? It was a delicate and difficult situation made all the more so by the fact that after John returned to France he had infrequent leaves. He abhorred the thought of being insensitive, but he had few opportunities to declare his feelings. What should he do? He turned to Nancy for advice. She tried to prepare Violet for a visit John paid early in July 1915, but the reality still came as a shock. Violet had, she told Nancy, always looked on Captain Astor as a friend, and had no idea that he regarded her in any other way. 'I am only too too sorry he should ever give me a thought,' the widow explained later that day. 'I have always liked Captain Astor but as you know I think of nothing but my darling Charlie and that longing to have him back becomes at times almost unbearable.'[41] Poor John had jumped the gun but he persevered, and ten months later was overjoyed when Violet responded to his advances. Old William Waldorf could not have been more delighted with his favourite son. Not only had John been wounded fighting for king and country, not only was he now marrying the widow of another war hero, whose late husband's father, Lord Lansdowne, he was anxious to court for personal reasons, but John's chosen bride came from one of the most blue-blooded families in the realm. The Elliot family tree positively bristled with aristocratic connections. He hastened to make an extremely generous settlement on Violet.

The couple wanted to be married as soon as possible, but that depended on John's being able to get leave. The originally planned July date passed, and eventually the wedding was a hurried affair on 28 August. After a week John returned to the front. Nancy had suggested to him that perhaps now he should let Waldorf pull some strings and get him a safe job, but he would not hear of it. Violet now added her entreaties. She had lost one husband on the western front and was at times paralysed with fear at the possibility of losing another. 'We must all try to get John some job for the winter. He simply can't spend another in France,' she wrote in June 1917, when she had received a particularly depressing letter from the trenches.[42]

Undoubtedly, John's attitude had changed as the war progressed, but he felt an overwhelming commitment to his job and, particularly, to his men. He knew only too well the contempt the ordinary soldier felt for the headquarters staff, who lived in luxurious safety while they were going through hell. He was immensely proud of his squadron and his letters home were full of praise for his 'fine bunch of fellows'.

In the second half of the war his dominant feeling seems to have been one of boredom rather than horror at the carnage. He wrote home describing the futility of being moved from A to B and then back to A again without any apparent reason. Much of his time when his squadron was away from the trenches was spent organizing sports and other amusements to keep up his men's morale. There were occasional moments of excitement, such as the time when he was sent forward with a detachment to find billets in a town. The area came under heavy attack, and he and his men found themselves lost, hungry and wandering the battle area with their kit on a handcart, through a confused countryside 'crawling with refugees and geese'. But three weeks later he was back to the old life, 'fishing, hacking about and finding amusement where we can'.[43]

At last, in September 1918, the long-promised 'big push' came. There was a concerted advance of ninety Allied divisions along a wide front. John, now with the rank of major, found himself in charge of a siege battery at Cambrai (scene of an earlier British tank victory). His position came under heavy attack and Major Astor was seriously wounded. His right leg was shattered by a shell and he was rushed to a military hospital in Paris. Violet hurried out to see him and must have been intensely relieved to find him in good spirits. She had, four months previously, given birth to their first child (and her third), a boy christened Gavin. John may have been badly mauled, but at least he was out of the war. The children would have a father.

John's injury (he subsequently received the Légion d'Honneur for bravery) and the birth of Gavin moved old William Waldorf deeply. His response was to vacate Hever immediately. He went to live in a Regency house in Brighton so that John and his family could make their home in the castle. Just how he felt about his younger son is revealed in a letter Lady Annesley, one of William Waldorf's few close friends, later wrote to John.

> He was so full of you and his grandson and the giving over of Hever to you. He said your Violet had made him such a beautiful present in his grandson that Hever was a little thank offering. He was never tired of talking about you. You were the dearest thing to him in the world and his great happiness.[44]

The war also brought changes to Cliveden. Waldorf and Nancy had three small children by the outbreak of hostilities and two more were born during the war, but this did not prevent them giving up their home to the national cause. As soon as war was declared they offered the house to the government to be used as a hospital, but it was, in fact, the Canadian army authorities who took up the offer. The covered tennis court William Waldorf had built for his children, together with the bowling alley, became a hospital for hundreds of wounded soldiers. Other buildings on the estate were occupied by staff, and the main house served as a convalescent home. Nancy was in her element as a hospital matron, jollying broken-spirited soldiers towards recovery.

She was also trying to heal the family's wounds. The conflict over the peerage worsened rapidly. Had the discussion remained at the calm and reasonable level reflected in William Waldorf's letter of 7 January 1916 quoted above, all might have been well, but soon things were said and written which lowered the debate to the level of invective. Waldorf went to see his father and there were further written exchanges. No record survives of exactly what passed between them, but it is not difficult to glean the main ingredients from other family correspondence. William Waldorf's attitude appalled both John and Pauline. From France John wrote to Nancy: 'What you hint at (if it really is what I think you mean) is more repellent, and revolting and altogether abhorrent and repulsive to me than I can possibly say. It makes me quite sick to think of it.' And his sister observed: 'I can't get over that letter you showed me yesterday – it was so *rude* and I feel so humiliated by my father's writing such a letter. I know that you are above bearing him a grudge for it but I can't help minding dreadfully.'[45]

William Waldorf made two things clear. One was that he blamed Nancy for his son's absurd egalitarian ideas and for the rift that had developed between them. The other was that he no longer considered Waldorf a suitable recipient of the bulk of the Astor fortune and that he would, accordingly, be making the appropriate changes to his will. Waldorf was banished from his father's presence and the old man told him he never wanted to see him again. Nor did he.

Nancy desperately sought to enlist the aid of Waldorf's siblings. Pauline responded by writing a firm but conciliatory letter to her father, although she had 'not much hope of its doing much good because I think that he likes to harbour resentment when he thinks he's got a grievance'. She added: 'I pity my father from the bottom of my heart and think it's almost impossible for us to realise the emptiness and the misery of the life he has made for himself.'[46] She underestimated William Waldorf's spitefulness. His response was to extend to her the ban he had imposed on Waldorf. John, suffering at the time the double misery of the trenches and his (as yet) unrequited love for Violet, felt impotent in this family crisis. As he told Nancy, any letter he might write to William Waldorf would only provoke the response 'mind your own business'; he pointed out that their father could be remarkably sensitive over some things and probably felt Waldorf's rebuff more keenly than the latter realized. In the end John did nothing. That inaction kept him in his father's good graces (and, as we have seen, parental favour was redoubled on the announcement of John's engagement) but soured his relationship with Waldorf for a time. Only a few weeks later Major Astor was sent out to France to inspect camp conditions. This included a visit to John's squadron. The younger brother looked forward to the event eagerly, laid on a parade and special events to mark the occasion and even singled out the best horse for Waldorf to ride. He was bitterly disappointed when Major Astor's party arrived in time for dinner and left after breakfast the next morning with scarcely a word exchanged between the brothers.[47]

Earlier biographers have exaggerated the rift which the granting of the peerage caused in the family, and some have blamed Nancy for perpetuating ill-feeling. The facts seem to be that all the younger generation were united in laying the blame squarely on their father. For a few years Waldorf's attitude towards his brother was cool, but time healed the wound. When, in August 1918, Waldorf and Nancy's last child was born, he was named John Jacob, not after the great pioneer, but after his uncle. This was a significant gesture, but it would be some years yet before the brothers were on affectionate terms once more. Nancy, meanwhile, tried to be friends with everyone. She resumed her correspondence with William Waldorf, though the exchanges were not as frequent or as cordial as before. She arranged for her children to visit their grandfather and this he greatly enjoyed. It was perhaps at his wife's instigation that Waldorf tried to salvage something from his relationship with his father. His overtures were met with civility rather than warmth:

My dear Son,

I thank you for your good wishes on my birthday and for your gift of an interesting volume upon Old New York. I already possess a copy but am glad to have a duplicate for Brighton.

With all my heart I hope that you may reach my age in as excellent health as mine today.

Your affectionate Father [48]

The financial consequences of this family row were complex. In dividing his estate William Waldorf clearly had two overlapping concerns in mind. His first responsibility was, as far as possible, to preserve the Astor fortune for future generations at a time when taxes on property, inheritance and unearned income were increasing on both sides of the Atlantic. His second objective was to give tangible expression to his disappointment in Waldorf. The first of these imperatives weighed the more heavily with him. He deliberately frustrated Waldorf's expectation that he would take over as head of the family and administrator of the estate. Waldorf had assumed that his father would follow the pattern of previous generations by making generous provision for all his children but leaving his elder son in overall control. He had envisaged himself taking over at Temple Place and probably moving in there with his family. William Waldorf reasoned that since Waldorf had declared himself opposed to the inheriting of titles, he was presumably also opposed to inheriting his position as head of the family. Very well, that being so, the old man decided to distribute the bulk of his estate *equally* between his two sons and their families, and in such a way that Waldorf and John would not be able to touch most of the capital. He created two trusts. One was set up in 1916 out of his American securities and investments (over $20 million) for his grandsons, the income from which could only be used for their education and maintenance during their minorities. The other (some $50 million) came from his American real estate and was established shortly before his death in 1919 and was divided between Waldorf and John.

Sad and momentous though these events were for the Astor family, everyone had more important things to think about during the second half of the war. In July 1916 Lloyd George became Minister for War in succession to Lord Kitchener, who was drowned when HMS *Hampshire* struck a mine off Scapa Flow. In the following months he was obliged to preside over the terrible first battle of the Somme, of which A. J. P. Taylor wrote, 'Not only men perished. There perished also the zest and idealism with which nearly three million Englishmen had marched to war.'[49] Spurred on by his frustration with the disastrous strategy of the generals, by the entreaties of radical parliamentarians and by his own ambition, Lloyd George finally challenged the country's leaders – men who, again to quote Taylor, were 'of excessive refinement – almost too fastidious for politics in peacetime, let alone at the turning point of a great war'.[50] The Astor press voiced the dissatisfaction of the Lloyd George camp. The British people, the *Gazette* observed, were tired of being exhorted to greater efforts by an incompetent administration.

> It would be more in accord with the facts if the public undertook the evangelising of Downing Street, for it is there that the signs of somnolence are most apparent. We require not words, but work from Ministers.[51]

After various intrigues and manoeuvrings, Lloyd George forced the issue by resigning on 5 December. Two days later he moved into Number 10 as Prime Minister.

For several hours he was closeted with his closest advisers to appoint his new team. Addison suggested (doubtless with a certain malicious glee) that Waldorf Astor might become Under-Secretary for the Local Government Board. This was a department which greatly interested him and in which he wished to see more radical reforms, but the 'fixers' knew that such an appointment would create friction. Six months later, Walter Long, who had just moved from the Local Government Board to the Colonial Office, warned: 'I hear there has been some idea of making young Astor President of the LGB! This would . . . be madness – Fisher [Sir Warren Fisher, Permanent Under-Secretary to the Treasury – i.e. head of the civil service] could not possibly stay and honestly I don't think he would be alone.'[52] This was the reputation Waldorf had among the stalwarts of the old guard. In fact, however, he was given a position even closer to the centre of political life – as parliamentary private secretary to the Prime Minister. Astor was appointed to this position at Lloyd George's right hand because of his proven character and abilities and his genuine support for a wide range of the Welsh wizard's policies. But the new (and still far from secure) leader was acutely conscious of the importance of Fleet Street, and it is likely that by his patronage of Waldorf he hoped to rally part of the Unionist press behind his coalition.

The next eighteen months were enormously busy and exciting. Essentially, Waldorf was Lloyd George's eyes and ears in the Commons. This was vitally important to the Prime Minister, whose vigorous conduct of the war kept him away from the chamber (and ultimately weakened his position). Waldorf liaised with government departments, chaired committees, drafted memoranda and continued to apply his mind creatively to those matters where he had already established an interest. He was unable to visit his constituency as often as he would have liked, but his absence was more than made up for by Nancy, who now became a prominent and much-loved figure in Plymouth. And, of course, there was the *Observer*, increasingly important to Waldorf as a mouthpiece for government war policy and for proclaiming the vision of the new society he and his friends had for post-war Britain.

Lloyd George worked with a small War Cabinet of five members, independent of the Cabinet proper, but the administrative nerve centre was the 'garden suburb', where he established his secretariat. It was so called because it was housed in temporary buildings erected in the garden of Number 10. Here Waldorf was in his element, for the team assembled by the Prime Minister consisted of young progressives, including fellow Round Tablers such as Philip Kerr and Edward Grigg. Lloyd George made an early gesture of friendship to the Astor family. In the 1917 Birthday Honours List, Baron Astor became Viscount Astor. The new Prime Minister wanted to bind to him influential people in all walks of life. Waldorf and his father were political figures. They also owned a newspaper.

All aspects of government business made up Waldorf's daily routine. He monitored American responses to the conflict, before and after the USA's entry into the war in April 1917. He wrote memos on housing, agriculture and other aspects of post-war reconstruction. He sounded out Labour leaders on their attitude towards Bolshevist Russia ('They would support allied intervention in Russia to restore a constituent assembly but not to revive Tsardom').[53] He made précis of Commons debates. He took the temperature of the lower house on the Irish issue. He reported on conditions in the munitions factories and on labour relations generally. His communications with Lloyd George were not couched in terms of sycophancy, nor were they expressed in formal civil service jargon. Astor spoke from the heart. He advised. He cajoled. He used his privileged position to advocate his ideas passionately.

For example, he urged a bold Irish policy based on imperial prerogative. Home Rule had been shelved for the duration of hostilities, and in Ireland there had been enthusiastic support for the war, with men enlisting in their thousands in both North and South. But the leaders expected a prompt reward for their people's loyalty – a permanent political settlement. All they received from Westminster was continued temporizing and fudge. The extremists, inevitably, took advantage of the situation. There was a nationalist rising in 1916 which was put down with perhaps unnecessary severity. Ulster's leaders became increasingly intransigent. The cause of Irish independence was encouraged both by German agents and by sympathizers in Australia and the USA. For Astor the answer, though not simple, was quite clear – federalism: one Ireland as part of a federated United Kingdom within a federated Empire. In a memo to the Prime Minister on 10 March 1917, he identified Ulster extremism as the main obstacle to be removed:

There is a general opinion in the House that the Irish Question cannot be left where it is without serious injury to the Government. I am also surprised at finding a critical feeling among many Unionists, amounting in some cases to an opinion, that Ulster, by its uncompromising attitude, blocks the way to the whole-hearted and united prosecution of the war. It would be most unfortunate if this were allowed to grow, as it would react in Ulster. We might find ourselves later with both Irish parties hostile to this country.

Belfast, Astor suggested, must be appealed to on the grounds of war emergency. If the northerners would soften their attitude they were uniquely placed to win concessions in terms of reduced legislative powers for a Dublin government or increased Ulster representation in such an assembly.

If Ulster is unable to save the situation and cannot yield at all, the German wirepullers will continue to hamper us in Ireland, in America and in Australia. If Ulster fails to come forward, the German plots must grow.[54]

A year later the situation had worsened. The Ulstermen had not yielded ground. As a sop to them Lloyd George had proposed to introduce conscription in Ireland. The Nationalist MPs had walked out *en masse*. The South was rent by strikes and demonstrations. The government responded with force but also promised to reconsider conscription. Thus was confusion worse confounded. Now Astor had a different reason for urging a rapid resolution of the Irish question:

Parliament must be free after the war to deal with (i) Imperial matters (ii) World matters (The League of Nations) (iii) India (iv) Trade. In preparation for this, domestic issues must be cleared out of the way. Why not introduce your Irish Bill and *immediately* set up a small Speaker's Conference or some other body to prepare a scheme for devolving certain powers to English, Scotch and Welsh Parliaments . . . Irish Nationalists and Ulstermen would find it more difficult to oppose a Bill which dealt with the whole of the United Kingdom, than if it touched Ireland alone.[55]

Days later he besought Lloyd George to 'act quickly on conscription'.[56] Compulsory military service was withdrawn in June, but it was too late. Mistrust and resentment were by now too deep-rooted to be eradicated. The

Irish problem would continue to take its toll of lives and resources. From time to time, also, the question of regional devolution within the UK would arise. There is no guarantee that the federal solution would have worked, but at least Waldorf and his Round Table friends had a clearly thought out manifesto which was free of Unionist dogma and Lloyd George's brand of Liberalism.

Despite Waldorf's intellectual independence, his relations with Lloyd George were very warm and cordial, at least on Waldorf's side. The Prime Minister was cautious in his personal dealings and made few close friendships. Many regarded him as slippery, even treacherous, but Waldorf remained a convinced and loyal admirer to the end of Lloyd George's life. One of his sons confirmed that, of all the political figures who visited Cliveden during the twenties and thirties, it was Lloyd George who was accorded the most respect. To the younger generation he was held up as a hero by their parents. In 1919 Waldorf's wife confided to a friend: 'There is no doubt that his heart is with the underdog, and I feel that he, more than anyone else, will fight for the right thing.'[57] A typical Nancy Astor telegram of 1936, pressing the former Prime Minister to come and stay, has more than a grain of truth amidst its flamboyance: 'Will not take no. John Davies, Philip Lothian, Tom Jones, you and I can settle all the problems in the world.'[58] Throughout the war years the formal relationship between the Prime Minister and his PPS was lightened by social encounters – in particular relaxed dinner parties at 4 St James's Square, at which 'all the problems in the world' were freely discussed. For instance, on the evening of 12 December 1917 Christopher Addison, Lloyd George, Lord Milner and Victor Fisher (a Labour MP) retired to Waldorf's fireside after their meal to talk about the issues of war and peace, freed from the constraints of party politics. This varied group agreed on the need to forge a statement of Allied aims as the basis for eventual peace talks with Germany while at the same time preparing an extensive programme of social reform. They were already aware that a different Britain would emerge from the conflict. 'A good many old distinctions are dim these days and the country is ready for a bold move forward under state inspiration,' Addison recorded in his diary after the meeting.[59] Quite clearly, as Waldorf approached his fortieth year his links with traditional Unionist policy had become very tenuous. He might almost be called a revolutionary, for he looked to achieve major changes in both public institutions and attitudes.

Throughout his time in the 'garden suburb' Waldorf took part in two crusades on issues about which he felt passionately. One he was able to see successfully concluded; the other failed. The first was the establishment of a Ministry of Health. By the beginning of 1918, aided by his various committees and study groups, Waldorf had drafted a bill which he placed before the

Prime Minister. At the same time he went public with his proposals. A letter to *The Times* over the signatures of Astor and nine colleagues outlined the bill and stressed the need for its urgent introduction:

Sir, In view of the war wastage of manpower and of the public and unchallenged statement of a Minister of the Crown that 1,000 baby lives are unnecessarily lost every week, we desire to urge upon the Government the importance of creating a Ministry of Health without delay, in order not only to end this lamentable waste of man-power, but also to secure that co-ordination of health powers which is urgently needed.[60]

By the summer the government was ready to present the measure to Parliament. But the traditionalists and the Local Government Board caucus were determined to give it a rough ride. When Waldorf attempted to raise it in an adjournment debate in July, it was talked out by its opponents. Those same opponents had tried hard behind the scenes to prevent Lloyd George appointing 'that dangerously progressive Astor fellow' to his new position as Parliamentary Secretary to the Department of Food. The new bill had to wait until after the November election before running its parliamentary course. When it became law the following year Christopher Addison was appointed Minister with Waldorf as his Parliamentary Secretary.

For Waldorf and his colleagues, it was a major triumph, one of the few permanent governmental reforms to survive the war years; but Astor's battle with obfuscation and administrative red tape in the cause of state-led social reform was not over. One of the first campaigns launched by the new ministry was building the 'homes for heroes' Lloyd George had promised to returning servicemen. Addison provided house-building targets for local authorities and was determined they should be met, but local councils were not accustomed to being dictated to in this way. Several dug their heels in. Among the most recalcitrant was Plymouth. Waldorf found himself involved in a long-running and often acrimonious debate with his own constituents. A man of principle rather than a politician, he did not hold his fire in the interests of electoral advantage. He had a model made of some of the town's worst slums and put it on display in the public library. And he challenged the civic fathers in the local press: 'Plymouth [council] is slow and backward by comparison with others. It gives me no satisfaction to announce this publicly now. But it won't help in the provision of houses in Plymouth if local patriotism causes people to say that the Plymouth Town Council have done as much as they could . . . when in fact they have not.'[61]

The issue in which he failed was his attempt to introduce prohibition. To understand his stance on this we have to trace the stream of his social consciousness back to its moral and religious spring. Waldorf was brought up as a serious, very ethical young man who imposed a rigid discipline on himself. More than one person who knew him has described him as a 'saint', referring, presumably, to his almost ascetic self-control, his modesty, his generosity and his dedication to public service. The religious basis for his actions and beliefs was the reserved, stiff-upper-lip Anglicanism of his public school. With Nancy it was different. Reared in a more aggressive strain of Protestantism, she had an utter abhorrence of 'papistical superstition' and most moral issues presented themselves to her garbed in clear-edged black and white. About the 'evils of drink' she felt particularly strongly – and not without reason. She witnessed two brothers and a husband destroyed by alcohol abuse. After her marriage to Waldorf she impressed upon him the importance of total abstinence. As an undergraduate he had been a modest imbiber, but he found himself easily convinced by Nancy's arguments. Alcoholism was a serious problem in Britain in the early years of the century, and it was logical that one could only campaign against it if one set an example oneself. Waldorf found no difficulty in cutting out all consumption of strong drink completely. Perhaps his self-denial contained an element of rebellion against his father. One of the traits he disliked in William Waldorf was his fastidious connoisseurship in matters of food and drink. When he entered public life it seemed natural to Waldorf that one of the things he had to work for was a restriction of the nation's drinking habits.

There was more to it than that, however. As a young woman who had passed through several crises Nancy needed a source of inner strength which her highly moral and theologically well-defined church did not provide. This unconscious quest reached a crisis point early in 1914 when she was taken seriously ill and needed surgery. At that time the most successful current renewal force sweeping America was Christian Science, which laid special emphasis on healing. Nancy was introduced to it on her sickbed, responded wholeheartedly to its teachings, made a rapid recovery and was committed to it for the rest of her life. Most mornings she 'did the lesson' (the appointed daily Bible reading), and she made sure that her children did too. The tenets of her faith became the foundation stones of her thinking on all matters. She sought to convert all who came within her ambit. Her most notable success was Philip Kerr, who accepted Christian Science shortly after Nancy and remained a lifelong devotee. Waldorf did not succumb for several years (probably his conversion occurred in 1924), but he was deeply influenced by the atmosphere of religious certainty which pervaded his home.

His fight against 'the demon drink' was thus more than a campaign against a social evil. During the war it became a major strand in his plan for national salvation. Most unbiased commentators recognized that excessive consumption of alcohol was a major cause of low efficiency in the armed forces and the munitions industry. Milner claimed that, in the early months of the war, it counted for more wastage than enemy action. George v gave the nation a lead when he signed the 'king's pledge' and foreswore alcohol for the duration. Lloyd George set up a Central Liquor Control Board, on which Waldorf served, and several of its suggestions became law. Licensing hours were reduced. The sale of grain and spirits to the brewing industry was cut drastically so that these commodities could be available for food and munitions factories respectively. In the Carlisle area an experiment in state ownership of the liquor trade was tried. There were major armaments works in this district, and it was believed that tighter controls and weaker beer would make an appreciable impact on absenteeism. There is some evidence that the Carlisle scheme succeeded in this respect.

Waldorf Astor was not content with these achievements. Whether talking with army officers in training camps, writing memos to the Prime Minister or speaking in his constituency, he went at his task with the zeal of an evangelist. And, like an evangelist, he interpreted as martyrdom the attacks against him by the drink trade and politicians claiming to defend individual liberty. His work at Southern Command and on the Control Board brought him constantly into contact with examples of alcohol abuse, and other campaigners sent him their horror stories. These went into his files and were used for ammunition as opportunity served:

> A CO on the Western Front was determined to have his whisky cask brought into his dug out, no matter what the cost might be. Accordingly two of the men (privates) were despatched to a certain place to fetch the whisky; in doing so they were dangerously exposed to the enemy's gun fire. They succeeded in getting to the place, but while returning one of the men was hit and killed by a bullet . . . I wonder how the parents of the boy, who was not merely 'Killed in Action' but was, in my opinion, cruelly murdered, would feel did they only know how and why their boy fell.[62]

Waldorf was profoundly shocked by such reports and outraged by the growth of drunkenness and the related sexual immorality. He paid to bring a Methodist minister over from the United States to tour the country lecturing on prohibition. He believed it was important that people should know the facts about total proscription 'considering how the trade there and *here* is lying about it'.[63] Waldorf became convinced that prohibition was the only real answer. Early in 1917 he and Milner presented a report to the War Cabinet setting out in detail the savings that would be made in materials, human resources, shipping capacity and efficiency if there were a total ban on alcohol sales. Predictably, their proposals were rejected; prohibition was too much of a political hot potato. They were invited to draft a bill for state ownership of the liquor trade, as had been tried in Carlisle, but this too the government decided to drop under pressure from the Tory brewers' lobby. Waldorf was bitterly disappointed at the want of moral will on the part of the nation's leaders and even contemplated resigning over the issue.

On 20 February 1918, he *did* tender his resignation – not over the drinks question, although this still clearly rankled. Waldorf had come to believe that his political position was incompatible with his proprietorship of the *Observer*. 'It is most important', he wrote two weeks later, 'that the influence of the Press should be maintained. The public have lost confidence in Parliament and many newspapers. The time may come – will probably do so – when the *Observer* can give you and the Government greater help in prosecuting the war if there is no official connection between the two.'[64] Lloyd George disagreed and pressed him to stay. Not until July, after further exchanges of correspondence, as well as private conversations, was Waldorf able to extricate himself and pursue the course of action on which he was clearly resolved.

His motives were more mixed than his formal letters to the Prime Minister indicated. Certainly the relations between press and government had become very difficult. Lloyd George devoted considerable energy to winning the support of newspaper proprietors and editors for his conduct of the war. His attitude was 'if they can't be squared they must be squashed'. His attempt to square Northcliffe the previous autumn by offering him a cabinet post had brought a public rebuff in *The Times*: 'in the present circumstances I can do better work if I maintain my independence and am not gagged by a loyalty that I do not feel towards the whole of your Administration.'[65] Thereafter, Northcliffe's dislike of Lloyd George became obsessive, and his opposition, through his newspapers, was eventually maniacal. Waldorf had no government post, but he genuinely believed that Garvin's freedom of expression was compromised by his closeness to the Prime Minister. It was not just his editor's independence that concerned him. He wanted a freer hand to pursue in the Commons his own ideas on Ireland, social reform and, above all, drink. Waldorf Astor was determined to be his own man. Just as he had refused to be constrained by official Unionist policy, so now he valued his freedom of speech and action above his privileged position at Number 10. Though he was pledged in broad outline to Lloyd George's policies, he had become convinced that the government had run out of steam. In May he urged the Prime Minister to go to the country as soon as possible. 'It is becoming increasingly difficult for this stale House to pass any Bills,' he told Lloyd George.[66] And six months later, on 8 November, he admitted in an article for the *Western Press* that there was 'a great and wide gulf between the present House of Commons and the country'.

Waldorf Astor was too independent ever to become a career politician. Perhaps that was his loss. Perhaps it was also his country's loss. His swift rise to prominence at Westminster and his effective use of his position had given promise of what might have been a long and valuable parliamentary career. It was not to be. For the time being, however, he remained at the centre of things. He was returned to the Commons again in the November 1918 election and soon embarked with enthusiasm on his new work at the Ministry of Health.

While one generation of Astors was preparing for a new, different post-war life, another was facing the end of life. Although latterly a prey to gout and rheumatism, William Waldorf enjoyed excellent health throughout most of his seventy-one and a half years. He certainly cosseted himself and took regular 'cures' at continental spas. However, soon after the armistice he fell ill and required the care of an attendant nurse. Though he was not seriously incapacitated, his moods fluctuated. Now he lived permanently in his house at Brighton. Sometimes he happily entertained grandchildren there and made plans to get back to Sorrento for the first time since 1914. At others he resigned himself to infirmity:

> . . . I thank you for your good wishes as to my wretched health, but have small expectation of improvement, the machine being worn out. But I have delightful recollections to look back upon, not having failed in anything to which I seriously applied myself for the last thirty years which is more than most Royalties can say.[67]

Perhaps it was necessary for him to believe that lie, if what days remained to him were to be tolerable. He spent his waking hours with his books, his wines and the exquisite meals prepared by his chef. On fine days he walked out from his house along the sea front, to sit on the pier, looking at the grey Channel swell and dreaming of the Mediterranean. Sometimes John and Vi came to visit him. The others had to rely on their reports of the old man's health. Pauline wrote to ask if she could come to help look after him. Her letter brought a curt response: 'I told you three years ago that I did not wish to see you again. There is no reason for me to change my mind.'[68] No one knew how ill William Waldorf really was. Thus, when the end came, it was a great shock. He died on Saturday 18 October 1919. He had insulated himself against the affection of family and friends and, at the last, he did not even have the consolation of his magnificent collections. It seems that he never did discover an adequate reason to thank God for his creation.

Despite or possibly because of the recent estrangement, all William Waldorf's children grieved. Perhaps the loss was worst for Waldorf: he had not seen his father since January 1916 and had been unable to give or receive forgiveness. Reconciliation frustrated by death is a bitter, debilitating emotion and it must go some way towards explaining Waldorf's health and behaviour over the next couple of years. The funeral service at St George's, Hanover Square, was a quiet affair. Then the first Viscount's body was cremated and his ashes taken to Cliveden, to be placed in the ornate, Romanesque chapel which he had created from a neo-classical temple high up on the estate with dramatic views of the Thames.

As those closest to him came to terms with his death their common feeling was one of sadness for a man they would have loved to help but who put himself out of reach of human sympathy. It was left to Nancy to put what they all felt into words. Replying to a letter of condolence from Gerald Tharp, who had also suffered a recent bereavement, she wrote:

I don't believe that people like your mother ever are really lonely. The lonely people are the people like my poor father-in-law ... Do you know what keeps people apart – 'Fear' – our hearts are sometimes so cold and worldly or so selfish that we daren't show them ...[69]

And to a friend in Plymouth:

One's heart just cries for that poor, old gentleman, who, had he been born with 2 *sous*, I feel would have become a great man. Waldorf gets many of his fine traits from him.[70]

It was a perceptive comment by one transatlantic immigrant upon another.

CHAPTER 8

'All the substantial delights that vast wealth could procure'

In 1884 Mark Twain published *Huckleberry Finn.* Not only was this his finest work; it was the work which finally announced that the American novel had come of age. The developing culture of the new land had produced many writers of talent and genius. James Fenimore Cooper, Nathaniel Hawthorne and Herman Melville were great novelists, worthy to stand beside the best in the language. They all carried American literature away from its European origins and towards a completely new identity. But, as Ralph Waldo Emerson observed, 'We all lean on England.' *Huckleberry Finn* breathed the life of the United States heartland. In colour, language, characterization, philosophy it was uniquely American. Where the cultural avant-garde led, others, more cautiously, followed. Throughout the nineteenth century the arbiters of fashion and aesthetic taste had relied on the Old World for their inspiration. Even now it would be several decades before there would be any full flowering of the American arts. The best of Mark Twain's contemporaries, such as Henry James and William Dean Howells, were still, in part, 'bridge' figures, spanning the Atlantic. The distinctively American works of Scott Fitzgerald and Ernest Hemingway, and composers Charles Ives and Aaron Copland, together with the birth of ragtime, jazz and Hollywood, were yet to come.

The links between the Old World and the new were still strong. Those who wished to be in the height of fashion praised everything European and, as we have seen, made frequent trips across the ocean to refresh themselves at the wellsprings of 'civilization'. So, when William Waldorf made his historic decision to settle in England, he was following fashion just as surely as his Aunt Caroline was through her social rule book. He chose to base himself in London and Naples; she tried to recreate Paris and London in New York. Neither had much affinity with truly American culture. The separation, bordering at times on hostility, that occurred between the two branches of the Astor family therefore was not just a matter of three thousand miles of salt water. John Jacob III and William disliked each other and met rarely. Caroline's airs and graces exacerbated the rift. As for the sons of the next generation, sixteen years separated William Waldorf and John Jacob IV. The latter was still in his teens when his cousin left New York for his first long sojourn in Europe. The two men never really knew each other. So, for reasons part personal, part accidental, the two halves of the family drifted apart and led very different lives.

To say that the American Astors were dogged by misfortune would be a massive understatement. The married life of William and Caroline was basically non-existent. He spent progressively more time in Florida – or, more precisely *off* Florida aboard his boat, where prying eyes could not observe the activities of the owner and his friends. About 1890 he sold the *Ambassadress* and took delivery of the biggest and most luxurious steam yacht in the world. He called it *Nourmahal*. The word means 'light of the harem' and comes from the erotic oriental romance *Lalla Rookh*, by the Irish poet Thomas Moore. The name and the way of life it implies is symptomatic of William's rejection of the hollow pieties of polite society. New York's élite (or at least its feminine members) took the moral and religious example of Queen Victoria's court as their ideal:

> Going to church was a social function. Everyone was religious. The more successful in business you were during the week, the more devoutly you attended church on Sunday. Pierpont Morgan took up the collection at St. Bartholomew's, the Vanderbilt men roared out the hymns untunefully at Saint Thomas's. Everyone lionised the popular preachers, they were invited to the smartest houses in New York.[1]

Wealthy men who could not stomach such public piety or found it impossible to live up to it in their private lives – men like the Prince of Wales and the explorer Richard Burton – made careful arrangements for the discreet exercise of their vices. William Astor had found the best possible answer to the problem. Of course, tongues wagged about the 'goings on' aboard the *Nourmahal*, but nobody really *knew* what Mr Astor and his guests did as the yacht steamed indolently past the Keys or moored in the aquamarine waters of the Gulf of Mexico.

Caroline, frenziedly absorbed in organizing the Four Hundred, simply shrugged off the salacious stories about her husband.

> The rumours grew more and more exaggerated as they flew from mouth to mouth. Everyone wondered what Mrs Astor, giving her stately dinners and 'musicales' at her Fifth Avenue house, thought of it all, but their curiosity was never satisfied. When someone would ask tentatively after her husband she would reply placidly: 'Oh, he is having a delightful cruise. The sea air is so good for him. It is a great pity I am such a bad sailor, for I should so much enjoy accompanying him. As it is I have never even set foot on the yacht; dreadful confession for a wife, is it not?' And her smile would hold nothing but pleasant amusement over her inability to share her husband's interests.[2]

In fact, Caroline had much to be grateful for. William's constant presence in New York would certainly have cramped her style and, unlike some other husbands, he at least committed his indiscretions far away from home and family. And the 'queen' had a very effective way of silencing gossip: she simply withdrew her favour. Humiliated tittle-tattlers swiftly came to heel if they were forced 'out of circulation' for a few weeks. Nor should one exaggerate the strangeness of this marriage relationship, for it was far from unique: the story of Grace and Neily Vanderbilt closely parallels that of Caroline and William. In both America and Europe the high society machine was driven and maintained by women (who, after all, had nothing better to do, since they employed others to look after their homes and children). Husbands spent their non-working hours in all-male clubs and exclusive brothels, at the card tables and the race track. With varying degrees of enthusiasm they escorted their wives to those functions at which their presence was required.

The real sorrows that beset the American Astors came via the children. William and Caroline had four daughters to bestow in marriage – and with them princely dowries. They thus faced, in quadruplicate, the old problem which confronted all Astor parents – how to protect their girls from fortune hunters and from their own hearts. Emily, Helen, Charlotte and Caroline were guarded carefully during their impressionable years and more than one unsuitable romance was nipped in the bud. The eldest, Emily, was twenty-one before a 'possible' suitor appeared in the shape of James Van Alen. At least, Caroline thought this son of an elegant Civil War general was 'possible', William did not. For some reason, he disliked the Van Alens and refused his consent. There were angry scenes. Emily gave way to tears and tantrums. Her father flew into a rage and simply tied tighter the Gordian knot of his disapproval. It was Van Alen senior who sliced through it. The old soldier claimed that his family's honour had been besmirched and he called Mr Astor out. That had the desired effect. After a great deal of huffing and puffing, William climbed down and apologized. On 14 March 1876, with all appropriate extravagance, Emily and James were wed. Their happiness was short-lived: five years later Emily died during her fourth confinement.

Helen made a match of which no one could complain. She married a Roosevelt. James was the half-brother of Franklin Delano, and a nephew of Laura Astor (William's sister). Helen and James made a quiet, cultivated couple and soon moved to England to lead a life of leisure on a country estate near Ascot. This relationship, too, was doomed. Helen died in November 1893 at the age of thirty-eight.

The youngest girl, Caroline (known as 'Carrie'), did not have a smooth path to the altar. She fell in love at sixteen. That was bad enough – but even worse, the object of her affections was a son of 'new money'. The Wilsons had made their fortune from Civil War profiteering and were systematically marrying their way up the social ladder (they were known as the 'marrying Wilsons'). Richard T. Wilson had run cotton through the Union blockade and obtained inflated prices for it in England. After the war he had moved to New York from his native Georgia and bought 'Boss' Tweed's mansion on Fifth Avenue. His wife then set about arranging suitable matches for their daughters. One daughter married a Goelet, a second a Vanderbilt and the third ensnared the Hon. Michael Herbert, brother of the Earl of Pembroke. It was the Wilsons' son, Orme, who paid court to Carrie. No family could have been more *arriviste* and less suitable. Mrs Astor moved in with her usual determination – but this romance refused to be extinguished. Financial inducements were tried. They failed. Carrie was refused permission to see her lover. She languished alarmingly. Caroline eventually gave way. She told her friends that it was the sight of the young couple emerging from church hand in hand and completely absorbed in one another which had finally softened her heart. The truth may be that she had learned from experience or that she no longer had the necessary energy for a protracted domestic campaign. Even so, the couple had to pay a price for parental approval: they were not permitted to marry until 1884, when Carrie was twenty-three. Mrs Orme Wilson lived to the age of eighty-seven. She was the only one of William and Caroline's five children to reach old age.

The girl who caused her parents the greatest embarrassment and distress was their third daughter. Charlotte Augusta was named after her aunt but certainly lacked her serene and steady nature. In October 1879 she married James Coleman Drayton and set up home with him in Bernardsville, New Jersey. Over the next ten years she presented her husband with two boys and two girls, and there seemed no reason to believe that the Drayton domestic scene was not a happy and contented one. But there were underlying strains in the relationship and Charlotte turned for consolation to a neighbour, Hallet Borrowe. For several months the matter was kept within the family. When Drayton appealed to his in-laws, William informed his daughter that, if she did not stop making a fool of herself, he would disinherit her (a threat he carried out). Charlotte was by now too far adrift on a sea of turbulent emotion to be able to grasp the lifeline of reason. Whatever passion there was in the affair seems to have been largely on her side. Borrowe acted, if not honourably, at least sensibly; he took ship for England and thither the headstrong Charlotte pursued him. She had by now cast aside not only her feelings for her husband but also those for her children. She left Drayton money for their upbringing before setting sail for Europe in March 1892.

Charlotte was followed across the Atlantic in different vessels by both her husband and her father. Drayton tracked the couple to a London hotel. Here he challenged the 'seducer' to a duel, an invitation which Borrowe declined on the grounds that there was no legitimate cause of dispute between them. If Drayton could not keep his wife within doors or prevent her rushing off with a head stuffed full of romantic notions that was his affair. While these unsavoury exchanges were taking place, Charlotte travelled to Paris to join her father. In doing so she moved from scandal to tragedy. On 25 April 1892, William Astor died of a sudden heart attack in his hotel suite.

New York society and the press on both sides of the water were hugely enjoying the Astors' discomfiture. Not even William's unexpected demise brought a respectful silence. For a time it seemed that the queen of the Four Hundred would be forced to abdicate. She and her daughter were vilified in the gossip columns. She was accused of bribing Drayton to keep his mouth shut. Some columnists even opined that Charlotte's loose morals were no more than could be expected of the daughter of a notorious libertine like William Astor. Attendance at Mrs Astor's functions dwindled. In the event this crisis proved to be Caroline's finest hour. Charlotte returned to New York with her father's body and the family enjoyed a brief respite during their period of mourning.

However cool relations had been between Caroline and her husband, the news of his death came as a shock. It could not have arrived at a worse time. Everything seemed to be going wrong. Not only was she embarrassed by her daughter's behaviour, she was soon plunged into conflict with her nephew who, at the end of 1892, informed her of his intention of pulling down the neighbouring house to build a hotel. The timing of William Waldorf's decision may not have been accidental. His Victorian prudishness allowed him to feel no sympathy for his aunt's predicament. Neither in America nor in England did he and Mamie give any support to their Astor relations at this time of crisis. Adding to Caroline's discomfiture by virtually forcing her to move house may have been mere thoughtless insensitivity but is more likely to have been a deliberate gesture. The head of the Astor family was distancing himself from the unseemly behaviour of his relatives and doing his best to disperse the court of the self-appointed 'queen'. For some months the need to consult with architects and supervise the plans for a magnificent new residence did, at least, distract Caroline from her other anxieties and gave her an excuse for reducing her social engagements. The mourning household was, temporarily, left in peace.

Then public attention was roused again by the divorce proceedings. Interestingly, it was not the wronged husband who sued for divorce. The one who went on the offensive was Caroline. Charlotte had convinced her mother that no adultery had taken place, an assertion Borrowe was only too happy to corroborate. Since there was no question of Charlotte returning to her husband, Caroline urged her to have the matter out in court. Thus it was *Mrs* Drayton who obtained a divorce on the odd-sounding grounds of her husband's 'cruel suspicions as to her marital fidelity'. The verdict was handed down in the spring of 1894 and Charlotte Augusta was once again a free woman. Drayton retained custody of the children. Borrowe disappeared completely – and doubtless thankfully – from the scene.

What effect had all this had on Caroline's standing in society?

> Everyone wondered what Mrs Astor would do. Would she who had hitherto turned her back on anyone who had come before the divorce courts, apply her rigid code to her own daughter? The first reception at the Astor house after the case was crowded to the very doors. Every friend of the family was there to support, or condole, as the necessity might be. But whatever it was, the Queen could do no wrong. They would follow her faithfully. Their eyes turned anxiously towards her as they entered the salon . . . then they sighed with relief. Mrs Coleman Drayton was standing by her mother, calmly helping her to receive her guests.[3]

And where the faithful courtiers led, the hangers-on followed. The threat to the throne had been averted.

Nevertheless Charlotte's continued presence in New York could only be an embarrassment, and she herself wanted to escape from wagging tongues and sidelong glances. She returned to London within a few months and took a house in Hertford Street, Mayfair. In the summer of 1896 an unknown Scotsman appeared among Mrs Astor's Newport guests. The arrival of George Ogilvy Haig, of the celebrated whisky distilling family, occasioned little interest – distinguished British visitors were a common feature in the life of the *haut monde* – so for once the gossips were caught completely off guard. Not until the beginning of December did the *New York Herald* break the news that the mysterious Mr Haig was to be Mrs Drayton's next husband.

The wedding took place quietly in London on 17 December and was attended by about thirty members of the aristocracy and the diplomatic corps, the US Consul General signing the register as witness. The *New York Herald* pronounced: 'The wedding comes in the nature of a happy relief from an embarrassing situation whereby society was split up into opposing factions.'[4] The couple moved into a splendid house in Berkeley Square and George became a Member of Parliament. It was soon clear that Charlotte had inherited her mother's flair as a hostess and was intent on using it in the furtherance of her husband's career. Describing an entertainment given by Mrs Haig in July 1899, a London newspaper declared that Charlotte had 'thrown herself into the world of London with a heart and a half'.

> After the generous fashion of her country – which is the most hospitable in the

world – Mrs Haig gave an entertainment which was delightful. She had a concert that was better than any you could get for love or money, even at St. James's Hall.[5]

The writer went into ecstasies over the top international artists hired for the occasion at a cost of more than £400 and the sumptuous supper laid out in a marquee to the rear of the house. Perhaps the party was not quite up to her mother's standard, but it certainly impressed London society. Charlotte Augusta, it seems, had, at last, found her *métier*. Alas, her happiness was to be short-lived. In 1905, six years later, George Haig was taken ill and died.

One name that never appeared on Charlotte's guest lists was that of her cousin. William Waldorf was not a forgiving-and-forgetting sort of man. He kept his family quite separate from Mrs Haig and her set. It may therefore have been with some mortification that he watched one of Charlotte's relatives by marriage become a popular hero, and it was undoubtedly as well for his peace of mind that he never lived to see the names of Astor and Haig once more joined in matrimony. George Ogilvy Haig had a younger brother named Douglas, who had chosen a military career. William Waldorf's son John must have known him, for when he was a very junior captain in India, in the Viceroy's entourage, Lieutenant General Douglas Haig was chief of the general staff. In 1915 he was given command of the British Expeditionary Force in France. During the next, appalling three years Haig's reputation survived the hideous toll of casualties, the bungling of colleagues and the personal attacks of politicians and he emerged as commander of the largest British army that had ever been sent into battle. In the spring of 1918 the major German offensive of the war was launched against the Allied lines on the western front. Haig nerved his men with an order of the day which has become almost as famous as Nelson's at Trafalgar: 'With our backs to the wall and believing in the justice of our cause we must fight on to the end. The safety of our homes and the freedom of mankind alike depend upon the conduct of each one of us at this critical time.' The line held and in subsequent months the British and French forces launched the devastating counter-attacks which brought the war to an end.

In the aftermath of the conflict a grateful king and nation bestowed upon Haig an earldom, a gift of £100,000 and a country mansion. Just as pleasing to this essentially quiet, humble man was the birth of a daughter in 1919. Appropriately, she was christened Irene – which means 'peace'. Aunt Charlotte Augusta was one of the godmothers, although the girl was destined never to know her, since Mrs George Ogilvy Haig died the following year. Several years later Lady Irene Haig married a grandson of William Waldorf Astor.

Meanwhile, back in New York, the Astors were glad to put the years of trauma behind them as the old century rattled to a close. Caroline, who turned seventy in 1900, had emerged triumphant. Her new French Renaissance-style palace at 840 Fifth Avenue was one of the city's sights and the entertainments given there were more sumptuous than ever. The mansion was, in effect, a double residence, for Caroline's son, John Jacob IV, lived in part of it with his family. Here, as a newspaper had declared in its obituary of William, they continued to enjoy 'all the substantial delights that vast wealth could procure'. But misfortune had not finished with the American Astors.

From the start the cards were stacked against John Jacob IV (or 'Jack', as he was usually known). He grew up with a domineering, doting mother, four elder sisters and a father usually conspicuous by his absence. As if that were not bad enough, he was physically unprepossessing – tall, thin, gangling and almost uncoordinated. To the casual observer, he looked like what the press delighted in labelling him – an idiot. One not particularly ingenious reporter dubbed him 'Jack-Ass' and the name stuck. It is hardly surprising that he became shy, introverted and gauche. Few people were intimate with Jack Astor, because he found it difficult to relate to others, yet someone who did know him wrote that 'one cannot imagine anyone simpler, kinder or more considerate'.[6] Jack was one of those people who are referred to as 'accident prone'. For such unfortunates we tend to feel a muted sympathy: we are sorry that everything seems to go wrong for them; yet we have a sneaking feeling that they bring most of their troubles on themselves. Like some sort of psychic magnet, Jack attracted disaster. It is utterly in keeping with everything else about this malfunctioning human being that history remembers him – if it remembers him at all – not for his way of living, but for the manner of his dying. Yet both his life and his death were full of consequence for the dynasty – tragic consequence.

As a boy, he escaped whenever he could from the feminine chatter of the Astor household. Sometimes he simply retreated into himself and conjured up a dream world of fantasy and adventure. He also spent time with his father and particularly loved the country estate, Ferncliff, on the Hudson. He showed, early on, a talent for things mechanical. He liked pottering in the workshops at Ferncliff, bringing his vivid imagination to bear on the possibilities of copper tubing, wires and electric currents. Later he built his own laboratory, in which he produced inventions which were far from ridiculous – a bicycle brake, a new kind of marine turbine engine, a machine for removing surface dirt from roads. Inevitably, he was one of the first Americans to own a motor car. In 1894 he published a Jules Verne type science fiction novel entitled *A Journey into Other Worlds* in which he predicted future developments such as aeroplanes, television and space travel. It was not well written or startlingly original, but it proclaimed an enquiring mind.

It could be argued that two of the major events that shaped his life happened in the wrong order. In 1891 Jack got married, and in 1892 his father died. Had he entered into his inheritance first and become fully his own master, he might not have made the disastrous mistake of taking as his wife Ava Lowle Willing. Ava was darkly beautiful and of impeccable lineage. When she was introduced to New York society in 1890 she took it by storm. In the narrow, fashionable world in which they moved Jack and Ava were the most eligible bachelor and spinster of the year. When they were increasingly seen together it was eminently suitable – a vindication of everything the Four Hundred stood for. Caroline was delighted and ensured that her son's wedding was the most talked about event of the year.

It did not take John Jacob very long to realize the enormity of his error. A French observer of the New York scene described Ava as '*nonchalante et froide*'. She was self-willed, arrogant and insolent. Having landed the richest husband in America she was determined to spend his money as she pleased and give as little as possible in return. Nine months after the wedding she gave birth to a son – Vincent. It was almost eleven years before she had a second child – Alice – and there were strong rumours that Jack was not the father. Ava filled the house with her own friends, drawn from a very wide circle, and with them indulged her own pleasures irrespective of her husband's wishes. And those pleasures constantly changed. Where Caroline had been the mistress of fashion, Ava was its slave. She took up every new craze with enthusiasm, then abandoned it for the next to appear. Mah-jong, tennis, skiing followed each other in quick succession. Early in the new century bridge was all the rage. Jack could only watch his chameleon of a wife with mounting irritation. A contemporary chronicler has given us a picture of a man who was not master in his own house, even during a weekend house party in the country:

> Ava Astor invariably invited people like herself, ardent devotees of bridge, and from the moment they arrived they would have their noses glued to the card table. Their host, who detested bridge and was far more at home going at top speed in his new racing car or at the helm of his yacht in a storm . . . shambled from room to room . . . in a vain search for someone to talk to.

If he found consolation in playing a pianola, Ava would send a message asking him to stop, as it disturbed the players.

> He would go up to his room and dress faultlessly for dinner, come down, prepared to talk and entertain his guests, and find everyone scurrying upstairs to make hasty, last-moment toilets. Of course, they would all be late, which annoyed him intensely, for he made a god of punctuality, and the probability of a spoiled dinner in consequence did not serve to improve his temper, for he was a notable epicure. The house party would come down to find him watch in hand, constrained and irritable.
>
> Dinner was not an enjoyable meal . . . he had to listen to interminable post-

mortems – 'You should have returned my lead ...' 'I was waiting for you to play your queen ...' ... And immediately after dinner they would return to the card tables.

Matters did not improve on Sunday:

He would come downstairs ready for church in cutaway coat and immaculate topper, only to find rubbers in progress already. So he would sit alone in his front pew, come back to lunch off a tray in his study, and return to New York in the afternoon ...[7]

Small wonder that Jack lavished attention on the *Nourmahal.* He gave the yacht a complete refit – which included installing a sixty-seat dining saloon – and spent an increasing amount of time aboard. It was William and Caroline all over again – but with a significant difference. Jack's parents had been content to go their own ways, to put a brave face on their semi-detached relationship, and to be civil to each other in public. Jack and Ava, by contrast, had frequent furious rows regardless of whether there were servants or guests present.

Then, in 1898, John Jacob was presented with a golden opportunity to exchange, for a time at least, the domestic battleground for a real military confrontation. America went to war and Jack was in the thick of it. Like his uncle thirty years before, he volunteered for active service – and for very similar reasons. He was impelled by political conviction and a romanticized sense of adventure. He believed that it was incumbent on leading citizens to play a prominent part in great events. Yet underlying all this there was a need to prove to loud-mouthed critics – and perhaps to himself – that he was not just an empty-headed playboy.

The occasion for Jack's military interlude was the Spanish–American War. The dramatic rise of prosperity in the second half of the century forced upon the United States a new role in international affairs. She had emerged by 1895 as a major exporting nation and the world's third naval power. This inevitably brought clashes of interest with old colonial powers such as Spain and Britain, and other emerging industrialized countries like Japan. America was being groomed by events to play a new, more prominent part in the drama of world history, but her citizens were not agreed on what that part should be. Some – and John Jacob Astor was among their ranks – had no hesitation in demanding an imperialistic future for the USA. Continued progress, they argued, demanded the possession of secure overseas bases. Others opposed such expansionism on the grounds that it was antithetical to all that America stood for. She was not an enslaving power; she was the champion of free people everywhere. In the Cuban crisis of 1898 these two constituencies found common cause.

The people of Cuba were fighting for their independence from tyrannical

Spanish rule. America had considerable investments in the island and was inevitably damaged by the conflict. Self-interest and philanthropic principle combined to urge Washington to intervene on behalf of the nationalists. The government was determined to restrict its activity to diplomatic channels and this it did with an impressive degree of success for three years. Then, on the night of 15 February 1898, all pacific intentions were obliterated in a violent explosion which rocked the port of Havana. The US battleship *Maine* was destroyed – probably by a mine – with the loss of over 260 lives. War fever now swept the nation. 'Remember the *Maine*! To hell with Spain!' was the popular cry. Idealistic and glory-seeking young men flocked to the colours, and John Jacob Astor was determined not to be found wanting.

He hurried to Washington to seek out his distant relative, Theodore Roosevelt, who had recently been appointed Assistant Secretary of the Navy. Teddy was a jingoist and a man after Jack's heart, although they had not always seen eye to eye politically. As a member of the reformist wing of the Republican party, Roosevelt had been engaged, on and off, for seventeen years in a campaign against boss rule in New York. Now, however, his aid and that of other influential friends was invaluable to Jack. While seasoned officers complained bitterly, Astor bought himself a commission by dint of lending *Nourmahal* to the navy and providing a $75,000 artillery battery for use in the Philippines, another theatre of war in the conflict with Spain. In June Jack sailed with the bulk of the army to Cuba, as a member of the headquarters staff.

The Cuban campaign was brief and relatively bloodless. The US Navy had command of the sea and, thanks largely to the incompetence of the Spanish command, the defenders' ground forces were outclassed and outnumbered. The only major actions were fought for possession of Santiago, Cuba's second city. On 1 July the battle of San Juan Hill took place. With immense bravura Teddy Roosevelt personally led his own corps of 1st US Volunteer Cavalry (the 'Rough Riders') in a charge on the Spanish gun emplacements. It was hot work involving sorties from various vantage points under heavy fire. Only after several hours was the hill taken.

Astor watched with other officers and a bevy of newspaper correspondents from what was adjudged – inaccurately as it transpired – to be a safe distance. The war artist Frederic Remington described how their position soon became too hot for comfort:

> It was thoroughly evident that the Spaniards had the range of everything in the country. Some gallant soldiers and some as daring correspondents . . . did their legs proud there. The tall form of Major John Jacob Astor moved in my front in jack-rabbit bounds. Prussian, English, and Japanese correspondents, artists, all the news, and much high-class art and literature, were flushed, and went straddling up the hill.[8]

Jack certainly had his share of excitement in the battle for Cuba, but even before the brief conflict ended with the capitulation of Santiago on 16 July, he had been forced to withdraw ingloriously from the fray. The novel discomfort of sleeping under damp canvas brought him out in a mild fever. He was sent home to carry dispatches to Washington and to recuperate.

Poor Jack. Even his most glorious episode only presented him to the newspaper-reading public as a figure of fun. He proudly used the title 'Colonel' for the rest of his life (he ended up with the rank of lieutenant-colonel), but no one regarded this as anything other than an affectation. It was the same with his magnificent yacht. Jack had made it into one of the wonders of the seven seas, but the only news about the *Nourmahal* that made the headlines was the accidents in which it was frequently involved. The most celebrated was a collision with the Vanderbilt yacht off Newport which delighted the press by leading to a lengthy and acrimonious court case.

As William Waldorf had already discovered, by the 1890s anything a member of the Astor family did was sure to be presented in the worst possible light. John Jacob actually managed his property portfolio more creatively than either his father or grandfather had done. It may have been because he was spurred on by his cousin's success, but he showed a definite interest in commissioning impressive buildings on Manhattan's chief thoroughfares. One edifice which he did *not* erect showed New Yorkers that John Jacob Astor was not quite the fool he was taken for. He owned the Schermerhorn Building, an office block on lower Broadway. In 1895 the American Surety Company acquired the neighbouring site and began to construct what was then one of the tallest buildings in the city, rising to twenty-one storeys. This, of course, diminished the value of the Schermerhorn – but not for long. Jack let the American Surety Company complete their work and then announced that he was going to emulate them by raising an equally tall building on his land. This would have completely blocked the windows on one side of the splendid new edifice. There was only one way the developers could prevent this: they were obliged to lease the Schermerhorn Building for $75,000 a year.

But the St Regis was Jack's proudest accomplishment. The hotel he built at Fifth Avenue and 55th Street deliberately continued the social revolution begun by the Waldorf-Astoria. More and more the priestesses of fashion and their acolytes were performing their rituals in public. Instead of 'going calling' they met for lunch in the city's restaurants, and those same restaurants became the venues for theatre parties and elaborate dinners. Towards the end of the century Caroline Astor bestowed her benediction on the changing mode by dining at Sherry's – and what a sensation that caused! Next morning the gossip pages were full of it:

ilbert Stuart's first portrait of John Jacob I (above left) did not please the young businessman.
:rhaps the artist read the ambitious and ruthless Astor's character too well. A later portrait (above
:ht) made Astor appear almost benign.

eorge Astor's musical instrument business grew from modest beginnings. He began as a flute-
aker but by the turn of the 19th century he was building organs and pianos. This impressive
uare piano was made for Thomas Jefferson's house at Monticello.

In the years when John Jacob I was establishing himself as one of the city's leading businessmen New York was a modest port town of around 50,000 inhabitants surrounded by farmland. Broadway (below), on which Astor already owned property, was the only impressive thoroughfare.

By the time of John Jacob I's death in 1848 New York had expanded to a city of half a million people. Astor now owned several blocks of property in the area bounded by 5th Avenue, 42nd Street, the Hudson and Central Park.

Fort Astoria (below), John Jacob I's visionary Pacific coast settlement, did not survive conflict with the British and the Indians. Yet the unoccupied site was restored to the USA after the War of 1812 and was an important factor in enabling the government to lay claim to Oregon Territory in 1846. Astor thus saw his dream realized before his death.

William Backhouse Astor. His father prophesied of him that he would not make a fortune but that he would not lose one either. He proved an efficient but unimaginative steward of the Astor millions.

John Jacob Astor III *was a man of cultured tas who did his duty by the family business and was, according to his son, too diffident to take up a public career.*

;aroline Astor used the fortune she married to establish herself as the undisputed 'queen' of New 'ork society. Her French Renaissance-style house on Fifth Avenue (above and below) housed a ·vish collection of antiques and works of art bought in Europe. Her annual ball was the highlight ' the social season (opposite below). The four hundred couples who received invitations constituted ıe élite of Manhattan.

Two cousins who warmly loathed each other gave New York a new generation of luxury hotels. The genteel and severe William Waldorf (left) despised John Jacob IV *(right), the playboy who was dominated by his mother and his wife, Ava.*

'he carriage entrance of the Waldorf Hotel on 34th Street brought a touch of Parisian elegance to Ianhattan (opposite below). When the Waldorf was linked with John Jacob IV*'s rival concern next oor, the Waldorf-Astoria provided fashionable New Yorkers with a new social experience. The umptuous tea room (below) became a venue at which to see and be seen. If this was the apogee f old world elegance, Waldorf's Hotel Astor, opened in 1904, set the tone for the future. The Astor ıbove), on what became Times Square, was soon* the *New York meeting place.*

William Waldorf, an austere widower after his wife's death in 1894, never really knew how to rela to his children. This photograph (c. 1900) shows him on a Scottish holiday with Waldorf, John and Pauline.

Nothing better demonstrates William Waldorf's romantic yet severe nature than the Renaissance-style business headquarters he built at Temple Place. This lofty baronial hall was his office.

Nancy Shaw was the most extraordinary phenomenon ever to marry into the Astor family. A beautiful, vivacious Virginian, she brought with her a young son, Bobbie, by a previous, disastrous marriage. Augustus John caught her mercurial temperament in this sketch for a painting (above). Between Nancy and Bobbie (shown here as a World War I *officer) there was an obsessive, destructive bond.*

William Waldorf's second son, John (above left), returned from the First World War minus a leg and plus a devoted wife, Violet (daughter of a viceroy of India). They brought up a family of five at Hever (above right). The castle and estate were a paradise for children. This long-vanished worl[d] of luxury and privilege is well illustrated by Philip de Laszlo's Gainsborough-esque portrait of John and Vi's second son, Hugh (below right). Hugh spent most of his childhood prostrate with tuberculosis. The photograph of Violet (below left) shows her in ATS uniform during the Second World War.

Cliveden, Waldorf and Nancy's Buckinghamshire home, became, between the wars, famous for its political house parties. Many of the great and powerful assembled in this sumptuous mansion with its superb views along the Thames. Here, according to the left-wing press, was born the 'Cliveden Set', a pro-Nazi cell. 'Hitler's Friends in Britain' was a scurrilous pamphlet produced by the Communist Party.

During the Second World War the Astors served in a variety of ways. Waldorf and Nancy put heart into the citizens of blitzed Plymouth (she was MP; he was Lord Mayor). Among other activities, they organized dances on the Hoe to raise morale (above). Michael and Jakie (inseparabl as youngsters) took up arms like the other Astors of their generation (below left). Meanwhile, in the USA, Vincent (below right) did valuable work in naval intelligence.

After years of happy marriage and political partnership, Waldorf and Nancy drifted apart in their later years. The main cause of friction was Waldorf's insistence that his wife should give up her parliamentary career. She left the House of Commons in 1945 after twenty-six years of service (below). The portrait of Waldorf at his desk (above) is by John Mac Lure Hamilton.

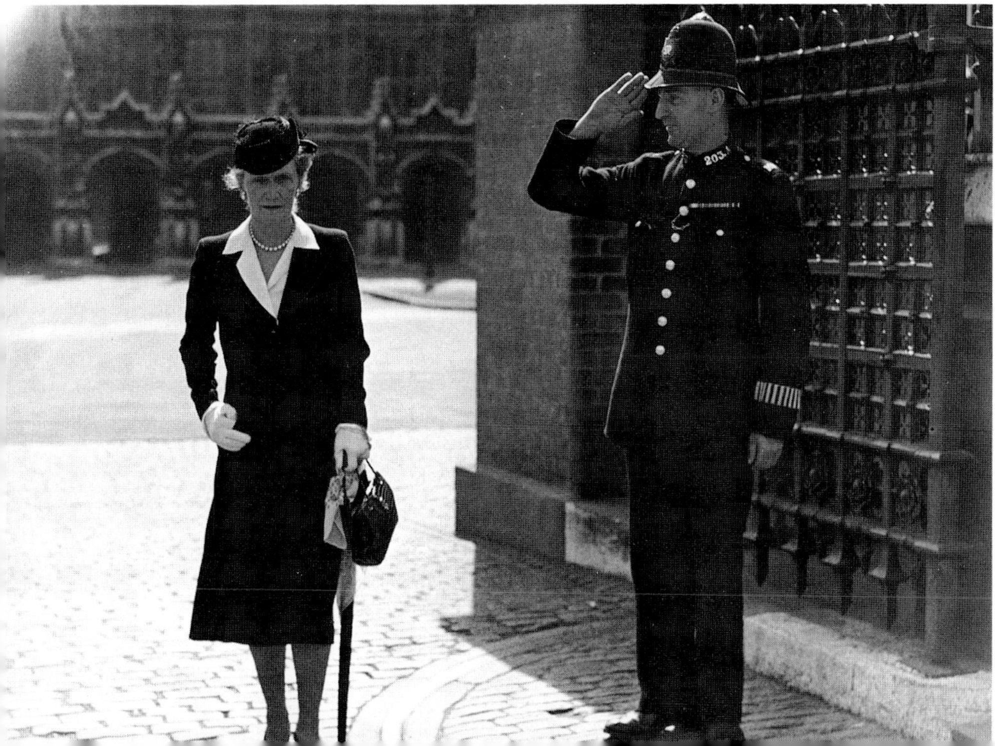

In the post-war years the idyllic world of Hever was coming to an end. John still pursued his various hobbies with enthusiasm. A family friend made gentle fun of Baron Astor passions for archery and painting (above). But in 1963 changes in the tax laws forced him to leave the country. As an elderly exile he used a buggy to get round his much smaller estate in France (centre). His son, Gavin, continued to run Hever but two disastrous floods in 1958 and 1968 (below) hastened the day when the castle and grounds had to be sold.

THE OBSERVER
· 1791 ·
22, Tudor Street, London, E.C.4
Fleet Street 9991
SUNDAY, NOVEMBER 4, 1956

EDEN

WE wish to make an apology. Five weeks ago we remarked that, although *we* knew our Government would not make a military attack in defiance of its solemn international obligations, people abroad might think otherwise. The events of last week have proved us completely wrong: if we misled anyone, at home or abroad, we apologise unreservedly. We had not realised that our Government was capable of such folly and such crookedness.

Whatever the Government now does, it cannot undo its air attacks on Egypt, made after Egypt had been invaded by Israel. It cannot undo the deliberate employment of haste so that our nearest allies had no opportunity to express disagreement. It can never live down the dishonest nature of its ultimatum, so framed that it was certain to be rejected by Egypt.

Never since 1783 has Great Britain made herself so universally disliked. That was the year in which the Government of Lord North, faced with the antagonism of almost the whole civilised world, was compelled to recognise the independence of the American Colonies. Sir Anthony Eden has the unenviable distinction of leading the first Administration since the days of George III to reach such an isolated moral position. His eighteenth-century predecessors succeeded in losing us an empire. Sir Anthony and his colleagues have already succeeded in losing us incalculable political assets.

So long as his Government represents this country, we cannot expect to have a good standing in the councils of the nations. It has attempted to prove those councils futile by rendering them futile. This it has done by, first, frustrating the Security Council of the United Nations through the use of the veto, and then by defying an overwhelming vote in the General Assembly. The Eden Government has become internationally discredited.

*

EVER since 1945, there have been two cardinal features of British external policy. The first has been to uphold the rule of law with special reference to the United Nations. The second has been the steady progress away from imperialism, exemplified in the full emancipation of Burma, India, Pakistan, Ceylon, West Africa and the West Indies. Neither of these cardinal features of our national policy was sincerely endorsed by the leaders of the Conservative Party, as we now see. In the eyes of the whole world, the British and French Governments have acted, not as policemen, but as gangsters. It will never be possible for the present Government to convince the peoples of the Middle East and of all Asia and Africa that it has not been actively associated with France in an endeavour to reimpose nineteenth-century imperialism of the crudest kind.

In these circumstances, what should be done? Is there any way of retrieving, in some degree, the errors of the last six days? In our view, there is one essential. Sir Anthony Eden must go. His removal from the Premiership is scarcely less vital to the prospects of this country than was that of Mr. Neville Chamberlain in May, 1940. Then the decision rested—as it does now—with the Conservative Party. Then, to their everlasting credit, some forty Conservative members marched through the lobby in opposition to their party leader. By their vote on that summer evening, they changed the course of British history and rescued their party from utter disgrace.

We are, of course, aware that in last week's Commons debate there was only one dissentient voice on the Conservative Benches. But this certainly does not mean that the whole Conservative Party, inside and outside Parliament, is solidly behind the Prime Minister. It is already evident that many loyal members of the party view the actions of the last week with the deepest disgust. It is for them to make their voices heard, as Mr. Nutting has already done. It should be made abundantly clear that the disastrous policy upon which the Government has embarked is opposed, not only by the Opposition parties, but by a great body of Tory opinion as well.

*

WHETHER the Conservative Party can save itself from obliteration for a generation now depends on whether it produces an honest parliamentary rebellion that contributes to retrieving the national situation. But whatever the Conservative Party may do, it is essential that the world should know that the Eden Administration no longer has the nation's confidence. Unless we can find means of making that absolutely clear, we shall be individually guilty of an irresponsibility and a folly as great as that of our Government.

The Eden Administration has, throughout this summer, shown that it does not understand the sort of world we live in. It is no longer possible to bomb countries because you fear that your trading interests will be harmed. Nowadays, a drowning man on a raft is the occasion for all shipping to be diverted to try to save him; this new feeling for the sanctity of human life is the best element in the modern world. It is the true distinction of the West. Our other distinction is our right of personal independence and responsibility in politics—a right that must be exercised.

It is for every individual in this country who is against the Government's attack on Egypt to say so by writing to his Member of Parliament, lobbying him, demonstrating in every legitimate way. Nations are said to have the governments they deserve. Let us show that we deserve better.

Under David Astor (below) the Observer *emerged as a radical Sunday paper which fearlessly attacked injustice and stood up for oppressed minorities. Many believe that the newspaper's 'finest hour' was when it fiercely denounced Anthony Eden over the Suez crisis of 1956. It was a brave move but it cost the* Observer *dear in lost circulation.*

A typical picture of Bill Astor (3rd Viscount) (left). He was a fun-loving man who liked to se[e] others enjoy themselves and was generous to a fault. This, couple[d] with a lack of wisdom over the choice of friends, helped to land him in trouble during the Profumo crisis.

After his father's early death, William became Viscount Astor. He is a leading member of the House of Lords and is shown here, as the Queen's representative, receiving President Gorbachev on a visit to Britain (below).

Even in the palmiest days of the Waldorf-Astoria one never saw the very ultra people dining and breathing the same air as . . . the 'middle classes'. Now and then people who were on the tip-top, and who had good sense enough to enjoy themselves and go wherever they pleased, would drop into the Waldorf-Astoria . . .

But I never dreamed that it would be given to me to gaze on the face of an Astor in a public dining-room.[9]

It was the thin end of a very thick wedge. Bold trend-setters appeared at restaurant tables in dresses which displayed bare necks and shoulders. 'Shameless! Disgusting!' muttered other diners. When a lady took her Parisian vanity case out in public to adjust her make-up the head waiter of Sherry's rushed across to ask if she was ill and required conducting to the ladies' room. But when another avant-garde young woman calmly lit up a post-prandial cigarette, that was too much for the establishment; she was asked to extinguish it or leave. Of course, it was only a matter of time before even this risqué behaviour was tolerated also.

Jack Astor's eighteen-storey St Regis, opened in 1904 at a cost of $5.5 million, was intended to cater for this liberated smart set. It bristled with innovations designed to provide the maximum luxury for guests. It was the first hotel to have air-conditioning; the first to provide telephones in every bedroom; the first to have mail-chutes in the halls. There was even a library of leather-bound books for guests to browse in. It had a top floor skylight ballroom and, of course, an immense dining room. Harry Lehr once hosted a meal there for 150 guests, all seated at one table. It was so long that the hotel staff, laying out the silver, crystal and porcelain, communicated by telephone from one end of the room to the other. The fittings were of marble and bronze and – ultimate concession to the new cult of casualness – there was an open café spilling on to the pavement. The St Regis was Jack Astor's pride and joy, yet the hotel had been an afterthought. His original intention had been to construct a discreet office block on the site. Only subsequently did he decide that a hotel would be more profitable, more fun – and one in the eye for the Vanderbilts. The railway millionaires had established themselves so securely on this stretch of Fifth Avenue that it was known as 'Vanderbilt Alley'. Jack's nautical confrontation with Cornelius Vanderbilt still smarted, and he therefore took a particular delight in establishing a very public Astor presence in the middle of 'enemy' territory.

At the same time as the St Regis, Jack built the Knickerbocker Hotel where 42nd Street intersects with Broadway. It was a slightly downmarket establishment to cater for those who could not quite afford the luxury of the St Regis. Yet the decor was every bit as exclusive and the interior designers, Trowbridge and Livingston, made extensive use of stained glass, murals, tapestries and sculpture.

Jack's interest in building extended to his own country home. At Ferncliff he constructed a vast indoor sports complex which housed a marble swimming pool, a tennis court, two squash courts, a billiard room, a bowling alley and even a rifle range. It seems that not all Ava's guests were slavish devotees of bridge. Mrs Astor, emancipated young woman that she was, loved exercise. She was one of the first ladies to sport a tennis skirt which revealed a daring expanse of ankle. She also led the fashion for winter sports in Switzerland. She made frequent trips to the Continent, alone, while Jack pottered with his yacht and his fleet of motor cars.

When William grew apart from his wife he took his pleasure with professional women and discreet ladies who went aboard the *Nourmahal* knowing precisely what they were letting themselves in for. Jack was unable to submit to such a frank dichotomy in the intimate side of his life. His sexual frustration showed itself in clumsy advances made to the sisters, daughters and wives of his friends. Once again, such action only made him look ridiculous. As the new century established itself the only thing that kept Jack and Ava together was Jack's mother. In December 1905 Caroline had a stroke. Although she recovered most of her faculties, there could be no question of subjecting her to the distress of a second Astor divorce. The 'queen' of the Four Hundred breathed her last on 30 October 1908 at the age of seventy-eight. Almost immediately her son and daughter-in-law set in hand secret arrangements for the dissolution of their marriage. It was one of the most successful manoeuvres of Jack's life. The lawyers handled the proceedings in closed session in November 1909 and the press knew nothing about it until Colonel Astor issued a public statement.

For months Jack was like a man released from prison. He ordered a new yacht. He carried out enormous alterations at 840 Fifth Avenue. He entertained lavishly. He went out and about in society. And society, now more tolerant and easygoing, seemed disposed to forgive and forget – until this silly man committed what appeared to many to be the ultimate silliness. He became involved with a girl who was not only almost thirty years his junior, but was the daughter of a small-time Brooklyn businessman. Like Jack she was the victim of an ambitious mother. Mrs Force was very conscious that her family had come down in the world since the days when her grandfather, Thomas Talmage, had been Mayor of Brooklyn. She was determined to regain her rightful place in society, and the way to do it was to parade her daughter's very obvious charms. She was immediately successful. At the age of sixteen Madeleine ensnared William Dick, heir to a sugar fortune. A wedding was imminent, but then a very much larger fish swam into the pool. Jack Astor met the pretty Madeleine Force in the summer of 1910. The following year he married her in the ballroom at Beechwood, his house at Newport. A few weeks later Colonel Astor proudly presented his bride to Manhattan society – and was roundly snubbed. Almost twenty years had passed since Charlotte Augusta's indiscretion. It had taken all Caroline's authority and force of character to brazen out that scandal. But Caroline was no more, and the wealthy matrons who had done obeisance to her were not going to have an ill-bred chit of a girl foisted upon them in her place.

Jack hastened to remove his beloved Madeleine from the poisonous atmosphere of committed snobs and false friends. He decided to show his wife the sights of Europe and Egypt. In March 1912 Madeleine discovered herself to be pregnant. Her considerate husband decided on an immediate return to New York. The birth of another Astor was an important event. If the baby turned out to be a boy he would stand to inherit half his father's fortune, which already stood at about $90 million. Come the autumn Jack would have to change his will. With huge sums like that at stake, it was important to keep all the legal strings neatly tied. It was not only his wife's condition that inspired the decision to travel home immediately. This lover of things nautical and student of technological progress was naturally excited at the possibility of crossing the Atlantic on the world's newest, most luxurious and up-to-date liner, which was about to make its maiden voyage. With eager anticipation he booked passages for himself and Madeleine aboard the *Titanic*.

When disaster overwhelmed the vessel in the small hours of 15 April 1912 Colonel Astor was one of the first passengers to be informed. Such evidence as there is insists that the tall American was calm throughout the crisis. He roused his wife, helped her into her life-jacket and saw her safely stowed in one of the boats. He asked if he might accompany Madeleine because of her condition but was firmly told that the rules were strictly 'women and children first'. When the terrified girl cried that she did not want to leave him, he gently insisted. He kissed her, promised to see her soon and waved as the boat was lowered from the already sloping deck. He helped some other women into the next lifeboat – the last to get away from the ship – and nothing more is known of him. The Astor millions were no use to him as the *Titanic* upended itself and plunged to the bottom of the Atlantic, and he was no use to the Astor millions. Dying without making full provision for his widow and his as yet unborn son was Jack Astor's final misfortune. It ensured the ultimate dispersal of the family riches into other hands.

CHAPTER 9

'Trying to keep their feet against the strong currents of reaction and selfishness'

During the inter-war years virtually all the British Astors were involved in politics. They exercised undoubted influence in national and international affairs. How extensive and of what nature was this influence? Some observers found it irritating. Some considered, or affected to consider, that it was sinister. Only by tracing the relationship of members of the family with the makers of policy and the organs which helped to frame public opinion can we obtain a clear picture of the Astors and their 'set'.

The immediate aftermath of war saw the most politically involved member of the family actually stepping back from his position in the forefront of national life. On the death of the first Viscount Astor in October 1919, Waldorf was obliged to forsake the Commons and assume his father's title, which he did with extreme reluctance. Ever since the 1918 election he had thrown himself into the work of reconstruction. In his constituency, as we have seen, he was actively campaigning for 'homes for heroes'. This meant more than battling with the local council over their building programme. He personally examined the availability of suitable sites and put up £20,000 of his own money to get one housing scheme off the ground. He was involved in programmes to provide playing fields, to examine juvenile unemployment, improve education and provide nursery school facilities for working mothers.

There was a great deal to be done at the Ministry of Health. A whole new administrative machinery had to be set in motion. The forces of reaction had to be confronted or assuaged, for it was not only the Plymouth councillors who regarded the extension of state control as 'back door socialism'. But more important was the actual work of the department – 'getting things done', as Waldorf said. This involved him in committee work, writing reports and speaking in various parts of the country on subjects as diverse as regulations to ensure the purity of milk and measures to combat the spread of venereal disease. In September 1919 he toured Belgium and Germany with Addison to see how those countries were coping with the problems of reconstruction, particularly with regard to housing, trade and transport.

His letters home reveal a sensitivity not common among his countrymen in the early days of their victory over the Boche:

> It really makes one shudder to transpose oneself and to picture England occupied by the Germans. Troops billeted in all the villages – swarming in Manchester and Birmingham – sentries with fixed bayonets guarding the big hotels.
>
> I'm told that the Germans were prepared to accept with reasonable equanimity all our troops but that what has really upset them has been the arrival of the English wives. To have their Cologne occupied by women – to see the English officers strolling about with their womenfolk really makes them feel they are down and out.
>
> One hardly sees any children of from one year to four. It is said the babies died thro' lack of food . . . it does seem a pity to see so many of our troops just idling and becoming confounded loafers hanging about. The French are hated – I'm told they are very insolent and overbearing.[1]

These scenes of a defeated and demoralized people deeply affected Waldorf's attitude towards the Versailles settlement and the later political developments in central Europe.

But the main reason for the visit of Waldorf and his colleagues concerned domestic not international affairs. One of the recommendations they brought back was that the government should emulate their continental neighbours in the development of 'garden suburbs', where work in agriculture and light industry could be locally available and residents could be encouraged to a measure of self-sufficiency by cultivating allotments. The minister and his aides envisaged between twenty and thirty such 'garden cities' of 4,000 houses each, built by private developers on land bought by the government.[2] A start was made on this policy (most notably in Welwyn Garden City, Hertfordshire), but the country was not yet ready for such an extension of centralized control.

Waldorf's closest political allies were very interested in his first-hand observations on continental recovery. Like him they were appalled by the protracted and labyrinthine nature of the peace negotiations, and the draconian solutions to complex issues of national sovereignty imposed by the victorious powers. It was the serious limitations of European diplomacy which led the Round Tablers to a new initiative. They were appalled by the prospect of rival statesmen trying to settle thorny, passion-rousing problems without adequate knowledge of the relevant facts and without the backing of instructed opinion in their own countries. Philip Kerr, one of their number, was present in Paris throughout the negotiations as Lloyd George's personal adviser on foreign affairs. It was actually Kerr who drafted the 'war guilt' clause of the treaty, which totally humiliated Germany (and which he later came to regret bitterly). Astor was therefore closely informed on everything that was happening at the peace talks and he was profoundly disturbed by what he heard. It was at his instigation that the Royal Institute of International Affairs was set up, chaired by himself, assisted by Lionel Curtis. In its London home, Chatham House, it became an independent body for the collection and objective dissemination of facts. Over the years its library, its conferences and its own publications would be used by students, statesmen and administrators from all over the world.

Waldorf was, of course, interested in the moves towards international co-operation which emerged after the war. In the summer of 1918 he had been appointed British representative of the Allied Food Council, whose potential power was as extensive as its avowed aims were philanthropic. It had come into being as an agency of the Supreme War Council, set up on America's entry into the war, but Astor was already looking beyond its immediate strategic function. In a memo to the Cabinet he prophesied that the council would

> enable the Allies to secure almost complete control of the world's supplies of food outside the Central Empires and Russia. Not only will a new war weapon be forged but the organisation will also be the means through which the enemy countries will ultimately obtain supplies and therefore an effective instrument will have been created for carrying the world through the trying period of reconstruction, when an effective association between nations in economic matters will be the strongest and most essential foundation for the re-establishment of permanent peace and order throughout the world.[3]

Such a view presupposed a high degree of collaboration between the world's main producer nations and was bound in with the widely shared hope for the establishment of some kind of 'world parliament' such as President Woodrow Wilson had recently projected in his 'Fourteen Points'. His experience on the Allied Food Council in 1918 might have caused Waldorf to reflect on the likelihood of such a utopian scenario. He experienced considerable difficulty with Herbert Hoover, the chairman (later US President). America was, of course, vital in providing the food aid which the European allies and other war-ravaged countries desperately needed (she eventually weighed in with 18.5 million tons), but Astor found Wilson 'difficult to handle' because he was advised by Hoover that Britain was not pulling her weight in the war effort. 'Hoover has formed strong views on war strategy on insufficient general knowledge as a result of talks to Pershing and Foch,' he complained to Lloyd George. 'He thinks Britain is opposing the big break through on the western front . . . because she won't make the necessary sacrifices (domestic).'[4] These problems largely disappeared with the armistice, but they foreshadowed the suspicion and isolationism which were to keep America out of the League of Nations.

On this subject, too, Waldorf had well-informed, well-thought-out, detailed views. In January 1919, while the statesmen were still discussing the terms of the Covenant of the League of Nations, he ran off on the *Observer* presses a pamphlet entitled *Co-operative Basis for a League of Nations*, in which he stated that the proposed body would only be effective if it had considerable powers – and not just political powers. Waldorf realized that arrangements for the policing of boundaries and the settlement of international disputes would not save the world from more atrocities unless there was an international forum for dealing with fundamental social grievances and economic development. Such a forum, he insisted, would have to have teeth. It must, for example, be able to regulate all international transport, impose high standards of health control, standardize working conditions and establish universal rights in industrial relations. Such ideas seemed dangerously progressive to people in comfortable Britain who had little understanding of the basic instability of many contemporary societies. Some disgruntled readers doubtless reflected that Mr Astor's proposals posed a greater threat to personal and national freedoms than the manifesto of the Communist International, which was produced a few weeks later.

Involved as he was in all these world-changing events, Waldorf had given little thought to what he would do when his father died. He was advancing his career at Westminster with considerable success and had clearly been marked as a young man with a brilliant political future. He had no reason to believe that Viscount Astor's death was imminent. He had not met his father for almost four years and can only have envisaged him as a well-cosseted man who habitually enjoyed rude health: none of the family, as we have seen, realized the seriousness of William Waldorf's last illness. Even when he did speculate about the future, Waldorf may well have been inhibited from calculating, and certainly from discussing with Nancy, his reaction to the death of a father from whom he was estranged. Even so, there is something startling about the confusion which fell upon Waldorf in the second half of October 1919. His grief at losing a parent with whom he was never reconciled was very real. For once Nancy does not exaggerate when she writes: 'I *never* remember going through a darker week. Never in my life. Waldorf's and Pauline's suffering was hard to see,' and 'I know how you will feel for Waldorf . . . it has been the most soul-trying week of his life.'[5] What made it worse was that he was unable to devote himself entirely to the formalities attendant on the funeral arrangements, public notices, reception of condolences, and so on – formalities which are important in the purging of emotions. Now he *had* to take careful and concentrated thought about his future. As soon as the first Viscount's death was announced sections of the press were speculating on whether Nancy would take over her husband's parliamentary seat. The issue had first been raised earlier in the year when a Hull MP had died and there had been some talk of his widow stepping into his shoes. However, the couple never entertained the idea of Nancy making a career in the Commons. They talked with friends and colleagues in Devon and London, but mostly they brooded over the situation alone at Cliveden. Writing to J. J. Judge on 25 October Nancy expressed her fervent prayer that Waldorf would not have to 'give up Plymouth'. 'Never in my life have I seen anyone so wholeheartedly long to do what is right . . . so he will be shown the way,' she observed. By now the constituency party had asked her to accept nomination, but husband and wife were agreed that a different course of action must be explored first. The idea of standing for Parliament was, as she told Gerald Tharp, 'a thing I really dread'. Since neither of them wanted to face that possibility, they turned, desperately, to the only other feasible solution. 'You will be glad to hear that he is going to bring in a Bill into the H. of Commons to try and divest himself of the title.' Only if this plan worked, Nancy declared, would she accept nomination, and then only to keep the seat warm till 'Waldorf got free'. Unfortunately for them, enquiries revealed that constitutional changes could not be made quite so simply. Waldorf could not introduce a measure in the Commons because he was no longer a member. He would either have to find a sponsor or bring a bill into the upper house, which would be a cumbersome process. By now, the Astors were being inundated with sympathy and advice. Other commentators were not so friendly. One elderly Unionist recoiled from the prospect of 'Lady Astor MP', because 'the woman is sure to get in' and prove an embarrassment to the party. On 26 October the nettle was grasped; Nancy telegraphed her acceptance to Plymouth. However, as she told J. J. Judge next day, she was '*cheered*, as I really believe Waldorf will divest himself of his title and then all would be well'. She hoped the other parties would not oppose her, 'but we shall see, perhaps they won't'.[6] Such was the 'campaign' which placed the first woman in the British Parliament.

In one sense it was an obvious solution. Nancy was well known and liked in the constituency. She was involved in the running of several charitable projects. She had blossomed as a public speaker whose orations more than made up in entertainment value for what they lacked in attention to details of policy. She had, in fact, spent more time in Plymouth than her husband during the war. And those who were closer to her knew that her personal generosity was prodigious. The following letter is typical:

Dear Mr Judge,

Will you do me a favour? Could you sometime go to the top of 66, Higher Street and see an old man called Rogers? It is, I think, a most pitiful case. He used, I believe, to work for the *Mercury* and still works for the *Independent*. I do not like to give him anything myself direct, but I want you to get the things for him. I think what he really needs is a mattress and blankets, and above all some books. Perhaps you could have a little talk with him, and find out what kind of books he wants, and then let me know the amount in which I am indebted to you . . .[7]

Nancy was a compulsive do-gooder – in the days before that expression was robbed of all meaning by cynics unable to take spontaneous benevolence at face value. The stories are legion of her spur-of-the-moment impulses to help people. Once, riding with the children near Cliveden, she encountered an erect, elderly woman dressed in black. Nancy accosted her. 'You shouldn't be walking on the road. Where are you going?' The stranger, obviously very poor and very proud, intimated that her destination was none of her ladyship's business, but Nancy persisted and eventually learned that the woman was destitute, had no family and was on her way to the workhouse. 'No you're not,' Lady Astor ordered. 'You're to go along this road until you come to the big gates. I'll meet you there.' Having issued her instructions, Nancy hurried back to make impromptu arrangements for the reception of her new 'guest'. The end of the story was that the old woman spent the rest of her days at Cliveden – fed, clothed and comfortably housed. During one of her visits to America in the 1950s Lady Astor happened to see on television a news item about a GI bride stuck on a run-down farm somewhere in the South and desperately unhappy. Nancy was touched by the tale. She determined to do something – and do it personally. She found out the address, had herself driven to it, went in and introduced herself to a perfect stranger and presented the young woman with an open airline ticket so that, if ever she felt the need to go home, she could do so. For Nancy Astor helping people – in her own way – was a Christian duty because she was rich; it gave her pleasure; but, more than that, it was second nature to her. Having her own Commons seat would, she believed, enable her to extend this charitable activity and champion causes to which she was passionately committed.

Over against all this was the sheer novelty. The principle of votes for women had been conceded in the Representation of the People Act of February 1918. This statute, which introduced the major constitutional change of adult male suffrage free of property qualification, gave the vote to women, but only those over thirty. Thus, half the population were still discriminated against, and radicals like Waldorf Astor were quick to point this out. In July 1919 he wrote to Bonar Law urging him to bring in a government bill equalizing the political rights of women: 'Most of us (ministers as well as the rank and file of the coalition) gave undertakings to this effect during the election . . . It would be most unwise for the Cabinet to alienate the five million voters concerned.'[8] But the Unionist leadership, fearing that the Labour party would be the main beneficiary of a further extension of the franchise, resisted the logic of change. Bonar Law's curt reply stated: 'It never occurred to me that it would be right for the government to agree a complete alteration of the Franchise Bill so soon, and I cannot think that this would be desirable.'[9] However, the logic of admitting women to the Commons could not be denied, and a bill to effect this was hurried through in time for the 1918 election. Though several ladies contested seats, only one was successful, but she never took her seat in the house. The Irish Nationalist, Countess Markiewicz, as a member of Sinn Fein, bore no allegiance to the Crown and therefore would not be sworn in. By October 1919 a year had passed without a member of the distaff side jostling her way across the threshold of the oldest gentlemen's club in London. Was Nancy Astor prepared to storm this particular bastion?

She might well 'dread' assuming this role. She might express her very real forebodings to her friends, discuss the situation fervently with her husband and give herself to ardent prayer and searching of the Bible, but the fact is that the script might almost have been written with her in mind. Nancy was a born actress. Wherever she was, she automatically created a stage for her own performance. As a young woman she had revelled in being the centre of attraction of the Leicestershire hunting set. She was in her element among a supporting cast of prominent politicians, literary giants and *hommes d'affaires* at her Cliveden house parties. She thrived on election meetings, where her rough-and-ready wit was more than a match for hecklers and her unpretentious warmth made voters feel that Mrs Astor was 'one of us'. Now, she was being thrust from the wings on to the stage of London's longest-running show.

Nancy went to the hustings to defend her husband's majority of 11,756 in the Sutton division of Plymouth (the town had been split into three electoral areas in 1917). The contest, inevitably, attracted enormous press interest. When the result was announced Nancy was found to have outstripped the Labour candidate by 5,203 votes. It was less than half Waldorf's majority – but she was home and dry. Meanwhile, in furtherance of the agreed plan, Waldorf took urgent steps to have himself set free from his ermine straitjacket. He persuaded a friend, the Labour MP James Thomas, to seek leave to bring into the Commons a bill 'to empower His Majesty to accept a surrender of any peerage'. Waldorf's proxy argued the case with skill and enthusiasm, but a Unionist-dominated house was not ready to respond to the revolutionary cry of '*à bas les aristos*', no matter how muted. Thomas's motion was resolutely defeated. That, to all intents and purposes, brought to an end a flourishing parliamentary career.

It has never been satisfactorily explained why this should have been so, why Waldorf should have moved completely into the background after such a momentous and successful first decade in politics, but that is precisely what he did. As Nancy's star waxed, his waned. Theirs became a team effort in which Waldorf was the silent, though stronger, partner. His son Michael described this strange relationship as follows:

> He would, I believe, have found more edge to life in the rough and tumble of active politics rather than conducting matters from his elevated and secluded plane . . . [He was] pleased to allow his remarkable wife to occupy the centre of the stage. As soon as she entered the arena of public life she did so not in a supporting role, in order to further his aims, but in her own context and in her own right. He helped her to do this, and admired her performance; and his restraining hand was always there to avert a crisis. Time and time again he came to her rescue when her tongue ran away with her and she found herself in difficulties. When it came to an issue, in the final analysis it was my father's will that prevailed, not hers.[10]

There was no reason why membership of the House of Lords should have debarred him from high office. He had the vision, the industriousness and the mental clarity to attain cabinet rank. He would have made a distinguished Minister of Health, or Agriculture – perhaps even Home Secretary. It was not lack of talent that kept him from the upper rungs of the political ladder, nor the opposition of his party hierarchy. It was his own self-denying ordinance. If we want to know why he imposed it on himself we have to look to his deeply ingrained modesty, which was a pale reflection of his father's reclusiveness. He readily – perhaps too readily – accepted a back seat when he saw that he could perform a valuable role supporting others. He gave up one position in order not to cramp Garvin's editorial style. He relinquished another to allow his wife to fill it more flamboyantly. He sometimes used to remark that he had spent the greater part of his life 'managing' two difficult and talented personalities, J. L. Garvin and Nancy Astor. 'Being associated with two geniuses', he remarked to a friend in 1938, 'is a never ceasing problem especially as one and occasionally both resemble a box of Brock's fireworks producing quite unexpected displays.'[11] It was a joke in which there was more than a grain of truth. Waldorf, if pressed to say why he stepped out of the sawdust ring, would doubtless have stressed his democratic principles. The idea of someone not answerable to the public holding high public office was something he found hard to accept. But he also believed, or persuaded himself, that he had a vital task to perform in supporting two more talented 'up front' performers.

Yet there were deeper, emotional reasons for his complete change of lifestyle. He was very depressed after his father's death. As well as his grief he had, or thought he had, financial worries to contend with. The realization that he was not to be the principal beneficiary under William Waldorf's will brought both anger and anxiety. He sold his sporting estate at Glendoe, overlooking Loch Ness, even though Pauline offered to pay for its continued upkeep. In the summer of 1919 he contemplated selling Cliveden. He spent most of 1920 sorting out family affairs. This involved protracted correspondence with lawyers and a long visit to America. All this undermined his health and certainly did not improve his temper. He became uncharacteristically tetchy. For example, he turned a misunderstanding with John over the future of Temple Place into an unnecessary quarrel.

He had little time to devote to politics, and when he did turn his mind to national and international affairs it was only to regard them with cynical, world-weary despair. The return of peace had ushered party wrangling back into the forefront of life at Westminster, and Waldorf went through a long phase of disillusionment with the way national affairs were handled. Despite his involvement in politics, he perhaps shared, deep down, something of his father's disdain for wheeling and dealing. Because he was not dependent on the Unionist leadership he had never found it necessary to kowtow to the party organizers. He had been able to throw himself into politics in the years of the wartime coalition because party issues had been pushed into the background and he had been working under a radical Prime Minister for whom he had profound respect. Though adored by their constituency party, neither Waldorf nor Nancy was ever really *persona grata* with the Tory leadership, either centrally or in the South West. Unfortunately, party strife was soon reasserting itself as the oxygen of British politics. After the 'coupon' election of 1918, which theoretically maintained the coalition, the old fissures began to open up again. The Unionists (or Conservatives as they were again called after the 'settlement' of Ireland in December 1921) were the largest group in the Commons and began flexing their muscles. Lloyd George's friends witnessed the unedifying spectacle of their leader manoeuvring unscrupulously and doing deals with anyone who would help him stay in office. Reformist legislation went to the wall as those who traditionally held the reins of power and influence tried to steer Britain back towards pre-war 'realities'. 'These are indeed trying times', Waldorf complained in March 1921, 'to all who are trying to keep their feet against the strong currents of reaction and selfishness which at the moment are sweeping over the country.'[12] Probably what sickened him most of all was the treatment meted out to Christopher Addison. The zest with which the Minister of Health carried through the 'homes for heroes' programme resulted between 1919 and 1921 in 213,000 houses funded by local and central government, and made available at pre-war rents. Unfortunately, Addison became a victim of his own enthusiasm and the urgency of the problem. Unscrupulous builders took advantage of the sudden bonanza of public funds. Incompetent and inexperienced officials added to the drain on the exchequer. There was a serious waste of taxpayers' money. Reactionary MPs who had never approved of the extension of state control, urged on by the Northcliffe press, bayed for blood. In March

1921 Lloyd George threw Addison to the wolves by sacking him from the Ministry of Health. Later in the year he was dismissed from the Cabinet.

For Waldorf, the treatment of his friend was a disappointment and an outrage second only to the circumstances which had brought about his own removal from the Commons. It contributed to a crisis in his political thinking which led him to relinquish his last government post as assistant at the Ministry of Health. He claimed medical reasons for this decision, but this does not appear altogether convincing when we look closely at Waldorf's movements in the period leading up to the final breach. In the late summer and autumn of 1920 he spent several months in America, largely on matters concerned with the estate and his father's will. He returned suffering badly from sciatica and, in October, placed his provisional resignation before the Prime Minister, suggesting that the ministry's heavy workload needed a more able-bodied man. Lloyd George was, once more, unwilling to lose his services, so we find Waldorf corresponding frequently with his personal secretary, A. P. Hughes-Gibb, about the situation in Whitehall and Westminster. The reports made depressing reading:

> The Miscellaneous Provisions Bill has been so violently attacked in both the Press and House of Commons that probably no serious attempt will be made to carry the majority of its 26 clauses . . .
>
> The Patent Medicines Bill has not yet been taken in the Lords and there is not the remotest chance for the Milk Bill this session . . .
>
> Licensing . . . involves new duties upon, and expenditure by, the Local Authorities, and in the present mood of the House of Commons it would unite the farming and financial reactionaries with also, perhaps, the opponents of all kinds of control . . .
>
> As regards a new Health Bill . . . whatever chances a big Bill had will be greatly diminished by the hostility in certain quarters both to the Minister personally and to any increased expenditure . . .[13]

Waldorf received this gloomy news – as well as reports from Garvin and others about the right-wing backlash – in Algeria. He had been sent there by his doctor, Lord Dawson, to rest and obtain some winter warmth. In January 1921 Lord Curzon enquired tetchily why Viscount Astor was not back at his post after the Christmas recess. Waldorf explained that he had now been obliged to press Lloyd George to release him from his obligations, adding, 'You can imagine how I hate being on the shelf during these difficult times.'[14] We could take that protestation at its face value were it not for Waldorf's subsequent correspondence with Christopher Addison. It is clear that the minister hoped to lure back to his desk the man who, more than any other, had supported his public health work from the very beginning. But in March Waldorf explained that this was out of the question. His doctor had told him that his back would not be fully recovered for several months, so, with deepest regret, he would have to part company with the Ministry of Health. What he then did was send a copy of this letter to Lord Dawson so that, if the latter should bump into Addison, he would not say anything at variance with the version of Waldorf's recovery that Waldorf had given.[15]

It would be a misreading of Waldorf's character to assume that he was exaggerating his ailments to distance himself from the government's unpopular policies (policies which he had played a significant part in framing). He was prepared to fight, and fight hard, for the things he believed in. What happened was that the two sides of his character – private reticence and public duty – were always in conflict, and in 1920–21 the private side won. He was dispirited by the political trends, grief-stricken by the death of his father, and worried about money. When, on top of all this, he suffered the debilitating pain of sciatica, he lost the will to continue the political battle – or, at least, to be in the forefront of it. In future, he would be, not the battery commander, but the quartermaster, providing supplies and equipment to Nancy, Garvin and other front-liners.

The years 1919–21 were a watershed. Thereafter, Waldorf stopped trying to frame policy and devoted himself, instead, to influencing policy framers. Friends sometimes appealed to him to come out of this self-imposed retirement. 'It is the very devil,' Lionel Curtis complained, years later, 'arguing with a man who . . . seems completely devoid of personal ambition. One can only appeal to your sense of public duty and beg you to realise that in the general interest you ought to be playing a larger part in public affairs.' Curtis had canvassed the views of others who, like himself, were alarmed that the vacuum created by the departure of men like Astor was attracting lesser men to high office. Astor's friends were motivated, Curtis insisted, by a 'desire to get you even against your inclinations into the more leading position in the country which you ought to fill, in times when the country can ill afford to have a man like you on a back shelf'.[16] To all such entreaties Waldorf turned a deaf ear. Commitment to a government job, he increasingly realized, would inhibit his freedom: not only to travel widely – America, Europe, winters in St Moritz, autumns on the beloved island of Jura estate which he bought in 1919 – but to associate freely with men and women of all political persuasions and to promote those causes closest to his heart. Some of his ideas were naïve, some impracticable and some simply ahead of their time. They could never have been made to square with any Tory manifesto. Viscount Astor in office would have been even more of an embarrassment to the party leaders than the maverick Nancy Astor on the back benches of the Commons.

An election in 1922 brought the Conservatives to power, and after the sudden death of Bonar Law they were led by Stanley Baldwin, an unimposing man against whom factions were soon intriguing. Writing at the beginning of 1924 to John St Loe Strachey, editor of the *Spectator,* Waldorf explained in a cynical letter why he declined to throw his weight behind another candidate:

The real strength of Baldwin is *not* his honesty (the electors began to get bored with that) or his 'grip' (which so far has been conspicuous by its absence . . .) or his imagination in framing policy. His strength lies in the absence of any outstanding personality to take his place. There are at least three competitors for his job. No one could say any of them was a Napoleon. So why change?

It's policy which is going to settle our fate and the leadership. What's the good of oiling the engines if you have no petrol to put in . . . Baldwin's speech at the Cecil was typical of our recent Tory leadership – 'Gentlemen we must be keen on Social Reform. We *are* keen and have been keen. But unfortunately the voters won't believe us (hear, hear). Look at our record. It's true you seem to have to look a long way back. Luckily we can always appeal to the name of Disraeli (hear, hear).'[17]

By this time there was another member of the family in Parliament. Waldorf's brother John (John Jacob Astor v) decided soon after the war that he was not content simply to sit at Hever and manage his Kentish acres. It was his responsibility to help shape the new Britain. Perhaps it would be truer to say that, like many of his class and time, he wanted to restore the *old* Britain, Kipling's Britain, with its firm roots deep in tradition, Hever's Britain rich in history, Elgar's land of hope and glory, ruling over all the bits of the globe proudly shaded red, a Britain of order, discipline and fixed relationships – landlord and tenant, master and servant. John was almost the epitome of the English country gentleman: slim, with cropped moustache and erect military bearing, undemonstrative, yet carrying an aura of quiet authority. He was his father's son in his conservatism, his shyness and his self-control. Nothing illustrates the latter more effectively than his conquest of his disability. For John Astor it was not good enough just to 'get about' on his artificial leg; he wanted to be fully mobile, even athletic. It was not long before he could once again beat younger men at squash.

When he bethought himself how best he could serve his country in peacetime he found a ready model in his brother. Waldorf exercised a degree of leadership, or at least influence, through Parliament and the press. John decided to do the same. He admired his brother and had a genuine affection for him. The coolness between them was certainly only on Waldorf's side: the surviving correspondence between the brothers reveals a warmth on John's part which was answered by a kind and thoughtful, but austere, elder-brotherliness. For example, in December 1919 we find John writing to ask Waldorf's advice on dairy farming. The new owner of Hever found that he could not, as his father had done, simply use the estate to meet the needs of the castle. He had to make the farmland pay. Enthusiastically he outlined his plans and invited the more experienced Waldorf's suggestions. He ended his letter with a plaintive plea, 'Won't you and Nancy come down here soon? I wish you would!' From Cliveden came back a helpful, considered reply and the generous offer to give John his head dairyman. To the invitation Waldorf made no response.[18]

Two months later John was again asking advice, this time about his political career. He had approached Conservative Central Office and had been enthusiastically endorsed by the party. A wounded soldier, a man of property and aristocratic connections, he was an ideal candidate, and had been offered the safe seat of Maidenhead. But his father's death had affected him profoundly, and in February 1920 he was very run down. His doctor diagnosed delayed shock and absolutely forbade any undue excitement, such as electioneering. What did Waldorf think he should do? Waldorf's reply has not survived, but since John turned down the Maidenhead offer it seems likely that the elder brother counselled him to put his health first. (It may also be that Waldorf did not want him operating in a constituency not far from Cliveden.) Months later John was invited to contest a by-election in Dover.

This should have been a straightforward matter of making a few speeches and then sitting back while the Tory faithful performed their customary task of voting their man into Westminster. In January 1921 events did not turn out like that. John stood as the official Conservative candidate in support of the coalition government. He was shocked to find himself up against the 'Anti-Waste League'. This was nothing less than an organ of the mighty Harmsworth brothers, Lords Northcliffe and Rothermere. Rothermere founded the league to back independent candidates opposed to the domestic policies of the coalition, particularly the 'waste' of taxpayers' money implicit in the post-war recovery programme. Rothermere's candidate, Sir Thomas Polson, successfully rode the wave of public outrage at the 'homes for heroes' scandal and, after a particularly vicious campaign in which he castigated John as an 'American' and was supported by the drunken demagogue Horatio Bottomley, Polson took the seat.

In fact, Major Astor only had to wait for the Conservatives to sort out their internal differences, which they did in the autumn of 1922, when Bonar Law and his colleagues decided to distance themselves from Lloyd George. John stood again for Dover in the resulting general election, but his entry to the House of Commons was still not straightforward. He was faced with the task of unseating Polson. The incumbent no longer had the backing of the Anti-Waste League, for that ginger group, having achieved its objective of breaking the coalition, had ceased to exist. But Polson, so it was rumoured, now had the support of no less a person than Lord Salisbury. The fourth Marquess, son of the great Victorian Prime Minister, was extremely right wing; he was the Conservative leader in the Lords, and the chief moving spirit in Parliament behind the destruction of the coalition. Writing in some consternation to Bonar Law, John observed that if this formidable figure did back Polson 'he would certainly not add much lustre to the name of Cecil'.[19] His lordship evidently did not trust Astor's political stance, but he was persuaded not to rock the boat and the official party candidate was safely installed as MP for Dover. However, there was a strong sub-plot running through these manoeuvrings. The party leadership had a very compelling reason for endorsing Major Astor's campaign: Major Astor had recently become the owner of London's leading daily newspaper.

On 14 August 1922, Lord Northcliffe died at the age of fifty-seven. Towards the end, this power-hungry newspaper tycoon and would-be statesman had lapsed into insanity. Driven by megalomania, he increasingly used his newspapers as vehicles for personal policies and vendettas (in particular against Lloyd George). In 1919, he sacked the editor of *The Times*, Geoffrey Dawson, because he would not execute the proprietor's more outrageous instructions (just as he had tried to oust Garvin from the *Observer* years before for displaying too much independence). Waldorf and Nancy also had a battle with the Harmsworths over ownership of influential Plymouth newspapers. They tried, unsuccessfully, to wrest the *Western Daily Mercury* and the *Western Morning News* from the control of the great press barons. Under a more amenable executive *The Times* energetically attacked the coalition, though its long-suffering employees were frequently driven beyond the bounds of prudence by the verbal (and sometimes physical) abuse of Northcliffe, who was determined to write Lloyd George's political obituary before going to his appointment with the grim reaper. He failed in this ambition by just two months.

Under the terms of Northcliffe's will a first option on *The Times* was to be offered to his one-time co-proprietor, John Walter. Walter was anxious to resume his association with the paper, which had been run by his family ever since it had been founded by his great-great-grandfather. Unfortuntely, he lacked the money (variously estimated at between £650,000 and £1 million) necessary to buy it. Various bidders now appeared, including at one point a backer who proposed to install Lloyd George as editor. Soon, however, the field was reduced to two runners, Lord Rothermere and Major J. J. Astor. The latter was successful because he was prepared to pay over one and a half million pounds to prevent *The Times* falling back into Harmsworth control. He became co-proprietor with Walter and held a 90 per cent shareholding.

We need look no further than John's declared objective in seeking his motive for this expensive investment. Writing a few months later for the *Empire Review*, he declared that he had been concerned 'to secure as far as possible the continued independence of one great journal, and through it the perpetuation of the highest standards of British journalism'.[20] He must have enjoyed a certain satisfaction in putting one over on the founder of the Anti-Waste League. In addition, he had achieved something of which his father would have been proud. Furthermore, his acquisition of 'The Thunderer' put him on more than equal terms with Waldorf. But his commitment to rescuing a fine newspaper was paramount and quite unfeigned. Unfettered, objective journalism was important to him. Later he became a conscientous president of the Empire Press Union. In 1923, when a committee was set up to draft regulations and procedures covering the new phenomenon of radio broadcasting, Major Astor was a member. He thus helped to thrash out the complex problems associated with the inauguration of a new public information and entertainment service (the BBC). This involved the consideration of fundamental principles of public taste, private property and the ethics governing a medium capable, in time, of being transmitted into every home in the land.

The clearest indication of John's determination to be a very different kind of *Times* proprietor was his decision to reinstate Geoffrey Dawson in the editorial chair. Dawson was a long-term friend of the Astors, a Round Tabler and a frequent visitor to Cliveden and St James's Square. His background was an unusual one for a journalist. After Eton and Magdalen College, Oxford, he became a Fellow of All Souls, and served as private secretary to Milner in South Africa before becoming involved with newspapers. He was a committed imperialist and internationalist. He was a thinking, but often passionate, controversialist who was on personal terms with most of the country's leaders. He delighted in being summoned to Chequers for meetings with Baldwin, in attending dinners with members of the royal household, in the intellectual stimulus of Round Table 'moots', in invitations to shoot over aristocratic grouse moors or attend exclusive country house parties. Dawson was never reticent about giving his opinion to politicians of all parties and he certainly exercised a considerable influence. It is an interesting coincidence that both Waldorf and John in their capacity as newspaper proprietors were served by remarkable editors.

Dawson's first task on arriving at Printing House Square was to draft a long memorandum (it went through three revision stages before reaching its final form) setting out the terms under which he was prepared to operate. In words reminiscent of Garvin's statement of journalistic principles to Waldorf, he asked for complete separation of editorial and management roles and a large measure of freedom from control by the proprietors. But this 'freedom' was not precisely defined and no contract was drawn up. As Dawson stated:

> I have never, myself, been able to see that any 'contract' with an Editor over a period of years can be devised except on conditions which will involve his 'writing to order'

when he differs from the Proprietors or their complete abdication. All that is possible in practice is that Editor and Proprietors should have confidence in one another, and a clear understanding to work in the constitutional manner suggested in this Memorandum'[21]

There was little risk of a rift between Astor and Dawson. The new owner believed that, traditionally, two principles had guided *Times* policy: non-adherence to any party or individual; and, in general terms, support for the government of the day whatever its political composition. Such high-minded impartiality was difficult to maintain in practice. Since John liked to describe his politics as 'enlightened Conservatism' and Dawson thought of himself as 'the secretary-general of the Establishment', the tone of the paper was clearly set. *The Times* found it much easier to support the government of the day when that government was Tory. For the next two troubled decades no relationship on Fleet Street was more cordial than that between Geoffrey Dawson and John Astor, largely because the latter never 'interfered' with the editorial content of the paper, and the former always kept a weather eye on the major shareholder's opinions.

Total impartiality in newspaper editorials is a fiction and John Astor was quite aware of this, but critics who complain that during his proprietorship *The Times* became a tame lapdog of Tory Central Office grossly oversimplify the truth. John was concerned above all to prevent his newspaper becoming an official organ of a political party (like, for example, the socialist *Daily Herald*) or a megaphone for broadcasting the views of a rich owner, like Northcliffe or William Waldorf Astor. To this end he appointed a body of trustees whose consent would always be required in any subsequent transfer of ownership. He was concerned to keep news and comment distinct within the pages of *The Times* so that, whatever readers thought of its editorial, they could trust its reporting. He was fortunate in having a clear-headed and experienced editor who, at least in the early years, tried to create a fair-minded forum of debate on all major issues. As time went by, Dawson, like Garvin, became too entrenched in both his opinions and his job. He fell into the trap of slanting news and trying to use the paper to influence public opinion by bombast and innuendo rather than a rational assessment of the facts. John's failure was in not applying pressure to his editor at that point, as Waldorf applied pressure to Garvin. Yet the fact remains that, in the twenties, the change at Printing House Square was both symptomatic of and contributory to wider, deeper changes in the world of London journalism – changes which were, for the most part, beneficial.

John was never the political animal that Waldorf had been at the outset of his parliamentary career. He seems to have been content to be the conventional, rural Tory MP who attended the right functions, met the right people and appeared at meetings whenever invited to do so by the local Conservative hierarchy. He had no great love of public speaking and cannot be said to have got to grips with the real problems of his large constituency (which comprised the greater part of eastern Kent). During the 1921 election he wrote in an offhand way about his political activities.

> We put in a good week at Deal last week, golf every morning and 2 or 3 meetings and concerts etc. every afternoon and evening. It is interesting and in parts amusing and I enjoy my outings there now.[22]

His casual approach scarcely varied after he became an MP. In December 1923 there was another general election. Since Major Astor was unopposed he saw no reason even to present himself to the voters. He took his wife to Egypt for a winter holiday. Returning after the start of the new parliament (the first Labour administration), he discovered, after a few days, that there had been some technical irregularity about the proceedings and that this voided his election. So the Dover voters were obliged to turn out again. And yet again – for in October Ramsay MacDonald went to the country. Thus, in less than four years, John Astor, who disliked campaigning, had to face five elections. Not that there was any doubt about the outcome after 1922: the dutiful electors of east Kent were never going to return anyone except the official Conservative candidate. As Bob Brand remarked, when congratulating John in November 1922, 'Dover ought to be yours for life if you want it.'[23]

John retained the seat for a quarter of a century. He became extremely popular among his constituents, and his wife, who probably appeared more often than John on public platforms, was greatly loved. John's was a more relaxed style than Waldorf's or Nancy's, and one that was perhaps better suited to his very different constituency. Compact, self-conscious Plymouth had obvious social problems which called for energetic and sometimes belligerent action. The farmland villages and small towns of Kent were happy with an MP who assumed a traditional, patrician benevolence. John took on this particular leadership role because it was expected of a man of his class and upbringing. The people of Kent understood this and accepted it. As for the House of Commons, John spoke there no more than four or five times during the turbulent quarter of a century of his membership. He preferred to sit quietly, listen to his colleagues and vote as the whips directed.

That charge certainly could not be levelled against Nancy. She was involved in mild controversy on her very first day. Ignorant of the labyrinthine rules governing members' conduct, she stopped to chat to a friend on the floor of the house and had to be called to order by the Speaker. She managed to remain silent in debate for her first few weeks. Then, on 24 February 1920, she made her maiden speech. The house was packed with MPs and visitors, come to be present at what was for some a historic moment and for others a curiosity. The first woman to raise her voice in Pugin and Barry's august chamber elected to speak not, as was the convention, on some fairly non-controversial topic, but on the subject closest to her heart – drink. She opposed a motion which sought to remove the restrictions on the sale of alcohol which had been imposed during the war. It was a theme she was to return to over and over again in the ensuing years. Nancy's first foray into parliamentary debate was hailed as a success, even by those members who represented the brewers' lobby.

It is very difficult to exaggerate the courage and strength of character which Nancy possessed – and had to possess – in order to survive her early years in the House of Commons. The rules and customs of the chamber had been made, over the centuries, by men and for men. The first woman had to learn the ways of this alien establishment and then learn how to use them to her advantage. It would have been easy to sit quietly in a corner and allow her party bosses to define her role for her. Nancy Astor was not that kind of a woman. The majority of members were courteous to her, but some certainly resented her presence and a few went out of their way to be unpleasant. Winston Churchill told her to her face that he found the sight of a woman in the house both an intrusion and an embarrassment. Years later he confessed that he had done his best to 'freeze her out' in the belief that the sight of Lady Astor retreating, humiliated, from the parliamentary arena would deter others of her sex from emulating her audacity. Nancy, however, knew only too well that the hopes of millions of women were focused on her and that she was ushering in a new era in British politics.

Having said that, it must be admitted that her initiation would have been easier had it not been for her impatience with the conventions of the Commons. She found the multitude of unwritten, petty regulations and meaningless ceremonies faintly absurd. Though she did not go out of her way to flout them, she did the next worst thing in many men's eyes – she openly registered her amused astonishment that they could take them so seriously. One storm in a teacup in her first months as an MP typified her clash with parliamentary tradition. She took a gangway seat in the chamber to avoid having to clamber over colleagues. Most members considered this a reasonable courtesy to offer to the only woman in the house. Not so Sir William Joynson Hicks, a particularly pompous and self-important Tory (later Home Secretary). He regarded the seat as 'his'. Although he was abroad at the time, as soon as he heard of the usurpation he wrote a letter of protest to Waldorf. There followed an acrimonious correspondence, and a ridiculous altercation between the rival claimants when Joynson Hicks returned, from which neither side emerged with much dignity.

Most women would probably not have survived in this alien environment. It took a thick-skinned 'tomboy' like Nancy Astor to establish beyond all doubt that not only did women have a *right* to sit as MPs, they also had a valuable contribution to make to the life of the Commons. In her early years, she inevitably concentrated on issues concerning women and children (and her enormous postbag showed how many wives and mothers appreciated the fact that there was now someone at the centre of things who they felt understood their problems). She concerned herself with the introduction of women to the police force (and sat on the Home Office committee which gathered information on the subject), the guardianship of infants, widows' pensions, juvenile courts, female unemployment and sweated labour, child abuse, housing and education. But she also served on the joint parliamentary committee on criminal law amendment and spoke in debates on wider issues such as the League of Nations.

Waldorf's hand can be seen in all her major speeches. It was he who spent time in the patient gathering of facts and statistics – a chore for which Nancy had no taste. He was always available to discuss complex issues with her and help her clarify her own thinking. (The arrangement worked both ways: as an MP Nancy could always obtain written or verbal answers to parliamentary questions on which Waldorf wanted information.) She became, and for many years remained, a star performer in the Commons because she could combine her own emotional intensity with a solid grasp of relevant detail and present her arguments in such a humorous way that even her opponents were reduced to laughter. All her statements were made with conviction, her arguments buttressed by moral and spiritual certainty. But it was not so much her set-piece speeches which cheered her supporters and outraged her foes, as her irreverent Commons style. She soon captured the record for interruptions when she disturbed the oratory of fifteen consecutive speeches. On countless occasions she sailed close to the wind by using unparliamentary language about her opponents. She referred to one MP as 'the village donkey' and to another group as 'loud-speakers and big-mouthed fellows with flapdoodle hearts and no heads'. Her unpremeditated interventions in debate, during which she not infrequently wandered off the point, were less impressive than her prepared addresses – but considerably more entertaining. Even political journalists who opposed most of what she stood for were open and generous in their admiration. The socialist *Clarion* declared on 19 May 1934:

> Always quarrelling and always making it up, she romps her way through political life, leaving a breath of fresh air behind her, but making surprisingly little difference to the conduct of affairs. Courage she has, love of a fight, readiness of speech ... She adds to these, boisterousness, inconsistency, irresponsibility, the fixed belief that generosity with one's own spare thousands can justify an oppressive social system.

This belief stands like a bar between her and reality, teaching her to rely on sympathy in place of political faith, on a miscellaneous assembly of convictions instead of a philosophy.

That very perceptive piece of not unfriendly journalism gets very close to the mark. In later years, when the Astors' attitudes towards fascism and communism came under frequent public scrutiny, Nancy's stock response was that neither she nor Waldorf was built 'on party lines'; they cherished their independence. But 'independence' tends to be a Humpty-Dumpty word, and it certainly meant whatever Lady Astor wanted it to mean at whatever moment she used it. She was certainly free of party dogma. Loyalty to the Conservative cause had, for her, a very limited meaning. Her most constant enemies were the grandees of her own party, hand in glove, she believed, with the drink trade. She was certainly independent of her own pronouncements and quite capable of changing her stance on issues at short notice. The reason for this is that she was intuitive rather than rational. Her outbursts in the Commons were as spontaneous as her instant generosity to people in need. (This was not only displayed in Plymouth. Whenever she went to America, Miss Ada Kindersley, Waldorf's exceedingly efficient PA, had to ensure that sufficient cash funds were available for Nancy's casual bounty.) The motors that powered her politics were emotion and prejudice.

A fact which earlier biographers have failed to grasp is that in many of her basic loves, hates and attitudes Nancy was poles apart from Waldorf. Both were Conservatives by accident rather than conviction, but whereas Waldorf's wellspring lay in nineteenth-century radical Liberalism, his wife was by instinct right wing. Before the war, when Waldorf was backing Lloyd George's reforms, Nancy complained to a friend: 'How dreadful the present situation looks all over the country. A fine mess these brilliant Reformers have made of things; they have created more hate in 8 years than a Caesar could.'[24] When Lady Astor declared herself a devotee of social reform, as she frequently did, and pointed out, as she enjoyed doing, that the Tories were in this regard the true inheritors of the Liberal tradition, her thinking was cast in a thoroughly paternalistic mould. The idea that social justice might require fundamental changes in the social fabric was anathema to her. It was not so for Waldorf. His thinking moved steadily leftwards. Writing to Lloyd George in 1934 he could say: 'I've dropped my Toryism on the questions of public ownership of land and of land taxes! It looks as if I were more advanced than you on this today.'[25]

Towards individuals and their views Viscount Astor was supremely tolerant. He enjoyed surrounding himself with people of all political, religious and social persuasions. When, in 1938, he had to defend himself against the charge of heading a clique of pro-Nazi sympathizers, one of the strongest parts of his armour was that his home was and always had been the resort of British and foreign politicians espousing a wide range of opinions. It was because he enjoyed listening to the views of such men and women that Waldorf developed and modified his own political thinking. Nancy, too, liked to be at the centre of a circle of talented guests, but what mattered to her was that members of her court should be 'interesting', and willing participants in her harlequinade. She could also be vicious. When a member of the Commons presumed to criticize her conduct in a debate, she turned on him with the words, 'Only a Jew like you would *dare* to be rude to me.'[26] Her pet aversions also included Roman Catholics and brewers.

It is important to be clear about the differences and potential tensions in the relationship between Waldorf and Nancy at this stage if we are to understand the development of that relationship. In the twenties there was much to hold the couple together. There was, of course, the family. The children were very important to both of them (perhaps, in Nancy's case, too important). There was their circle of friends. Although hundreds of guests passed through their homes every year, there was an inner core of intimates with whom they were very close over many years. These ranged from the famous, such as George Bernard Shaw, through lesser luminaries like Lionel Curtis and Bob Brand (who married Nancy's sister Phyllis) to such relative unknowns as 'Judie' Judge, the Plymouth newspaperman and social reformer. But always in a special category was Philip Kerr (who in 1930 succeeded his cousin as Marquess of Lothian). He and Nancy were very close, and she found in him a friend to whom she could confide her deepest thoughts. Perhaps what helped the marriage most of all, apart from Waldorf's skill in handling his quicksilver wife, was their separate but overlapping spheres of activity. They were both involved in politics, but Lord Astor's activity centred on the Lords, Chatham House and frequent visits to overseas capitals, while Nancy spent most of her working life shuttling between Plymouth and the Commons. It was an ideal arrangement in that it allowed them periods of separation in between which they could catch up on each other's news.

John Astor's arrival in the Commons did not help family relations. He and his brother-in-law, Bertie Spender-Clay, had an unfeigned affection for Nancy, but they found the lady MP's conduct an embarrassment. They seldom acknowledged her in the house. She, for her part, did not seek them out. There was no 'family feud', but inevitably the worlds of Cliveden and Hever diverged. Certain differences did arise between the brothers when they had to sort out their father's estate. The most taxing problem was the disposal of 2 Temple Place. Waldorf had always assumed that the building would come to him and he planned to use it as his town house as well as continuing to oversee the Astor estate from it. However, thanks to William

Waldorf's testamentary dispositions, there was precious little estate to administer and the magnificent building was left to John and Waldorf jointly. For a while the elder brother contemplated buying out his sibling and was annoyed when he heard (incorrectly) that John had invited Messrs Knight, Frank and Rutley to auction the house and contents. Eventually Waldorf agreed that the property should be sold – but who would want to buy such a highly individualistic building in a period of post-war depression? Number 2 Temple Place stood empty for three years before going, at the virtually knock-down price of £50,000, to the Sun Life Assurance Company in November 1922. (It changed hands three times in the ensuing years and was badly damaged during the Second World War. It was sensitively restored and then extended in a style in keeping with the original. The main part of the building stands today much as William Waldorf Astor left it.)

Once the distressing events surrounding William Waldorf's death were past, Waldorf and John were able to reach an amicable understanding. They corresponded, met to discuss family business and occasionally socialized. But the lives of the two households were very different. Nancy's success as a hostess had something to do with it. She overawed the other Astor women, who knew that they could not possibly compete. 'How you manage I don't know,' Vi once wrote, thanking her sister-in-law for a weekend at Cliveden. 'I saw more people in 36 hours than I usually do at Hever in a month.'[27]

In fact, Hever was the centre of a social life scarcely less energetic than that of the more famous Astor home. John and Vi were very conscious of the beauty of their Kentish castle and its superbly kept grounds and felt a responsibility to share these delights with others. 'Others' did not just mean men and women from the same social background, for 'class' was never a very prominent factor in John's thinking. His American heritage, combined with the experience of wartime camaraderie, enabled him to value men and women for themselves rather than for their ancestry or their wealth. The present Lord Lansdowne (Violet's eldest son) remembers the warm relations between servants and family at Hever. The staff were free to enjoy the tennis courts, golf course and other amenities when the Astors were not using them, and often the footmen could be heard running down to the lake in the early morning for a dip before commencing their duties. The annual staff dance was always a fancy-dress affair so that no servant should feel out of place for lack of a sufficiently splendid gown or suit. On one such occasion the chef appeared as an oriental potentate swathed in Mr Astor's silk dressing-gown and no one enjoyed the joke more than Mr Astor. Guests at Hever included charity workers, constituency activists and anyone John and Vi thought might benefit from a relaxing weekend at the castle.

The highlight of every year was '*Times* Day'. On a Saturday in July the entire staff of the newspaper and their families were brought by special train to Hever, where each guest was presented with an elaborately printed programme setting out the available entertainments. There were lunch and tea in gaily decked marquees. There was dancing to the strains of a military band. There were tours of the house and a variety of competitions – golf, shooting, tennis and photography. There were swimming and rowing races and even a baby show. Viewed from the standpoint of our very different age this may look like benevolent paternalism, yet, as far as John Astor was concerned, there was nothing condescending about it. It was the proprietor's way of saying 'thank you' for all the hard work that went into the paper over the year. It showed that Major Astor cared about his employees. If the house magazine of *The Times* is anything to go by, they were equally interested in him and his family. Weddings, anniversaries and special events were always noted and the more important happenings marked by presentations from the staff.

It was partly this close relationship between employer and employed which underlay the remarkable role played by *The Times* during the General Strike of 1926. The TUC called on workers in key industries to withdraw their labour on 3 May. That summons included print operatives. Determined that his presses should not be halted, John Astor took personal control of the situation and, for nine days, ran a quasi-military campaign. As well as the basic problem of operating complex and sensitive machines with largely unskilled labour, Astor had to fight a war on two fronts. Not only did he have to face opposition and possible sabotage from the pickets; he also had to fend off the government, in the person of Winston Churchill, who wanted to commandeer newsprint and technical staff for the official broadsheet, the *British Gazette*. John spent the week of the strike rushing between Westminster and Printing House Square. Afterwards, he wrote some abbreviated notes on the progress of the campaign.

On Day 1 he brought members of his own staff to the *Times* office – two secretaries, two typists, eight gardeners and one driver, plus a lorry from Hever. Before the striking men went (many of them reluctantly) off shift, he addressed them:

> 'Situation beyond us. Part as friends and hope to meet as such before long. The *Times*, being above party or class, does not recognize the right of anyone to dictate policy or course of action, and will carry on ... as long as possible. Goodbye and good luck.' (Loud applause) (Tongue in cheek?)

Day 2 was spent marshalling non-union men, family employees, friends and union members, who managed to find a loophole which allowed them to carry on, to run off 70,000 copies of a single-sheet paper on cumbersome multigraph presses. This was the day that pickets were posted outside the building. 'To my surprise they touched their hats to me, and continued to do so throughout.'

Astor was determined to get the rotary presses turning, and much of Day 3 was spent bringing in retired, skilled staff and setting up a steam-powered generator in case the electricity supply was cut. The general confrontation was now becoming ugly. Newspaper offices were attacked and saboteurs tried to set fire to the *Times* building by pouring petrol under a back door. Despairing of adequate police protection, Astor organized his own guards who patrolled twenty-four hours a day. As darkness fell, the *ad hoc* newspapermen gathered anxiously to see if the production process could be made to work.

With an occasional ebullience of molten metal, and a certain amount of overlapping of effort, the plates were duly cast and trimmed. One hardly dared watch operations on the Printing Machine – but we all did, greatly to the annoyance of Tanner, upon whom the strain appeared considerable. Allah was with us. The machine worked. The baby was safely delivered.

Seventy-eight thousand copies of a four-page newspaper were printed, bundled and rushed to the fleet of cars and volunteer drivers outside. Scuffles broke out as pickets tried to impede the process. Four helpers 'each stopped something hard with their heads. Two strikers were arrested, each with a thick ear.'

On Day 4 so many would-be helpers appeared that some had to be turned away. Inside the building, life was getting better organized. The board room became a canteen. This service provided a moral dilemma. It was funded by the *Times* workers themselves.

Yet now the pickets were outside and could not get in: the sandwiches and beer were inside and could not get out. There was no logical reason why the two should not come together, and in due course they did, at intervals.

The delivery vehicles which left Printing House Square with the next edition were bristling with 'guards' packed on the running boards. This time there were no scuffles.

By Day 5 the strike was already crumbling and Astor had more trouble with the *British Gazette* than with the trade unionists. Jealous of *The Times*'s success, Churchill made difficulties over supplies of newsprint and tried to force 'The Thunderer' to restrict its number of pages. These problems had to be ironed out over the next two days in the intervals between agreeing terms with the strikers. On Day 7, 'for the last time in this crisis, the *Times* was printed and published, to a very great extent, by lawyers, legislators, financiers and gentlemen of leisure'.[28]

The strike over, Astor thankfully retired and left *The Times* once again to its managerial staff. There remained only one more task to perform: the proprietors had five hundred silver match boxes made, inscribed with *The Times*' masthead and the date 3 May 1926, and presented one to each member of the volunteer army. Thanks to them the newspaper had maintained an unbroken publishing tradition and had, in fact, been the only London newspaper produced on rotary presses during the strike.

For John Astor such excitements were rare. His brother continued to be much more emotionally committed to the rough and tumble of current events. The Round Table remained the cornerstone of the Waldorf Astors' political alliances. Its members were no longer the young idealists of pre-war days. They now occupied prominent positions in business, journalism and academia. Bob Brand was on the board of Lazard's Bank. Tom Jones ('TJ') was assistant secretary to the Cabinet. Sir Edward Grigg had left *The Times* and was now a Liberal MP, and the only professional politician in the group. Dawson, of course, was editor of *The Times*. Lionel Curtis remained at All Souls and lectured on colonial history. Philip Kerr left politics in 1921 to devote himself to Christian Science and to United Newspapers Ltd, and to write occasionally for the Liberal *Daily Chronicle*. They were all men who combined knowledge and eagerness to serve with lack of government responsibility. They were influential in various walks of life and were frequently consulted by the nation's leaders. Therefore, they were regarded with suspicion in many quarters. The *Morning Post* on 10 April 1923 described them as 'a group of idealists who take a much greater part in the politics and policy of this country than is generally suspected'. They were widely regarded as being pro-German and, later, pro-Nazi (although one Munich newspaper denounced them as communists!). Such charges were usually levelled by commentators who had not waded regularly through the rather solid prose of the *Round Table*, and were addressed to a public who certainly had not. The facts were more complex. The Round Table members were intellectuals, to whom disagreement was more familiar than consensus. There was no 'party line' on Germany or any other issue. On the contrary, the group saw their responsibility as trying to steer people away from prejudice and entrenched attitudes. As Germany sank into political extremism and began to rearm in defiance of international treaties, the Round Tablers were agreed on the need to help people *understand* what was happening as a basis for finding a peaceful solution to the problems of Europe. They were by no means agreed on what those solutions should be. They were not conspirators. If they were guilty of anything, it was of supposing that complex and highly emotive issues could be dealt with on the level of even-handed common-room debate. Viscount Astor saw no contradiction in making a visit to Russia in 1931, during which he had a long conversation with Stalin, and the following year joining the committee of the Anglo-German Association. The public at large found such behaviour difficult to comprehend.

The main issue of foreign policy in the twenties was disarmament, and the Astors contributed both to public debate and to private discussion in high places. These were years of golden optimism. Germany had been disarmed and was admitted to the League of Nations. The League successfully resolved several minor disputes between member states. In 1927 all leading nations signed the Kellogg Pact forswearing war as a means of settling conflicts of interest. It seemed as though much of what Waldorf and his friends had striven for since 1910 was coming to pass. World trade was booming and the USA was emerging as an economic superpower. The only major threat to peace was Bolshevik Russia which refused to enter any agreement with capitalist states, but provided that the non-communist world kept together, there seemed little that the cohorts of Marxist-Leninism could do.

The linchpin of what we might call the Astor–Kerr foreign policy was Anglo-American solidarity. If the British Empire and the world's leading industrial nation pursued common aims and provided an example of settling differences by arbitration, then the security of the world would be ensured. Britain would have to take second place in international commerce, but it would be a thriving second place. To bring about this desirable state of affairs the USA had to be wooed out of its isolationism. It was all very well for Secretary of State Frank Kellogg to provide world leaders with noble sentiments and fine words (and to be awarded the 1929 Nobel Peace Prize for so doing), but America must be prepared to help turn principles into reality. Idealistic and nationalistic confrontations in Europe and Asia were very real and would take more than optimism to resolve. Another necessity was for statesmen to stop being bogged down in disarmament talks. Careful balancing of sizes of armies and navies was not the way to prolong peace. Philip Kerr summed it up in a letter to Garvin in October 1928: 'Our only line is independence, that is, friendship with France, Germany and the United States; ententes and alliances with nobody.'[29] Kerr was constantly crossing the Atlantic advocating these attitudes to highly placed politicians. Cliveden and St James's Square played their established role in housing meetings between international policy-makers. Nancy bore the brunt of the speech-making, both in the Commons and elsewhere, delivering addresses carefully prepared by her husband and her friend. Thanks to the unique position she had won for herself in public life, people listened. Waldorf's brains and Nancy's personality made a formidable combination.

The Astors were public property; that was their strength and their weakness. In an age when most leading politicians were too drab to excite much interest, Waldorf and Nancy had something of the glamour of Hollywood stars. The man in the street was familiar with Lord Astor from his racing triumphs. Waldorf was known as the luckiest man on the turf. Between the wars he won every classic except the Derby, in which race his horses were placed second five times. (The final tally of his horse-breeding career was eleven classic winners and over two hundred victories in other races.) Ascot week was always the highlight of the social calendar at Cliveden. There was invariably a large house party. John and Vi, Pauline and Bertie would usually be there, together with a dozen or more close friends and one or two royals, diplomats and foreign visitors. It was interesting that Nancy should throw herself into celebrating this particular event, for she did not altogether approve of horse racing: it was a pastime which lured the lower orders into gambling and drinking. One day when Waldorf and his youngest son, John Jacob (always known as 'Jakie'), who was then about twenty, were setting off for Kempton Park to watch one of the Astor horses run, Nancy called after them, 'Don't forget racing attracts the worst from every class!' Jakie, the only member of the family who could match her for instant repartee, wound down the car window and shouted back, 'Yes, just like the House of Commons!' It was one of the few occasions on which Lady Astor was rendered speechless.

The public knew of Nancy because of her parliamentary activities. The press followed her avidly; she was always good copy. And then there was all that lavish entertaining. The comings and goings at Cliveden and St James's Square were assiduously reported by the gossip columnists. As well as the house parties, there were three or four balls during the season and frequent dinner and lunch parties, often for thirty or forty people. Then there was impromptu entertaining. 'I came up on Monday,' Nancy wrote from London in June 1922, 'as I had some rather important work to do, but hadn't been here very long, when I received a message that the King and Queen would like to go to Cliveden for tea, so had to rush back.'[30] Most celebrities from the world of entertainment, literature, politics and social and religious affairs received invitations to the Astor homes. Most of them were flattered to be asked, enjoyed themselves and hoped to be asked again. Charlie Chaplin, Evangeline Booth, Hilaire Belloc, Joachim von Ribbentrop, Sean O'Casey, T. E. Lawrence, Stanley Baldwin, Mahatma Gandhi, Neville Chamberlain – the net was cast extraordinarily wide because, between them, Waldorf and Nancy had an extensive range of interests. It was not just Viscountess Astor who surrounded herself with 'interesting' people. Her husband, for different reasons, was a compulsive entertainer. A relative noted about one hastily contrived dinner party:

> Aunt N ... hurriedly assembled all the League of Nations delegates and various ambassadors! She is a remarkable woman! But it's Uncle Waldorf who makes her give that sort of party. He has a sort of self-bestowed sense of Host of England that

makes him collect celebrities and it isn't snobbish really, he thinks it's his duty. Quite beyond me.[31]

Sometimes Nancy pursued prospective guests relentlessly. Towards the end of 1921 she secured the scalp of a member of the Bloomsbury Group, Lytton Strachey. The initial meeting was obviously a success, since for the next ten years she bombarded him with frequent invitations, her heavy humour sometimes scarcely masking her desperation: 'Dear *Poet*. Will you come back to us again. What of New Year? Would that suit Your Highness? I beg to remain Yr. Highness's Most Humble Servant'; 'Could you come here and dine with Bobby Shaw and me next Thursday ... Don't disappoint your devoted admirer, who is not as bad as the papers make out!!!' The poor man's attempts to escape were likely to bring an outraged telegram: 'Your excuse is appalling. Shall expect you.'[32] Not everyone enjoyed the Astors' style of hospitality. On a visit to Cliveden in 1930, Harold Nicolson, husband of Vita Sackville-West, sardonically observed in his diary: 'After dinner, in order to enliven the party, Lady Astor dons a Victorian hat and a pair of false teeth. It does not enliven the party.'[33]

Nancy added George Bernard Shaw to her list of Cliveden star attractions in 1926. The dramatist, critic and professional personality was then seventy and past his prime, but he was still a formidable and entertaining conversationalist. An unlikely but firm friendship developed between the Shaws and Nancy which lasted till Shaw's death. Throughout the years leading up to the Second World War, he and his wife Charlotte were among the most frequent visitors to Cliveden and St James's Square. The fact that Shaw and Nancy were poles apart politically did not matter. They were both outrageous exhibitionists and their performances seemed to strike fire from each other. Shaw, to the dismay of his socialist friends, enjoyed being cosseted at the Astors' homes and fêted in the Astors' social circle. Nancy revelled in her acquisition and convinced herself that she had a God-given role to play as his protector (in the last years of his life she became positively possessive towards him).

It was with Shaw that the Astors made a much-publicized visit to Russia in 1931. Just who originated this is not, now, clear. Shaw, because of his frequent defence of Bolshevism, had often been invited by the Soviet leaders, but he resisted, as he said, until the Astors 'suddenly took it into their heads to see for themselves whether Russia is really the earthly paradise I had declared it to be ... and challenged me to go with them'.[34] Other sources insist that the initiative came from Shaw. It matters not; everyone involved was eager for the trip. Waldorf was impelled by his desire to gain first-hand information, and much the same can be said for Philip Kerr and the Astors' second son, David, who were also in the party. Nancy went as a crusader, to attack the irreligion of infidels who opposed capitalism.

Europe was fast becoming a confused ideological battleground. The war and the peace treaties had bequeathed economic dislocation and political disorder. Demagogues of the right and left pointed their followers towards different gilded futures, whose only common feature was that the road which led to them was ankle-deep in blood. Idealists in Britain, and to a lesser extent America, were caught up by fascist or communist rhetoric without understanding its implications. Shaw, for example, somehow managed to be an admirer of both Stalin and Mussolini. Less impressionable politicians became sympathizers with the new order emerging in Berlin or Moscow, according to their own right-wing or left-wing proclivities.

The travellers saw what their hosts intended them to see, and those who had gone with fixed attitudes returned with their own beliefs and prejudices enhanced. At Shaw's request the Astors were permitted to accompany him to an audience Stalin had reluctantly been persuaded to grant his honoured guest. Nancy was not overawed. Writing to a friend a few days later, Waldorf commented:

> David and I frequently shuddered at her audacity. She seemed to look on herself as a missionary for Capitalism, and to hope that she might convert the Communists, whilst when we saw Stalin she simply could not resist talking to him about his shooting political prisoners.[35]

In later years Nancy recalled that when Stalin, doubtless to turn the conversation away from her opinion of Russia, asked her to what she attributed Britain's imperial success, she replied, 'When the English people translated the Bible into the common language they became an uncommon people because they learnt justice and mercy.'[36] She then went on to harangue the Soviet leader about his persecution of Christians. While Nancy irritated and bewildered the Moscow bureaucrats and Shaw fawned on them, Waldorf, Philip and David kept a low profile. The correspondent of the *New York Times* reported of Waldorf, 'He keeps his own counsel for the most part, but asks shrewd questions about the mechanism of State industry, finance and business, and the reasons for or against collectivisation from the peasants' angle.' The same reporter, after a chat with Philip Kerr, considered that the visitor had quickly achieved an understanding of the Soviet system which accorded completely with his own views, formulated during a ten-year residency.[37]

David, who was nineteen and between Eton and Oxford, was already very interested in politics. On his return, he wrote a long letter to 'Judie' Judge giving his impressions of the progress of Russian society. It is full of an inexperienced young man's hesitancy, but he does seem to have grasped remarkably clearly the point the revolution had reached:

> . . . the proletariat imagine 'real communism' – with equal or nearly equal wages – is just round the corner . . . those at the head of affairs either don't believe this or, half-subconsciously, don't desire it.

He thought that among party activists Bolshevik idealism was rapidly giving way to career communism.[38] David's political leanings were towards the left but, having been brought up in an atmosphere of constant, open debate, his critical faculty and powers of observation were already well-honed.

Of course, the British and American public, or, rather, the hacks of the popular press who fed them with their ideas, could not accept the Russian visit at face value. Tory die-hards seized on heavily censored accounts from Moscow which associated the Astors with Shaw's eager approval of the Russian system. 'After you have seen Bolshevism on the spot,' GBS was reported as saying, 'there can be no doubt that Capitalism is doomed,' and 'To describe [Stalin] as a great man is to use too mild a term. There is nobody like him in Western Europe.'[39] To the reactionaries the Astors had become fellow-travellers, traitors to country and class. But this did not mean that they had won friends on the left. Socialist writers castigated Nancy for her rude and uncomprehending outbursts against her Soviet hosts.

On their return the Astors did not enter into the public debate, and the leader writers soon had more important events to comment on. But, at the end of the following year, Waldorf and Nancy were back in the headlines. The First World War was still haunting international relations. At the peace conferences swingeing 'reparations' had been imposed on the aggressor states. Collecting them had proved quite impossible, had undermined the German economy and brought international repercussions. By a series of agreements payments had been reduced and then, in the summer of 1932, stopped altogether. This left Britain and France in difficulties. They needed the money from the defeated nations in order to repay the United States for the funds they had borrowed to prosecute the war. (In 1930 Britain was repaying the war debt at the rate of £34 million a year.) In 1931 French and British statesmen negotiated a moratorium but, on 15 December 1932, payment was due to be resumed. The European nations asked for an extension of the freeze. The Americans, shocked by the severity of the Great Depression, were insistent that the Europeans should meet their commitments, and the more strident elements in the press complained that Britain was squealing about paying her debts. That was the situation at the beginning of December, when Lord and Lady Astor paid a visit to Washington.

They were staying with Nancy's relations in Virginia and were scheduled to make a brief stop in the capital, during which they would make a courtesy call at the White House. Then, apparently out of the blue, they were invited by the Senate Foreign Affairs Committee to appear before them and give their views on the debt issue. This extraordinary request reveals something of the esteem in which the couple were held in the USA. The frequent trips to the New World for business and family reasons always attracted press comment. One of their sons recalled, years later, that the family were always given VIP treatment. On arrival at docks or airports they were always whisked through immigration and customs to a waiting car with the minimum of delay. The American public found Nancy as intriguing as did the public on the other side of the Atlantic, while in official circles she and her husband were regarded as unofficial ambassadors.

They were *not* so regarded in Westminster. When news of the Astors' impending appearance before the Senate committee broke on 6 December, there were furious protests in the Commons. A Tory member demanded to know, to the accompaniment of cheers, whether the interview had an official nature, and if not, whether steps would be taken to advise the US government of the undesirability of hearing evidence given 'by members of the Briish Parliament'. In reply, Anthony Eden, Under-Secretary at the Foreign Office, said that no member of either house had been authorized to appear before the Senate. It was an embarrassing situation and one which had to be resolved quickly. The situation was saved when the committee decided to postpone its meeting, ostensibly because a group of hunger marchers had encamped in front of the Capitol. (Unfortunately, the arbiters of protocol had not got their excuses sorted out, because when the Astors were asked why they were not appearing before the Senate committee they claimed that their schedule was too crowded.)

Notwithstanding this diplomatic retreat, the Astors' reception in Washington had about it something of the atmosphere of a modern royal walkabout. R. J. Cruikshank, reporting for the *News Chronicle* on 8 December, wrote:

> Across the grounds of Capitol Hill this morning I saw that bustling, trim, masterful figure which is commanding all eyes in Washington these days – Lady Astor, England's best known American and America's best known Englishwoman.
>
> Southern Senators, wearing Robert E. Lee hats and Bohemian ties, made sweeping bows of old-fashioned chivalry as she sped by.
>
> Children waved to her, Congressmen beamed, hostesses dashed after her with invitations to lunch.
>
> Lady Astor has returned and seen and conquered.

The Astors' meeting with President Hoover was brief (fifteen minutes) but cordial. In fact, Hoover was on his way out, having just been defeated in the presidential election. The economic crisis and divisions in his own party had resulted in victory for the Democrats and Franklin D. Roosevelt. When pestered by reporters to know what had been said in the White House Nancy was, for once, reticent, though she could not help having a dig at the American electoral system. She found it odd, she said, that the President and his whole team of advisers and officers should be sent out into the wilderness leaving the incoming administration bereft of their counsel. Then she led the way to the hunger marchers' camp for what we would now call a 'photo opportunity'. Over three thousand victims of the Depression – men, women and children – were camped on waste ground just outside the city, ringed by a large cordon of police. One officer tried to dissuade her from going too close, for her own safety. 'Do you call this alarming?' she replied. 'I've fought communists all my life! What I find alarming is that you haven't woken up to the need for social legislation over here.' Then she waded into the crowd, talking earnestly with the women and replying sharply to cries of 'Down with capitalists!' – just as if she had been electioneering in Plymouth.

The visit had its serious side. Waldorf, as usual quietly in the background, talking with officials, gathering information and trying to influence those in a position to 'get things done', was keenly aware of the need to get the two nations to understand each other. On the war debt issue he believed that America was making the same mistake that many British right-wingers had made over German reparations. Forcing nations in financial difficulties to 'pay up' could only have devastating international consequences. Writing to Ada Kindersley, he observed: 'Over here I have to try and explain European events and points of view. When I get back to England, I shall have to try and explain the American situation and point of view.'[40] In a speech during the tour Nancy expressed more trenchantly the concern they both felt: 'The terrible nationalism which grips many nations is a menace to progress. We are going to get another war unless we get rid of some of these foolish ideas.' That, she insisted, was what Britain was trying to say; she was not just 'squealing about the debt'.[41]

It would be impossible to overemphasize the energy and enthusiasm with which the Astors played the role of unofficial ambassadors to the USA, and scarcely less difficult to exaggerate their effectiveness, certainly in America. Nancy, the Virginian who had staked a claim for womankind in the British Parliament and was in the process of teaching the Old World the *real* meaning of democracy, was a heroine in the United States. Waldorf commented during a visit to Arizona and California in 1926 that the western newspapers gave more coverage to Lady Astor's doings than to the rest of the European news. She was deluged with invitations to speak, even when she crossed the Atlantic on purely private visits. She grabbed these opportunities with a sense of 'mission', convinced that world peace depended heavily on the unity of the English-speaking nations, that isolationism was indefensible, and that America must join the League of Nations, 'not necessarily this League, but the League as a means and symbol of international goodwill and co-operation'. She understood, as only an American woman could understand, the reasons behind the USA's reluctance to become enmeshed again in the problems of Europe. In an interview for the *Observer* on 4 June 1922 on her return from one visit, she remarked:

> It is natural, after all ... that a rich country, like a rich man, should have at least occasional suspicions of its poorer neighbours' designs. I have urged that America is great enough and strong enough to rise above the fear of 'entanglement'. American mothers have no wish to send their sons to fight foreign wars in remote countries, on behalf of strange peoples, for possibly unworthy causes. But that is not Europe's claim on America. I have tried to show that Europe needs the moral support of America even more than her money or her men.

It is remarkable how accurate, almost prophetic, Waldorf, and even Nancy in her more reflective moments, were. Summarizing his feelings about the 1932 visit, Waldorf observed that Americans were more panic-stricken about the Depression than they needed to be, simply because they had got it into their heads that prosperity was destined to continue. Unemployment was worse, proportionately, in Britain, but its impact was greater in America because there were no labour exchanges and no national insurance. He believed that the Depression had passed its nadir and that the world economy would have recovered (though not to the boom levels of the early 1920s) by the end of 1933. Yet recovery would be wasted, he warned, if nationalism was not held in check. A few days later Adolf Hitler became Chancellor of Germany.

Having travelled widely and visited all the leading nations of the world, no one saw more clearly than Waldorf the issues which could shatter all dreams of peace and prosperity. He took every opportunity to make people aware of the dangers. Unfortunately, because of his self-imposed exile from government, his opportunities were few. It was to a YMCA conference in Torquay in October 1933 that he issued a passionate warning. He spoke of the idealism that fired people, especially young people, in Russia, Germany and Italy. He described vividly the regimes of terror that obtained in those countries where people were afraid to speak openly to foreign visitors, where zealots tried to 'dragoon or terrorise men into paradise ... by the firing squad, physical torture, police espionage, and its accompaniment of imprisonment without trial'. In the face of all this

> he would be a blind optimist who did not see the real drift towards war as well as the imminent danger to the individual liberty of mind.
>
> It might well be that in the near future the peoples of the world might have to decide whether they cared for liberty even to the extent of protecting their rights

against those systems which would if possible stamp liberty out. This liberty of conscience and freedom of mind might assume the greatest importance. He doubted whether it was possible to have complete spiritual liberty in a State where political and civic freedom were denied.[42]

It is ironical that this was the man who, a few years later, would be labelled a friend of Nazism and an arch-appeaser.

Waldorf and Nancy were as prominent in debates on domestic issues as they were in matters of foreign policy. Unlike his father, the new Viscount Astor interpreted his peerage politically. Thus, although Waldorf entered the House of Lords reluctantly, he was a diligent member of the upper chamber and held in contempt the 'backwoodsmen' who only appeared in emergencies to defend their ancient privileges. Apart from the day-to-day work of the house – listening to and occasionally speaking in debates and sitting on committees – he used his position to advance those causes he believed in, through speeches and articles and through obtaining access to influential people and organizations. The Lords was, in fact, a more congenial arena than the Commons for Waldorf's style of oratory. It was less partisan. Arguments could be presented on grounds of principle, in an atmosphere less clouded by party rancour. For twenty years Waldorf interested himself in a wide range of topics, bringing to them a mind well trained in the marshalling of facts and firmly grounded in faith and ethics. As he was fond of saying, 'the major issues of our day are spiritual'. It was almost inevitable, therefore, that he would be both a visionary and an advocate of lost causes. That is to say, he saw clearly the social and political changes that were necessary, but such changes were usually of too radical a character to be implemented in his lifetime. He advocated government works and training programmes to alleviate unemployment. He opposed the introduction of a betting tax because it would lead, inevitably, to the appearance of high street betting shops. And in the struggle with Hitler he pressed for the development of a propaganda machine to counter the very effective organization headed by Goebbels.

There is space here only to discuss three policy areas to which Viscount Astor devoted his attention throughout his entire parliamentary career. Agriculture interested him as a landowner and farmer, and also as a politician who had, since before the war, grappled with the problems of national health and the food supply. The need to put the nation's agriculture on an efficient basis was the springboard for Astor's 'socialism' or, at least, his move away from Tory free enterprise in the direction of greater state control. Farming, as Waldorf knew personally from the fortunes of White Place, the Cliveden home farm, was always vulnerable to the vagaries of weather and market forces. Comparatively small-scale private enterprises could not escape the cycle of boom and slump. This meant that many of them were poorly placed to benefit from those developments which, potentially, should have enabled them to improve the quality and quantity of farm yields, and therefore profitability. Scientific research, mechanization and vastly improved transport facilities were beacons pointing the way to modernized agriculture, and the war had underlined the importance of making Britain self-sufficient in foodstuffs. Over the years he and the various committees he chaired produced a stream of reports, but Waldorf's own thinking was crystallized in three books of which he was co-author – *Land and Life* (1932), *The Planning of Agriculture* (1933) and *British Agriculture: The Principles of Future Policy* (1938).

British Agriculture, which Astor wrote in conjunction with the Quaker industrialist and social reformer B. Seebohm Rowntree, was the result of work by a distinguished panel of experts and made recommendations which, for the 1930s, were breathtakingly radical. The writers advocated public ownership of farmland – not, as they were anxious to point out, from doctrinaire devotion to socialist ideology, but because many landlords 'are unable to discharge their historic function of supplying agriculture with ... long-term capital improvements'. They called for government-appointed marketing boards with powers to fix prices, fair to both producer and consumer, and also to enforce stringent quality controls. They looked for the development of larger, more efficient agricultural holdings, better housing for rural workers and parity of wages between farm and factory workers. Small wonder that the Astors were regarded by some as 'traitors to their class'; nothing could have been more alien to the traditionalist, fiercely independent landed interest than *British Agriculture*. Yet there was an inescapable logic in the book's arguments, and some at least of its proposals were taken up during and after the Second World War.

Another cause which Viscount Astor championed made no progress in his lifetime, though in later years steps were taken towards reform. From the moment he set foot in the House of Lords he was determined to change its composition. Four times he introduced bills aimed at admitting peeresses to the chamber. Now that women were in the Commons it seemed to him patently absurd to preserve the upper house as an all-male club. It was tilting at windmills, although on one occasion in May 1925 his measure failed by only two votes. But Waldorf's activity did not stop there. He aimed at the complete overhaul of the institution. To this end he twice introduced legislation himself, and supported measures introduced by others. The main flaw in the existing system, as he pointed out in a pamphlet in 1931, was the hereditary principle. It was, he suggested, in one of his more colourful passages of prose, like the Old Man of the Sea who fastened upon Sinbad.

The actions of the Lords are cramped by the ugly, sinister weight it bears on its back. Moreover Sinbad himself does not always turn a deaf ear to the evil promptings of his incubus, and one must admit that out of date and out of touch die-hard sentiments are too often enunciated in the House of Lords . . .[43]

Waldorf was anxious that the Tories should bring in the measure in order to defuse the 'people v. peers' arguments used by the other parties ('The House of Lords should be conservative not Conservative'). He advocated life peerages, nominated by the Commons, for prominent men and women in every walk of life. And, of course, his proposals were backed by an impressive body of research. Waldorf compiled facts and figures on the composition of every bicameral legislature from the Soviet Union to India and from the USA to New Zealand. He was still urging the need for reform on Churchill in 1947.

But the windmill against which Lord Astor – and his wife – tilted most ardently was the demon drink. They argued for continuing reform through restriction of pub opening hours, limitation of licensed premises and, above all, nationalization of the liquor trade. What angered Waldorf even more than the social effects of alcohol consumption was the wealth, power and tactics of the brewers' lobby. Nancy spoke contemptuously of the members of the upper house as the 'beerage', and Waldorf claimed that the Conservative party was riddled with those who were actively involved in the drink trade and those whose support had been bought:

Lord Stout, Sir W. Distiller and Mr Brewer represent the reactionary right wing of Toryism and hold that Party back on social reform, just as . . . the intoxicants they sell tend to blunt the ideals, independence, and ambition of the public.[44]

In this, as in health, land reform and other issues, it was, in Astor's view, the money-grubbing die-hards of the Tory Establishment who opposed reforms and set their own wealth and privileges before the good of the nation. There were no dirty tricks to which the liquor tycoons would not stoop. The only way to defeat them, therefore, was to confront them head on. Waldorf looked to an extension of the Carlisle system by which production and distribution of beer and spirits would be controlled by the local authorities. This he envisaged as being achieved not by central government diktat but by local referenda. When the people in a given area voted for change a process of compulsory purchase would swing into operation.

Nothing would have such a far-reaching effect on our public life as changing the drink trade from a profit-seeking self-interested competitive basis to a system of supervised public ownership . . . We want the change for the nation's sake.[45]

The campaign was, of course, doomed to failure. By 1930 the temperance movement had passed its peak. Earlier achievements had been won largely by appealing to public sentiment during the 1914–18 War. Without such a stimulus the moral crusaders found themselves deprived of allies in their war against vested interests who possessed a large repertoire of corrupt practices. The Astors did, however, notch up some successes during their long siege of the brewers' citadel. They did not ally themselves with the extremists, such as the member for Dundee who urged that all bottles containing alcohol should be labelled 'Poison', but thanks to their pressure Parliament refused to sanction a return to pre-war pub opening hours, and Nancy's private member's bill of 1923 outlawed the sale of alcohol to anyone under the age of eighteen.

CHAPTER 10

'Everything is political'

Since Lord and Lady Astor were such controversial figures and since their home was a busy centre of political activity, it was inevitable that the world of Cliveden and St James's Square should be a strange, intense, 'busy' one for children to grow up in. At the heart of it was the relationship between Waldorf and Nancy. Bob Brand once jokingly compared it to the kind of rapport which exists between a good animal trainer and a dangerous wild beast. As best he could, Waldorf 'managed' his wife. His love for her was total and intense. He admired her courage and audacity. He encouraged and helped her in all her enterprises. He was her greatest fan and regarded her as 'my primadonna'. He was always ready to spring to her defence. David remembers how Waldorf explained the 'facts of life' to him as a teenager: 'You will find that your mother is liked and admired by a lot of people and also criticised by a lot of people. The ones who like and admire her are the ones with a larger outlook. Those who attack her are petty-minded and usually don't like her for all the wrong reasons.' When necessary, however, he put his foot down, usually to save her from herself. Nancy, for her part, generally accepted his authority, although her feminism and her strength of will sometimes made it hard for her to do so.

Emotionally the relationship was one-sided. 'You always seem to be so understanding with everyone else and with me to be sitting just trying to find fault.'[1] So Waldorf complained one day in the hot summer of 1913 when he was sweltering in London, fulfilling a round of political and charitable engagements while Nancy was relaxing in Scotland with, apparently, nothing better to do than write him highly critical letters. Waldorf's comments were just. Nancy was profligate with her time, money and care on behalf of others, but she never felt herself to be fully a part of the 'Astor brood', as she sometimes called them. She clung to Bobbie Shaw, her son by her first marriage, with results which were not good for mother or son and tended to set up barriers within the family. Waldorf and *his* sons received scant encouragement. To some extent Nancy resented her husband's celebrity and success, which increasingly cast her in a mere supporting role. Later, when it was she who received star billing, the relationship worked much better. Yet always its basis was unsteady because Waldorf did most of the giving and Nancy most of the taking.

Inevitably, this profoundly affected their family life. By the end of the war that family was complete and consisted of four sons and one daughter, in addition to Bobbie Shaw. Both Waldorf and Nancy intensely desired to be good parents. In many households where the adults are wealthy and busy, children live on the periphery of parental affection, their needs ignored. It was not so in the Astor home. Waldorf and Nancy took a close interest in their children's schooling as well as their wider education. They arranged frequent holidays and took the youngsters to America and all over Europe. Every summer the family went to Scotland. In 1919, having given up the Glendoe property, Waldorf bought 40,000 acres on the island of Jura in the Inner Hebrides. He chose this wild spot with its house (Tarbert Lodge), providing only basic amenities, very deliberately. 'I have five boys (including my stepson, Bobbie Shaw),' he explained to his lawyers. 'I am very anxious periodically to get them away from civilization and all its comforts and luxuries. In addition to ordinary sport, such as deer, grouse, salmon and trout, there is sea fishing, seal shooting, lots of lobsters, oysters, etc ... I am sure it will be excellent for the boys to rough it for a few weeks every year.'[2] Waldorf provided the earnest, dutiful element in the children's upbringing. He impressed upon them the responsibilities of their position: 'You are lucky enough to be wealthy so you must have a care for people who are not so lucky.' Being a man of austere habits himself, he was determined that his sons and daughter should not grow up as rich men's spoiled brats. Inevitably this means that he projected a rather austere image. The only member of the younger generation who was able to get on easy terms with him was Bobbie.

It was Nancy who provided the gaiety and spontaneity in the lives of the growing Astors. Her immense vitality filled the home. Michael remembered cosy afternoons by the nursery fire when his mother would tell hilarious stories, enacting each character with a different voice and mannerisms. The daily Bible reading, the Christian Science 'lesson', might sometimes end up in laughter and chaos. Even with the children, Nancy was a performer. There was a strong strain of mimetic talent in the Langhorne family. Nancy's sister Nora was a first-rate entertainer, and it was Nora's daughter, Joyce Grenfell, who showed the world the family talent for portraying characters. However, as Michael explained, Nancy's clowning, which might be spontaneous or prepared, outshone everyone else's. The characters she invented

> usually appeared on the slightest pretext in the dining-room when the conversation looked like becoming monotonous and my mother wished to escape from ordinary-

life conversation and jump into another element ... There was the little Jewish business man, and in order to do him justice she would hurry upstairs and a few moments later appear again wearing trousers, a tail coat, and a bowler hat crammed over her ears. This character had no name or any name. He was in business, any sort of business. He was excitable, affectionate, gigglish, a family man devoted to his wife and children: he was confidential, persuasive, but really suffered from terrible anxieties which at times rendered him hysterical. Then there was the horsey English lady who hunted in Leicestershire. The false teeth were enough to do her justice. This character went hard to hounds, swore a bit, and suffered from no anxieties whatsoever. There was also the lady of infinitely good breeding and no brains, conventional and vague, who found Americans common ... And there was the frightened mean old lady with no teeth in her head, her skin all wrinkled and her hair pulled down over her face, who looked shrewd and canny and who was deeply suspicious of her neighbours. In the library these characters came to life; sometimes to give a recital of their experiences but usually to carry on conversations with everyone in the room. It was more than a talented performance. My mother knew the whole range of the business instinctively. Turning her back on an audience she could indicate by a walk the lady whose feelings had been slighted but who still retained her pride; or the heroic old body who joined the women's services at the outbreak of war and whose only thoughts were blind patriotism and loyalty to the flag.[3]

Inspired by Nancy's lead, other members of the family circle gave uninhibited performances of their own. Bobbie Shaw's repertoire was more limited than his mother's, but his satire of an earnest village clergyman made frequent appearances. One Langhorne sister and three nieces settled in Britain and were frequent visitors to Cliveden. They could always be relied on to keep a party going. As the Astor children grew up they all played their parts in these amateur theatricals, though, by common consent, Jakie was the most talented of the younger generation. If ever the expression 'never a dull moment' meant anything, one feels it certainly applied to the Astor home. There was always something, either serious or comic, happening at Cliveden and Nancy was sure to be at the centre of it. Whatever it was, everyone was expected to participate – with gusto.

The ground bass upon which the other activities – fancy-dress balls, tennis, riding, staff sports, concerts, etc., – formed embellishments was *talk*. Talk of political, religious or social issues – but always talk with a high moral tone. Outside Oxbridge common rooms there can scarcely have been anywhere else in the kingdom where intellectual debate was such a constant. For the children, especially the younger ones, mealtimes could be an ordeal, but as they grew up and became gradually aware of how privileged they were to be on easy terms with such 'greats' as George Bernard Shaw, Lloyd George, Balfour and Sean O'Casey, they found the conversation stimulating. Again, the atmosphere has been well caught by Michael Astor:

Were there ever such talkers brought together in one place? Bernard Shaw commanded an audience and his talk demanded one. But J. L. Garvin, Walter Elliot, Lionel Curtis and Geoffrey Dawson had to compete. Garvin would go ten minutes without eating when he was talking, otherwise he lost his place. Lionel Curtis on a Federated Europe evoked a sense of timelessness, of something inexorable which had to be stated and had to be heard, impervious to Bobbie's aside, voicing our unspoken thoughts, of 'Can't anyone tell him to shut up?' which carried to his end of the table and roused my mother to ask Bobbie to shut up, and through the various requests of 'shut up' Lionel boomed on, noble and unbowed.[4]

Every biographer of Nancy Astor has drawn attention to her besetting sin – possessiveness. She clung to her children, her relatives, her constituency and her friends with talons of jealousy, emotional intensity and moral outrage. It was a tragedy for her and for them. Nancy had to organize people and could never be deflected from her conviction that she and she alone knew what was best for them. The other side of her genuine philanthropy and concern for people was an unmasterable passion to interfere in their lives. GBS, after the death of his wife, had to be emphatically rude to prevent Lady Astor coming to look after him. Joyce Grenfell had to fight against Nancy's objection to her following a stage career. It was, of course, worst for the children. They were ensnared by their mother's enchantments. She tried to direct the course of their careers. She became inordinately jealous when other women appeared in her sons' lives. She tried to make them into good Christian Scientists. In the 1920s her letters were full of news of their progress and their little triumphs. But as they grew up they inevitably needed to break free from her spell, and in the 1930s the tone of her correspondence changed to one of bitter resentment because they were defying her will and deliberately trampling on the things she held sacred.

Yet even in the midst of estrangement there remained fascination, admiration – and humour. David recalls an incident in the 1930s when he and his mother were scarcely on speaking terms. He went to Cliveden for the weekend but determined to leave on Sunday, instead of Monday morning, pleading an important engagement. Nancy tried to persuade him to stay over but eventually gave way with the comment, 'Well, if you must, you must. By the way, if you bump into your mother give her my regards. I'm told she's a very pleasant woman.'

It was not just Nancy who wound maternal coils around her offspring. Cliveden – and by extension 4 St James's Square, Rest Harrow and Tarbert Lodge – were havens, sanctuaries, but they also became spiritual prisons from which escape was difficult. They were gardens of earthly delight where desire for the outside world was dimmed, magic places which exercised a mesmeric power over those who grew up there. In 1934 Joyce Grenfell and her husband, Reggie (whom she had married in 1929, with Waldorf and Nancy holding the reception in St James's Square), moved into Parr's Cottage on the Cliveden estate, which Nancy let them use because they were hard up. The couple lived on the periphery of the regular regimen at the 'big house' but were often included in it. Joyce's partial detachment and keen sense of observation make her assessment of Cliveden particularly valuable.

> When one hasn't been to C. for a while its strange restlessness smites you, I find. Too much goes on. Too many people, too much talk, too much food. The fires are lovely, so are the flowers and it is fun in some ways but oh, how glad I am to get down to my quiet little drawing room . . .
>
> . . . there are times when the atmosphere of C. strikes me as being so darned poisonous that I have to get out at once. The odd thing is that I sincerely believe Aunt N. thinks the house has a rarefied and good air to it. It's always struck me as significant that Uncle W. escapes to the somewhat chill but ever happy atmosphere of his Munnings-hung room upstairs!![5]

Cliveden was an enchanted kingdom and Nancy was its queen. For years she bound her children to her with spells of vitality and humour. Yet, eventually, the years came when mounting discontent and the need to develop their own identities drove them to challenge her rule. Then there was nothing for her to do but break her wand and go away.

The family that grew up here in the 1920s and 1930s consisted of five boys and a girl. First there was Bobbie Shaw. Many years later Bobbie pronounced his own succinct epitaph – 'I've had a very full, empty life.' From childhood, Nancy's first son was extremely good looking. To go with his physical appeal he developed immense charm, a sense of fun, a disregard for danger, and the Langhorne theatricality and panache. He was nine years older than the first Astor child, and his stepbrothers and sister hero-worshipped him. For them he was a breath of fresh air blowing through the stuffy moral rectitude of Cliveden. Bobbie had an extraordinarily easy relationship with his stepfather which Waldorf's own sons were never quite able to achieve. Perhaps more important in their eyes, Bobbie was deliciously wicked. Not only did he say outrageous things, for which they would have been seriously castigated, but he would get away with escapades they would never have dared try.

Nancy both revelled in Bobbie's audacity and warned her younger children not to take him as an example. She doted on her eldest son, and there was between them an intense bond that neither of them was ever able or willing to break. Nancy indulged Bobbie, but at the same time she regarded him as a possession. In emotional terms she gave him everything and yet denied him the freedom to be his own person. The end result was that he could not live without her, but that very fact built up inner tensions and resentments. Nancy was caught up in Bobbie's life in a way that was never true of her relationship with the Astor children. Her attitude frequently drove Waldorf to despair. 'You owe it to the rest of the family', he once protested, 'not to let Bobbie affect you so much. It deprives the little boys and all of us of your help.'[6] Nor was Nancy's protectiveness good for her son. Any attempt by Waldorf to bring parental discipline to bear was completely vitiated by his habitual appeal to his mother. At a very early age he became a genius at playing one off against the other.

Waldorf, for his part, found it difficult to strike the right balance in his relationship with his stepson. On the one hand, he made a special effort to be the father that Bobbie never had and to make up to him for the years of childhood insecurity. On the other he saw the need to 'make a man' of Bobbie and instil in him a sense of purpose. For this reason the young man, unlike the Astor boys, was sent not to Eton but to Shrewsbury, because it was felt that the tougher regime of Dr Alington would do him more good. The experiment failed, largely because Bobbie felt he had been discriminated against and resented it.

Waldorf next encouraged his stepson to take up a military career. After some hassle with the army establishment, which was not at all sure about this unconventional, 'un-British' young man, he secured for Bobbie a commission in the Horse Guards in December 1917. Here Robert Shaw was in his element. He got on well with all ranks and was a superlative horseman. The activity he excelled in above all others was steeplechase riding. He was twice winner of the Military Gold Cup, a prize almost as prestigious in its day as the Grand National and competed for over a course which was almost as formidable. There was, of course, little time for such activities during the First World War. Towards the end of the conflict when it was clear that Bobbie would have to join his regiment in France, Nancy was beside herself with worry. While Waldorf insisted that the young man must go and take his share of danger, and while Lieutenant Shaw himself was eager for the fray, Nancy surreptitiously pulled strings to try to keep her son in England. Eventually Bobbie spent the last five months of the war on the western front and returned unscathed.

His military career was soon interrupted by scandal – scandal, by the standards of the time, of the most serious kind. Bobbie was homosexual. An incident occurred in 1919 and was discovered, and Lieutenant Shaw was removed from the active list. For the sake of all concerned the facts were hushed up. It was given out that Bobbie had been found drunk on duty and that this was the reason for his dismissal. In order to distance him from wagging tongues, Waldorf sent Bobbie to Rhodesia. He hoped that a hard, outdoor life in the colonies would reform his stepson and help him to find a purpose in life. Once again, young Mr Shaw declined to co-operate in this programme of rehabilitation. Within a short time he was home again, much to his mother's relief.

Something else that Waldorf tried was to involve Bobbie in the Jura estate. When it was set up as a limited company in 1919, he gave the young man a £20,000 stake in it. Bobbie liked the rugged island but he was not prepared to spend long periods of time there. He was essentially a city person and he had no intention of being separated from his favourite haunts.

Later the ne'er-do-well was provided with a farm at Wrotham in Kent. He never put his back into agriculture, but simply used the house as a base conveniently near his friends and centres of entertainment in London. As a fun-loving young man of independent means he saw no reason why he should not just amuse himself. In the 1920s and 1930s he lived the carefree man-about-town kind of life satirized by P. G. Wodehouse and Noël Coward. People who knew both men saw some distinct similarities between Bobbie Shaw and his near contemporary, the Prince of Wales (later Edward VIII). They moved in the same circles and had several friends in common. Both were handsome, popular and outspoken. Both had little regard for convention. Both eventually found it impossible to suppress their own inclinations in order to do what was expected of them.

Waldorf despaired of ever getting his stepson to make something of his life; then, somehow, the Horse Guards were persuaded to give Bobbie a second chance. Doubtless he made solemn promises to behave himself, and doubtless his parents used all their influence in high places to get him reinstated. For a few years he returned to the pleasant camaraderie of the officers' mess and to the work with horses which he loved. It was at this time that he made a name for himself as an utterly fearless steeplechaser. A racing event in 1925 illustrates well the relationship which existed between him and his mother. One day in January, he asked Nancy to come and watch him ride at Plumpton. She asked Waldorf and he said 'No', but Nancy 'suddenly felt compelled to go', despite her dislike of racing, and this was one of the few occasions on which she defied her husband. She reached the course in time to witness Bobbie's race and was horrified to see him fall at the water jump. She almost had hysterics when her son was carried 'bleeding and unconscious' from the course. She went with him to Lewes cottage hospital and summoned the family doctor from London to attend him. This august professional diagnosed what the local GP and probably even a competent nurse could have observed: Bobbie looked a great deal worse than he was; there were no serious injuries and nothing that a few days' rest would not put right. Writing from the patient's bedside, Nancy commented: 'I sit in his room by day and have come here to sleep by night. Shall move him to Cliveden Sunday. It's only been 2 days but it seems 2 years.'[7] One might expect such maternal solicitousness for an injured and badly shaken child. For a twenty-six-year-old soldier it seems a little excessive.

After a few years the tensions in Bobbie's personality began to tell. He went through bouts of bitterness and resentment, and doubtless his suppressed sexuality was at the root of his problems. In his moments of depression he, naturally, vented his rage on the person he loved most – his mother. He was still keeping from her his awful secret. He knew that if it became public the revelation would disgust her and cause her serious public embarrassment. In 1931 it did become public. He was arrested for importuning young men. The police had no desire to prosecute and with their connivance the family were able to whisk Bobbie away to Paris. But he refused to stay there. He told his friends, 'I could never live outside England,' and he disdained to run away. He returned and faced trial as a practising homosexual. While Waldorf and Nancy went off on their Russian trip, Bobbie was sent to prison for five months (he served four). In the event, the scandal did not harm the Astors because it was kept out of the papers. The family used their influence with the press. In particular, Nancy, Bertie Spender-Clay and Garvin made individual appeals to Lord Beaverbrook, the proprietor of the *Daily Express*, who was no friend of the Astors. He suppressed the story but kept their letters on his files. The day would come when he would demand his pound of flesh. The only note that appeared in the newspapers was the bald statement in *The Times*' 'London Gazette' on 17 August, that Lieutenant R. G. Shaw 'having been convicted by the civil power, is removed from the Army, his Majesty having no further occasion for his services'. No mention of Bobbie's offence. Of course, there was no reason why most people should connect 'Lieutenant R. G. Shaw' with the famous Astors. Nancy penned a note of thanks to 'the Beaver'. It must have been hard for her to go cap-in-hand to a man she loathed and whom she loved to ridicule as 'Been-a-crook'. In her letter she said that she had only sought silence for the sake of the other children, and that she was really proud of Bobbie because he had refused the chance given him by the police and chosen to return and face the music.[8]

Bobbie's character disintegration continued. He often took refuge in drink from his feelings of frustration and despair. What had been a wicked sense of fun became cruelty. His wit was distorted into bitter cynicism. The family continued to be supportive and when he tried he could still be charming, but with the passage of the years he tried less often. 'His conversation is so tinged with bitterness and cynicism', Joyce Grenfell reported to her mother, 'that it pervades and fouls the atmosphere. He can't resist bullying the children and uses the most low methods of attack.'[9] He was an unhappy and deeply pathetic figure. It is worth leaping ahead a few years to illustrate this from a letter he dashed off to Nancy in 1947. A fellow MP and friend of hers, Mavis

Tate (not a particularly close friend of Bobbie's), had died of an overdose of barbiturates. Bobbie wrote:

> Oh Mother Darling, Mavis committed suicide in her poor little house yesterday. What is this life? Perhaps it's only a sort of dream anyway. Death to me is so final, suicide to me so tragic, as say what people may, I know the black misery that proceeds the thoughts of life being no use to one any more and all hopeless. I know them only too well, poor, poor creatures who are driven by despair . . . Oh Mother, what should I do, when, and if, I am some day separated from you for ever.[10]

Those words were written by a man in his fiftieth year.

Yet it would be quite wrong to stereotype Shaw as a degenerate misfit who got on everyone's nerves. He had many friends, and throughout the thirties he remained an extremely important member of the Astor circle. He was, moreover, intelligent and a very astute judge of character. Bob Brand, undoubtedly the cleverest member of the circle, once remarked that anyone aspiring to cabinet rank should be obliged to submit to a couple of hours' grilling by Bobbie Shaw in order to determine his suitability for high office.

William Waldorf (Bill) was the first child born (in 1907) to Waldorf and Nancy. He was destined to fill the role of the elder brother in the biblical parable, the major difference being that there were three 'prodigal sons' rather than one. Quiet, though not withdrawn, by nature, Bill of all the Astor children was the one most affected by his mother. This was because he was the one who received least affection from Nancy. In fact, it would scarcely be an exaggeration to say that she rejected him. Perhaps because Bill was the first Astor child, or the first child born after the adored Bobbie – whatever the reason, he and his mother never established a loving rapport. This had two results: Bill gravitated more towards his father, and at the same time worked desperately hard to win his mother's favour. For instance, he accepted CS indoctrination and, to please Nancy, kept up a pretence of belief in it long after it had ceased to have any meaning for him. He did not 'fit in' completely. One of his brothers recalls that Bill was never comfortable with the constant badinage that was part of Astor life. As the boys grew up, they naturally broke the chains of parental guidance and control. Except Bill. He suppressed or hid a young man's natural 'vices' from his disapproving parents. This inner rebellion and outward conformity set up tensions which were, at times, intolerable. He once commented to Violet Astor's daughter Margaret, 'I wish I had your mother instead of mine.' At prep school Bill was easily bullied. Once his contemporaries suspended this 'rich boy' out of a window by his feet to see if gold would drop from his pockets. He suffered the usual disadvantages of the first-born: he was brought up to assume responsibility and to adopt a serious attitude to life. Despite a bout of illness, he enjoyed himself at New College, Oxford. He acquitted himself well academically, devoted an acceptable amount of time to hunting and polo, and discussed current affairs late into the night as a member of the exclusive Canning Club. Thereafter, the path was clearly laid out for him by the expectations of his parents and of society – travel, farming and politics (Conservative, of course).

Bill was brought up to continue the family tradition. He involved himself in various charities, interested himself in the life of Cliveden and the farm at White Place, with genuine pleasure, studied the management of the Astor racing stables, travelled abroad extensively and kept himself particularly well informed on Middle Eastern and Far Eastern affairs. Both his parents – but especially his mother – towered over him like giant oaks. While his brothers all veered away to find their own light and space, he determinedly stayed within his parents' shadow. Other people looked upon him as 'Waldorf and Nancy's son'. A parliamentary colleague, writing to Bill in 1945, undoubtedly believed he was paying him a compliment when he described him as 'less enthusiastic than your mother, less radical than your father'.[11] Bill conformed. He strove to please his parents. He ended up being caught between Nancy's irresistible force and Waldorf's immovable object. According to his widow, even as a fully grown man Bill's face would 'turn the colour of the ceiling when his mother entered the room'. Bronwen Astor is convinced that the aortic aneurism that killed her husband was the result of tension built up over his early years.

Even when it came to establishing his political identity his inheritance posed problems. During the thirties Nancy and Waldorf moved steadily further apart. Lord Astor's trend was idealistic and leftish, while his wife became more and more right wing. From Waldorf, Bill learned the careful and unimpassioned study of facts. He became a member of Chatham House, whenever possible preferred to see foreign situations for himself and built up a large number of overseas friends who helped to keep him well informed. But it was his mother's sheer emotional intensity that largely decided his own political stance. At Oxford he associated with the more reactionary elements in the university and eventually found himself well to the right of the party.

Soon after Bill came down, his father obtained a position for him on the League of Nations Commission led by Lord Lytton in 1932 which was set up to enquire into China's complaint of Japanese aggression in Manchuria (see below pp. 261–2). For a young man genuinely interested in Asian affairs it was a fascinating introduction to practical statesmanship and diplomacy – and it also helped bring him to the attention of the nation's political leaders. It was in the following year that the celebrated Oxford Union debate occurred which insisted that 'this house will not fight for King and Country'. Explaining this to an American audience shortly afterwards, Bill observed:

. . . the resolution was worded in a most provocative manner. But I do not think that that was altogether a bad thing as it showed quite clearly that the young people of the country were deadly serious in their desire for peace and the pacifism we profess is a constructive pacifism. We do not mean by it a mere indifference to politics in peace time and in war time a personal refusal to fight. We mean, rather, a sustained positive effort to see that the foreign policy of our country is conducted in such a way that it will avoid war, support the peace machinery of the world and enforce treaties.[12]

There was nothing remarkable in Bill's associating himself with what would later be called 'appeasement'; the abhorrence of a new outburst of total war was shared by most political thinkers.

Determined to keep up the family's parliamentary tradition, Bill began actively looking for a suitable seat in 1933. It took a long time. 'None of those I want look like falling due,' he wrote to a friend in October 1934. 'The ones they suggest are safe country seats in Essex or textile towns beyond Liverpool.'[13] With the economy in the doldrums this was not a good time for the Conservatives. Bill's brother-in-law James Willoughby only scraped home in a by-election in what had been one of the Tories' safest seats. This made Bill's eventual achievement even more noteworthy. In the general election of 1935, he recaptured against the prevailing trend the constituency of East Fulham, which Labour had won two years before. The following year, he became PPS to Sir Samuel Hoare, who was the First Lord of the Admiralty and, subsequently, Home Secretary. Hoare was one of the arch-appeasers in the Cabinet and, for a variety of reasons, one of the most unpopular members of the government. Being linked with him was not the most auspicious start to a political career. Yet Bill was loyal to his chief, and during the Second World War, when Hoare had been demoted to Ambassador in Madrid, went on record to defend a man who had 'one of the keenest brains in public life' and who had, while at the Admiralty, instigated the laying down of modern battleships and destroyers, and as Home Secretary had established the basis for Britain's system of civil defence.[14]

Bill was also following another family tradition. He showed a keen interest in the *Observer*, frequently wrote articles and took considerable pride in a paper that he fully expected, one day, to take over as proprietor. At this time he enthusiastically backed the *Observer*'s independent stance. The paper, he told a friend, 'is going against almost all the rest of the press. We are stressing the dangers of sanctions [against Italy], the perils to England if she gets into a clash with Italy and the harsh realities of the situation generally. We are like St. Athanasius "contra mundum".'[15] When he entered Parliament Bill was twenty-eight and showing no signs of getting married. The reason for this was that he nursed a deep passion for an American divorcée, five years his senior. Mary Stevens Baird was an intelligent and attractive member of New Jersey society. She and Bill had much in common, including a love of horses and opera. They corresponded regularly for over a dozen years and visited each other frequently. But Mrs Stevens Baird remained impervious to Mr Astor's protestations of love and resisted his oft-expressed determination to marry her. She urged him to seek the company of attractive young English ladies. His reply was that he was doing so but could find no one to compare with his New Jersey belle.

Nancy Phyllis Astor ('Wissie') was born in 1909. She had her father's dark good looks and her mother's impetuosity, but she was also highly sensitive and this was something that Nancy never made allowances for. Wissie came in for the same sharp criticism and lack of encouragement as the boys. For example, Nancy would make disparaging remarks about her dress sense in public. Few things are more calculated to cause embarrassment to a teenage girl than that. Wissie also became a victim of her mother's sense of Langhorne–Astor rivalry. Alice Perkins (later Alice Winn) was almost the same age as Wissie and was one of Nancy's Langhorne nieces. When Alice tragically lost both her parents Nancy virtually adopted her and she became part of the Cliveden household. There Nancy lavished more attention on her than she did on her own daughter. Only when Wissie was a young woman were she and Nancy brought dramatically together through a bad accident. One day when she was twenty, Wissie took a bad fall on the hunting field and her horse rolled over her. An X-ray revealed a severe spinal injury, necessitating immediate treatment. Valuable hours were lost while her parents argued with friends about whether her injuries should be placed in the hands of a Christian Science practitioner or a top orthopaedic surgeon. Eventually, and against their religious inclinations, Wissie was entrusted to medical science. She made a slow but almost complete recovery. The episode was certainly a shock to Nancy. Her relationship with her daughter had become increasingly stormy as Wissie learned how to stand up for herself. Now that she had come close to losing her little girl, Nancy grew more indulgent towards her.

Three years later James Willoughby d'Eresby, son and heir of the Earl of Ancaster, came into Wissie's life. He was a quiet, well-mannered young man (Joyce Grenfell described him approvingly as 'cosy' and believed he would help his beloved to 'calm down'). In 1933 he was at Cliveden for Ascot week, though on that particular occasion he had little interest in horses. He proposed and, after being kept on tenterhooks for a fortnight, was accepted. Wissie and James were married at Taplow church on 27 July. Interestingly, Wissie was marrying into another Anglo-American family; her mother-in-law, Eloise, Countess of Ancaster (*née* Breese), came from solid New York commercial stock. When the couple returned from their honeymoon in Biarritz, they were faced with a pleasurable ordeal that proved how very popular the Astors were in Plymouth. The city fathers had laid on in the Guildhall a reception for two thousand people in the newly-weds' honour. (Two years previously there had been similar celebrations to mark Nancy and Waldorf's silver wedding. The Astors were presented with a magnificent silver model of the *Golden Hind*.) The local press reported that Waldorf spoke entertainingly in introducing the couple but that, 'of course', everyone wanted to hear 'the Lady'. Nancy did not disappoint.

This was destined to be the only long-lasting first marriage in the family. All Wissie's brothers later experienced the pain of divorce. One must avoid the temptation of deducing too much from this simple statistic, but it is certainly true that Nancy tried to cling to and dominate her boys and that all her daughters-in-law had a tough time. Immediately after the wedding James was elected as prospective Tory candidate for Rutland and Stamford. He took his Commons seat in 1933 and held it in 1935, so Wissie remained in the thick of party politics.

Francis David (always known as David), born in 1912, was the most introverted and intense member of the family. At first, he quietly accepted the guidance of his parents and was prone, as a teenager, to searching self-analysis. He inherited his parents' strong social conscience and interest in politics. He followed Waldorf's austere personal regime and, like his father, loved Jura. In his early years he was a faithful devotee of Christian Science, and Nancy had hopes of his becoming an active proponent of the faith. The crisis came towards the end of his time at Eton, when he tried to assert his own individual identity and, in particular, expressed grave doubts about Christian Science. Instead of seeing this for what it was, natural adolescent rebellion, Nancy regarded it as 'betrayal' and 'rejection'. David had a minor breakdown.

It was agreed that, after the Russian trip and a three-month stay in Heidelberg to learn German, David would go to Balliol, rather than to New College like his father and elder brother. Balliol had a reputation for intellectual distinction and 'leftist' policies, and Waldorf hoped that its atmosphere would suit David's questioning and unsettled spirit. It should have done so. No one went up to Oxford better equipped to take advantage of its stimulating atmosphere. David's education in contemporary politics had been unique. For years he had met and talked with its leading exponents and had arrived at a personal commitment:

> ... it seems to me that politics is the most important pursuit of all as being the necessary setting for all good lives. 'Politics first and last' seems the creed. Everything is political and must be looked at politically ...[16]

He mixed with socialist undergraduates and joined the Labour Club. This was not only part of his rebellion; it seemed the natural course to follow. David shared his father's apprehensions about the developing international situation, and, as far as he could see, the people of the Left were the only ones who were taking it seriously. Everyone else seemed frivolous or reactionary, or both. In a letter to J. J. Judge he angrily and sweepingly dismissed the Oxford establishment:

I hate the beastly place and think its atmosphere vile. I think, in fact, that they are out of touch with the beauty of the universe and I loathe almost everything about them. Arrogance, puppyness, small-mindedness in a dozen forms, artificiality and hypocrisy but, first and last, pomposity.[17]

David's espousal of socialism, a creed she hated and denounced with increasing venom as the years passed, was, for Nancy, another example of his treason. In one sense it was even worse than his rejection of Christian Science, because it gave her political enemies a stick to beat her with. When the press hounded her, she was forced on to the defensive. It was 'rot' to suggest that her son had embarrassed her, she declared.

Even if he has joined the Socialists why should it embarrass me? So long as he is working to improve the world and not wasting his time I shouldn't worry if he joined the Communists. His mind is not really interested in party politics. It is the social problems that attract him.[18]

Behind that public façade the rift between mother and son became greater. 'Mother has just returned from Switzerland feeling like an avalanche,' Bill informed Mary Stevens Baird, 'and I've spent rather a trying day attempting to patch up a row between her and brother David, who resembles her far too closely to get on with her.'[19] The psychological impact of all this on the young man was severe. 'Keep my dear parents off the subject of me if they get onto it, as the less they think and talk about me, the happier for everyone'[20] – so David wrote to 'Judie' Judge early in 1933. Judge and Kerr had been brought in as mediators, because David liked both men and trusted their counsels. But neither they nor a psychiatrist whom David consulted were able to fend off another breakdown. Inevitably, his work suffered, and he left Oxford half way through his final year. Fortunately, he had come into his inheritance under his grandfather's will and was now able to set himself up independently in London. His relations with his father remained close and their political opinions converged to a remarkable degree, but, for all practical purposes, David remained outside the family for several years.

Michael Astor (born 1916) also rebelled, for reasons which were fundamentally identical though, on the surface, they appeared different. He jumped through the same educational hoops of Eton and Oxford and emerged with a degree in agriculture and political economy. He was cosmopolitan and artistic by temperament. In later years he became a very competent painter, and his autobiographical *Tribal Feeling*, reveals a literary talent which was destined to remain undeveloped. In his formative years he travelled widely, both in wild places, such as the forests and mountains of Canada, and the sophisticated capitals of Europe. This experience of a wide world coupled with the freedom of undergraduate life drew him away from what seemed to him the stifling atmosphere of Cliveden. In the 1930s there were basically two paths which young people might take who felt the need to reject the beliefs and attitudes of their parents' generation. Some challenged prevailing political assumptions and the class structure on which they were based. This was David's route. Others flouted 'Victorian' moral restraints. That was Michael's road. He was never a political animal and took as read the class assumptions of the Tory establishment. He became a member of the Oxford and London 'fast set' and earned the disapproval of his parents for such enormities as smoking, drinking, casual sexual relationships and, worst of all, rejection of Christian Science.

Michael's rows, which increased in frequency, were with his father rather than his mother.

He [objected to my being] unpunctual and sloppy. He would prefer it if I did not drink. Smoking, too, was a bad habit: it really showed a lack of self-control. He did not like to see me reading the glossy magazines: my spare time would be better occupied with a good and improving book. Had I yet made up my mind what I wanted to do? . . . My language, of late, he found distasteful. The words 'bloody' and 'damn' were offensive. He personally never used any word stronger than 'drat' . . . Stern, benevolent, judicial in his view, he reigned, for the time being, like Jehovah, a figure to fear, respect and increasingly to resent.[21]

This was no more than the commonplace phenomenon of the arrogance of youth coming into conflict with the arrogance of maturity. But there was something more behind it – the Cliveden factor. Michael had come to realize what lay behind the beauty, the gaiety and the fascination of the Cliveden which, as a child, he had loved.

The world of Cliveden . . . which existed behind the brilliant social façade, was the world of moral adjuration . . . the world in which our and everyone else's actions were judged on a moral basis, a world of denial and restraint which allowed little room for experiment o . . . self-expression . . . a world from which I was determined to escape.[22]

And escape he did, just as soon as he secured his financial independence. He left Cliveden, never to live there again, except for brief visits on family occasions.

John Jacob Astor VII (born 1918) was always known as 'Jakie', and more than one of his friends over the years made the rather obvious comment that 'Jokie' would be a more appropriate nickname. He was a lively youngster, full of fun and very quick-witted. Most of the troubles of the other children between the wars washed over him. As the youngest he was the last to go to Eton and thence to New College. As Nancy desperately tried to keep the old Cliveden atmosphere going in the late thirties, especially on set-piece occasions such as Christmas and Ascot week, he was her willing aide, enthusiastically organizing charades or doing his own party turn. Horses were always his first love: he had ambitions to be an amateur steeplechase jockey. Certainly at Oxford racing and polo took up much more of his time than books. His father remonstrated with him (forgetting, as fathers are prone to do, that in his day he himself had been a far from model student) and eventually took away Jakie's horse. It was too late; academic failure stared him in the face. 'I may have to come clean,' he confided to Michael, 'and tell father the only thing I've passed this term is water, and not much of that.'[23] Retribution, if retribution there was, was brief, and Jakie was spared the soul-searching his brothers had gone through. By this time the world was teetering towards another war, and there was no time to indulge in introverted speculation about one's true place in the scheme of things.

Waldorf watched the thirties tragically unroll, and for him the pain was worse, because he saw, more clearly than most, the direction in which world affairs were heading. For him the euphoria of the Locarno era had evaporated early. He was actually present, in September 1931, when the covenant system of international co-operation began to come apart at the seams. Waldorf had always been a firm supporter of the League of Nations, though he felt it should have greater power and knew that it was, perhaps fatally, weakened by the non-membership of the USA. In the early post-war years he kept in close touch with Edward House, who as personal adviser to President Wilson had been a principal architect of the League. Both men hoped to see a change of attitude in America and watched with sadness its descent into isolationism. In the autumn of 1931 Waldorf was first appointed one of the British commissioners to attend the annual assembly of the League in Geneva. During the next few years he gave a large amount of his time to the international organization. It was while the 1931 meeting was in progress that Japan invaded Manchuria. In Geneva this provoked furious exchanges between the two Asiatic delegations, and demands from several representatives for economic sanctions to be applied if the Japanese failed to withdraw. This was the first real test of the League of Nations. Waldorf's letters home reveal little of the tension or importance of these events. There is about them a certain aloofness and a distinct sense of British superiority. Thus the head of the Portuguese delegation looks like 'a very fat carp' and the chairman of the council resembled 'a pork butcher, and is about as competent to deal with a ticklish situation as a pork butcher would be'. The 'Latins' made conditions in the conference hall difficult for everyone by insisting that the heating be turned on full. The French tried to pull a fast one by submitting an ambiguous resolution and were foiled by the Italians – 'it requires one Latin mind to catch out the subtleties of another'. All in all, Waldorf declared, 'I am inclined ... to agree with that person who said that you leave the white race when you cross the Channel.'[24]

This chauvinism concealed a growing disillusionment with the League of Nations. Waldorf arrived in Geneva having spent several weeks witnessing at first hand the harsh reality of the political situation in Germany and Russia. The subtle manoeuvrings and pompous posturings of the conference seemed to bear little relation to these ominous happenings. While in Geneva he sat in on the disarmament talks, which had been in progress for years and which, soon afterwards, foundered on Hitler's demands that the German army should be raised to the same level as those of other leading nations. Waldorf observed sourly that so many delegates wanted to have their say that the committee's report was complicated to the point of incomprehension. He was still committed to the ideals of the League, which was why he was frustrated to see it being successfully elbowed aside by aggressive nations.

It was Bill who became closely involved in the Manchuria episode. Like his father, he had a passion for amassing facts and also for seeing situations for himself. In January 1932 Lord Astor obtained an invitation for Bill to observe the crisis in the Far East at first hand. The Earl of Lytton welcomed Waldorf's suggestion and urged Bill to come as his personal secretary on the League of Nations commission of enquiry to Manchuria. Naturally, the twenty-four-year-old accepted the honour eagerly, and his appointment was endorsed by Geneva with a salary of 1,000 Swiss francs a month. In fact, the expedition turned out to be a more arduous adventure than young Astor had bargained for. In addition to the long voyage, the delicate diplomacy, the deliberately over-generous hospitality provided in Tokyo and Peking and the collecting of on-the-spot evidence, Bill had to act as nurse when Lord Lytton was taken ill in July. His companions had to borrow a plane and hurry the peer to the German hospital in Peking. The commission completed its work, but afterwards Lytton had to make his way home in easy stages, and Bill, as his secretary, went with him.

Having accompanied the commission's leader in the summer, Bill had to go to Geneva for discussions on the commission's report in the autumn. Lytton was not strong enough to attend the assembly, so Bill had to go in his stead to keep him informed on the Manchuria debate.

It was a depressing experience, but an important lesson in fence-sitting diplomacy. Despite talk of sanctions, the League's only real power lay in such moral pressure as could be brought to bear by a majority of its members. If it failed to make its decisions effective, its very existence might be under threat. Conscious of this, the Lytton report made no attempt to change the *status quo* in Manchuria. It did condemn Japan for resorting to force but conceded that she had received provocation. It was unlikely that this face-saving attempt to please the League and the two combatants could succeed. Japan threatened to leave the organization unless the report was modified. American observers backed China in wanting the League to take a tougher line. When Sir John Simon, the British Foreign Secretary, spoke in support of Lytton's work, the speech was interpreted as being pro-Japanese and did not enhance already strained Anglo-American relations. Bill found himself scurrying round behind the scenes trying to keep various delegations on speaking terms. The behaviour of some of the representatives did not help matters. 'In walked Matsuoka and his two generals . . . in extravagant form, banged the table, asked why the League did not condemn Japan like they obviously wanted to and then Japan would get out.' Astor was convinced that Germany was encouraging this truculence. Meanwhile, the brother of the head of the Chinese mission 'is here with a French mistress, and takes her out dancing every night, and the Chinese are terribly upset as they think everyone will think that it is their chief delegate who is out on the tiles of Geneva seven times a week!'[25] Simon returned home in mid-December convinced that all was well. It was an optimism Bill did not share – and he was right. The assembly adopted the Lytton report and Japan walked out, becoming the first important member state to leave the League.

Over the next few years Germany and Italy, as well as Japan, dismissed the League as an irrelevance while they pursued their territorial ambitions. Waldorf, as his letters show, was depressed and apprehensive about the situation long before most other people saw the danger signals. For the principle of collective security to work, the League of Nations had to enjoy, and when necessary enforce, universal respect. When potential aggressors were tempted to strike, they had to know that an immense weight of moral, political and economic pressure would be applied to them. Without the full involvement of the United States this was not possible. Waldorf watched in dismay as the assembly degenerated into a sometimes absurd talking shop, as its representatives temporized and finally capitulated over Manchuria, and as European dictators took their cue from Japan's success.

In 1935 Mussolini declared his intention of annexing Abyssinia. First Anthony Eden, the Minister for the League of Nations, and then Samuel Hoare, the Foreign Secretary, came up with compromise plans. They were rejected, and Italian troops marched into Haile Selassie's kingdom. Hoare resigned, and in December Eden was appointed to take his place. A guest at Cliveden reported Waldorf's reception of the news:

Looking grave, Lord Astor came to breakfast this morning, saying that war was nearer, Eden appointed Foreign Minister and the French fleet moved. He had shaken his head on Friday night when Lady A mentioned Eden's name, and speaking later to me said that Eden was in part to blame for the situation, having said that Musso was bluffing.[26]

Waldorf disapproved of Eden because of his hawkish attitude. As he later wrote to Nancy: 'Anthony's manner always gets Hitler and Musso on the raw – It's no good lecturing people or talking down to them if you want to improve relations or avoid a war.'[27] Belligerent talk without military or economic backing was bluff. It could only provoke counter-bluff. Ultimately the forces of international justice would have to back down – again – or bolster their words with force. The tragedy of the League's failure, as Waldorf clearly saw, was not that it made war *likely* but that, sooner or later, it made war *inevitable.* Simply swapping belligerent slogans with the likes of Hitler and Mussolini was not the mark of a statesman working for peace.

But much as Waldorf disliked Eden's stance and his naïve reliance on economic sanctions, he was not prepared to see the man pilloried, and this became one of a growing number of issues which created friction with Garvin. Astor was finding his obdurate editor more and more of a problem. In April 1936 he wrote:

We have got on splendidly for many years because we were sensible as well as having real feelings of affection. I have not abused my position as Chairman of the Observer Company and you have respected my views. I am determined that nothing shall prejudice our spirit of co-operation if I can avoid it but there must be the same willingness on your part as there has been hitherto . . . I wrote to you specifically last week about Eden. I was frankly disappointed when I read the *Observer* today. It is and sh'd be quite easy to criticise the official policy when such a course is necessary without seeming to have a personal vendetta against him. Do see about this.[28]

Garvin was quite unrepentant. What he had written, he insisted, was the 'truth', and he implied that nothing the proprietors did would prevent him from telling it.

Such differences always ended up with Garvin digging his heels in, and this became increasingly frustrating for Lord Astor; but this did not stop the two men keeping up a lively and frequent (sometimes daily) correspondence. They were both passionately concerned about the international situation. Europe was a complex of fragile relationships and there were no simple or obvious ways of sustaining peace. In a twenty-two-page letter on 18 May

1936, much of which was in energetically scrawled note form, Waldorf went over all the options. Italy, surely, was the real threat to the Empire and to Europe. Might it not be best to stop Mussolini now, by military means if necessary, while Britain could still count on the goodwill of other nations? But 'What of Germany? Where does she stand? What will she do? Presumably she wants either influence over a substantial portion of Central and S. Eastern Europe – [or] ownership of some of it.' Would that be so terrible? 'Is a strong Germany in Central Europe a greater danger to our Empire than a powerful Roman Empire dominating the Mediterranean and Red Sea? . . . We must settle with either Germany or Italy if it is not possible to settle with both.' For the objective must be 'an assured peace – not a *short lived* peace because that is not peace – not a peace at any price because that is neither worthwhile nor real'.[29]

Garvin's scarcely less brief reply reveals a more astute analysis of the situation:

> Musso . . . does not want acute enmity with either Britain or France and assuredly not with both at the same time; but he does not want to be dependent on either of them; and he would prefer a solid adjustment *with* Germany for a term of years . . . And this is what Berlin too would prefer . . . Hitler [whose medium-term objective is annexation of Austria] . . . *does* want the largest and strongest anti-Communist bloc that he can form in Central Europe, Italy necessarily being one of the solid portions of that nucleus.

He insisted that there should be no talk of rushing into a conflict:

> . . . it would be a madness never exceeded in the whole of history to precipitate any unavoidable war whatever without gaining at least another year's time, for preparation *if we can*. We are still only sixth in the list of air-powers.[30]

'Appeasement' is a blanket term, and it meant different things to different people. For Waldorf, although he never owned the word, it meant not giving in to tyrants, but trying to rediscover for the benefit of generations to come a world where disputes were resolved by peaceful means. He was not optimistic about the chances of avoiding war, precisely because he made it his business to understand the conflicting aims and ambitions of the European states. What he and Garvin agreed on was that the British public (and those of its leaders given to knee-jerk reactions) were ignorant of the complexities of the situation. Waldorf was concerned, by speeches and through the press, to rouse a nation which had its head firmly embedded in the sand. The majority of the population could not or would not recognize just how real the threat of war was. On 5 February 1937 he wrote an article for the *Western Morning News*, entitled 'Causes and Dangers of Unrest in Europe'. Basically, he observed, the reasons for instability fell into two categories. One, the growth of Russian communism, was something for which other nations could not be blamed. However, it constituted the greatest potential threat to world peace because its long-term aims were aggressive and it was pledged to the overthrow of all capitalist systems. The other was a state of affairs for which all the signatories to the Versailles peace treaty (but principally France) were largely responsible. Germany had been encircled and humiliated, and this had made the emergence of Nazism inevitable. Versailles had also created the problem of small states containing ethnic minorities whose integrity was guaranteed by the major powers, thus setting up a situation as nonsensical as it was nightmarish. For example, Czechoslovakia would be fully justified in expecting British soldiers to shed their blood in order to prevent a breakaway movement by the Hungarians within its borders. Waldorf believed, as Philip Kerr both believed and deeply felt, that, borne along by post-war bitterness and righteous indignation, the Allied leaders in 1919 had made some terrible mistakes which were now rebounding on their originators.

From 1936 onwards Nazi Germany became progressively bolder in 'rectifying' these mistakes by main force. The Rhineland, Czechoslovakia and Austria were 'liberated', and foreign powers were compelled to recognize Germany's need for *Lebensraum*. Winston Churchill and a handful of other belligerents insisted that those who used military might to breach international agreements should be answered in the same coin. The Astors were among those who regarded such talk as both wrong and dangerous. It was wrong because one could not ask British servicemen to lay down their lives to defend treaties which were morally and politically flawed. It was dangerous because it would confirm the dictators' creed that justice only comes out of the barrel of a gun, because it was virtually impossible that a war in part of Europe could be contained, and because such a war would certainly do nothing to help the small nations on whose behalf it was launched. There was still an alternative, and that was for the world's leaders to consider carefully and sympathetically the grievances of which Germany and her neighbours protested and to deal with those grievances by peaceful means. It was an unfortunate and unpalatable fact that this would mean dealing with Adolf Hitler.

Waldorf was under no illusions about the German Chancellor. The Prime Minister, Neville Chamberlain, and other leaders who visited Berlin were almost all taken in by Hitler, who could appear disarmingly friendly and reasonable while telling straight lies and concealing hideous plans. But Waldorf was treated to a display of the dictator's real self and it made a considerable impression. He went to Germany as part of a Christian Science delegation and had an interview with the Führer. Hitler deliberately turned the conversation to politics and asked why it was that Britain was so unfriendly towards him. As an individual, with no diplomatic responsibility, Waldorf gave a straight answer: 'It cannot be otherwise as long as you persist in your policy towards the Jews.' At that, Hitler literally went berserk and had to be calmed down by his aides. Lord Astor saw Nazism as a disease which the German people should be encouraged to eradicate. He did not, like many British right-wingers, regard it as a necessary counter-balance to the greater threat of communism. He was quite clear that it was oppressive, undemocratic, vicious and a threat to civilization. It might be that a crusade would have to be launched against it; but that should only be after all other alternatives had been tried.

It seems very likely that what he most ardently hoped was that the Germans themselves would see Nazism for what it was and rise against it. Despite the reports of mass hysteria and hero worship coming from the Third Reich, such a hope was not altogether forlorn. During these years Waldorf was growing emotionally and politically closer to his son David. David had many friends in Germany, most of whom were, secretly of course, opposed to Hitler. One young man to whom he was particularly close was Adam von Trott zu Solz, who moved in government and diplomatic circles and who testified that there existed at the highest levels an anti-Nazi movement which, as well as being fervent, was organized. On visits to England in 1937 and 1939 Trott both canvassed support for the rebels and encouraged his contacts to believe that an end to the Nazi regime was a distinct possibility. Official circles in Britain did not really take this young enthusiast seriously, but for the Astors Trott's confidential information added weight to their conviction that the military option should be resisted as long as possible. Nancy, who was still on bad terms with David and disliked or affected to dislike his radical friends, quickly took to Trott. The young German was a Rhodes scholar – a group in which she had a special interest – and he impressed her by the quality and strength of his character.

The man who had the misfortune of steering the ship of state through the mine-strewn waters of the late 1930s was Neville Chamberlain, who became Prime Minister in May 1937. Neville and his wife, like his brother Austen and other members of the family, were friends and occasional guests of the Astors, and Nancy, in particular, backed the Prime Minister to the hilt until almost the last days of his premiership. Waldorf was less uncritical. By 1940, if not earlier, he had come to see Chamberlain as an 'egoist', a 'mediocrity' and 'honestly obstinate'.[31] There is no doubt, however, that, like the bulk of the British people, both the Astors supported his two-pronged policy of seeking negotiated agreements with Hitler while at the same time, albeit lackadaisically, building up the nation's armaments. The only member of the Cabinet who opposed Chamberlain's handling of the crisis was Eden. The conflict between the two men had as much to do with personality as policy. The Foreign Secretary was apt to take a high moral tone in official exchanges with other states, but when it came to negotiation he was just as ready to compromise as his predecessor, Hoare. Chamberlain regarded him as unhelpfully provocative and sometimes went behind his back in dealing with foreign governments. This not unnaturally riled Eden. It was clear that this situation could not continue for long. In February 1938 Eden was somewhat shabbily elbowed out of office and replaced by Edward Wood, Viscount Halifax. Edward and Waldorf had gone through Eton and Oxford together and were still warm friends. The Astors were therefore never closer to the process of policy-making than they were in these crucial years.

Everyone in Britain was anxiously aware of Chamberlain's toings and froings to meet Hitler. Time and again the Führer obtained concessions and made promises, only to break his word and make fresh demands. This activity culminated in the ill-fated Munich agreement of September 1938, when Chamberlain seemingly plucked the brand of 'peace in our time' from the livid coals of imminent war.

Bill was in his seat in a packed House of Commons on 28 September when Chamberlain announced the Munich agreement and the apparent climb-down by the German leader, and he described to a friend in America the euphoric and relieved cheers with which the news was greeted. Bill prophesied that the world would now draw back from the precipice of war. He located the only possible threats to peace, not in Berlin, but closer to home: a lack of determination to build up British armaments and 'a really deep hatred of Nazism in many people who really do not want friendly terms with Germany'.[32] Most of Bill's countrymen shared his stubborn optimism. But he was right in identifying a groundswell of horror at the stories of atrocities emerging from Nazi-controlled territories, of distrust of the German Chancellor and conviction that war was the only way to halt his growing power. Those swayed by such feelings remained in a minority – until 15 March 1939. The day Hitler marched into Prague was the day that the fragile structure of appeasement came crashing to the ground. Almost within hours the population, angry, fearful and crushingly embarrassed at having been duped, turned against the architects of false hope.

Daily life went on against this troubled background. For the Astors it was perceptibly changing. Sorrow came early in 1937 with the death of Phyllis, Nancy's much-loved sister who was the wife of the Astors' close friend Bob Brand. At about the same time Waldorf supervised the funeral arrangements of Bertie Spender-Clay, and Nancy had to find the emotional energy to comfort Pauline and her two daughters. Eighteen months later Buck Langhorne, Nancy's own last brother, passed away in America. In 1937, for the first time, Lord and Lady Astor did not preside over the Christmas festivities. They went to Florida for Waldorf's health. In fact, the heart was going out of the family gatherings at Cliveden. Bill did his best to keep up the traditions, but David and Michael seldom came. 'Deserted' by her family, Nancy found it difficult to summon up enthusiasm. As for Waldorf, every year he surveyed his mounting tax bills and wondered how much longer he could keep his queen in her magic kingdom.

There were, of course, still many glittering occasions, and Nancy was not to be cheated of her determination to bring happiness into the lives of other people – even the royal family. In March 1938 she arranged a very special children's party at 4 St James's Square.

> The upstairs dining room was transformed into a market green, with artificial grass on the floor, stalls all around – fruit & flowers, sweets, toys, fancy balloons – and draped in scarlet and white canvas. At one end there was a floodlit Punch and Judy theatre! In the ballroom was a three-piece orchestra. A wandering musician with an accordion wandered around in gipsy costume! Then there was a tea of major proportions. All the usuals plus angel cake, meringues fashioned into birds, ice cream of two sorts and dozens of little cakes, etc.
>
> The invitations said 'Country or Peasant Costume'. This was fairly widely adhered to. Princess Elizabeth was a Dutch Peasant. What a charming child she is. She has lengthened out a lot and has now got quite a lovely little face, really graceful arms and generally is very attractive. She has a quiet poise that makes her remarkable among the other children. My word, she and Princess Margaret are well brought up. They have such unobtrusive manners and are natural – surely an achievement in their position – always being watched and concentrated on . . .
>
> After the tea and presents there was dancing and games in the ballroom. Bill is surprisingly good with children and had them all Follow-My-Leadering all around the room and through the two drawing rooms and back again.
>
> Both Queens were there. Mary in regal grey and Elizabeth in old rose . . .[33]

But on the whole the late thirties were sombre years in both private and public life. Nancy felt bitterly the estrangement from her sons and this was made worse by the growing understanding between Waldorf and David. The married life of the Astors was becoming increasingly 'semi-detached'. Now that the family had grown up, husband and wife frequently took separate holidays. Every summer Waldorf went to Jura, and Nancy to Sandwich. He had by now ceased to be her political mentor. Rarely did she ask him to write her speeches or give her advice or gather information and statistics. She developed her own style and approach to issues. She entertained ambassadors, statesmen and foreign dignitaries in her own right. Without Waldorf's restraining hand, Nancy's public (and especially parliamentary) performances became more eccentric and outrageous. Her contributions to debates were still sometimes telling, but the house which had once been amused by her antics now tended to regard them as tiresome. She and her husband were, as ever, easy targets. At the end of 1937 they encountered a new enemy.

Claud Cockburn was a left-wing Irish journalist who, in 1933, parted company with *The Times*. He decided to join the prevailing fashion of producing a weekly political broadsheet. He called it *The Week*. It was cheaply produced and had a modest circulation, but it caught on in influential circles. Cockburn latched on to the well-known stratagem of providing his readers with inside – or supposedly inside – information. The public loves exposés, the idea that they are being made privy to the secrets of the people who control their destiny, that they are discovering what *really* goes on in high places. Cockburn was, doubtless, partly influenced by frustration. Fleet Street was being gagged. Many proprietors and editors, under pressure from Westminster, had fallen into the habit of suppressing or colouring information which might 'embarrass the government' in a time of international tension. Opponents of official foreign policy were denied newspaper space. Alternative voices were simply not being heard. Cockburn was determined to fight this conspiracy of silence and to find ways of stirring anti-fascist sentiments. There was, inevitably, a limit to the amount of genuine inside information at his disposal – but lack of evidence has seldom inhibited newspapermen. It certainly did not inhibit Cockburn. What he did not know, he surmised, and what he did not surmise he invented. Because he wanted to rouse his readers against the prevailing appeasement policy he conjured up a group of conspirators and called it the 'Cliveden Set'.

The members of this cabal were Halifax, the Astors, Lord Lothian, Geoffrey Dawson, his deputy editor Robin Barrington-Ward, and other individuals well known to be Astor hangers-on. They were 'appeasers'. They were pro-Nazi. Over the weekend of 23–24 October at Cliveden, Cockburn claimed, they hatched a plot which involved sending Halifax to Berlin to offer Hitler a free hand in Europe in return for the abandonment of his colonial ambitions. Their devious plots included neutralizing members of the Cabinet who might not easily fall in with their schemes, notably Anthony Eden. *The Week* ran articles, short on substance and long on innuendo, intermittently for a year. At first they made little impact. Then the idea was taken up by a few other editors. In March, the Communist party published a scurrilous penny pamphlet, its title emblazoned in startling red, white and black, *Hitler's Friends in Britain*. Twenty thousand copies were soon in circulation.

Week-end parties at Cliveden House [it trumpeted] have made and broken British Cabinet Ministers. Decisions taken there have brought Europe to the verge of war. Friends of Hitler and enemies of the people are welcome there. Many of the 'National' Government's betrayals of peace have begun with a Cliveden week-end party. The Cliveden Set ... their power reaches through British banking, transport, journalism – through Britain's Parliament, across the seas to International Fascism . . .

The authors of the pamphlet did not trouble themselves with accuracy or consistency. They portrayed John Jacob Astor I as a man who had made his fortune out of selling liquor to the Indians. Determined to cap Cockburn's scoop about the October house party, they invented a weekend gathering at Cliveden in January 1938 at which the downfall of Anthony Eden had been plotted. They were hard put to it to show how giving in to Hitler's demands had brought Europe to 'the verge of war', but then truth and logic were not their objectives. They were improving upon Cockburn's conspiracy theory to stir Britain's 'workers' against the upper classes, against America and against the forces ranged worldwide in opposition to communism.

The Cliveden Set myth would quickly have sunk into the quagmire of public apathy had it not been for the changing mood in the country. Cockburn helped the opponents of appeasement to find a focus for their anger. By the time Czechoslovakia fell and the nation wanted someone to blame for its predicament the scapegoats had been clearly marked out. When people asked themselves and each other how they could have been so easily deceived by Hitler the answer was ready to hand. It was not their fault at all; there was a diabolically clever Hitlerite cell at work. It had infiltrated government, the press and big business. The real culprits were the members of the Cliveden Set.

Once the myth was up and running it developed both speed and stamina. Within six months it was all over the world and, once established, it clung stubbornly to its hold on men's convictions. In January 1939, Philip Kerr (now Lord Lothian) reported from Chicago:

> The Cliveden Set yarn is still going strong everywhere here. It symbolises the impression spread by the left and acceptable to the average American that aristocrats and financiers are selling out democracy in Spain and Czecho-Slovakia because they want to preserve their own property and privileges. Chamberlain is their tool.[34]

The Astors' inclination was to ignore the smear. They were used to being sniped at by enemies on the right and the left. Nancy found it hurtful to be dubbed 'the member for Berlin' in the Commons, but such barbed ribaldry was no worse than she herself indulged in. Soon, however, it became apparent that this particular calumny had staying power. Even the respectable newspapers were having to give it space. There was a permanent posse of press photographers outside 4 St James's Square to record the comings and goings of Astor guests. The story was used to good effect in by-election campaigns. And it was provoking strong reactions from all over the world. In an interview for the *Saturday Evening Post* a year later, on 4 March 1939, Nancy admitted:

I get letters from hundreds of people I've never seen – from Australia, Canada, Hong Kong – everywhere. They call me Nazi, pro-Fascist, traitor, and worse!

This is what they say: That my family and friends ought all to be taken out and shot! That I'm the center of a vicious and degenerate gang which, in some mysterious fashion, has got control of England's foreign policy, and uses it to keep tight hold of their own fortunes, at the expense of England's honor and to the destruction of the Jews.

In March 1938, when Waldorf and Nancy returned from a visit to the USA, it was obvious that silence would not stifle the accusations and that the charges must be answered. Nancy's reaction was flippant but not without point. She sent out to prominent people who had enjoyed Cliveden hospitality over the years group photographs in which they appeared. With each one went the following note: 'Cliveden weekends have become so world famous that you might like to have a photograph of one which you graced with your presence.'[35] The implied blackmail was obvious: there were very few people in high society who could afford to point the finger at the Cliveden Set, since to do so might attract attention to their own involvement. Waldorf took a more serious line. He sent copies of the offensive propaganda to the nation's leaders, including Queen Mary at Marlborough House. He wrote to leading newspapermen round the world. He appealed to Conservative Central Office for an official repudiation. It may well have been with some satisfaction that Douglas Hacking, the chairman, wrote to decline this suggestion on the grounds that it would be bad for party publicity. For three decades the Astors had shown scant regard for orthodox Tory policies and discipline. They had from time to time attacked the die-hards of the Conservative Establishment. Now they wanted help from the party machine. Well, they could go on wanting.

On 5 March Waldorf published a long letter in *The Times** repudiating the Cliveden Set 'fiction' and issuing a counterblast against its authors, whom he identified as communists who 'attacked and misrepresented anyone who aimed at replacing international suspicion, fear and ill will, by a sense of good will and confidence' and 'a weak and disunited opposition ... [who tried] to discredit the motives of a Prime Minister who was new to his office and to injure the reputation of a new Foreign Secretary'. Waldorf was easily able to pull the rug from beneath the main arguments on which the Cliveden Set myth rested. There *had* been a house party at his country home on 23–24 October, but it was not used to plan the details of Lord Halifax's forthcoming visit to Berlin, since these had already been settled. Surprisingly, he did not add that Halifax was not present at the gathering in question. As for the

* See Appendix, p. 408.

conspirators seeking to undermine the Foreign Secretary, that would have been difficult because Anthony and Beatrice Eden were among his guests on 23–24 October. The meeting of the cabal in January was easily disposed of: during that month Cliveden was shut up and its owner was in America.

There was no Cliveden 'Set', if that word is taken to mean a body of intriguers. The contemporary refutations by Waldorf and Nancy, supported by George Bernard Shaw and other friends, discredited all the evidence for a conspiracy. Later writers have gone into the incident in detail* and there is no need to reiterate all the arguments. Nancy's own disclaimer in her 1939 article for the *Saturday Evening Post* is the central pillar of the Astors' defence:

> . . . we do not entertain with any plan or plot. With a purpose yes, for our life has a purpose; but not a plot or a plan. I am too impulsive to plot or even to plan long ahead. Naturally, we entertain politicians, and politicians include peers and paupers. But they are only some of the guests. They're mixed up with Labor men, social workers, writers, our American friends, religious teachers, temperance workers – all sorts . . . The object of our parties is just that – to give people of all sorts a chance to get together and hear one another's views.

It had, for three decades, been the Astors' self-appointed mission to foster understanding by talking with and bringing face to face people of opposing views. Waldorf could honestly assert in *The Times*: 'Lady Astor and I are no more Fascists today than we were Communists a few years ago when we supported the trade agreement with the Soviet.' Yet it was precisely because of their chosen and very public lifestyle, and their desire to affect the course of national and international events, that people were ready to regard them as exercising a sinister influence. Here were two inordinately wealthy (and foreign!) people, only loosely attached to the political system, who were on close terms with British and European royalty and with the US President, who owned newspapers and who were intimate with leaders of government, finance and business. Moreover, this couple had several causes, ranging from teetotalism to pro-Germanism, about which they felt strongly and which they advocated openly. The Astors would have denied none of this. It was their profound wish to change the world in certain ways. To do this they exercised influence, though they would have called it benign rather than sinister.

However, the line cannot always easily be drawn between influence and conspiracy. Consider a letter written on 24 June 1938 from one member of the Astors' inner circle, Lionel Curtis, to another, Lord Lothian:

> Your long and persistent efforts were largely responsible for the replacement of

* See, for example, C. Sykes, *Nancy: The Life of Lady Astor*, 1972, chapter 18.

Vansittart–Eden, by Halifax. Though Chamberlain and Halifax may have diverged from your lines you still exercise the most powerful influence on their policy outside the Cabinet.[36]

In the light of that let us review the events of the autumn and winter of 1937–8. Neville Chamberlain had taken office in May. Under the previous administration the Astors had enjoyed easy access to the Prime Minister via Tom Jones, who was Baldwin's principal adviser. Chamberlain, of course, looked to his own men for counsel, and Sir Horace Wilson became his main confidant. Nancy and her friends worked hard to rectify the situation. By late September she could report some success to Lothian: 'I believe TJ has got into touch with the PM, in fact I know he has which is really good news, but don't give me away!'[37]

Someone else who was feeling excluded from the new regime was Sir Robert Vansittart. This seasoned civil servant had, until recently, been the permanent under-secretary at the Foreign Office. He was violently opposed to Hitler and Mussolini and constantly urged a policy of 'standing up to' the dictators; though he was unclear about exactly what that meant and what its results might be. So strongly was he opposed to government policy towards Germany that he passed information to Winston Churchill, its principal critic. Not surprisingly, Chamberlain excluded him from office and appointed him to the high-sounding but less powerful position of chief diplomatic adviser to the Foreign Secretary.

Meanwhile, plans were progressing for the Cliveden house party of 23–24 October. Eden was invited and accepted. When Nancy wrote urging Lothian to come she stressed that it was important because Sir Nevile Henderson would be present. Henderson was the very pro-German British Ambassador to Berlin. Among the twenty or so other guests who eventually assembled on the famous weekend were the old Round Tablers Lionel Curtis, Bob Brand and Geoffrey Dawson, together with two Foreign Office officials, Sir Alexander Cadogan, the deputy under-secretary, and Sir Philip Nichols, who was married to Phyllis Spender-Clay (Bill's cousin). The Astors and their guests spent long hours discussing the European situation. If there was a hidden agenda it had nothing to do with planning Halifax's trip or plotting Eden's downfall; it had everything to do with apprising the Foreign Secretary, who took a high-handed attitude towards the Nazi leader and had never been to Germany, of the actual situation in Berlin and the need for a cautious approach. It became clear that Eden was unlikely to moderate his views and that Vansittart had redoubled his efforts to urge him and the Prime Minister to a more forthright policy.

Shortly after this, Lothian left for a trip to the Far East and Australia. Any direct influence he brought to bear on the nation's leaders, therefore, must have been largely by letter. Nancy, on the other hand, met frequently with Chamberlain, Halifax and their close colleagues. She kept her friend informed. 'Neville seemed . . . very wise about America and quite determined about Germany,' she reported after one tête-à-tête; 'I am particularly struck with his patience.' By contrast Vansittart and his allies were working 'violently and subtly' to undermine the Prime Minister's endeavours. It seems quite likely that the thwarted civil servant was Cockburn's principal informant. When Halifax returned from his trip to Berlin, Nancy was eager to pass on to Philip his impressions. 'He liked everyone he met . . . particularly Goebbels. What struck him most was the attitude to the League of Nations and anything like Collective Security. He said that he felt he was speaking a completely different mental language but he realised that it was absolutely necessary for us to get on with them.'[38] On 19 December Waldorf and Nancy left for Florida. They were still away when Eden was manoeuvred into resigning.

For three of the 'arch-conspirators' to be absent during the crucial weeks leading up to the disclosure of their machinations seems remarkably indolent. For them to have failed to install their nominee at Chamberlain's right hand (for TJ, as Jones was always called in Astor circles, never supplanted Horace Wilson) shows a certain lack of Machiavellian determination. Clearly there was no plot. But, just as clearly, there was an enthusiastic wielding of influence. And, if we are to believe Curtis's letter of 24 June, quoted above, that influence did not fail in its objective.

In all democracies an important part of the political process is lobbying. Interest groups go to considerable trouble and expense to make sure that governments know their opinions and are provided with such facts as are pertinent to matters in which they are concerned. These pro and anti groups are rather like competing tugs, nudging the ship of state in opposite directions and having an influence on its ultimate course. The lobby system is capable of abuse in many ways. There is the possibility of bribery, particularly in subtle forms, of manipulation of the press and even of blackmail. And it is undeniably a system that favours those organizations and individuals who have the deepest purses. One could say that the political establishment is one big lobby, for many are the 'understandings' reached in gentlemen's clubs, on golf courses and over expense-account lunches. The Astors themselves complained about the power and corrupt dealings of the brewers' caucus. Cliveden and all that it represented was part of this system; it was a multi-purpose lobby, devoted not to a single but to several national and international causes. There is no evidence that the Astors and their friends behaved in ways that might be considered reprehensible, but that they strove mightily to influence the course of affairs is undeniable.

Nomenclature is vitally important in the creation of myth. Easily remembered slogans and titles help to fix ideas in the public consciousness. They remain as trip-switches capable of activating reaction long after the events and attitudes to which they relate have been wholly or partially forgotten. Cockburn knew this when he coined the sobriquet 'Cliveden Set'. It haunted the family for years. Even the Astors' friend President Roosevelt let the phrase slip in a wartime statement. When Nancy protested, Eleanor Roosevelt replied, on behalf of her husband:

> Of course when Franklin spoke to the press, he was speaking generically – in general terms and certainly without any reference to you or your husband.
>
> We have had and still have people in Washington who continue to have much the same theory as those who belonged to the Chamberlain school of thought from 1937 to 1939. They have been proved wrong, but continue in their wrong-headedness, whereas you and your husband did not. We do not consider these people here as unpatriotic or subversive, but they can be classified as thoroughly mistaken in view of the fact that they have been proved wrong in the past.
>
> Right or wrong, the term 'Cliveden Set' has become a symbol in the country of not just appeasement, but a failure to evaluate the world situation as it really was.[39]

There could be no clearer statement of the power of myth.

Nancy did achieve one small revenge against the man who had blackened the Astor name. Sometime during the war she was attending a political function in London when a friend of hers, a Labour MP, told her that Cockburn was present and offered to introduce her. For the first time vilifier and victim confronted each other. The journalist extended his hand. Nancy spat in his face.

Something that still confuses the issue when the Cliveden lobby is discussed is its country house image. Harold Nicolson complained in April 1939 about the effects of expensive entertainment in glamorous settings:

> The harm which these silly selfish hostesses do is really immense. They convey to foreign envoys the impression that policy is decided in their own drawing-rooms. People such as Simon and Hore-Belisha* (who are middle-class individuals flattered by the adulation of what they suppose – with extreme incorrectitude – to be the aristocracy) are also impressed by the social efficiency of silly women such as Mrs Grenville and Lady Astor. Anybody who really knows the latter understands that she is a kindly but inordinately foolish woman. Yet these people have a subversive influence. They dine and wine our younger politicians and they create an atmosphere of authority and responsibility and grandeur, whereas the whole thing is mere flatulence of the spirit ... Lady Astor ... must realise that her parrot cries have done much damage to what (to do her justice) she must dimly realise is the essence of her adopted class and country.[40]

The political house party was a nineteenth-century phenomenon. In the

* Sir John Simon, currently Chancellor of the Exchequer, and Leslie Hore-Belisha, Secretary for War.

days when most parliamentarians were men of means who drew no salaries for their attendance at Westminster, affairs of state could as easily be discussed in country mansions as in spacious town houses, and much more comfortably than in the anterooms of the Commons or the Lords. The fate of nations in those days often was decided over the port at the end of a day's shooting or in the scented rose garden as the sun dipped behind the ancient cedars. By 1920 that world had passed away. The social composition of the House of Commons was very different. Many large estates had been broken up under the assaults of war and taxation. But at Cliveden, and perhaps half a dozen other rural mansions, the old ways seemed to live on. Here the lavishness and the graciousness of the entertainment were on a Victorian scale, and the nation's leaders frequently gathered to meet with diplomats, foreign statesmen, press barons, bankers and businessmen. But any suggestion that such houses were centres of power was an illusion. The work of government was increasingly complex and was handled by a growing army of civil servants in offices which reproduced themselves, amoeba-like, along the length of Whitehall. Gatherings at Cliveden or 4 St James's Square were occasions peripheral to the task of running the country. The hospitality was sumptuous, the hostess amusing, the other guests were usually interesting and there might be useful opportunities to discuss with well-informed people the major items on the government's agenda; but no affairs of state were settled there.

To outsiders it could look very different. The man in the street knew the Astors as a wealthy couple who hobnobbed with royalty and foreign statesmen, who acted as self-appointed unofficial ambassadors and who were frequently in the thick of political controversy. Of such people it was possible to believe almost anything, and certainly that they were pro-Nazi arch-conspirators. For minor politicians and officials brought into the glamorous world of Cliveden the experience could well be dazzling and, because Nancy was an excellent hostess who paid close attention to all her guests, they might feel they were very important and were present at a highly significant occasion. The unintentional deception was most marked among visitors from other countries. There is no doubt that Germany's leaders had a very imperfect understanding of the workings of the British social system. Ribbentrop, Hitler's Foreign Minister, who had been the German Ambassador in London, believed that the English 'nobility', and especially those who enjoyed easy access to the royal 'court', were a major power in the land. When Astor, Lothian, Hamilton, Londonderry or some other 'lord' expressed pro-German sentiments, Ribbentrop took this as evidence of an influential caucus capable of influencing government policy. All the brouhaha about the Cliveden Set only served to reinforce these impressions. Clearly such miscalculations in Berlin helped to convince Hitler that Britain would never go to war against him; but the Astors can scarcely be blamed because German diplomats did not do their homework properly.

All this publicity inevitably rebounded on Bill. There was a strong Labour presence in Fulham (the neighbouring constituency was represented by Dr Edith Summerskill, one of the most formidable socialist MPs) and the local press kept up a constant nagging attack on Mr Astor's 'pro-German sentiments'. Like his father, Bill always wanted to see things for himself. In the autumn of 1938 he went to Czechoslovakia and Sudetenland and, on his return, gave a generally favourable report to the Commons. The *Fulham Gazette* reacted speedily. Was the member for Fulham East defending a regime of savages? Was he sympathetic towards Nazi dictatorship? Would he cheerfully accede to Herr Hitler's future demands – for the return of the former German colonies, for instance? Bill's reply on 25 November showed that in policy matters he was, like his mother, still firmly within the Chamberlain camp:

I endorse and have endorsed the policy of one person only, the Prime Minister. I endorse also his attitude on colonies as expressed in the House of Commons. I endorse the belief that we must continue to try to settle all disputes by peaceful means and not by the terrible arbitrament of war.

An altogether more complex and serious matter was the Astor press and the extent to which it was or was not used to influence policy. The transgressions of *The Times* and the *Observer* in the late 1930s were sins of omission rather than commission and they shared culpability with most other leading newspapers. The stark fear of seeing a well-ordered world torn apart by a total war, to which air power would add a terrifying new dimension, paralysed Fleet Street's editors. They believed they were being responsible when they closed their columns to dissidents such as Churchill, whose intemperate language threatened the delicate balance of relationships with the continental dictators. Nor was there any political incentive for them to challenge the administration. Chamberlain's government, like every government since 1931, was a coalition, so party allegiance scarcely entered into the reckoning of Fleet Street editors. All commentators, except those of the extreme right or left, had got out of the habit of being seriously critical. Above all, proprietors were concerned with circulation. What the public wanted from their newspapers in troubled times was reassurance. When, for example, the *Sunday Times* grew critical of Chamberlain's handling of foreign affairs many readers angrily cancelled their orders. As ever, the country was getting the press it deserved.

It was, however, sad to see the Astor papers losing their independent cutting edge as a result of the decline of once great editors. On 3 January 1938 the *Evening Standard* cartoonist, David Low, depicted Dawson and

Garvin among other Cliveden Set notables as the 'Shiver Sisters' obediently going through their balletic paces under the direction of Dr Goebbels. It was one of the artist's most memorable and effective lampoons. Dawson and Garvin failed in the final crisis for opposite reasons; one had become out of touch with the politicians, and the other had become too closely involved with them. In 1938 Garvin was seventy and still clinging to power. Moreover, his appearances in the office had become infrequent: he ran operations from his house at Beaconsfield. Even there the *Observer* became something of a hobby, for the great editor devoted most of his time to work on a large-scale biography of Joseph Chamberlain. Inevitably Garvin was less in touch with political leaders than some of his own subordinates were. His appearances at Cliveden gatherings certainly became less frequent. Yet his belief in his own judgement never faltered. He allowed editorial policy to be guided neither by his journalists nor by his proprietor. Waldorf, who had always backed to the hilt Garvin's right to independence, was in a cleft stick. He had immense respect and liking for the old man but knew that his powers were failing and wanted him to resign or, at least, to share his authority. Waldorf was also trying to help his second son, David, to sort his life out and find a purpose. Like Bill, his second son also displayed a considerable interest in journalism and politics – though the two young men were poles apart in many of their opinions. Bill was now well settled in a parliamentary career, and Waldorf thought that active involvement in the *Observer* would constructively channel David's energies. He tried to persuade Garvin to make room for him on a permanent basis; but, while making flattering remarks about the young man's ability, the wily editor firmly resisted the thin end of that particular wedge. Waldorf tried to exert himself when Garvin's contract came up for renewal, but the old lion was morally and legally well ensconced. His contract actually gave him a 'life editorship' which could only be terminated if he publicly repudiated the views of the proprietor – an unlikely eventuality.

Until the end of 1938, Waldorf did not have any real policy difference with Garvin. The *Observer* editor had never been a very committed member of the 'Shiver Sisters' troupe. While stressing the need for negotiation with Hitler and sympathetic attention to his grievances, Garvin believed, as he told a friend as early as May 1935, 'There will be no war if Germany knows us strong enough to clinch the issue.'[41] After Munich he launched an energetic campaign for conscription and full-scale rearmament. Later, Waldorf acknowledged his editor's courage and prescience over these emotive issues:

> Old Garve has been proved 100% right when one looks back. The *Observer* alone has demanded more energy and drive at the Air Ministry; it has also consistently asked for national service, a Ministry of Supply and a smaller War Cabinet. The *Times* has been too much a sounding board for 10 Downing St. and Kelmsley

[proprietor of the *Sunday Times*] and Camrose [owner of the *Daily Telegraph*] have vied with each other to boost Neville to the damage of the country ...[42]

By this time, as we shall see, the Astors had performed a belated volte-face on the subject of Neville Chamberlain. Now, a real policy rift opened between them and their editor because Garvin refused to be openly critical of the government in case this should reveal to Germany a serious failure of confidence in the leadership of the country.

Geoffrey Dawson, Garvin's counterpart on *The Times*, was in a strange position: he was employed by John Astor but was always much closer to Waldorf. On the crucial issues of the late thirties he was in complete accord with other members of the Cliveden lobby. That does not mean that his friends were uncritical of his editorial stance. As early as 1928, Waldorf, Tom Jones, and Kerr pressed Dawson's deputy, Robin Barrington-Ward, about *The Times*' undue deference to the government. Barrington-Ward loyally defended his boss but admitted in his diary that the paper was 'much too subservient to the Foreign Office, Admiralty (especially) and conventional club view'.[43] Dawson immensely enjoyed being on first-name terms with ministers of the Crown, meeting intimately on a daily basis with the great and powerful and providing the establishment with a solid buttress. In 1937–8 *The Times* led the Fleet Street convoy as it made full steam under the appeasement banner. There were moments when it even sailed ahead of the government. This occurred most notably in September 1938, when the paper came out openly in support of the dismemberment of Czechoslovakia and the right of the Sudetenland Germans to seek incorporation in the Third Reich. This provoked an official Foreign Office disclaimer and a chorus of press protest, but Halifax seemed unmoved and Dawson remarked smugly in his diary that the Foreign Secretary lunched amicably with him next day at the Travellers' Club. Dawson was genuinely appalled by the prospect of Britain being stampeded into a war in which she might have little support from the Empire and none from the USA, and in which her only ally would be France, whose military preparedness was very questionable. He believed that it was his responsibility to do all he could to prevent such an eventuality – including one-sided reporting and the 'doctoring' of news items. When Chamberlain returned from Munich on 30 September there were a few people who did not join in the delirious applause of a nation delivered from the threat of war. One was Alfred Duff Cooper, First Lord of the Admiralty. He resigned and made a Commons speech attacking the Prime Minister for permitting a tyrant to dominate the Continent. The lobby correspondent of *The Times* was Anthony Winn, Nancy's nephew. He duly filed his copy, only to have it spiked by Dawson, who substituted for it a brief report which dismissed Duff Cooper's stance as irrelevant. Winn immediately resigned and joined the *Telegraph*. It was a small incident in the life of the family, but it may have helped to wake them up to the shortcomings of the Astor press. John Astor had long since fallen into the habit of total non-interference with his editor. The basic principle of a proprietor not using a newspaper to further his own views was sound, but if John had occasionally taken action to prevent 'The Thunderer' being muzzled by its own editor the result would have benefited the press and perhaps the nation.

There was certainly no question of his not being aware of the mounting tide of criticism directed against *The Times*. At regular board meetings and during informal visits to the office he saw some of the adverse correspondence which grew in volume month by month. And his own mailbag was not immune from angry protests like the following:

> Sir, many besides myself have been disgusted with the recent activities of the 'Times', the latest specimen of which has been even noticed in parliament. One can only trust that the paper's circulation will follow its reputation. And, if you are not a native born, some of us would be glad if you returned to the land of your origin – or any other you may obviously prefer – to enrich it, and yourself, by your labours.[44]

By the time of Munich, John also had his own doubts. A few days after Chamberlain descended from his aeroplane triumphantly brandishing his agreement with Hitler, he spent a weekend at Hever. John's second son, Hugh, described one after-dinner conversation:

> I couldn't believe that Munich was real, that it was going to stick. I remember, over the port, objecting in a rather childish way. And Chamberlain said, 'But this really *is* peace in our time.' He obviously accepted it as a fact. But I looked at my father and I could see that he didn't.

The comings and goings at Cliveden were so headline-grabbing that few commentators noticed what was happening at Hever. In this very different Astor home there were also frequent weekend house parties. John's political friends, who numbered back-benchers and also several of the nation's leaders, travelled down to Kent to relax by the lake or on the tennis court. Many of the same names appear in the visitors books of both Cliveden and Hever. Baldwin and Chamberlain were guests of John and Vi, as were Anthony Eden, Geoffrey Dawson, Halifax and Harold Macmillan (married to Vi's cousin Dorothy). But John liked to mix his house parties and so there was always a smattering of celebrities from the world of journalism and the arts – J. M. Barrie, A. P. Herbert, Bernard Miles, and Philip Laszlo, the portrait painter, among others. But it was not only the famous who enjoyed the relaxing atmosphere of Hever. John and Vi were equally generous to constituency and charity workers, *Times* employees and the staff of the Middlesex Hospital. The connection with the Middlesex went back to 1918. When

John was severely wounded on the western front it was an RAMC colonel, Alfred Webb Johnson, who saved his life by amputating the lower part of John's already gangrenous right leg. Webb Johnson subsequently became Dean of Middlesex Hospital. Thereafter, the Middlesex became John's major charitable interest. He provided a nurses' hostel (Astor House) and donated considerable sums of money for other purposes; but his support was never just a matter of writing cheques. He maintained close personal links, and bringing hard-pressed doctors and nurses out to Hever for restful weekends was one way of helping them in their work.

Undoubtedly, the most interesting guest at Hever was Winston Churchill. He often used to drive over from his nearby house at Chartwell to spend a day painting. John was also by way of being an amateur artist and this shared hobby forged a close friendship between the two men which was stronger than their political differences. These were the wilderness years for the future Prime Minister, and John shared the common view that the maverick MP was brilliant but lacking in judgement. He backed Chamberlain to the hilt in the appeasement debate and, indeed, faithfully supported the Tory leadership on all major issues. It was the three Astor boys (Gavin, Hugh and John) who – perhaps because they had been spared the horrors of 1914–18 and were therefore not numbed by the obsession with peace – were able to make an independent assessment of Churchill. 'Winnie' was always a great favourite with children. He could talk to them on their own level, play games with them and help them sail their boats on the lake. They trusted him instinctively and, as they grew up, they easily found reasons for confidence in him. Hugh Astor recalled hearing him talk with foreign visitors at Hever during the late 1930s.

> I used to be enthralled by him because he seemed to be the only person who made any sense at all. Foreign heads of state would come over and go to Downing Street and do the political rounds but at the first opportunity they'd talk to Churchill because he kept his finger on the pulse. He knew how many divisions the Germans could muster and how many troops the French could field. It always seemed to me that he knew all about everything.

Winston was certainly a better painter than John. In fact, it was he who persuaded John to abandon the delicate precision of watercolours for oils. He gave his friend a set of paints and invited him over to Chartwell. Hugh was present when Churchill went out to examine the results of several hours' novice labour.

> My father had spent the whole day using his oils as if they were watercolours, putting every leaf on every tree, one by one. Winston roared with laughter. 'That's no good John,' he said, gesturing extravagantly. 'You want to make a piggery of it!'

John Astor took up painting, as at various stages of his life he took up golf, archery and playing the organ, because he had an abhorrence of inactivity. He inherited his father's iron will and the trait was reinforced by his determination to master his disability. One of his friends observed: 'John achieves anything he puts his mind to. He'd grow another leg if he could be bothered but he doesn't really feel he needs it.' It was certainly by solid application that he acquired political skills. By temperament he disliked crowds and, at the beginning of his public career, was very awkward on public platforms. In the early days his wife was a more accomplished speaker, probably because, as a girl, she had often watched her father addressing meetings. His stepdaughter remembers John getting in a 'terrible tizz' over unveiling a war memorial at Hever around 1920. But this 'disability' he also laboured hard to overcome, and eventually he became a relaxed and amusing speaker, much in demand at political and business functions.

In parliamentary terms all he ever wanted was to be a good constituency member and a reliable back-bencher. He seldom spoke in debates and never sought office. His disinclination to be a career politician stemmed in part from a realization of his own limitations and interests and also from his involvement in other areas – *The Times*, his chairmanship of Middlesex Hospital and his directorship of several large companies. John's was the paternalism of the conscientious officer, part of whose duty it is to look after the 'other ranks'. He took up the causes of the men and women he represented, worked hard on their behalf and attended public functions at the behest of his local Conservative association – and they loved him for it. Whereas Waldorf, in his Commons career, took up great causes, John expended his energy caring for individuals and groups. He never questioned that this, like his enormous amount of charity work, was a responsibility he carried as a wealthy member of society. Not unnaturally, he took a particular interest in those who had suffered in the war. Hugh remembers this activity well.

> He got involved as president of things like limbless ex-servicemen's organisations which deliberately created jobs for people who couldn't really do a job. The chap who was a lodge keeper at Hever had lost an arm, so his job was to open and close the front gates and he was given a free house and wages for doing it. And another man had been blinded. My father had been told that a blind man could look after chickens, so he started chickens, to provide the fellow with a means of earning a living. Frequently jobs were created just to give people employment.

But in a changing age marked by increasing state intervention Major Astor was not exclusively committed to private charity.

> He made a point of always claiming his disability allowance, which I think was 10s.

a week, and he did it for a reason. He found a great reluctance among the war wounded to accept what they believed was 'charity'. So my father used to collect his dues and say 'Look I'm collecting my 10s. a week, why don't you?'

Violet was equally energetic. Running Hever and entertaining were very time-consuming and, in addition, she had constituency responsibilities and a wide range of charitable concerns. Like John, she was keen on sport: riding, swimming and tennis were her regular activities, as was golf, played on Hever's nine-hole course or the public links at Oxted.

Hever was a paradise for children. There were fields and woods for outdoor games and pony riding. There was the lake on which the family kept two dinghies – *Kate* and *Duplikate.* There were the jumbled roofs of the 'village' over which the youngsters used, somewhat perilously, to scamper, and the service passages beneath, which they transited on their roller skates. There were tennis and squash (18 Carlton House Terrace was one of the few London houses to have its own squash court). Some winters the moat would freeze and the children could then don ice skates. And, when John thought his brood were not getting enough exercise, he would equip them with axes and saws and lead them into the hardwood plantation to thin the trees. The family acquired extra acreage at nearby Chiddingstone so that they could farm properly and also run a good shoot. In the summer holidays they usually went up to Meikleour, a Scottish estate held in trust for George Mercer Nairne, Violet's son. When they were in London they were able to enjoy the large residence in Carlton House Terrace which, apart from its other attractions, was an ideal vantage point for watching royal processions in the Mall. As the youngsters grew up, Hever became a wonderful place for dances and parties to which their friends came as well as their (older) cousins from Cliveden and Ford Manor (the Spender-Clays). Although the Hever Astors used to enjoy their exciting visits to Cliveden, Waldorf and Nancy's children used to find the atmosphere at their cousins' home much more relaxing.

Five children grew up together at Hever. The first two, Margaret (now Lady Margaret Myddelton) and George (now Lord Lansdowne), were Violet's son and daughter by her first marriage. John, like Waldorf, inherited a family when he married; but there the comparison ends. There was no attempt to over-compensate Margaret and George. The Mercer Nairnes were completely incorporated into the life of Hever. Neither John nor the Astor boys ever made them feel like stepchildren. Margaret grew up as the responsible elder girl in a rumbustious household of boys, but she had several unofficial 'sisters'. Three of her cousins often stayed for long periods and shared lessons with her. They were the two daughters of the Earl of Cromer, who served in the colonial service in Egypt, and the daughter of the Duke of Devonshire, Governor-General of Canada. Margaret was also very close to Wissie, her exact contemporary, and in the 1930s the two girls travelled to Europe together.

Like so many who had suffered in the First World War, John and Violet were destined to raise sons who would be just the right age to be sent off to fight in the second. Gavin (his parents deliberately shunned the traditional family names) was born in 1918. He had all the graces. He was naturally athletic, had a good eye for a ball and was a first-class shot; there was no game in which he did not excel. He also possessed considerable artistic talent. 'Gavin had all the charm in the world,' Hugh recalls. 'He was always a tremendously popular figure, very gregarious. Probably he was too trusting – and, yet, it was very difficult to cheat Gavin. He wouldn't expect you to; so you didn't.'

Hugh (born 1920) was, as a fine painting by Philip Laszlo suggests, a very attractive, bright, astute child. Then, at the age of six, tragedy struck. He was diagnosed as having TB in his right hip. In those days, understanding of the disease, especially in its non-pulmonary forms, was very limited. Immobility and fresh air were the usually prescribed 'cures', so young Hugh spent the remainder of his childhood inactive. 'He used to be on a sort of mobile bed with his feet higher than his head,' Lady Margaret recalls. 'He was pushed about in the garden in all weathers. Even when it was cold they didn't cover him up. I remember one day when I had been ice skating and was frozen I went over and put my hands on his tummy to warm them up. He had to live completely in a room on the ground floor and when the rest of us went to Scotland, poor Hugh had to stay behind because it was too difficult to get him up there and, anyway, there would have been nothing for him to do.' At the age of fourteen he was clear of the disease, though slightly disabled. Like his father, he was determined not to let a physical handicap restrict him more than was absolutely necessary. He insisted on going off to Eton with his elder brother.

Hugh and Gavin were joined at public school shortly afterwards by John (born 1923) and the family was able to claim the unusual distinction of having three brothers in the same Eton house at the same time. John was the brainy member of the trio, always able to pick up academic distinctions without seeming to work for them. But before he could complete his intellectual development and emerge into the adult world, that world came to him. Like all the Astor men of his generation, he was soon fighting for king and country.

As we have seen, the Astors, like most of their fellow-countrymen, were behind the government in wishing to preserve peace at almost any price. Almost to a man, they backed Chamberlain and were suspicious of Churchill. That does not mean, however, that their perceptions were identical. During the crucial months between Munich and the outbreak of war each of them assessed the changing situation and came round, at his or her own pace, to a different view. Immediately after Munich, Bill, as we have already mentioned, paid a visit to Germany and Czechoslovakia. On his return he prepared a confidential memorandum for the Cabinet. It is, in many ways, a remarkable document – concise yet wide-ranging, shrewd and very clear in its recommendations. Bill painted a picture of a Third Reich in which the masses were solidly behind a violently unstable leader; a leader who, urged by idiots like Ribbentrop, was determined to press Britain to the point of war if necessary; a leader who had only reluctantly allowed himself to be dissuaded from conflict at the time of Munich and who had then prophesied, 'If we don't fight now we will fight later.' With such a potential enemy, gentlemen's agreements were meaningless. War was still not inevitable, but 'we must never get again into the position of making threats or promises we cannot fulfil to the full ... we must make it clear at what point we would fight ... We must, when on good ground, be prepared to use the threat of force.'[45]

However, Bill remained one hundred per cent behind Chamberlain. In his correspondence with his American friends, he derided scaremongers and 'jitterbugs' and assured them that the British government was well in control. At the end of February he reported that the Prime Minister had been 'as gay as a cricket' on his recent visit to Cliveden, and added: 'I feel pretty optimistic really. I don't think the Germans want a war and I don't think the Italians will dare try it on.'[46] Weeks later his mood had changed, but not his underlying conviction: 'War seems certain – but I believe it unnecessary and perhaps disastrous.'[47] By mid-May he had enlisted with the Royal Naval Volunteer Reserve and was on his way to Cairo. Although far removed from the political scene he still had faith in Chamberlain's ability to resolve the crisis. Like most Tories Bill remained loyal to the 'old firm' until the end.

Nancy's conversion was slow, painful and reluctant. As the banner of Hitler's limitless ambition was unfurled for all to see, it was particularly hard for her to accept the inevitable: that Churchill was right and Chamberlain wrong. Their mutual animosity was personal and had ancient roots. In a famous series of exchanges with him in the Commons in October 1938 she had screeched at him, 'Don't be rude about the Prime Minister!' As late as November 1939 she was still wavering. After hearing Chamberlain speak about the war, Nancy reported to Lothian:

> The whole thing was so absolutely lacking in Statesmanship, uplift or vision of any kind, it really got me down for the moment ... its effect on me was to make me wish that Winston were P.M. (This was only momentary, and I know it was wrong, but that was my reaction.)[48]

Six months later, however, she had the courage, along with thirty-two other Tory MPs, to vote against the government in the crucial division which resulted in Winston Churchill becoming Prime Minister.

Waldorf's reassessment of the situation was altogether swifter. He had pinned all his hope on Chamberlain reaching an honourable and workable accord with Hitler. When Lothian, in Sydney, heard that Chamberlain was on his way to Munich in September 1938, he was alarmed at the possible outcome and cabled to ask whether the Astors thought he should return immediately. Waldorf replied with optimistic brevity: 'ADVISE YOU GAMBLE ON PEACE – WALDORF.'[49] Seven months later, on 14 April 1939, he stood in the House of Lords to admit that he, like the majority of his countrymen, had been wrong to put any faith in the words of dictators. 'But', he added, in a veiled reference to Eden and those given to making empty threats, 'there are others who have made mistakes of a different sort.'

> They have believed that passing a resolution, whether of sympathy for a nation that is threatened or of condemnation against a potential aggressor, carried some weight.
>
> Words unless supported by action, resolutions unless supported by adequate power, are a snare and a delusion, as we now see.
>
> You cannot answer power politics by diplomacy; you can only answer them by the willingness and the ability to exercise similar or superior power.

Waldorf was critical of the government for not providing the vigorous lead the people expected. He had by now completely revised his opinion of the Prime Minister. 'It is amazing', he wrote to Kerr a year later, 'how two men, Hitler and Chamberlain, can affect the lives of millions of innocent people – one a genius as energiser and organiser, with a new technique of treachery and deceit called propaganda; the other an egoist, a mediocrity, honestly obstinate.'[50] The new crisis called for Britain to be equipped and ready for war and Waldorf backed Garvin's strong demands for military preparations. The country also needed men of stature to lead it. He wanted to see Lloyd George back in the Cabinet as a minister without portfolio – a sort of free-ranging elder statesman. He also wanted to have Viscount Trenchard recalled. Trenchard was the man who had, almost single-handed, established the Royal Air Force as a highly trained fighting entity in the twenties and thirties. As for Churchill, Waldorf now realized that the belligerent maverick who had wanted to involve Britain in senseless conflict against the Bolsheviks in 1919 and the Turks in 1922 was an essential ingredient of the team needed to rally the nation against Hitler. He spent several months in 1939 with Halifax winning all-party support for Winston's inclusion in the government.

Viscount Astor, with the prescience gained from years of studying world problems from an uncommitted distance, saw that a cataclysmic change was in the air. That change might or might not involve war, but it would come. Events on the international scene were reflected in his own domestic circumstances. Bowed at last by the burden of taxation, in August 1939 Waldorf drastically reduced the number of staff at Cliveden and closed the house up. Nancy spoke of reopening it for Christmas, but Waldorf knew that they had come to the end of an era. It was time for the gates of the magic kingdom to be shut once and for all. Joyce Grenfell, reviewing the life of Cliveden in the 1930s, wrote: 'The more I see of people brought up in the easy way the more I lean towards socialism. I needn't worry; we're hurtling in so called ... easy stages towards it. Things will never, can never, *mustn't* ever be the same, as they were before the war.'[51] Waldorf would never have expressed himself in that way, but it was a sentiment that, in his heart, he shared.

CHAPTER 11

'A famous and wealthy New Yorker [and] an old friend of mine'

Like his cousins, Vincent Astor was a child of a new age. He was a hitherto unknown phenomenon in America: an Astor with a highly developed social conscience. When his father went down with the *Titanic* in April 1912, the heir to the family millions was seven months short of his twenty-first birthday. William Vincent Astor was born in November 1891 and grew up a lonely child in the home of estranged parents. His earliest memory was of being dressed by his nanny in a smart sailor suit in order to be 'presented' to his mother in the drawing room. Ava took one look at the nervous little boy and shrieked, 'Nanny, take him away! He looks perfectly horrid!' That early rejection haunted him for the rest of his life. At first he was effectively an only child, for his sister, (Ava) Alice, was not born until he was almost eleven. He developed into a tall, lumbering, clumsy youth who seemed to be cursed with two left feet. He was still in his teens when Colonel Jack and his wife were divorced and he acquired a stepmother who was a few months younger than himself. All in all, the experiences of his formative years were not designed to negate that difficulty with human relationships which seems to have been an inherited Astor trait.

The problem was made no easier by the fact that in his early quest for affection he had gravitated towards his father, only to be deprived of him suddenly and tragically. Ava actively disliked her son, who did not conform to her image of American youth: outgoing, handsome, athletic. In her eyes, Vincent had inherited his father's gaucherie and she despised him for it. However, she had custody of the children and so Vincent had to spend a large part of each year with her in Britain. In fact, Ava never bothered with him, and he passed most of his time at boarding school and in the company of tutors and companions, with one of whom he made enjoyable tours of the Continent. His happiest days were the holidays spent with his father at Ferncliff or aboard the yacht. As to his stepmother, there could be no question of a maternal relationship with a woman the same age as himself. No question, either, of friendship. He scarcely knew Madeleine and had been highly embarrassed by his father's second marriage and the social ostracism which followed it. For Vincent the one positive outcome of his father's death was that he was absolved from the responsibility of developing a relationship with the second Mrs Astor. Madeleine soon went her own way, taking with her her husband's posthumous son, John Jacob Astor VI, who was born in September 1912.

Vincent's youth ended with a sickening jolt of finality. Not only did he become, suddenly and unexpectedly, the head of the family, he also occupied that position in lonely isolation. He immediately left Harvard to shoulder his obligations. The first was the traumatic duty of presiding at his father's funeral. Jack Astor's was one of the bodies that had been recovered from the icy waters of the Atlantic after the loss of the *Titanic.* Vincent had it brought back to New York and decently interred. Days later he reported to the estate office to learn all he could about the disposition of the Astor millions. A few months after that he came of age and those millions were his. Few men can ever have come into such an immense fortune so tragically and unexpectedly.

The lives of Colonel Jack's ex-wife and widow read like the worst kind of American blockbuster, romantic fiction. After 1912, they moved to the periphery of the Astor story, yet from there they continued to cast bizarre light and grotesque shadows over the lives of their marital relatives. Both women were, of course, comfortably provided for financially. Ava emerged from the débâcle of her marriage with over two and a half million dollars. Madeleine enjoyed a marriage settlement of $1,695,000. In addition she had the use of Jack's two homes in Manhattan and Newport plus the interest from a $5 million trust fund, as long as she remained unmarried. These sums were, of course, paltry by Astor standards, but perfectly in line with the established practice of keeping the fortune in the male line of the family and preventing it being dissipated by marriage. The *exception* to the Astor rule lay in the treatment of the infant John Jacob. There existed for him a $3 million trust fund, presumably set up by his father as an interim measure until such time as the sex of his unborn child was determined. Madeleine and her son would always claim, probably correctly, that it had been Colonel Jack's intention to divide his estate *per stirpes*, that is more or less equally between his surviving sons. In fact, Vincent inherited the bulk of his father's fortune – $87,218,000. Furthermore – and this too was unique in the annals of Astor testamentary practice – the money was all his, upon his majority, to do with precisely as he wished. It was not encumbered by any 'leapfrogging' trust arrangements such as those by which his ancestors had sought to preserve their wealth for future generations.

After her divorce, Ava spent most of her time in England, where she moved in the highest circles. In February 1919, at the age of fifty, she married Lord

Ribblesdale. Thomas Lister, fourth Baron Ribblesdale was, at sixty-five, still tall, athletic and handsome. He was a keen sportsman and an excellent rider to hounds (he had been Master of the Royal Buckhounds from 1892 to 1895). He was wealthy. He had an ancient title together with an imposing country seat and five thousand acres at Gisburne Hall, Yorkshire. He was one of the most popular figures in English society and famed for his sardonic wit. Ribblesdale, who was Asquith's brother-in-law, was politically active. He frequently attended the House of Lords as a Liberal peer, although he affected disdain for the upper chamber. 'When we disagree with the elected House of Commons,' he observed, 'we are presumptuous; when we agree with it we are superfluous.' On the earlier burning issue of home rule for Ireland he claimed to have been converted to the cause during an unplanned train journey between London and Holyhead in the company of Charles Stewart Parnell, the nationalist leader. He was a secure member of the Establishment, very popular in court circles and had been a lord-in-waiting to Queen Victoria in the 1890s. Yet he frequently opened his London home to radicals and socialists. It is not difficult to see why Tom Lister appealed to Ava Astor: not only did he provide her with unimpeachable social standing; he was also unconventional and able to 'sit loose' to the advantages of wealth and class which were his by birth.

Ribblesdale's marriage to an American divorcée may have been yet another gesture to the Establishment. It certainly provided a further cord connecting the Astors to the British aristocracy. By 1920 William Waldorf was a viscount; his brother John was related by marriage to the Mintos and the Lansdownes; Charlotte Augusta was sister-in-law to Earl Haig; and now Jack's ex-wife was a baroness. Yet it is undoubtedly too cynical to view this marriage purely in terms of dynastic calculation. For all his good humour Ribblesdale's life had carried more than its fair share of tragedy. His first wife, Charlotte (Margot Asquith's sister), had died comparatively young in 1911. Both his sons had opted for military careers. Thomas, the eldest, was killed while fighting in Somaliland in 1904. Charles died of wounds sustained during the Dardanelles campaign in 1915. Tom had the comfort of three devoted daughters, but it was cruelly appropriate that he who had always been scathing about the English peerage was destined to be the last Lord Ribblesdale. In his declining years he wanted a beautiful and fun-loving woman at his side.

Whatever happiness he and Ava found together was doomed to be of short duration, for Tom Lister died in October 1925. Thereafter Ava spent most of her time on the Continent. She had a house in her beloved Geneva, where she was frequently visited by her fashionable friends and was able to watch them indulging in winter sports, even if she could no longer participate herself. She was still living there at the outbreak of war in 1939. Despite

Switzerland's neutrality, she felt insecure. Early in 1940 she managed to obtain a passage to New York. As Lady Ribblesdale she had no desire to stand with her fellow-countrymen against the seemingly unstoppable Nazis. Ava renounced both her title and her British citizenship. As plain Mrs Ribblesdale she lived out the rest of her long life at 720 Park Avenue, dying there in 1958. By her will she bequeathed $3 million – none of it to members of the Astor family.

Madeleine Astor's life was no less eventful. She determined not to be ensnared by the terms of her late husband's will, and in 1915 she married her childhood sweetheart, William Dick. As the wife of a sugar tycoon she lacked for nothing. Her husband was not in the same financial league as Jack Astor, but she had only moved from the ranks of the fabulously wealthy to the ranks of the very wealthy. Life for her still meant houses in the town and the country, foreign travel, yachts, jewellery and a busy social calendar – for now that she had 'regularized her position' she was once again welcomed to the tables and the opera boxes of the élite. This did not stop her doing her utmost, through the courts, to secure what she considered to be her infant son's patrimony. Vincent rebuffed all such approaches and the law was on his side. But young John Jacob was well provided for in his new home. He grew up in a wealthy household, with two younger stepbrothers, the promise of a $3 million inheritance, plus interest, at the age of twenty-one, the prospect of some share in the Dick fortune and the hope that, in due course, his half-brother Vincent would prove more generous.

It was his mother's continuing amorous adventures which now clouded John Jacob's life. In 1934 Madeleine's younger sons persuaded their father to engage a young Italian pugilist to teach them the noble art of self-defence. Enzo Fiermonte was handsome, muscular and determined to get rich quick. Madeleine Dick was just turned forty, wealthy, bored and susceptible. There followed a sordid affair, a divorce and, for Madeleine, swift disillusionment when she realized that Enzo was only after her money. Her lover deserted her and returned to Europe. Distracted, Madeleine followed. There was a short-lived reconciliation, but soon Madeleine accepted the inevitable; her marriage to Fiermonte was dissolved in a Florida court in 1939. By now she was destroyed socially, estranged from John Jacob, and had gone through most of her money. She died in Palm Springs in March 1940 at the age of forty-six. It is to Vincent's credit that he raised no objection to his stepmother's dying wish that her body should be brought to New York and buried next to her first husband, Colonel Jack.

Vincent could only contemplate all these matrimonial adventures and misadventures with revulsion. He was intensely jealous of the Astor name and honour and determined to rescue it from the accusations of extravagance and exploitation and the derision heaped by the press upon playboys, dilettantes and gold-diggers. Even before he entered upon his glittering inheritance in 1912 he let it be known that a wind of change was arising to blow through the Astor estate office. It would be his responsibility, he insisted, 'in every way to attempt to aid mankind'.

This volte-face takes some explaining. Certainly the Manhattan social circus had not struck its big top and gone out of business. The passing of 'Queen' Caroline had not left the throne vacant for long. It was occupied for several years by Grace Vanderbilt, the vivacious wife of Cornelius ('Neily') Vanderbilt III. Grace did not command a fraction of the fortune Mrs Astor had been able to lavish on her sumptuous entertainments – during the Newport season she was even obliged to rent Beaulieu from William Waldorf – yet she provided New York society with the mistress of ceremonies it needed. She approached the task with the devotion of her predecessor – spending hours planning entertainments and drawing up guest lists but, above all, devising coups. These were the stock-in-trade of successful hostesses, and Grace proved herself unsurpassed in the audacity of her innovations. She brought the New York hit musical *Wild Rose* to Newport for one night, which involved cancelling two performances at the Knickerbocker Theater, transporting the entire cast and scenery and constructing a special auditorium on the lawns at Beaulieu. She cultivated foreign notables such as Grand Duke Boris of Russia and Prince Henry of Germany. She used Neily's *North Star*, the magnificent rival of *Nourmahal*, as a travelling HQ. She visited Cowes, Kiel, St Petersburg, Biarritz, Monte Carlo, Athens to establish and strengthen her contacts with the crowned heads of Europe. It mattered not that the Vanderbilt yacht had to be kept moored in England because the seamen's wages there were lower than in America. The important thing was that Grace Vanderbilt could indulge, as Theodore Roosevelt observed, 'in a kind of perpetual fairy tale'. To one correspondent she wrote:

> As soon as the King [of England] entered he looked around the house and . . . pointed me out to the other royalties . . . And they all said I had the most beautiful jewels in the house that night . . . Is it not kind of him to recommend me to the Italian King and Queen? . . . On Sunday the Emperor is to be received by the Pope and on Monday His Holiness is giving us a private audience!!!! . . . did I tell you old Grand Duke Michael sent me his photo?[1]

Grace's letters indicate that the 'court' life of Manhattan was – or seemed to be – as enclosed, introverted and secure as ever.

Vincent Astor was not a very committed courtier. He went through the motions – dutifully appearing in his box at the Metropolitan Opera's diamond horseshoe, gracing the tables of hopeful matrons who seated him next to their no less ambitious daughters, hosting the annual Astor ball – but his heart was not in the social round which had been his grandmother's life. Partly this was because New York high society was a matriarchy, and Vincent was a lonely bachelor with no mother or wife to plan his calendar and approve his guest lists. He was free to choose his own friends and make his own amusements. Not unnaturally, he preferred the company of people who shared his enthusiasms for motor cars, yachts and all things maritime. Vincent was captivated by the sea and ships. He had implored his father to allow him to go to naval college, but Jack had insisted that only Harvard could provide a fitting education for an Astor and to Harvard Vincent had gone. But it was soon observed that, as well as dashing young men who could talk knowledgeably about the contenders for the America's Cup or the merits of the latest Hispano-Suiza, Vincent was inviting to his table writers, politicians, religious leaders and charity organizers. As the gossip-writers began to get the measure of the new head of the Astor family they realized that he was, at bottom, a very serious young man.

It would be an exaggeration to say that Vincent had a 'vision' or that he saw clearly the brittle absurdities on which wealthy society rested. But he was influenced by and became part of a reform movement that reached its peak in America in the years just before the First World War. Woodrow Wilson observed during his early days in the presidency: 'It is only once in a generation that a people can be lifted above material things. That is why conservative government is in the saddle two-thirds of the time.'[2] Such sporadic bouts of reform take decades to bring to the boil. In America the heat had been building up since about 1880.

As the population of the United States grew, so the differences between the few thousand wealthy families and the multitudes of the poor became more marked. It was difficult to equate the America of the closing years of the nineteenth century with Lincoln's definition of a country 'conceived in liberty, and dedicated to the proposition that all men are created equal'. The experiment of unrestrained capitalism had, in a few generations, created in the New World those conditions that the nation's founders had denounced in the old – a class system based on inherited wealth, economic exploitation and government corruption. Among the results were urban slums and the spread of crime, vice, disease and despair. Conditions were worst in the big cities. New York, with over a million of its poorer inhabitants crammed into 32,000 tenements, had a greater population density than Calcutta. Municipal authorities – even those not dominated by a self-seeking establishment – lacked the powers and the funds to provide adequate education, health care and sanitation. The existence of squalid slums within a few minutes' walk of the palaces of the Astors, Vanderbilts, Belmonts, Rockefellers and their friends excited mounting protest.

First it was the journalists who denounced political corruption. Then came the writers with their more detailed analyses; men like Jacob Rüs who, in 1890, described the New York tenements in his *How the Other Half Lives*:

> Be a little careful, please! The hall is dark and you might stumble over the children ... Not that it would hurt them; kicks and cuffs are their daily diet. They have little else. Here where the hall turns and dives into utter darkness is a step, and another, another. A flight of stairs. You can feel your way if you cannot see it. Close? Yes ... All the fresh air that ever enters these stairs comes from the hall-door that is forever slamming, and from the windows of dank bedrooms that in turn receive from the stairs their sole supply of the elements God meant to be free, but man deals out with such a niggardly hand.[3]

Such wilderness voices were followed by bold political spirits who challenged the bosses and the Tammany caucus on their own ground and occasionally succeeded in putting the crooks behind bars. Last of all came the leaders thrown up from the ranks of the oppressed – socialists, anarchists, men who had nothing to gain from the existing order and nothing to lose from change. By the turn of the century these various strata had compressed into a movement for progressive reform, a movement which possessed its own idealism – not much different from the idealism of the founding fathers – its own political programmes, its own propaganda, and which attracted men and women from all social levels.

Among its ardent devotees were members of the Roosevelt family – Vincent's relatives. The Astor heir was not yet ten years old when, in September 1901, Theodore Roosevelt became president on the assassination of William McKinley. Throughout most of his teenage period 'Teddy' and his 'square deal' held sway. Roosevelt, one of the most red-blooded and popular presidents in American history, pursued a liberal programme of modest government intervention to fend off working-class demagogues and to control the plutocrats whose greed provided the agitators with their ammunition. He attacked commercial monopolies. He initiated factory reform. He began to make respectable the notion that even in a free enterprise economy the activities of the rich and powerful have to be curbed. He initiated what another Roosevelt would call 'the struggle for the liberty of the community rather than the liberty of the individual'.[4]

Franklin Delano Roosevelt (ten years Vincent's senior) was one of the many Americans to fall under the spell of Teddy Roosevelt, who was a distant cousin. Though his family were traditionally Democrats, FDR avidly supported the Republican ticket in the presidential election of 1904. By this time he had decided on a public career. Although he could have slipped easily into the life of a country gentleman, the influences brought to bear upon him at school and at Harvard urged him towards a more service-orientated life. These inclinations were confirmed by his marriage in 1905 to Teddy's niece. Eleanor Roosevelt was a serious-minded young woman, educated in England and committed to social justice. When Franklin began courting her, she had him meet her in Lower East Side tenement buildings so that he could see for himself the conditions she and her friends were fighting against.

Over the next few years the name Roosevelt was scarcely ever out of the newspapers. FDR worked his way, via the New York state legislature, to Washington. He became widely known as a progressive, anti-Tammany Democrat. Meanwhile, Teddy, having retired from office in 1908, was angered to see the Republican party fall back under the control of the big corporations and the money men. He roared out of retirement to fight the election of 1912 at the head of his own new party, the Progressives. His campaign speeches tapped the new idealism:

> The man who wrongly holds that every human right is secondary to his profit must now give way to the advocate of human welfare, who rightly maintains that every man holds his property subject to the general right of the community to regulate its use to whatever degree the public welfare may require it.[5]

Theodore stood little chance against the major political groupings. The man who won the race to the White House was a radical Democrat, an academic liberal by name Woodrow Wilson. One of the first acts of the new president was to appoint F. D. Roosevelt Assistant Secretary to the Navy. It was the office which had provided Theodore with a springboard to greater things at the time of the war with Spain.

These were the personalities and the public movements which went to shape the thinking of young Vincent Astor. The Roosevelts, as well as being relatives, were friends and neighbours. They too had a Manhattan house and an estate on the Hudson at Hyde Park, a little to the south of the Ferncliff estate at Rhinebeck. FDR – good-humoured, witty, urbane, popular – was Vincent's boyhood hero. He actually had much in common with his elder cousin. Franklin too had a passion for the sea. He too had wanted to attend the naval college at Annapolis, only to be diverted to Harvard by his parents. He too married a woman who confirmed the serious side of his nature.

Vincent's wife, to whom he was wed in 1914, was Helen Dinsmore Huntington, an attractive, intelligent woman of impeccable ancestry. The two had known each other since childhood and their fathers had been close friends. Helen was quiet, loved music, enjoyed visits to Paris and London, and was a considerable patroness of charities. She had no time for the more extravagant excesses of Manhattan society. She preferred intimate dinner parties to elaborate balls, and when she did entertain lavishly it was frequently in aid of some worthy cause. For many years Helen and Vincent lived happily together. The only thing missing from their relationship was children.

For this fact we have to blame another of those cruel blows of fate which befell the American Astors. Up to this point the direct male descendants of John Jacob I had never been numerous: in each generation there had been just one or two males to share the fortune. That meant that while there were enough to ensure that the money stayed in the family, there were not so many that the inheritance became widely diffused. All that was about to change in the nation where the Astor fortune had been made. Vincent and Helen's wedding was announced at the end of 1913 but had to be postponed several months because the groom fell ill. When it did take place, on 30 April 1914, Vincent was still in a wheelchair. A honeymoon spent on the *Noma* restored him to full health – with one exception. The disease which had laid him low was mumps. As sometimes happens, it left a permanent mark on the victim's life: Vincent was infertile. The only Astor now left who was capable of prolonging the line was Vincent's half-brother, John Jacob VI (Jack), but though he had the name, he did not have the fortune to go with it.

The fortune was with Vincent and he systematically set about increasing it. He became the first Astor in over twenty years to attend the estate office in person. He familiarized himself with his holdings; he studied the market; and he concluded that successful property management was no longer a question of sitting tight and watching property values rise. Every square inch of Manhattan was now built over and the interest of architects and builders was moving away from spreading outwards to thrusting upwards. The skyscraper era had dawned. It would be a few years yet before office blocks and company headquarters would penetrate the cloud layer, but demolition and rebuilding were in vogue and Vincent realized that this was where the money was to be made. For fifteen years he devoted himself to property development.

He concentrated on modest, tasteful buildings and, to help pay for them, he divested himself of some of his more prestigious holdings. Several central Manhattan edifices were sold off – the Schermerhorn, the Longacre in Times Square and the site of the Paramount theatre. His father's proud achievements, the St Regis and Knickerbocker hotels, went too; the former sold, the latter turned into an office block. Most of Vincent's attention was centred further out in the residential areas bordering Central Park. His architect, Charles Platt, designed the very latest in apartment blocks on West 89th and 95th Streets and, across the park, on East 81st and 86th Streets and East End Avenue, overlooking the East River, where John Jacob I's country residence had once stood. Vincent saw the East Side as a fashionable new district and, in 1926, he moved there himself. Caroline's Renaissance palace was sold off and demolished, and Vincent and Helen took up residence in a much more modest house on East 80th Street. But it was no longer a matter of establishing *the* smart quarter. New York's leading families did not rush to become the

Astors' new neighbours. Nor did the Astors wish it to be so. Although all Vincent's buildings were individually designed and finished to a high standard, prices varied. Next to prestigious apartment houses on East 88th and 89th Streets stood 'Poverty Row', deliberately designed for shallower pockets. He wanted to bring tasteful surroundings within the range of a wider clientele. One experiment failed. At the corner of 95th and Broadway he constructed the Astor Market. The covered area was laid out for relaxed, leisurely shopping. The walls were decorated with colourful murals by William Mackay. The object was to create an environment in which the average family could shop at reasonable prices. Vincent was defeated by the shopkeepers, who thought that fancy surroundings entitled them to seek higher profit margins. The customers stayed away and America's first high-class shopping mall closed down.

Part of Vincent's property campaign involved putting an end to the Astors' slum landlord image. An early attempt to root out vice on his inherited holdings ended in farce. He dispatched a fleet of private detectives to prowl around the most depressed areas sniffing out evidence of prostitution. The snoopers were soon run out of the neighbourhood. However, Vincent remained very sensitive to charges that he was enriching himself by exploiting the poor. He realized that he would have to take more radical action to distance himself from the notorious tenements described in *How the Other Half Lives*. One motive for his East Side development was to replace some of his run-down holdings and to raise the general tone of the area. Later he sold other local tenement blocks to the city authorities (having first rehoused the occupants) at less than the current market value. Vincent was helped in his rehabilitation of the family name by the fact that the slum problem was moving. It was now parts of Brooklyn, Queens and the Bronx which provided the most scandalous examples of decrepit, insanitary accommodation. But Vincent was determined, not only to clean out his own Augean stables, but to be seen as a public benefactor. He chose to build a new, spacious apartment complex in the Bronx with an integral play area for children. At Rhinebeck he set up a home for underprivileged children and gave a thousand acres to the government for agricultural research. All these projects spanned many years. They were tumultuous years in the life of America and the world.

The 1914–18 War made its first impact on precisely that stratum of society to which the Astors belonged. The emergence of the great ocean liners had reduced transatlantic crossings from weeks to days. Frequent visits to Europe were *de rigueur* for New York's social élite, and many wealthy American families had second homes in London, Paris and the fashionable Mediterranean resorts. They had close friends and relatives in the Old World. They hired their staff from European agencies. When war broke out they could not remain emotionally detached from it. Some were actually (like William Waldorf Astor) travelling on the Continent and fled back to safety with hair-raising stories to tell. Even those who heard the dismal news from three thousand miles away were not immune to the inconveniences of war. In the second week of August Grace Vanderbilt had planned a dinner in honour of the German Ambassador, Count Bernsdorff, at Beaulieu. Mrs Vanderbilt hastily ascertained that, given the changed situation, her guests were still prepared to come. They were. What she had left out of her reckoning was her kitchen and dining room staff, who, almost to a man, were French, English and Belgian. The soup was served and consumed. The hostess rang for the next course. Nothing happened. After ten minutes of increasing embarrassment, a maid entered bearing a note from below stairs. It read:

> We the undersigned regret to inform you, Madam, that we cannot any longer serve the enemy in our respective countries. We have thrown the rest of the dinner into the dustbin and we have all left your service. There is nothing else to eat in the house. We hope you all enjoyed the soup, for we took good care to spit well into it, every one of us, before it went to the table.[6]

America was officially neutral and many citizens hoped and prayed that she would remain so, but some of the Astors' friends and relatives could not stand aloof while those they knew and loved were suffering in Europe. They crossed the water to help run Red Cross hospitals and drive field ambulances, to look after refugees, to open their homes to soldiers on leave from the front. Even Harry Lehr, the cynical high priest of the *haut monde*, returned to Paris in 1915 to do what he could. Thousands of wealthy Americans who did not themselves travel to the sundered continent sent money and supplies and petitioned their government for direct action. Such demands increased after 7 May 1915, when 128 US citizens went down with the torpedoed *Lusitania*. Franklin Roosevelt did all he could to persuade Wilson to declare war, but the President spent another two years bringing diplomatic pressure to bear on the belligerents, determined that his administration would be able 'to come into the court of history with clean hands'. Vincent contacted Franklin Roosevelt to assure him of his support. He suggested setting up an Atlantic patrol, composed of armed pleasure yachts, to help counter the U-boat menace. He contributed substantially to relief funds. He provided the New York militia with a seaplane, having first learned to fly one himself. For this energetic young man in his mid-twenties, the prospect of active involvement in the war was not only something he approved in principle; he also welcomed the prospect of real 'naval' action.

His chance came with America's commitment to the Allies in April 1917. He was immediately commissioned. He gave *Nourmahal* to the war effort and sailed in her to the French coast. He was appointed port officer at Royon, where his main task was control of shipping in and out of the Gironde estuary. Helen went with him and took a house in Bordeaux where she and a friend, Ethel Harriman Russell, set up a YMCA canteen. The couple spent most of the remainder of the war in south-west France. They were visited there by FDR in August 1918 and the Assistant Secretary to the Navy had nothing but praise for Vincent's work and, particularly, his successful laying of a communications cable from Royon to Pauillac. Roosevelt saw other Astors on this tour, for he stayed at Cliveden in July and was impressed by Nancy's hospital and the splendid unostentatious war work she and Waldorf were doing.[7] Vincent ended the war with the rank of lieutenant. He saw no active combat but he suffered as a result of his service. In 1918 he was ordered to return to America in command of the captured German submarine, U 117. On the crossing, because the vessel had been deliberately sabotaged before being surrendered, it filled with gas. The bronchial damage inflicted on Vincent lasted the rest of his life.

After the war he returned to his various commercial interests. The English Astors were eager to realize some of their Manhattan assets. Together with the head of the American family, they planned what the newspapers called 'the greatest real estate auction ever held'. It was part of Eden Farm. When John Jacob I had acquired it for $25,000, it was described as 'the farm at Bloomingdale, near the four mile stone ... consisting of about twenty-two acres'. A hundred years later it was a piece of downtown land extending from 43rd Street and Broadway to 12th Avenue and 51st Street, on which were sited twenty-three theatres and three hotels, as well as hundreds of other properties. The Astors selected for sale 141 lots around Times Square. They sold for a total of $5,159,075, and that still left the bulk of Eden Farm intact.[8] Property development was only one of Vincent's activities. He was the first real businessman the family had had since John Jacob I. He had the natural entrepreneur's flair for seeing where money could be made. At Ferncliff he built up, with expert help, a prime herd of Aberdeen Angus beef cattle, which were sold both for meat and for breeding stock. He also had a large range of hen batteries which produced eggs for the St Regis Hotel, where the management's boast was that no egg was served more than twenty-four hours old. The St Regis was something he took an immense interest in, perhaps because his father had built it and had been particularly proud of it. Although he sold it in 1929, he reacquired it five years later, gave it a half-a-million-dollar face-lift and made it once more a major centre of Manhattan social life. Vincent frequently dined there when he was in town and sometimes stayed there, even though his own house was only a short cab ride away. He was always thinking up improvements for the hotel and his constant presence kept the staff very much on their toes.

The 1920s were boom years for the American economy. Opportunities for investment were legion. Vincent never had any need to go in search of places to put Astor money to work; he was frequently approached with 'sure fire' deals. He had an almost unfailing ability to distinguish good investments from bad. Nothing shows this more clearly than his one venture into the film business. In the twenties Hollywood was developing fast. From simple one-reelers the industry was moving into ever more ambitious projects. In 1925 MGM was looking for backing for one of the first great movie epics, *Ben-Hur.* They approached Vincent. He assessed the property and agreed to put up almost a quarter of a million dollars. The film was an immense and immediate success on its release the following year. It gave Vincent a quick gross profit of over $370,000. With his capital and business acumen he was invited on to the boards of several companies. Among the many with which he became actively involved were the Western Union Telegraph Company, the Chase National Bank, the International Mercantile Marine Company, the North Atlantic Steamship Corporation and four railway companies. Real estate played a diminishing role in his business life. He had no interest in the skyscraper craze which swept New York in the post-war years, and in 1929 one of the most significant events in the Astor story took place. Together with his English cousins Vincent sold the Waldorf-Astoria for $15,120,000. The gracious old hotel was bulldozed and on its site was raised a tribute to the new, brash age – the Empire State Building.

Vincent belonged to the 'work hard, play hard' school. He pursued his leisure activities with the same devotion he applied to business. His early passion for fast cars evaporated, but he remained a keen member of the Aero Club of America. He delighted in taking guests for rides on the miniature railway he built at Ferncliff. But his first love remained yachting. In 1926 he ordered a new *Nourmahal*. She was more like a mini-liner than a yacht. She could reach speeds of twenty knots and travel a third of the way round the world without refuelling. She carried a permanent crew of forty-two, was equipped with the most up-to-date navigational aids and even had her own operating theatre. It goes without saying that she was the ultimate in luxury. She could accommodate up to twenty voyaging guests in well-appointed state rooms, and her suite of superbly fitted saloons included a large, panelled dining room. It became Vincent's custom to go off on six-month cruises almost every year to various distant locations. His favourite spot, however, was the Galapagos Islands. He often took naturalists with him to this famed zoological paradise and brought back specimens of rare wildlife (he was a trustee of the New York Zoological Society). But Vincent's passengers were not restricted to men of science. They included distinguished people from every walk of life. The most distinguished of all was the man who was four times President of the United States of America.

In 1921 Franklin D. Roosevelt was crippled with polio, the disease which, had it not been for his iron will, would have put an end to his political ambitions. Although out of office, he remained active in the affairs of the Democratic party, but most of his efforts were directed towards overcoming the partial paralysis with which he was afflicted. One element of the treatment was swimming in warm water, and he paid frequent visits to Florida and Warm Springs, Georgia. However, he had to spend much of his time in New York. It was then that he made frequent use of the heated pool at Ferncliff. This was the period during which Franklin and Vincent became really close. Roosevelt never fully recovered the use of his legs, but he coped with his handicap so successfully that, by 1928, he was able to resume his climb up the political ladder. In that year he was elected Governor of New York. Vincent Astor backed his campaign and would continue to support him in the years ahead.

Vincent was now an accomplished businessman in his mid-thirties with a wide network of friends in many fields – politics, philanthropy, science, finance, education, journalism, law, industry, diplomacy, sport, publishing. He travelled widely, had a finger in many pies and was intensely interested in world affairs. He was wealthy, sociable and successful. but there was nothing to suggest that he would play a significant role in the life of his country. Then came The Room. In 1927 he and a small group of other influential men got together to form what was a cross between an exclusive gentlemen's club and a private information-gathering agency. They called themselves 'The Room', met once a month for dinner and conversation in an unpretentious apartment on East 62nd Street, occasionally welcomed visiting speakers such as Somerset Maugham, and kept their gatherings secret. The members thought alike on the major national and international issues of the day and, because of the positions they occupied, they were extremely well informed. Some, indeed, were or had been active in military and naval intelligence. In its origins The Room had no specific political orientation, nor did its members seek to be active, as a body, in government affairs. But somebody who knew about their activities and realized that they could be useful was Franklin D. Roosevelt.

FDR was never a member of The Room, but Teddy's sons, Kermit Roosevelt and Theodore junior, were, and so were several other of the governor's friends. He was particularly close to four of its core members – Vincent and Kermit Astor, Frederic Kernochan, a Supreme Court judge, and the philanthropist William Stewart. These four sometimes met on the *Nourmahal*, either for fishing trips or just to get away for a few hours to drink, play cards and talk. A few years later, when the walls of the White House had closed round him, Roosevelt described Vincent's yacht as 'the only place I can get away from people, telephones and uniforms'.[9] As the 1920s came to a close, Roosevelt was on the brink of becoming the most autocratic President in the history of the United States, and the man who would engineer the country's recovery from its worst crisis since the Civil War. In the capacity of national saviour he needed friends with whom he could relax and private sources of intelligence. In Vincent and his 'Room-mates' he found both.

In 1929 the great party came to an abrupt end. For a decade America's domination of world markets had brought her citizens unprecedented prosperity. Agricultural and industrial exports reached record highs; business expanded; investment soared to dizzy heights, blasted off by easy credit. On 29 October the overheated stock market exploded. Billions were wiped off the total value of shares. The Great Depression had begun. In the next three years five thousand banks went out of business; foreign trade fell from $9 billion to $3 billion; agricultural output fell by two-thirds; there were countless bankruptcies and massive unemployment. Americans lost their life savings and – what was in some ways worse – their confidence in their country. The unbelievable had happened – the USA had gone broke.

For three years Hoover's Republican administration grappled ineptly with the problem, too dependent on the moguls of finance and industry to take the draconian measures necessary to get America back to work. FDR won the Democratic nomination for the 1932 election and promised the nation a 'New Deal' (although he was far from specific about the details of his recovery package). Vincent backed him to the hilt. He became a member of Roosevelt's finance committee. He contributed heavily to campaign funds. He gave his friend constant encouragement and passed on any information he thought might be useful. Thus, in August 1932, he advised Roosevelt to expose the false optimism the Republicans were trying to generate on the basis of a current stock market recovery. Roosevelt took such advice seriously: 'I agree with you entirely about the present market and the little investors,' he replied.

> I had a very interesting example given me the other day. In a village in upstate New York sixty people had speculative accounts in 1929 and all were wiped out except one fellow who sold out before the crash in order to get married. These people were interviewed ten days ago and only five out of the sixty had enough money, i.e. four or five hundred dollars or more, to speculate with if they wanted to. The other fifty-five were broke and are irritated at the thought of the market going up.[10]

In the presidential election later that year Roosevelt won an overwhelming victory with a seven million lead over his rival in the popular vote and a record 413 majority in the electoral college.

In February 1933 the President-elect took a cruise on the *Nourmahal*. It was to be part work, enabling him to speak in a few coastal towns, but largely an opportunity to relax before embarking on the rigours of office. The party stopped in Miami for an open air rally. The motorcade reached the park and FDR addressed the crowd. It was when he had finished and was being helped down from his specially raised car seat that a deranged bricklayer with a grudge against the rich and powerful stepped forward and fired a revolver from close range. A woman beside the assassin grabbed his arm and the bullets missed Roosevelt. Some, however, struck his companion, Anton Cermak, the reformist Mayor of Chicago. Cermak was having some success in cleaning up a city which had long been ruled by Al Capone and other gangleaders, and this led to speculation that he had been the real target. It seems, however, that the assassin, Giuseppe Zangara, was a loner and not a gangland hit-man. Vincent from his vantage point in the motorcade saw the whole appalling incident. With others, he tried to persuade FDR to speed back to the *Nourmahal* and safety, but Roosevelt, with total calm, insisted on taking Cermak to hospital before thinking of himself. The President-elect seemed quite unmoved by his brush with death. That night, aboard the yacht, he drank a whisky and slept soundly, while Vincent and the Roosevelt aides sat up late trying to calm their jangled nerves. Days later, when he wrote to thank his host for the trip, Roosevelt was relaxed, even jaunty, and reported that Cermak was making a good recovery. On this point he was mistaken; the Mayor of Chicago died of his wounds.

Vincent's personal feelings for FDR remained warm even when, as increasingly happened, he was unhappy about some of the New Deal policies. Their correspondence combined serious discussion of important topics with cheerful banter and private jokes. Thus, in August 1933, Astor, writing to arrange a forthcoming boat trip, explained that Western Union was having difficulty meeting the tough demands of the new industrial policy. The company president, Mr White, he reported, had had a very unsatisfactory meeting with a member of the government.

> It has seemed to me that your most miraculous achievement has been the rebirth of courage and confidence throughout industry, and I am just wondering whether such 'discussions' may not undermine much of that . . . it would seem to me that maybe the wrong sort of whip is being cracked; a whip of fear, and rather panicky fear at that. Probably a lot of coercion is going to be needed to deal with dilatory industries, but couldn't it be done better by other methods – like moral persuasion and publicity – rather than by just scaring them to death?[11]

The President replied immediately:

> Dear Vincent,
>
> Your deck-hand and his duffle bag stand ready to be shanghaied at the Dutton

Lumber Company dock on Thursday August 31st, any time after twelve noon. Do you want to send a radio to Kermit to rescue him from the Haitian natives? If so, telephone it to Naval Communications, Washington, to send to USS *Raleigh* by my directions ...

I wish much that Mr White could have a talk with Dean Acheson [Under-Secretary to the Treasury] himself. I am sure that a little common sense on both sides can straighten out that code ...

Affectionately yours,
FDR[12]

Roosevelt was adamant about the level of control government had to maintain over the business and financial sectors if the country was to escape from the economic doldrums. He deliberately appealed over the heads of the rich and powerful to the mass of less affluent American citizens. Fighting speeches, such as his acceptance of the Democratic nomination in 1936, sent shivers down the spines of many of Astor's friends and colleagues:

... out of this modern civilization economic royalists carved new dynasties. New kingdoms were built upon concentration of control over material things ... There was no place among this royalty for our many thousands of small businessmen and merchants who sought to make a worthy use of the American system ... Against economic tyranny such as this, the American citizen could appeal only to the organized power of Government ... These economic royalists complain that we seek to overthrow the institutions of America. What they really complain of is that we seek to take away their power ... In vain they seek to hide behind the Flag and the Constitution ...[13]

The realities of the New Deal made many enemies for the administration. One was Raymond Moley, who was a member of the presidential entourage and one of FDR's principal speech-writers. During Roosevelt's first term the two men grew further and further apart. Moley was also a close friend of Vincent's and, in 1934, joined him in a new enterprise that was to become very important for both men. Soon after taking office, FDR offered Astor a post which, bearing in mind two of its former incumbents, had great personal significance. He asked his friend to become Assistant Secretary to the Navy. Vincent declined. Perhaps he felt that he was not cut out for a political life. Perhaps he did not want to be forced into a position in which differences of opinion might spoil his relationship with the President. But, though he shunned public office, he did want a public voice. He saw how his English cousins helped to shape popular opinion through their newspapers. In this generation the breach between the two branches of the family was healed. There were frequent visits between the Astors of Manhattan, Cliveden and Hever. In 1933 Vincent became the proprietor and major shareholder of *Today*, a glossy weekly. Moley was appointed editor. Vincent took a stand similar to Waldorf's in allowing his editor a very free hand, while discussing policy regularly and expecting to be consulted on major issues. This meant that, as the gulf between Moley and Roosevelt widened, *Today* became increasingly critical of government policy. This alienated the President from his former speech-writer but, interestingly, it did not spoil his relations with Astor. Vincent managed to remain close friends with both men. He certainly continued to support Roosevelt and to vote for him. Basically, he liked to think of himself as a political independent, a fact he demonstrated by appearing on the platform of Joseph McKee when the latter was running, as an independent, for the mayoralty of New York in 1933.

The occasional boat trips continued, although now they were, of necessity, complicated by the fact that arrangements had to be made to keep the President in touch with affairs of state. Thus, when Astor and Roosevelt were fishing in the Bahamas in March 1934, a temporary White House was set up in Miami which maintained radio contact with the yacht via the destroyer *Ellen*. However, FDR soon had another use for the *Nourmahal* and its owner.

A successful dictator – and Roosevelt had assumed powers that were not far short of dictatorial – needs a good spy network. The White House was equipped with an information service, but the President needed to supplement it with his own intelligence sources. He wanted to know how bankers, businessmen and union bosses were reacting to his policies; what caucuses were being formed to frustrate his plans for national recovery. He even needed informants to maintain a watching brief on his own staff. This was where The Room was important to him. Everything which cropped up at the monthly meetings which might be of use to the President was passed on by Astor or Kernochan, as were snippets of information which arrived from day to day. But it was intelligence of a different kind that Astor specialized in. As the 1930s advanced, international developments added to Roosevelt's worries. The activities of Germany, Italy and Japan needed constant monitoring, and the President was not content simply to rely on information arriving through State Department channels. He had ambassadors and foreign correspondents relay news directly to the Oval Office and he set up his own secret intelligence unit headed by Washington journalist John Carter. In addition, he dispatched personal fact-finding missions. Some of these were commanded by Vincent Astor.

The innocent pleasure cruises of the *Nourmahal* provided a perfect cover for espionage. On his trips to the Caribbean and the Pacific coast of Latin America, during which he made frequent landfalls to be entertained by politicians and other local worthies, Vincent probed, pried and reported back. But what was more interesting to Roosevelt was Japanese activity on the Pacific islands they held under League of Nations mandate. He asked Astor to explore farther afield.

In February 1938 Vincent and Kermit set off on a 'scientific expedition' to the Marshall Islands. Roosevelt provided letters of introduction describing Astor as 'a famous and wealthy New Yorker', 'an old friend of mine' and 'widely known as an ichthyologist'. The letter pointed out that, to acquire specimens, Mr Astor would need to deal directly with island fishermen, and asked that any misunderstandings which might arise from Mr Astor's unfamiliarity with the Japanese language be overlooked.[14] Vincent attended a briefing with the director of naval intelligence and made arrangements for *Nourmahal* to be linked with the navy's radio network. He installed a direction-finder aboard the yacht in order to locate Japanese transmitting stations. *Nourmahal* spent several weeks among the Marshall Islands, during which time Vincent and Kermit made visual observations, interviewed local people and intercepted radio messages. On his return, Astor was able to give the President an accurate picture of the use Tokyo was making of these imperial outposts, including the location of naval bases, communications centres and airstrips.[15]

By this time *Today* had folded. It had never lived up to its expectations and, in 1937, Vincent acquired the well-established *Newsweek* and merged the other journal with it. He became sole proprietor of the magazine and discarded Moley as editor (although he continued to contribute). Vincent grew passionately attached to his journal and moved his personal office to the Newsweek building at 152 West 42nd Street. *Newsweek* and the St Regis were now Astor's principal concerns in New York. There was still real estate to administer, but very much less than when he had come into his inheritance. Even so, increased land values meant that what was left was still worth in the region of $80 million.

The gap between Vincent and the two other American Astors progressively widened. This was partly because they had been brought up separately and partly because he disapproved of the lifestyle they chose for themselves. His sister Alice lived with her mother, although it would be truer to say that she lived in the same house as her mother. She was six when her parents divorced, and nine when her father died. No man ever appeared in her life to fill Colonel Jack's parental role, and by the time Ava married Lord Ribblesdale (who was old enough to be Alice's grandfather) Alice was seventeen. In the intervening years she had been dragged around Europe by her pleasure-seeking mother. Her life, thus, had no pattern, no stability, no discipline. In addition to all this, she was a rich young lady in her own right, with the interest of a $5 million trust fund to live off. Not unnaturally, she attracted many suitors. Ava had ambitious plans for her, but Alice resisted them all, and as soon as she was twenty-one married an impecunious Russian prince, dispossessed by the revolution. Everyone who met Serge Obolensky, including Vincent, liked him. He was intelligent, cultured and had impeccable manners. Vincent gave the couple a large chunk of the estate at Ferncliff on which to build their own country mansion; but if he hoped that they would settle down he was soon disappointed. The only life Serge and Alice knew was that of the roving fast set. They flitted from Rhinebeck to St Moritz, to Paris, to Hanover Lodge (their London house overlooking Regent's Park), to the Riviera. Seeking, at all costs, to escape boredom they made every day a party day – and found it boring. In 1932, after six years of marriage, and despite the efforts of relatives and friends, they were amicably divorced. From that time on, although he continued to be friendly with Serge (and even helped him to obtain custody of his son, Ivan) Vincent had virtually nothing to do with his sister. Alice lost little time in getting married again, this time to Raimund von Hofmannsthal, the son of the Austrian poet and dramatist Hugo von Hofmannsthal (who wrote the libretti for several of Richard Strauss's operas, among them *Der Rosenkavalier*). She had a talent for finding charming, talented and intelligent husbands, but not, alas, for achieving happiness with them. In 1940 Alice's second marriage also ended in divorce.

Jack Astor likewise failed to win the approval of the head of the family – not that he tried particularly hard. The two had had little contact for years. Jack lived in Florida with his mother and stepfather. Helen had originally wanted to adopt the boy, but neither Madeleine nor Vincent showed any enthusiasm for the idea. Madeleine's notorious amorous misadventures alienated him from her – and also from his Dick half-brothers, who stood by their mother. In 1933 he came into his inheritance and he, too, lived life in the fast lane, for a time. He enjoyed travel (he had a special passion for trains), nightclubs and women, and he developed into a notable connoisseur of art. The press, of course, loved to chronicle (and exaggerate) his exploits. Thus it was confidently asserted that when he came into his millions Jack rushed out and bought ten cars, an untrue story frequently repeated by later writers. This was what particularly aggravated his half-brother. Vincent was inordinately proud of the family name, and Jack seemed (whether intentionally or not) to do nothing but bring it into disrepute. Still, he was an Astor, and Vincent tried to groom him to assume eventual responsibility for part of the family fortune. He secured a job for him with one of his companies, so that the young man could make his way up from the bottom of the ladder, learn what working life was really like and develop a healthy respect for money. Jack stuck it for a few months then quit, saying that he did not like the hours; he sometimes did not get home until six o'clock, and that seriously cut into his evening. Once more, the newspapers went to town. In 1934 Jack married

Ellen Tuck French ('Tucky'), an eighteen-year-old Newport belle, and the following year he was a father. Perhaps now he would settle down. Or perhaps not.

CHAPTER 12

'The only foundation for world peace ... close co-operation between the British Commonwealth and the United States'

It took the pressure of attempted world domination by alien philosophies – Nazism and Marxist-Leninism – to force Britain and America into the 'special relationship'. That development went a long way towards the realization of the vision the Round Tablers had long held of a worldwide community led by the Anglo-Saxon nations. Writing in June 1939, Philip Kerr, Lord Lothian, summarized what he and his friends had been urging for years:

> There have only been two long periods of world peace in history. One was created by the Roman Empire. The other was the great Pax of the nineteenth century which was created by the British Navy. That is why I have always believed that the only foundation for world peace was close co-operation between the British Commonwealth and the United States for the restoration of the nineteenth century British system operated not by Britain alone but the whole English-speaking world. With that as a nucleus, I think you can achieve the ideals of the League and in no other way.[1]

Now that rapprochement with the Third Reich was impossible, Kerr believed that the transatlantic imperative had become even more important. As soon as he had rejected appeasement, he took up with equal enthusiasm the crusade of Anglo-American solidarity against the common foe.

In August 1938 he had been appointed British Ambassador to Washington (the post to be taken up one year later), and this added point to the private, already planned, visit he made to America early in 1939. He had a long talk with the President and reported to Nancy that FDR was quite clear that the next major world struggle would be between the USA and Hitler.[2] Roosevelt's recollection of the meeting was rather different:

> Lord Lothian ... started the conversation by saying he had completely abandoned his former belief that Hitler could be dealt with as a semi-reasonable human being, and went on to say that the British for a thousand years had been the guardians of Anglo-Saxon civilization – that the sceptre or sword or something like that had dropped from their palsied fingers – that the USA must snatch it up ... I got mad

clear through and told him that just so long as he or Britishers like him took that attitude of complete despair, the British would not be worth saving anyway.[3]

Roosevelt was in a very difficult position. His own inclinations, supported by what he learned through his official and private intelligence agencies, made him want to support the stand against Nazism; but neither in Congress nor in the nation as a whole did he enjoy majority support over the issue and, in 1940, he was due for re-election. In the circumstances he did not take kindly to being preached at by a British aristocrat. When news of the President's displeasure reached London, Lothian's enemies, who believed that he was still tarred with the appeasement brush, made a vain attempt to get his appointment quashed.

Meanwhile Kerr kept the Astors informed of American attitudes, as he evaluated them. He detected that isolationism was slowly declining. The people were bitterly opposed to Hitler but were not going to be hustled into an anti-Nazi commitment by 'lefties and Jews'. Moreover, comment on Britain was far from uncritical: the UK was definitely 'off its pedestal for not going to the rescue of Czecho-Slovakia as it did of Belgium [in 1914]'.[4] At this time of crisis, the Astors felt the strength of their transatlantic ties even more acutely than their old friend. With one exception, all the members of the family committed themselves wholeheartedly to the Allied cause between 1939 and 1945.

For the English Astors phase one of the conflict lasted until December 1940. The first half of that period was, as for everyone else in Britain, a time of uneasy calm – the Phoney War. Gas masks were issued, public shelters built, air-raid wardens trained, children evacuated from the major cities to the countryside – but nothing happened. The Luftwaffe did not make its expected strikes against London and the south-eastern ports. Hitler, too busy with Poland, did not invade France. The British Expeditionary Force dug in on the Franco-Belgian border and fired scarcely a shot in anger. Chamberlain's government, 'moving into war backwards with their eyes tightly closed',[5] as one historian has put it, complacently asserted that an over-stretched Reich would collapse as a result of economic blockade. But most people knew they were only experiencing the lull before the storm, and were now impatient with leaders who provided no leadership. In the spring of 1940 Chamberlain's false optimism was shattered. Denmark, Norway, the Netherlands and Belgium fell to rapid German strikes. As the victorious armies rolled on, the French government collapsed and Chamberlain's party forced him to resign in favour of Churchill. One of the first acts of the new administration was to bring the troops back from France, and the Prime Minister's reputation received an early boost from the successful evacuation of over 300,000 men from Dunkirk. By the end of June, France, complaining of her ally's treachery, capitulated and a puppet government was set up under Marshal Pétain at Vichy to govern the unoccupied southern part of the country. Britain was alone and, in August and September, sustained the merciless aerial bombardment which was meant to be the precursor to invasion. Few neutral observers expected the UK to survive. When the RAF emerged victorious from the Battle of Britain and Hitler called off Operation Sealion to concentrate on his invasion of Russia, it was clear that a new stage in the war had begun.

Waldorf was using every political and diplomatic channel open to him to play his part. He hoped to see his friend Halifax become Prime Minister, but the peer correctly assessed the mood of his parliamentary colleagues and stood aside for Churchill. Lord Astor campaigned even more enthusiastically for Lloyd George. 'He still has his flair, resource and energy,'[6] Waldorf reported in June 1940. Garvin agreed with him; in an exasperated letter about the nation's leaders in May 1940 he dismissed Chamberlain as a man with 'no political foresight, hindsight or eyesight of any kind', and Halifax as 'splendid in high, moral and spiritual expression' but 'nowhere near big enough as a man of action in a business like this'. Britain only possessed one statesman of international stature: 'L.G. is the card, I'm sure.'[7] This, too, came to nothing. Churchill was not prepared to share the limelight with the hero of the First World War. Waldorf's uneasiness about Winston never completely abated. Three years later he could still say of Lloyd George, 'I wish he had been in the saddle in this war.'[8] Yet it was Winston who now made the gesture of friendship and confidence which no Prime Minister had made since 1920. As he gathered his team around him, he offered Viscount Astor the post of secretary to the Board of Agriculture. It was too little, too late to tempt Waldorf back into government. He declined on the pretext that his ideas were at variance with those of the new Minister of Agriculture, but it is unlikely that that was the real reason. Avoidance of national office had become a habit. Even had he wanted to break that habit, and even if he had been prepared to work under Churchill, Waldorf knew that he no longer had the stamina for the task.

The relationship with Philip Kerr was vitally important to the Astors. The new ambassador spent his last seven days in England with them at Rest Harrow, their house at Sandwich, before sailing to take up his new appointment, and wrote to them a few days later from the *Aquitania* to say how badly he felt about leaving Britain at such a time and how much he hoped to achieve something useful in the USA.[9] He kept up a vigorous correspondence with his friends, which reveals how hard the ambassador was working to engage America's active participation. Churchill made no secret of his desire to see the USA fully committed to the armed struggle with Nazism but, failing that, he wanted money and material sent across the Atlantic. As leader of a neutral power, Roosevelt had had to place an embargo on the supply of munitions to the belligerent nations. Lothian assured his friends that the President had taken this step reluctantly and that he hoped for a shift in public opinion in order to be able to remove it – 'There is no doubt that he is not a neutral about Hitler and Hitlerism!'[10] Yet the President was assailed with all kinds of conflicting advice. What some Americans feared even more than Nazism, Lothian made clear, was communism. Informed feeling in Washington was that the ultimate beneficiary of the European conflict would be Stalin and that the nation should be girding itself for a confrontation with the USSR. In such a scenario, the fate of Britain was of small consequence. Others, including Joseph Kennedy, Lothian's counterpart in London, insistently pointed out that Hitler's victory over the UK was only a matter of time and that the USA would soon have to do business with a very altered Europe. As for the bulk of the American people, they simply hoped that their boys would not be expected to fight in a war three thousand miles away. 'The United States, like all other nations, will only act when its own financial interests – which include its ideals – are menaced,'[11] Lothian reported. Roosevelt would not be free until after the 1940 election to pursue a firm foreign policy line. For the time being the maxim was 'wait and see'. However, he did persuade Congress to lift the arms embargo in November 1939. 'That is very satisfactory,' Lothian enthused, 'and must be a bitter blow to Hitler and Goering.'[12]

What might be termed the Astor–Lothian undercurrent of unofficial diplomatic activity continued on a regular basis. Nancy, in particular, kept up a frequent correspondence with her friend – her letters, typically, rambling from political affairs of high moment to family matters and social trivia. Thus, on 12 January 1940, she reported on a long conversation with the new US Ambassador, complained about an abscess in her ear – 'The pain is a result of painful thought about those darned children of mine' – and included the superb throwaway line about a recent 'small' dinner party in St James's Square, 'we had just Bobbety [Robert Cecil, Marquess of Salisbury and leader of the Tory peers], Geoffrey Dawson, Anthony Eden, Tom Jones, the Archbishop of Canterbury and myself.'[13] Early in 1940 Lothian arranged for Nancy to appear in a radio broadcast to tell the Americans how British women were facing up to the anxieties and hardships of the war. In March he asked her to arrange a lunch for Churchill to meet David Gray, the new US Minister to Ireland. Three months later Waldorf wanted Lothian to redouble his efforts to persuade the President to ship planes and guns to Britain urgently. Military supplies were coming through but not nearly fast enough. By the same letter he raised another concern that carried echoes of the First World War:

> Can you bring any influence to bear on Ulster to come to terms with de Valera [Eire's *Taoiseach* or head of government]? They are obstinate but Southern Ireland as a base for air or submarines would increase our difficulties. De Valera is doing his best but a united Ireland would strengthen his hand.

De Valera had proclaimed Eire's neutrality, but Astor remembered the aggravating diversion the country had been during the last conflict and feared that extremists might push Dublin into pro-German activity or giving succour to enemy agents. In July Waldorf asked his friend's opinion of a scheme he had devised to send US Red Cross units into Vichy France to distribute food. As well as having propaganda value, such an arrangement would provide London and Washington with fresh information channels.[14]

Waldorf had only recently come to appreciate the value of propaganda and counter-intelligence. This was, partly, a natural development of the work he had been involved in for years through Chatham House and the Round Table, which had been concerned with the gathering and dissemination of *accurate information*. The Nazi propaganda machine, under the diabolically clever Josef Goebbels, was now showing the world just how effective a programme of *disinformation* could be, using radio, film, posters, rallies and all the resources of modern communications technology. Waldorf interested himself closely in the work of gathering intelligence and attempting to counter the leadership's lies in occupied Europe.

In the summer of 1939 it seemed to Waldorf and his friends and associates in the Royal Institute of International Affairs that, at a time of worsening foreign relations, Chatham House might have a useful role to play. Accordingly, a group was set up in Oxford called the Foreign Research and Press Service. This secret, semi-official organization, on which Lionel Curtis was Lord Astor's representative, had various functions. At one level it was, purely and simply, an intelligence-gathering agency. Information from a variety of civilian sources – academic, social, cultural, diplomatic – was collected, translated, sifted, evaluated and passed on, as applicable, to the relevant authorities. The FRPS was also concerned to operate the system in reverse order to weaken the Nazi party's hold on the citizens of the Reich. As Curtis said, 'as long as the Germans continue to feel that Versailles or something worse (the disintegration of Germany) will follow an Allied victory . . . opinion there will remain solid behind Hitler and Goebbels.'[15] Therefore, it was important to disseminate as widely as possible the true objectives of the Allied powers. But what were those objectives? In the summer of 1940 all thoughts at Westminster were concentrated on survival. *Winning* the war was, at best, a remote possibility. Shaping the peace was something no one had time to speculate about. It was this that the Chatham House people, including Waldorf, were basically interested in. They wanted to be able to brief government, at the appropriate time, on the possible structure of a new Europe. This thinking went right down to the historic roots of the Royal Institute of International Affairs. It had grown from the poisoned soil of the 1919 peace talks, when wrong decisions were made by prejudiced and ill-informed delegates inflamed by an ignorant public opinion. It was vital that outrage against the aggressors should not, again, be the dominant factor after the present conflict. So the FRPS prepared reports, talked with ministers, and provided the press with positive propaganda. It was inevitable that MI5 and MI6 should look askance at the FRPS as a bunch of idealistic, intellectual amateurs who used up valuable government funds and would probably do more harm than good. Right-wing elements certainly wanted the group suppressed because it was not making the right kind of bellicose noises. In August 1940 these critics were threatening to have the unit closed down. That was when Waldorf took a firm hand. He went straight to Halifax. As a result the Foreign Secretary and the FRPS leaders met for dinner at 4 St James's Square. This led to a series of meetings with Treasury officials which put the workings of the group on a secure basis.

On a day in July 1939 a small car stood parked on a side road just north of Berlin. Its two occupants gazed across a level turnip field to the gaunt walls and massive iron gates of a concentration camp. 'This is what Nazism amounts to,' Adam von Trott said to his friend David Astor.[16] David became another important influence on his father in these years. It would be truer to say that their thinking existed in symbiosis; for Waldorf's liberalism had been the stock up which David's developing ideals had climbed, and the older stem now drew fresh strength from the new, vigorous growth. Since his stay in Germany in 1931 David had developed friendships with several academic families in Heidelberg. He disagreed radically with Bill's assessment of the Reich as a nation of automata, who would bow to Hitler's will come what may. Through his friendship at Oxford with Adam von Trott and other young Germans he knew that there were strong counter-currents. He spent the greater part of 1939 and 1940 trying to persuade people in high places that there was an alternative to war as a means of bringing down the Hitler regime. What Trott and his co-conspirators were asking for was time. They wanted the British government to go on talking to the dictator so that all the pieces of the plot to overthrow him could be put in place. War would be catastrophic, not only because it would restrict the activities of the resistance, but also because it would transform Hitler into the heroic leader of the nation; an attack upon him would be seen as an attack on Germany. David arranged meetings for his friend with several politicians, including Chamberlain. In June 1939, von Trott had dinner at Cliveden with Halifax and Lothian. But what the ardent young Hessian was proposing was now totally at odds with feeling in the country. By now the British were not only expecting war, they were spoiling for war. To the Astors' enemies this idea of 'keeping Hitler talking' was the last desperate gamble of the Cliveden Set, and von Trott was, in all likelihood, a Nazi spy.

Trott went on to America, where Lothian arranged some interviews for him. They achieved nothing. From London David gave him vigorous support. He paid for other like-minded men to cross the Atlantic – such as the 'young man who is an intimate of our mutual friend ... [and] is married to an American'.[17] He gathered around him a few other young men, known as the Europe Study Group, whose task was to develop a vision of a Europe without Hitler but in which Germany had an honourable part to play. By disseminating these ideas in Britain (through the press and broadcasting) and in occupied Europe (by aerial leafleting) they hoped to win the battle for people's minds and shorten the war. In thinking ahead to what might lie beyond armed struggle and planning a propaganda campaign they were very similar to the FRPS, and Waldorf was greatly in sympathy with them. He was the only Astor who was. David wrote to Lothian on 20 October 1939: 'I have sat through some pretty painful meals at the family table. My father is the only one in the family whose ideas are firmly against this atmosphere produced by Khaki.'[18] David's strong connections inside Germany attracted the attention of the Secret Intelligence Service and he was interviewed with a view to a job in Intelligence. But he had little stomach for either the people or the work. In May he joined the Royal Marines. Adam von Trott, meanwhile, had returned to Germany, despite David's earnest pleadings. He was executed in July 1944 for complicity in a plot to assassinate the Führer.

The fact that Waldorf, like David, rejected the prevalent gung-ho militarism does not mean that he was either unpatriotic or naïve about the real situation. He was clear-headed and never underestimated the complex problems created by the war. For example, through his work in Plymouth he became involved with French sailors detained in Britain after the fall of their country. The Vichy government ordered the return of all ships and men, but Churchill had no intention of allowing such an augmentation of the Axis navy. Thus, wherever possible, ships were impounded and their crews provided with British 'hospitality'. The question was, where did the loyalty of such men lie? They were under orders from their legally constituted government. Their families were at risk in occupied territory. Some were certainly not well disposed towards Britain, especially after 3 July 1940, when the Royal Navy opened fire, in Oran harbour, on French warships whose officers had refused to place themselves under British orders, destroying three vessels and killing twelve hundred men. Waldorf made strenuous efforts on behalf of the detainees. He talked with French officers. He invited their leader, Admiral

Cayot, to Cliveden. He arranged private hospitality for the sailors in local homes. He set up clubs. He organized English lessons. He suggested to Ernest Bevin, the Minister of Labour, the setting up of a French pioneer corps, which would work in forestry and agriculture. But it was not just the men's social welfare that concerned him. As he repeatedly explained to the Cabinet and the Admiralty, it was important to counter Vichy propaganda, obtain volunteers for the navy and train agents who could return to France as spies and saboteurs. The Admiralty, of course, had its own routines for dealing with the problem. They did not satisfy Viscount Astor, as he explained in a very confidential memo to Churchill's confidant, Brendan Bracken, at Number 10:

I am not at all happy. I consider the French liaison officer, who has been here through the winter, dangerous. I have misgivings lest our own C. in C., with his tradition of naval honour between officers, may be hoodwinked by the French. I fear he may wait on the course of events instead of anticipating them. People from the Ministry of Information have been in Plymouth with Nancy talking to French sailors. Nancy can give you more information that I care to put on paper.[19]

On 12 October Lord Lothian returned home for a short visit. He experienced the Blitz at first hand when the London hotel in which he was staying was rocked by a bomb. The Astors laid on a special dinner for him at Cliveden with as many of his Round Table friends as could be reached. The guest of honour addressed the gathering on the subject of Anglo-American relations. He prophesied that the United States would soon be standing shoulder-to-shoulder with the British and that the two nations would play a major role in reshaping the world. Meanwhile, President Roosevelt was elected for a third term. In his inaugural address he underlined the ambassador's words: 'There are men who believe that ... tyranny and slavery have become the surging wave of the future – and that freedom is an ebbing tide. But we Americans know that this is not true.'[20] Lothian returned to his post. Early in December he fell ill with uremia, an eminently treatable complaint. In accordance with his religious convictions he sent for a Christian Science practitioner and not a doctor. On the night of 11 December, he died. He was fifty-eight.

Mike and Jakie were both called up last week and Aunt N says that Jakie looked just like an hors d'oeuvres in his khaki. We saw Michael and he was heart-rendingly handsome in his.[21]

So wrote Joyce Grenfell to her mother the day after war was declared. All the Astor boys saw active service. Bill, the oldest, was the first to enlist. He joined the navy in May 1939 and spent the early part of the war working for naval intelligence in Egypt – stationed for most of the time in Ismailia. There was a great deal of work for a Middle Eastern specialist to do in that complex theatre of war, assessing the political activities and conflicting loyalties of Palestinians, Iraqis, Syrians, Iranians, Turks and Trans-Jordanians in an area where Britain, Vichy France, Germany and the USSR all had colonial or economic interests. It was not all work. Violet heard, in May 1942, that Bill had met up with her son George for a few weeks' swimming and sailing in Lebanon and commented to Nancy, 'Isn't it nice how the Astor family cling together.'[22] Bill returned home in the autumn of 1942 to resume his parliamentary activities. In November he made a long speech to the Commons about his experience of the campaigns in the Mediterranean and North Africa. Half a century later, it reads like a very pompous, jingoistic address: The British Tommy is doing a splendid job; the war has proved the solidarity of the British Empire; Britain and her dependencies are bound together by bonds of love and respect for those national virtues of honesty and fairness which no people on earth can match; these are the things we must all strive to preserve. Doubtless, at the time, it struck a common chord.

For Bill's brothers the war had scarcely yet begun by 1942. Michael had joined the army's reconnaissance unit, usually known by its code name 'Phantom', and found that service life seemed to mean perpetual 'training', which he regarded as organized boredom. Inactivity, however, did have its compensations. Stationed in Sussex, he was able to renew his relationship with an old friend, Barbara McNeill, who was working for Archibald McIndoe, the plastic surgeon who did such remarkable work repairing the faces and lives of burn-scarred airmen. After a typical wartime 'live for today' romance, Barbara and Michael were married. It was not until after the D-Day landings of 1944 that Captain Astor saw active service. He went ashore in the second wave and spent the remainder of the war as a liaison officer between various British, American and Canadian headquarters. His closest confrontation with death came when an artillery unit to which he was attached was heavily bombed, by mistake – by RAF planes. As a liaison officer Michael rarely came under enemy fire, though carrying messages between Field Marshal Montgomery and senior Allied officers who shared a mutual dislike could be almost as harrowing. He was awarded a Bronze Star by the Americans. The citation referred to his 'energy, intelligence and diplomacy' and commented that his 'generous spirit, uncommonly fine personality and rare sense of humour' had helped to maintain a good relationship between the British and US armies.[23] It cannot be often that those particular qualities have been singled out in the awarding of a military medal. Michael ended the war on Monty's staff and was actually present at the historic moment when the German chiefs-of-staff arrived at Montgomery's HQ on Lüneburg Heath to present their formal surrender. It was typical of Michael's oblique, rather cynical view of life that he found something else to comment on about this great moment: 'The sight of two of my colleagues saluting German generals, practically clicking heels, dancing round them like blackcock in the spring of the year performing the steps of their courting display, left me with the feeling that the requirements of etiquette could be carried too far.'[24]

Jakie, who was commissioned in the Life Guards before the war, also transferred to the Phantom unit in 1940. He was employed in a liaison capacity with various Canadian forces, but saw more front-line action than Michael because he commanded a Phantom squadron and went into battle with various SAS and Commando units, which involved arriving at the operational zone by parachute or amphibious craft. He was present at one of the most hazardous and criminally pointless engagements of the war. On 19 August 1942 an Anglo-Canadian attack was launched on Dieppe. In so far as it had any strategic justification, it was conceived to discover the problems which would be faced when the Allies launched their second front in occupied Europe. Plans for the raid were bungled. It was made with inadequate air support and naval backing. The attackers found themselves making a head-on assault against well-sited gun emplacements. The casualties were fearful. Probably half of the Canadian contingent were either killed or captured. Jakie was one of the lucky ones. He never got ashore from his destroyer.

Bobbie Shaw went to Edinburgh in an attempt to join the Scots Greys, the only regiment still using horses, but his age and health prevented him joining up. He 'did his bit', however, as a member of a Home Guard unit in Kent. In this capacity he received 'war wounds' in October 1940 – but only because the pub in which he happened to be drinking was hit by a bomb. Several people were killed. Bobbie was luckier, though both arms and one leg were damaged and he lost a lot of blood. By mid-November, he was back at Cliveden recuperating. Of course, his mother was very worried – and proud, because in his report from hospital Bobbie had been careful to conceal the *location* in which he had sustained his injuries.

Gavin, the oldest Hever boy, was not so fortunate. He too joined the Life Guards. He too became bored with the Phoney War and volunteered for the Commandos. His first taste of action was in Iraq. Early in 1941, Rashid Ali el Gailani became Prime Minister, overthrew the pro-British royal family and cast his lot with the Axis powers. On 18 April, Iraqi forces, backed by artillery, launched an attack on the British air base at Habbaniya. After a week, the garrison troops, outnumbered three-to-one by the enemy, were in a parlous state. It was at this point that reinforcements from Egypt were airlifted into Habbaniya. Gavin Astor was part of the relief force which, within a few days, completely reversed the situation. By the end of May the rebel forces were defeated on the ground and el Gailani had fled the country. In 1943 Gavin rejoined his regiment and took part in the invasion of Italy. One day in the following year he went off with a driver and a jeep to reconnoitre ahead of the advancing army, ran into an enemy patrol and was captured. He spent the rest of the war in a prison camp.

John Astor was only sixteen when the war broke out, but he was determined to get into the action and, as soon as possible, he volunteered for the RAF. He went to Canada for his training and proved to be an excellent aviator. He passed out top of both the pilot's course and the navigator's course. He returned to Europe just in time to see service, with Coastal Command, on flying boats.

Ironically, the member of the family who had the most interesting war was the one who, because of his disability, was debarred from front-line service. Hugh Astor, Gavin's younger brother, served in military intelligence, worked in Europe and Asia, and, by 1945, had achieved the rank of lieutenant-colonel. Right up to the end of the war in Europe, Hugh was a member of a specialist team which operated a network of double agents throughout the Continent who gathered vital information about military activity and, perhaps more importantly, supplied the Germans with bogus intelligence.

The most important agent Hugh ran personally was a man code-named 'Brutus'. When the Germans overran France, British Intelligence was left with not a single operator in the country, then they suddenly began picking up radio signals. They investigated and discovered that the transmitter was a member of the Polish air force who had been awarded the Virtute Militari, the highest Polish award for gallantry. He had been caught in France by the invasion, left his unit and gone underground in Paris. With the aid of a friend, he built his own wireless and made contact with London. Once they were satisfied with his bona fides, the British spy-masters sent him money and equipment. Soon Brutus had established over a hundred agents throughout France, most of whom were providing enormously valuable information. He was brought to England for a briefing visit in autumn 1941, but shortly afterwards he and his whole organization were betrayed to the Nazis by a jealous girlfriend. It looked like the end. That it was not was due to the reputation Brutus had established as an agent and to his cool resourcefulness. Under interrogation he actually managed to persuade his examiners that his real enemy was Russia and that he would do anything to help Germany crush the communist menace. He tricked the Nazis into thinking that they might be able to turn him and send him to England as a double agent. They put the suggestion to him, and the prisoner was so clever that he was even able to impose conditions: he would work for the Germans if they would guarantee not to execute his collaborators. Brutus's 'escape' to Britain was engineered and he reached London towards the end of 1942.

A few months later Hugh assumed responsibility for running Brutus and spent some time carefully building up his credibility with the Germans, who soon believed him to be one of their most effective agents. Once this had been achieved the stage was set for the implementation of Fortitude South. This was the plan to persuade the enemy that the main Allied invasion would be in the Pas de Calais area. In order to feed the Germans with disinformation the intelligence operators concerned had to know what the real invasion plans were. This was, of course, extremely restricted information provided only to members of the privileged coterie known as 'Bigots'. Hugh became a Bigot at the end of 1943.

Over the next few months the architects of Fortitude South worked hard and long to build up a detailed and ingenious structure of misinformation. The British, American and Commonwealth forces, it was suggested, were going to capture a dozen Channel ports and harbours between Ostend and Boulogne through which to land troops and keep them supplied. To confuse the enemy they proposed to make a feint at Bordeaux (Operation Ironside); although if this proved successful they would develop their southern landing into a secondary attack. Fortitude South was a complete success. The only heart-stopping moment came three weeks before D-Day when information reached London that a crack Panzer division was being moved up to Normandy from the south. Through another of his agents, 'Bronx', Hugh was able to convince the Germans that the Bordeaux attack was imminent and the troop movement order was immediately reversed.

In the final year of the war Britain had to face Hitler's most appalling weapons, the long-range V1 and V2 rockets. Hugh reported the development of these devices to the War Cabinet months before the first ones were fired. Unfortunately, the government chose to believe, instead, its own scientific advisers, who confidently told them it was impossible to build a projectile capable of covering the necessary distances. When the rockets did begin to fall, doing considerable damage in and around London, Hugh's section was called in to suggest some way of minimizing their effectiveness. British Intelligence knew that the V1s were targeted on Charing Cross and that they had an accuracy radius of about two miles. Operators at the launch sites relied on reports from their people in England as to how effective the bombing was – but the agents they listened to had been turned by Intelligence. Accordingly, false estimates were relayed back to Germany and the rockets began falling more and more to the south of the capital. This was hard on some of the inhabitants of Kent and Surrey but, as Churchill observed, 'if they're going to fall somewhere, they might as well fall where they can do less damage'.

Hugh Astor was involved in operations throughout Europe from Britain to Sicily right up to VE Day. Then he was transferred to south-east Asia to work against the Japanese. After that he was seconded to the British military mission in Indo-China and was involved in the early stages of the civil war there before returning to civvy street in 1946.

In the 1940s intelligence work was not the highly technical activity involving satellites and electronic surveillance equipment that it was later to become. It was still, at the upper levels at least, a game – a very serious game, no doubt, but a game nevertheless – played by intelligent men trying to outwit each other. The obvious recruits for this type of work were men from families like the Astors – men who were much-travelled, spoke foreign languages and had social and business contacts in many lands. Such were the members of The Room in New York who performed valuable services for President Roosevelt. When war broke out in Europe they were even more important to him.

Roosevelt was in a cleft stick. Ideologically he stood alongside the European democracies. From the point of view of practical politics he knew Hitler had to be stopped, since victory in the Old World would encourage the dictator to turn his eyes towards the new. He would have a powerful Atlantic fleet, would take over former British colonies in the West Indies and seek to install puppet regimes in Latin America. On the other hand Roosevelt could not intervene without a popular mandate and, as he explained in a secret interview with the British Ambassador in 1938, even were his personal stock at an all time high he would be powerless to invest his nation's men and money unless Hitler actually invaded Britain. The only escape from this dilemma was somehow to wean the American people from their isolationism while at the same time remaining in office. In this delicate situation he needed every intelligence source he could acquire.

In 1939 The Room was renamed The Club and concentrated largely on monitoring the activities of embassies and agents in the USA and neighbouring countries. Vincent and his friends were soon involved in clandestine activities that defied federal laws, such as tampering with the mails, intercepting international cables (which Astor was able to do through trusted employees in Western Union) and even opening diplomatic bags. The members of The Club were prepared to take risks because every one of them was strongly pro-British. Some had been educated in England; others had transatlantic marriage ties; all had close and valued friends across the ocean. Kermit Roosevelt was, in fact, not active in The Club, because he hurried to Britain in 1939 to enlist in the army. (He died in 1943 while working for military intelligence.) Others were committed to the war effort in different ways. David Bruce went to London to direct American Red Cross relief. The banker Winthrop Aldrich organized the British War Relief Society and funded a secret organization which trained British pilots in the USA.

Vincent Astor had several strings to his espionage bow. He obtained confidential information from Chase National Bank about foreign accounts being used to fund agents and saboteurs in America. One such was operated by the Antorg Corporation, a cover organization for Soviet intelligence. Chase National had other uses. When the Japanese government asked the bank to send a commission to Tokyo to advise on certain economic affairs, Vincent reported the development to Roosevelt, adding that 'such a commission might be of great value to us in obtaining valuable information, provided that certain individual members were wisely chosen and adequately educated in advance as to what to look for'.[25]

Vincent was hand in glove with UK agents in New York and Bermuda (where he owned property). British Intelligence in Manhattan was run by Sir James Paget and Walter Bell under the cover of the passport control office, and from them Vincent discovered useful information about Nazis operating through Spanish embassies in the Americas and the existence of a vigorous anti-American cell in Mexico City. There was always the risk that such illegal activity, if discovered, would be blocked by enemies in Congress. This happened in the summer of 1940, when State Department bureaucrats complained about The Club's violation of United States neutrality. All Vincent's intelligence work was directed by the President, who issued his instructions during frequent private meetings. Very little was committed to paper and, officially, FDR knew nothing of the activities of Astor and his friends. He could not, therefore, support them against formal complaints from the Capitol.

Relations were, similarly, not easy with the American intelligence services, who knew something about Astor's amateur set-up and resented it. In June 1940 Vincent appealed to his friend for help: 'I do hope that I shall have a chance to come down and talk with you for a little while about the "club", which I am up to my neck in; and also the suggested Chase Bank mission to Japan.' Referring to complaints by Naval Intelligence, he commented, 'Maybe I shall need you to protect me from a firing squad!' In such a case, in which he was protected by departmental secrecy, the President *could* act. He sent a memo to the chief of naval operations informing him: 'I have requested [Mr Astor] to co-ordinate the Intelligence work in the New York Area, and, of course, want him given every assistance . . . I would like to have great weight given his recommendations on the selection of candidates because of his wide knowledge of men and affairs in connection with general Intelligence work.'[26] Early the following year, although his official counterparts were still unhappy, Vincent's omni-competence within the New York area was confirmed and further defined. He had powers 'to control all local intelligence functions undertaken by the Military Intelligence Division of the US Army, the Office of Naval Intelligence, the Justice and State Departments and liaison with other information-gathering agencies'.[27]

By now, however, events were moving rapidly. Roosevelt had been safely elected for his third term and could pursue his policies more openly. The war situation had become complex and necessitated a drastic overhaul of US intelligence services. The President had no time, in those critical days, for trips aboard the *Nourmahal* and Vincent saw much less of him. Then, in December, came the attack on Pearl Harbor and America was in the war. During the summer Astor was ill. When he returned to his desk he discovered that he was no longer in touch with fast-changing events. Roosevelt had set up a new central intelligence bureau (the forerunner of OSS – the Office of Strategic Services) under the command of Colonel 'Wild Bill' Donovan. Some members of The Club were employed by the new organization, but there was no room now for gentlemanly amateurs.

As soon as the war became 'official', Vincent re-enlisted in the navy and rose eventually to the rank of captain. For the first couple of years he remained largely deskbound. From an office in the Eastern Sea Frontier HQ he helped to organize Atlantic convoys and anti-submarine patrols. His post as area intelligence controller for New York was never officially revoked, and he involved himself in several counter-espionage activities including secret radio monitoring of vessels close to the coast. He maintained the strongest links with members of the secret service, most notably with William Stevenson ('Intrepid'), for whom he provided the St Regis as a safe house. Gradually, however, his effectiveness in this aspect of the war effort waned and he had a longing to get back to sea. In 1944 he became directly involved in convoy operations and was kept fully occupied by these duties during the vital months when men and supplies in vast quantities were being shipped to Europe for D-Day and its aftermath.

Alice, Vincent's sister, was in England at the outbreak of war, her second marriage having just run its course, and she elected to stay there. Whatever character defects she may have had, she did not lack courage. She identified herself totally with the beleaguered Londoners during the worst days of the Blitz. She worked in an electronics factory by day, and at night she drove an ambulance through the bomb-cratered streets, or took a mobile canteen to anti-aircraft gun sites. On one of these mercy missions she fell in love again, this time with a soldier, Philip Harding. They were married in 1940. This strange, intense, tall creature, described by her sister-in-law as having 'the look of a Persian princess, with a rather secret oval face and coal black hair',[28] could slip easily from the rough and cheerful company of an ack-ack platoon to the sophisticated world of the London artistic and literary set. Throughout the war she gave parties in her elegant Regent's Park home to guests who included Edith and Osbert Sitwell, Aldous Huxley and Frederick Ashton. She was devoted to the theatrical and musical life of the capital and a generous benefactress to Sadler's Wells Ballet Company. Alice was very much her own person, which may explain why she never found anyone with whom she could share her life. In her forties she was still beautiful, with an aura of mystery. She had her own very distinctive and stylish way of dressing which always stopped just short of eccentricity. Joyce Grenfell described her as turning up to one of Nancy's parties looking like a Chinese pagoda. Yet beneath her oddities, she was enormously warm-hearted and generous. She genuinely loved her husbands, had children by each of them, and intended to make a success of every marriage. By the end of the war she had parted company with Philip Harding, and in 1946 she married David Pleydell-Bouverie, a cousin of Lord Radnor. While all this was going on, her first husband, Serge Obolensky, had joined the US paratroopers, at the age of fifty plus.

The one member of the family who was not involved in the fighting during the Second World War was Jack Astor. Years later Bill reported to the family's New York lawyer a conversation he had had with Vincent about his half-brother:

> Vincent was furious because Jack had taken no part in the war, and he told me that Jack had deliberately faked mental disability in order to get rejected by the Draft Board before whom he was called and succeeded in doing so. Vincent was so annoyed that he even took up the matter personally with President Roosevelt who had, however, no power to reject the opinion of a Draft Board about an individual.[29]

Whether or not this was true, Vincent believed it. For one so patriotic this must have been the last straw. From this point on he had nothing to do with his half-brother. Vincent's second wife, Mary, or 'Minnie' as she was known to most people (Vincent and Helen had obtained an amicable divorce in 1940), tried to put a stop to this 'silly' feud, but where Jack was concerned Vincent was quite implacable.

The feeling was mutual. Jack was perfectly content not to be on speaking terms with Vincent. He parted company with his first wife in 1946 in order to marry twenty-one-year-old Gertrude Gretsch. One of Jack's problems was that he simply could not keep away from beautiful women. He consorted with them quite openly and never attempted to hide his liaisons from his wife. Once he planned a trip to Europe with his latest girlfriend. When Gerty protested, 'You should be taking me,' Jack replied, 'I've taken you three times; it will be more fun to go with someone else.' There was something totally anarchic about Jack's eccentricity. He refused to acknowledge that his conduct should be in any way modified to make it harmonize with the ideas or feelings of others. Gerty's honeymoon was spent travelling through Canada in a private railway coach, listening to her husband prattling on about locomotives, track, construction dates and hundreds of other statistics with which his mind was well stocked. He could be immensely generous – but always on his own terms. On Gerty's twenty-fifth birthday he gave her $25,000 to go out and buy herself whatever she wanted. She found a small Monet painting that she particularly liked. Jack took one look at it and laughed. 'Impressionist rubbish!' he declared. 'Let's take it back and I'll buy you some jewellery.' Jack Astor always reckoned he owed life nothing. If he was inconsiderate to others it was because no one had shown consideration for him. His father had been thoughtless enough to get killed before Jack was born. His stepfather had never cared for him. His mother had shown him little affection and had finally embarrassed him by her absurd relationship with an Italian thug. Fate had not gone out of its way to please Jack Astor, so Jack Astor would please himself.

This did not mean a constant round of love affairs and wild parties. He was intelligent, well-informed and read voraciously. He had inherited something of his father's interest in things technical and scientific. As well as railways and cars, he made a close study of meteorology. He loved paintings and had an excellent eye. Over the years he built up a fine collection of modern works, often buying before an artist came into fashion. Donning khaki and shouldering a rifle were activities that simply did not enter his scheme of things.

In Plymouth there are still many people who hold the name of Astor in high affection. These feelings, in most cases, have their roots in the wartime activities of Nancy and Waldorf. In 1939 an almost unprecedented tribute was offered to Viscount Astor when he was appointed lord mayor with the unanimous backing of all parties. He was re-elected unopposed every year until 1944. Poor health (he had a mild stroke in 1942) restricted his movements and he was not able to be in the city as much as he would have wished. However, he continued to identify with the problems of the people and, particularly, with the work of reconstruction. Discovering, in 1940, that less than 20 per cent of the young people belonged to any kind of youth organization, he set up the Junior Service Corps, which was soon taken up by government and made into a national scheme. We owe it to our serving men and women, he insisted, to see that their children are brought up to be the right kind of citizens to create a new Britain and a new Europe. With Nancy, he took on the local authorities in a battle to get younger children evacuated to Scotland. To Waldorf it was obvious that Plymouth, with its important naval and civil dockyards and nearby military installations, would be a prime target for the Luftwaffe, and so it proved. Early in 1941 a series of devastating air-raids began which laid waste a large part of the city. Eleven hundred people were killed and thousands more were injured. Every major civic building and half the schools and churches were destroyed. Waldorf's immediate priority was relief work. He worked tirelessly with local services to provide for the injured and the homeless and he was constantly battering on the doors of central government for aid. Other towns and cities had also been devastated and there was fierce competition between civic leaders for the limited financial resources available from Westminster. This brought him into close contact with Clement Attlee (Lord Privy Seal and, later, Deputy Prime Minister) who was in charge of the home front. The two men worked well together and shared many ideals. It was in large measure thanks to their friendship that Plymouth maintained a high place on the government's agenda. But Waldorf was not content merely to react to the war situation. As in 1914–18, he looked to the future and immersed himself in the work of reconstruction. He gathered around him a team of planners and architects and drew up a revolutionary scheme for a new city centre. He was determined that Plymouth should emerge from its harrowing experience, not just patched up, but with a new civic 'heart' of which its people could be proud and which would pioneer new concepts of inner city design. He had had a deep interest in town planning (perhaps the fascination with building was inherited from his father) ever since the aftermath of the First World War, and he grasped eagerly this opportunity to turn his ideas into reality.

Revolutionary schemes inevitably provoke opposition. Waldorf's proposals were altogether too radical for the Conservative majority on the city council. Planning smacked of socialism and the Tory members ganged up against him. Waldorf fought them every inch of the way, even when Nancy refused her support. In the end they 'deposed' him from the office of lord mayor in 1944. Up to that point the Conservatives had been happy to renominate him every year, and the Labour councillors had waived their right to put up an alternative candidate, so great was their respect for Waldorf. Now Viscount Astor was removed by his own party. But he had the last laugh. Their objective had been to ditch the Plymouth plan. In fact, with Labour support, he had already steered through the council a resolution which committed it to all the essentials of the plan. In 1947, King George VI opened the first part of the redeveloped city centre.

But what mattered more to the people of Plymouth during the worst days of the war was that the Astors were *there*. Within the city they had come to love, Waldorf and Nancy were the equivalent of royalty. Just as George VI and Queen Elizabeth boosted the morale of Londoners by touring the blitzed areas of the capital and talking with the homeless, the bereaved and the wounded, so Waldorf and Nancy – but especially Nancy – frequently appeared among the ruins, in the hospitals, the air-raid shelters and the emergency treatment centres. Like the royal family, who refused to move out of Buckingham Palace even when it was hit by bombs, the Astors frequently lived at their house on The Hoe, which also sustained damage. Here they continued to give dinners and parties for local people as though nothing had changed. Nancy organized dances, concerts and other events to keep people's spirits up. And when she was not in Plymouth she was usually in Westminster cajoling and bullying government for more aid for her battered constituency. Nancy had a large heart, and a major part of it was given to Plymouth. Half a century later there are those who remember her telling jokes and performing impromptu caricatures to make people laugh or sitting for hours with a mother weeping over the death of her child.

Cliveden, as in the First World War, was handed over to the Canadian Red Cross for use as a hospital. Taplow Lodge, also on the estate, became a wartime government orphanage. Responsibilities in Plymouth and Westminster meant that Nancy could not be as involved in the work there as she had been in 1914–18, but when she was around her presence was certainly felt. One of Joyce's letters recorded:

> I've put in quite a lot of time lately giving a hand down at Taplow Lodge with the settling in of the eighty-one babies. There are actually eighty-two tonight, for Aunt N. discovered an eighteen-month-old boy in Kentish Town whose mother was having another this week and had seven more besides so she bundled him into the car and brought him down to join the rest.[30]

Cliveden was not taken over entirely for war work. It remained a home and Waldorf spent a great deal of time there. Family members still came down from time to time, and friends, but there were no elegant house parties. Gaiety of a different kind took over – concerts and impromptu cabarets arranged by Joyce, Nancy, the Winns (Alice, Nancy's niece, and her husband, Reginald), and others, dragooned in to entertain the wounded troops. George Bernard Shaw and his wife came fairly often and the soldiers were most impressed to meet such a celebrity. Life at Cliveden in the war years was an odd mixture – a luxurious stage set across which moved aristocrats, actresses, literary figures, harassed nurses and crippled men in khaki. Joyce's letters captured the jumbled, exhausting life of this bizarre place.

> I had a very early lunch on Tuesday in order to be at the hosp. by 1.30 as I was taking a party of three [patients] to the movies in M[aidenhead] ... We followed the show by tea here and rounded off the evening by a view of the big house and a box of candies to be shared among 'em from Aunt N., who had just returned from Devon that day. I dined up there that night ... One soon gets out of practice with the family I find and when they suddenly reunite it is a very strong dose and takes quite a lot

of digesting. The thing I find the hardest to endure from them is their abnormalcy! Not one of them fits in to the ordinary world.[31]

In 1942 Waldorf made a far-seeing and drastic decision. He offered Cliveden to the National Trust. Its upkeep had become ruinous and he felt very deeply that it had long since ceased to provide a family *centre*. Michael and David kept away from the place, and it could not be maintained for Bill and Jakie to use for occasional hunting and shooting. Far better to avoid the death duties which would otherwise prove an immense burden to his sons. The arrangement he reached with the National Trust was that his heirs could go on renting the house in perpetuity should they wish to do so. He had another reason for offering control to a charitable concern:

It has been a place where men and women of all types, Ministers, M.P.s, businessmen, trade unionists, educationalists, civil servants, etc., have foregathered. In offering this property my hope is not only to preserve the amenities of the place for the public, but also to make it possible for Cliveden in times to come to continue to be used for similar purposes.[32]

It was a bold move. Waldorf, unlike other rich men burdened by the upkeep of stately homes, did not hang on till the last moment or look for commercial ways to make Cliveden pay its way. He made a clean break. It was one that was not altogether appreciated by those most closely involved, despite the release given to the press, which declared that the decision had been made 'with the full approval of Mr William Waldorf Astor MP, . . . who has returned from the Middle East with reinforced faith in the future of the country'.[33] (Some years later, when John Astor was wondering what to do with Hever, he briefly contemplated following his brother's example. Representatives from the National Trust came to discuss the possibilities. John found their attitude insufferably arrogant and eventually brought the meeting to an abrupt close with the rebuke, 'I was under the impression we were trying to reach a gentleman's agreement. As far as I can see, there is only one gentleman present.' From quiet, amiable John, those were strong words.)

The world of politics to which Bill returned at the end of 1942 was one in which the Conservatives found themselves in difficulties. The government of national unity had brought into office several Labour members of outstanding ability, such as Clement Attlee, Stafford Cripps, Ernest Bevin and Herbert Morrison, and others of the party had been given junior executive positions. Throughout the country and among the armed forces the prevailing mood was for social change. People were looking for a different Britain after the war. It was clear to informed observers that the Labour party would be more strongly placed than ever before to win votes and form a government at the next election. Early in the conflict, a leading economist, Sir William

Beveridge, was invited to provide a blueprint for post-war recovery and, in mid-1942, he produced his *Social Insurance and Allied Services*, always known as the Beveridge Report. It was to be one of the most important documents in twentieth-century British history, for it marked out the ground plan of the welfare state. Labour MPs were strongly behind the report's sweeping proposals. The Tories were, at best, lukewarm.

Bill Astor took much the same line that his father had taken during the First World War: reform was not only essential, but failure to endorse it would be political suicide for the Conservatives. He became a founder member with forty colleagues of a ginger group, led by Lord Hinchingbrooke and called the Tory Reform Committee. He helped draft its manifesto, published in October 1943, which opposed the party die-hards 'whose political ambition is to return to the conditions which existed between the wars, or who regard the party merely as a convenient organization for exposing the fallacies of Socialism'.[34] The manifesto was called *Forward – by the Right!* but only succeeded in giving the impression of a platoon shuffling uncertainly along and looking anxiously to both right and left. It broadly endorsed the Beveridge plan and attempted to claim that it was in line with age-old Tory policy. It accepted the need for greater government control in the work of reconstruction, while rejecting the shibboleth of 'state planning'. It called for national unity and a taxation system in which all contributed to the common purse, but rejected the socialist ideal of ironing out class differences.

On the list of members of the TRC Lady Astor's name appears. It would be the last time that she was publicly associated with the progressives. She always thought of herself as 'liberal', but in fact she was moving rapidly and erratically towards the right wing of the party and events in her own family circle hastened the process. Waldorf was foursquare behind the group. For him it must have provided an experience of acute *déjà vu*: it was the Unionist Social Reform Committee all over again. Certainly, he was not a whit surprised to discover the party leadership reacting exactly as it had done thirty years before. He explained to Ronald Tree (another member of the group) that Conservative Central Office always tried to control every aspect of research and policy development and (in a fine mixture of metaphors) that if the TRC could not find a member of the hierarchy to 'hold an umbrella over the progressives' they would end up 'having their throats cut by the Right Wing'.[35] Waldorf had, by now, totally cut himself adrift from the party. He had never had much sympathy with confrontational politics, but he had remained in the ranks, if only in a support role, as long as he believed in basic Tory principles. The impulse of his own radicalism had now carried him beyond the point at which he could, with conviction, support Conservative policies. Now a sick man in his mid-sixties, he was determined to retire from the fray.

The war years brought profound changes to the Astor newspapers. At *The Times* there was a distinct transformation of tone when Geoffrey Dawson retired from the editorial chair in September 1941. John Astor remained loyal and supportive to the end, thanking him for 'making and keeping the *Times* the world's best newspaper' and insisting that he accept a generous pension of £4,000 per annum.[36] However, the paper's whole stance changed after Dawson's departure. The proprietors and the new editor, Robin Barrington-Ward, were determined to fling off the Tory lapdog image *The Times* had acquired in the Chamberlain era. Colonel Astor, who had relinquished his parliamentary seat in 1939, became more involved in the day-to-day running of the newspaper. He still did not control editorial policy, but he maintained closer contact, made suggestions, passed on ideas. He was, for several years, a very active president of the Empire Press Union. This brought him into contact with owners and journalists the world over and obliged him to keep his ideas fresh about the responsibilities of a good paper – especially in wartime. For example, 'propaganda' was something everyone had become very aware of. The Nazis were past masters at it. Every day they poured out wildly exaggerated statistics of German successes and Allied losses. The British press, under government censorship, exercised the 'negative propaganda' of concealing information which might help the enemy or weaken morale at home. John believed there was a case for using news for deliberately calculated effect – to stir up the Americans, for instance. In the spring of 1941 Britain was desperately hoping that the USA would enter the war.

> Has not the time come [he suggested] to disclose every now and again particulars of American munitions, manufactured and despatched under the Lease and Lend Act, which have been sunk by German action? ... The workers in the US recently contributed a Spitfire. If this had been sunk by enemy action [and reported] ... the fact would have had a very definite and helpful reaction on public feeling in US ... Newspapers can do much to 'play up' the news.[37]

John was now more prepared to 'lean' on his editor if he felt it necessary. On one occasion Barrington-Ward was taking a highly critical line on the conduct of the City. Some members of the *Times* board thought he had got his facts wrong and suggested it might be helpful if the editor would meet them over dinner. Barrington-Ward was outraged at the suggestion, which he interpreted as an attempt to interfere with his editorial integrity. It was then that Colonel Astor took a hand. He had a chat with Barrington-Ward and, in his usual quiet way, pointed out that his colleagues had no intention of dictating the paper's policy, but simply wanted to enlighten him on the economic situation as it appeared from their point of view. The dinner party took place and was, it seems, a success.

John had acquired a number of company directorships and he had widespread contacts in politics and the armed forces. The crisis of the war encouraged many prominent and informed people to come to him with their comments, questions and ideas. John Astor had become a sort of 'elder statesman' of the journalistic world, and he was sought out by people who thought he could bring influence to bear on public opinion and government policy. So, for example, we find Viscount Trenchard making suggestions about the most effective use of British air power, and Lord Melchett, head of ICI, complaining about civil service interference in industrial war production. Such matters were 'discussed with Mr Barrington-Ward' or 'drawn to the attention of our editor'.[38]

Such exalted issues had to be considered in the intervals between confronting the problems of producing a daily newspaper in a city sporadically under siege. Just before 2 a.m. on 25 September 1940 the *Times* editorial and business offices took a direct hit and were totally demolished. In Berlin Goebbels crowed that the London *Times* had been put out of action. In fact, the presses were not damaged and not a single issue was lost, and this in itself was important for national morale. John Astor was determined that a newspaper which had not been silenced by the combined efforts of British trade unionists in 1926 was not going to be gagged by a mere German dictator. With shortages of manpower and newsprint, bombed-out staff sleeping in dormitories, a subterranean canteen providing meals and shelter, and delivery vans carrying the finished copies through blacked-out streets hazardously strewn with rubble, 'The Thunderer' thundered on. And it was now a more vibrant, independent newspaper, no longer tied to the government's apron strings.

The exigencies of war also called upon Colonel Astor's military experience. He became commanding officer of the 5th City of London (Press) Home Guard battalion. The veteran troops in this last line of national defence were, of course, never called on to fire a shot in anger. Their activities were confined to training and ceremonial duties (such as providing the guard of honour at the Guildhall when Churchill received the freedom of the city). But had it ever come to it, these men would have had the responsibility for defending the nation's capital. With that in mind John Astor worked them pretty hard. Meanwhile his wife had also donned uniform as London controller of the women's army, the ATS (Auxiliary Territorial Service).

The departure of Dawson from *The Times* was accompanied by gentlemanly pleasantries on all sides. By contrast the passing of Garvin was highly traumatic. Not only did it indicate editorial differences on the *Observer*; it tore the Astor family apart. David's interest in journalism developed rapidly. After his initial Marine training, he obtained, in 1941, a posting to the Combined Operations HQ in London as press officer. He had gathered around him a coterie of radical young friends and, through his father's mediation, had persuaded a reluctant Garvin to accept from the group a number of articles of a distinctly 'leftist' flavour which sought to persuade readers that the real issue behind the war, and the peace which would follow, was the ongoing struggle against world fascism.

In the meantime, Waldorf's long-standing differences with Garvin had grown more intense. The editor, who had been unwilling to confront Chamberlain through the newspaper's columns, now refused to print constructive criticism of Churchill's government. The disagreements between proprietor and editor increased until they were scarcely on speaking terms. In May 1941, feelings were so bitter that Garvin wrote an editorial disagreeing with the substance of a letter that Lord Astor had written to *The Times* suggesting that, able as Churchill was, it was a mistake for him to combine the roles of Prime Minister and War Minister. It was around this time that Waldorf had a mild heart attack. In 1942 Garvin was seventy-four and at the beginning of that year his contract came up for renewal. The terms were always negotiated through a small 'tribunal' whose membership was mutually agreed between editor and proprietor, and Lord Astor put it to this body that the time had come for Garvin to assume a different role so that there could be a gradual transition to a new regime. Garvin refused to relinquish any of his power, accused the Astors of an anti-Churchillian plot and sought the support of friends in high places. From Number 10 Brendan Bracken urged the aged editor to stand firm against 'the decadent descendants of Wall Street toughs'.[39] The situation had reached the point where someone had to break. In the event it was Garvin. In a self-destructive gesture of defiance, he virtually forced the tribunal to request his resignation by publishing another editorial opposing the Astor 'line' on the Churchill administration. The only contractual lever the proprietor had was the right of dismissal if the editor publicly opposed his known political opinions. This lever Waldorf now, reluctantly, used. At the end of February Garvin left the desk he had occupied for thirty-four years. A new editor was installed, but David now became much more involved on the journalistic side of the *Observer* and it was understood that he would take over as editor when he was eventually released from military service. Waldorf underlined this by making over to his son 49 per cent of his shares.

All this was unpleasant enough, but the ramifications in the family were much worse. There were three reasons for this. First of all, Bill had expected to inherit the *Observer*. He was away in the Middle East when the vital decisions were being made. He returned, at the end of 1942, to be presented with two *faits accomplis*: his father was giving the *Observer* to David, and Cliveden to the nation. Secondly, Nancy was jealous of the closeness between Waldorf and David. Thirdly, the political gulf between Lord and Lady Astor had become wider.

Across this emotional and political fault line the contending parties assailed each other in what became increasingly a dialogue of the deaf. Bill, egged on by his mother, tried to assert his claim to his 'rightful inheritance'. Waldorf and David resisted. The shock to Bill was profound. He was genuinely committed to the family newspaper and, though his parliamentary work had absorbed most of his time after 1935, he had always assumed that the *Observer* would be there for him when his Commons career came to an end. His disappointment was exacerbated by the political gulf which existed between him and his brother. David was not a 'good little Conservative'; indeed, from Bill's standpoint, he seemed to have some odd and quite disastrous ideas:

> ... it is very dangerous to leave [the *Observer*] entirely in the hands of one person, David, who is brilliant, but emotional and sometimes erratic ... If the general line of the paper is to be that of the last six months I am sure it can't work.[40]

David was equally adamant about keeping his brother at arm's length from the *Observer*:

> I am perfectly in agreement that the kind of Liberal-Conservative attitude of my father ... should always be strongly represented ... My anxiety about Bill is that I don't think he does represent this point of view. I fear that he has always been a Right Wing Tory with a certain amount of impatience with mild progressives and an almost violent antagonism towards radical progressives ...[41]

Waldorf was absolutely firm in his decision. He had made his assessment of his sons' varied abilities and decided that the political independence of the *Observer* would be safest in David's hands. But, of course, he did not want a family row, and he did his best to resolve the fears expressed by Bill and Nancy. The solution that was found for the running of the paper was to appoint a trust (financed largely by the Astor shares), which would own the *Observer* and have the power to appoint and dismiss the editor. This avoided the unwelcome possibility of David becoming both proprietor and editor. In setting up this arrangement, Waldorf expressed the hope that Bill might become a director and assist his brother on the business side. This he eventually did, though there is no doubt that the *Observer* affair rankled with him for a long time.

While these negotiations were going on David had a taste of military action. In the summer of 1944, as the Allied forces moved inland from the

Atlantic and Channel ports, he became part of a Special Operations Executive unit whose task it was to liaise with various resistance groups. David had already worked with the Free French military staff in London (for which he was subsequently awarded the Croix de Guerre). He was now flown into south-east France to make contact with some of the Maquis. His party ran into a German ambush and was raked with machine-gun fire. They escaped but David was wounded and had to be hospitalized. That was, to all intents and purposes, the end of his war. But a conflict awaited him at home which was, in its own way, almost as unpleasant.

The fact that Bill seemed prepared to come to terms with the *Observer* situation only served to rouse Nancy to more determined opposition. As the Conservatives girded themselves for the first post-war election she became more and more extreme. She was frenetic in her denunciations of socialism, which in her eyes was synonymous with communism: 'Socialism and Communism are blood brothers ... if socialism goes on at the rate it is doing now it will kill the spirit which has made this a Christian country.'[42] When she was not attacking left-wing politicians, she vented her wrath about the international Roman Catholic conspiracy, of which she claimed to see evidence everywhere. Her diatribes in the Commons and on public platforms had always been stronger on emotion than reason; now they often descended to the irrational. She had become what Waldorf had always disliked most intensely – a virulent reactionary. To have a 'red' son running the family newspaper was more than she could bear. Being Nancy, she made no secret of her feelings. She spoke freely about her anger with David and Waldorf, and as we have seen, she threw in her lot with Plymouth friends who were opposing Lord Astor's rebuilding plans. The family rifts were thus affecting the Astors' private and public life, and it was clear to Waldorf that something would have to be done. Nancy's behaviour was becoming a very public embarrassment. It was under these circumstances that he made a hard but firm decision. He asked her not to stand for re-election to Parliament and made it clear that if she did she would not have his support.

Waldorf has often been criticized for terminating his wife's political career, and it is important to see his decision in the proper context. There were four things that mattered to him more than anything else – Nancy, his family, the *Observer* and Cliveden. The strains placed by the war upon his never robust health convinced him that he must, as a matter of urgency, make the best possible provision for all of them. He had taken care of the house and the newspaper. He helped and encouraged each of the boys (in so far as they would accept his guidance) to discover his appropriate niche. It remained only to steer Nancy into a new course because her Commons career had passed its peak. He delivered his bombshell only after long thought and after discussing the subject with the boys. Their basic reason for wanting Nancy to retire gracefully was to save her from herself. Jakie recalls that he agreed with the decision because 'her memory was not as sharp as it used to be, and she was becoming more and more aggressive, and it would have been sad to watch her decline after such a historic career'. Of course this is not what they told Nancy. Waldorf pleaded his poor health and his desire to escape from party politics. Probably the nearest he got to the painful truth was in a letter he wrote her in March 1944:

> When I urged you not to go on in the parliamentary arena without me I was activated mainly by my pride in and care for you. In so far as I asked for my own sake, it was to relieve me of worries which were wearing me down. I do need and love you.[43]

He suggested they could do effective work as a team in other areas.

Nancy would have none of this. She went into a state of deep shock from which neither she nor her marriage ever recovered. All she could see was that she was being 'ordered' (that was the word she frequently used to explain her husband's attitude; she being, of course, a 'dutiful wife', had had to obey) to give up what had become the centre of her life. She loved the Commons, but even more she loved Plymouth, and the bonds which bound her to her constituency had become steel-hard during the war. It was, she convinced herself, all because Waldorf – under David's evil influence – had become a socialist. Her reaction was to 'walk out'. The Astors were never officially separated, but from now on they spent almost as much time apart as together. Nancy very rarely went to Cliveden, where Waldorf lived an almost bachelor existence. When he holidayed in Scotland, she went to Sandwich. She made trips to America without him. Whatever the legal situation, and whether they were together or apart, from this time they were emotionally and psychologically almost divorced.

Waldorf was shaken by her reaction and by her continued sniping at him and David. Although convinced that he had been right, and not allowing her to think that he regretted his decision, he never gave up pleading for a return to normal relations:

> ... you have repeatedly told me and your family that you were going away because you could not direct the *Observer* – or because you could not bear to see your son make a success of the paper – and because you were not in parliament. All this you repeated over and over again till one saw that it had got a sort of mesmeric obsession over you ... You told me that under no circumstances would you return if I had anything to do with the unfortunate David. I told you then and I repeat now that if you insist on this choice naturally I come to you and leave David to do as best he

can ... I think he needs and wants our help but it must be done tactfully and lovingly and not by telling everybody that he is the worst judge of everything and is bound to make a mess of everything. That is not very CS [Christian Science].[44]

Peace came to an exhausted world in September 1945. It did not come to the Cliveden Astors.

CHAPTER 13

'Napoleon is back from Elba'

1945 was the year of the 'great betrayal' (at least in the minds of those on the right of British politics). The electorate voted out of office the man who had led the nation through five harrowing years of war. They looked, not to the Conservatives – associated in many people's minds with the economic hardships of the 1930s – but to Clement Attlee and the disciples of radical social change. Among the seats which fell to the Labour party were Plymouth Sutton and Bill's Fulham constituency. Looked at from different angles, the result could be seen as bearing out the prophecies of Waldorf and David that post-war Britain would be looking for a different ordering of society (hard though it might be to define the characteristics of the new order), and also the fears of Nancy that the country was rushing pell-mell into communist revolution. (As she was fond of declaiming from public platforms, 'The welfare state is the farewell state.') The ideological conflict in Britain was only a pale reflection of what was happening on the world scene. Speaking in the USA in March 1946 Churchill coined the phrase 'iron curtain'. The Cold War had begun.

The election shock of July 1945 did nothing to assuage Lady Astor's bitter disappointment. Within days, she wrote to an old friend: 'I still feel that I should be in the House of Commons. I am trying not to be resentful but to be reconciled to what has happened.'[1] Her efforts were not conspicuously successful. When she wrote, she and Waldorf were undergoing their first period of painful separation – he on Jura, she in Sandwich and Cornwall. It was a situation Lord Astor was anxious to bring to an end. In September he wrote to tell her that he was coming to Sandwich, just because he wanted to be with her.

What you don't realise is that I admire and appreciate your good qualities more than ever and want to get back the real Nancy. You sometimes seem to think that people who give you advice you don't like are not fond of you. It's because we love and admire you that we occasionally go through the very unpleasant experience of firmly speaking to your mortal mind ... What I did not do and could not honestly do was to say that I thought it would be a good thing for you to stand . . . I was much too fond of you to be able to do that honestly.[2]

There was a reconciliation and early the next year the couple spent several months touring the eastern side of the USA. During this holiday Waldorf was in the best of spirits and wrote an amusing journal for family consumption. They travelled out in January on a small cargo ship and he took great delight in watching and recording the various shades of green through which his fellow passengers passed. On the train between Washington and Miami he was highly amused to see his wife totally outgunned in a dispute with the sleeping-car attendant upon a subject on which she regarded herself as a definite expert – the Bible.

The darkie on the train was a nice old man. He came in whilst Mother was studying her Bible and observed that he was also a student. This immediately gave Mother an opening and her missionary spirit rose as she saw a chance of bringing a burning brand into the true faith. But the attendant . . . soon took charge of the conversation. He could refer Mother to various chapters and verses and explain them to her. When she tried to interrupt and regain a footing, he would say, 'No, Ma'am, you just wait for the point I'm coming to' – For 1½ hours he monopolised the talk with great fervour. Never have I seen Mother completely nonplussed in a theological argument. Every now and then he would clap his hands and reiterate, 'Yes Ma'am, glory be to God,' as he pursued his argument and his position.[3]

Everywhere they went Nancy was fêted and asked to make speeches. When she was not doing that she was playing energetic rounds of golf or attending parties and dinners till late into the night. Waldorf was delighted to look on from the ringside, retiring to bed early while his wife was still in full flood. Sometimes he helped her with her speeches. It was just like the good old days. Nancy certainly seemed to have regained her former zest. Passing through Savannah, Georgia, she found the town untidy – and complained publicly till the authorities promised to take the matter in hand. And she was both flattered and highly amused when, on one South Carolina golf course her caddy enquired, 'Is you a queen? The other boys say you is a queen.'

But back in England it soon became apparent that the stitches applied to her emotional wounds had failed to hold. After the war she and Waldorf had exchanged 4 St James's Square for a house in Hill Street, Mayfair, but instead of staying to establish a new home, Nancy was soon off on a barnstorming tour making anti-socialist speeches. Waldorf protested:

What *is* the good of putting me in a large house and then running away to be soothed and flattered by distant admirers. You can't really expect me to go on alone either here or at Cliveden. I only hope that you are enjoying the commiserations showered on you for your hard lot in life.[4]

A few days later, he urged her to accept a different kind of political role:

taking a position in the wings, helping and supporting a new generation of leading actors.

> Yes, I repeat supporting, not directing, and doing so even if you don't get any kudos yourself ... There is much to be done – not of the fireworks and volcanic kind connected with the blare and publicity of party politics – But just solid, constructive quiet help and guidance of others.[5]

If Waldorf was hoping that Nancy could slip into the kind of role that had come so easily to him over the years, he was asking for the moon. The greasepaint and the applause were in her blood; she could not give them up. So the estrangement continued. A few weeks later Waldorf was pleading with his wife to come to Cliveden, just for *part* of the summer. Failing that, how about a trip abroad together in the winter? 'Why not ... just lead more of a normal Christian life – I believe you w'd be happier and benefit.'[6]

When she was not speaking from the platforms eagerly provided by a clamouring public she was descending on Ayot St Lawrence to 'look after' George Bernard Shaw, now a widower in his nineties. Lady Astor was convinced that nobody understood the aged writer better than she, and was intensely jealous of his other companions. Shaw wrote to her, very directly, to ward off her mothering and smothering:

> If you will not let me manage my work and my household in my own way you must not come at all ... You need looking after far more than I do; and nobody knew this better than Charlotte, except perhaps your own unfortunate secretaries. You must upset your own household, not mine.[7]

It did little good. Still she came – fussing, reorganizing, quarrelling with the old man's nurses and attendants. And she was present during Shaw's last few days, in 1950.

She was still adept at 'upsetting her own household'. Michael and David had escaped her clutches, but the other boys had remained close to her. However, in 1944, Jakie did something which, in her book, was unspeakable. He announced his engagement to the daughter of the Argentinian Ambassador, the beautiful Ana Iñez Carcano. What was wrong with that? The girl was a Roman Catholic. Nancy was furious. She and Waldorf announced that they would not attend the wedding. Nor did they. Jakie, of course, was deeply hurt. He told his mother that if she did not come to his wedding, he would have serious reservations about being present at her funeral. But, as Jakie now comments wryly, she had the last laugh: in her will she requested her youngest son to preside over her obsequies.

January 1948 found Waldorf and Nancy making another American trip together, this time to California and the Mid-West. Once again they enjoyed travelling, meeting old friends and making new ones. Once again their relationship seemed on the mend. Once again Lord Astor gave his wife unstinting support, privately and publicly. At one point on the tour, he had to leave her in order to fulfil some engagements in Washington, New York and Boston. On the train between Houston and New Orleans he discovered that he had two celebrated co-passengers in the shape of film comedians Bud Abbott and Lou Costello (the names meant nothing to Waldorf until someone explained them to him). When they reached Atlanta the train was invaded by reporters wanting to interview the movie stars. When they realized that an English lord was aboard, some of them turned their attention to Waldorf and asked him about himself. He replied, 'My claim to fame? Just put me down as the husband of Lady Astor. I'm proud to be that and let's leave it there.'[8] That typically modest answer concealed the fact that he was on his way to attend a lunch given in his honour by leading New York newspapermen, to be the guest of honour at a publishers' convention in Boston, and to discuss the forging of closer Anglo-American educational links with Senator William Fulbright, one of Congress's leading internationalists. The Astors returned home on the *Queen Mary* in April, but after only a few weeks Nancy went back to the United States.

The basic problem was still the *Observer.* David's influence had been steadily increasing and he had spent the post-war years toning up his journalistic muscles. In 1948 he took over as editor. To Nancy this was like the final turning of the key in the lock, although in fact the door had long been firmly closed against the *Observer*'s becoming a more overtly Conservative paper. In 1944 Waldorf had laid down that it was to be an *independent* weekly. He saw this, not as a new departure, but as a return to the traditional values of the best kind of quality newspaper. This is quite clear from a letter he wrote to his brother in June 1948:

My dear John,

Am I right in believing that the policy of the Times, as annunciated last century, was to be independent of party and on the whole to support the elected Government of the day, but to reserve the right to criticise the government at any time or even of turning against it altogether?

If I am correct, I wonder whether you could tell me where this policy is laid down and can be referred to and quoted. I imagine that this must have been done more than once in books, and that you will have no difficulty in giving me one or two references.

As you probably know, I am trying to run the Observer on the above lines and want to strengthen my hand in this policy.

Yours ever,
Waldorf[9]

Explaining his policy in more detail to Jakie, he made it clear that his overriding consideration was for the *quality* of the *Observer* as an honest, intelligent paper, free from the tub-thumping of politicians and proprietors:

... I want the Observer to be an independent paper ... The Trustees I chose include Air Marshal Portal (whom Eisenhower put at the top of all English leaders whether Air, Naval or Army), Arthur Mann, a leading ex-Editor, Oliver Franks, our Washington Ambassador who stood out among the men brought to the Civil Service during the War.

Though the Trustees have political views they agree that the Observer should be independent of Party. This is one of the reasons why I could not appoint your choice Rab Butler.

I also want to re-establish editorial authority.

Northcliffe prostituted journalism by destroying this.

Geoffrey Dawson, like the great editors of The Times such as Delane and Monypenny, was entirely responsible for its policy. This also applied to another outstanding modern journalist, C. P. Scott of the Manchester Guardian.

Unfortunately, a less good type now enters the London Press and provincial papers ...

Kemsley and Camrose run decent newspapers, but both call themselves Editors-in-Chief which means that their so-called Editors are not fully responsible for the policy of the paper. Kemsley has provincial papers, e.g. Newcastle and Sheffield, but he, being Editor-in-Chief of all his papers, the citizens of those cities are misled in believing that their local journal is of the same independent character as the Scotsman or Glasgow Herald, whose editors are *really* editors.[10]

The new-style *Observer* very rapidly established itself. David had a talent for recognizing and attracting high-calibre journalists. He was excellent at sub-editing other people's copy so that the paper quickly achieved a recognizable style. Its editorial line was clear and firm – radical, probing, questioning. And the control at the top was strong but benign. One feature writer recalled how, knowing the boss's passion for verbal economy, he slaved long over his very first article, especially the initial paragraph. Nervously, he showed the result to David. The editor complimented him on a good piece of work – then drew his pen through that precious first paragraph. '"It's like a cough before a speech, isn't it?" he said, "you have to get it over with before you begin."'[11] Among some sections of the intelligentsia the *Observer* became almost a cult newspaper. A recent writer has neatly summarized the reasons for its success:

it was the product of a thoughtful, serious generation which had fought through the Second World War, and had also seen – and in some cases experienced – the miseries of Depression and the failure to combat Fascism in the 1930s. To this generation ideas about politics, disarmament and world peace were serious issues. Such ideas were also in a considerable state of flux, which gave this generation the opportunity for constructive thinking about the world and its difficulties that had been denied to an earlier generation, and was to be denied to a later one brought up on the fixities of the Cold War. The Observer spoke for that generation of the middle classes which searched for ideas about and solutions to the problems of their earlier life.[12]

Within the first three years of David's editorship, circulation had trebled, advertising revenue was very healthy and the paper was showing a respectable profit. Bill and Jakie recognized its success and its journalistic integrity and both served happily as directors. This open-mindedness was not shared by their mother.

Napoleon (mama) is back from Elba (USA) firing from all guns. She is in good health but still disinclined to stop chewing the political bone. She is as controversial as ever.[13]

So wrote Jakie to J. J. Judge in August 1948. Nancy's main target was the *Observer.* She kept up a constant campaign – attacking it in public, arguing with Waldorf, cajoling her sons. She kept on talking about going back into politics, until her husband wearily responded that if that was what she really wanted she could go ahead and he would watch the fiasco from the sidelines. She made no serious attempt to find a new political role. Age was beginning to tell and she found positive thought and action progressively more difficult. As Jakie observed to his father in 1951, she just seemed to be accumulating dragons to slay and her current selected adversaries were 'Socialism, Roman Catholicism, Psychiatry, the Jews, the Latins and the Observer'.[14]

The faults, of course, were not all on one side. Waldorf was equally obstinate and unyielding. When the bullets were flying between him and Nancy, their sons usually kept their heads down. When, on one occasion, Jakie emerged from the dugout to suggest that his father might soften his attitude and consider changes of policy at the *Observer*, he was told quite bluntly to mind his own business. The newspaper issue was settled and his mother should be given no encouragement to think otherwise.

I believe most sincerely that you are wrong in thinking your Mother cannot be expected to accept what has been done. This brings me to your further belief which I hope is also illusory, that your Mother cannot have a major interest outside politics because in your view she must begin the day by a hymn of hate against the Socialists whilst she and you believe I am no longer 'a good little Conservative' . . .

You are wrong if you think Mother has not a great opportunity for service outside the political arena, work where I could giver her 100% support.

Please show this letter to Chiquita [Jakie's wife] whose intelligence is greater than yours![15]

Waldorf was now seventy-two and growing frail. Yet still the flow of letters to Nancy – dignified, firm, unyielding, but basically plaintive and sad – continued in a hand ever more shaky and indistinct:

It's for you, not for me, to decide if you really want to live at home with me in harmony . . . I pray for it but you must decide.

We have done so much together. Life without you would have but little purpose. That's why I pray and pray that you will want to arrange your purpose so that we do have the same active purpose. I have been waiting for over 5 years for you to come along. I just ache for this ... I am waiting and waiting for you. Much, much love. Waldorf [16]

By now Lord Astor had had his bed brought to a downstairs room at Cliveden. Nancy was rarely there, and when she was the atmosphere was tense. Visits to Sandwich, London (Waldorf had made 35 Hill Street over to her) and America filled much of her time. In the end Waldorf gave up hope of any emotional and psychological reunion. In the last year of his life he stayed much of the time with Bobbie or David, unable, eventually, to face the barrage of complaints he was subjected to when he and Nancy were together. Their letters became remote, formal, concerned with practicalities. Waldorf could not resist the occasional jibe:

You will be interested to hear that hundreds, literally hundreds of orders are coming in for the pamphlet which will contain the special articles that have appeared in the *Observer.* People are very glad to have some constructive, original thinking. Your Sandwich golf friend just doesn't seem to have a clue as to the intricacies of world problems. Even the head of a big Bank has written in congratulating.[17]

Waldorf wrote these words on 27 August 1952. He had recently, while living with David, survived another heart attack and knew that the end could not be far away. Despite everything his thoughts were now all with Nancy. Setting aside his son's protests he insisted on going back to Cliveden, which was still officially the matrimonial home, because 'It will distress your mother if I die anywhere else.' Five weeks later he was dead. At the end Nancy was with him. What passed between them we cannot know. It would be pleasant to think that in their last hours together they rediscovered something of the tumultuous, frenetic decades of happy common purpose rather than the last, soured years of pain.

it was impossible not to be stimulated and attracted by his charm, his perfect manners, his vitality, his gaiety and sense of fun ... That his married life was not a success was no doubt his own fault. His fantastic vitality and love of people sought outlets in too many directions ... If one accompanied him on journeys, one saw the conscientiousness with which he visited ... community centres ... orphanages ... schools and the numerous philanthropic activities ... with which he was actively associated ... He did good work on various U.N. committees ... and was a valued member of the British Commonwealth group ... showing tact, vision, political insight and above all, common sense.

Those are extracts from a *Times* obituary Bill Astor wrote in 1960 for his friend of twenty years' standing, Prince Aly Khan. In more muted colours they could stand as comments on his own life. There was no sense in which Bill modelled himself on the much more famous international figure, but he admired Aly enormously, their lives touched at several points and the similarities between the two men are striking. Aly was a playboy, the friend of film stars and jet-setters with a passion for fast cars, horses and beautiful women. But there was an equally well-established Jekyll to his Hyde – a man keenly interested in international affairs, an intelligent diplomat and a generous supporter of charitable causes among his own Ismaeli community.

In the same way, Bill Astor had two sides to his nature, although they were not so well integrated, a fact which ultimately brought him to grief. He possessed immense *joie de vivre*. He led an active social life and his wide circle of friends included men and women from several countries, and from many different worlds – politics, sport and the arts as well as the 'top' British families. He liked to travel and acquire new experiences. He enjoyed music and the theatre and, in later years, tried to get to Salzburg for the festival as often as possible. He revelled in many kinds of sport – hunting, polo, shooting, sailing, swimming, skiing, skating. But his great love was horses. He took a personal interest in the work of the Astor stud and loved to go racing. Throughout the winter he hunted every week when he was in England. And in the summer there was polo. Sitting in the arid heat of the desert at the grimmest moment of the war he reflected wistfully on what had been:

> I can hardly believe that it ought to be Ascot week, with a big party at Cliveden: tennis and riding in the morning: and all the girls in their best dresses and the men in grey top hats fixing on buttonholes and sprays of flowers in the hall at 12 and the cars all lined up and the Royal Procession and Father's colours on the course and polo in the evening and swimming and all the rhododendrons out and for once my parents forgetting politics and giving themselves over to social joys! I hope that I won't find a new order when I get back: I enjoyed the old order so much![18]

Bill believed in making life fun – for himself and for other people. During his long bachelor years there was little to inhibit his enjoyment of life. His hopeless devotion to Mary Stevens Baird (during the war he made a will naming Mary as principal beneficiary in the event of his remaining unmarried) prevented him from forming a deep attachment to any other woman, but doubtless he had his discreet amorous adventures. There is nothing to suggest that there was anything odd about his sex life – contrary to later scurrilous allegations by some journalists and writers.

Coexisting with this fun-loving aspect of Bill's character was a very serious side. His interest in and knowledge of Asian and Middle Eastern affairs was considerable. He threw himself into politics with enthusiasm and commitment. Returning to the Commons in 1942, he explained to his beloved Mary: 'If you want to be an effective MP you can't do anything else – and unless you are an effective one, then one might as well not be there at all. So I devote all my time to Parliament.'[19] Bill was never content to be back bench lobby-fodder. During the thirties he paid long visits to the Manhattan estate office, learning about the family's property investments – something his brothers were happy to leave entirely in his hands. He became quite an effective speculator in real estate and equities. But the acquisition and enjoyment of wealth never fully satisfied him. His upbringing had impressed upon him that wealth also carries responsibilities. He was active in charitable work from an early age and inherited from his mother the gift of spontaneous generosity. His widow recalls how he impressed upon her that she could spend whatever she liked on herself as long as she gave away an equivalent sum. Few things gave him more pleasure than helping someone in financial need – money to buy a house, or complete a son's education; he even paid for one couple's honeymoon.

Several years after his death, someone who knew him very well described Bill Astor as follows:

> Guileless perhaps to the point of naivety . . . He loved life and he lived fast. He loved people and he helped them . . . He loved pleasure and did so with zest. He just had an immense zest for the whole of life. Perhaps sometimes too easily led, and certainly too modest to defend himself against mean criticism . . . he was, as I remember him, straight as a die.[20]

Yet there was something out of kilter about this uncomplicated character. The different aspects of his personality did not dovetail. Overawed by his parents and his inheritance, he never achieved the independence of mind that had been so characteristic of Waldorf and Nancy. The other boys proved that they were, indeed, their parents' sons by breaking out, experimenting, discovering their own values. Bill was never able to do that – or, at least, he was never able to do it with an easy mind.

In his political opinions he was greatly influenced by his mother, by right-wing friends he made at Oxford and by his own innate conservatism (with a small 'c'). He was deeply suspicious of any threat to the traditional order of things. Speaking in America in 1949, in the wake of the communist takeover in China, spy trials on both sides of the Atlantic and the beginnings of the McCarthy witch-hunts, he described Europe as going through a spiritual crisis brought about by a rampant communism which sought

> to destroy all existing values, all tradition, all moral standards, all political and religious belief and to plant doubt, skepticism and cynicism . . . The phrase that poverty is the cause of communism is a dangerous half-truth, if not a fallacy . . . The communist adept is . . . a person of some intellectual standards or pretensions who lacks a standard of values – religious, patriotic or ethical . . . [the] battle for the cause of freedom . . . is to my mind the supreme battle of our age . . . but the latent spiritual power of

America is as great as its physical power and if it rises to assert it, the forces of enslavement, the gates of hell, will not prevail.[21]

It might have been Nancy speaking.

Yet there was always a vital difference between Bill's politics and that of his parents. He lacked their total seriousness born of religious conviction and ethical certitude. Bill drifted away from Christian Science and did not rediscover faith until late in his life. Waldorf and Nancy could speak with total independence and from a secure philosophical pulpit on a wide range of issues, knowing that their convictions were sincere and carefully formulated and reinforced by the standards they applied in their own lives. They could extol Anglo-American solidarity because they worked hard for it on both sides of the Atlantic. They could seek greater restrictions on betting and drinking because they did not gamble or consume alcohol. They could talk with conviction about Germany and the Soviet Union because they had been to those countries to see for themselves. It was partly because they were morally unassailable that people wanted to assail them (most notably over the Cliveden Set). When Bill tried (or was expected by others) to step into their footprints in the snow he found that their strides were too long for him.

Bill was what neither of his parents had ever been, a conventional politician. For him high principle was always muted by pragmatism and party loyalty. He was blessed (or cursed) with the realization that national and international affairs are painted in varying shades of grey, that compromise is of the very essence of politics and that principles can, at times, be an embarrassment. Thus, in 1943, addressing a Commons Middle Eastern affairs sub-committee, he had no qualms about suggesting:

There is a fairly simple solution to the Palestine question provided that we have the courage to declare that the British administration in Palestine shall be permanent and that there shall be no further question of either a Jewish or an Arab state.[22]

Bill took a particular interest in imperial policy and spoke quite often in debates on foreign and colonial affairs. He belonged to the house's Imperial Affairs Committee and chaired its Middle East sub-committee. He had a passionate commitment to the British Empire, but his was not the Round Tablers' ideal of an English-speaking union playing a leading role in an international community of free nations. Intensely moved by the sight of colonial contingents going into battle beside British Tommies, he looked to preserve the glories of an imperial past. He did not see that the very war which had brought troops from across the oceans to fight the common foe had also given an immense impetus to the forces working for independence. Soon after the war David began championing, in the *Observer*, the cause of self-determination for colonial peoples. It was not a viewpoint Bill shared:

Disraeli, when he said that the key to India was ... in London, saw that we could only play a great beneficent part in the world if we were worthy of playing it. We will maintain our position, we will make the British Commonwealth of Nations a force for good in the world, if we, in England deserve it ... and if we can continue to send to serve the Empire men whose integrity is absolute, whose courage is clear and whose personalities and characters arouse honour and respect.[23]

Bill lost his Fulham seat in the Labour landslide of 1945. Suddenly, he had no occupation. He continued to work for the Conservative party and to plan his return to Parliament but, for the first time in his adult life, he had no public responsibilities. He had, however, now acquired pressing private responsibilities. Immediately after the end of the war in Europe he got married. After a dozen years he finally accepted that his courtship of Mary Stevens Baird was doomed to failure. He was thirty-eight. His brothers and his sister were all married and Bill felt, doubtless urged by his mother, that it was time he took the same step. When he did so, it was in a headlong rush. Amidst all the euphoria of the victory celebrations and the hectic preparations for the forthcoming election campaign, his eye lighted upon an attractive party worker, Sarah Norton, twelve years his junior, and they were married weeks later. 'She is immensely sweet and immensely sensible, most lovely and charming and has the same air of breeding that you have,' he told Mary.[24]

For some years the relationship seems to have been happy enough, although the couple had no children. They lived in a lovely house near Oxford from where Bill farmed and gradually took over more and more responsibilities at Cliveden. In the 1950 election he contested High Wycombe and came within 476 votes of unseating the Labour member. The following year he was more successful. 1951 was doubly happy for Bill. Not only did he get back into Parliament, Sarah presented him with a son and heir who was christened William Waldorf (the present Viscount Astor).

From this high point life began to fall apart. Within a year of taking his Commons seat Bill had to forsake it. His father died and Bill was automatically translated to the Lords. At the same time that he was sorting out Waldorf's affairs and assuming his new responsibilities, Sarah left him for a younger man. To add to these traumatic experiences, his doctor diagnosed very high blood pressure and ordered Bill to cut down his activities drastically. Among those to whom the new Viscount Astor turned for sympathy and support at this difficult time was his osteopath, a strange but talented practitioner by the name of Stephen Ward.

Waldorf, unlike his own father, left the bulk of his estate to his eldest son. Not that by now there was anything like William Waldorf's fortune left to distribute: by 1950, Viscount Astor's total UK assets were about £2 million. Increased taxation on inheritance and unearned income on both sides of the

Atlantic had seriously diminished the benefits the Astors derived from their investments. Between the wars the philosophy behind taxation changed in both countries. The argument that levies should be based on ability to pay had long been accepted as a socially just basis for the individual's contribution to the expenses of government, but after 1918 this broadened into the concept that taxation might properly be used as a means of social levelling. This had two principal effects on the way revenue was actually collected. The balance shifted from indirect to direct imposts (basically, to a graduated income tax), and high rates of estate duty were levied specifically to prevent the accumulation of large family property holdings. In Britain and the USA both inheritance and income taxes were higher than in other western nations (for example, direct taxation accounted for well over 50 per cent of government revenue in America and the UK, as against 32 per cent in Germany and 26 per cent in France). Nor had Waldorf and Nancy made any real attempt to cut their coats according to their diminished amount of cloth. For some years they had been living on capital – his capital; Nancy kept her own income from her marriage settlement and various Langhorne and Shaw trusts quite separate. The boys had been well looked after by their grandfather. The only way, therefore, that Waldorf could try to 'keep the family fortune intact' was to leave as much as possible to his heir. Accordingly, Bill inherited those parts of Cliveden not assigned to the National Trust, White Place, a large amount of money, and was also given charge of the remaining American interests. He shared the bloodstock with Jakie, who also received a house in Plymouth. David had already received the major shareholding in the *Observer* (and he had passed it on to the new governing trust). Nancy inherited the London house as well as 3 Elliot Terrace and the family jewels. All the boys had shares in the Jura estate. Michael seems to have come out as the least favoured in his father's will: because he was 'interested in painting', Waldorf gave him a Munnings and one of the old masters from Cliveden.

Bill now had to make a new life for himself. After his divorce came through in 1953, he was able to concentrate on his new responsibilities. For the sake of his health he abandoned confrontational party politics. He found that he enjoyed the House of Lords, where the pressures were far less and where he could champion those causes he believed in without bringing the wrath of the whips down on his head. In fact, he was probably better equipped to be a diplomat than a politician. He made friends easily and had a knack of being able to get people to work together.

At this time Bill reached a deliberate decision to devote the greater part of his energies to charity. He became actively involved in the Overseas Relief Committee, the Save the Children Fund, the Ockenden Venture, Lifeline, the Peabody Trust, the MacMillan Teacher Training College, the Royal Naval Volunteer Reserve Officers Association and, nearer to home, he was a member of the Windsor Hospital Group committee and was to be seen frequently talking with staff and patients. Through the Worshipful Company of Musicians he commissioned two modern works. His most creative activity at this period was the setting up of the William Waldorf Astor Foundation. This was basically an expression of his family's commitment to Anglo-American relations. Lord Astor set aside $500,000 (later raised to $2 million) from his New York assets to establish a fund for the benefit of British scholars who wished to study in the USA. After the war America had research and development resources Europe lacked, and Bill saw his foundation as a way of enabling finance-starved specialists to cross the Atlantic to keep in touch with the latest developments in their fields. Because grants from the fund were available in dollars the recipients were able to travel without being hampered by the existing stringent exchange control regulations. The first to benefit were nuclear physicists, and the Astor scheme was eagerly supported by a government anxious that Britain should not fall behind in the study of atomic power. But the scope of the foundation widened rapidly. Other branches of science benefited from Astor money, as did medicine, oriental studies, linguistics, archaeology, music, education, among other disciplines. Grant recipients now travelled all over the world and funds for specific projects were also made available to libraries and to university departments. In its first ten years the foundation dispersed almost half a million dollars and its work continued to expand.

Bill's day-to-day concerns were largely taken up with White Place, his transatlantic business interests and the Astor stud, which he ran without a manager. But life was not all work – far from it. Lord Astor wanted to have FUN. He knew a large number of people ranging from British and foreign royalty to film stars, from statesmen and diplomats to nightclub owners. Now, at Cliveden, he possessed the perfect setting in which to entertain them. An added attraction was that his mother steadfastly refused to live there. Bronwen Astor recalls that Bill hardly ever organized a *party*, because life was just one long party. There were always friends staying or dropping in. The old life of Cliveden had come to an end in 1939 and Bill wanted to revive it, to restore its *raison d'être*. He filled his house with celebrated guests and entertained them lavishly; but his Cliveden house parties were not like those organized by his parents. Politicians and statesmen still appeared on the guest lists, but they came to relax. There was no underlying seriousness of purpose, no attempt to set the world to rights, no pompous academics holding forth across the dinner table, no earnest debates about the international situation. At a time when most stately homes were falling into decay or being opened to the public to preserve their fabric, Bill Astor managed to sustain in his house a way of life that had almost disappeared.

In 1955 he had another stab at matrimony. It proved disastrous. His bride, Philippa Hunloke, was another beautiful and much younger woman. She was the daughter of a very old friend and the goddaughter of Harold Macmillan. Their marriage did not survive the honeymoon. By the time the couple returned Philippa was pregnant and she and her husband were sleeping apart and virtually living apart. Philippa was, in due course, delivered of a daughter and almost immediately went home to mother. Bill attempted a reconciliation, but it was a lost cause. Bill and Philippa were divorced in 1957. Exactly what went wrong is difficult to say. Certainly, Philippa was not prepared to be the Cliveden hostess Bill wanted. She did not like the house and she did not like many of Bill's friends. That is not altogether surprising. Lord Astor was generous, gregarious and a poor judge of character. He tended to be uncritical of people's faults, and not all the varied people he brought to his home were such as would appeal to his wife. Furthermore, in the background there was always Nancy, who certainly never made life easy for her daughters-in-law.

In the wake of the later Profumo scandal sensationalizing writers pounced on Bill's two failed marriages as evidence of a quirky or lascivious sex life. It is therefore important to try to understand the lifestyle of the man who became the third Viscount Astor. There was nothing sybaritic or even hedonistic about it. There were women in his life, but his underlying attitude to sex remained essentially rather prim. He was never a roué, because he was more concerned to give pleasure than to take it. If he had a sneaking admiration for the 'freedom' of Aly Khan and other jet-setters, it was because he could never give himself up completely to their excesses. A glance through his correspondence with Aly Khan illustrates this attitude. The two men enjoyed a common interest in horse racing and often shared one another's boxes at Newmarket or Longchamps. Aly was often at the now-resumed Cliveden Ascot week parties. Recalling an incident in the Oaks when Astor's mare narrowly beat his friend's, Bill illustrated the relaxed nature of their rivalry:

> I suppose that Aly would have lost £17,000 in stakes, £25,000 off the value of the mare, as well no doubt as a very large bet running into thouands. But his immediate reaction was to turn and hug me and give me a kiss and say, 'I couldn't have been happier if I had won myself.'[25]

Aly and other friends often made use of Bill's New York apartment when he was not using it, and Aly's many houses around the world were always open to Bill. They met at St Moritz for skiing and at other exotic locations from time to time. In March 1955 the prince invited his friend to join him in

California for 'the time of your life'. He promised attractive female company, but this was only because Bill was, at the time, unmarried. He should enjoy a 'fling', Aly suggested, 'before you get yourself into any permanent situation again'. In October 1957, writing from Kenya, he urged Bill to join him in Paris, where he would shortly be giving a dinner at Maxim's for the President of Pakistan. In November 1959 he regretted that he did not have much 'girl news' to impart but urged Astor to join him in Paris or Vienna or New York with a female companion, so that they could all have a good time together.[26] Once again, this was at a moment when Astor's latest marriage had broken down and the prince was anxious to provide him with a diversion. Aly was one of the few really close friends that Bill had. Many people enjoyed Bill's generosity and hospitality; some exploited his good nature. Bill always saw the best in people. He seemed incapable of believing that some of those who clustered around him, enjoying his bounty, were motivated by anything other than genuine affection. Perhaps his early religious training was partly to blame. Christian Science does not recognize the existence of objective evil: evil exists only in the mind, and the devotee is urged to free his thinking of it. Bill needed people around him. At root he was still a dislocated personality who found it difficult to establish deep relationships. That is probably one reason why he surrounded himself with people and tried hard to give them a good time. He gave a lot of pleasure and a lot of help to a lot of people. In doing so he brought disaster upon himself. One of the beneficiaries of his kindness was Stephen Ward.

Bill's regular forays onto the hunting field inevitably involved him in occasional falls. In 1949 he had a particularly bad one and injured his back. As a result he was in constant pain and the doctors did not seem to be able to give him any relief. Bill therefore responded eagerly when Bobbie Shaw recommended an osteopath he 'swore by'. Stephen Ward was a free spirit who enjoyed cocking a snook at 'respectable', dull convention. Like most free spirits he considered himself above the petty moralities and decencies that bound other people – and, indeed, superior to other people. He was self-absorbed and regarded the men and women around him as legitimate ingredients for him to use in the life that he was making for himself. That life became increasingly complex. He was a social climber who employed his skills (he was an accomplished portrait painter as well as an osteopath) to gain access to the wealthy, the powerful and the famous. Satisfied customers recommended him to their friends. Before Bill met him, Ward already had many clients in the entertainment world, politics and even the outer circles of the royal family. He was sometimes seen in public with celebrities and was already beginning to appear in the gossip columns. He was a very agreeable and amusing companion – charming, witty, a good conversationalist and a *bon viveur*, but also a very sympathetic listener. This was the public Ward.

There were other aspects of his life which were not so obvious. His sexual relationships were bizarre. He dabbled in drugs. In so far as he had any political sympathies, they were of an extreme left-wing variety. In later years he toyed with occultism. But there were more serious flaws in his character. As his political and social contacts increased so did his fantasies. He saw himself as wielding behind-the-scenes influence; as an important player in the game of politics, diplomacy and espionage. Not unconnected with this was his deliberate manipulation of other people. He enjoyed 'handling' people's lives just as he enjoyed handling their dislocated limbs or damaged muscles. As with his osteopathy, much of this activity was beneficial. At the time of his trial several friends testified to the help they had received from Stephen. Yet it is no exaggeration to say that his controlling and directing of the destinies of men and women was, at root, sinister; for it was having power over others that was his motive force. Stephen delighted in surrounding himself with beautiful young women, including several from very humble origins. This was not basically to satisfy his own sexual appetite or even to enhance his prestige. He got a kick from acting as 'Professor Higgins' and grooming the girls for entrée into high society. He also used his protégées as a means of placing 'important' men in his debt by introducing them to agreeable sexual partners.

It is hard to appreciate now the degree of power that Ward exercised over people. One story may serve to make this clear. Bobbie Shaw had many frailties, but one thing no one could accuse him of was being a coward. He was a man who knew his own mind and was not afraid to speak it. At one time he was suffering from a poisoned arm and Ward was tending it for him. When Bobbie's half-brother David heard about it he told him that he ought to go to a 'proper' doctor. 'It's OK,' Bobbie replied, 'Stephen's treating it.' 'But Stephen's an osteopath,' David protested. 'You need medical attention, not manipulation. Go and see a specialist.' Bobbie was very worried by the suggestion. 'I couldn't do that; Stephen would be upset.' It became clear that Bobbie was afraid to defy Ward. Eventually he agreed to follow David's sensible advice as long as David would explain the situation to Ward. David, accordingly, telephoned Stephen. There ensued a very difficult conversation during which Ward did not disguise the fact that he was put out by this 'interference' in the patient–doctor relationship.

If we are to put Lord Astor's involvement in the 'Profumo affair' in proper perspective, we need to be clear about his growing relationship with Ward. Allegations were later made that the two men were close friends and that Bill was to some extent involved in the seamier side of Stephen's life. Lord Astor's papers now make quite clear for the first time that this was not the case. It was not in Ward's interest to run the risk of shocking Lord Astor, from whom he derived money and access to Bill's social circle. Both were vital to him.

The relationship began as a purely doctor–patient one, but one from which Bill derived immediate and considerable relief. Soon the consultations were taking place on a regular basis. Ward gave Bill a massage at Cliveden after every outing during the hunting season. At other times Bill called at Ward's London surgery. When the doctor wanted to acquire new professional premises, Bill readily lent him money. This became the first of many appeals for financial help to which Lord Astor invariably responded. In April 1952, Ward, who was appallingly bad at managing his affairs, was facing bankruptcy proceedings. He approached Bill, and he did not approach in vain. During the following weeks Bill gave Ward two gifts, totalling £1,250. There were several future occasions on which Astor handed over smaller sums. His widow recalls that Ward only had to ask for money and Bill would write a cheque, without asking what it was for. It had been readily assumed that this indicates that Ward had some influence over his patron. Such an interpretation is superfluous because, as we have seen, Bill Astor was incredibly generous. He was also extremely grateful for Ward's professional ministrations. Writing to his solicitor in April 1952, Bill made this quite clear:

> Dear Mr Wooding,
>
> My osteopath, Dr Ward, has got into a financial jam. As he cured my neuritis I want to help him. I have asked him to put his solicitor in touch with you. I gather £500 will clear things. Will you cope with things up to that amount – or thereabouts . . . If you knew how much pain he saved me when he cured my neuritis you'd realise that I want to put him out of *his* pain . . .[27]

Despite his many acts of spontaneous generosity, however, Bill made it clear that his purse was not a bottomless well to which Ward could return at will. Bill's financial affairs were extremely well organized. His accountants, therefore, kept careful note of all sums paid to Ward. They wrote frequent reminders to Ward about the repayment of Lord Astor's original loan. The arrangement was that the doctor could pay it off in treatments to Bill, his family, staff and friends. Ward was not allowed to get away with being casual about the arrangement. He had to present proper invoices to show how the loan was being worked off.

The relationship between Astor and Ward was mutually advantageous. A development in the summer of 1956 seemed, at the time, to suit both of them admirably, though it was to lead to the most appalling consequences. Ward discovered Spring Cottage, a partially derelict building on the Cliveden estate close to the river. He asked Astor if he could rent it for use as a weekend retreat. Bill readily agreed. It made a great deal of sense: Stephen would now be available to offer his professional services to Bill's family, staff and guests more frequently.

There always remained an element of formality about the relationship between Astor and Ward. When Ward arrived at Cliveden to give a treatment his visits were professional and brief. If he brought a ladyfriend she would be deposited in the hall with a glass of sherry and collected by Ward on his way out. He was seldom invited to meals – nor, when he was, were relations between host and guest always cordial. On at least one occasion they had a fierce row, as Bill later explained:

> ... one Christmas he got into an argument after dinner with Lady Grantley, who is half Hungarian, in which he attacked the Hungarians who had revolted against the Communists and said that there was nothing to choose between them and Castro. Lady Grantley was very upset, as indeed I was, having been deeply concerned with the Hungarian problem at the time. I got very angry and told him that if he felt like that he had better go and live somewhere else, and I went into the next room. My Mother, who was there, followed me out later and said that I could not have a row with a guest in my house. I went upstairs to bed and later Dr. Ward came up and apologised saying that he had only meant that he disliked all violence.[28]

Ward often expressed communist sympathies, but this probably reflected his basic anti-Establishment attitude rather than a well-thought-out political philosophy. It must have amused him to express left-wing views under the roof of his ultra-Tory patron. Some see Bill as an innocent victim falling under Ward's diabolical spell. Others regard Lord Astor as a wealthy Establishment figure who took Stephen up, used him and then dropped him when he became an embarrassment. The truth is much less tidy than such easy value judgements would suggest. In the early days of their relationship it is probably true that the inadequacies of the two men interlocked. Both experienced difficulties with women. In 1949 Stephen's wife left him after only six weeks. He had previously attempted suicide after another failed romance. Before long Bill's marriage was also coming unstitched. The rejected husbands had suffered severe blows to their self-esteem and their shared experiences drew them together. When, in 1956, Bill was again in a state of matrimonial turmoil, it was Stephen whom he asked to try to patch things up between himself and Philippa. Shortly afterwards, their roles were reversed. Stephen was in love with a young woman and wanted to marry her. The lady in question was hesitant, and it was Bill who talked over the situation with her at some length. She eventually went off and married a wealthy American – though whether or not as a direct result of Bill's advice is not known.

Did discussion about marital problems lead on to shared sexual adventures? In the aftermath of the 1963 scandal various young ladies attempted to cash in on public interest in the 'Astor–Ward circle', knowing that of the two central characters one could not and the other would not confront them in public. Some claimed that Lord Astor had been involved in assignations or orgies. The truth is that Bill became close to *one* woman introduced to him by Stephen Ward. She was not a call girl or a participant in Stephen's more grotesque sexual activities. She was, in fact, a respectable woman and, although fond of Bill Astor, she eventually married someone else. It was partly to protect this lady's reputation that Bill never spoke publicly about his relationship with Ward. In private he told family members and close friends that he knew nothing about the seedier side of his osteopath's life.

In one of his letters from New York after his appointment as head of Pakistan's UN delegation, Aly Khan described to Bill a conversation he had had with Sir Gilbert Laithwaite, Under-Secretary of State for Commonwealth relations:

> I told him how I thought the British Government was completely wasting your exceptional qualities and qualifications for a high office. He completely agreed with me, but seemed uncertain whether you would accept a post if offered it. So bear this in mind when next you see him, if it is of any interest.[29]

It was a friend's gentle way of trying to nudge Bill back into public life. The early fifties had been both busy and unpleasant. Just when he had been settling back into his stride in the Commons his father had died, and upon Bill fell the responsibility of looking after his mother. In the following months he had had to sort out the second Viscount's affairs in Britain and America, make plans with the family for Nancy's future and cope with his own divorce. Much of 1954 he had spent travelling in Asia, including several weeks relaxing with Aly Khan in his Bombay palace. That had been followed by the giddy romance with Philippa which had restored his vitality and zest for life. The rapid collapse of his second marriage was therefore doubly hard to bear. It is scarcely surprising that, during these years, he had little time or inclination to seek new spheres of public service. Overtures had in fact been made to him, but he had felt unable to respond to them. He was on the council of Chatham House but he was not very active. In his view (and many members agreed with him) the institute had become moribund. He issued a hard-hitting memo to this effect in which he indicted a secretariat composed of 'second-class brains' and a membership which had 'a heavy backlog of bores, fools, cranks and persons who come to pass the time of day, and people who, after retirement, have nothing else to do but clutter up places like Chatham House'.[30] It was the dramatic events of November 1956, one of the great crisis months in modern European history, which gave Bill a new purpose in life.

Before we deal with that, we must look at the lives of other members of the family during the early 1950s. After the war Michael and Jakie, with varying degrees of unenthusiasm, found themselves in Parliament. Michael emerged into peacetime life a self-confessed dilettante, torn between his basic passion for art and a sense that he ought to 'do something' in public life. He decided to present himself to Tory Central Office as a prospective candidate, was offered the safe set of East Surrey and was duly elected. He was not a very active MP; indeed, some members of his constituency party took him to task over his Commons attendance. But he was personable and intelligent; he had an unassailable majority and the name Astor. These were enough to ensure a parliamentary career. One friend, expecting promotion when the Tories returned to power, offered him the position of PPS. He did stand again in 1950 but decided not to contest the next election. He later wrote: 'I did not enjoy the game of politics enough to play it convincingly. I needed, above all, to discover a little more about the source and impulse of ideas before attempting to suggest to other people which way they should think.'[31] Perhaps this trial run in politics was something he had to do to work the last bit of 'Astordom' out of his system.

Jakie and his wife acquired a farm near Cambridge and settled there very happily to grow cereals and breed horses. After 1945 and the shock of seeing Plymouth Sutton 'go socialist', Waldorf and Nancy both asked Jakie to contest the seat at the next election. Very reluctantly, and largely because he believed that this would help to reconcile Nancy to the loss of her Commons seat, he agreed. In 1950 he won the constituency back for the Conservatives and in 1951 he increased his majority. His victories, however, did nothing to aid his parents' reconciliation and he never really enjoyed the life of an MP. Like Waldorf and Nancy, he had no great love of the Tory Establishment, and the feeling was mutual. After being returned again in 1955, he made it clear that he would not stand for re-election at the end of the current Parliament. In November 1956 he had no compunction about opposing the party leadership on the floor of the house.

David frequently asserted that what the *Observer* was about was searching for sense in a world ruled by nonsense and insanity. We can trace a distinct line back to the thinking which led Waldorf and his friends to found Chatham House against the background of impassioned ignorance at the time of the Treaty of Versailles. What the Round Tablers aimed to do was provide *facts*, to help people see beyond prejudice and party slogans to the real meaning behind things. It seemed perfectly clear to David that this was the sort of task a Sunday paper had the opportunity and the responsibility to carry out. Between 1945 and 1950 he made the *Observer* the first quality newspaper to look seriously at Labour party policy and consider issues such as the national health service and nationalization schemes on their merits. He opened his columns to writers who had a fresh viewpoint or a trenchant style – writers who would make people *think*. David was a great believer in psychology. He had regular psychoanalysis himself and was convinced that one service the *Observer* could perform was to help people *understand* what made public figures tick instead of (or, at least, before) passing judgement on them. In the 1950s taking such an attitude towards murderers, demagogues and international businessmen was considered by many to be dangerously free-thinking and morally neutral. 'Neutral' the *Observer* certainly was not. Some of its campaigns – notably those in favour of the state of Israel and the civil rights of black South Africans – were fought long, hard and with conviction.

In the early 1950s, David and his paper fell foul of Lord Beaverbrook. The Astors had always maintained a polite distance from 'the Beaver', disliking both his politics and the way he ran the *Daily Express* group. David had met the celebrated newspaper proprietor some years before in a box at Covent Garden and, as they shook hands, the tycoon had commented, 'So you're the fellow who's going to take my place on Fleet Street?' David still recalls how he recoiled and thought, 'Good God! I hope not!' His opinion of Beaverbrook was, and still is, that he was 'not an easy person to take seriously because he wasn't serious. I think he was a great entertainer but he was an unprincipled person who produced a school of journalism which excelled in the low game of gossip. Politically he was an opportunist. Even his contribution to the war effort was suspect. He got planes built [Beaverbrook was Minister of Aircraft Production in 1940–41] but only at the cost of causing havoc in other departments by stealing resources from them.' What David and 'the Beaver' both knew was that in 1931 the *Express* had responded to Astor appeals not to publish the story of Bobbie's arrest and imprisonment. Beaverbrook believed that this placed the family and the family's newspapers perpetually in his debt. David did not.

In 1951 the *Observer* ran a profile on Lord Beaverbrook. It was not an exposé; it was a critical assessment of one of the most influential journalistic and political figures of the age. Beaverbrook was furious. In an almost incoherent memo to his editor, he drew attention to the Shaw incident of twenty years before:

> Look that all up and let's have a look at it. That was suppressed, of course, at the request of the Editor of the *Observer*. There they are – a sanctimonious lot and dragged us into the gutter. Having suppressed the story they now make a feature of attacking us.[32]

Days later Beaverbrook removed from the 'secret' files at the *Express* office one marked 'Notes on Lady Astor'.[33] From that point on he pursued a personal vendetta against the ageing Nancy and against the *Observer*. He caricatured the Sunday paper as anti-Semitic and anti-Catholic on the slender grounds that its trust deed included a clause stating that the editor must be 'of the Protestant religion' (a clause included to placate Lady Astor and, years later, removed by her son). It was all petty and personal, though underneath symptomatic of the clash of two schools of journalism. Years later Jakie expressed a desire to be introduced to the now aged Beaver. The latter refused. He could not, he claimed, believe that any Astor would want to meet him without having some devious ulterior motive.

In November 1956 two events shook the world. Britain and France, in collusion (as it later transpired) with Israel, invaded Egypt, whose President Nasser had nationalized the Suez Canal. Taking advantage of the attention focused on this by outraged international opinion, Russia sent troops into Hungary to suppress a popular revolution against communist rule. Both military operations were fraught with significance: one, the last gasp of an old imperialism; the other, the defiant roar of a new one. Both threatened world peace. Scaled down to a personal level, both were important in the lives of the Astors.

Over the preceding weeks Fleet Street had divided sharply into two camps. The majority supported the Prime Minister, Anthony Eden, in taking a tough line, including military force if necessary. The *Observer* led the minority press which rejected 'gunboat diplomacy' as a solution to twentieth-century problems. The British public was similarly split. The international community was not. Through the UN and diplomatic channels, America, Russia and many smaller nations criticized Anglo-French belligerence. Eden denied that he was contemplating invasion, while at the same time confirming the military battle plans. On 1 November the attack began. The following Sunday, the *Observer* published what was to be its most famous leader.

EDEN

We wish to make an apology. Five weeks ago we remarked that, although we knew our Government would not make a military attack in defiance of its solemn international obligations, people abroad might think otherwise. The events of last week have proved us completely wrong; if we misled anyone, at home or abroad, we apologize unreservedly. We had not realized that our Government was capable of such folly and crookedness.

Whatever the Government does now, it cannot undo its air attacks on Egypt, made after Egypt had been invaded by Israel. It cannot undo the deliberate employment of haste so that our nearest allies had no opportunity to express disagreement. It can never live down the dishonest nature of its ultimatum, so framed that it was certain to be rejected by Egypt . . .

The Eden Administration has, throughout this summer, shown that it does not understand the sort of world we live in. It is no longer possible to bomb countries because you fear that your trading interests will be harmed. Nowadays, a drowning man on a raft is the occasion for all shipping to be diverted to try to save him: this new feeling for the sanctity of human life is the best element in the modern world. It is the true distinction of the West. Our other distinction is our right of personal independence and responsibility in politics – a right that must be exercised.

It is for every individual in this country who is against the Government's attack on Egypt to say so by writing to his Member of Parliament, lobbying him, demonstrating in every legitimate way. Nations are said to have the governments they deserve. Let us show that we deserve better.

It was a bold and risky line to take, but David believed he had no option. Matters had reached the point that Waldorf had envisaged they could reach, at which a truly independent paper had to turn against the government. The ultimate example of editorial freedom is when a newspaper takes a stance which may well result in its own loss of support and revenue. That certainly happened to the *Observer.* Three trustees resigned. Angry letters arrived by the sackful. Subscriptions were cancelled. Advertisers withdrew their orders. From this point (though not entirely for this reason) the paper's economic viability declined.

The extraordinary fact is that Suez united the family as no other political crisis, including Munich, had ever done. From their widely differing standpoints and quite without any collusion, the four brothers came to the same mind. In the Commons emergency debate four days later, Jakie was one of only eight Conservatives who dared to run the gauntlet of his colleagues by opposing the government's action. In the upper chamber, Bill also denounced the Anglo-French invasion. Michael made it clear that he backed them to the hilt. He later wrote that if he had still been in Parliament he would have resigned over the issue. Bill, Jakie and Michael all stood well to the right of David politically, but the Suez fiasco was an outrage against all that the brothers had been brought up to believe in. They had been taught to reason out their attitude to political issues. They had never been gung-ho imperialists, knee-jerk reactionaries or unthinking members of the Tory Establishment. Their international and, particularly, their transatlantic connections prevented them from seeing the Suez incident from a narrowly nationalist or patriotic viewpoint. By 1956 the Astors' political influence was well on the wane, but for a brief moment it shone forth brighter than ever before.

For Bill it was the other major event of those autumn weeks which was to have a more profound influence. The atrocities in Hungary had led to a serious refugee problem. Men, women and children were fleeing, or attempting to flee, from their Soviet oppressors across the Austrian frontier. Lord Astor was already interested in the problems associated with refugees. He had experienced them in the Middle East. He had also been to Hong Kong and studied at first hand the difficulties of dealing with people escaping from the communist regime in mainland China. He now involved himself in the plight of the Hungarians. Apart from anything else, he was glad to have something to occupy his mind. Philippa had just left, taking their baby with her. The prospect of a lonely Christmas at Cliveden held no attractions.

As soon as it was realized that Hungarians were escaping across the border in hundreds, then thousands, western relief agencies went to work and made urgent appeals for aid. Stories were relayed of brave little bands stumbling through snow pursued by brutal guards firing machine-guns. Soon, volunteers were rushing to Austria. It was one of those situations which appealed to people in the free world on several levels – political, humanitarian, romantic. There were idealistic students, nurses and doctors who had skills to offer, even some people who saw themselves as latterday Scarlet Pimpernels.

Bill's first contacts with the rescue operations were with Alec France, an American Fulbright scholar studying in Paris for the diplomatic corps, and retired Household Cavalry Major Derek Cooper and his wife, Pam. Alec was – very undiplomatically – organizing a team of foreign volunteers at Andau, an hour and a half's drive south-east of Vienna. He was joined at the end of November by the Coopers, who arrived with their Land-Rover. His friends sent Lord Astor vivid descriptions of the rescue operations and the appalling conditions in the makeshift camps. They reported the urgent need for four-wheel-drive vehicles – the only ones capable of covering the frozen terrain in the remote areas through which the escape routes passed. Once again, Bill decided to 'see for himself'. He believed that if he could combine first-hand information and his wide circle of wealthy contacts he could make a useful contribution. Here, at last, was a cause to which he could devote himself. With his chauffeur and a Cliveden estate Land-Rover he set off for Austria in mid-December.

He spent a week, over Christmas and New Year, at Andau, personally involved in the rescue work, and a second week visiting the whole frontier as far south as Burgenland. Later, he wrote up his experiences as part of a fund-raising exercise. He explained that many of the refugees came by train disembarking as close to the border as they dared, then trudging – always by night – over the frozen flatlands of the Kis Alföld, their babies drugged with Seconal to prevent them crying with the cold. So, eventually, they arrived near Andau, often frostbitten and in the last stages of exhaustion.

> Here there was a canal, both banks of which were actually in Hungary. The bridge had been blown up. We used to go out with a rubber boat at night and lie on the banks of the canal. The guides would bring refugees to the other side and we would see the dark figures slowly coming out from the trees and emerging in the snow. The American and Norwegian boy ... would then paddle the rubber boat across. The volunteers would bring the refugees over three at a time, collect them together on our side until a Land Rover came to take them back to Andau.

There were two little dramatic moments that stick in my mind. One was on Christmas Eve, a mother and baby arriving quite alone when I was single handed. The baby doped, with a frost-bitten foot, but it was saved. The other was when a big party of refugees had reached the edge of the canal, and we had got about a dozen of the women and children over. Suddenly a Tommy gun was fired into the air and a Security Patrol appeared on the other side of the Canal, firing shots and Very lights into the air, and driving the rest of the refugees back. They knelt and wept and prayed, but were driven off at gun point when they were only 50 yards from freedom, the Security Guards firing a few shots at us for good measure. We were left with children separated from their parents, women separated from their husbands, in a state of complete collapse and agony. After waiting for an hour or two, one little figure suddenly emerged – a young woman who had jumped into a ditch, escaped the patrol and had come back to rejoin her fiancé.[34]

As soon as Bill reached home he began sending off appeals – to celebrities such as Douglas Fairbanks Jr, to religious leaders such as the Chief Rabbi in London and Cardinal Spellman in New York, to diplomats and UN officials. By now the relief work was being brought under the control of established charities. Alec France was rapped over the knuckles by the US Ambassador in Vienna for embarrassing Washington and violating Austrian neutrality. He was ordered back to Paris and for a while his scholarship was in jeopardy. The time for amateur efforts had passed. Lord Astor, through his friend Princess Schwartzenberg in Vienna, was already in touch with the Austrian Priory of the Knights of Malta who had long experience on both sides of the border. They had the facilities, the buildings, the organization and the personnel (most of whom were bilingual and spoke Magyar) to deal with the problem effectively. He channelled aid through the order.

Within days he was flying to New York, cajoling the wealthy in private (Henry Ford II donated a bus) and appearing on chat shows to stir the public. He even allowed himself to become fodder for the gossip columns. On 2 February 1957 Elsa Maxwell reported in her *America* column:

Had a small dinner for Ali Khan at the Colony the other night and took him to see *Auntie Mame* . . . Baronne Jean de l'Espée and Lord Astor were with us . . . Lord Astor has been quietly but seriously plunging into Hungarian refugee relief . . . Lord Astor did not accompany Ali to Caracas, as I previously stated. Instead he spent New Year's and Christmas on the Hungarian border helping the Knights of Malta . . . [with] our mutual friends, the brave young Counts Alexander and Freddy Pallavicini. Bill . . . has already gotten close to $100,000. I am proud of him!

In fact, by 1959, Bill had raised nearly $116,000, as well as several vehicles (of which he personally contributed three Land-Rovers) and other aid in kind. In March 1957 he was awarded the Grand Cross of the Knights of Malta. It was an honour of which he was particularly proud.

1956 was also significant for the Hever Astors. On the first day of that year,

John was elevated to the peerage as Baron Astor of Hever. Other press lords had regarded such honours as no less than their due. William Waldorf had courted ennoblement. It was typical of John that he considered long and hard whether he ought to accept the title. What he questioned was whether doing so might call in doubt the independence of *The Times*. He decided (and was perhaps so advised by those he consulted) that, since he did not direct editorial policy, his acceptance could not be misconstrued.

In fact, John had already begun the slow process of withdrawing from involvement in the paper – theoretically. In 1954 he handed his 90 per cent shareholding to his eldest son, it having been agreed with John Walter that Gavin Astor would eventually take over as sole proprietor. But Lord Astor never resigned his own position as joint chief proprietor and was never able totally to relinquish policy-making to his son. Gavin took over as chairman of the *Times* board in 1959, but John was far from inactive during the fifties. His diaries, now preserved in the *Times* Archive, reveal a full schedule of activities with or on behalf of the staff of the newspaper. One of his particular delights was the weekly *Times* lunches at which he entertained a wide cross-section of leading figures from every walk of life. Names culled at random from his guest lists include John Betjeman, Selwyn Lloyd, England cricket captain Peter May, Vice-President Richard Nixon, A. P. Herbert, radio and TV personality Wilfred Pickles, Yehudi Menuhin, Lord Beaverbrook, Viscount Montgomery, Ralph Richardson, Evelyn Waugh and Bernard Miles. John and Violet still entertained at Hever, but to some extent these more modest gatherings took the place of the pre-war house parties. In his later years John spent more time painting and managed to combine it with yet another new interest – yachting. In 1957 he took delivery of a ninety-nine-foot boat which he christened *Deainiera* (an almost-anagram of the names of two of his daughters-in-law, Irene and Diana). At £60,000 it was the biggest and most luxuriously equipped craft for which a British customer had placed an order since before the war. For John it became a floating studio. He used to invite other artistic friends and they would go off on painting cruises.

Hugh Astor, John's second son, was also involved with *The Times* during these years, in both its managerial and journalistic life. He served an apprenticeship on the *Glasgow Herald* before joining *The Times*, and worked first in London and then in Cairo as an assistant foreign correspondent covering Middle East affairs. Later, he joined the board as a director and became deputy chairman. Adventure seemed to follow Hugh, like an embarrassingly faithful dog. For almost a decade he was involved in reporting from some of the world's political hot spots. In Palestine, during the last days of the British mandate, he was hit by a sniper and had to be invalided home. As a result of this escapade he lost the kneecap of his 'good' leg. This in no way deterred him from visiting the area. Quite the reverse. In 1956 he planned a tour of Israel and some of her Arab neighbours because 'my antennae had persuaded me that something was going to happen'. Shortly before his departure, he received a surprising invitation from King Ibn Saud of Saudi Arabia to visit Riyadh – surprising because relations between the two countries were poor and there were, at the time, no direct diplomatic links between them. Hugh was actually in Bahrain when Israel invaded Egyptian territory. He cabled Riyadh to ask whether, under the circumstances, the Saudis would prefer to postpone his trip. Back came the reply, 'No, all the more welcome.' Thus began a bizarre couple of weeks. Hugh was in a Muslim country as both an enemy and an honoured guest. He was given red-carpet treatment throughout the crisis but was unable to leave and was never quite sure whether or not he was a hostage. It was a surreal experience:

> I dined every night in the palace with the king. He sat at the head of the table with all his nephews and cousins all the way down both sides. They were all ministers of government departments. And at intervals through the meal people would come in and give the latest news on the Suez campaign. Much of it was propaganda, making wild claims for the victorious Egyptian forces. After each report I would be invited to comment. Being as diplomatic as possible I would reply 'Well, your Majesty, I should need confirmation of that before commenting.'

In his unique position Hugh could not voice his real opinions. Although he had many Arab friends and sympathized with the Arab stance, he admired the Israelis' efficiency and thought that in this campaign they were pulling the Anglo-French chestnuts out of the fire by toppling a troublesome Egyptian leader. Not being *au courant* with events in London, he accepted the official line that European troops were only being brought in to stop the conflict between the two Middle East neighbours. From the *Times* office the situation looked very different. Eden had placed the editor, William Haley, in an impossible position. Trusting in the paper's support for government policy, the Prime Minister had given Haley prior warning of the troop movements. The editor was shattered by Eden's duplicity, but *The Times* could not go on the attack with the proof that the government had been deceiving the nation without revealing the source of its information. The paper had a scoop which it could not and (with one eye on circulation) which it dared not use. It was numbed into an unsatisfactory neutrality.

By this time Britain had embarked on a period of technological and social revolution which challenged every aspect of newspaper production. The next quarter of a century was a difficult one for Fleet Street (indeed, Fleet Street itself ceased to be the 'home' of the national press). This was, in large measure, due to the traditionalism which afflicted the industry from board room to shop floor. Editors were obsessed by newspaper 'image'. Directors were loath to sanction expenditure for new plant. Union leaders dug their heels in over labour-saving printing methods. Yet change had to come, if for no other reason than because a new breed of wealthy, predatory tycoons was appearing. They possessed the ambition of the Harmsworths of old coupled with the wealth derived from multi-national corporations, and they were intent on building up personal empires in the communications media. The quality newspapers were especially vulnerable. They were competing for a restricted readership and they lacked the resources to maintain the necessary pace of change. In their quest for increased revenue they were caught on the horns of a dilemma: their principal advertisers, who were producers of expensive products, such as prestige cars, perfumes and designer clothes, placed their orders with the papers which reached the largest number of 'top' people; but the papers could only significantly push up their circulation by going further 'down market'. In this new atmosphere of harsh commercialism, newspapers like *The Times* and the *Observer* could only survive by shedding their 'gentlemanly' image.

Gavin and Hugh Astor were intelligent young men who shared many of the ideals and aspirations of their generation – a generation which emerged from a horrifying war committed to the principle of change and hoping to construct a better world. They read, fairly accurately, the writing on the Printing House Square wall and sought to introduce the necessary wide-ranging innovations before it was too late. They were up against the conservatism of their 'elders and betters', particularly their father ('*The Times* is the world's best daily paper – why try to change it?'). Even when, later, John was living abroad (see below pp 396–7) he exercised a strong influence on the board through members who were sympathetic to his views and kept him well informed. Soon there were conflicts between family, directors, management and editor as each tried to preserve territory and exclude trespassers. In a long memo in July 1958, Lord Astor tried to head off the threatened conflict:

> Various questions have been raised recently, e.g. what does the term 'editorial policy' cover? How far do the duties and responsibilities of directors extend? What is the position of the Manager in relation to the Board? . . .
>
> Minutes of past meetings show that matters of business have frequently been discussed which touched both the Editor's and the Manager's province. The success or otherwise of the editorial policy pursued in *The Times* can hardly fail to affect the economic position of the Company and this in its turn must affect the resources available to the Editor.
>
> In the early years of the Company conditions in the newspaper industry were comparatively easy. Our meetings consisted largely of the Manager's (Mr. Lints Smith) report on routine matters. Decisions were rarely called for . . .

> In recent years we have had a succession of important and difficult problems to deal with ...
>
> It was found that Directors were frequently expected to take important decisions without having previously been provided with relevant and adequate facts and information ...
>
> In my view the Articles of Association of '23 as amended and embodied in those of '54 correctly interpret the spirit and intentions of the original gentleman's agreement between J.W. and myself. Both the spirit and intention have always been carefully observed and this rather loose set-up has worked satisfactorily, I believe, because we have been guided by commonsense and reasonably wide interpretation. I feel that to attempt definitions beyond the guiding lines indicated in Sections 108–121 of the 1954 Articles of Association would only lead to confusion and misunderstanding – and unnecessary difficulties.[35]

Lord Astor simply could not sense the rapidly accelerating pace of change. Gavin and Hugh sensed it all too clearly, but, in the last analysis, were unable to convey their sense of urgency to their boardroom colleagues.

As early as 1956 the Astor brothers were exploring the possibility of abandoning the hot-metal process in favour of electronic and facsimile typesetting. They studied the new techniques being pioneered in America by such papers as the *Milwaukee Journal* and proposed a scheme which would not only improve cost-efficiency and news delivery (for example, the paper could have been 'put to bed' three or four hours later each night), but would make it possible to sell their services to other newspapers. In 1956 Hugh got to know Roy Thomson when they both toured Australia for the Commonwealth Press Union (the old Empire Press Union). The Canadian businessman had recently begun his assault on the British communications industry by buying *The Scotsman* and was currently bidding for the Scottish ITV franchise. He suggested that *The Times* might broaden its base by acquiring one of the commercial networking companies. This seemed to Hugh and Gavin to be another direction in which the newspaper should be heading. Long before the days of weekend supplements, the Astors saw the need for a different kind of *Times* on Saturday, which would take a leaf from American journals such as *Time* and *Newsweek*, produce analytical articles, have a much better leisure coverage and therefore attract both readers and advertisers. It would also enable them to make better use of their already existing (and expensive) team of foreign correspondents. Unlike the editor, the young Astors believed that content of the paper *could* be improved, that sport, women's issues and other interest areas could be better covered. Many of their ideas were put to the board in a long and wide-ranging report. It never emerged from the jungle of claustrophobic establishment foliage, suspicious interest-group predators and the pervading miasma of Lord Astor's disapproval. Changes certainly were made. The most obvious one to readers was that, for almost the first time in over two hundred years, *The Times*' front page was devoted to news instead of classified advertisements (which now went to the back page). At the same time the building at Printing House Square also received a facelift. An extensive programme provided *The Times* with new print works and replaced the old rabbit warren of offices with a more open-plan arrangement in keeping with the needs of a modern newspaper. Such changes might divert, for a time, the rising flood waters of commercialism: they would not prove very effective under storm conditions. Whether the radical changes desired by Gavin and Hugh could have saved the existing *Times* operation is, perhaps, doubtful. Thanks to the conservatism of their father and his like-minded colleagues on the board, the new men were never given the chance to try their ideas.

In 1958 Hever provided its owners with a real-life allegory. The castle stands amidst meadows at a height of 117.5 feet above sea level and its site has always been prone to flooding. William Waldorf took this into account in his gargantuan earth-moving operations. He diverted the river Eden, deepened the existing moat, built an outer moat and created a thirty-five-acre lake with lock gates to control the level of water around his refurbished property. For over half a century these precautions proved a hundred per cent effective. Then, on 5 September 1958, a prolonged storm delivered three inches of rainfall in twelve hours; river, moats, land drains and lake rose, spilling flood water over the estate to an unprecedented level of 121.8 feet above sea level. A yard-deep muddy sea swirled through the ground floor of the castle and village, damaging floorboards, wainscoting, antique furniture, hangings and carpets. Some of the spoliation proved irreparable. It was a devastating experience for John and Violet to see their home so ravaged, but there was nothing to do but patiently set about a three-year task of getting castle, village and grounds back to normal. In addition, they had to ensure that there could never be a repetition of the disaster. So, at enormous expense, embankments were raised, the river was widened and new pipes were installed to convey flood water away from the site. The normal river flow past Hever is about 15 cubic feet per second. In the 1958 flood it was 2,750 cubic feet per second. The new precautions were designed to cope with a seemingly impossible water surge of 3,300 cubic feet per second.

All this work made considerable inroads into the Astor fortune. Yet it is indicative of the size of that fortune, and of John's unabating generosity, that he continued his lavish support of several charities. Bernard Miles, the actor and theatrical impresario, recalled a visit he made to Lord Astor's office in 1958 when he was trying to raise funds to build the Mermaid Theatre at Blackfriars. His host indicated a pile of letters on his desk, some three or four inches high. They were the appeals for money that had come in over the last few days. However, he wrote a cheque, put it in an envelope, sealed it carefully and handed it over with the words, 'That will give you a start.' On the way down in the lift, Miles hurriedly opened the envelope. The figure on the slip of paper was £3,000, and Lord Astor topped that sum up with more when the Mermaid project passed through subsequent crises.[36]

In 1961 he and Violet took Gavin and some of the grandchildren to visit Astoria, Oregon, where they were to be the guests of honour at the city's sesquicentennial celebrations. The English visitors were shown the historic sites and modern amenities of the thriving metropolis which had grown up on the location of John Jacob I's doomed settlement. The younger members of the party climbed the extraordinary 123-foot Astoria Column, a replica of Trajan's more famous architectural monument, paid for by members of the family and the North Pacific Railroad in 1926. Lord Astor was impressed and moved by the experience. So was Gavin, who had developed a considerable interest in family history. John decided to mark the event with a spectacular gift from the English Astors of $100,000, to which sum he was the leading contributor (the money was used to build a library). As he explained to his youngest son (though not quite accurately), 'For historical and sentimental reasons I regard Astoria as a sort of symbol of the creation of our fortunes. A good deal of fur, tea and silk must have passed through Astoria and led to ships, railways and land which continues to appreciate.'[37]

CHAPTER 14

'An outrageous piece of nonsense'

Something which did not continue to appreciate – or, at least, not to the benefit of the Astors – was that part of the fortune which belonged to the American branch of the family. In 1953 Vincent's second marriage broke up. Although of much shorter duration than the first, it followed a similar pattern. He and Minnie drifted apart because their interests and their choice of friends diverged, and also because Vincent was increasingly given to moods. At times he had a Puck-like exuberance, but then he would lapse into depression and could appear distant and rude. It was in one of his more impetuous spells that he met an old friend, Brooke Marshall, at a dinner party. Brooke was in her late forties and very recently widowed; in fact that evening was one of the first social engagements she had accepted since her husband's death. Vincent talked to her very earnestly after the meal, almost monopolizing her for the latter part of the evening, and insisted that she come for a weekend to Ferncliff. During her brief stay at the Astors' country place, Vincent took her for a drive in his Mercedes. Suddenly, he stopped the car and announced, 'Minnie wants to leave me and, up to now, I have refused to give her a divorce, but now that I have met you I will give her a divorce if you will marry me.'[1] Utterly stunned, Brooke could only decline to give an immediate answer. She went back to her life as features editor for *House and Garden* magazine. But Vincent kept up the pressure, and when he went off on a two-month trip to Japan he wrote to Brooke five times a day, sometimes more. In October they were married at a very private ceremony in a friend's house.

In July 1956, Alice Astor died at the age of fifty-four. She had returned to America after the war and spent most of her time in the house she and Serge had built at Ferncliff. Her eccentricities had increased with the passing of the years and, despite Brooke's efforts, Vincent could only take his sister in small doses. They were complete opposites. Alice covered her basic unhappiness with gaiety. She was gregarious and devoted much of her time to entertaining her artistic friends from both sides of the Atlantic. She was inventive and imaginative. In her last years she was much interested in Egyptology and believed herself to be a kindred spirit – perhaps even a reincarnation – of some member of the royal line of the Eighteenth Dynasty. Vincent, by contrast, was methodical – a creature of habit who mistrusted what he could not understand and shunned too much company. It was inevitable that his sister's death should fill Vincent with sorrow and remorse. She had been his only close relative (he never established a real relationship with his mother) and, as so often happens in such cases, he felt that he had never made the effort he should have made to understand her.

The initial shock was made worse when, the day after Alice's death, two people claiming to be her friends turned up at Ferncliff suggesting that she had committed suicide and offering to have the fact hushed up for a 'consideration'. Vincent's reaction was to throw them out and then order an immediate autopsy. The examination confirmed that Alice had died of a heart attack.

Meanwhile, Jack Astor's rejection of inconvenient formalities had landed him in a real legal tangle. By 1954 he was separated from his second wife, Gertrude. One day she was surprised to read in a newspaper that he had married again. Naturally, she had her lawyers find out what was going on. It transpired that Jack had found another beautiful young woman, called Dolores (Dolly) Fullman (he was now forty-two), obtained a Mexican divorce from Gerty and promptly married his latest love. Since Gerty had not been a party to the divorce, it was not valid. Jack was thus a bigamist. His troubles did not stop there. Within a few weeks, Dolly walked out. He was now having to maintain two wives, with neither of whom he was cohabiting. Each demanded financial support and had her claim upheld by a different state judiciary. Jack tried to wriggle out of his commitments to Dolly on the grounds that the invalidity of the Mexican divorce meant that he was never legally married to her, but Dolly's representatives demolished that argument. The various cases went on for years, doing little more than enriching the lawyers involved. It was Gerty who finally shifted the log jam by obtaining a 'proper' divorce. By doing so, she established that she *had* been married to Jack Astor and that she *was* now free to remarry. It only remained for Jack to disentangle himself legally from the lovely Dolores.

Through all these expensive complexities Jack never lost his sense of humour. On one occasion he phoned Gerty to ask how she had got on in court. She brightly replied, 'I made the front page of the papers with President Eisenhower.' Jack riposted, 'If they'd let me appear in court I'd have made the front page and Eisenhower would have been on page two.' Years later, when he was trying to lay his hands on part of Vincent's estate, he called her again to say, 'Give me the name of your lawyer. He was great against me and I want to use him.' Nor did Jack bear any grudge against the women with whom he was doing legal battle. Years after these events, he went to Europe, bought a brand new Opel car, had it shipped back to America and gave it to Gerty. Eventually all the matrimonial threads were untangled. Instead of being warned off the whole institution, Jack took a fourth wife. This time it worked out. He and Suzanne had ten happy years together, which were only terminated by her tragic early death.

Too old – and, as ever, totally disinclined – to change his ways, Jack Astor continued on his charming, easy-going, self-absorbed way. He was casual and impulsive about everything, even his fine collection of pictures. On one occasion, while riding in a taxi up London's St James's Street he caught a glimpse of a painting on the back wall of an art gallery. He stopped the cab, rushed in and bought the picture. He could, just as unpredictably, part with his treasures, though sometimes he regretted it afterwards – as was the case with a Courbet and a Turner, both of which ended up in public galleries. Just how laid back he could be is indicated by the story of fifteen paintings stored in a London bank vault for over twelve years. When he recounted the tale in 1976, this little cache was worth about $700,000, but the paintings were certainly suffering from neglect:

> ... in their flight from Miami to London in November of 1963 ... they were supposedly put in a heated baggage compartment, but were apparently put in an unheated compartment. At 40,000 ft. the air temperature in November over the North Atlantic could have easily been as low as 60°F. below zero. On my last trip, I delayed far too long before inspecting these paintings ... I came with two flashlights and two screwdrivers ... and I got two men who I think were tellers to help me unscrew the crates. The screws were very sharp, and 45 to each cover! These men were not used to using a screwdriver, and had no gloves to remove the screws. I opened the crate containing the best one – a painting known as 'Entretat' – as that was the one I was most interested in, by George Inness. It had badly peeled in the lower portion. I feel that was caused by the extreme cold in the plane and that the canvas must have shrunk, breaking loose from the paint, or vice versa, and I am anxious to find a good man who can restore these without bankrupting me. There was no peeling on the next two I opened. We only had time to open three. The next time I go back I will take at least two carpenters and plenty of equipment, electric screwdrivers, etc.[2]

In the autumn of 1958 Vincent and his wife visited Europe. Brooke had been invited by Cardinal Spellman to go to Rome for the election and coronation of a new pope (John Paul I, the man who summoned the Second Vatican Council and revolutionized the Catholic Church). Vincent had no taste for such things, so he went straight to London, where he met up with Brooke and had appointments with his tailor and shoemaker. Then the couple spent a weekend at Cliveden. Vincent liked Bill and the two men had much in common. They swapped naval reminiscences and talked a great deal about their charitable interests, which were extensive. In 1948 the American millionaire had set up the Vincent Astor Foundation, whose object was expressed, with simple, sweeping grandeur as 'the alleviation of human misery'. In the previous year, Vincent had subscribed generously to Bill's Hungarian appeal.

In his latter years the public-spirited side of Vincent's nature triumphed over the businessman. This emerged quite clearly in the matter of the last great American Astor building project. Vincent had been steadily divesting himself of property and transferring his capital into stock exchange investments, but, in 1955, he decided to dazzle New York with another new construction. It was to be Astor Plaza, a forty-two-storey office block on Park Avenue between 53rd and 54th Streets, equipped with a heliport and all the latest commercial mod. cons. Almost from the beginning, however, he was in two minds about the venture. He enjoyed visiting the site and planning fresh eye-catching features, such as a bright mosaic map of Manhattan Island on the pavement in front of the entrance. But on other days he worried about the amount of money he had tied up in the scheme, and would say to his wife, 'Pookie, we have to get rid of that damned building, otherwise we will have to sell almost everything we own. It will be the death of me, and you, poor Pookie, will be left with a paltry sum, no foundation and a thousand worries.'[3] Eventually, Vincent did get rid of 'that damned building'. The site was acquired by Citibank for their prestigious headquarters. Thus ended the Astors' long history of contributing to the townscape of New York. Vincent preserved the bulk of his fortune in liquid assets in order to be able to devote it to charitable causes. Only with *Newsweek* did he still think in terms of business expansion. He wanted to add a sister journal in order to broaden coverage of current events and issues and further develop editorial talent.

During the Astors' visit to Britain Vincent was taken ill and Brooke had to have bulky X-ray equipment brought to their London hotel suite. However, he recovered sufficiently to be able to travel back to America on the *United States* as planned. During the voyage there was an incident which brought out all Captain Astor's patriotic fighting spirit. The *QE II* had recently come into commission and was intent on capturing the Blue Riband for the fastest transatlantic crossing. One lunchtime the British ship was sighted, gaining on her rival. Vincent took one look at her and rushed off, telling Brooke, 'I'm going to the bridge.' Brooke recalled: 'Within five minutes, as I was sipping my coffee, the whole ship began to shake and the passengers, bewildered, jumped up to see what was happening. I went out on deck, and hanging onto the rail, watched as the *Queen Elizabeth* disappeared below the horizon, behind us.'[4] Soon Vincent rejoined her, smiling with satisfaction. Thanks to his intervention the *United States* hung onto her record. Back home, doctors diagnosed a cardiovascular complaint. Vincent's condition fluctuated over the next five months. On 3 February 1959 he and Brooke lunched at their usual table at the St Regis. That night the head of the American Astor family had a sudden heart attack and died.

The contents of his will came as a shock to everyone. Half of his $130 million estate went to the Foundation, which Brooke was to administer. Vincent's widow received an outright bequest of $2 million and a life interest in the remainder of the fortune, which was hers to devise as she wished at her death. Jack received not a penny and neither did Alice's children. Months later the St Regis and *Newsweek* were sold. It is a cliché but a true one: this really *was* the end of an era.

Jack lost little time in contesting the will on the grounds that towards the end of his life his half-brother had not been in full command of his faculties and had fallen under the influence of bad advisers. The family lawyers wrote to all those who, they hoped, might be able to help ward off Jack's claims. Viscount Astor's reply was quite unequivocal:

> I know from repeated conversations that [Vincent] had a very low view of Jack and disliked him. He felt that his deportment and conduct were not in accordance with the traditions of the family, nor likely to redound to its credit. He had taken no part in public or charitable work and his married life had been unfortunate. Particularly Vincent was furious because Jack had taken no part in the war . . . He had no contact with Jack and I would, indeed, have been most surprised if he had left him anything . . .

As to Alice's children (one boy and three girls):

> I think he probably thought that they were adequately provided for by their mother. It has never been a tradition in the Astor family to leave large sums of money to daughters, as it has always been felt that very rich women are seldom very happy ones.[5]

Jack's claim for half the Astor estate failed. There would be no vast inherited wealth to pass down the surviving male line to his son, William or his grandson, Billy.

Being impulsive and determined in matters of the heart seems to have been something of an Astor trait. Vincent's courtship of Brooke was certainly matched by one of his English cousins. Bill was at St Moritz for New Year 1958, and one of the talking points among his friends was a fashion show at which the models had decided to 'send up' what was usually a solemnly chic event. The 'ringleader', it was said, was a statuesque twenty-eight-year-old brunette by the name of Bronwen Pugh. Bill was intrigued. He always wanted to be up to date with what was happening among the jet set, so he set out to meet Bronwen. First of all, he tried for an introduction through a mutual friend. Miss Pugh refused the bait. So Bill telephoned and asked to meet her. Bronwen was equal to this sort of thing: models spend a fair amount of their time fending off advances from middle-aged men. Although she had a fun-loving streak, she was the daughter of a Welsh judge and, at root, a serious-minded young woman. But Bill persisted. At the third attempt Bronwen agreed to have lunch with him – but was careful to arrange another appointment for 2.30, so that she had a genuine reason to make good her escape. In fact, the 'ordeal' did not turn out at all as she had expected. 'It was one long laugh from beginning to end. He was the most entertaining, the most wonderful host. I kept being in fits of laughter the whole way through lunch. At the end of it, I thought, "You could never be scared of this man." ' But that reaction was a very long way from any positive feeling of wishing to encourage Bill's pursuit. Bronwen was, in fact, in love with someone else at the time and was going through an emotional crisis which pushed middle-aged peers well to the edge of her vision.

It is at this point that a spiritual element enters into the Cliveden story which constitutes one of the vital keys to the tragic and mysterious events of the next few years. In the three months between that lunch and Bill and Bronwen's next meeting, Bronwen had a profound mystical experience which immeasurably deepened her Christian faith and made it, for her, a matter of daily commitment. As a result she put an end to her existing romance and sensed that she was waiting for God to direct her life into a new channel. The next time she went out with Bill she was very struck by what were almost his first words, 'My goodness, you've changed.' Over the ensuing months, as their feelings for each other deepened, they, naturally, opened up to each other aspects of their lives – physical, intellectual and spiritual. Gradually, Bill felt his way back to Christian faith. A few years later he underscored this by seeking confirmation in the Church of England and remarking to his friend and director, Bishop Gordon Savage, that by so doing he was nailing his colours to the mast and wished to be 'listed as among those who are *practising* members of their church'.[6] Bill and Bronwen were married in October 1960.

It would be facile to say that Viscount Astor found in his third wife a replacement for his mother. Nancy and Bronwen were very different in many ways. Yet there were similarities that Bill, perhaps unconsciously, must have recognized. Both women were immensely fun-loving and deeply religious. Bill needed these two elements in his own life, and he needed them to be balanced. As a result of Nancy's withdrawal of maternal love the two had got out of kilter. When Bill rediscovered faith, he already had a sound basis of biblical knowledge to build on – thanks to those daily Christian Science lessons in the nursery long ago.

The background to these events was one of considerable busyness for Bill. His achievements in obtaining aid for Hungarian refugees and publicizing their plight had marked him out as an obvious leader in a much more extensive crusade. Indeed, the very success of the 1956 operation had drawn attention to larger problems upon which the world had hitherto turned a blind eye. There were still 162,000 refugees in Europe, but the situation was much worse in other areas. There were over a million dispossessed Arabs in the Middle East, a similar number of Chinese in Hong Kong, 10,000 dispersed White Russians, and several millions who had fled from persecution in India, Pakistan, Korea, South Vietnam and elsewhere. In the middle of 1958 Bill was one of a group of British people which came together and decided to take an initiative. The result was World Refugee Year (June 1959 to May 1960), an international campaign of fund-raising and publicity. As well as activating his contacts worldwide, Viscount Astor succeeded Lady Elliot as chairman of the executive committee of the Standing Conference of British Organizations for Aid to Refugees. This body drew representatives from the fourteen leading aid agencies in Britain and co-ordinated the UK contribution to World Refugee Year.

It was a role that demanded considerable orgnizational and diplomatic skills and it took up most of Bill's time. He had to liaise with the royal family over the most effective contributions various members could make, and with government over their promised contribution of £100,000 and their pledge to receive a quota of refugees. He had to organize the making of films, the publication of books and the production of a variety of promotional literature. He planned a Mansion House dinner and a film première. He organized press releases. He set up a number of concerts at which many international performers gave their services. He cajoled bankers, industrialists and trade union leaders. He spoke at innumerable functions and signed thousands of letters. In subsequent years the world grew familiar with major charity events and the paraphernalia associated with them. In the 1950s an event on such a scale as this was quite new. The amount raised in the United Kingdom was £9,119,349, out of a global total of over £35 million.

Bill was very proud of this achievement, but it was quite evident that the work could not stop there. The funds gathered had to be allocated and their distribution and use supervised. Despite all that was done, the overall problem did not diminish; each new civil war or international crisis added to the number of displaced persons. Therefore the work of the Standing Committee continued. Bill spent February to April 1961 in the USA alerting agencies there to the *new* problems which World Refugee Year workers had brought to light, such as the special needs of physically handicapped refugees, and the 180,000 Algerians who would need repatriating when the war with France came to an end.

1962 was a particularly hectic year. It ended with a major effort (unsuccessful) to persuade the government to waive tax on a charity record produced by the UN High Commission for Refugees featuring the leading popular singers of the day (among them Bing Crosby, Maurice Chevalier and Ella Fitzgerald) even though he confessed to finding their music 'revolting'.[7] Between May and October Lord Astor, sometimes accompanied by his wife, visited Bavaria, Austria, Lebanon, Syria, Jordan, Israel and Hong Kong on behalf of the Standing Committee, to assess the progress being made with relief work. His observations were detailed and wide-ranging. Everywhere the fundamental truth was that, while much had been accomplished, much more remained to be done. Thus, 3,000 people a year entered Austria from Yugoslavia. Many were given asylum until they were able to move on to countries of final settlement; but if the funds needed to provide travel money were not increased, more people would be sent back where they had come from, and for many that would mean prison. In Lebanon 'an old Turkish barracks built to accommodate 600 soldiers at pre-1914 standards ... now contains 3,600 refugees. The barrack rooms are divided by concrete blocks, with a passage between, which is just wide enough for one person to move, and are swarming with humanity.' In Hong Kong the situation was complicated because there was no means of distinguishing between refugees and residents. An intolerable strain was being placed upon the colony's employment market and public services. Most children were receiving education, but many were too undernourished to benefit from it.[8] By November, Viscount Astor was back to speak in a House of Lords debate on the refugee problem. During the course of it many peers paid tribute to Bill's quiet, persistent and dedicated work.

As well as the heart-rending human suffering, the refugee problem involved a bewilderingly complex tangle of legal and political complications. One issue to which Bill addressed himself was the German law on the indemnification of victims of Nazi persecution. The government in Bonn had accepted responsibility for helping those who had been dispossessed or rendered incapable of returning to a normal life by the Hitler regime, but legal loopholes prevented some 20,000 refugees from receiving government aid. Lord Astor and his teams researched and collected hundreds of distressing case studies, such as that of Erik Balasz, a Polish gipsy.

> He and his family were arrested in 1940. They owned a travelling circus and lived in a caravan. For a time the boy and his mother were together. She was later shot,

the rest of the family disappeared. During his imprisonment the boy contracted TB, and was treated in a prison hospital.

His claim for loss of health, due to 70% disability, was rejected on the ground that the criminal police had stated that at the time of his arrest he was without proper means of support, living by begging and stealing, and of asocial character. As he was not arrested on racial grounds, but under a Nazi law of 1933 for the purpose of controlling gipsies, he was not eligible for compensation ... No reference was made to the destruction of his home or the killing of his family.[9]

Lord Astor raised a petition against such legal loopholes, signed by hundreds of prominent people from all walks of life. In February 1963 he discussed the matter from every angle with officials in Bonn, and in May he returned for an interview with Chancellor Adenauer.

Another, often unsung, achievement of Lord Astor's at this time was the setting up of the International Disaster Relief Committee. It occurred to him (in the small hours of one morning, as his widow remembers) that every time there was a major catastrophe somewhere in the world it took days for governments and charitable organizations to send the necessary aid. Not infrequently, relief work was hampered by duplication of effort and inadequate information. Bill brought together representatives of all the major relief agencies to form a committee empowered and funded to dispatch task forces to disaster areas at a few hours' notice in order to assess what aid was needed and how it might be most effectively channelled.

When Bill was not involved with some aspect of work for refugees he was an active member of the House of Lords. In 1961 he was a founder member of the parliamentary campaign for British entry into the Common Market. He interested himself in legislation concerning the police and the working of the law courts. In 1962 he sponsored a bill to permit the introduction of lie-detectors, which had proved valuable in the USA. And he continued his father's campaign on House of Lords reform, speaking in favour of the creation of life peers and attempting unsuccessfully to introduce an amendment to the bill which would have made it easy for MPs to renounce peerages. He did not, however, always allow parliamentary business to interfere with his social obligations. In May 1963, he complained to Lord Shackleton:

Really, to have your Division on Divorce on the Friday of Ascot week is very difficult, because clearly most of the Peers who have sympathy for the Division are likely to be at the races. However, I will do my best ... The best moment would be 7 p.m. which would allow one to get up from the races and go out after.[10]

Lord Astor also continued his private charity work. To his extensive commitments he added donations to several refugee organizations. He supported a vocational training centre in Palestine, aided Russian refugee families in Germany. But he had many other concerns. He was, for example, chairman of the Great Ormond Street Hospital Institute of Child Health. All these pursuits constituted Bill Astor's major activities between 1961 and 1963, and not the ones that made the newspaper headlines.

Bronwen was installed as the chatelaine of Cliveden in the autumn of 1960 and loved it. She adored the house and the estate. She liked meeting Bill's friends. She was in her element acting as hostess to the groups of guests who passed through the Italianate portals. At last, Bill had found the ideal partner who shared his pride in the family home and was equally dedicated to helping other people enjoy it. As far as Bronwen was concerned, there was only one fly in the ointment. From her modelling friends she had heard about Stephen Ward – the word was that he was trouble. She was therefore appalled to find him ensconced on the estate. When she met him she quickly came to the conclusion that he was 'evil' and she tried to persuade Bill of this. He laughed off her apprehension. It did not take long for her hostility to communicate itself to Ward. One cannot help wondering whether this lay at the heart of the trouble which broke over Cliveden in the following summer. For four years everything had been going well for Ward. Spring Cottage, introductions to Lord Astor's guests, the freedom to impress his own visitors with the beauties of the Cliveden estate – these had been important elements in his mounting success. Fundamental to all of them was his influence over Lord Astor. Now, he must have sensed that this was under threat. Some of his extraordinary actions over the next couple of years may well have been designed either to reassert his position or to exploit to the full his relationship with Bill Astor while he still had the chance. He was, in any case, becoming more and more unstable. The licentiousness of this middle-aged roué took increasingly extreme forms and his Walter Mitty fantasies moved further and further away from reality.

The tragic sequence of events which led to what became known as the 'Profumo affair' began early in 1961 when Ward met Captain Eugene Ivanov, Soviet naval attaché and, like several embassy officials, an agent of the GRU, Russian military intelligence. This was a time when East–West tension was at its height and the governments of the leading powers were gripped by spy-fever. In 1960 the Soviets had captured Gary Powers, the pilot of an American U2 spy plane shot down over the Urals. Western intelligence scored a counter-coup by turning the Russian agent Oleg Penkovsky. Investigations were still going on into the Burgess and Maclean network and led to the unmasking of Kim Philby and Anthony Blunt in 1962 and 1963. Everyone in the security services was jittery and there was much talk of 'moles' and 'double agents'. Ward now experienced the thrill of being on the fringe of this exciting, secret world. The osteopath was useful to Ivanov because he had access to several top people and because he possessed, or claimed to possess, discreditable information about the private lives of some of them.

The next incident occurred one evening in the summer of 1961. It seems both trivial and odd, but when he was called upon to give evidence in camera to an official inquiry, Bill thought it worth recalling and believed it to be significant. Stephen, he recalled, 'pressed' him to come down to Spring Cottage for a drink after dinner. When he arrived he was surprised to discover one of Ward's girls, Valarie Holman, scantily dressed and doing a dance to entertain the company. Bill claimed that he left after half an hour. He later reflected:

> I cannot help but note a resemblance between this meeting and the occasion on which Mr Profumo met Miss Keeler. In both cases Dr Ward engineered a meeting after dinner when one was mellowed by food and drink on a summer's night, in which one was suddenly confronted with a young lady scantily dressed.[11]

On two or three subsequent occasions Bill saw Miss Holman in Ward's company. Once she expressed admiration for a pair of trousers being worn by another of Stephen's girls and Bill gave her about £20 to buy herself a pair.

Why did Bill draw attention to this particular example of minor generosity when it was his custom to keep his benefactions very private? The answer can only be that he was anxious to clear his name when details about his life were being twisted, exaggerated and fabricated. He was being 'revealed' to the world as a man who engaged in sexual romps with young women provided by Ward. His problem was that he could not deny *all* knowledge of Ward's activities. He *had* been to Spring Cottage. He *had* enjoyed the company of some of his tenant's alluring companions (though only, he always insisted, on an innocent level). And he *had* (by his own submission only on this single occasion) given one of the girls money. Knowing that the unadorned facts stood little chance of being accepted by the public, Bill kept silent, but he tried to make his version of events clear to the official inquiry.

It was his contention that he often called at Spring Cottage, usually to ask Ward for treatment (there was no telephone connection with the house). He therefore met several of Stephen's friends – of both sexes. He claimed that he did not like some of them, that he never knew any of them very well and that he made a point of not interfering in Ward's private life. Can we really believe that Lord Astor was that naïve? Most of those who have written about the Profumo affair have certainly found it difficult to swallow the degree of detachment claimed by Bill. The tendency has been to go too far the other way. Some have asserted that Cliveden was open house to Ward and his friends, and that Bill often enjoyed the delights proffered by Ward at Spring Cottage. While being cautious about Bill's protestations, we must be equally wary about 'revelations' of scandal. One major weakness in all the accounts of Bill's involvement in lascivious goings-on at Cliveden is that they betray a lack of understanding of what life at Cliveden was like. It was a small community of indoor servants, outdoor servants, tenants and neighbours. Everyone knew everyone else's business. There was little privacy and much gossip. Therefore, one of the ground rules at the 'big house' was *pas devant les domestiques*. Lord Astor was not so stupid as to behave in a way that would set backstairs tongues wagging or to outrage and risk losing his best servants.

Another fact that we must grasp if we are to set the events of July 1961 in their proper context is that life at Cliveden was well organized. On such a large estate it had to be. This meant that records were kept and that staff knew who had permission to enter the house and its environs at any particular time. The access of Ward and his guests was strictly limited. In June 1963 Bill could state quite categorically, 'Our records show that, in the last three years, he has only had four meals at Cliveden.'[12] Stephen Ward only entered the house when invited to do so, and usually in a professional capacity. In view of Bronwen's dislike of him, his social calls were not very frequent. He had permission to use the swimming pool but was expected to check, before doing so, that it was convenient to the Astors. This was a privilege he shared with a few other tenants and neighbours. It was something that had to be policed rather carefully. Obviously Bill and Bronwen did not want to have hordes of visitors crowding the pool and there were times when they wanted it to themselves. Moreover, it was overlooked by staff quarters, and they did not want their servants to be disturbed by thoughtless or rowdy parties. Bill once had to remonstrate with Stephen about late-night bathing sessions after his butler, Washington, had ejected a Spring Cottage group at 2.30 a.m.

This brings us to the oft-recounted events of 7–9 July 1961. The composition of the weekend house party was, as usual, very mixed. International and national celebrities mingled with more ordinary mortals. John (Jack) Profumo, the Minister for War, and his wife arrived on Friday evening. Nine other guests came on Saturday and stayed the night. Various other people appeared for lunch or dinner on the two days. Among those coming and going (not all of whom were present at the later publicized events) were Viscount Astor's aunt Pauline Spender-Clay, various members of the House of Lords, an Eton schoolmaster, a horticultural expert (the Profumos were keen gardeners), Nubar Gulbenkian, Lord Mountbatten (a close friend), an Oxford don, a judge and two schoolgirls. The guest of honour, who came in time for lunch on Sunday, was General Ayub Khan, President of Pakistan, who arrived with members of his suite. The Profumos had for some years been patients of Ward, and during the course of the weekend they received three treatments from him, the first probably being on Friday evening. Ward therefore knew the minister was at Cliveden, he knew Profumo's weakness for nubile young women and he probably knew who the other principal house guests were. With this knowledge under his belt, he could easily have arranged for Christine Keeler and Captain Ivanov to be among his own weekend visitors.

The suggestion has been made, without much in the way of concrete evidence, that Ward was being used by MI5 to entrap Ivanov so that he could be turned. This theory does not fit in with the subsequent events in which Lord Astor was involved with the osteopath and the Russian. It seems unlikely that Ward was acting under carefully formulated orders in his dealings with Ivanov, and much more in character that on that hot July weekend he was behaving like a small boy with a chemistry set – putting various components together in a test tube to see what would happen.

What did happen was that after dinner on Saturday evening several members of the Astor party enjoyed the cool late evening air. Bill was particularly anxious to show everyone a new bronze which he had commissioned; it was near the swimming pool and that was why he led the way in that direction. Walking ahead of the others, he and Jack Profumo went through a door in the wall flanking the drive which led to the open-air pool. There they saw Stephen Ward and his three guests who had come up from the cottage. The party included one of Stephen's girls, Christine Keeler, and she had been running around the edge of the pool, stark naked. It was obvious that the party was in a highly 'relaxed' mood. Miss Keeler hurriedly clambered into a costume. The rest of the Astor guests arrived. They stayed for a while, then returned to the house, and the Ward party was invited to join them. Such are the agreed facts. From this point the versions of interested parties diverge widely.

According to Lord Astor's version, nothing untoward happened that evening that he was aware of. He and his guests entered the pool area to find about six

> people swimming, all of whom were either in bathing costumes or wrapped in towels, and at no moment did my wife and myself, or any other people in our party, see anyone without a bathing costume. According to Miss Keeler's account she went to the far end of the pool and put on a bathing costume, and this would tally with my recollection of some of those present being at the far end of the pool. I was not in sight of the pool all the time as I went to change into a bathing costume and to dress afterwards. Most of the dinner party, including the ladies, were at the pool at the time and no one saw any action to which anyone could take exception.[13]

Christine Keeler's accounts, which began to appear eighteen months later, present a very different picture, and they were the ones which came to be widely believed. According to her, Astor and Profumo chased her naked round the pool, switching on the floodlights to obtain a better view. Only after the arrival of the ladies was she able to get into a bathing costume. When the whole party went back to the house, Profumo pursued her through rooms and corridors and ended up dressing her in a 'suit of armour' in which she paraded to the general amusement of all.

Which narrative are we to believe – the 'plain' or the 'coloured'? On closer investigation the latter account falls down because it is uncorroborated and riddled with improbabilities. One would imagine that anyone else who was present would have remembered seeing two middle-aged men chasing a nude teenager, and that same teenager clanking around the great hall encased in steel. Yet there was never any corroboration from either guests or servants, despite press inducements to 'tell all'. Nobody else present seems to have registered anything unusual about the weekend. The Keeler version might just conceivably have credibility if it was only *one* version, but in fact her subsequent accounts differ on points of detail. In one, the party from the house are very formally garbed: the men in tails, the ladies wearing tiaras. In another white ties have disappeared in favour of dinner jackets. Some exaggerations are so obvious as to be absurd. When Profumo chased her round the house (and such activity would have been confined to the ground floor) Keeler discovered Cliveden to be 'bigger than Buckingham Palace'. As to the dressing up episode, the question that springs immediately to the sceptical mind is 'what armour'? William Waldorf had accumulated many sets of combat and tournament armour for display at Hever and Cliveden. They were heavy, cumbersome and unyielding. The idea of a slip of a girl, encased in one of these, being able to stagger more than a couple of steps is absurd. It is quite clear that these heavily embellished narratives are the invention of a working-class girl, thrust into a wealthy and glamorous milieu and subsequently paid large sums of money for her reminiscences. Those reminiscences were coloured by an over-stimulated imagination and a desire to 'tell a good story'. It may well be that Profumo did get fresh with her, though his scope for horseplay would have been somewhat inhibited by the presence of other, highly respectable guests – not to mention his wife. And Christine may have tried on one or two pieces of armour. That was quite a common entertainment at Cliveden (among Nancy Astor's photographs there is one of Waldorf fitting a helmet on a young female guest). Anything beyond that is sheer embroidery.

On the Sunday afternoon, Ward's party, now joined by Ivanov, were once again at the pool. Also present were two or three groups of neighbours with their children. Profumo spent a long time there, and he and Ivanov vied for Christine's attention. Bill had a short swim and then took President Khan on a tour of the gardens. Christine's version of this, as printed in the *News of the World*, was that they had all engaged in pretty physical high jinks and that Ayub Khan had joined in. The latter allegation came close to sparking off an international incident in 1963, when the Pakistan government threatened to call off a presidential state visit to London unless an official apology was forthcoming.

These distortions and their repercussions were still in the future when the Cliveden house party broke up and everyone carried on with their lives as usual. The immediate aftermath was that Keeler became sexually involved with both Profumo and Ivanov. Bill knew nothing of this at the time. He was not closely involved with the minister and only met him occasionally at social functions.

Ivanov was a different matter. Part of his brief was to gather information on Anglo-American relations. International affairs were reaching a point of high crisis over Berlin. Since 1949 East Germany had lost over two and a half million citizens to the West, mainly through the divided ex-capital. Moscow was worried and wanted tighter border controls. A meeting of the Warsaw Pact was planned for early August to decide on the new measures. The NATO powers had made it perfectly clear that they would brook no interference with their rights of access to Berlin and the legitimate movements of German citizens. While the Kremlin openly pursued a defiant brinkmanship, Soviet agents were set to discover the strength of American resolve and the degree of common purpose between London and Washington. Ivanov had long since marked out Lord Astor, with his many transatlantic connections, as an obvious source of information. He asked Ward to arrange a meeting. After considerable badgering, Bill agreed, and the two men came to lunch at Cliveden. It was a tedious meeting. Lord Astor had to listen to all the well-aired Soviet arguments and then submit to being quizzed about whether the Americans would fight and whether the British would support them and risk European war. Bill was careful to follow the official government line and was relieved when the arrival of some visitors, come to see the Astor stud, enabled him to make his escape.

After further thought he decided that he ought to draw the attention of the security forces to Ivanov's activity. On 2 August he wrote to the Foreign Office:

> I have a friend called Stephen Ward who is a leading osteopath and has a small weekend cottage here. He is also, incidentally, a talented artist who does weekly portraits in The Illustrated London News of celebrities including your Secretary of State. He has become a friend of the assistant Russian Naval Attaché, Captain Eugene Ivonof, who is always asking him questions about the general political intentions of the British. What strikes Stephen is how few contacts the Russian Embassy seem to have in this country, and how hard they seem to find it to assess British opinion and intentions accurately.

I have met Ivonof who is, according to Ward, an absolutely dedicated Communist and also a nice person.

It occurred to me, after talking to Ward, that if you wished to ensure at any particular moment that the Russian Embassy was absolutely correctly informed as to Western intentions this might be a useful chap. Ward would pass on information himself or could very easily arrange for Ivonof to meet, at a meal, anyone you wish.

I have suggested to Ward to emphasize to Ivonof that the Americans, rightly or wrongly, are absolutely determined to stand firm over their access to Berlin, even at the risk of an all out war.

If you, or anyone else, wish to get hold of Ward his address is:—

38, Devonshire Street, W.1. Telephone WEL 3082.

And his home telephone number is BAY 8564

His address for the weekend is The Springs Cottage, Cliveden, Maidenhead, Berks. but there is no telephone.

I am off to Jura on Monday so if you wish to get hold of me I suggest you communicate direct.[14]

Much has been made of Bill Astor's wartime intelligence work and his friendships with senior officers in MI5 and MI6. It has been suggested that he was still working for the security services and that he was using Ward for the purpose of entrapping Ivanov. But an active agent would have had no need to write such a letter. He would simply have passed on the relevant information to his superior. Even if there had been a reason to write, someone involved in intelligence work would have known whom to write *to.* He would have known that the intelligence services are answerable directly to the prime minister and not the Foreign Office. It was because his message had to be passed on that he did not receive the following reply for about a fortnight:

... Contacts of this sort are becoming increasingly common and we believe that the Russians are making a particular effort at present to estimate public opinion about the Berlin crisis and to find indications of dissension amongst the Western Allies.

I think it would be helpful if Ward could take a robust line with Captain Ivanov and I will arrange for one of our people to have a word with him ... I am very grateful to you for your suggestion.[15]

Four days after the writing of that letter the Berlin Wall began to go up. If this was the extent of Bill's espionage activity we must conclude that he was wielding a decidedly threadbare cloak and a very blunt dagger. For over a year after this, Lord Astor had no dealings with Ivanov, except for occasionally seeing him in Ward's company.

Their next encounter, in October 1962, was generated by an even graver East–West crisis. President Khrushchev had upped the stakes by sending Soviet nuclear missiles to Cuba. The CIA had had no difficulty in discovering them and Washington demanded their removal. It was the most dangerous moment in the entire Cold War; the ultimate confrontation in which neither side could walk away without losing credibility, and neither side could stand its ground without provoking World War III. Ivanov had been building up his contacts, with and without Ward. Now, they suddenly became more important than ever. Moscow was urgently looking for a way out of the mess it had got itself into. Ivanov was ordered to open possible unofficial channels which might lead to negotiations. Ward, now excitedly at the centre of world events, turned once more to Lord Astor. Bill was not pleased.

> I again emphasized that I was out of all active politics and was not interested in passing on any information between the Russian Embassy and the British government. However, after considerable persuasion, again I had them to lunch alone, and on this occasion Ivonof's line was that Khruschev had got into an impossible position in Cuba, that he wished to extricate himself from it without losing face, but there was grave danger of war if this was not done and that England should call a conference to which Mr Khruschev would be delighted to come so that he could save his face and get some quid pro quo. I answered first that I was convinced that America would fight, secondly, that in my opinion there was no possible chance of England being separated from America or taking any separate initiative on this matter . . . I said that I refused to be a channel between him and Foreign Office and told Dr. Ward that he should ring up the Private Secretary of Sir Harold Caccia who was then Permanent Under-Secretary for Foreign Affairs and ask to be put in contact . . . He also wished to get in touch with the Press, so I mentioned this to Lord Arran, who I regard as a very responsible journalist.[16]

It is difficult to know how much weight Ivanov's information carried. It was clear to western intelligence from several sources that Khrushchev would have to back down. The CIA had already established that the USSR lacked the nuclear strike capability to support Khrushchev's bluff. On 27 October Ward and Ivanov went to Cliveden for dinner, at Bill's invitation, to discuss the situation further with Lord Arran, a fellow guest. It would seem that Astor, despite himself, was caught up in the unofficial toings and froings involved in this tense situation. It was while they were actually together that the news came through of Khrushchev's complete, and unconditional, withdrawal. Bill commented of Ivanov's reaction, 'I have never seen a more astonished man.'

As far as Lord Astor was concerned, that was the end of his involvement in the security aspects of the Ward–Ivanov–Profumo triangle. But much worse was to follow. Six weeks later Christine Keeler was involved in a sordid scene with a jealous lover who came after her with a gun. This event opened the Pandora's box that released a flood of evils upon scores of people who had become involved with Stephen Ward.

Bill's first, generous, impulse was to phone Stephen to ask if he could be of any help. He recommended a solicitor to represent Christine Keeler at the impending trial. It was early in the New Year that the fatal mischief was done. Keeler started being stupid, Ward panicked and Astor made wrong decisions. The sequence of events was as follows: In their investigations, the police, inevitably, stumbled upon details of Ward's life and his dealings with prominent people. Intriguing truths, half-truths and rumours reached the press. Newspapermen hounded Christine Keeler. She suddenly saw the chance to make a great deal of money. The first information Bill had of all this was on 28 January, when Stephen Ward telephoned to tell him that Keeler had agreed to do a series of articles for the *Sunday Pictorial* in which, among other things, she would present a highly coloured account of the events at Cliveden in July 1961. When Ward had given him some idea of the distortions which were likely to appear in the paper, Bill decided on a two-pronged course of action to get the feature suppressed. He contacted his solicitors so that they could make legal representation to the *Pictorial*, and he gave Ward £500 to enable his lawyers to collect the information necessary to prove to the newspaper that Keeler's story was unreliable. By now Bill knew that Profumo had had an affair with Christine and that if this became common knowledge it would damage his married life and his career. He immediately arranged an interview with the minister 'and advised him strongly to see the Attorney General or Minister of Defence that very day and put himself completely in their hands'.[17] At this time there was no thought in Bill's mind that the threatened scandal had any security aspect. He was concerned for the reputation of a member of the government and for the reputations of himself and his other guests. That was, on the surface, how matters stood on 1 March, when Bill went to America for six weeks.

During his absence matters became more complicated and more unpleasant. Ward, rightly worried at the prospect of Christine Keeler being cross-examined by a clever counsel, wrongly arranged to get her out of the country. The money he had had from Bill paid for this, and it was soon being alleged that Lord Astor was involved in the plot. Bill always categorically denied this: 'If I had ever heard of it I would have strongly advised against and never been a party to such an addle-pated scheme of trying to get a witness to disappear.'[18] Meanwhile, the security services were becoming alarmed. Ivanov had been whisked back to Moscow at the first sign of trouble, but MI5 were concerned that, in all the fracas of court cases and press exposés, Ward's fringe intelligence activities might be revealed. It was decided to discredit him. The police were authorized to make an exhaustive investigation of all his affairs and dig up as much dirt as possible. The osteopath's patients and friends were grilled, with the result that his practice dwindled rapidly.

Eventually the police managed to cobble together enough evidence to make a case against Ward of living on immoral earnings. But it was not only reporters and policemen who were sinking their teeth into the rotting carcase of Stephen Ward's affairs; politicians were also on the prowl. George Wigg, the Labour chief whip, scented an unprecedented opportunity to bring down the government. He pursued Profumo relentlessly, hinting that his connection with Miss Keeler, who had also been consorting with Ivanov, constituted a grave security risk. The minister's reaction was to lie forthrightly, first to his colleagues, then to the House of Commons.

By the time Bill returned on 11 April, his name was being splashed across the newspapers with every kind of innuendo that Fleet Street's libel lawyers thought they could get away with. The *Daily Express* was particularly vicious, as Lord Beaverbrook pursued his ancient vendetta with great relish. A friend reported to Bill that 'Max Aitken told him that his father, Lord Beaverbrook, had his knife into me. He asked him why and received the cryptic reply, "Wouldn't you like to know." He says that Lord Beaverbrook is rampaging against me, putting round the idea that I am a callous libertine.'[19] Also, facts were coming to light of orgies Ward had held at Spring Cottage and in London which genuinely surprised and shocked Bill. He told his brother David, 'I thought I knew Stephen but I was obviously wrong.' A meeting with Ward was one of his first priorities. There is disagreement about what passed at that encounter. Ward claimed that Lord Astor demanded that he relinquish the cottage. Bill claimed that Ward had immediately offered to give it up, but added, 'I was very glad he had done this and I had intended to ask him to do so if he had not.'[20] Bill gave Ward £200 to cover the improvements he had made to the cottage. Later writers were quick to seize on this as evidence that Astor was coldly turning his back on his friend.

Nothing could be further from the truth. Stephen Ward had very obviously abused Bill's generosity. Bill knew it. Stephen knew it. More to the point, everyone at Cliveden knew it. There could be no question of him remaining on the estate. There was equally no question of Bill rejecting his friend. He guaranteed a £1,500 overdraft so that Ward's lawyers could properly defend him and also take action against his detractors, and less than a month later he responded positively to yet another pathetic appeal. Ward's letter on this occasion was certainly not couched in the tone of someone who felt he had been deserted by a friend.

Dear Bill,

I should very much like to see you. It seems probable that I cannot continue my actions because of lack of money. I might obtain some sort of settlement and apology anyway. In the meantime I have reached an absolutely desperate financial situation.

Fortunately there are signs of revival in my practice. Can you help me sort out some of my problems, and save something from the ruin. Anyway I desperately need your help or I shall go completely under.

Stephen[21]

Bill immediately sent another £200.

It would have been perfectly understandable if Bill had washed his hands of Stephen Ward. Several of the osteopath's other patients and 'friends' were doing precisely that. The garbled mixture of truth and falsehood which the nation was daily consuming with its cornflakes and toast, throughout the summer of 1963, was proving an enormous embarrassment to the Astor family. Jakie, typically, made a joke of it by saying that with all the publicity the Astors were getting he was thinking of changing his name to Shaw. The scandal was beginning to bite hard. Several of Bill and Bronwen's 'friends' turned their backs on them and some of the mud stuck to other members of the family. One American newspaper confused 'Viscount Astor' with 'Lord Astor of Hever' and received a broadside from John's solicitors.

As far as his public stance was concerned, Bill was placed in an impossible position. He had three alternatives. He could confront his detractors in the news media – within the restraints imposed by certain matters being *sub judice*; he could go into hiding; or he could go about his life as normally as possible to show the world that the sordid events of Dr Ward's life had nothing to do with him. Whichever course he chose had its pitfalls. Like any calumnied public figure he was in an impossible situation. In the event, he took the latter path, continuing his work and his social obligations and, whenever pressed by reporters, offering a smiling 'no comment'. Of course, the press, denied anything more positive to report, fell back on accusing him of using Ward for his own lecherous purposes and then dropping his friend at the first sign of trouble.

What seemed to give point to this charge was that Bill did not speak up for Stephen at his trial. It is clear from those who were close to him at the time that he was genuinely shocked and surprised to learn of some of Stephen's excesses. And his correspondence bears witness to his bemused reaction on learning of three-day orgies and the cavorting of masked libertines. Yet he remained convinced that Ward was no pimp. He was also convinced that the specific accusation brought by the police was not only nonsense but vicious nonsense. An embarrassed Establishment and a corrupt constabulary were determined to make an example of an outsider who had done so much damage to the Conservative government. Bill could not conceive of the charges being made to stick and was appalled by the way the court proceedings were handled. Ward had ranged against him, not only the prosecuting counsel, but also the judge, the press and the public. Bill's opinion was reinforced by friends in the legal profession and by Bronwen's father, a county court judge, who described the summing up from the bench as an absolute travesty of justice. Bill was certain that, even if Ward were convicted, he would be freed on appeal because of the irregularities in the trial. Why, then, did he not stand up in court for the falsely accused Ward?

The simple answer is that he was not cited as a witness – either for the defence or, perhaps more significantly, for the prosecution. Bill followed the advice of his solicitor, and that advice was to remain silent. But had Lord Astor been summoned to appear in court he would have had to go. In fact, he deliberately stayed at his town house during the early days of the trial in case he was called. The press chose to ignore this and to put the worst construction on his 'silence'. Bill's very real dilemma is made clear by papers in the possession of Bill's widow and his son, and by those who knew Bill closely. It was this: in the summer of 1963 there were two men 'on trial', Stephen Ward and Jack Profumo. The minister had been forced to resign, and the Master of the Rolls, Lord Denning, had been appointed to carry out an inquiry into the security aspect of the whole affair. The dilemma for Bill and his legal advisers was that if he was placed on the witness stand there was little he could say that would help Stephen, and if he was cross-examined he might be manoeuvred into making potentially damaging statements about Profumo. It seemed clear that Ward would either not be convicted or that his conviction would be quashed on appeal. If that had happened he would have been able to rebuild his life, and there is no doubt that Lord Astor would have helped him to do so. No one could foresee that events would take a sudden, tragic turn.

Although Bill kept silent on the charges against Stephen Ward, he did not keep silent on the more important aspects of the case which, it was alleged, affected national security. As early as 12 June he wrote to the Prime Minister's office offering to give whatever help lay in his power to unravel the Ward–Profumo–Ivanov relationship. The supposed ramifications had become incredibly complicated, as the scandal provoked intelligence chiefs to near paranoia. It was all happening at the same time as Sir Anthony Blunt, KCVO, Surveyor of the Queen's Pictures, was being unmasked as the 'fourth man' of the Burgess and Maclean spy ring (though his treason was kept secret by the security forces for several years). No one could be sure that the entire establishment was not worm-eaten by Soviet spies. Feverish, ill-co-ordinated activity was going on behind the scenes. The old rivalry between MI5 and MI6 and their mutual mistrust of Scotland Yard were exacerbated. It was suggested that Ward was part of a communist cell with scores of contacts in high places. Bill was cited to appear before Lord Denning and he knew that it was his responsibility to help establish the truth.

It was a costly decision fraught with inner conflict. His spiritual director records how Bill came to him daily for counsel:

> . . . the consequences he most feared were not on himself but on his family and also on those whom he might need to incriminate through direct questioning, by the full answers he was expected to give. I remember so well him saying as the enquiry proceeded, 'You see, Bishop Gordon . . . if I answer fully and truthfully that question, think of the hurt the possible publicity will give to X or Y.'[22]

In his deposition, Bill set out, as clearly as possible, the details of his contacts with Ivanov during the Berlin and Cuban crises. He deliberately played down any suggestion that Stephen was a communist:

> I have . . . been told by a friend that Dr. Ward, under the influence of alcohol, said to my friend's wife that he was a Communist and looked forward to the Russians coming to this country. My impression was rather that Dr. Ward was rather naive and a Left-winger as regards politics and that Ivonof was a very strong subtle character who may well have exercised an influence over Ward and have used him for his own purpose.[23]

A few weeks after Bill wrote those words in preparation for his appearance before Lord Denning, Ward was dead.

He did not wait for the jury's 'guilty' verdict. His world had fallen apart. His fantasies had all exploded. He took an overdose of Nembutal in the early morning of 31 July. He was rushed to hospital in a coma but the doctors were unable to save him. This new turn of events provided the press with yet another stick to beat Lord Astor with. Ironically, he had written to a relative only four days before:

> I have a feeling that the worst of our troubles are behind us now, though one never can be sure. The whole thing is an outrageous piece of nonsense but for the moment I have to suffer in silence.[24]

Bill was genuinely upset at the news and immediately penned a letter of condolence to Peter Ward, Stephen's brother. Wissie, holidaying in the South of France, correctly divined Bill's feelings – feelings she did not share. Her comment on hearing that Stephen had been rushed into hospital was:

> Knowing you, I bet you are sad that dodger Ward tried to kill himself – but for myself, I am anti creeps, however talented and entertaining they may be.[25]

The same newspapers that carried the headlines of Ward's death also blazoned photographs of a smiling Lord Astor at 'Glorious Goodwood' and did not fail to draw the 'obvious' conclusion that Lord Astor was enjoying himself at the racecourse while his friend lay dying. Once again the press got it wrong, as Bill explained to his lawyer:

I gave up the first day of Goodwood to preside over the Emergency Disaster Committee of the British Voluntary Organisations which I have succeeded in forming and which was in operation for the first time over the Yugoslav earthquake. Incidentally a statement on this put out over the signatures of Lady Limerick, who is Vice-Chairman of the Red Cross, and myself was ignored by the Press. Bronwen and I were staying with Mr. and Mrs. Maze in their cottage near Midhurst. We went racing on the Wednesday and as we left the Course we saw in the evening paper that Ward had taken an overdose of drugs and accordingly we decided not to go to the races any more, staying quietly with the Mazes on Thursday and coming home to Cliveden on Friday.[26]

The Profumo affair and its ramifications rumbled on into the autumn. It played a major part in bringing down the Macmillan government in October. The sufferings of Bill and his family abated only slowly. There was the inevitable crop of obscene letters and at least one attempt at blackmail (immediately reported to the police). David advised his brother to tailor his schedule of public activities and keep a low profile for a couple of years. Bill's reply was that none of his charitable and social engagements was headline-grabbing; that he believed them to be important and that he would carry on with them as long as he had the strength to do so. He and Bronwen (now expecting their second child) went to Salzburg for the festival in August, as planned, and then to the Jura estate for a few weeks in September to try to relax and recover from the traumatic events of the past months. Even there they were not protected from the persistence of Fleet Street. Reporters from the *Daily Mail* and the *Daily Express* pursued them to the Hebridean haven. For most people such an intrusion might well have been the final straw, but Bill preserved his equanimity. As he told his solicitor afterwards, he preferred to regard this as an opportunity to rebuild bridges, since no private individual can ever emerge victorious from a prolonged conflict with the press. He took the reporters to the local bar and spent the evening there drinking with them.

Eventually the day came when the news media had wrung every last drop of copy from the Profumo affair and had moved on to harass other unfortunate victims. The activities of Stephen Ward and his clients passed into history. In a later, more liberal age most people would be inclined to wonder what all the fuss was about. Political students eventually came to agree with Lord Denning that the Profumo–Keeler–Ivanov link involved no breach of national security. Now that Lord Astor's papers have become available it is possible to agree broadly with his assessment of the whole business, as he expressed it to his solicitor in August 1963:

... I really do apologise for this awful mixture of stupidity, unwisdom, and chance and misplaced kindness and heaven knows what all which produced this situation.[27]

Earlier chroniclers of the events of 1961–3 have laboured under crippling disadvantages. They were like jigsaw puzzle solvers working with only half the pieces and, to make matters worse, some of the wrong pieces. They had no access to intelligence files and no access to Bill Astor's papers. Their main sources were Stephen Ward's material, trial transcripts, and interviews with Ward's 'girls', some of whom had already perjured themselves in court or published inaccurate stories for gain. We still do not possess all the facts. But now we can see the whole sequence of events from Bill's perspective. We may not be able to reveal the complete picture but we can obtain a far clearer image of Lord Astor and his involvement, and that means that we can dismiss some of the earlier theories that have been advanced. Bill was not a guilty libertine who threw his friend to the wolves in order to get them off his track. He was not a semi-official intelligence operative playing complex entrapment games. He was not these things, basically, because he was too simple and straightforward a character to have been able to carry off either role convincingly. He was gullible. He sometimes lacked common sense. He was generous to a fault. He was a poor judge of character. These failings led him into a compromising relationship with Stephen Ward and prevented him from being able to extricate himself from it (though it is difficult to see how anyone could have disentangled himself from the various coils which rapidly assumed Laocoon complexity and strength). But no one who knew Bill Astor ever charged him with deviousness. The man who was described as 'straight as a die', the man who daily prayed and studied the Bible with his wife; the man who continued to give Ward money even though it might look bad, the man who insisted on going about his daily life as normally as possible – could not have set 'honey traps' or covered up a sordid sex life or convincingly lied at the Denning inquiry.

It was Viscount Astor's misfortune that, while he would not or could not speak up for himself, others in a position to know the truth failed to come to his aid. With so much moral and political shrapnel flying about, everyone remotely concerned stayed under cover in their trenches. The man who knew more than anyone about what was really happening was Harold Macmillan and he, certainly, was not disposed to help Bill. He had disliked Nancy. He had recently fallen out with the Hever Astors. He was the godfather of Bill's ex-wife and now he was reeling from the damage done through Profumo's exposure. With his own ship sinking beneath him, the Prime Minister derived a certain grim satisfaction from seeing Lord Astor struggling in the water.

For the Astor family, the Profumo affair was an embarrassment which is still keenly felt three decades later. For the second time this century, the name of Astor had been pilloried by the press and, quite unjustly, held up for public humiliation. The scandal came at a time when Bill and his siblings were already under other pressures. Bobbie's problems only seemed to intensify with age. Nancy was not the easiest elderly mother to deal with and, quite apart from anything else, her children had to mount an almost military campaign to prevent her hearing about the Profumo business – difficult when it appeared in frequent broadcasts and newspapers. Basically, everyone felt sorry for Bill and outraged at the way he was misrepresented, but, inevitably, these emotions were tinged for some members of the family with the feeling that he should have seen through Stephen Ward or that he might have conducted himself more intelligently in the latter stages of the crisis by keeping a lower profile. Much of their distress tended to become focused on Cliveden. The house itself seemed to stand for so much that had gone wrong for the Astors. Bronwen had the mansion and Spring Cottage exorcised, but for some members of the family the place had acquired an ineradicable aura.

CHAPTER 15

'The cloak of inherited attitudes falls away'

In 1963, at precisely the time when the name Astor was daily appearing in the headlines and members of the family were feeling acutely embarrassed by the publicity, they were taken aback to discover that a book about themselves had suddenly appeared in the shops. It presented the world with a detailed insight into life at Cliveden since the thirties and the relationships between its inhabitants. The new revelation was not by a sensation-seeking journalist nor by an academic who had been remarkably lucky with his publication date. In either case the Astors could have distanced themselves from the work. What made any reaction to *Tribal Feeling* so difficult was that it was written by one of themselves.

Michael Astor, the third son of Waldorf and Nancy, had become the most detached member of the family. He was living in London with his second wife, devoted much of his time to painting and had made for himself a Bohemian, dilettante style of life. His attitude to the family was ambivalent. He had not changed those habits relating to sex, drink, smoking and 'dubious' company that his parents had disapproved of, yet he had been reconciled to his father during Waldorf's last years. He had distanced himself or become distanced from his brothers but always remained on affectionate terms with his sister, Wissie. Throughout their early years Michael and Jakie had been virtually inseparable, but now this relationship, too, had deteriorated. Jakie felt, or Michael believed he felt, that his emancipated lifestyle was something of a pose, a kind of pseudo-intellectualism masking an adolescent defiance of convention. Yet, despite all this, it was Michael who was, in some ways, the most protective of the family name. From time to time, when would-be biographers had appeared wanting to write 'the Astor story', he had strongly advised against their being given any help by the family. He believed (in some cases correctly) that writers looking from outside would trivialize or sensationalize, and that anyway they could never really understand the Astor phenomenon. It was partly to sort out his own jumbled thoughts that Michael decided to write his autobiography.

When he embarked on *Tribal Feeling* it was probably with no intention of publication. He simply needed to express his own feelings and get them out of his system. However, when the manuscript was complete, he felt, justifiably, rather proud of it. He offered it to a publisher who eagerly accepted it and the book appeared in the shops in 1963. It was honest and, though written with affection, it catalogued what Michael felt had been the shortcomings in his and his brothers' upbringing. He explained to the world how hard it had been to grow up in the shadow of great parents and the even deeper shadow of Astordom; how difficult and yet how necessary it had been to withdraw from that penumbra and find the light and space to grow. All young men, he concluded, need to rebel.

> If later, as their inner lives begin to grow, they come to see that what they dislike is only the veneer – the postures in living – rather than the true expressions of life, then at last they begin to live. The cloak of inherited attitudes falls away, and they can respect the memory of their forbears without experiencing any need either childishly to venerate their personalities or pathetically to imitate their performances.[1]

The unheralded appearance of *Tribal Feeling* shook the family. In retrospect David Astor believes that the autobiography was basically a *cri du coeur*, a plea for understanding, an attempt to bridge the gaps that had grown between Michael and his siblings. If that was its author's intention, it singularly failed. Jakie was particularly incensed by the book and told his brother that anyone with an ounce of tribal feeling could not have written it. As for the head of the family, he had already had a disagreement with Michael over whether or not some of Waldorf's letters should be destroyed. Now Bill, doubtless concerned for his mother, was not at all happy about *Tribal Feeling*. This lowered still further the temperature of the brothers' relationship. Michael genuinely found this difficult to understand. 'I had the impression', he wrote in May 1964, 'that you carried a feeling of deep injury. And I wondered what it was about. About my book? Or about father's letters? Or did you think I could have done more for you last summer?'[2]

Michael seems to have seriously wanted to build bridges. In the aftermath of the 1963 scandal, he insisted that since the name of Astor was not particularly popular at the moment the brothers ought to pull together. Nothing seems to have come of it. Michael was soon complaining that, on matters of common concern, Bill and David made decisions without consulting him. If this was the case it was largely because Michael had kept himself at a distance for so many years that his brothers had got into the habit of making their own arrangements. As is the way with family squabbles, little things easily came to assume importance and could lead to angry exchanges of letters. One such storm in a teacup was over which brothers should have priority in planning holidays on Jura. The end result was that Michael continued to go his own way.

In affairs of the heart he was as impetuous and almost as unfortunate as his eldest brother. In 1957 he obtained a divorce from his first wife in order to marry Pandora Clifford Jones. He and Barbara had four children aged between five and fourteen and the proceedings were harrowing. They were arranged by lawyers on the basis of a fictitious technicality, as Michael later described: 'I confessed to an adultery I had not committed, with a lady whose name I never discovered, and whose charms were not apparent to me the first and only time we met.'[3] He was in the dangerous forties, his marriage seemed to have gone stale and he was looking for a fresher, more exciting, experience. He did not discover it with Pandora – or, if he did, it did not last very long. Within a few years his quest had begun again. One day, Judy Innes, a *Daily Mail* journalist in her mid-twenties, received a telephone call at her office. It was Michael Astor. He had heard about her through a mutual friend and wanted to meet her. Would she have lunch with him? With mixed feelings, she agreed. Her responses were even more confused when she arrived at the fashionable restaurant decided on for the meeting. When she asked for Mr Astor's table, the head waiter (acting under instructions) looked nonplussed. Judy was left, red-faced, looking around the room for her host. Only after Michael had had a good look at her did he come to her rescue. That did not look like an auspicious start to a relationship, but Michael and Judy were subsequently married. They had a daughter and an adopted son, and in the bosom of this new family Michael found the happiness that had eluded him for so many years.

Yet, apart from his home life, he was still unable to find anything which fully utilized his talents and brought him complete satisfaction. There was always something *more* – the Grail that eluded him no matter how many different paths he explored in his quest for it. He wrote another book, a novel called *Brand*, and he continued with his painting. He was, for a few years, a member of the Arts Council and in 1978 he joined the executive of the National Trust. He enjoyed everything that he did by the simple expedient of doing very little that he did not enjoy. He was a witty and charming host and he had a very wide circle of devoted friends. Yet he never settled to make his mark in any one area of life. In his last years he observed the public recognition achieved by Bill, David and Jakie and he felt something of a failure. His brothers were easily identified with specific things – newspapers, horses, refugees. David was respected throughout the world as an outspoken commentator and as a supporter of important causes. Jakie had been a steward of the Jockey Club and was a member of the Horseracing Betting Levy Board. He had served the farming community as a member of the Agricultural

Research Council and as spokesman on the National Economic Development Council. These activities had brought him a knighthood in 1978. It seemed to Michael that, by comparison, he had nothing to show for his life.

That was not a view shared by others. In 1980 Michael died of cancer at the age of sixty-four. When his memorial service was held, St James's, Piccadilly, was packed with people from many walks of life and several paid tribute to the ways in which this renegade Astor had helped them. Perhaps it was in being a renegade that he had achieved his real success. Family history had shown that it was a difficult thing to break away from Astordom and establish an independent identity. Michael had done it.

If the early sixties were traumatic years for the Cliveden Astors, they were catastrophic for their Hever cousins. In 1962 John and Violet received a terrible shock. Section 28 of the Finance Act extended liability for British estate duty to property owned overseas by British subjects domiciled in the UK at the time of death. The provision was meant to close a loophole in the existing law and stop wealthy men salting away assets beyond the reach of the Inland Revenue. The Hever Astors did not come into this category but they were caught fair and square by the new legislation. William Waldorf had created settlements from his American real estate in favour of his grandchildren. Waldorf's children had come into their inheritance on his death, but as John and Pauline were income beneficiaries for life it was deemed that their estates would be liable for duty at the rate of 80 per cent if they died in Britain.

When the full implications of this came home, the wound was sharp and deep. The funds in question had been accumulated by an American, in America, and were still being managed by American trustees. Moreover, under US law there was no way of escaping liability. The terms of the trust could not be altered. John and Pauline could not renounce their life interest, nor could the property be sold and the capital be repatriated. What made it even harder to bear was that this legislation had been brought in by a *Conservative* government – and one led by Harold Macmillan, a close friend of the family.

Anxiously, the Astors considered all the possibilities. They came down to two. Either future generations would be deprived of the bulk of their inheritance or John and Pauline would have to emigrate. Within three months, three elderly people were hustled out of the land of their birth. Pauline, at eighty-two, moved to the Channel Islands, where she acquired a small house and devoted the remainder of her life to creating, from scratch, another superb garden. John was seventy-six and his wife was already in poor health. They left for the South of France. Among the hurried and emotional farewells one did *not* take place. When Violet went to call on her dear friend Dorothy Macmillan, the Prime Minister's wife, John did not accompany her. They settled quickly into the life of a village near Cannes. John had his painting and his yacht, and friends from Britain often came to stay. But it was difficult to adjust to a new scale of life, to be suddenly confronted with the sort of restrictions that the less privileged have to live with – such as not having several acres in which to exercise the dogs and having to be careful not to allow them to stray on to the road.

There was something very symbolic about the enforced exile of this most English of all the Astors. Society was changing, and changing more rapidly than ever before. There was still, and always would be, a place for people of wealth. Wealth still carried, and always would carry, special privileges. But it was now made increasingly difficult for the enjoyment of wealth to be based on hereditary and class factors. Meritocracy was replacing aristocracy. Society was becoming more open. The possession of an ancient name and an impeccable pedigree counted for less where there were new and more glamorous paths to fame and fortune – television, sport, pop music, wheeling and dealing. Nor was it just that the ramparts of ancient ways were being attacked from outside. The rising generation of Astors were young men and women with modern attitudes, new ideas – about work, equality, social issues. One by one the representatives of the passing order left the stage, and their places were taken by actors and actresses who played their roles – and interpreted the drama – very differently.

Nancy Astor died on 18 April 1964. Perhaps the kindest way of describing her in her last years is to say that her body remained stronger and healthier than her mind. Her prejudices and eccentricities became more pronounced with the passing of time. Her family dutifully and affectionately provided for her. She visited them and stayed with them. Yet she preferred the company of her Langhorne niece Nancy Lancaster, and made a part-time home with her in the Lancaster house, Haseley Court, Oxfordshire. Her most frequent visitor was Bobbie, and she persisted in her conviction that she and her eldest son were quite distinct from the Astors. In January 1960 she wrote to her niece: 'Don't talk to me about the Astor boys ... I feel very strongly about them, but I can't say it before Miss Jones [her secretary].' And in another letter: 'In spite of my six children, I feel a stranger in a strange land.'[4]

She was frequently a trial to her children but adored her grandchildren and was adored by them. Her irreverence created for her an instant bond with young people. The present Viscount Astor recalls an incident when his father, Bill, had arranged a little tribute for her at Cliveden. He had new gates installed to the vegetable garden featuring Waldorf and Nancy's monograms. The staff was duly called together for the ceremonial opening and Bill made a little speech. Then Nancy pointed to one of the gardeners. 'Have you ever seen me in the vegetable garden?' she demanded. 'No, M'lady,' came the answer. 'And you,' pointing to another, 'have you ever seen me in the vegetable garden?' 'No, M'lady.' 'Or you? Or you?' She went down the row, eliciting the same response from everyone. Then she turned triumphantly to her son. 'So what a silly idea to put my name on the gate!'

When life peerages were introduced in 1959 she nursed the hope of at last getting back to Westminster. She had been the first woman in the Commons and she felt it would have been appropriate for her to have taken her place as the first lady peeress in the upper chamber. She was therefore very disappointed that Harold Macmillan did not recommend her for one of the new honours. By the time of the Profumo affair her mind was wandering. Despite the efforts of the family, in the various houses where she stayed, to keep the news from her, she did, at last, see a newspaper and insisted on being driven to Cliveden immediately. Fortunately, by the time she arrived she had forgotten the purpose of her journey. Bobbie remained a source of anxiety to her to the very end. In 1964, he took an overdose of pills and almost succeeded in ending his life. The family agreed to let his mother go to him but told her that her son had suffered a heart attack. She came away from his bedside very subdued and it may well be that she guessed the truth. Her own death came only a few weeks later. In accordance with her own and Waldorf's wishes, she was cremated, her ashes mingled with her husband's and interred in the chapel at Cliveden.

Bobbie did not long survive his mother. His bouts of depression became more frequent and when he was depressed he drank. For much of the time David took him under his wing and remained the member of the family who most easily related to him. To the others Bobbie was, by turns, a charming companion and a nuisance. Jakie commented that the pleasure of Bobbie's company palled when he had had to put him to bed for the third time. Though he lived quietly in his own house with a succession of male companions, the family never knew when he might 'break out' and need rescuing – as, for example, on an occasion in August 1963. He went drinking in Deal and Sandwich and made himself fairly offensive to a number of people. At last a friend was summoned who collected him and called a doctor to him. But Bobbie refused to have his freedom curtailed and, though far from sober, insisted on driving himself to London. His mother's death removed his only real reason for living. A couple of years afterwards he made another, and this time successful, attempt to end his unhappy life. Even then the family did not escape immediately from the repercussions of Bobbie's lifestyle. One of his friends threatened to make 'revelations' which would, he claimed, further embarrass the Astors. Only when Jakie got tough with the blackmailer was this menace disposed of.

Lady Violet Astor lived less than three years in her new environment. Leaving Hever had been an enormous wrench. Her life in Kent had involved so many responsibilities and brought her so many friends that giving it up was like losing a large part of herself. John's retirement from political life had been a signal for her to take it up, and from 1946 to 1951 she had been a Tory member of Kent County Council. Her involvement with the St John's Ambulance Brigade, the Kent Association of Youth Clubs and several other charities had continued until the very eve of her departure from Britain. Like her husband, she threw herself energetically into the life of Pégomas but it was not the same. She died in January 1965 and her body was brought back to Hever for burial.

John survived his wife by six and a half years. He, too, did not find the transition to France in his seventies an easy one; but he had overcome past handicaps and difficulties and was not going to be defeated by this setback. He threw himself into the life of Pégomas. The local boule championship was held in his garden. And he converted outbuildings into holiday homes so that doctors and nurses from the Middlesex could come out for holidays. Thus this quintessential Englishman lived the last nine years of his life under a foreign sun but managed to retain in exile something of the seigneurial air that he had so effortlessly exuded at Hever.

In America it was not until July 1992 that another living link with the past snapped. That was when Jack Astor died in Miami. It was eighty years since his father had gone down with the *Titanic*, with such disastrous results for the dynasty. Jack left a son and a grandson. Thus, ironically, it is only through the disowned, disinherited, posthumous son of Colonel Jack that the Astor line has been maintained in the USA.

After the Profumo affair Bill and Bronwen tried to put the pieces of their public life back together. They eventually had two daughters and Bill had his work. Judging by his enormous quantity of correspondence, it is clear, in fact, that his work was never interrupted. The refugee problem did not stop growing because a British minister got himself into difficulties and, as long as there was a problem, Bill remained active. In 1964 he addressed himself to the plight of Tibetan refugees in India and this led to the setting up of the Institute of Tibetan Studies at London University's School of Oriental and African Studies. In the same year he chaired a meeting to set up the Central African Relief Committee.

He was even more active in the House of Lords than before. He spoke forcefully on the Police Bill in 1964. Doubtless, he had vividly in his mind the way Stephen Ward had been persecuted, when he called for higher standards among police officers and deplored the fact that no university graduates had been attracted to the force since the war. In the following year he was demanding similar quality improvements in the treatment of juvenile offenders. What was needed, he insisted, was not special courts but better judges.

> As Christians, we owe to children and young people the very best. If we believe what we continually say, our Judges and Magistrates are the fairest and wisest, and our Courts the most humane imaginable, why do we increasingly propose to remove the young from their jurisdiction?[5]

His arguments and his passion reveal that he was now reaching the height of his powers – powers doubtless honed by his own harrowing experiences. His speeches and memoranda reveal a new depth of compassion and a new urgency in his demands for justice. Early in 1966 he was supporting the Abortion Bill because he wanted to see an end to back-street practitioners and the situation in which women's lives and futures were wholly in the hands of men. He proposed sweeping reforms to gambling legislation, including proposals to close down seedy casinos and to establish lotteries and football pools for the benefit of charities and medical research. And, of course, his work for refugees worldwide continued unabated. His son recalled that he was the only boy in his school who could return for the autumn term to report that a large part of his summer holiday had been spent in Austria – listening to opera and visiting refugee camps.

But Bill's letters were increasingly scattered with apologies for not being able to attend meetings: 'these damned doctors have put me into bed again for the moment, which is a great nuisance.'[6] His heart condition caused frequent interruptions to his schedule. Yet the end, when it came, was sudden. Bill died in the Bahamas on 7 March 1966, at the age of fifty-eight. Those closest to him believe that it was the loss of friends at the time of the Profumo affair which put the final pressure on his already overstrained heart. A few months later St Margaret's, Westminster, was packed to capacity for his memorial service. One cannot help wondering how many members of the congregation were driven thither by a guilty conscience.

It was not only certain Astor lives that were coming to an end. The financial position of *The Times* and the *Observer* was worsening year by year. By the mid-1960s it was clear that limited-circulation papers could only survive with the backing of large corporations. For a while David and Gavin explored the possibility of forming a consortium with the *Guardian* proprietors, which they hoped would bring the three quality newspapers under one roof, rationalize costs and enable *The Times*, the *Observer* and the *Guardian* to maintain traditional standards. But these negotiations came to nothing.

In 1963 Gavin acquired the last 10 per cent of the shares still held by the

Walter family. For the first time the Astors had total ownership of *The Times*, though John Walter (ninety-three) and Lord Astor (seventy-seven) both remained joint chief proprietors with Gavin. The older men, and John Astor particularly, found it very difficult to relinquish their connection with a great British institution which they had done so much to build up and, as we have seen, their influence was not always positive. Gavin was unable to modernize the newspaper as he would have wished and his reign was destined to be as brief as theirs had been long. In 1967 the newspaper was sold to Roy Thomson, who already owned the *Sunday Times*. The two papers were brought together under a new company, Times Newspapers Ltd, of which Gavin was honorary life president with a 15 per cent stake in the equity. So matters remained until 1981 when Rupert Murdoch acquired the company. Gavin then relinquished his life presidency in return for a seat on the board of Times Newspapers Holdings Ltd.

The end was in sight for David's *Observer* also. He clung on tenaciously for another ten years. The paper was in his blood in a way that was not true of Gavin and *The Times*. He baled it out with money from the family trust, thus becoming, in effect, major shareholder as well as editor. He and his staff worked hard to maintain the quality and independence of the paper's content. The *Observer* still found giants to fight and, though forced to make concessions to popular taste, it kept its sword sharp. But inflation took its toll of circulation figures and advertising revenue, while union power stood in the way of real economies. In 1975 David resigned as editor and will surely go down in newspaper history as one of the finest upholders of the tradition of independent journalism. In 1976 the *Observer* was sold, though the building in which it was produced remained in the ownership of the Astor Family Trust.

Waldorf, John and Bill had, each in his own way, gone to great lengths to preserve as much property and wealth as possible on both sides of the Atlantic so that the next generation of Astors could continue to live in luxury. In the end, their sacrifices achieved little. Bill's relationship with the National Trust was far from being a happy one. From time to time he toyed with the idea of giving up Cliveden and going to live in Ireland (where he kept some of his horses) for tax reasons. His early death prevented him putting this into effect and his estate was burdened with heavy death duties. His heir, William, the fourth Viscount, was only fourteen at the time of his father's death so, for the next seven years, all decisions were taken by the boy's trustees. William was desolate when they came to the conclusion that the tenancy of Cliveden must be given up. The Trust had to look for another tenant and the family urged them to bear in mind Waldorf's wish that the house should be used in some way to foster Anglo-American friendship. It seemed, therefore, an ideal solution when Cliveden was taken over, as a study centre, by Stanford University. For over twenty years Bill had managed the family's New York investments, and managed them very successfully. None of his brothers had his knowledge or shared his interest in America. They decided to liquidate their Manhattan interests. Between 1966 and 1972 most of the family's remaining real estate was sold off. Unfortunately, during these years US property values were just about at their lowest. Had the Cliveden Astors held on to their investments until the boom years of the eighties they would have seen the values multiply twenty or thirty times over.

When John and Vi left Hever, Gavin and his wife, Irene, moved in. The castle now embarked on its final phase as a family home. The new residents, consciously or unconsciously, modelled their lives on those of Lord and Lady Astor. Gavin, as we have seen, maintained his link with *The Times* as long as possible. He was prominent in the affairs of the Commonwealth Press Union and was elected president in 1971. Like his father, he held many directorships and served on the committees of several charities and voluntary bodies. He never stood for Parliament but he was a leading figure in county life and was Lord Lieutenant of Kent from 1972 to 1982. Irene was the youngest daughter of Earl Haig, the First World War commander-in-chief. Her father's second claim to fame, after his wartime generalship, was the founding of the Royal British Legion, and Irene associated herself very closely with his work, helping to run the women's section of the organization. She devoted many years of service to the British Red Cross and, from 1949 to 1980, was chairman of the League of Friends of Middlesex Hospital, a cause dear to her father-in-law's heart. Among her many other charitable activities she was vice-president of the Royal National Institute for the Blind.

Hever thus continued to be the centre from which the Astors served both locally and nationally in a wide variety of capacities. The new owners had five children and they found the old buildings and magnificent grounds as enchanting as their father and uncles had done. But Hever was not, nor could it be, the same. Gavin fought a running battle to cut costs and make the estate pay for at least some of its upkeep. The 'village' was turned into separate units which could be available for staff or let for income. The castle, which had only ever had one bedroom, was now converted to provide accommodation for the whole family. And, like so many stately-home owners, the Astors in 1963 opened their doors to the public. The castle did not happily lend itself to being both a home *and* a showpiece. At the beginning of every tourist season, for example, Irene was to be seen hurrying through upstairs corridors with armfuls of clothes, so that they could be stored in cupboards and the principal bedroom be left tidy for visitors. Yet the family agreed that sacrifices should be made in order to preserve Hever for future generations. It was therefore a particularly cruel blow when, almost ten years to the day after the 1958 storms, floodwater struck again.

The defences constructed after the previous devastation had been calculated to withstand a river flow of 3,300 cubic feet per second. On 15 September 1968 the storms which swept across Kent swelled the Eden until its waters were rushing past Hever at 7,000 cubic feet per second. Torrential rain fell for sixteen hours and resulted in the worst floods in recorded history. Once again, the buildings, 90 per cent of whose area is at ground-floor level, were inundated, this time to a depth of four and a half feet, with water, silt, fuel oil and sewage. All the furniture and furnishings had to be taken out. Some were restorable but much, including priceless items from William Waldorf's collection, had to be destroyed on health grounds. Months were spent removing floorboards and panelling, repairing plaster, replacing miles of electrical and telephone wiring. Then several months had to pass before the building was dry enough to permit the slow, careful work of putting the house back together again. This time the clean-up and repair operations took four years, and though the cost of most of the work was covered by insurance the loss of income was serious and the emotional drain on the family considerable. Gavin and Irene might well have decided that this latest misfortune was their signal to quit. Instead, they decided to carry on. Over the next few years further facilities were added to make Hever still more attractive to the fee-paying public. Soon after reopening, the castle welcomed its one-millionth visitor.

Every stratagem was tried to make Hever commercially viable. It was hired to film companies, made available for business conferences, and used by advertising agencies. But the sad fact was that the Astors were hanging on by their finger-nails. In 1974, to avoid death duties, Gavin made Hever over to trustees on behalf of his eldest son, Johnnie. It was only staving off the inevitable. The days of Hever as a family home were numbered. By this time all the children were grown up. Johnnie, the eldest, served for five years with the Life Guards in Malaya, Hong Kong and Northern Ireland, before spending some time with a London estate agency in preparation for starting his own property company. Of the three girls Sarah was married in 1975, Bridget was working as a professional photographer and Louise was nursing. Philip, the youngest, also served in the Guards and later read for the Bar.

By 1982 Gavin and Irene had devoted a considerable portion of their lives to maintaining Hever as a going concern. Lord Astor was now in his sixty-fourth year and no longer felt inclined to continue the effort. Johnnie, his wife and their three daughters now lived in France, which was where most of Johnnie's business was. He had made it clear that he could see no way of making Hever commercially viable in anything like its existing form.

Accordingly, the trustees put the entire estate up for sale. In the following year most of it was acquired by a Yorkshire-based property company.

Just at the time when the Hever Astors were severing their last links with their ancestral home, Viscount Astor was staging a comeback at Cliveden. As William grew into manhood he retained a deep affection for the home in which he had been brought up. He wanted to do all he could to ensure that it did not become merely an empty museum; that something of its 'life' should be retained. The National Trust, also, hoped that someone could be found to occupy Cliveden and save them the costs of maintenance. When Stanford University gave up their tenancy William tried to interest the Getty museum in taking on the house as a European base and showplace. This would, at least, continue Cliveden's Anglo-American association. When nothing came of that option, he developed another idea that he had been turning over in his mind for some time.

William was now in his thirties, married with a young family and living in a charming house in Oxfordshire. He had his own investment consultancy and took very seriously his membership of the House of Lords. His wife, Annabel (granddaughter of the writer Enid Bagnold, and daughter of Pandora Clifford Jones, who was, at one time, married to Michael Astor), was a jewellery designer and had her own business. The entrepreneurial spirit thrived in the Astor household and William now applied it to Cliveden. His vision was for a top-quality, exclusive country hotel. The mansion could be converted for such a purpose with the minimum of internal alteration and would be able to offer its guests a genuine taste of the gracious lifestyle of a bygone age. It was a very similar idea to the one that had possessed William's great-grandfather when he built the Waldorf-Astoria. But that had been in the 1890s, when the Astors could finance ambitious, exuberant projects with ease. In the 1980s the family fortune was much slimmer and William had to look for commercial partners. Eventually, the Royal Crescent hotel company showed an interest and, in 1984, a new company, Cliveden Hotel Ltd, was formed. It acquired a lease and began the work of careful refurbishment which would, as far as possible, maintain the atmosphere of a family home.

1984 was also the year in which Gavin Astor died and his elder son, Johnnie, inherited the title Baron Astor of Hever. Soon afterwards he and his wife established their principal residence in Kent, not far from the original family home. Johnnie also inherited from his father and grandfather an interest in Astor history. He studied the lives of his ancestors, especially John Jacob I, with fascination. He has collected autographed letters by the great furrier and other Astor memorabilia. He has visited many of the sites associated with his great-great-great-great-grandfather. In August 1986, for example, he was invited to view the reconstruction of Fort Union, the American Fur

Company's most distant inland post, set up in North Dakota in 1829. It is Lord Astor of Hever who has been the principal link between the English family, Astoria and Walldorf. The time has passed when the Astors could make large and frequent donations to the municipalities in Oregon and Baden, but the connections and the interest still exist and a visit by Lord Astor is still considered a major event whether in the Rhine Valley or on the Pacific coast.

The family's political tradition has also been maintained. Gavin Astor's youngest brother, John, was Tory MP for Newbury from 1964 to 1974. In 1987 the electors of Plymouth once again had the opportunity to vote for an Astor. Michael's elder son, David, stood in the Drake division – as a Social Democrat. There are now no Astors in the House of Commons, but Viscount Astor is a vigorous member – and one of the younger members – of the upper chamber. He has for some years been a government spokesman, and after the 1992 election he became the Lords' representative of the national heritage department.

The Cliveden ghosts were finally laid in November 1991 when Bill Astor's widow, Bronwen, hired the hotel for the wedding of her elder daughter, Janet, to Charles, Earl of March. Most members of the family gathered to see the couple married in the chapel in the grounds and to enjoy a lavish reception which ended with dancing late into the night. Those who could remember agreed that it was 'just like old times'. Those who could not were impressed with the way the house and grounds seemed to preserve the feeling of a long-past way of life. Even Jakie, who attended the function reluctantly and admits that he was very apprehensive about what he might find, felt that he had stepped back over half a century, and he appreciated the way Cliveden had been not only preserved but also brought back to life. Viscount Astor was particularly happy to have the approval of the family, for his hotel is not just a commercial enterprise; it is a labour of love. It also enables him, as he freely admits, to have his cake and eat it. 'I can give parties there whenever I like,' he says, 'but I don't have to pay the enormous upkeep costs.' Those, of course, are met from the hundreds of wealthy guests who pass through Cliveden every year and are happy to pay between £200 and £500 a night to be cosseted in impressive luxury, to bathe in *the* swimming pool (redesigned since the time that Profumo, Ivanov and Keeler splashed about in it), to hold business conferences in the Churchill Boardroom in the new leisure complex, or just to walk or ride through the gardens and wooded grounds.

A couple of months before the wedding at Cliveden another Astor luxury hotel reopened for the benefit of an even deeper-pocketed clientele. On 10 September 1991 Jacqueline Astor Drexel (daughter of the semi-reclusive Jack) cut the tape across the gilded portals of New York's St Regis Hotel. Its owners, the ITT Corporation, had just spent $100 million on a three-year restoration designed to make it the last word in luxury just as it had been when Colonel Jack had built it. The famous King Cole bar was restored as a period piece, together with its well-known mural. So was the skylight ballroom where Manhattan society had danced before the First World War. Its bedrooms and suites (claimed as the most spacious hotel rooms in New York) are equipped not only with gilded plasterwork and Louis XV furniture, but also with the latest computer and fax facilities – an echo of Colonel Jack's original 'advanced' concept which placed a telephone in every room. Jackie's verdict was, 'My grandfather would have been proud of how well it was done.'

The Astors are still remembered for their buildings. That is why their story may appropriately be thought of as a 'Landscape with Millionaires'. It is not just those who can afford to stay at the world's finest hotels who come into contact with this story. Visitors to Newport, Rhode Island, are invited by the publicity brochure to call at Beechwood and 'Step back in time to the Gilded Age, when THE Mrs Astor ruled as Queen of American Society. Actors and actresses portray Mrs Astor's guests and servants in a spirited living history re-creation of life in Newport in 1891.' More sedate English travellers may visit Hever Castle, where the new owners have retained most of the furnishings and features to create a major tourist attraction. Businessmen can hire for conferences the Tudor 'village' with its 'unique blend of Tudor appearance and Edwardian comfort'.

But, for those with eyes to see, these spectacular buildings are not the only visual impacts that generations of Astors have made on the landscape. The development of Manhattan and the very existence of Astoria owe much to John Jacob I. His Astor Library survives as a municipal theatre. Waldorf gave Plymouth its new city centre. Vincent made his contributions to the New York cityscape. Temple Place and the Villa Sirena still stand as reminders of William Waldorf's romantic imagination.

Yet it is their interaction with the 'landscape' of history that makes the Astors such a remarkable dynasty. Through two centuries that saw the United States of America grow from a fringe of Atlantic coast settlements to the richest and most powerful nation on earth; that saw the ebb and flow of culture between the Old World and the new; that saw Europe export its best political ideas across the Atlantic and then have its freedom saved by the new champions of democracy – through these tumultuous, formative years the Astors have been at the heart of the life of both continents. Through their social contacts, their political activities and their newspapers they have exercised unique influence. And, of course, they have been profoundly influenced themselves by the passage of events. That is why to study the Astor story is to obtain a new focus on the last two centuries of human history.

For three days in June 1988 Walldorf, in Baden, was *en fête*. The focal point of the celebrations was the unveiling by Lord Astor of Hever of a bust of his distant ancestor, who had left the town 209 years before. John Jacob VIII encountered John Jacob I (in effigy). The wheel had come full circle. Then everyone – the citizens of Walldorf, the American Consul, visitors from Britain, the representatives of Astoria – went on to enjoy the displays, the concerts, the dancing, the feasting and the fireworks. It was quite a party.

The same could be said of the life and times of the Astors.

REPRINTED FROM

THE TIMES

Thursday May 5 1938

THE "CLIVEDEN SET"

A COMMUNIST FICTION

SOME FALSEHOODS AND THE FACTS

TO THE EDITOR OF THE TIMES

Sir,—The fiction that has been written recently about an imaginary group described as the "Cliveden Set" was better ignored so long as it was the monopoly of irresponsible journalism. But now that it has figured in debates of the House of Commons, and is being used as a weapon in the Communist campaign against the Government, I may perhaps be allowed to place a few facts before your readers.

For years my wife and I have entertained in the country members of all parties (including Communists), members of all faiths, of all countries, and of all interests. To link our week-ends with any particular clique is as absurd as is the allegation that those of us who desire to establish better relations with Germany or with Italy are pro-Nazis or pro-Fascists. Lady Astor and I are no more Fascists to-day than we were Communists a few years ago when we supported the trade agreement with the Soviet, nor do we sympathize to-day with Communism because of a desire to preserve good relationships with the Russian dictatorship.

The story that a group meets at Cliveden for week-ends, and not only intrigues in the interests of Fascism but is able to force its views on to the Cabinet, originated in the imagination of the editor of a "Red" publication, who last autumn stated that at a Cliveden week-end of October 23-24 Lord Halifax's visit to Germany was planned, and that this project drove Mr. Eden to threaten resignation.

The writer had subsequently to produce some pretty lame explanations on discovering that Mr. Eden himself had in fact been staying with us at this particular week-end. Had the writer taken the trouble (as I did subsequently) to learn the facts, he would have discovered that the Halifax visit had been settled by the Government *before* the week-end of October 23.

Imaginary accounts of the "Cliveden Set" have also appeared periodically in the Communist organ, the *Daily Worker*. And in March the Communist Party issued another version in a pamphlet in which it was stated that

> late in January a week-end party took place at Cliveden. Among the guests were, in addition to the Astors, Lord Lothian, &c., &c.

The pamphlet intimated that decisions were taken at this January party which led up to certain events in February and March. It even went so far as to state that the

> evidence is so strong that no intelligent person with a shred of political understanding could fail to be fully satisfied as to the back-door wire pulling of the Cliveden Set.

What are the facts? In January our house was closed, Lord Lothian was in India, and Lady Astor and I were in the United States, from which I returned in March. The "fateful week-end party" in January never took place at all.

These publications adopt the known methods of Communism of stirring up class war and spreading suspicion by stating that the so-called "Cliveden Set" consists of pro-Fascist politicians, peers, millionaires, international bankers, and representatives of "Big Businesses" plotting secretly against British democracy.

But the aim of Communism is even more sinister than the creation of internal class war. It has been exposed by the British Labour Party as being

> to organize an armed struggle for the overthrow of the international bourgeoisie and the establishment of an International Soviet Republic as a transition to the complete abolition of the Capitalist State.

The last thing which Communism desires is an appeasement between Britain and Italy or between Britain and Germany. Communists have therefore attacked and misrepresented anyone who aimed at replacing international suspicion, fear, and ill will, by a sense of good will and confidence.

The story of the "Cliveden Set" was produced at a time when a weak and disunited Opposition were trying to discredit the motives of a Prime Minister who was new to his office and to injure the reputation of a new Foreign Secretary. Lord Halifax has suffered because he was not at once recognized as the Lord Irwin who made a reputation as a peace-loving Viceroy or as the Mr. Edward Wood who was a progressive President of the Board of Education.

So it is that we find Left M.P.s and certain newspapers which support Popular Front combination against the Government elaborating the tales of Fascist plots and putting it over more or less innocent Liberal and Labour M.P.s and others. The whole conception of a "Cliveden Set" is a myth from beginning to end.

I am, &c.,

May 3. ASTOR

Printed by THE TIMES PUBLISHING COMPANY, Limited, Printing House Square, London, E.C.4, England. 3545

Notes

(Place of publication is London unless otherwise stated.)

CHAPTER 1

1 A. D. Howden Smith, *John Jacob Astor, Landlord of New York*, Philadelphia, 1929, pp. 22–3.

2 Information about the Astor brothers' London business is found in *The New Grove Dictionary of Music and Musicians*, I, pp. 662–3; *The New Grove Dictionary of Musical Instruments and Makers*, p. 96; L. G. Langwill, *Index of Instrument Makers*, Edinburgh, 1974, p. 6. The dates given by these authorities do not all agree. I have interpreted them as best I can.

3 *Scribner's Monthly*, II, no. 6, April 1876, p. 883.

4 Quoted in K. W. Porter, *John Jacob Astor, Businessman*, 2 vols, Cambridge, Mass., 1931, I, pp. 26–7.

5 L. Kleinfeld (ed.), *Astoria, or Anecdotes of an Enterprise Beyond the Rocky Mountains*, vol. XV of *The Complete Works of Washington Irving* (ed. R. D. Rust), Boston, 1976, p. 12.

6 Quoted in Porter, op. cit., I, p. 31.

7 *Dictionary of American Biography.*

8 Kleinfeld, op. cit., pp. 15–16.

CHAPTER 2

1 British Library, Manuscript Room, Add. MS 41636, fol. 1.

2 Quoted in K. W. Porter, *John Jacob Astor, Businessman*, 2 vols, Cambridge, Mass., 1931, I, p. 115.

3 R. Walters, *Albert Gallatin, Jeffersonian Financier and Diplomat*, New York, 1957, p. 219.

4 Quoted in Porter, op. cit., I, p. 387.

5 Ibid., pp. 138–9.

6 Ibid., pp. 633–4.

7 Quoted in ibid., pp. 420–1.

8 Quoted in L. Kleinfeld (ed.), *Astoria, or Anecdotes of an Enterprise Beyond the Rocky Mountains*, vol. XV of *The Complete Works of Washington Irving* (ed. R. D. Rust), Boston, 1976, p. 23.

CHAPTER 3

1 F. Bunsen, *A Memoir of Baron Bunsen*, 2 vols, 1868, I, pp. 27, 39.

2 Quoted in K. W. Porter, *John Jacob Astor, Businessman*, 2 vols, Cambridge, Mass., 1931, I, p. 320.

3 Ibid., II, p. 1057.

4 Library of Congress, Madison Papers, lviii, Gallatin to Madison, 19 April 1816.

5 H. Adams, *The Life of Albert Gallatin*, New York, 1943, pp. 487–9.

6 New York Historical Society, Gallatin Papers, J. J. Astor to A. Gallatin, 9 August 1813.

7 Count Gallatin (ed.), *A Great Peace Maker: The Diary of James Gallatin . . .*, New York, 1914, pp. 85–6.

8 New York Public Library, Monroe Papers, J. J. Astor to J. Monroe, 22 July 1814.

9 Quoted in Porter, op. cit., I, p. 337.

10 Ibid., II, p. 947.

11 Ibid., II, p. 962.

12 Ibid., II, p. 964.

13 Ibid., II, p. 967.

14 Quoted in L. Kleinfeld (ed.), *Astoria, or*

Anecdotes of an Enterprise Beyond the Rocky Mountains, vol. XV of *The Complete Works of Washington Irving* (ed. R. D. Rust), Boston, 1976, p. 35.

15 Ibid., p. 39.

16 Ibid., p. 47.

17 Ibid., pp. 33–4.

18 Quoted in Porter, op. cit., I, p. 342.

19 New York Historical Society, Gallatin Papers, J. J. Astor to A. Gallatin, 22 December 1814.

20 Quoted in Porter, op. cit., I, p. 242.

21 New York Historical Society, Gallatin Papers, J. J. Astor to A. Gallatin, 7 March 1827.

22 C. A. Bristed, *A Letter to the Hon. Horace Mann*, New York, 1850, p. 16.

23 Porter, op. cit., II, p. 1184, Gallatin to James Barbour, Secretary of War, 30 June 1826.

24 Gallatin, op. cit., p. 80.

25 New York Historical Society, Gallatin Papers, J. J. Astor to Hannah Gallatin, 2 August 1815.

26 Loc. cit., Astor Papers, W. B. Astor to J. A. Smith, 29 December 1815.

27 H. Zimmern, *Schopenhauer, His Life and Philosophy*, 1932, pp. 35–6.

28 Porter, op. cit., II, p. 969.

29 Adams, op. cit., p. 584.

Chapter 4

1 F. Bunsen, *A Memoir of Baron Bunsen*, 2 vols 1868, II, p. 274.

2 New York Historical Society, Astor Papers, W. B. Astor to J. A. Smith, 19 January and 21 March 1816.

3 Loc. cit., Gallatin Papers, J. J. Astor to A. Gallatin, 3 March 1817.

4 G. S. Hellman (ed.), *The Letters of Henry Brevoort to Washington Irving*, 2 vols, 1915, II, p. 43.

5 New York Historical Society, William Kelby, 'Notes on the Astor Family' – affidavit sworn 10 November 1818.

6 Loc. cit., Gallatin Papers, J. J. Astor to A. Gallatin, 14 March 1818.

7 Archive of Lord Astor of Hever, John Jacob to William Backhouse, n.d., (1818).

8 Loc. cit., John Jacob, 12 September 1818.

9 New York Historical Society, Gallatin Papers, J. J. Astor to A. Gallatin, 19 September 1819.

10 New York Public Library, Monroe Papers, J. J. Astor to James Monroe, 5 April 1820.

11 R. Walters, 'The James Gallatin Diary: A Fraud?', *American Historical Review*, July 1957, pp. 878–85.

12 Count Gallatin (ed.), *A Great Peace Maker: The Diary of James Gallatin*, New York, 1914, p. 52.

13 E. L. Didier (ed.), *The Life and Letters of Madame Bonaparte*, 1879, p. 61.

14 New York Historical Society, Gallatin Papers, J. J. Astor to A. Gallatin, 16 June 1817.

15 Loc. cit., J. J. Astor to A. Gallatin, 20 August 1821 and 2 December 1821.

16 Loc. cit., J. J. Astor to A. Gallatin, 9 September 1822.

17 H. Adams, *The Life of Albert Gallatin*, New York, 1943, p. 584.

18 Gallatin (ed.), op. cit., p. 229.

19 New York Historical Society, Gallatin Papers, J. J. Astor to A. Gallatin, 19 September 1819.

20 Didier, op. cit., p. 117.

21 New York Historical Society, Gallatin Papers, J. J. Astor to A. Gallatin, 18 October 1822.

22 Loc. cit., J. J. Astor to A. Gallatin, 9 January 1823.

23 Didier, op. cit., 1879, pp. 162–3.

24 K. W. Porter, *John Jacob Astor, Businessman,* 2 vols, Cambridge, Mass., 1931, II, pp. 1175–6.

25 Didier, op. cit., p. 188.

26 New York Historical Society, Astor Papers, J. J. Astor to L. Bradish, 28 December 1825.

27 J. D. Haeger, 'Business Strategy and Practice in the Early Republic: John Jacob Astor and the American Fur Trade', *Western Historical Quarterly*, XIX, no. 2, May 1988, p. 201.

28 Porter, op. cit., II, p. 776.

29 R. Baird, *Transplanted Flowers or Memoirs of Mrs Rumpff . . . and the Duchesse de Broglie*, Glasgow, 1839.

30 New York Historical Society, Gallatin

Papers, J. J. Astor to A. Gallatin, 17 March 1827.
31 Loc. cit., J. J. Astor to A. Gallatin, 30 November 1832.
32 Porter, op. cit., II, p. 1225, John Jacob to W. P. Hunt, 4 May 1834.
33 Ibid., p. 940.
34 Ibid., p. 1162.
35 L. Kleinfeld (ed.), *Astoria, or Anecdotes of an Enterprise Beyond the Rocky Mountains*, vol. XV of *The Complete Works of Washington Irving* (ed. R. D. Rust), Boston, 1976, p. 356.
36 H. M. Lydenberg, *The History of the New York Public Library,* New York, 1923, p. 3.
37 Ibid., p. 4.
38 Porter, op. cit., II, p. 1117.
39 Ibid., p. 1118.
40 *Illustrated London News*, 22 April 1848.
41 H. Mann, *A Few Thoughts for a Young Man*, Syracuse, New York, 1850, p. 60.
42 *New York Herald*, 5 April 1848.
43 C. A. Bristed, *A Letter to the Hon. Horace Mann*, New York, 1850, p. 9.

CHAPTER 5

1 F. Bunsen, *A Memoir of Baron Bunsen*, 2 vols, 1868, II, p. 382.
2 Ibid., p. 435.
3 New York Historical Society, Astor Papers, J. J. Astor III to S. Ward, 27 December 1840.
4 S. W. Sears (ed.), *The Civil War Papers of George B. McClellan*, New York, 1989, p. 608.
5 Archive of Lord Astor of Hever, John Jacob III to William Waldorf, 31 March 1865.
6 E. D. Lehr, *'King Lehr' and the Gilded Age*, Philadelphia, 1935, p. 57.
7 Ibid., pp. 11–12.
8 Ibid., p. 77.

CHAPTER 6

1 Archive of Lord Astor of Hever, Gavin Astor, a memorandum, 'The First of the British Astors'.
2 Ibid.
3 Archive of Lord Astor of Hever, Notes written by John Jacob Astor V.
4 Loc. cit., Gavin Astor, op. cit.
5 Ibid.
6 Library of Congress, Astor Papers, William Waldorf to Amy Richardson, 22 September 1904.
7 W. W. Astor, 'A Secret of Olympus', *Pall Mall Magazine*, December 1904, p. 447.
8 Archive of Lord Astor of Hever, Gavin Astor, op. cit.
9 J. C. Bossidy, *On the Aristocracy of Harvard.*
10 Archive of Lord Astor of Hever, Notes written by the Hon. Pauline Astor.
11 Loc. cit., Gavin Astor, op. cit.
12 Ibid.
13 Ibid.
14 Ibid.
15 Quoted in A. M. Gollin, *The Observer and J. L. Garvin 1908–1914*, 1960, pp. 301–2.
16 Henry James, 'A Passionate Pilgrim', in *The Tales of Henry James*, 1978, II, pp. 42–3.
17 Ibid.
18 Quoted in J. W. Robertson Scott, *The Life and Death of a Newspaper*, 1952, p. 376.
19 Ibid., pp. 378–9.
20 Ibid., pp. 379–80.
21 'Cliefden Lights and Shades', *Pall Mall Magazine*, XXI, May–August 1909, p. 517.
22 *Pall Mall Gazette*, 29 December 1892.
23 Archive of Lord Astor of Hever, Notes written by the Hon. Pauline Astor.
24 W. E. Cheal, *A Family Business*, n.d., p. 11.
25 Library of Congress, Astor Papers, William Waldorf to Amy Richardson, 11 January 1909.
26 Ibid.
27 Archive of Lord Astor of Hever, Notes written by the Hon. Pauline Astor.
28 Ibid.
29 Michael Astor, *Tribal Feeling*, 1963, pp. 17–18.
30 Archive of Lord Astor of Hever, Notes written by the Hon. Pauline Astor.
31 *Pall Mall Magazine*, XXII, September–December 1900, p. 530.
32 H. Avray Tipping, 'Hever Castle, Kent', *Country Life*, 19 October 1907, p. 560.
33 Robert Gathorne-Hardy (ed.), *Ottoline* –

the Early Memoirs of Lady Ottoline Morrell, 1963, p. 291.

34 Library of Congress, Astor Papers, William Waldorf to Amy Richardson, 13 June 1905.

35 Michael Astor, op. cit., p. 20.

36 New York Public Library, Astor Family Papers, 295, 13 November 1906.

37 Library of Congress, Astor Papers, William Waldorf to Amy Richardson, 18 June 1909.

CHAPTER 7

1 W. W. Astor, 'The Vengeance of Poseidon', *Pall Mall Magazine*, XL, January–June 1910, p. 5.

2 Michael Astor, *Tribal Feeling*, 1963, p. 47.

3 Reading University Library, Astor Papers, 1416/1/3/6, William Waldorf to Nancy, 14 July 1915.

4 Loc. cit., 1416/1/3/4, John to Nancy, n.d. (May 1916); 1416/1/3/18, Pauline to Nancy, 12 February 1916.

5 Library of Congress, Astor Papers, William Waldorf to Amy Richardson, 1 January 1908.

6 *Evening Standard*, 8 June 1929.

7 *Western Morning News*, 24 November 1911.

8 'Nationalism and Liberty', *The Round Table*, no. 17, December 1914, pp. 52, 69.

9 Archive of Lord Astor of Hever, Gavin Astor, a memorandum, 'The First of the British Astors'.

10 Library of Congress, Astor Papers, William Waldorf to Amy Richardson, 23 December 1909.

11 Waldorf to J. L. Garvin, 27 December 1912, quoted in A. M. Gollin, *The Observer and J. L. Garvin 1908–1914*, 1960, p. 364.

12 K. Garvin, *J. L. Garvin, A Memoir*, 1948, p. 58.

13 J. L. Garvin to Waldorf, 2 August 1911, quoted in Gollin, op. cit., pp. 341–2.

14 House of Lords Record Office, Bonar Law Papers, 24/2/8, Waldorf to Bonar Law, 14 November 1911.

15 Waldorf to J. L. Garvin, 12 November 1911, quoted in Gollin, op. cit., p. 361.

16 House of Lords Record Office, Bonar Law Papers, 26/4/9, 24 May 1912.

17 Cambridgeshire Record Office, Tharp Papers, R84/29, Lord Curzon to W. W. Astor, 11 July 1910.

18 *Dictionary of National Biography.*

19 Viscount Astor's Archive, Waldorf to an unnamed friend, n.d.

20 Loc. cit., William Waldorf to Waldorf, 6 March 1913 and 6 January 1913.

21 Waldorf to J. L. Garvin, n.d., quoted in Gollin, op. cit., pp. 417–18.

22 Gollin, op. cit., p. 427.

23 William Waldorf to J. L. Garvin, 28 March 1914, quoted in ibid., p. 424.

24 S. M. Alsop, *Lady Sackville, A Biography*, 1978, p. 196.

25 Ibid., pp. 189–96.

26 Reading University Library, Astor Papers, 1416/1/3/6, William Waldorf to Nancy, 14 August 1914.

27 William Waldorf to Waldorf, 1 January 1915, quoted in Stephen Koss, *The Rise and Fall of the Political Press in Britain*, 2 vols, 1984, II, p. 260.

28 Reading University Library, Astor Papers, 1416/1/3/6, William Waldorf to Nancy, 14 August 1914.

29 *Pall Mall Gazette*, 13 March 1914.

30 C. Addison, *Four and a Half Years*, 1934, I, p. 52.

31 West Devon Record Office, 94/113. Nancy Astor to J. J. Judge, 14 May 1914.

32 *Pall Mall Gazette*, 9 December 1915.

33 Archive of Lord Astor of Hever, Notes written by the Hon. Pauline Astor.

34 Loc. cit., W. W. Astor to the Management of the Walldorf Voluntary Fire Brigade, 2 December 1892.

35 Reading University Library, Astor Papers, 1066/1/17/A119, 2 March 1920.

36 Viscount Astor's Archive, Waldorf to J. L. Garvin, 15 December 1916.

37 House of Lords Record Office, Lloyd George Papers, F/83/1/6, 21 April 1917.

38 Viscount Astor's Archive, Waldorf to J. L. Garvin, 15 December 1916.

39 Reading University Library, Astor Papers, 1416/1/3/6. William Waldorf to Nancy, 7 January 1916.

40 Archive of Lord Astor of Hever, Notes written by John Jacob Astor v.
41 Reading University Library, Astor Papers, 1416/1/3/5, Violet to Nancy, July 1915.
42 Loc. cit., 1416.1.3.5, Violet to Nancy, 4 June 1917.
43 Loc. cit., 1416/1/3/4, John to Nancy, 13 April 1918, 5 May 1918.
44 Archive of Lord Astor of Hever, Priscilla Annesley to John Jacob Astor v, 20 October 1919.
45 Reading University Library, Astor Papers, 1416/1/3/4, John to Nancy, 18 February 1916; 1416/1/3/18, Pauline to Nancy, 12 February 1916.
46 Loc. cit., 1416/1/3/18, Pauline to Nancy, 12 February 1916.
47 Loc. cit., 1416/1/3/4, John to Nancy, 16 February and 1 March 1916.
48 Loc. cit., 1416/1/3/6. William Waldorf to Waldorf, 31 March 1916.
49 A. J. P. Taylor, *English History 1914–1945*, Oxford, 1965, p. 61.
50 Ibid., p. 67.
51 *Pall Mall Gazette*, 24 November 1916.
52 House of Lords Record Office, Bonar Law Papers, 82/1/18, 20 June 1917.
53 Loc. cit., Lloyd George Papers, F/83/1/24, n.d.
54 Loc. cit., F/83/1/4, 10 March 1917.
55 Loc. cit., F/83/1/18, 9 May 1918.
56 Loc. cit., F/83/1/19, n.d.
57 West Devon Record Office, 94/115, Nancy Astor to J. J. Judge, 16 September 1919.
58 House of Lords Record Office, Lloyd George Papers, G/141/3/6, 15 July 1936.
59 Addison, op. cit., I, p. 459.
60 *The Times*, 10 January 1918.
61 *Western Evening Herald*, 5 December 1919.
62 House of Lords Record Office, Lloyd George Papers, F/83/1/25, n.d.
63 West Devon Record Office, 94/114, Waldorf to J. J. Judge, 12 March 1919.
64 House of Lords Record Office, Lloyd George Papers, F/83/1/12, 5 March 1918.
65 Stephen Koss, op. cit., II, p. 313.
66 House of Lords Record Office, Lloyd George Papers, F/83/1/20, 15 May 1918.
67 Reading University Library, Astor Papers, 1416/1/3/6, William Waldorf to Nancy, 14 July 1919.
68 Archive of Lord Astor of Hever, Gavin Astor, op. cit.
69 Cambridgeshire Record Office, Tharp Papers, R84/29, Nancy Astor to Gerald Tharp, 25 October 1919.
70 West Devon Record Office, 94/115, Nancy Astor to J. J. Judge, n.d. (October 1919).

Chapter 8

1 E. D. Lehr, *'King Lehr' and the Gilded Age*, Philadelphia, 1935, p. 65.
2 Ibid., p. 73.
3 Ibid., p. 74.
4 *New York Herald*, 18 December 1896.
5 Archive of Lord Astor of Hever, report from an unknown newspaper dated 29 July 1899.
6 Lehr, op. cit., p. 149. A quotation from Harry Lehr's diary.
7 Ibid., pp. 149–50.
8 S. E. Morison, H. S. Commager and W. E. Leuchtenburg, *A Concise History of the American Republic*, Oxford, 1983, p. 487.
9 Lehr, op. cit., p. 71.

Chapter 9

1 Viscount Astor's Archive, Waldorf to Nancy, 18 September 1919.
2 House of Lords Record Office, Lloyd George Papers, F/2/7/12, n.d.
3 Loc. cit., F/2/7/2b, n.d.
4 Loc. cit., F/2/7/1, 14 August 1918.
5 Cambridgeshire Record Office, R/84/29, Nancy to Gerald Tharp, 25 October 1919; West Devon Record Office, 94/115, Nancy to J. J. Judge, n.d.
6 West Devon Record Office, 94/115, Nancy to J. J. Judge, n.d. Also ibid., 95/115, Nancy to J. J. Judge, n.d. (separate letter), and S. Koss, *The Rise and Fall of the Political Press in Britain*, 2 vols, 1984, II, p. 363. Some of these letters are undated but the reconstruction of their sequence has been possible from internal evidence.

7 West Devon Record Office, 94/114, Nancy to J. J. Judge, 17 October 1923.
8 House of Lords Record Office, Bonar Law Papers, 97/5/8, 6 July 1919.
9 Loc. cit., 101/3/117, 8 July 1919.
10 Michael Astor, *Tribal Feeling*, 1963, p. 48.
11 Bodleian Library, Oxford, Dawson Papers, 69 fols 67–86, n.d. (1922).
12 West Devon Record Office, 94/116, Waldorf to J. J. Judge, 21 March 1921.
13 Reading University Library, Astor Papers, 1066/1/710/S125, A. P. Hughes-Gibb to Waldorf, 25 November 1920.
14 Loc. cit., 1066/1/22/S32, Waldorf to Lord Curzon, 17 January 1921.
15 Loc. cit., 1066/1/20/S132, Waldorf to C. Addison, 3 March 1921; Waldorf to Lord Dawson, 4 March 1921.
16 Bodleian Library, Oxford, Curtis Papers, 12 fols 191–206, Lionel Curtis to Waldorf, 6 July 1938.
17 House of Lords Record Office, Strachey Papers, S/1/3/6. 18 February 1924.
18 Reading University Library, Astor Papers, 1066/1/13/S107, John to Waldorf, 23 December 1919; Waldorf to John, 30 December 1919.
19 House of Lords Record Office, Bonar Law Papers, 115/4/16, 29 October 1922.
20 J. J. Astor, 'The Future of *The Times*', *Empire Review*, 1923, p. 945.
21 Bodleian Library, Oxford, Dawson Papers, 69 fols 67–86, n.d. (1922).
22 Reading University Library, Astor Papers, 1066/1/20/S107, John to Waldorf, 29 January 1921.
23 *The Times* Archives, Bob Brand to John Astor, 17 November 1922.
24 West Devon Record Office, Judge Papers, 94/111, Nancy to J. J. Judge, 29 July 1914.
25 House of Lords Record Office, Lloyd George Papers, G/141/3/1, Waldorf to Lloyd George, 2 December 1934.
26 Nigel Nicolson (ed.), *Harold Nicolson's Diaries and Letters 1930–1939*, 1966, p. 326.
27 Reading University Library, Astor Papers, 1416/1/3/5, Violet to Nancy, n.d. (1938?).
28 *The Times* Archives, Notes by J. J. Astor, 1926.
29 Scottish Record Office, Lothian Papers, GD 40/17/240/243–4, Philip Kerr to J. L. Garvin, 24 October 1928.
30 West Devon Record Office, Judge Papers, 94/115, Nancy to J. J. Judge, 14 June 1922.
31 James Roose-Evans (ed.), *Darling Ma: Joyce Grenfell's Letters to her Mother 1932–1944*, 1988, pp. 10–11.
32 British Library, Manuscript Room, Add. MS 60656/80, 82, 85, Nancy to Lytton Strachey, 15 July 1926, 10 December 1926, 25 April 1928.
33 Nicolson (ed.), op. cit., p. 60.
34 Michael Holroyd, *Bernard Shaw*, vol. 3, *The Lure of Fantasy*, 1991, p. 233.
35 West Devon Record Office, Judge Papers, 94/118, *Western Independent*, ? August 1931.
36 Loc. cit., Astor Papers, 186/19/16, Nancy speech to Rotary Club, 26 October 1955.
37 Loc. cit., Judge Papers, 94/118, *Western Independent*, ? August 1931.
38 Loc. cit., 94/114, David to J. J. Judge, n.d. (August 1931).
39 Loc. cit., 94/118, *Western Independent*, ? August 1931.
40 Reading University Library, Astor Papers, 1066/1/85A, Waldorf to A. M. Kindersley, 6 December 1932.
41 Loc. cit., 1066/1/85A, Report in the *Yorkshire Evening News*, 3 December 1932.
42 *Western Independent*, 22 October 1937.
43 Reading University Library, Astor Papers, 1066/1/712, Draft pamphlet, 1931.
44 Waldorf Astor, *Progressive Reform*, a pamphlet published by the Temperance Council of the Christian Churches of England and Wales, 1927.
45 Ibid.

Chapter 10

1 Viscount Astor's Archive, Waldorf to Nancy, 3 August 1913.
2 Reading University Library, Astor Papers, 1066/1/13/A119, Waldorf to Charles A. Peabody, 10 December 1919.

3 Michael Astor, *Tribal Feeling*, 1963, pp. 76–7.
4 Ibid., p. 79.
5 J. Roose-Evans (ed.), *Darling Ma: Joyce Grenfell's Letters to her Mother 1932–1944*, 1988, pp. 252, 270.
6 Viscount Astor's Archive, Waldorf to Nancy, n.d.
7 British Library, Manuscript Room, Strachey Papers, Add. MS 60656, 70–2, Nancy to Lytton Strachey, 22 January 1925.
8 House of Lords Record Office, Beaverbrook Papers, BBK/C/15, Various.
9 Roose-Evans (ed.), op. cit., p. 42.
10 Reading University Library, Astor Papers, 1416/1/3/11, Bobbie to Nancy, n.d.
11 Viscount Astor's Archive, Hugh Molson to Bill, 16 September 1945.
12 Loc. cit., speech given by Bill Astor, n.d.
13 Loc. cit., Bill to Mary Stevens Baird, 9 October 1934.
14 Loc. cit., 'Sir Samuel Hoare', an appreciation by Bill Astor.
15 Loc. cit., Bill to Mary Stevens Baird, 9 October 1935.
16 West Devon Record Office, Judge Papers, 94/114. David to J. J. Judge, n.d.
17 Ibid.
18 *Western Morning News*, 18 December 1933.
19 Viscount Astor's Archive, Bill to Mary Stevens Baird, n.d. (1933).
20 West Devon Record Office, Judge Papers, 94/120, David to J. J. Judge, n.d. (1933).
21 M. Astor, op. cit., p. 119.
22 Ibid., pp. 121–2.
23 Ibid., p. 131.
24 Reading University Library, Astor Papers, 1066/1/9/4, Waldorf to Nancy, 28 September 1931.
25 Viscount Astor's Archive, Bill to Lord Lytton, 16 December and 12 December 1932.
26 West Devon Record Office, Judge Papers, 94/114, J. J. Judge to W. Welling, 23 December 1935.
27 Quoted in Christopher Sykes, *Nancy, The Life of Lady Astor*, 1972, p. 388.
28 Viscount Astor's Archive, Waldorf to J. L. Garvin, 26 April 1936.
29 Loc. cit., Waldorf to J. L. Garvin, 18 May 1936.
30 Loc. cit., J. L. Garvin to Waldorf, 21 May 1936.
31 Scottish Record Office, Lothian Papers, GD 40/17/398/320, Waldorf to Philip Kerr, 6 June 1940.
32 Viscount Astor's Archive, Bill to Lindsay Bradford, 14 October 1938.
33 Roose-Evans (ed.), op. cit., pp. 47–8.
34 Reading University Library, Astor Papers, 1416/1/4/58/14, Philip Kerr to Nancy, 5 January 1939.
35 Loc. cit., Astor Papers, 1066/669–70, April 1938.
36 Bodleian Library, Oxford, Curtis Papers, 12 fol. 177, Lionel Curtis to Philip Kerr, 24 June 1938.
37 Reading University Library, Astor Papers, 1416/1/4/56, Nancy to Philip Kerr, 24 September 1937.
38 Loc. cit., 1416/1/4/56, Nancy to Philip Kerr, 27 November 1937.
39 Viscount Astor's Archive, Eleanor Roosevelt to Nancy, 27 May 1942.
40 Nigel Nicolson (ed.), *Harold Nicolson's Diaries and Letters 1930–1939*, 1966, p. 396.
41 S. Koss, *The Rise and Fall of the Political Press in Britain*, 2 vols, 1984, II, p. 548.
42 Scottish Record Office, Lothian Papers, GD 40/17/398/230, Waldorf to Philip Kerr, 6 June 1940.
43 Koss, op. cit., II, p. 480.
44 *The Times* Archives, T. Panton to J. J. Astor, 4 April 1939.
45 Viscount Astor's Archive, 'Memorandum by Mr W. W. Astor, M.P., on the Situation in Germany and Czechoslovakia'.
46 Loc. cit., Bill to Mary Stevens Baird, 28 February 1939.
47 Loc. cit., Bill to Mary Stevens Baird, n.d. (April 1939).
48 Reading University Library, Astor Papers, 1416/1/4/58/14, Nancy to Philip Kerr, 23 November 1939.

49 Loc. cit., 1416/1/4/56, Waldorf to Philip Kerr, 29 September 1938.
50 Scottish Record Office, Lothian Papers, GD 40/17/398/230, Waldorf to Philip Kerr, 6 June 1940.
51 Roose-Evans (ed.), op. cit., pp. 247–8.

CHAPTER 11

1 A. T. Vanderbilt II, *Fortune's Children: The Fall of the House of Vanderbilt*, New York, 1989, p. 311.
2 F. Freidel, *Franklin D. Roosevelt, A Rendezvous with Destiny*, Boston, 1990, p. 23.
3 S. E. Morison, H. S. Commager and W. E. Leuchtenburg, *A Concise History of the American Republic*, Oxford, 1983, pp. 505–6.
4 Freidel, op. cit., p. 21.
5 Morison, Commager and Leuchtenburg, op. cit., p. 527.
6 E. D. Lehr, *'King Lehr' and the Gilded Age*, Philadelphia, 1935, pp. 250–1.
7 E. Roosevelt (ed.), *Franklin D. Roosevelt, His Personal Letters*, New York, 1950, II, pp. 388, 437–8.
8 *New York Evening Post*, 1 April 1931.
9 Roosevelt (ed.), op. cit., II, p. 394.
10 New York Public Library, Vincent Astor Papers, F. D. Roosevelt to Vincent Astor, 23 August 1932.
11 Ibid., Vincent Astor to F. D. Roosevelt, 3 August 1933.
12 Ibid., F. D. Roosevelt to Vincent Astor, 4 August 1933.
13 Freidel, op. cit., p. 202.
14 New York Public Library, Vincent Astor Papers, n.d.
15 Information in this section is based on J. M. Dorwert, 'The Roosevelt–Astor Espionage Ring', *New York History*, July 1981, pp. 307–22.

CHAPTER 12

1 J. R. M. Butler, *Lord Lothian (Philip Kerr) 1882–1940*, 1960, p. 234.
2 Reading University Library, Astor Papers, 1416/1/4/58/14, Philip Kerr to Nancy, 5 January 1939.
3 F. Freidel, *Franklin D. Roosevelt, A Rendezvous with Destiny*, Boston, 1990, pp. 312–13.
4 Reading University Library, Astor Papers, 1416/1/4/58/14, Philip Kerr to Nancy, 5 and 18 January 1939.
5 A. J. P. Taylor, *English History 1914–1945*, Oxford, 1965, p. 466.
6 Scottish Record Office, Lothian Papers, GD 40/17/398/230, Waldorf to Philip Kerr, 6 June 1940.
7 Viscount Astor's Archive, J. L. Garvin to Waldorf, 9 May 1940.
8 House of Lords Record Office, Lloyd George Papers, G/1/9/15, Waldorf to Lloyd George's secretary, 5 March 1943.
9 Reading University Library, Astor Papers, 1416/1/4/58/14, Philip Kerr to Nancy, 23 August 1939.
10 Loc. cit., Philip Kerr to Nancy, 18 September 1939.
11 Scottish Record Office, Lothian Papers, GD 40/17/398/216–17, Philip Kerr to Bill, 18 December 1939.
12 Reading University Library, Astor Papers, 1416/1/4/58/14, Philip Kerr to Nancy, 3 November 1939.
13 Ibid., Astor Papers, 1416/1/4/59/15, Nancy to Philip Kerr, 12 January 1940.
14 Scottish Record Office, Lothian Papers, GD 40/17/398/228–9, 235, Waldorf to Philip Kerr, 1 June and 26 July 1940; Reading University Library, Astor Papers, 1416/1/4/58/14, Philip Kerr to Nancy, 20 October 1939.
15 Bodleian Library, Oxford, Curtis MSS, 21 fol. 23, Lionel Curtis to Waldorf, 6 June 1940.
16 R. Cockett, *David Astor and the Observer*, 1991, p. 55.
17 Scottish Record Office, Lothian Papers, GD/40/17/398/214, David to Philip Kerr, 6 November 1939.
18 Cockett, op. cit., p. 63.
19 West Devon Record Office, Astor Papers, 186/21/12, Waldorf to Brendan Bracken, 30 June 1940.
20 Freidel, op. cit., p. 364.
21 J. Roose-Evans (ed.), *Darling Ma: Joyce Grenfell's Letters to her Mother 1932–1944*, 1988, p. 140.
22 Reading University Library, Astor

Papers, 1416/1/3/5, Violet to Nancy, n.d.

23 British Library, Manuscript Room, Add. MSS. 50528 fols 106–7.

24 Michael Astor, *Tribal Feeling*, 1963, p. 171.

25 J. M. Dorwert, 'The Roosevelt–Astor Espionage Ring', *New York History*, July 1981, p. 314.

26 Ibid., pp. 317–18.

27 Ibid., p. 319.

28 Brooke Astor, *Footprints, An Autobiography*, New York, 1980, p. 299.

29 Viscount Astor's Archive, Bill to W. S. Gaud of Carter, Ledyard and Milburn, 27 July 1959.

30 Roose-Evans (ed.), op. cit., pp. 140–1.

31 Ibid., p. 311.

32 West Devon Record Office, Astor Papers, 186/17/7, Waldorf to the National Trust, n.d.

33 *Western Independent*, 10 December 1942.

34 *Forward – by the Right!*, 1943, p. 1.

35 Viscount Astor's Archive, Waldorf to Ronald Tree, 25 August 1945.

36 Bodleian Library, Oxford, Dawson Papers, 82 fols 111–12, 116, 177–8; 83 fols 1–2, John Astor to Geoffrey Dawson, August–October 1941.

37 House of Lords Archive, Beaverbrook Papers, BBK c/14, John to Lord Beaverbrook, 23 April 1941.

38 Archive of Lord Astor of Hever, Correspondence of John Astor with Viscount Trenchard, October 1941, and Lord Melchett, February 1942.

39 Cockett, op. cit., p. 86.

40 Ibid., p. 121.

41 Ibid.,, pp. 120–1.

42 West Devon Record Office, Astor Papers, Letter from Nancy in *Western Independent*, n.d.

43 Viscount Astor's Archive, Waldorf to Nancy, 21 March 1944.

44 Reading University Library, Astor Papers, 1416/1/3/11, Waldorf to Nancy, 17 June 1947.

Chapter 13

1 West Devon Archive, Astor Papers, 186/19/10, Nancy to J. J. Judge, 2 August 1945.

2 Viscount Astor's Archive, Waldorf to Nancy, 13 September 1945.

3 Loc. cit., Waldorf's travel journal 1946, n.d.

4 Reading University Library, Astor Papers, 1416/1/3/11, Waldorf to Nancy, 2 June 1947.

5 Loc. cit., 1416/1/3/11, Waldorf to Nancy, 11 June 1947.

6 Loc. cit., 1416/1/3/11, Waldorf to Nancy, 13 July 1947.

7 M. Holroyd, *Bernard Shaw*, vol. 3, *The Lure of Fantasy*, 1991, p. 472.

8 Viscount Astor's Archive, Waldorf's travel journal 1948, n.d.

9 Archive of Lord Astor of Hever, Waldorf to John, 7 June 1948.

10 Viscount Astor's Archive, Waldorf to Jakie, 3 March 1951.

11 Anthony Sampson, quoted in R. Cockett, *David Astor and the Observer*, 1991, p. 173.

12 Cockett, op. cit., p. 133.

13 West Devon Archive, Judge Papers, 94/10, Jakie to J. J. Judge, 17 August 1948.

14 Viscount Astor's Archive, Waldorf to Evelyn Heywood, 12 March 1951.

15 Loc. cit., Waldorf to Jakie, 3 March 1951.

16 Loc. cit., Waldorf to Nancy, two letters 1951, n.d.

17 Loc. cit., Waldorf to Nancy, 27 August 1952.

18 Loc. cit., Bill to Mary Stevens Baird, 21 June 1941.

19 Loc. cit., Bill to Mary Stevens Baird, 6 June 1943.

20 An appreciation by Bishop Gordon Savage, given to the author by Bronwen, Lady Astor.

21 Viscount Astor's Archive, Speech by Bill, n.d.

22 Loc. cit., Paper by Bill for the Commons Middle Eastern affairs committee, 17 March 1943.

23 Loc. cit., Memorandum by Bill to the Commons Imperial Committee 1945, n.d.

24 Loc. cit., Bill to Mary Stevens Baird, 15 June 1945.

25 Loc. cit., Bill to James Leasor, 20 February 1962.

26 Loc. cit., Aly Khan to Bill, 5 March 1955, 22 October 1957, 26 November 1959.
27 Loc. cit., Bill to R. A. Wooding, 17 April 1952.
28 Loc. cit., Bill's draft deposition to the Denning inquiry.
29 Loc. cit., Aly Khan to Bill, 24 May 1958.
30 Loc. cit., Memo, 'Post-war reconstruction of Chatham House', n.d.
31 Michael Astor, *Tribal Feeling*, 1963, p. 209.
32 House of Lords Record Office, Beaverbrook MSS, BBK/C/15, Memo, n.d.
33 Ibid.
34 Viscount Astor's Archive, Bill to John Davies, 9 October 1957.
35 *The Times* Archive, Memo of Lord Astor of Hever, 8 July 1958.
36 Archive of Lord Astor of Hever, Lord Miles to Gavin, July 1980.
37 Loc. cit., Lord Astor to John, 17 March 1961.

CHAPTER 14

1 Brooke Astor, *Footprints, An Autobiography*, New York, 1980, p. 266.
2 Archive of Lord Astor of Hever, Jack to Gavin, 30 April 1976.
3 Brooke Astor, op. cit., pp. 310–11.
4 Ibid., p. 319.
5 Viscount Astor's Archive, Bill to W. S. Gaud of Messrs Carter, Ledyard and Milburn, 27 July 1959.
6 An appreciation by Bishop Gordon Savage, given to the author by Bronwen, Lady Astor.
7 Viscount Astor's Archive, Bill to Lord Dundee at the Foreign Office, 27 January 1962.
8 Loc. cit., Reports made by Bill, 1962.
9 Loc. cit., Report, 'Some Rejections of Claims for Compensation Selected From a Large Number', March 1960.
10 Loc. cit., Bill to Lord Shackleton, 28 May 1963.
11 Loc. cit., Bill's draft deposition to the Denning inquiry.
12 Ibid.
13 Ibid.
14 Loc. cit., Bill to Sir Frederick Hoyer Miller, GCMG, CVO, 2 August 1961.
15 Loc. cit., David Moynahan to Bill, 13 August 1961.
16 Loc. cit., Bill's draft deposition to the Denning inquiry.
17 Ibid.
18 Loc. cit., Bill to Lord Denning, 18 August 1963.
19 Loc. cit., Bill to W. M. Mitchell, 1963.
20 Loc. cit., Bill's draft deposition to the Denning inquiry.
21 Loc. cit., Stephen Ward to Bill, n.d. (1–4 May 1963).
22 Bishop Gordon Savage, op. cit.
23 Viscount Astor's Archive, Bill's draft deposition to the Denning inquiry.
24 Loc. cit., Bill to Nancy Lancaster, 27 July 1963.
25 Loc. cit., Wissie to Bill, August 1963.
26 Loc. cit., Bill to W. M. Mitchell, 10 August 1963.
27 Loc. cit., Bill to W. M. Mitchell, 14 August 1963.

CHAPTER 15

1 Michael Astor, *Tribal Feeling*, 1963, p. 220.
2 Viscount Astor's Archive, Michael to Bill, 30 May 1964.
3 Michael Astor, op. cit., p. 155.
4 Viscount Astor's Archive, Nancy to Nancy Lancaster, 18 and 21 January 1960.
5 Loc. cit., Speech by Bill, n.d.
6 Loc. cit., Bill to Edward Heath, 9 November 1965.

Further Reading

(Place of publication is London unless otherwise stated.)

The present volume has largely been written from primary sources, all of which are listed in the chapter notes. The secondary works consulted are also cited, as appropriate, in the notes. There are a handful of general Astor histories. Unfortunately, none of them is sufficiently critical in its utilization of sources, nor did the authors concerned have the benefit of access to the more recently opened archives. The reader requiring more information would be better advised to consult those works which deal with specialist areas of the subject. The purpose of the following notes is to draw attention to some books which I have found most helpful.

Of the dozen or so biographies of John Jacob Astor I, most were written either in praise of his success or in denigration of his methods. For example A. D. Howden Smith in *John Jacob Astor, Landlord of New York*, Philadelphia, 1929, blamed John Jacob's un-American meanness of spirit on his Germanic origins. Most writers tended to repeat the anecdotes of earlier biographers, many of which were unattributed. A useful starting point for anyone wishing to research in detail the life of John Jacob I is J. D. Haeger's bibliographical essay, *John Jacob Astor and the Historians: Old Myths and New Interpretations*. A copy is available at the New York Historical Society. The most comprehensive study is K. W. Porter, *John Jacob Astor, Businessman*, 2 vols, Cambridge, Mass., 1931. Porter's study concentrates on John Jacob's commercial dealings, and its division of the material is somewhat bizarre but it is copiously annotated. For a more modern assessment, see J. D. Haeger, 'Business Strategy and Practice in the Early Republic: John Jacob Astor and the American Fur Trade', *Western Historical Quarterly*, XIX, no. 2, May 1988. H. W. Lanier's *A Century of Banking in New York 1822–1922*, New York, 1922, sets Astor's financial activities in context. James Parton's *John Jacob Astor* appeared first in *Harper's Magazine* in the 1860s. It was reprinted in 1967. It should be read with care. Count Gallatin (ed.), *A Great Peace Maker: The Diary of James Gallatin, Secretary to Albert Gallatin*, New York, 1914, is a very entertaining account of diplomatic life in Europe in the years before and after the fall of Napoleon, but utterly unreliable about the character of John Jacob Astor. Two biographies of Gallatin help to set the diplomat's relationship with Astor in a broader context: H. Adams, *The Life of Albert Gallatin*, New York, 1943, and R. Walters, *Albert Gallatin, Jeffersonian Financier and Diplomat*, New York, 1957. Washington Irving's *Astoria, or Anecdotes of an Enterprise Beyond the Rocky Mountains* (ed. L. Kleinfeld), forms vol. XV of R. D. Rust (ed.), *The Complete Works of Washington Irving*, Boston, 1976. Though obviously biased in Astor's favour, it is a comprehensive account of the great venture based on documents most of which have long since vanished. The political background is covered in F. F. Beirne, *The War of 1812*. G. S. Hellman (ed.), *The Letters of Henry Brevoort to Washington Irving*, 2 vols, 1915, provides useful background information. R. Baird, *Transplanted Flowers or Memoirs of Mrs Rumff . . . and the Duchesse de Broglie*, Glasgow, 1839, is an idealized account of the later years of John Jacob I's youngest daughter but the only one we have.

For family activities in the second half of the nineteenth century we have to rely largely on references in American newspapers and then make allowances for journalistic hostility. However, there are a few other sources. In 1905 Burton Hendrick, a Pulitzer prizewinner, wrote 'The Astor Fortune' for *McClure's Magazine*. It is a hostile account of how the family, in Hendrick's view, enriched themselves at the expense of their fellow citizens. Much the same is true of Gustavus Myers's *History of Great American Fortunes*, 3 vols, Chicago, 1911. The New York Historical Society possesses a remarkable manuscript scrapbook of collected details catalogued as William Kelby, 'Notes on the Astor Family'. The political background is covered in D. Rothman, *Politics and Power* and L. D. White, *The Republican Era, 1865–1900*. Most of William Waldorf's literary and antiquarian writings appeared first in the *Pall Mall Magazine*, but some of his stories were collected and published separately as *Pharaoh's Daughter and Other Stories*, 1900. His novels were *Valentina*, 1886, and *Sforza*, 1889. He kept assiduous notes on his various houses, some of which survive and are available for research purposes. The collected documentation about Cliveden is in the possession of Viscount Astor. Articles on the house and estate appeared in *Country Life* on 11 and 18 July 1931, 24 February and 3 March 1977, 10 July 1984 and 13 July 1986. The story of Hever was covered in the same magazine on 12 October 1907, 25 October 1919 and 3 January 1969. Gavin, second Baron Hever, published a valuable précis, *Hever in the Twentieth Century*, in 1973. Gavin researched his family history extensively and the results appeared mostly in privately published pamphlets and small books such as *The Astors of Hever*, 1982, and *The Astor Family*, 1970. Brief descriptions of 2 Temple Place have been published: *Incorporated Accountants' Hall: Its History and Architecture*, 1935; *2 Temple Place, Headquarters of Smith and Nephew Group of Companies*, n.d. (*c.*1973).

On the Astor newspapers the most useful books are: A. M. Gollin, *The Observer and J. L. Garvin 1908–1914*, 1960; R. Cockett, *David Astor and the Observer*, 1991; S. Koss, *The Rise and Fall of the Political Press in Britain*, 2 vols, 1984; I. McDonald, *History of the Times*, 5 vols, 1973–84.

Several books have been devoted to Nancy Astor. Probably the best are: C. Sykes, *Nancy: The Life of Lady Astor*, 1972, and E. Langhorne, *Nancy Astor and Her Friends*, 1974. References to Waldorf's political life are much more scattered. He contributed to various published works on agriculture: Viscount Astor and K. Murray, *Land and Life*, 1933, and *The Planning of Agriculture*, 1933; Viscount Astor and B. Seebohm Rowntree, *British Agriculture*, 1938 and *Mixed Farming and Muddled Thinking*, 1946. Valuable background for Waldorf's Commons career is found in C. Addison, *Four and a Half Years*, 2 vols, 1934; T. Jones, *Lloyd George*, 1951; W. M. Aitken (Lord Beaverbrook), *Politicians and the War 1914–1916*, 2 vols, 1928–32, Lord Beaverbrook,

The Decline and Fall of Lloyd George, 1963. Anything written by Beaverbrook is, of course, coloured by his antipathy towards Lloyd George. Several articles and pamphlets appeared under the names of Waldorf and Nancy (most of the research was, in fact, carried out by Waldorf). Among them are: Lady Astor: *Why Students Should be Interested in the Drink Question*, 1922; *Are Temperance Reformers Cranks?*, 1922; 'The English Law Relating to the Sale of Intoxicating Liquors', *Annals of the American Academy of Political and Social Science*, Philadelphia, September 1923; Lord Astor: 'Reform of the House of Lords', *Contemporary Review*, May 1927; *The House of Lords*, 1933. Waldorf contributed frequently to *The Round Table* (though anonymously as the custom was in that journal), which is useful as a barometer to the thinking of Astor and his circle on international affairs. J. R. M. Butler, *Lord Lothian (Philip Kerr) 1882–1940*, 1960, is quite useful on the Astor–Lothian connection.

Michael Astor's *Tribal Feeling*, 1963, is obligatory reading for anyone who wants to obtain the flavour of life at Cliveden. Joyce Grenfell's correspondence in J. Roose-Evans (ed.), *Darling Ma: Joyce Grenfell's Letters to her Mother 1932–1944*, 1988, provides a delightful and perceptive oblique view of Cliveden before and during the Second World War.

The nearest thing to an inside look at the life of the twentieth-century American family is Brooke Astor, *Footprints, An Autobiography*, New York, 1980. Serge Obolensky's autobiography, *One Man and His Time*, 1949, is rather disappointing in its detail on Alice Astor and her family but valuable on the international lifestyle of the wealthy in the 1930s. Much has been written about New York high society. Some of the books which may be scanned for Astor detail are: T. Beer, *The Mauve Decade: American Life at the End of the Nineteenth Century*, New York, 1926; S. Birmingham, *America's Secret Aristocracy*, Boston, 1987; A. Churchill, *The Upper Crust: An Informal History of New York's Highest Society*, New Jersey, 1970; J. D. Gates, *The Astor Family*, New York, 1981; E. D. Lehr, *'King Lehr' and the Gilded Age*, Philadelphia, 1935; G. Myers, *History of the Great American Fortunes*, New York, 1936; H. O'Connor, *The Astors*, New York, 1941; D. Sinclair, *Dynasty: The Astors and Their Times*, 1984; V. Cowles, *The Astors*, 1979; A. T. Vanderbilt II, *Fortune's Children: The Fall of the House of Vanderbilt*, New York, 1989. On the more serious aspects of Astor life in America, mention should be made of W. Andrews, *Architecture in New York*, New York, 1969; C. Gray, 'Astor Places: The First Family of Manhattan Real Estate', *Avenue*, May 1990; R. Jarman, 'What Parties They've Thrown Here!', *Saturday Evening Post*, 2 January 1954; J. M. Dorwert, 'The Roosevelt–Astor Espionage Ring', *New York History*, July 1981. Political background will be found in F. Freidel, *Franklin D. Roosevelt*, 4 vols, New York, 1952–73; G. Ward, *Before the Trumpet*, New York, 1985, and *A First Class Temperament*, New York, 1989; E. Roosevelt (ed.), *Franklin D. Roosevelt, His Personal Letters*, New York, 1950.

Several journalists, authors and ghost writers cashed in on the Profumo affair. Two books appeared a quarter of a century after the scandal and made a cooler appraisal of the evidence. They were P. Knightley and C. Kennedy, *An Affair of State: The Profumo Case and the Framing of Stephen Ward*, 1987, and A. Summer and S. Dorril, *The Honeytrap: The Secret World of Stephen Ward*, 1987. Both have points to prove and, indeed, axes to grind and should therefore be read with caution.

Index

The honorific titles of people mentioned in this index are those they enjoyed at the period then referred to and not necessarily those they later acquired.